SOCIAL MOVEMENTS
IN A GLOBAL CONTEXT

SOCIAL MOVEMENTS
IN A GLOBAL CONTEXT
Canadian Perspectives

Rod Bantjes

Canadian Scholars' Press Inc.
Toronto

Social Movements in a Global Context: Canadian Perspectives
Rod Bantjes

First published in 2007 by
Canadian Scholars' Press Inc.
425 Adelaide Street West, Suite 200
Toronto, Ontario
M5V 2C1

www.cspi.org

Every reasonable effort has been made to identify copyright holders. CSPI would be pleased to have any errors or omissions brought to its attention.

Canadian Scholars' Press gratefully acknowledges financial support for our publishing activities from the Government of Canada through the Book Publishing Industry Development Program (BPIDP).

Library and Archives Canada Cataloguing in Publication

Bantjes, Rod
      Social movements in a global context : Canadian
perspectives / Rod Bantjes.

Includes bibliographical references and index.
ISBN 978-1-55130-324-6

    1. Social movements--Textbooks. I. Title.

HM881.B365 2007   303.48'4   C2007-900773-2

Cover photo: "Police bodies in riot gear." Copyright: laryn pkb
Cover design, interior design and layout: Aldo Fierro

Printed and bound in Canada

Canada

MIX
Paper from
responsible sources
FSC
www.fsc.org   FSC® C004071

For my mother June, who, when she had been robbed of so much,
held on to her sense of humour and her love of the printed page

TABLE OF CONTENTS

PREFACE

I did not write this book out of any particular quarrel with existing texts in the area of social movements. I was quite happy teaching from readings that I had collected myself and made available on reserve, in "course packs," or, increasingly, found already available online. World events seemed, in the first years of the 21st century, to be outstripping analysis. It takes time for good academic research to get published and even longer for it to filter into standard texts.

Megan Mueller, editorial director at Canadian Scholars' Press Inc., discovered, by reviewing Web sites for social movement classes taught across Canada in 2003, that I was not alone. Many of us had given up on the idea of using a textbook. That told her that there was a need here for a book with a new approach. She somehow got the idea from the content of my Web site that I might be the one to fill that need.

She contacted me by e-mail. Of course I had other projects in mind. Still, I took her idea to my students, who enthusiastically supported it. My partner and oft-times collaborator, Maureen Moynagh, who is a much more serious academic than I, convinced me that there is no shame in writing a textbook. I was particularly attracted to the idea of trying out some new ideas, so I wrote and submitted a prospectus.

The reviewers for Canadian Scholars' Press Inc. liked the look of what I was proposing and made some very helpful suggestions for improvement. From the very start Megan has been an enthusiastic advocate of this project. There have been times, past deadline, when I have dreaded her e-mails, but she has always been the most supportive and understanding of editors. This book owes its existence almost entirely to her.

I would also like to acknowledge John Thompson, an excellent teacher, whose courses on sociological theory and social movements helped to seduce me away from philosophy. He gave me my first job teaching in sociology and my first experience at a young age in writing textbooks. He set me on the path to this work and it certainly bears the marks of his influence.

Others who deserve acknowledgement are the students of Soc 212 (Social Dissent) and 312 (Social Movements), who read and made, on the whole, approving comments on early drafts of chapters. I also would like to thank those in all my classes who have done their best over the years to teach me how to make obscure ideas clear and how to cut to the heart of complex issues.

A Note from the Publisher

Thank you for selecting *Social Movements in a Global Context: Canadian Perspectives*, written by Rod Bantjes. The author and publisher have devoted considerable time and careful development (including meticulous peer reviews at proposal phase and first draft) to this book. We appreciate your recognition of this effort and accomplishment.

Teaching Features

The author has enhanced the book by adding extensive pedagogy. Each chapter contains a thorough introduction, concise conclusion, detailed reference list, critical thinking questions, annotated further reading, and annotated relevant Web sites. The art program features chapter-opening photographs and numerous boxed inserts and engaging case studies throughout.

INTRODUCTION

I suspect that most students do not read introductions to textbooks and that I am likely addressing a colleague, perhaps one considering whether he or she should assign this book for a course. I have always hated choosing texts. No one ever writes them exactly the way we want or expect them to be written. Inevitably, their fatal inadequacies become evident only when you try to teach from them. I know that some have found this book, in outline, to confound their expectations. It does not seem to be organized by the major theoretical approaches in the subdiscipline or by movements arranged according to theme, contemporary relevance, or historical chronology.

SOCIAL MOVEMENT THEORY

The organizing thread is the development of social movement theory. What might be a little misleading is that I understand theory as what Imre Lakatos calls a "structure of problems." The ongoing debates within theory revolve around persistent and recurring problems such as the paradox, posed and persuasively answered by Marx and Engels, of how "the powerless" could possibly challenge modern structures of power. These debates have always responded to changing historical context. To help students make sense of how social movement history has shaped theoretical debate, I have organized the chapters roughly chronologically. The first chapter begins not with the labour movement so much as the Marxist paradigm for understanding it because so much of subsequent social movement theory is a debate with the ghost of Marx (and Engels).

Unlike Kuhn and his followers, I do not believe that theoretical paradigms supersede one another in a sequential history. Theoretical approaches remain alive, and their proponents re-enter debates, albeit on "altered ground." Consequently many chapters also have a synchronic dimension. So, for instance, the opening chapter on the Marxist paradigm moves backwards and forwards in time comparing, among other things, conditions of Engels' working-class

Manchester and modern "sweatshops" and informal settlements in the developing world, and asking students to think about the relevance of Marxist analysis in the present. My intent here is both to represent the realities of the current debate (Marxist analysis is not dead) and to engage students interested in contemporary relevance.

I introduce theoretical traditions sequentially. However, since they remain active in debate, I recall them periodically in later chapters. So, for example, I introduce new social movement theory in Chapter 3 (Movement Innovations in the 1960s: Resource Mobilization?) and develop it, in successive layers, in chapters 5 (Culture and the Politics of Identity), 6 (Bureaucratization and Anarchist Resistance), and 11 (Coalition Politics). I treat new social movement theory as a cluster of theories around a new "problematic." My priority here, as with all theory discussions, is to introduce students to the problems it raises as much as the solutions it proposes. These problems include, for instance: What is (or should be) the role of class as the basis for organized dissent? How are political "collective actors" constituted (and to what extent can we appeal to the "logic of capital" to understand this)? How, more generally, is "representation" of social constituencies accomplished by the bodies that purport to speak for them?

In order to represent the Marxist tradition as an ongoing theoretical debate, I have referred outside social movement theory proper to include liberalism: from Adam Smith (Chapter 1), through liberal-democracy (Chapter 3), to neoliberalism (chapters 7, 8, 11, and 12). In Chapter 11 (Coalition Politics) I discuss neo-Gramscian approaches to "counter-hegemonic culture" favoured by many Canadian academics. Because of my interest in the intersection between state and movement, I introduce students to Foucaultian theories of "governmentality" (Chapter 2). In every chapter I explicitly address spatial problems related to the translocal, transnational, and "global" dimensions of movement activism. No nameable tradition of spatial theorizing has yet developed. However, throughout, and particularly in chapters 10 (Beyond Nation-State Sovereignty: Indigenous Peoples' Internationalism), 11 (Coalition Politics), and 12 (In Search of Global "Public Space"), I highlight theories/theorists that emphasize the "geographic turn."

My hope, in taking a problems-based approach, is to help students see points where divergent theoretical discussions intersect (and, of course, clash). I aim to encourage not theoretical allegiance so much as theoretical problem solving. For this I think students need encouragement to try out different theoretical tools. It helps also to adopt a somewhat irreverent stance that permits innovation. Such skills I see as critical in a period like the present when the grounds upon which struggles for social change play out are shifting so radically.

NOVEL THEMES AND REPETITION

The understanding of contemporary social movements as well as social movement theory requires a tremendous amount of conceptual groundwork. Second-year students tend not to have a clear grasp of basic concepts like: capitalism, the state, civil rights, civil society, liberalism, neoliberalism, colonialism, mobility of capital, economic globalization, etc. My strategy is to introduce these, as well as more complex concepts like alienation or autonomization of power, early and come back to them often, providing repetition and layering of complexity and context. I return to theoretical problems raised earlier in the text as students learn of theoretical developments or changing historical contexts that cast new light on the problems. I also make links to material, whether conceptual or empirical, in previous chapters. These sorts of repetition provide for reinforcement and an element of continuity.

I place somewhat more emphasis than most sociologists on the intersecting themes of violence, the representation of violence, and the relationship between movements and the state. The question of how to explain states' varying responses to social movements—from opposition to co-optation to violent repression—is central and one that merits returning to, albeit through very different case studies. Some have noted an apparent repetition between chapters 4 and 7 dealing with terror. Chapter 4 problematizes the "terrorism" debate by looking first at state terror. However, my focus here is on explaining the resistance to state terror. The social movements at the centre of this case study are human rights and peace movements, quite different from the FLQ and al Qaeda cases dealt with in Chapter 7. Violence more generally and representations of violence play complex roles in claims-making about legitimacy, strategies of power, and relations between states and movements. The theme bears repeated treatment (it is an important thread in chapters 1 through 3, as well as 4, 7, and 12).

There could hardly be a more thoroughly sociological theme than Weber's problem of bureaucratization and oligarchization that thwarts so many popular attempts at social innovation. However, it appears to have been largely dropped from contemporary sociological discussions of social movements. This seems to me to be rather odd, especially as so many young activists today see themselves as anarchists, motivated by the dream of freedom from centralized or system authority. In Chapter 6 (Bureaucratization and Anarchist Resistance) I have resurrected the debate around this problem. While the question is sociological, I have reached beyond the discipline for new approaches to addressing it.

In Chapter 8 (Consumer-Citizen: The Market as a Social Movement Tool) I address a theme that until recently has received little academic treatment and almost no systematic theorizing. That is the increasing use of market strategies by social movement activists. Drawing on Naomi Klein's work, I offer an argument to the effect that features of the neoliberal revolution and the "new economy" provide favourable conditions for the deployment of this strategy. On reading the prospectus for this book, one of the reviewers argued that the theme did not merit a full chapter. On seeing the final draft he was persuaded, as I hope others will be, that it is "of great import."

METHODOLOGICAL APPROACHES

Many of the problems within social movement research demand a political economy approach. Here the method I favour is comparative case study. In Chapter 4 (Resistance to State Terror) I provide an illustration of a systematic use of the method. I also explicitly discuss the logic of comparative analysis as a social science method. I apply comparative analysis in chapters 2, 7, and 9, albeit more loosely.

Throughout the text I pay attention to questions of identity formation and the construction of meaning, both of which demand more interpretive approaches. These get extended treatment in chapters 5 (Culture and the Politics of Identity) and 9 (Discourse and the Power of Constitution:

"Speaking for" the Environment). In Chapter 5 I also make a plea for not divorcing culture from structure in theory or method of analysis.

Both interpretive and comparative methods require case studies, preferably featuring "rich description." Accordingly, in each chapter I have highlighted at least one such case described in detail. The result is chapters that are longer than they might otherwise be. I have written up the cases in such a way that, I hope, students will find the narrative thread inherently engaging and will not resent the extra reading. They will also gain a much richer sense of "the real," which they can use as a basis for critically applying theory.

INCLUSION OF SPECIFIC SOCIAL MOVEMENTS

With some exceptions, such as the anti-sweatshop movement, I take the position that theory defines the importance of movements. New movement innovations become especially relevant when they confound theoretical expectations. I have selected movement case studies mostly on this basis. The fact that social movement theory, particularly in Canada and Europe, has wrestled with the ghost of Marx has meant that movements of the left get privileged attention both in the literature and in this text.

I think that all of the 20th-/21st-century movements important from a left perspective get some play in this text. A few, like the labour and women's movements, are featured in more than one chapter. Others, like the civil rights movement, make briefer, although often repeated appearances. The only movement that I regret not having found proper space for is the disability movement.

Right-wing movements, or what resource mobilization theorists call "counter-movements" to the left, are arguably a more prominent feature of the U.S. and European landscapes than the Canadian. Nonetheless in Chapter 9 (Discourse and the Power of Constitution: "Speaking for" the Environment) I have included a case study of the U.S.-based Wise Use movement and its Canadian counterpart, which attempted to mobilize a largely working-class constituency to a right-wing anti-environmentalist cause. It was a corporate-sponsored movement and so allows students to explore a further dimension of co-optation. The case also raises complex questions about what are genuinely "popular" movements. It enriches later discussions of labour/environmental alliances as well as the problem of "hegemony" (Chapter 11, Coalition Politics). I have also devoted a part of Chapter 7 to the anti-Enlightenment al Qaeda movement.

Any single-authored text that attempts to cover such a wide field as this one does is bound to suffer in some way from the author's limitations. I appeal to the readers and users of the book to point out those limitations and make suggestions. I am already, in Hegelian fashion, looking at the finished object with a critical eye and thinking of changes. The second edition, if there is one, will be a different book and a better one with your contributions.

Chapter 1

WORKERS OF THE WORLD, UNITE!

INTRODUCTION:
THE ANTI-CAPITALISM OF
MARX AND ENGELS

A common accident for workers in cotton mills was to get caught in the wide belt that carried power from spinning drums on the ceiling down to the machines on the floor of the factory, especially when these belts had buckles—they could easily catch a person's clothing or hair and catapult them to the ceiling and back "with such force that there is rarely a whole bone left in the body"(Engels 192). Friedrich Engels records this grisly image as part of his exposé of the exploitation suffered by the working class in England in the 1840s. He tells us with disgust that the factory reports from which he gets much of his information attribute many of these accidents to the fact that children fail to pay attention when working with the machines, or that workers clean the machines while they are still running. Why then, asks Engels, do capitalists hire children if they know that they will put themselves in danger?

The reason was that child labour was cheaper than that of adults—about half the price. Yes, workers do clean the machines while they are running, but, Engels points out, if they do not, then their employers require them to do it during their breaks in order to save time. Finally, why not redesign the machinery with safety in mind or, at minimum, provide some protective housing for dangerous moving parts? The answer, of course, was that this would add costs to production and factory owners were driven to minimize costs in order to survive in their competition with other factory owners—this is the logic of capitalism. The cost of injury was greater to the worker, but not to the factory owner. Injured workers rarely received pay or any compensation once they were off work. Their wages were insufficient to cover medical treatment. Those who survived encounters with belts or pulleys typically died from lockjaw, which meant that their wounds were not being properly treated for infection.

Workers' bodies could be treated like disposable factors of production, their use determined by a purely economic calculus. As Karl Marx, Engels' sometime collaborator, would put it, their labour, and therefore their lives, which they could hardly separate from their bodies or their work, was treated as a commodity. Marx understood this as a perversion that did violence not just to the body but also to the soul, or the very essence of what it means to be human. It diminished both the employer, forced to treat people as things, and the worker, who had little choice but to submit to such treatment.

Marx was a romantic. His moral indictment of capitalism is important because it has inspired anti-capitalist sentiment throughout the 20th century and continues to do so in the 21st. Early in his career, however, he set out to prove that he was not a romantic in the sense of being a dreamer, but had a workable plan for changing the world. His analysis of worker exploitation and class struggle became one of the most enduringly influential models of how people could and would organize to resist capitalism. In this chapter we are going to assess that model and its continuing relevance, if any, for the 21st century.

First we will flesh out some of Marx and Engels' basic concepts. Then we will see how well they apply to a case study of worker resistance in two New England towns in the 20th century. The great challenge for Marxism—and Marx understood this from the beginning—was to understand not how workers would fight this or that local struggle, but how they would take on the might of international capitalism. They failed, under Marx's direction, to create a lasting international organization in the 19th century.

We will see why in the 21st century the need is even greater and the challenges more complex. The global reach of firms and dynamism of modern capitalism have allowed multinational firms to outpace efforts of organized labour to challenge them. We will look at new approaches to mounting that challenge and ask how relevant Marxism is to understanding them.

Living Conditions under Capitalism

The workers Engels described earned in the range of 1–2 shillings (12–24 pence) a day. Of course this is meaningless until you know what sort of living conditions they could buy with that amount of money. Engels answers this question with a tour of working-class neighbourhoods in the great industrial cities of England such as London, Manchester, and Glasgow. Here is an example of a "working men's quarter" in Manchester called "Little Ireland." The neighbourhood is "surrounded on all four sides by tall factories and high embankments, covered with buildings." There are no trees or grass.

> The cottages are old, dirty, and of the smallest sort, the streets uneven, fallen into ruts and in part without drains or pavement; masses of refuse, offal and sickening filth lie among standing pools in all directions; the atmosphere is poisoned by the effluvia of these and laden and darkened by the smoke of a dozen tall factory chimneys. A horde of ragged women and children swarm about here, as filthy as the swine that thrive upon the garbage heaps and in the puddles. (Engels 93)

Notice that there is no garbage collection here. Why? Engels would argue that this failure comes from trying to organize social life, a community, purely on the basis of private ownership. Who could make a profit collecting the garbage in Little Ireland (except perhaps the owners of the pigs)? Similarly for other community or public goods like paved roads, street lamps, sewers, or water-treatment plants. No one will invest in them unless they can make a profit from that investment. How would you make money from building or maintaining a sewer? Even now we do not pay per flush, or get charged every time we dump dishwater down the drain. Municipal governments can and do own this sort of infrastructure and pay for it through collecting taxes. But that is public ownership with the aim of fulfilling a collective need, quite different from the capitalist principle of private ownership motivated by profit.

Engels was also disgusted by how landlords, bound by few legal requirements and little moral concern, crammed buildings together, spent as little as possible on maintenance, and charged the maximum rent that the market would bear. The result was overcrowding.

> ... what must one think when he hears that in each of these pens [i.e., the cottages], containing at most two rooms, a garret and perhaps a cellar, on the average twenty human beings live; that in the whole region, for each one hundred and twenty persons, one usually inaccessible privy is provided. (Engels 93–94)

If you know about the "informal settlements" that surround 21st-century megacities in the developing world—São Paulo, Mexico City, Mumbai, Calcutta, Dhaka—you experience a kind of *déjà-vu* in reverse when reading Engels. In the largest urban slum in Africa—Kiberia, Nairobi—neighbourhoods can have as few as 10 pit latrines for 40,000 people. Desperate people resort to using "flying toilets." They relieve themselves in plastic bags, tie them off, and toss them "on to the nearest roof or pathway"(Salmon). There is no running water, little in the way of garbage collection, and "open sewers filled with stinking, raw sewage" (Vidal). Dwellings are made from "found" materials, flattened oil drums, salvaged wood, plastic sheeting. Up to five people will live in a single windowless room.

Engels and his contemporaries thought that crowding and lack of fresh air and sunlight was a key cause of ill health for urban workers of his time. The real killer was the lack of clean water and sewage disposal. Add to this the fact that many workers could afford only one set of clothes. Without being able to change clothes or find clean water to bathe, it is not surprising that injured workers died from infection. In places like Little Ireland and Kiberia, otherwise healthy people die from water-borne diseases like cholera. In the 21st century Kiberia is not an isolated example. In Africa, Asia, and Latin America, according to one United Nations estimate, a little over a *billion* people (one-sixth of the human population) lack "a good water supply" and a little under a billion are without "decent sanitation"(IRC). Other estimates are higher, up to 2.5 billion worldwide.

Clearly many workers were not able to buy a very high quality of life with the few shillings that they earned. But Engels is a little loose in the way he maps the conditions of working-class neighbourhoods with the conditions in the workplace. Are the residents of the worst neighbourhoods like Little Ireland actually working in the factories? Or are they getting by, like so many in present-day slums, with even less desirable and less lucrative forms of employment at the margins of the wage economy—casual labour, street vending, scavenging, prostitution, or even petty crime? Engels mentions the occupation of only one of the inhabitants of Little Ireland—a handloom weaver—who lives in a cellar with clay walls that seep so badly he has to bail water out onto the street every morning. Handloom weavers were being squeezed

out by competition from the big factories that could produce cloth more cheaply, so possibly this independent operator was making less than factory workers.

Let us consider the present situation. We know that over a billion people earn less than U.S.$1 per day; two billion earn less than $2 per day. Many of these people will be found among the billion or so in the worst of the new urban slums. If the factory workers who assemble cellphones, designer jeans, and Barbie dolls for consumers like us are making even close to U.S.$6 a day, they are likely not among the poorest slum dwellers. Many people argue that we should not feel any guilt about the low wages these so-called "sweatshop" workers receive from their involvement in global capitalism since the alternatives for them are so much worse.

The Reserve Army of Labour and Worker Exploitation

Marx and Engels argued that the fates of the industrial workers and the mass of marginally employed and unemployed were tightly bound together by the economic logic of capitalism. Slum dwellers then as now are mostly migrants from the countryside. What they are escaping is unemployment and underemployment caused by the capitalist development of agriculture or rural "development" projects like dam building, which involve the expropriation of land. Capitalist agriculture relies on mechanization, which in turn requires fewer people to work the land. Small farmers cannot afford the costs of the new technologies and, depending on their tenure, are either evicted from their land or bought out by large operations. The result is always the same: displaced people who must choose between living in rural misery or migrating to the urban slums to live in misery with at least the hope of better employment.

Currently about 160,000 people migrate from the country to the urban margins every day (Vidal). Just as in 19th-century England, there are always more than can be absorbed into the formal wage economy, but their presence shapes the formal economy nonetheless. Marx and Engels called them a "reserve army of labour." The idea is that the employers can "enlist" them when necessary to replace workers who object to factory conditions. A reserve army of people desperate for work shifts the balance of power in favour of employers over their employees. The extent of workers' fear of being fired can be gauged by the levels of abuse that they endured.

In addition to intense work schedules, women workers were often forced to submit to their employers' sexual advances. As Engels put it, for many a factory owner "his mill is also his harem" (Engels 177). Women were required to work into the final months of their pregnancy and if they dared to sit during their 12-hour shift, they could be fined half a day's pay. Workers put up with abuse and humiliation not because they wanted the job so much as because they feared the alternative. The point for Marx and Engels was that both "options" facing the worker were produced by capitalism. Capitalism created a situation in which superficially people had the freedom to choose, but the reality as experienced by the worker was one of coercion.

Capitalism and Alienation

So far what we have been discussing—low wages for long hours of difficult and dehumanizing work, rents for desperately inadequate living conditions—can be categorized under the heading of economic *exploitation*. Engels was equally interested, and Marx perhaps more interested, in a related concept

that they called "alienation." We have seen it already in the way that people get treated like things or the way in which they lose human qualities like the capacity to freely choose in situations of economic necessity. Marx was particularly interested in how it worked within the new factory workplaces.

Adam Smith, the great theorist of free trade and the market, tells the following story to illustrate how workers have contributed to innovation in the design of machinery.

> In the first fire-engines [i.e., steam engines], a boy was constantly employed to open and shut alternately the communication between the boiler and the cylinder, according as the piston either ascended or descended. One of these boys, who loved to play with his companions, observed that, by tying a string from the handle of the valve, which opened this communication, to another part of the machine, the valve would open and shut without his assistance, and leave him at liberty to divert himself with his play-fellows. (Smith)

What Smith does not tell us is what happened to the boy and his fellow valve operators when the installation of connecting rods made their jobs obsolete.

Marx would point to two important consequences. One is that the boy's ingenuity, a combination of what Marx would see as the essentially human qualities of skill and creativity, becomes built into the machine. The other is that the benefits—cost and time savings that the boy wants to convert into play and leisure—do not accrue to the worker. He will be forced either to find another 12-hour-a-day job or starve. The cost savings accrue to the firm whose owners reinvest it in raw materials, more machinery, the purchase of more labour time, or perhaps even more low-grade "cottages" that can be used to gouge rent from workers.

To use Marx's abstract terms, it becomes "capital," the very force that in so many aspects of the boy's life will oppress him and rob him of freedoms. Here is the core irony of alienation: a free and creative act by a human being takes on alien and non-human form—the machine and abstract capital. Transferred to these alien forms, human qualities act back upon the person who created them, depriving him of their benefits, as well as the very qualities themselves. Machines and abstract systems take on some of the powers of humans while humans, by losing those powers, become a bit more like machines.

In the case of mechanized workplaces, like the ones being created in the new factories, it is possible to think of the entire operation—including the building, the floor plan, and the way in which job assignments are designed and coordinated with one another—as comprising a single mechanism or machine entity. This is the idea that we invoke with the familiar metaphor of the worker as a "cog in the machine." Factory interiors were often designed to make it easy for a single person to keep an eye on many workers at once. Surveillance enables discipline, so that the employer knows, for example, who to fine half a day's pay for sitting down for a moment's rest.

Surveillance also has a disciplinary effect in itself, in that workers will conform when they know that they are being watched. You can still see this sort of design in modern workplaces where, for example, the supervisor's office may be raised with a commanding view of the shop floor. However, employers now rely less on architecture and more on electronics. Most people who have worked in the service or retail sectors will be aware of the video cameras trained on them

or else know that the machine they work on, whether it be a cash register, a computer terminal, or even the cab of a truck, can automatically record their every move or transaction, comparing their speed and mistakes with those of all other workers.

Disciplinary features can be physically designed into the workplace environment in other ways. Many employers, rather than relying on fines, simply removed chairs or designed workstations so that it was impossible to sit down (the idea being that standing kept people alert). To get people to work faster, one could integrate the human task with some machine function—like the boy and the piston—so that the speed of the person could be governed by setting the speed of the machine. This type of solution became widespread after the invention of the assembly line in the early 20th century. These are all instances of alienation in which people are treated as irresponsible and/or lazy, and the moral qualities of responsibility and enthusiasm for work are designed into inanimate things.

The artificial environments of the new factories were marvels of intelligence and ingenuity, coordinating machine and human effort. One of the earliest innovations employed to coordinate human effort—the division of labour in detail—had the ironic effect of depriving workers of their own ability to exercise intelligence and ingenuity. The idea was to take a single task, the making of a shoe or, in Adam Smith's famous example, the making of a pin, and break it into its component operations, standardize each operation, and assign it to a separate worker to perform repeatedly and exclusively.

The division of labour in detail is not quite the same thing as specialization. A chef could specialize in a style of cuisine, but he or she would still engage in a full range of activities from planning the menu to selecting ingredients to adjusting the seasoning.

To see an illustration of the division of labour in detail in cooking, you would have to look at fast-food assembly lines where a worker can be tied to a standardized task requiring almost no skill or discretion—flipping a burger patty when a light goes on to tell them it is done. The division of labour in detail almost always involves "deskilling," the designing out of any discretionary elements that demand thought, creativity, or specialized knowledge on the part of the worker.

Adam Smith encouraged employers to capitalize on this new innovation for three reasons. First, it increased workers' dexterity and speed. There is a striking image of this in some old film footage of women folding small boxes on an assembly line. They are smiling at the camera, obviously not even having to think about what they are doing, but their hands are moving almost faster than the eye can follow. Second, workers do not waste time moving from one task to another. Third, once tasks are so simplified that people can do them in a machine-like way, it becomes easier to design machines to automate them completely (he gives the boy at the steam engine as an illustration of this).

He does not make explicit two additional reasons that have continued to be powerful motivators to employers to divide labour in detail. The first is that it allows them to hire unskilled workers to do what was formerly skilled work. Since unskilled workers can be paid less, this is called "the cheapening of tasks." Unskilled workers are also more replaceable and are therefore much more vulnerable to the competitive threat of the "reserve army of labour."

Smith recognized how damaging to people's potential this sort of work could be. He writes:

> The man whose whole life is spent in performing a few simple operations, of which the effects, too, are perhaps always the same, or very nearly the same, has no occasion to exert his understanding, or to exercise his invention, in finding out expedients for removing difficulties which never occur. He naturally loses, therefore, the habit of such exertion, and generally becomes as stupid and ignorant as it is possible for a human creature to become.

Notice here that he is saying not so much that it is an insult to the worker's intelligence, as that it shapes the worker's mind and undermines his intelligence. Marx, reading this, saw again the perverse irony that is alienation. We invest our inanimate production systems with human intelligence and in the process rob actual people of it.

DIALECTICAL THEORY: CAPITALISM CREATES WORKER RESISTANCE

Engels concludes his survey of the condition of the English working class by arguing that the only way that the workers can preserve their humanity in the face of growing exploitation and alienation is through "hatred and rebellion" against their bourgeois oppressors. He documents a growing history of clashes between workers and capitalists. Some of these were political demonstrations, where workers came out in the streets in force; occasionally these clashes were strikes, although there was no legal requirement for employers to negotiate with strikers. Often these actions were met with violence. Frequently the workers resorted to violence themselves. Engels describes locked-out brickmakers in 1843 advancing on their factory "... in military order, the first rank armed with guns" (Engels 252).

What to the bourgeoisie seemed acts of "disorder" were, as Engels and Marx correctly perceived, evidence of new forms of order among the workers that were neither created nor sanctioned by the bourgeoisie.

Working-Class Community

At the same time that workers were being forcibly organized into the new industrial machine, they were organizing themselves outside of the factory walls. While their work dulled their minds, and the bourgeois state provided them little or no formal education, they were educating themselves. They created their own "mechanics' institutes" where they read books, went to lectures, and discussed ideas. Engels was impressed to observe "... working-men, whose fustian jackets scarcely held together, speak upon geological, astronomical, and other subjects, with more knowledge than the most 'cultivated' bourgeois in Germany possess" (Engels 265).

They also read the best literature and political theory, including the anarchist Proudhon and the socialist Robert Owen, both of whom outlined visions of more just and egalitarian societies. Independently, Marx was witnessing the emergence of a similar working-class culture in that most revolutionary of cities, Paris. Here the reading list would have been similar, although the French socialist writers, such as Charles Fourier, were particularly popular.

In the working-class neighbourhoods where capitalism failed to provide the necessary infrastructure for decent living, and the state provided no "external" institutional services, people created spontaneous order. Mothers, forced to work in the mills, learned to rely on neighbours to look after the children too young to work themselves. When illness or industrial ac-

cident threw workers' families on to hard times, other workers shared what little they had. As the canon of Manchester observed in 1841, "the poor give one another more than the rich give the poor" (Engels 154). Workers built on these informal networks of mutual aid to create "friendly societies," which pooled resources to provide social services such as paying for funeral costs. Where capitalism could not provide services for a profit, people began to help one another out for free.

This sort of mutual aid, spontaneous and freely given, creates powerful emotional ties and guarantees further commitments among people to support each other and help one another in times of crisis. This sort of "solidarity" is an element of "community." Community often refers also to a place, a neighbourhood, a physical container of the meetings, exchanges, and interactions that make up community networks. Physical proximity guarantees face-to-face relationships that facilitate common concern.

Even if your neighbour is an unskilled Irish labourer who is living in squalor and would be desperate enough to do your job for less money, you face her every day and are forced to recognize your common humanity. Working-class neighbourhoods were physically bound to the factories, since workers could only afford to travel by foot and had to be close to their places of work. But they provided a principle of organization parallel to the workplaces where people from different factories with different skill levels and occupational histories mingled and found common cause.

Working-class communities were the sites within which locals of workers' unions, political, educational, and social organizations were created. Marx saw them as spontaneous expressions of the communist spirit. They represented a collective coming together, uncoerced by external, alien structures of capital or the state. Their aims were the public good rather than individual profit; but at the same time they became expressions of what he thought was people's natural love of sociability.

> When communist artisans form associations, education and propaganda are their first aims. But the very act of associating creates a new need—the need for society—and what appeared to be a means has become an end. The most striking results of this practical development are to be seen when French socialist workers meet together. Smoking, eating and drinking are no longer simply a means of bringing people together. Company, association, entertainment which also has society as its aim, are sufficient for them; the brotherhood of man is no empty phrase but a reality, and the nobility of man shines forth upon us from their toil worn bodies. (Marx, qtd. in McLellan 87)

The French socialist workers eventually succeeded in overthrowing the government in Paris, establishing the Paris Commune and trying to implement some of their socialist experiments. Their revolution was short-lived and they were defeated and brutally suppressed by the French state. Thirty-thousand communards were shot by troops, while 45,000 were arrested, many of whom were executed. Events like this underscored to all communists and socialists the fact that not only the powers of the capitalist system, but also the powers of the state were ranged against them. The situation posed a theoretical problem to which Marx and Engels offered an ingenious solution.

Increasing the Numbers and Organization of the Workers

The problem was a fundamental and recurring one in the study of social movements. How can the powerless find the power to change their circumstances? The solution hinges on the irony of unintended consequences. Marx and Engels theorized that in the very attempt to consolidate and expand their power, capitalists would find that, despite themselves, they created an equal and opposing force in the form of the organized proletariat. In a nutshell, capitalist development resulted in greater numbers and greater organization of the proletariat.

Let's start with the second principle—organization. Yes, worker associations were spontaneous, but they grew out of a setting—the factory neighbourhood—that capitalism helped to create. Capitalist agriculture drove the "reserve army of labour" from the countryside to the cities where its presence depressed wages for all workers. Industrial capital (in the form of the new factories) was drawn to wherever the cheapest labour could be found—hence to the cities. Marx refers to this as the "centralization of capital."

Factory districts and the associated factory neighbourhoods grew, bringing larger and larger numbers of workers into contact with one another. Capitalism provided the setting for organization. It also provided the motive by failing to secure for workers the necessary means of existence within the working-class neighbourhoods. Finally it supplied some of the tools for organizing. Marx and Engels thought, for instance, that the "military order" that the bricklayers exhibited in rebellion was a reflection of the military order learned in the factories.

You could easily get the impression from reading Marx and Engels that most workers in England and Europe in the 1840s were factory operatives. These were in fact a tiny minority. However, Marx and Engels predicted that they would grow into a majority, as capitalism "created" more of them. Economic logic pointed in that direction. The division of labour in detail did allow commodities to be produced quickly and cheaply, as did many of the new machines. The ability to buy raw materials and sell commodities on a large scale also brought down the unit price of factory-made goods. The factories could therefore drive smaller workshops and independent producers out of business.

In the process craft workers and what Marx called "petty-bourgeois" producers were forced out of work and often found themselves as semi-skilled or unskilled factory operatives. The petty bourgeoisie were those who owned their own businesses and workshops and did the work themselves or with the help of family or a handful of employees. Many small capitalist firms were being replaced by a few big ones. Marx refers to this as the "concentration of capital." The key outcome is that, proportionally, capitalists become fewer and their enemies, the workers, become more numerous.

The Self-Defeating Capitalist Economy

Bankruptcies came in cycles and created brief periods of economic crisis where large numbers of people faced business failure or unemployment together. People in these circumstances buy less, so those businesses that relied on their custom also faced a financial crunch that left the smaller and weaker of them bankrupt. In addition to dividing capitalist societies into two opposing classes, Marx predicted that as these crises became worse they would create moments of social instability and intense dissatisfaction with the capitalist system, and an opportunity for workers to rise up in revolt.

Neither Marx nor Engels lived to see the Great Depression of the 1930s, but it provided a partial illustration of their prediction. Capitalism had created a situation where millions of people were out of work and unable to buy the necessities of life while industrial plants sat idle, capable of producing these necessities, but unable to do so because no profit could be made. Anti-capitalist sentiment was widespread throughout the Western world. However, Marx and Engels were wrong in that this moment of weakness of capitalism did not spark a proletarian revolution like the ones they had seen in Paris in the mid-1800s. Workers never even attempted, in any large-scale fashion, to use their numbers and organizational strength to bring down the capitalist system. A great deal has been written attempting to explain why not. This is certainly a question worth considering for a student of social movements such as you.

Workers did, however, organize to fight their employers and the state in an effort to improve their position *within* the capitalist system. Their success varied relative to their ability to create strong organizations based on solidarity and working-class culture. This process of "class formation" did in some ways follow Marx and Engels' model, as we shall see in the following case study. Historian John Cumbler compared class formation in two industrial towns in Massachusetts between 1880 and 1950. The economy of Lynn, Massachusetts, was based on the shoe-making industry; Fall River's was based first on textiles, then in the 1920s increasingly on electronics components for General Electric. In each town changes in the industries shaped the "built environment" in which people worked, lived, and interacted with one another. Just as Adam Smith and Karl Marx would have predicted, these physical structures shaped social relations.

CLASS FORMATION: LYNN AND FALL RIVER CASE STUDY

The Structure of Capitalist Industry Influences the Structure of Community

Shoe making in Lynn was initially done by skilled craftsmen working in small shops without the assistance of power-driven machinery. Merchants in Boston, who contracted out to these shops, controlled production. For them it increasingly made economic sense to centralize production. Mechanization became a priority when the sewing machine was introduced in 1852. Survival in this industry required quick responses to fluctuations in demand for shoes. It helped to be close to the city's warehouse district to access raw materials, to the working-class neighbourhoods for a ready supply of labour, and to the financial district to arrange the loans necessary to finance production. Real estate firms erected multi-storey factory buildings in the centre of town and leased whole floors to shoe-manufacturing companies. Capitalist development of the shoe industry resulted, rather like Marx would have predicted, in a centralized industry and a town where work, residence, and public life for the working class all focused on the downtown core.

The cotton mills in Fall River were centralized initially. They clustered around a waterfall on the Quesquechan River in order to harness it for power. Fall River, like many early industrial towns, grew up around this natural power source. However, the capacity of the falls was finite and expansion required a shift to steam power in the 1880s and 1890s. The new steam mills required a lot of space—they could not be stacked in multi-storey buildings like the shoe factories. They

also required a ready supply of water. For these reasons, they were built on the town's periphery, often several miles from the falls.

Textile companies built accommodation for workers surrounding the mills. These residential areas took shape as loosely connected villages with names like Mechanicsville, Border City, and Flint Village. Labour demands were more stable in this industry, and it was not as necessary to be able to access a single flexible labour pool as it was in the shoe industry. The end result, by the beginning of the 20th century, was that while workers were sorted into exclusively working-class neighbourhoods, these were decentralized, unlike what had been predicted by Marx.

Working-class solidarity developed in both Lynn and Fall River, but in Lynn it proved more enduring and encompassed the whole industry. Those who shared the tenements and working-class streets found themselves drawn together through common neighbourliness and mutual aid in domestic tasks. To avoid the high prices charged by private shops, people set up and ran their own co-operative stores.

The main labour organization in Lynn, the Knights of St. Crispins, was designed to be more than just a labour union. It also sponsored social and community activities. "After work," says Cumbler, "workers would drift over to the union hall to play cards, pool, and billiards and to sing union songs and listen to old-timers' tales of past struggles" (Cumbler 431). As was the case for the French workers Marx observed, people's politics became their social and leisure activities as well.

Urban form was important to sustaining class-based community networks. Neighbourhoods were exclusively working class in both towns, but in Lynn they all clustered within walking distance of the town centre, which had a public square that became a more general community focus than the residential neighbourhood. Central Square was a public space of interaction where people's paths crossed going to and from work or when they wanted to relax or socialize in the pubs or cafés. It was the kind of place that many cities still have, where you can always go and find something happening, and lots of people out on the street.

One worker recalled it to Cumbler in the following terms:

> If you were to come down to central square in Lynn, the place was full of people, always a friend, if you go to a restaurant and have a cup of coffee, there was half a dozen friends at least, who were sitting down, having a cup of coffee or what not, something like that. (qtd. in Cumbler 432)

It was the place to hang out. And hanging out inevitably meant talking shop, finding out what was going on in your own industry—the dirt on the latest management plan, the cause and consequences of shifts in the shoe market, or tips on job openings. It also meant framing the world—municipal affairs, government policy, the capitalist economy—from a uniquely working-class perspective. Workers were suspicious of news that came from "moneyed men or capitalists" and relied on their own information networks to make sense of the world (Cumbler 435).

Immigration Tests Class Solidarity

In both Lynn and Fall River the sense of common identity and solidarity that workers constructed was tested by successive waves of immigration. While capitalist agriculture developed if anything more

quickly in North America than in Europe, the "excess" rural population that it created did not necessarily flock to the cities. Displaced rural people could as easily head out for the frontier. American capitalists often had to "import" workers from the reserve armies developing in other countries. The textile workers needed to staff the first wave of expansion in Fall River came from some of the cities that Engels had observed in northern England.

In Lynn, the shoe companies recruited Irish workers in the 1860s; English, French-Canadian, German, and Scandinavian workers in the 1870s and 1880s; and after 1905, Polish, Russian, Italian, and Greek workers. The general sequence was similar for Fall River and many other places in North America: immigrants from the British Isles followed by northern Europeans, then southern and eastern Europeans. It reflected a 19th-century hierarchy of prejudice according to which the British were believed to be the most and eastern Europeans the least desirable "races." The challenge for workers was to overcome these societal prejudices in themselves as well as to integrate the newcomers into an emerging class-based culture so that they began to identify primarily as workers rather than Catholic, francophone, Greek, or what have you. To use Marx's language, they sought to free themselves from exclusive ethnic or national prejudice in the name of a universal "brotherhood of man."

Immigrants dealing with a foreign language and culture always find comfort in the company of others dealing with the same "culture shock" and frequently congregate in the same neighbourhoods and recreate familiar cultural institutions and traditions from "home." Those who found themselves living in Lynn near Central Square quickly discovered that they could also experience a sense of belonging in the cafés and union halls of their fellow

workers. Ethnic-based community organizations tended to be short-lived. In Fall
River, immigrants tended to congregate
in the separate neighbourhoods and "villages" dispersed at the edges of town. Since
there was no central meeting area, ethnic
exclusiveness tended to persist.

The French Canadians were brought in to
Fall River in the 1870s as strikebreakers, so
initially they were doubly resented as cheap
foreign labour and as "class traitors." Textile
companies continued to recruit them to the
mills up until the turn of the century. They
tended to work in separate mills and live in
their own neighbourhoods close by—"Little
Canada" or "French Village" in town and
"Globe Village" on the southern edge of
town. Still, English and Irish workers made
special efforts to integrate them into the
social life and formal organizations of the
union movement. And as one observer put
it, "... after some years the genius of unions
took hold upon them." They were encouraged
to take positions of authority within union
organizations and sat alongside English and
Irish workers on the strike committee in the
walkout of 1884. In the strike of 1889, they
were on the forefront of organizing and
"were active in the formal parades, dances,
rallies and other activities during the strike"
(Cumbler 437).

Decentralized urban form made it difficult but not impossible to maintain worker
solidarity in Fall River. However, successive
waves of immigration from Poland and Por-
tugal eventually overwhelmed the capacity
of working-class institutions to integrate the
newcomers. The long walk from the outlying
"villages" to the centre of town inhibited
the ongoing face-to-face contact that builds
acceptance and trust. It was in these outlying areas that weaknesses in solidarity first
began to show. Workers here were the last to
respond to calls to strike or march in demonstrations, and were the first to capitulate and
return to work. These sorts of "betrayals"
made it increasingly difficult for the English,
Irish, and now the French Canadians to overcome their ethnic prejudices. The Portuguese
and Poles were seen as irredeemably "other."
"Poles and Portuguese, who live in crowded
tenements," complained one worker, "will
sleep and eat according to the needs of the
employers" (Cumbler 438).

The Labour Process and Class Divisions Based on Skill

Cumbler argues that it was not just immigration and decentralization that undermined
working-class solidarity in Fall River, but also
the labour process. To illustrate this, he again
compares Fall River and Lynn. The shoemakers in Lynn were subject to division of labour
in detail and deskilling. By 1880 the work
had been subdivided into 33 separate tasks
assigned to different workers. Nonetheless,
the work still involved more skill than textile
manufacture. Also, while a shoe operative
might do a single task on a sewing machine,
he or she still set the speed of the machine,
unlike workers on the huge spinning "mules,"
which were powered from a central source.
The shop floors were relatively small in the
shoe factories, and the workers, unlike the
cotton workers, were able to interact as part
of the work and were also able to chat with
one another while they worked.

Deskilled work in the textile factories offered lower pay, and Fall River families were
much more likely to rely on the wages of
both parents as well as the children to make
ends meet. Pay was based on piecework; in
other words, people were paid by the amount
of cloth produced rather than the number
of hours worked. Like the English workers
whom Engels observed, workers were responsible for cleaning and maintaining their machines and would often do this during their

breaks. While Lynn workers would typically be hanging out in the lunchrooms or cafés in Central Square talking politics, Fall River workers would be bolting their lunches next to their machines, anxious to get back to work. To make things worse, toward the end of the century textile manufacturers in Lynn began to feel the pinch of competition from the southern U.S. Instead of modernizing their plants, they demanded "speed ups and stretch outs" from their workers. People were required to manage more looms, up to 16 at a time when these were fitted with semi-automatic devices. They were also required to work longer hours.

Workers in the textile industry had little time during their workday or after hours to socialize or engage in political activities. The work was physically exhausting, but also mind-numbing for the reasons that Adam Smith had identified. Exploitation and alienation might have given Fall River workers more reason to resist, but left them with fewer resources to do so. It sapped their energy, dulled their minds, and robbed them of time both on and off the job.

Cumbler confirms the effect of labour process on class formation when he shows how even in Lynn when the labour process changed, "the strong community oriented labour movement of the shoe workers" was undermined. In the 1920s the shoe industry went into decline, and a General Electric plant took up the slack. GE designed its plant on the basis of "Taylorism," a new approach to workplace design that applied "scientific" principles to increasing worker surveillance and deskilling. Former shoe workers describe the new workplace as like being "in prison" (Cumbler 438).

Cumbler's case study points to an important principle of social dissent that Marx and Engels were not sufficiently aware of. That is, misery is not enough to incite social dissent. People must also have some means at their disposal to enable them to act. Lynn workers were more militant in part because they still had some control over their lives. Time and energy were essential, but having at least some money to spare for union causes must also have been important. How else would they have rented union halls, printed pamphlets, and bought the books that their members used to educate and inform themselves?

Other historians have exposed this mistake more clearly. Where Marx thought that the Paris uprising of 1848 was the first truly proletarian revolution, George Rudé has shown, by meticulous sorting through such sources as police records of those arrested, that "masters, shopkeepers and independent craftsmen ... may have outnumbered the wage earners by as much as two to one" (Rudé 236). Furthermore many of the violent class conflicts that Engels documented did not originate in the most overcrowded and destitute neighbourhoods that he describes in the *Condition of the Working Class*, but rather in the more settled and prosperous working-class districts. Again, the participants tended to be skilled artisans, not deskilled factory operatives.

Craft workers were very likely motivated by the threat to their independence that the new forms of industrial capitalism posed. The growth of alienation in factory work and the visible evidence of misery in the worst neighbourhoods no doubt shaped the politics of the relatively better off. While the tour of misery through the great industrial cities could spark moral outrage and sympathy in an industrialist's son like Engels, for a worker these emotions would likely have been mixed with identification that came from the knowledge that "there but for the grace of God go I." Workers often did create common cause despite real differences in their circumstances.

As the labour movement developed, it nonetheless remained a great temptation for skilled workers to organize separately from the unskilled. Skilled workers always had more clout because they were less replaceable and therefore harder to fire. Unions of the skilled, so called "craft unions," could even become means to exclude other workers—the unskilled, women, ethnic minorities—from the benefits they could win for their members. Notably in Lynn, where unions sprang out of neighbourhood and community that included all workers, skilled shoe workers repeatedly resisted efforts to organize craft unions. They maintained solidarity with their unskilled "brothers" even when craft unions offered much better wage contracts. This is an interesting element of solidarity that we will see again—the idea that solidarity involves a willingness to self-sacrifice in the interests of some larger identity—the brotherhood of shoe workers, or perhaps the "brotherhood of man."

Marx clearly imagined that worker unity would eventually be based on the elimination of differences. Independent craftsmen would become wage earners, skilled work would become deskilled, the cheapening of tasks and competition from the reserve army of labour would drive wages down until all workers were equally impoverished. This is the theory of "emiseration." Marx also expected that the culture of mutualism and class solidarity would erode what he saw as meaningless ethnic, religious, and other cultural differences among workers. But does unity have to depend upon the elimination of differences? This is a particularly important question for workers in the 21st century. While alienation and exploitation affect millions of workers, there are still enormous differences in the levels of skill, autonomy, legal rights, and economic benefits that workers in different jobs, industries, and countries enjoy. There are also huge differences in workers' experiences and opportunities depending on their gender, race, or nationality. Can workers fight together for change while accepting their differences? If so, how would the model of organizing differ from the one outlined by Marx and Engels?

GLOBALIZATION AND CROSS-BORDER CLASS FORMATION

The principles of class formation that we have so far discussed are local. They depend upon ongoing face-to-face interaction to build familiarity and trust between people who might otherwise be suspicious of one another because they compete for work, because they have different levels of skill that give differential advantages in this competition, because they are from different cultural and ethnic backgrounds. The first step in local class formation is the making of community.

The interactions that form the basis of community are bound by two physical "containers": the shop floor delimited by building walls, and the neighbourhood by a collection of streets and squares within convenient walking distance of one another. These define the "local." Before workers could afford cars (this did not happen for most until the postwar prosperity of the 1950s), workplace and neighbourhood tended to be physically close and the networks they defined overlapping. People who worked together tended to live in the same neighbourhoods, reinforcing bonds of community among them.

Distanciated Relationships of Capitalism: The Cash Nexus

From its very beginnings the principles of order in capitalism, by contrast, were not merely local. Adam Smith distinguishes between the ways in which what he calls "trifling manufactures" and "great manufactures" are organized under capitalism. The former is organized on the shop floor.

> ... the whole number of workmen must necessarily be small; and those employed in every different branch of the work can often be collected into the same workhouse [i.e., workshop or factory], and placed at once under the view of the spectator [i.e., supervisor]. (Smith)

In this case relationships are local and rely on face-to-face surveillance to coordinate them.

In the case of the great manufactures, he tells us, "... it is impossible to collect [all the workers] into the same workhouse. We can seldom see more, at one time, than those employed in one single branch." The workers in different branches and different specializations are spread out in different workplaces, often in distant cities or even other countries. They are related, but intangibly. Smith recognizes that this is difficult to visualize, so he gives an extended example of what he means by looking at the manufacture of a coat.

> The woollen coat, for example, which covers the day-labourer, as coarse and rough as it may appear, is the produce of the joint labour of a great multitude of workmen. The shepherd, the sorter of the wool, the wool-comber or carder, the dyer, the scribbler, the spinner, the weaver, the fuller, the dresser, with many others, must all join their different arts in order to complete even this homely production. How many merchants and carriers, besides, must have been employed in transporting the materials from some of those workmen to others who often live in a very distant part of the country? How much commerce and navigation in particular, how many shipbuilders, sailors, sail-makers, ropemakers, must have been employed in order to bring together the different drugs [chemicals] made use of by the dyer, which often come from the remotest corners of the world? ... Were we to examine, in the same manner, all the different parts of his dress and household furniture, the coarse linen shirt which he wears next his skin, the shoes which cover his feet, the bed which he lies on, and all the different parts which compose it, ... if we examine, I say, all these things, and consider what a variety of labour is employed about each of them, we shall be sensible that, without the assistance and co-operation of many thousands, the very meanest person in a civilized country could not be provided, even according to, what we very falsely imagine, the easy and simple manner in which he is commonly accommodated. (Smith)

No one person does, or could very easily, oversee this "joint labour of a great multitude." How is this activity coordinated? What motivates those involved to "co-operate" and assist the poor day-labourer? Certainly it is not caring for him and his need for a coat, since they will never know him. Nor are most of them likely to meet or come to know one another. We will use the term "distanciated" to refer to these sorts of impersonal relationships from a distance.

In this passage Smith indicates that technologies of communication and transport make distanciated relationships possible. These technologies are not used to create long-distance personal relationships, but to facilitate impersonal contracts to buy, sell, and ship commodities for money. The web of contracts is coordinated by the competitive dynamic of supply and demand that Smith calls "the market." What motivates the players in this complex is not concern for the wearer of the coat or for anyone else but themselves and the prospect of personal economic gain. Smith thought it was a marvel that the "co-operation of many thousands," unknown to one another and dispersed across vast distances, could be founded on individual self-interest in this way.

He helped to define "liberalism," which is the faith that the market will coordinate distanciated relationships in the best way possible, in a way that is the most advantageous to all. Marx saw the market as the epitome of alienation. Here was an impersonal system entrusted with the social function of coordinating our collective endeavours, under which flesh-and-blood people were expected to act in an asocial, selfish, and competitive fashion. The market, he and Engels wrote, "... left no other nexus between people than naked self-interest, than callous 'cash payment'" and "egotistical calculation" (Marx and Engels). It removed moral considerations from people's relationships; indeed, the competitive pressures of the market not only permitted, but also required that employers exploit their workers, and workers accept exploitation and alienation.

Writing in 1848, Marx and Engels saw, even more clearly than Smith, the growing transnational character of modern capitalism. The way they wrote about it makes it sound very like the "globalization" that is so much a feature of our present reality.

The bourgeoisie has, through its exploitation of the world market, given a cosmopolitan character to production and consumption in every country.... All old-established national industries have been destroyed or are daily being destroyed. They are dislodged by new industries, whose introduction becomes a life and death question for all civilized nations, by industries that no longer work up indigenous raw material, but raw material drawn from the remotest zones; industries whose products are consumed, not only at home, but in every quarter of the globe. In place of the old wants, satisfied by the production of the country, we find new wants, requiring for their satisfaction the products of distant lands and climes. In place of the old local and national seclusion and self-sufficiency, we have intercourse in every direction, universal inter-dependence of nations. And as in material, so also in intellectual production. The intellectual creations of individual nations become common property. National one-sidedness and narrow-mindedness become more and more impossible, and from the numerous national and local literatures, there arises a world literature.

Worker Internationalism and the Problem of Coordinating Difference

They admired this internationalism and sought to ensure that worker resistance was transnational as well. Their model for how this would happen is clever as it hinges on the ways in which capitalism provides workers with the tools of resistance. The union of the workers, they wrote,

... is helped on by the improved means of communication that are created by Modern Industry, and that place the workers of different localities in contact with one another. It was just this contact that was needed to centralize the numerous local struggles, all of the same character, into one national struggle between classes. But every class struggle is a political struggle. And that union, to attain which the burghers of the Middle Ages, with their miserable highways, required centuries, the modern proletarians, thanks to railways, achieve in a few years.

Still, railways, printing presses, and steamships were only technological means of conquering distance. What social or organizational principle, other than the market, could coordinate relationships between millions of workers across great distances? Marx and Engels had seen the outlines of a model of local class formation in the spontaneous forms of order that sprang up in factory neighbourhoods. But these had been based on the principle of face-to-face caring and concern for others. National and transnational class formation would bring together people, most of whom could never meet face-to-face even once, never mind on an ongoing basis. The problem was how to create international unity without creating "external" organizational structures that people found abstract and distant from them, and over which they felt they had little control.

Workers' first experiment with organizing internationally—the International Workers Association (IWA or "First International")—showed just how difficult this could be. The internationalism of the IWA encompassed only the industrializing countries of the 19th century in western

Europe and the United States. (In 1862 when the IWA formed, Canada, like many other countries, was integrated into the worldwide capitalist economy, but not as an industrial player with a significant urban proletariat.) Nonetheless worker experience varied enough from country to country to create tensions within the new organization. Some governments, like the French, were responding to the threat of worker activism with violence and repression, while others, like the English, were beginning to learn that efforts to co-opt the workers were likely to yield a mutually beneficial détente.

English workers were very gradually gaining basic civil rights—the right to vote, to hold office, to organize. In France and other European countries, workers still had to organize illegally, in secret. Property requirements for voting or holding office excluded millions of workers from the democratic process. Where the parliamentary process was so blatantly designed to serve the interests of the propertied classes, the appeal of revolutionary violence was much greater for workers. But the English saw the promise of eventual inclusion in that process and had begun to see some of the results of state intervention on their behalf. Intense lobbying had resulted in 1847 in the passage of the 10-Hour Bill, which limited the length of the workday for women and workers under the age of 18. Municipal governments had begun the public works in water treatment, sewage, and urban planning that were to transform life in the cities. Engels was to report in 1892 that the ugly conditions he had seen in Little Ireland had been swept away by urban reform (Engels 24).

For workers from these different contexts, the promise of worker internationalism varied. Workers who faced jail or the firing squad for their activism relied upon international networks to provide them with safe haven. English workers aided their French comrades subject to persecution, held mass demonstrations against slavery, and suffered near starvation to support a boycott of cotton made using slave labour in the southern United States (Foster 46). But many English trade unionists saw internationalism as a kind of "foreign policy" instrument to defend their own trade union gains from being undermined by immigrant workers (in the way that the workers brought in from other countries were to undermine unionism in Lynn and Fall River, Massachusetts). English delegates to the IWA were increasingly interested in preserving and "exporting" the trade union and parliamentary model that they felt had so much potential in their own country.

Many French and European delegates were more likely to follow Bakunin or Marx, who saw a role for the IWA in "smashing the capitalist state." There were also ideological differences among those who supported violence. Bakunin's followers called for acts of violence to be committed immediately. These, they thought, would quickly escalate into an orgy of destruction of all "bourgeois" institutions of government and make way for spontaneous "outbreaks" of co-operation among working people. Marx stressed the need for slowly building up the organizational capacity of workers—through spontaneous mutual aid, formal unions, co-operatives, and political parties—to provide both the strength to carry out a successful revolution as well as a set of skills, socialist values, and institutions that could form the basis of a new society.

Proudhon, another anarchist within the IWA, advocated non-violent means of defeating capitalism. Workers were already beginning to form co-operatives in which they collectively owned their own workshops and ran them democratically. Proudhon thought that the entire economy could gradually be transformed in this way from one based on competitive private enterprise to one based

on co-operative public enterprise. The result would be a democratically run economy and a decentralized political system in which federated workers' councils could manage political affairs without the need for a central government. He, like Bakunin, was very sensitive to the "tyranny" that centralized political organizations could exercise, regardless of whether they were run by workers or capitalists. These ideas are all very intriguing in and of themselves, but what I want to focus on is how this diversity of opinions and interests was managed within the IWA. Marx played a key and telling role here.

Marx took part in the formation of the First International, apparently with the aim of ensuring that it followed what he thought was the correct ideological path. He drafted the IWA's first statement of principle. In its wording you can see the outlines of his agenda. The first line asserts:

> That the emancipation of the working classes must be conquered by the working classes themselves; that the struggle for the emancipation of the working classes means not a struggle for class privileges and monopolies, but for equal rights and duties, and the abolition of all class rule. (Foster 51)

He is ruling out the type of unionism that defends special privileges for English workers or for workers in skilled crafts. The "abolition of all class rule" means the abolition of the "bourgeois state" that English workers are beginning to view as a legitimate institution to work with rather than against. Still, the document was general enough in its wording to accommodate differences of political interpretation.

However, once delegates within the IWA had signed on to this general statement of principles, Marx conducted an ideological war against what he derisively labelled the "sects" led by "amateurs" like Bakunin and Proudhon. He saw that petty bourgeois workers were drawn to co-operatives, sometimes as a way to collectively improve their access to capital or markets. He felt that if the petty bourgeoisie dominated the socialist movement they would never be able to relinquish their interest in the ownership of capital. This is why he always insisted on the leadership role of the proletariat in any truly liberatory movement. Marx dismissed Proudhon's vision as "bourgeois socialism" that would result in a "bourgeoisie without a proletariat."

International Organization and the Risk of Bureaucratization

Marx had great prestige among workers and his followers within the IWA eventually came to dominate its General Council. In 1871 this body passed new resolutions that strengthened their power relative to the national and local affiliates, and made "political action" aimed at a "social revolution" and the "abolition of all classes" central to the association's program. By this time it was clear that "political action" was code for Marxist political action as against, for example, the "economic" strategy of change through the co-operative movement or trade unionism. Marx had defeated the "sects," but left many feeling disaffected and excluded from the association. He had helped to create an institutional structure that many felt was imposing an ideology and program from the top down without sufficient regard for the differences of opinion among participants and the autonomy of member organizations. It was a difficult problem because at the same time as being inclusive, to be effective an organization must have a common goal and program.

The result was a series of defections that led to the demise of the First International in 1872 (Drachkovitch 32 ff.). Although Marx would never have seen it in these terms, in a sense his efforts resulted in a form of "alienation" in a place that one would hardly expect it—a workers' organization—and for which he had no theoretical explanation or remedy. The failure of the First International points to an ongoing problem for social movements. That is, how is it possible to organize large numbers of people, particularly if they are spread out across great distances, without sacrificing tolerance for diversity, active local participation, and autonomy? This is often referred to as the problem of "bureaucratization."

Unions, in their efforts to unite workers beyond the bounds of the local, have tended to fall prey to bureaucratization. In the late 1970s Ford workers in different European plants sought to share information about Ford strategies because they suspected that the company was attempting to play one group of workers off against another. Their unions were affiliates of the International Metalworkers Federation (IMF) with headquarters in Geneva. In order for Swedish workers to communicate with Spanish workers, they discovered, the bureaucratic procedure was as follows:

> [First] you must ask your union official; that official goes to the international representative of your union; he sends a letter or telegram to Geneva; Geneva distributes it to the different national unions in the different countries; they ask the convenor or maybe the union official at the specific plant, and the information eventually gets back to Geneva, and from Geneva to your union. It may take about 4 to 6 months to get an answer, if at all. (Huws et al. 61)

While it would have been easier to just pick up the phone and talk worker to worker, that would have been against the rules. It is very common for bureaucracies to require that information travel "vertically" in this way—up the hierarchy and then back down the hierarchy. The idea is that the national unions or federations speak *for* the members and must be accountable for what gets said in their name. Therefore, there must be centralized control over communications at the higher levels. Here the model of international relations between workers has little to do with "horizontal" worker-to-worker relations, but is instead about relations between national union bureaucracies.

National union federations like the Canadian Labour Congress and international union federations like the International Metalworkers Federation also collaborate on international issues through affiliation with international trades union bodies such as the International Convention of Free Trade Unions (ICFTU). The ICFTU acts as a voice for labour in intergovernmental affairs—the UN, multilateral trade agreements such as the WTO, and the like. It lobbies for agreements on international labour standards, and helps to expose abuses of labour rights worldwide (see its Web site at www.icftu.org). While it claims to speak for 155 million workers worldwide, many of these are scarcely aware of its existence, never mind actively engaged in its work. It is a vertical structure perched atop vertical structures. There have been numerous calls recently for new models of labour internationalism that are innovative, flexible, and responsive to worker input (Waterman).

The idea is that the labour movement must match the flexibility and innovation that corporations have discovered in the latest round of globalization. In Marx's time something as simple as a coat was assembled from components manufactured at different points on the globe and traded as "commodities" across borders. Workers, too, whose labour power had become a commodity, crossed borders and oceans to sell their labour in distant places like Fall River, Massachusetts. The 19th century was an unusual period of "free trade" and open borders for commodities and labour.

That openness has been renewed and expanded in the decades leading up to the 21st century for many commodities. However, instead of "importing" cheap labour to work in assembly plants in the industrialized countries, firms are increasingly able to "export" the assembly plants to countries where not only is labour cheaper, but taxes, labour legislation, and other "costs" of doing business are lower. This capacity of firms to easily relocate aspects of their production process to wherever in the globe is advantageous is called the "mobility of capital."

The mobility of capital has created new "proximities" between workers at opposite ends of the globe in the sense that they can now compete with one another for the same manufacturing jobs. The threat to organized workers is similar to that faced by textile workers in Fall River when non-union French Canadian workers were brought in to take their places. The difference now is that competition from non-union workers anywhere on the globe—Mexico, China, or the new sweatshops in Toronto—can weaken union protection for similar workers anywhere else on the globe.

Since the 1970s employers have been closing down union plants and shifting production to countries or special regions called export processing zones or maquiladoras where workers are non-union and union organizing is difficult and sometimes dangerous for workers. This strategy has become so effective that management can often prevent workers from organizing unions or going on strike simply by dropping not so subtle "hints" such as posting a map with an arrow pointing from the plant site to Mexico (Klein 224).

Multinational corporations have made the world their "global village." Workers can use some of the same tools—cheap long-distance telecommunications, Internet, and jet travel—to shrink the distances between them. How they use these tools to build new forms of global resistance is still being worked out. Would it be possible or desirable to forge the sort of "solidarity" based on a common culture and class identity that was so effective in Lynn, Massachusetts? Can the organizational principle be bureaucracy, and at what cost?

Perhaps the best we can do is look at one or two examples of new forms of labour internationalism to see if any themes or principles can be identified. As you read the following case, think about the question of class and Marx's insistence on the leader-ship role of the proletariat. What social classes are involved here and what roles do they play? In what sense are "workers of the world" uniting here? Also, think about the relationship between the labour movement and the union movement. What are the pros and cons for workers of relying on non-union organizations, networks, and alliances?

BOX 1.1:

INTERNATIONAL SOLIDARITY WITH GUATEMALAN COCA-COLA WORKERS

In 1975 Coca-Cola bottlers succeeded in forming the first and only union (which they called by the Spanish acronym STEGAC) in any of the three bottling plants in Guatemala. This was an enormous demonstration of courage and solidarity in a country where union organizers were routinely tortured and murdered by company thugs or members of the army. Workers resisted efforts of the plant owner (not the giant multinational Coca-Cola but a subcontractor) to break the union. When 160 union members were fired, the workers staged a 16-day occupation of the factory, threatened a general strike, and won reinstatement. The company then hired "mobile military police" to intimidate the workers. In 1978 the killings began. By 1980 eight workers had been murdered and four "disappeared" by death squads. The union's leader and its first lawyer went into exile to escape death threats. Acts of cruelty and intimidation continued, including the torture and rape of the next lawyer's 16-year-old daughter.

Prior to exile, Guatemalan unionists had already found support from other unions, church groups, and human rights organizations in Costa Rica. Through these connections they were put in touch with two transnational allies, the Interfaith Centre on Corporate Responsibility (ICCR; www.iccr.org) and the International Union of Food, Agricultural, Hotel, Restaurant, Catering, Tobacco, and Allied Workers' Association (IUF; www.IUF.org). The ICCR represents "faith-based" institutions that own billions of dollars' worth of shares in multinational corporations. Sharehold-ers have a right to vote on company policy and the ICCR used this power to pressure Coca-Cola to investigate the Guatemalan bottler and establish a "code of conduct of labour relations" as a condition of licence for all of its subcontractors. This is an interesting example of using capitalist investment for social reform.

Although it is a large bureaucracy, the IUF became mobilized to support the Guatemalan cause in part because of the personal contacts of an individual official, general secretary Dan Gallin. Gallin became aware of the blatant abuses of labour rights when he toured Guatemala as a member of the human rights organization Amnesty International (www.amnesty.org) in 1979. Through his contacts with other international union federations he initiated campaigns against two targets. One was the Guatemalan government, which had been both a perpetrator and tacit supporter of anti-union repression. The Canadian Labour Congress pressured Ottawa to cut off aid to Guatemala; the Israeli labour federation, Histadrut, and the United Auto Workers in the U.S. lobbied their governments to end military support to Guatemala. Gallin also mobilized a European tourism boycott.

The other target was Coke, which continued to deny responsibility for the abuses of its sub-contractor. Workers staged industrial actions in Finland, New Zealand, and Sweden. European and American students got their schools to pull Coke from their campuses and a worldwide boycott was organized. This sort of anti-corporate activism became much more common in the 1990s. It hinges on corporations' sensitivity to their brand image, which they spend billions of dollars to promote. The old "Things go better with Coke" message would have been a bit tarnished by the alternate slogan circulating in the early 1980s: "In Guatemala, Coca-Cola is a name for murder."

International solidarity helped to create a space locally in which community-based union activity could survive. It gave workers relative immunity from persecution, which allowed them to stage another plant occupation without suffering reprisals. Coke had decided to close the plant in 1984 for "economic reasons." For 379 days the workers occupied the plant and kept up a "... daily routine of maintenance, assemblies, education and leisure activity." Like the Lynn and Fall River unions of the last century, STEGAC had always attended to a wide range of work and non-work needs of its members. In the end, the plant reopened under new management, most of the original workers were hired back, and laid off workers were given a total of $250,000 in back pay.

Sources: "Sweatshops and Coke, New Labor Battlegrounds," *Infopress Central America Report* 29, no. 44 (2002): 1–3; August 20, 2004, www.xyx.org; Max Fuller, "In Guatemala, Coca-Cola Is a Name for Murder," March 1, 1998, Columbia Solidarity Campaign Web site, August 16, 2004, www.columbiasolidarity.org.uk/Solidarity%2013/guatemala.html; Thali G. Kidder, "Networks in Transnational Labor Organizing," in *Restructuring World Politics: Transnational Social Movements, Networks, and Norms*, edited by Sanjeev Khagram, James V. Riker, and Kathryn Sikkink (Minneapolis; London: University of Minnesota Press, 2002).

Labour Responses to the Dynamism of Capital

> "Constant revolutionizing of pro-
> duction, uninterrupted disturbance
> of all social conditions, everlasting
> uncertainty and agitation distin-
> guish the [capitalist] epoch from
> all earlier ones. All fixed, fast-frozen
> relations, with their train of ancient
> and venerable prejudices and opin-
> ions, are swept away, all new-formed
> ones become antiquated before they
> can ossify. All that is solid melts into
> air ..." (Marx and Engels)

In this lyrical passage Marx and Engels acknowledge the dynamism of capitalism. However, they were not quite able to foresee how the "new-formed" *class* relations in which they put such store might also be transformed by this ceaseless change. Remember, their model of class formation was that the centralization of capital would bring together large numbers of people working and living in the same urban neighbourhoods. Faced with common oppression, these people would, over time, build a common culture, class identity, and array of formal organizations—unions being just one of these.

They did not foresee the degree to which workers would become mobile. Once workers were able to commute from private homes in the suburbs to workplaces anywhere in the city, the link between work and residential community became "disorganized" for many. Nor did Marx and Engels foresee how the mobility of capital would allow multinational firms to take flight just as soon as the culture of worker resistance began to "ossify" or develop strength and permanence in any one spot.

Suburbanization in Canada and other industrialized countries meant that increasingly workers' lives in common took place only at work. Union activity was only a small part of that life in common. Workers come and go. Continuity, in terms of values, understanding of and commitment to worker causes came increasingly from the union and its bureaucracy only, not from a working-class culture and identity nurtured by a surrounding community. In this context the union relies less on volunteer commitment and more on paid staff supported by union dues to ensure that it remains a permanent presence in workers' lives.

It becomes much easier for anti-union employers to represent unions as peripheral and external to workers' lives. Wal-Mart tells its managers that unions are "third parties," and that they "... are not a club, sorority, fraternity or social organization. They are a business, a big business that needs to make money.... Where do they get their money? Out of the pockets of their members!" (Mason)

The Challenge of Organizing the Service and Retail Sectors

The Wal-Mart memo goes on to warn that, "due to the decline in union membership in recent years, new members are more crucial than ever if unions are going to survive.... Wal-Mart is an attractive target for unions because of the large number of Associates [Wal-Mart's euphemism for employees] we employ and our growth in the grocery industry." This is true: Wal-Mart and a number of other giants within the retail and service sectors such as McDonald's and Sodexho Marriott have become targets of unionization drives in North America.

Capital flight from Canada and the U.S. has weakened the well-unionized industrial sector of the economy. The blue-collar jobs that have disappeared have tended to be the ones that were most "expensive" to employers—not just well paid, but full-time, long term, and covered by health and pension benefits. New jobs within the growing service and retail sectors are designed to be low skilled, part-time, and temporary. Wages and benefits can be kept to a minimum and turnover tends to be high. These jobs have also proven to be notoriously difficult to unionize. The big players like Wal-Mart and McDonald's pride themselves in remaining union free.

BOX 1.2:

WORLD BANK HIGHLIGHTS POSITIVE DEVELOPMENT IMPACT OF TRADE UNIONS

Brussels, February 12, 2003 (ICFTU online): The positive impact of trade unions in economic development, as well as evidence showing the role of trade unions in combating discrimination and in reducing inequality, are among the central findings of a new World Bank publication, launched today. According to the ICFTU, however, there is still a long way to go in terms of translating these findings into policy at the national level.

The report, "Unions and Collective Bargaining," reaffirms the Bank's support for the core labour standards "as important elements of a well-functioning labour market." Based on a survey of more than a thousand studies on the economic effects of unions and collective bargaining, the newly released book concludes that high unionisation rates often lead to lower inequality of earnings, decreased wage discrimination against women and minority workers, and improved economic performance. It finds that the positive impacts of unionisation tend to be greater in countries with highly coordinated collective bargaining than in countries where the labour movement is more fragmented.

The Bank's communiqué announcing the launch includes statements endorsing the positive economic impact of "sound industrial relations" from managing director Mamphela Ramphele. The lead author of the book, Zafiris Tzannatos, is quoted as stating that with the transformations brought about by globalisation, "labour standards can no longer be the concern of just individual governments but also of the entire international community. [...] Labour standards are now a prominent item on the international agenda and are likely to stay there for a long time to come."

Of particular significance on the eve of the eighth ICFTU World Women's Conference, which opens next week in Melbourne, is the fact that the publication also points to the marked benefits of unionisation for women workers. According to the report, union membership tends to reduce wage differences between men and women.

"Although it comes as no surprise to the ICFTU, this public acknowledgement by the World Bank, backed by in-depth research, is welcome," said ICFTU General Secretary Guy Ryder. "The Bank must now go on to translate these important findings into policy, which may involve a significant shift in its organisational culture. In contrast to the worker-friendly statements at the global level, country-level Bank staff still routinely advise governments to, in effect, violate the core labour standards by making access to unionisation and collective bargaining more difficult."

In follow-up to a high-level round of meetings between Bank officials and representatives of ICFTU affiliates and Global Union Federations which took place last October, trade unions around the world will be able to raise the findings of this latest report in their dealings with country-level representatives of the Bank.

"Unions and Collective Bargaining: Economic Effects in a Global Environment," which is 185 pages long, will shortly be available on the World Bank's web site (www.worldbank.org) in English only.

The ICFTU represents 158 million workers in 231 affiliated organisations in 150 countries and territories. ICFTU is also a member of Global Unions: www.global-unions.org.

Source: ICFTU. "World Bank Highlights Positive Development Impact of Trade Unions," February 12, 2003. ICFTU Online, August 27, 2004, www.icftu.org/displaydocument.asp?Index=991217201&Language=EN. Reproduced here with permission.

In Canada and the United States it is illegal for an employer to dismiss workers for attempting to organize a union. Wal-Mart has been indicted for doing this in the U.S. (Featherstone, "Will Labor"; UFCW) Mc-Donald's has gotten away with it in Canada. After workers filed for union certification in St. Hubert, Quebec, McDonald's closed the outlet ostensibly for economic reasons unrelated to unionization (Featherstone, "Burger International"). Not surprisingly there is now a pervasive fear among service and retail workers that forming a union will result in the loss of their jobs. Union organizers are looking for one or two signal successes to break this psychological barrier. However, fear is not the only reason unionization continues to fail. To understand what else is going on, consider the experience of Sarah Inglis, who attempted to organize her fellow McDonald's workers in Orangeville, Ontario, in 1993 (Inglis).

There was enough resentment about management's abuse of power in firings and allocation of hours as well as "verbal and sexual harassment" that a majority of workers signed union cards with the Service Employees International Union. Unionization is a highly

formal process governed by provincial laws. Once a certain percentage of workers signs cards, the organizers apply for certification with a labour board, which typically requires a formal election to be held. Once the union is certified, the employer is legally obligated to recognize it and bargain with it. At the first sign of union activity, managers at Wal-Mart or McDonald's are instructed to call a "hotline" that puts them in touch with staff and resources at the head office dedicated to dealing with this sort of "problem." Head office immediately despatched a management consultant to Orangeville to gauge the situation and advise the local managers.

The strategy they devised included subtle intimidation. Rumours began to circulate that management knew who had signed cards, and that people should sign an anti-union petition to demonstrate company loyalty. "Cam," one of the managers, held a "crew meeting" at which he gave a pep talk on the benefits of working for McDonald's, which included "paid breaks, two free uniforms and half-price food," and implied that workers might lose these if they unionized. He encouraged anti-union employees to speak up. Inglis was the only one with enough courage to defend the union idea, but only after being challenged by Cam.

A more interesting tactic was to evoke the fun, happy world of the McDonald's brand image in aid of management's cause. Cam hired a cartoonist to print up posters portraying him as superhero "Candid Cam" fighting the big bad union. "Crew events," regular company-sponsored fun, began to support anti-union themes. Inglis describes how on a tobogganing outing—"Olympic Bobsledding"—Cam "had people lie down in the snow in the form of 'NO' and the managers yell out 'Do we need a union?' The crew obviously was supposed to reply 'NO!' If you didn't lie down and scream 'No,' you were labelled a union supporter." At the Christmas party, management had great success with a "hysterical video of people goofing off at work." They followed this up with a similar slide show with the theme "Just Say No" to the accompaniment of tunes like "It's a Wonderful World" and "Shiny Happy People" (Inglis).

In order to give time for this magic to work, the McDonald's negotiating team delayed the certification process, and succeeded in requiring a vote, which the union organizers eventually lost. One has to admire the company's rapid mobilization of ersatz "community" for its captive audience of workers. It is quite ironic. While Wal-Mart claims that a union is a big business, not "a club, sorority, fraternity or social organization," here is an actual big business representing itself to workers as though it were some sort of club or social organization. There are no sites or occasions outside of work and company-sponsored events where all of these workers will be brought together to socialize and talk openly among themselves. Most workers are young with little experience of work or union culture. The company is in a position to control and define for them both the meaning of work as well as the meaning of worker resistance.

Even if workers do succeed in building an independent base of union knowledge and support, the high turnover rate makes their achievement very fragile. Sarah Inglis' story is typical; she worked for the Orangeville McDonald's for three years, then left to go to university. Her union knowledge and experience is lost to that work site, but the anti-union management consultants remain ready on call. High turnover helps to "disorganize" worker culture, and many firms design work in this way for this reason. In an economy more dynamic than even Marx and Engels imagined, time has become a strategic resource. Delay of the union vote was important in the Orangeville case. In other anti-union struggles, you will often see companies using legal challenges to extend that delay for months or even years because in terms of control of workplace culture, time is on their side.

The Challenge of Labour Flexibility and Global Subcontracting

The temporal reorganization of work also affects those manufacturing jobs "exported" to developing countries and export processing zones. I began this chapter by suggesting that 19th-century working conditions, as described by Engels, could be found today in the developing world. You might well ask whether 19th-century worker radicalism can be found there as well. For one perspective on this we are going to turn to Naomi Klein, the Canadian author who has become a kind of modern-day Engels touring the factories and neighbourhoods in the developing world where the kinds of things we buy in Wal-Mart are assembled.

In the export-processing zone (EPZ) called Cavite in the Philippines, she discovered a territory "within a kind of legal and economic set of brackets" where companies are exempted from normal taxes, rents, and the enforcement of labour laws. While officially the workday is eight hours, workers are typically required to work 12 hours and receive "bonuses" instead of overtime pay. The bonus for workers making IBM computer screens, Klein discovered, was "doughnuts and a pen" (Klein 211). The minimum wage is U.S. $6 a day, but most companies get official "waivers" that allow them to pay less.

Nineteenth-century belts and pulleys are no longer a hazard, but workers are exposed to new health and safety risks in the form of chemicals in, for example, the glues that they apply in poorly ventilated conditions (ICFTU, "World Union Report"). They are subjected to surveillance and military work discipline. While it is against Philippine labour law, Klein writes, "some employers ... keep bathrooms padlocked except during two fifteen-minute breaks, during which time all workers have to sign in and out so management can keep track of their non-productive time. Seamstresses at a factory sewing garments for the Gap, Guess and Old Navy told me that they sometimes have to resort to urinating in plastic bags under their machines. There are rules against talking, and at the Ju Young electronics factory, a rule against smiling" (Klein 211). Work follows a boom-and-bust cycle, and at peak periods is intense and exhausting. Shifts can be extended from 7 a.m. to 2 a.m. Workers are left, like they were in Fall River, with little time or energy for interacting with one another or organizing either in or off the job (see video interview with a Cavite worker: www.icftu.org/displaydocument.asp?Index=991218414&Language=EN).

When the work slows down, workers are laid off without pay. This casual relation that firms have with their employees is often called "flexibility." It is a feature of production that has increasingly allowed firms to adapt quickly to rapidly changing markets and to cut costs throughout their produc-tion system. The Japanese were the first to realize how new computer modelling systems could allow them to manage complex timing problems in their global operations in such a way as to cut out waste. They called their new approach "just-in-time." Previously auto parts, for example, would have been manu-factured and then warehoused until needed in the assembly plant. Now the timing of component manufacture, shipping, final assembly, and sales could be coordinated ex-actly so that the warehousing along the way could be minimized or eliminated.

Full-time workers often become "waste" in these new flexible production systems, but they are not as easy to get rid of as real estate. Big-brand multinationals like Nike, Coke, and General Motors have attempted to solve this problem by retaining only a core of full-time workers and then subcontracting out their flexible labour requirements to other firms. Most of the plants observed by Klein in the Philippines were run by Korean firms taking contracts from different multinational brands.

Subcontractors, as we have seen, deal with flexibility by alternately intensifying work and laying off workers without pay. They also hire workers on short contracts, typically five months in Cavite. These give the employer flexibility not to rehire and also enable them to deny rights and benefits associated with permanent status. From the perspective of worker resistance, when workers view their relationship to a company on a five-month time horizon, they are less likely to invest in improving conditions there. Klein argues that there is one final and important way that these employers destabilize any cohesive workplace-based worker activism. They prefer hiring young women from rural areas who are "scared and uneducated about their rights" (Klein 221). These young women are typically "retired" in their mid-20s by employers who consider them "too old." There are always others to take their place—rural children sent in search of wage work by their families whose farms are threatened by rural "development."

Employers have a dual motivation here. The first is to avoid paying maternity benefits. Women are (illegally) required to sign agreements that if they marry they will lose their job (ICFTU, "World Union Report"). Pregnant women are harassed into quitting. In other EPZs women are subject to humiliating scrutiny to monitor their periods. Contracts are limited to the length of a menstrual cycle, and those who miss a period are conveniently not rehired. Women in their mid to late 20s are considered too great a risk. The second motivation of employers is to allow worker turnover to constantly erode any culture of worker resistance before it takes shape and permanence.

In Lynn and Fall River generations of workers and their families lived in the same neighbourhoods and worked for the same companies. In this context it took perhaps 10 years for newcomers, desperate for work and uneducated in workers' culture of resistance, to discover the "genius of unions." In Cavite every 10 years, there is a whole new workforce, and often during that time many of the firms that employ it will have shut down, moved to other locations with even more favourable tax holidays and labour conditions, and been replaced by new ones. The key difference between 19th-century and 21st-century manufacturing work is this temporal dimension: the dynamism that ensures that, for worker resistance, "all that is solid melts into air." While Klein calls for consumers and citizens in the developed world to support the anti-sweatshop movement, her analysis implies that the prospects for *worker-led* resistance in the developing world are dim.

Klein did find locally based activism in Cavite, but it was sponsored by a non-governmental organization (NGO) connected with the Catholic Church. The Workers' Assistance Centre had set up an office and resource centre in the town just outside the EPZ. Its staff educated workers about their rights, health and safety risks, and unions. Like the cafés in Lynn, it had become popular with workers from Cavite as a place to "hang out, eat dinner and attend seminars" after their shifts (Klein 213). It may point to a new model of labour activism that some are calling "community unionism" that is neither workplace nor union *based* (although supportive of union activity). Consider a recent example from Toronto.

New Models of Labour Organizing: Community Unionism in Toronto

We often like to think that sweatshop conditions exist only in developing countries in places like Asia, Africa, and the Pacific Rim—what many call "the South." But increasingly, pockets of exploited labour can be found everywhere on the globe, including countries where workers are supposed to be protected, like Canada and the United States. Consisting often of migrants, illegal immigrants, and those working outside the formal economy, these workers form part of a "global South."

The word "sweatshop" was first applied to small, cramped workshops in tenements or people's homes where immigrant women and children manufactured garments. In Toronto, Jewish immigrants dominated the sweatshop industry in the 19th century; in the 1930s it was Italians. Sweatshops have returned, this time employing mostly women from southeast Asia. These are typically small, patriarchal enterprises run by men from the same ethnic community and often the same family as the women workers.

Global competition has led to the closure of many Canadian clothing manufacturers and the loss of jobs to overseas contractors.

Or rather the least skilled and least lucrative stage of clothing manufacture—final assembly—has been restructured in this way while firms like Calvin Klein and Alfred Sung continue to do the design, cutting, and marketing. Competitors for final assembly contracts must find some exploitive niche in order to survive in Canada.

Home-based sweatshops avoid real estate costs. They are relatively invisible and can operate in a grey area between the formal and informal sectors, avoiding health and safety inspections, making no Canada Pension Plan contributions, offering no vacation pay. Women working in their homes can save on child-care expenses. Toronto sweatshop workers are paid on a piecework basis and in 1998 earned an average of $4.50 an hour. Like the workers in Cavite, they work long hours—between 46 and 82 hours per week (Tufts 238).

The Ontario district of the International Ladies' Garment Workers' Union (ILGWU) has had to struggle with the loss of members' jobs and the growth of this new non-union workforce that is particularly difficult to organize. Many of these Southeast Asian women speak little or no English, and their primary allegiances are to their ethnic community, including the men who employ them. In addition, their workplaces are uniquely invisible and scattered—the opposite of the centralization predicted by Marx and Engels. It makes little sense to view the workplace as a site of organization.

Some of the initial interest and leadership in assisting these women came not from unions, but from women's groups seeking to address a wide range of needs of women within their communities. The ILGWU began to take up these women's issues under the leadership of a woman with a "progressive feminist" agenda. Previously the union hierarchy had been male dominated, and subject to pressures to protect its more privileged members

rather than reach out to cut-rate, non-union workers who "threatened" union jobs.

The ILGWU established contact with homeworkers by placing an ad in the local Chinese newspaper offering $10 to anyone willing to be interviewed. The interviews, mostly done in Chinese, helped the union to understand the women's needs from their own perspective, and to design a series of programs that could begin to meet those needs. They established not a union local, but a "Homeworkers' Association" as a social site, bringing workers together with activities such as "social teas and day trips" (Tufts 242). Union offices became a central locale where dispersed workers could come together for legal seminars, language education, and instruction on useful skills like sewing machine maintenance. In 1991 the ILGWU, religious, and women's rights groups in Ontario collaborated in lobbying for legislative changes that would clearly extend labour law protections to homeworkers and shift liability for labour infractions "upwards" to the truly powerful players in the industry—brand-name manufacturers and retailers rather than small subcontractors.

The final piece in the "community union" strategy was to engage consumers in the struggle. The ILGWU Clean Clothes Campaign, like all consumer-based anti-corporate activism, focused pressure on visible and powerful corporate players—in this case retailers that stocked clothing made under sweatshop conditions. They staged demonstrations at the Eaton Centre, a downtown mall that houses numerous retailers stocking brand-name clothes. Shoppers were handed "Clean Clothes Scorecards" that exposed the links in the exploitive chain between the brand and the immigrant workers. They were encouraged to send these to key retailers to register their protest. Retailers have proven very sensitive to pressure from educated consumers.

"Community," as the term is used in "community unionism," refers to the idea that the organizational site for workers is some nexus—an ethnic community, a women's advocacy network—outside the workplace. Within these alternate sites organizers attend to a correspondingly broad range of human needs, both work and non-work related. There is also an idea that support of labour causes involves a collaboration of "community" organizations, religious, consumers, human rights, and so on beyond union circles. While unions are involved, they may set aside traditional union tactics—getting locals certified as legal collective-bargaining units to specific workplaces—in favour of a broader range of social movement tactics borrowed from their NGO collaborators. Do you suppose these innovations could be effective in dealing with the two problems of dynamism we considered earlier: the rapid turnover of workers and the rapid mobility of capital? Within these new coalitions, could worker dissent ever become as radical as Marx and Engels hoped it would?

CONCLUSION

In this opening chapter we have used the ideas of Marx and Engels as a touchstone because they helped to define for generations of activists and scholars what social dissent should look like in capitalist societies. The world of Marxian analysis of social movements has become infinitely more complex than what we have presented here. But since this is meant to be your first introduction to all of this, I thought it best to stick to the basics of Marx and Engels' original formulation. We can use it later as an exemplar against which to compare what actually happens as well as other theories of how social movements should develop. Their central thesis is that the development of capitalism generates dissent as

an equal and opposite force. It creates reasons for dissent by perverting human potential through multiple forms of alienation and by deepening inequalities through exploitation. Capitalism also creates the tools for resistance by increasing the number of capitalism's enemies and providing them with the spaces and technologies to organize. This model of "class formation" is Marx and Engels' solution to the problem of how the powerless can gain power.

In addition to their critique of capitalism and analysis of class formation, Marx and Engels advocate a particular aim and program for working-class struggle. The aim is nothing less than total revolution: the replacement of capitalism with an economic and political system based on a culture of mutualism and decentralized democracy built up within working-class communities as capitalism lurches from crisis to crisis toward its final end. This anti-capitalist mission can only be entrusted to the proletariat because this is the only class that has no investment in capitalist ownership. The proletariat, they insist, must take a leadership role in all genuinely "progressive" social movements. How you evaluate these ideas depends on how you answer two questions. First, how persuasive are Marx and Engels' indictments of capitalism? Second, if you accept their criticisms, do you think the problems they identify can be overcome within a market economy driven by the profit motive; in other words, can capitalism be reformed?

I am most interested in Marx and Engels' theory of class formation. My main question is how relevant is it to the 21st century? Here are some concerns raised by our case studies. I think they have tended to underestimate the ways in which capitalism can weaken resistance. In those processes they identified as fuelling revolt, emiseration, and alienation, there is not always the promise of resistance. The worst off are often the least able to do anything about it. Other developments have emerged under capitalism that they simply did not foresee. First was the disorganization of the workplace-community bond. More recent are the disorganizations caused by 21st-century mobilities.

The mobility of capital means that many firms have loosened all geographic ties and feel little need to make commitments to or compromises with any government, workforce, or community. The new "labour flexibility" and consequent high turnover in many new industries disorganizes the workplace as a site of ongoing worker interaction and of commitment both to the job and to any worker collaboration to transform it. What you need to consider is whether the new tactics and alliances represented by "community unionism" can help workers overcome these handicaps. What other strategies might workers employ?

Marx and Engels also were unable to foresee the degree to which workers in the leading industrial countries would follow the British example and use their organizational power to push for reforms to their governments and national industries that fell far short of the ideals of total revolution and international solidarity. Now that the mobility of capital is eroding these national "islands" of labour security, there is a greater than ever need for solidarity between workers across borders. Workers both in the industrialized West and the newly exploited economies of the South are seeking new models of international solidarity. Our main question here is how can the labour movement mirror the global reach of the capitalist market and multinational firms without itself creating alienating transnational structures? Neither the Marxist paradigm nor the legacy of international unionism has provided satisfactory models for how to accomplish this without sacrificing diversity and local autonomy. Some suggest that the Internet, with its open and "horizontal" flow of information, can facilitate non-hierarchical networks across borders unlike any other communications medium. What do you think?

REFERENCES

Cumbler, John. "The City and Community: The Impact of Urban Forces on Working-Class Behaviour." *Journal of Urban History* 3 (1977): 427–442.

Drachkovitch, Milorad M. *The Revolutionary Internationals, 1864-1943*. Hoover Institution Publications. Stanford: Published for Hoover Institution on War, Revolution, and Peace by Stanford University Press, 1966.

Engels, Friedrich. *The Condition of the Working Class in England: From Personal Observation and Authentic Sources*. 1844. Introduction by E.J Hobsbawm. London: Granada, 1982.

Featherstone, Liza. "The Burger International," 1998. *Left Business Observer*, August 27, 2004, www.leftbusinessobserver.com/McDonalds.html.

———. "Will Labor Take the Wal-Mart Challenge," June 10, 2004, *The Nation online*, August 27, 2004, www.thenation.com/doc.mhtml?i=20040628&s=featherstone.

Foster, William Z. *History of the Three Internationals: The World Socialist and Communist Movements from 1848 to the Present*. New York: Greenwood Press, 1968.

Fuller, Max. "In Guatemala, Coca-Cola Is a Name for Murder," March 1, 1998, Columbia Solidarity Campaign Web site, August 16, 2004, www.columbiasolidarity.org.uk/Solidarity%2013/guatemala.html.

Huws, Ursula, et al. *Solidarity for Survival: The Don Thomson Reader on Trade Union Internationalism*. Nottingham: Spokesman, 1989.

ICFTU. "World Union Report Condemns Philippines' Consistent Record of Trade Union Rights Violations,"

September 28 1999, World History Archives, August 27, 2004, www.hartford-hwp.com/archives/54a/206.html.

———. "World Bank Highlights Positive Development Impact of Trade Unions," February 12, 2003, ICFTU Online, August 27, 2004, www.icftu.org/displaydocument.asp?Index=991217201&Language=EN.

Inglis, Sarah. "Witness Statement, 'McLibel' Trial," November 28, 1995, McSpotlight Web site, August 27, 2004, www.mcspotlight.org/people/witnesses/employment/inglis_sarah.html.

IRC. "Slums: World Habitat Day Highlights Water and Sanitation for Urban Poor," October 22, 2003, International Water and Sanitation Centre (IRC) Web site, August 24, 2004, www.irc.nl/page/5908.

Kidder, Thali G. "Networks in Transnational Labor Organizing." In Restructuring World Politics: Transnational Social Movements, Networks, and Norms, edited by Sanjeev Khagram, James V. Riker, and Kathryn Sikkink. Minneapolis; London: University of Minnesota Press, 2002.

Klein, Naomi. No Logo: Taking Aim at the Brand Bullies. Toronto: Random House, 2000.

Marx, Karl, and Friedrich Engels. Manifesto of the Communist Party. 1848. Edited by Rick Kuhn, based on the 1888 translation by Samuel Moore. August 20, 2004, www.anu.edu.au/polsci/marx/classics/manifesto.html.

Mason, Orson. "Labor Relations and You at the Wal-Mart Distribution Center #6022." 1991. United Food and Commercial Workers (UFCW) Web site, August 26, 2004, www.ufcw.org/docUploads/Wal%2DMartAnti%2Dunio nManuals%2EPDF?CFID=1037888&CFTOKEN=72023247.

McLellan, David. Karl Marx: His Life and Thought. London: Macmillan, 1973.

Rudé, George F.E. "The Growth of Cities and Popular Revolt, 1750–1850: With Particular Reference to Paris." In The Face of the Crowd, edited by Harvey J. Kaye. Atlantic Highlands: Humanities Press International, 1988.

Salmon, Katy. "Nairobi's 'Flying Toilets'—Tip of an Iceberg," August 26, 2002, Inter-Press Service (IPS) News, July 29, 2004, www.ipsnews.net/riomas10/2608_3.shtml.

Smith, Adam. An Inquiry into the Nature and Causes of the Wealth of Nations, edited by Edwin Cannan. London: Methuen and Co., Ltd., 1904. August 24, 2004, www.econlib.org/library/Smith/smWN.html.

"Sweatshops and Coke, New Labor Battlegrounds." Infopress Central America Report 29, no. 44 (2002): 1–3. August 20, 2004, www.xyx.org.

Tufts, Steven. "Community Unionism in Canada and Labour's (Re)Organization of Space." Antipode 30, no. 3 (1998): 227–250.

UFCW. "Welcome to Wal-Mart's War on Workers." United Food and Commercial Workers (UFCW) Website, August 27, 2004, www.ufcw.org/issues_and_actions/walmart_workers_campaign_info/worker_testimony/working_america_sp03.cfm.

Vidal, John. "Disease Stalks New Megacities." The Guardian, March 23, 2003, August 20, 2004, www.guardian.co.uk/debt/Story/0,2763,672665,00.html.

Waterman, Peter. "Trade Union Internationalism in the Age of Seattle." Antipode 33, no. 3 (2001): 312–336. November 13, 2006, www.antennaeul/~waterman/ageseattle.html

CRITICAL THINKING QUESTIONS

1. Does unity have to depend upon the elimination of differences? Can workers fight together for change while accepting their differences? If so, how would the model of organizing differ from the one outlined by Marx and Engels?
2. How can the labour movement mirror the global reach of the capitalist market and multinational firms without itself creating alienating transnational structures?
3. Do you suppose community unionism could be effective in dealing with the two problems of dynamism we considered earlier: the rapid turnover of workers and the rapid mobility of capital?
4. How persuasive are Marx and Engels' indictments of capitalism? If you accept their criticisms, do you think the problems they identify can be overcome within a market economy driven by the profit motive; in other words, can capitalism be reformed?
5. How relevant is Marx and Engels' theory of class formation to the 21st century?

FURTHER READING

Cumbler, John. "The City and Community: The Impact of Urban Forces on Working Class Behaviour." *Journal of Urban History* 3 (1977): 427–442.
     You know about this study from having read Chapter 1 of this textbook. It is simply the best analysis of North American labour activism that embeds it in the geography of local community life.

Galabuzi, Grace-Edward. *Canada's Economic Apartheid: The Social Exclusion of Racialized Groups in the New Century.* Toronto: Canadian Scholars' Press Inc., 2006.
     This book calls attention to the growing racialization of the gap between rich and poor, which, despite the dire implications for Canadian society, is proceeding with minimal public and policy attention. This book challenges some common myths about the economic performance of Canada's racialized communities. These myths are used to deflect public concern and to mask the growing social crisis. The author points to the role of historical patterns of systemic racial discrimination as essential in understanding the persistent overrepresentation of racialized groups in low-paying occupations.

Heron, Craig. *The Canadian Labour Movement: A Brief History,* 2nd ed. Toronto: James Lorimer, 1996.
     Heron has written a highly condensed and readable history of the labour movement in Canada. He focuses on many of the themes we pursue in this textbook: labour as an agent for social change; the role of the state in co-opting labour militancy; organized labour's political response to neoliberalism and the new economy.

Jackson, Andrew. *Work and Labour in Canada: Critical Issues.* Toronto: Canadian Scholars' Press Inc., 2005.

This original and timely book focuses on critical issues surrounding work and labour in Canada. It examines changes in the labour market and in workplaces, with a strong empirical component based upon the most recent Statistics Canada data.

MacDowell, Laurel Sefton, and Ian Radforth. *Canadian Working-Class History: Selected Readings*, 3rd ed. Toronto: Canadian Scholars' Press Inc., 2006.
This is an updated version of the reader that brings together recent and classic scholarship on the history, politics, and social groups of the working class in Canada. Some of the changes include better representation of female academics and nine provocative and groundbreaking new articles on racism and human rights, women's equality, gender history, Quebec sovereignty, and the environment.

Maheu, Louis. *Social Movements and Social Classes the Future of Collective Action*. Sage Studies in International Sociology 46. London, Thousand Oaks: Sage Publications, 1995.
This is a collection of essays all dealing with the question of how relevant class analysis is for modern social movements. You will find the writing challenging, but you will get a good introduction to some of the key theorists and theories (such as New Social Movement theory).

Raphael, Dennis. *Poverty and Policy in Canada: Implications for Health and Quality of Life*. Toronto: Canadian Scholars' Press Inc., 2007.
This book provides a unique, interdisciplinary perspective on poverty and its importance to the health and quality of life of Canadians. Central issues include the definitions of poverty and means of measuring it in wealthy, industrialized nations such as Canada; the causes of poverty—both situational and societal; the health and social implications of poverty for individuals, communities, and society as a whole; and means of addressing its incidence and mitigating its effects. All of this is placed within the context of the political economy literature concerned with the evolution of the modern welfare state in Canada.

Rudé, George F.E. *The Face of the Crowd: Studies in Revolution, Ideology, and Popular Protest: Selected Essays of George Rudé*. Edited and introduced by Harvey J. Kaye. Atlantic Highlands: Humanities Press International, 1988.
Rudé, a Marxist social historian, sifts through historical records to uncover the "face" of, or the identities of, those involved in popular uprisings of the 19th century. His results offer a surprising corrective to Marx and Engels' analyses of these events.

Shalla, Vivian. *Working in a Global Era: Canadian Perspectives*. Toronto: Canadian Scholars' Press Inc., 2006.
This progressive reader examines work in a global era. Divided into eight key parts with a total of 16 essential readings, this volume covers a great deal of ground: Fordist and post-Fordist methods of work organization; labour markets in transition; working in the free trade zones; migration, transnationalism, and domestic work; neoliberalism and the dismantling of the welfare state; education, training, and skills in a knowledge-based economy; and the labour movement in transition. All major issues surrounding work in Canada are covered.

Waterman, Peter. "Trade Union Internationalism in the Age of Seattle." *Antipode* 33, no. 3 (2001): 312–336.

You have to read Waterman if you are interested in the question of how organized labour can resist the power of global capitalism. He argues that labour must adopt some of the tactics and decentralized organizational style of the new anti-globalization movement.

RELEVANT WEB SITES

Global Solidarity Dialogue
www.antenna.nl/~waterman/dialogue.html

Here you will find a collection of writings by a number of well-regarded thinkers on the theory and practice of building international social movement networks that include workers and their organizations.

International Conference of Free Trade Unions (ICFTU)
www.icftu.org

Get the international news and current issues on labour rights and labour organizing. You will find it arranged by category: e.g., child labour, youth.

Labour Start
www.labourstart.org

Excellent collation of labour news worldwide from various sources—weekly world summary and daily by country.

Marxist Internet Archive
www.marxists.org

Huge repository of writings of most of the great Marxist, socialist, and even some liberal thinkers. Check out what Marx, Engels, Che Guevara, and Kropotkin actually said. I particularly recommend the *Communist Manifesto*, a rhetorical masterpiece and the most succinct statement of Mark and Engels' theory of class struggle. Because all the texts are searchable (you know, "ctrl-f") this is a good place to find specific quotes or passages on specific topics. (Go to www.marxism.org/ if you want to join a Marxist discussion list.)

Union Network International
www.union-network.org

Web site for a new trade union international formed in 2000 and focusing on workers' needs in a global information economy. Represents 900 unions with 16 million members. In 2006 they were addressing important themes like "building union strength in China and India."

Unite Here Canada
www.unitehere.ca

Union of garment and hospitality workers seeking to represent a vulnerable and underorganized sector of workers.

Chapter 2

STATE AND
CO-OPERATIVE MOVEMENTS

INTRODUCTION:
THE CO-OPERATIVE STRATEGY

Violent insurrection is on the mind of Bob McNair in the fall of 1901: "The only kind o' resolution that'll *get* anythin' is made o' lead and fits in a rifle breach! And I want to tell you, old man, if there ain't some pretty quick right-about-facin' in certain quarters, I'll be dashed if I ain't for it! An' I won't be standing alone either!" (qtd. in Moorhouse 24). The "old man" he is speaking to is W.R. Motherwell, one of the pioneers of the co-operative movement in the Canadian Prairies. What the two men along with the others McNair refers to are "riled" about is their powerlessness against the large corporations that dominate their lives as grain farmers.

They supply the global market with wheat, which, they have discovered, is one of the few products they can make any money from, so they have specialized in growing it and are now utterly dependent upon it for their livelihoods. Each fall tens of thousands of prairie farmers come to market with wheat that is useless to them and valuable only to those who can ship it to international buyers. So, when all the local "middlemen" offer them the same insultingly low price and say, "Take it or leave it," they have no choice but to swallow their pride and take it. They like to think of themselves as independent property owners, but feel as exploited as Marx's industrial proletariat.

Present-day "monkey wrenchers" and direct-action advocates could probably recognize the immediate trigger of McNair's frustration. That is the conviction that his own government is ready to support the interests of corporate capital against the interests and wishes of its own people. It was not as if the farmers had not already been seeking non-violent, democratic solutions. They had already organized and lobbied the government. And the government had made a show of acting on their behalf by setting up a royal commission, receiving recommendations, and passing legislation on the farmers' behalf.

It was now the law that elevator companies had to provide a special platform that farmers could use to load wheat directly into boxcars, and the railway companies had to allocate boxcars for this purpose. (Farmers had hoped that this way they could get a better deal by circumventing the local buyers and selling directly to milling companies in eastern Canada.) However, in the fall of 1901 the railway companies simply ignored the law and the state did nothing to enforce it, so McNair was ready to stage armed occupations of grain elevators to force the state into action. Motherwell advocated a different course of action that reflected a very different perspective on the relationship between movement and state.

Instead of trying to influence the state to act for the farmers' movement, the idea was for the movement to act on its own, to attempt to solve its members' problems, independently of the state, but in a way that was still legal and constitutional. A more decisive way to circumvent exploitive capitalist firms, according to this view, would be for the farmers themselves to form co-operative enterprises, which could do the same work that capitalists had done except now in the service of the farmers' needs. Prairie farmers embraced the co-operative strategy and were rewarded with a string of practical successes, but also a new attitude that replaced the sense of desperation and powerlessness expressed by McNair. They developed confidence that they themselves, with minimal government assistance, could transform an economic world that exploited them into one that they could control for the popular good.

Their first successes were with farmer-owned grain elevators that bought, stored, and sold their grain at cost. By the 1920s they were close to a much more ambitious aim of a "one hundred percent wheat pool" whereby the grain of tens of thousands of prairie farmers would be marketed as one. The idea here was a kind of people's monopoly, an equal and opposing force to the great corporate monopolies of the time that had the power to actually dictate prices.

Prairie farmers were in control of the co-operative strategy and many began to hope that with it they could eventually replace capitalism itself by an economy run by the people on co-operative principles. This was a surprising development since governments, the Catholic Church, and members of the economic elite had been promoting co-operatives as a way to channel the grievances of working people away from direct challenges to the capitalist system. In this chapter we will be looking at the reasoning behind these very different expectations for co-operatives. Then, by comparing three examples of the co-operative movement in Canada—one in Quebec, one in the Maritimes, and one in Saskatchewan—we will try to understand how and why the movement took a pro-capitalist direction in eastern Canada and an anti-capitalist direction in the Prairies.

CO-OPERATIVES: ANTI- OR PRO-CAPITALIST?

Farmers' co-operatives, like all co-operatives, were a type of "corporation." Corporations are simply human collectivities with the legal status to act, to enter into economic relations with others as "one body." Co-operatives differ from capitalist corporations in three fundamental ways. First, the owners are people who use the co-op's services. So, for example, farmers sold their grain to the elevators or bought supplies from the co-op stores that they owned. People often own shares in capitalist firms, but they typically want nothing more from the firm than a profit on their investment.

Second, shareholders in the co-op each have only one vote in decisions affecting how the co-op is run. Shareholders have votes in capitalist corporations proportional to the number of shares they own so that large shareholders normally dictate corporate policy. Capitalist corporations are more plutocratic (ruled by the rich) than democratic. Third, the raison d'être of a co-op is not the pursuit of profit, but the service of human needs—the needs of the members or the community to which they belong. Co-ops are a democratic form of "common property" or public rather than private ownership—that public property is meant to be put to work in the service of human need rather than the accumulation of profit.

BOX 2.1:

COMMON PROPERTY TRADITIONS

Like the workers described in the previous chapter, prairie farmers valued self-education. They sought news and analysis that challenged mainstream views they saw in the "capitalist" press and heard from public "experts." A popular text among "co-operators" was Kropotkin's *Mutual Aid* in which the author makes a case that co-operation is as "natural" an adaptive strategy in evolution as competition. Kropotkin argues that some of the oldest traditions of governance in Europe were based on local self-government and common property in "village communities." Many of these institutions and the values that animated them survived in pockets throughout Europe at the time that he was writing (1902).

For example, in Switzerland, writes Kropotkin:

> ... the village communities remain in possession of a wide self-government, and own large parts of the Federal territory. Two-thirds of all the Alpine meadows and two-thirds of all the forests of Switzerland are until now communal land; and a considerable number of fields, orchards, vineyards, peat bogs, quarries, and so on, are owned in common. In the Vaud, where all the householders continue to take part in the deliberations of their elected communal councils, the communal spirit is especially alive. Towards the end of the winter all the young men of each village go to stay a few days in the woods, to fell timber and to bring it down the steep slopes tobogganing way, the timber and the fuel wood being divided among all households or sold for their benefit. These excursions are real fêtes of manly labour. On the banks of Lake Leman part of the work required to keep up the terraces of the vineyards is still done in common; and in the spring, when the thermometer threatens to fall below zero before sunrise, the watchman wakes up all householders, who light fires of straw and dung and protect their vine-trees from the frost by an artificial cloud. In nearly all cantons the village communities possess so-called Bürgernutzen—that is, they hold in common a number of cows, in order to supply each family with butter; or they keep communal fields or vineyards, of which the produce is divided between the burghers, or they rent their land for the benefit of the community.

As an anarchist, Kropotkin was fascinated by these traditions because they represented communal order arising without "external" pressures from the state or market. While these forms of co-operative order are not exactly spontaneous, they rely on no legal framework or monetary exchange. In fact, Kropotkin argued that states, in order to consolidate their power, had jealously sought to eradicate these competing claims to "govern." This sort of analysis gave anarchists the faith that "smashing the state" would result not in chaos, but in a flowering of democratic, co-operative order. Both the idea that it is "natural" for humans to co-operate and that order in human affairs is self-forming continue to give inspiration to 21st-century "anti-globalization" activists that "another world is possible" and worth struggling to achieve.

Source: Peter Kropotkin, *Mutual Aid* (London: Heinemann, 1902), August 30, 2004, www.spunk.org/library/writers/kropotki/sp001503/.

Many committed "co-operators" thought that they were not just solving the practical problem of getting a better economic "deal" for farmers, but actually working toward the transformation of capitalism into a more humane system that they called the "co-operative commonwealth." While western

Canadians fervently embraced this idea, it was international in scope and origins. It had its roots in the utopian socialism of 19th-century Europe, and in particular the ideas of Pierre-Joseph Proudhon in France and Robert Owen in England.

Followers of Owen reluctantly gave up his

idea of building self-contained socialist communities separated from the larger society. They discovered it was much more workable to create co-operative institutions that could thrive within the capitalist framework but on the basis of non-capitalist and perhaps ultimately anti-capitalist principles (Birchall 4–5). Capitalism as they understood it was a system that replaced older common property traditions with private property and individual ownership. Co-ops could reassert common property on a modern institutional basis.

Capitalism replaced community-based forms of co-operation with individualistic and competitive competition. It also undermined the moral basis of economic activity. Indeed, Adam Smith, who defined what we call the "liberal" stance on capitalism, counselled people not to concern themselves with the public good, or with any morality other than material self-interest in their economic dealings. Co-operatives were businesses that could respond first and foremost to human need or to any ethical principle that the community of shareholders defined, even if that meant foregoing economic profit.

Proponents of the co-operative commonwealth believed that the spread of co-operatives would result in businesses that behaved differently from capitalist firms. They would be less likely to exploit, pollute, or oppress in the name of profit. Their spread would also bring with it a cultural transformation, allowing citizens to preserve and build upon their concern for others and non-materialistic values rather than the material self-interest demanded by capitalist competition.

CO-OPERATIVES:
THE ROLE OF THE STATE

The co-operative movement promoted public ownership, but not state ownership of what Marx would call the "means of production." Indeed many co-operators were strongly opposed both to state ownership and to state influence on their organizations. However, just like capitalist firms, co-ops are dependent on the state to define for them their legal status as corporate bodies. The legal apparatus of the state is important not only to "make real" the legal fiction of the "one body," but to enforce the obligations and rights of the participants in the event of bankruptcy, malpractice, and so on.

The first efforts to get the Canadian government to pass legislation mandating co-operative enterprises reveals a fascinating ambivalence on the part of "the state" about the meaning of co-operatives and the movement of which they were a part. I have put "the state" in quotation marks because it is not really a thing, but like all social institutions, an amalgam of legal fiction and networks of real people pursuing various and often conflicting agendas.

The instigator of the first bill at the national level (Bill no. 2, 1906) was a man by the name of Alphonse Desjardins. He had begun setting up caisses populaires in Quebec and was looking for a legal framework to support them. Caisses populaires are small lending institutions organized as co-operatives; they are called "credit unions" in English Canada. The legislation was brought forward as a private member's bill and contained provision for three types of co-operatives: co-operative banks (the caisses populaires), commercial co-operatives (including grain elevators and retail stores), and co-operative industries (Rudin 128). Discussions among elected representatives, senators, and lobbyists reveal a great deal about the attitudes of those who governed in Ottawa toward the working people who made up the majority of the Canadian population.

These groups came from different classes. Generally those in government relied for their livelihood on capital as investors, managers, or owners of firms or else by providing legal and financial services to firms. They were members of what Marx would have called the "bourgeoisie." Most Canadians at the time earned their livelihoods working with their hands in the primary resource industries: farming, fishing, forestry, and mining. In the cities there was a small and growing industrial working class doing manual labour in factories and small workshops.

Politicians' attitudes toward working people were often condescending, as you can see in this senator's choice of words. "It has been shown most conclusively," he argued, "that [the co-operative savings bank] has produced marvellous thrift, industry and temperance and all the virtues one can think of in the class of men who require some uplifting." Senators in particular (who are not elected) saw it as their role to give the people what they needed whether they wanted it or not. The role of the state, even in a democracy, was not so much to represent as to educate and "uplift" the population so that they could see what was "really" in their best interests. Judging by the debates over co-ops, it appeared that their best interests were in supporting capitalism, since most of the arguments for and against co-ops hinged on whether and to what degree they would promote or else threaten capitalism.

Lobbyists for the Canadian Retail Merchants Association argued that co-ops should be opposed because they were "dangerously socialistic [and] a kindergarten for all that is bad in these socialistic doctrines" (Canada 17) Note how they too see the co-op as a type of "school." While the merchants thought workers would learn dangerous skills, others argued that workers might, despite themselves, become educated in bourgeois virtues such as the "thrift, industry and temperance" mentioned by the senator. They quoted authorities to the

effect that "the loan association accustoms the workman to economize, to have order in his business, to be exact in his engagements, because otherwise he could not remain a customer-member of the association ..." (Canada 136). These skills of handling money and ordering and disciplining oneself according to the clock could be acquired from involvement in any formal business, co-operative or capitalist.

Bourgeois virtue also included a new sort of motivation that the sociologist Max Weber has called the "spirit" of capitalism. This spirit is the perverse drive to deny one's immediate sensual pleasures—to party, to drink, to slack off, and squander money and time on things that one enjoys—for the sake of a very abstract form of money—savings, credit, or "capital." Involvement in co-ops, particularly savings co-ops, could foster this spirit as well. In summary, the co-operative "education," according to one authority, "gradually makes [the worker] become a capitalist by means of the fund it obliges him to create, by the dividends he receives. Hence what better means of causing the antagonism between capital and labour to disappear than by transforming the labourer, himself, into a capitalist, than by supplying them, in the meantime, with the means of making his credit fill the void created by his lack of means" (Canada 136).

Representatives of the state clearly saw it as their duty to foster this bourgeois spirit and to minimize class antagonism. If co-operatives could help in this project, then they would be supported with enabling legislation. They promised an additional benefit in that they were self-forming and self-directing. Workers would be educating *themselves* in bourgeois virtues, "governing" themselves without any effort on the part of the government. This sort of delegation of governing to non-governmental agencies is what Michel Foucault calls the "autonomization of power." Foucault and others who follow his ideas have a tendency to view a lot of popular action that *appears* to be independent of government as actually extending in this way the project of governing or of what he calls "governance."

Another term that describes the use of social movements to further the aims of powerful groups is "co-optation." I apologize for introducing this term in a chapter on "co-operatives" since the two words sound similar but are completely different in meaning. Co-operatives are non-profit firms governed by community shareholders on a one-person, one-vote basis. Co-optation is the redirection of opposition to either neutralize it or enlist it somehow to further one's own agenda. It is a tremendously important concept that recurs again and again in the study of social movements. The question I am posing now is: Were co-ops used to co-opt workers into supporting capitalism? If this were so, of course it would be a great irony since the early co-operators thought that their movement would undermine and even replace capitalism.

To understand better what role co-operatives have played in Canadian society, I want to look more closely at three examples of co-operative movements: Quebec's caisses populaires, the Antigonish movement based in Nova Scotia, and the co-operatives of the western Canadian farm movement that contributed to the formation of a new political party known as the Co-operative Commonwealth Federation (CCF), which later became the NDP. The CCF is interesting in this connection because in its formative years (the 1930s and 1940s) it was explicitly socialist and anti-capitalist—just the sort of "danger" that the Canadian Retail Merchants Association feared that co-ops might lead to. However, elsewhere, particularly in Quebec, the co-operative path led away from CCF-style socialism.

QUEBEC'S CAISSES POPULAIRES

Alphonse Desjardins failed in his efforts to have Ottawa pass enabling legislation for caisses populaires. Instead he turned to the Quebec legislature where he found political elites sympathetic to his argument that co-op lending agencies would both benefit workers and help to preserve the authority of the Church and French-speaking elites in rural Quebec society. Ronald Rudin has shown that the caisse populaire movement was promoted and largely dominated not by workers but by the local bourgeoisie in rural towns and villages—"doctors, notaries, lawyers, clerics and small businessmen"—acting in their own as well as in the farmers' and workers' interests (Rudin 3).

Capitalist Development in Rural Quebec

In Quebec, like elsewhere in Canada, rural society was being transformed by capitalist agriculture. What this meant was that farm families grew less of their own food and produced fewer of their own necessities such as furniture, clothing, tools, and the like on their own farms. Increasingly they sold crops for cash with which they now bought the old necessities as well as new ones. They found they could not compete using equipment that could be made by local craftspeople, but required modern factory-made machinery from distant suppliers. For these larger purchases, they increasingly needed credit, which they sought from banks or other lenders located or owned by those outside the community. (You must remember that this is not a pattern of the distant past, but one that has repeated itself throughout the 200-odd-year history of industrial capitalism and continues to be evident in rural areas in

India, China, Africa, and the "developing" world generally in the 21st century.)

In turn-of-the-century Quebec, people's links were becoming increasingly translocal, connecting them with "anonymous people from Montreal and elsewhere" who were represented as neither French-speaking nor Catholic (it was true that Montreal finance and industrial capital was dominated by English-speaking Protestants) (Rudin 5). The local bourgeoisie and workers could be unified against a common threat of control from outside the cultural community, but also by the threat of the impersonality of capitalist relations in their pure form. Personal ties at the local level had tempered relations between the classes with ethical obligations, or so the story went.

"Desjardins and his colleagues," writes Rudin, "were fond of extolling the virtues of the local merchant, who recognized his responsibility to his neighbour by refusing to grant more credit than he believed his client could afford and by refraining from encouraging the consumption of luxuries that would only compromise the financial viability of the family, and, ultimately, the integrity of the community" (4). The local bourgeoisie recognized that capital represented power and hoped that the caisse populaire would be a means of investing capital locally under their control.

The way in which Desjardins and his Quebec counterparts attempted to frame the meaning of the co-operative movement cannot be simplistically represented in either pro- or anti-capitalist terms. There was an impulse simply to spread the skills and resources to control capitalism to the Quebec people. Desjardins liked to recount a story of how the first caisse populaire refused a loan to a member who hoped to use the money for a pleasure trip to visit family. Desjardin knew that the would-be borrower had "splendid" creditworthiness, but

wanted to see him use it only for productive investments—in seed, more land, new machinery—in short, "capital" (Rudin 12–13). For Desjardins, the role of the caisse was to teach the "spirit of capitalism." At the same time, he and his supporters were critical of the impersonality and moral indifference of capitalist relationships.

The Church's Response to Capitalism

Their stance probably owed more to Catholic teachings than to the intellectual debates within the international co-operative movement. Catholicism remained a dominant influence over culture and thought in Catholic communities throughout Canada. In sociological terms it was a "hegemonic" discourse in local communities in Quebec, Acadia (French-Catholic settlements in the Maritimes), eastern Nova Scotia (where Catholics of Scottish origin predominated), and Manitoba. The Catholic Church was an institution with extraordinary global reach. Its priests exercised authority at the local or "parish" level (a parish being a geographic unit small enough that one man could exert personal influence over its inhabitants). At the same time ideological conformity was enforced worldwide through a rigid hierarchy of authority under the command of a single voice and single truth represented by the Pope.

The myth that the Pope's word reflected God's eternal truth has always created tensions between the Church and a changing world. The Church has consequently changed much more slowly than the rest of society; its role has been fundamentally conservative or reactionary, rejecting the modern world and seeking to reassert earlier forms of social order and authority. Industrial capitalism everywhere sets in motion accelerated change both in the economic and social organization of societies as well as in their cultures.

Catholic thinkers have responded with profound moral objections to many of these changes, particularly to Adam Smith's "liberal" notion that social morality should be left to the market or, as Marx put it, the "cash nexus." Like the socialists, they condemned the way in which liberal capitalism led to materialistic and exploitive relations between and within the social classes, allowing the economically powerful to use others "as mere instruments for making money," and deepening economic inequalities between those who could exploit and those who found themselves being exploited (Alexander 54).

At the same time the Church viewed the labour movement as an equally suspect artifact of modern society, and socialism as perhaps one of its greatest evils. Militant unionism, with its adversarial stance toward capital, was seen as socially divisive like liberal individualism. The Catholic ideal was one of social harmony in which classes performed different but complementary roles, like organs in a body. The Church justified differences of power and material wealth so long as abuses were held in check by a sense of moral obligation to others and to the social good. This was a model drawn from an idealized "moral economy" of the feudal past. The Church was adamantly opposed to socialism. Part of the reason was the socialist attack on "private property," or individual ownership of the "means of production." The Church defended private property so long as ownership was morally bound up with social obligation—a land developer, for instance, would have no moral right to ignore the interests of the surrounding community or existing land uses before constructing a steel plant or a dam.

The Church also had difficulty with the degree of egalitarianism advocated by socialists, in terms of "property" but also in terms of authority. A deeply authoritarian institution itself, it was suspicious of the modern idea, shared by liberals and socialists alike, that ordinary people have equal capacity and should therefore have the right to think for and decide for themselves. Finally, it cannot have helped the socialist cause in Rome that many saw the movement as explicitly atheist, and at the same time a system of meaning and faith that was beginning to compete effectively with religion for people's allegiances.

Many of these Catholic principles were codified in 1891 by Pope Leo XIII in an encyclical on the modern world called *Rerum Novarum* (Alexander 53–57). He defines a Catholic "middle way" between capitalism and socialism. The vision of authority and harmony is, of course, backward looking. However, he does offer explicit support for "modern" organizations among the working class, so long as these do not advocate "class struggle" or socialist ideals. He also encourages Catholic engagement in social reform, in particular the eradication of poverty, as an "effective weapon against socialism." It is this ideological framework that informs the efforts of Catholics like Desjardins and, as we will see shortly, Father Moses Coady in Nova Scotia, and makes their Catholic countrymen (and women) more receptive to their message. Co-operatives, so long as they are not represented as leading to a socialist "co-operative commonwealth," fit well within the papal criteria for acceptable working-class organization. There was to be some common ground here between the Catholic perspective and the perspective of the bourgeois state.

One of the motives for Church-sanctioned promotion of co-operatives was the threat of competition from organizations that advocated class conflict or socialism. A similar principle motivated governments to move beyond merely providing enabling legislation toward more active promotion of co-ops. For example, in the 1920s the Fermiers unis (United Farmers) began to mobilize Quebec farmers on an explicitly class-conscious political agenda, demanding state intervention on behalf of the farmers to provide, for example, agricultural credit (Rudin 134–135). The Quebec government responded, as Canadian governments tend to, with a commission of inquiry.

The commission had a mandate to look into models for the delivery of agricultural credit. Perhaps, as legislators had anticipated, the co-operative movement was better organized than the Fermiers unis and made submissions opposing state-run agricultural credit. The recommendation in the end was for the state to support an increase in the lending capacity of the caisses by issuing government bonds to back larger loans. The state strengthened the co-operatives relative to the competing people's representative (the Fermiers unis) and at the same time empowered the co-ops to do what the government might otherwise have had to do itself. This is another example of the "autonomization" of power—getting popular organizations to govern more or less in line with state agendas.

THE ANTIGONISH MOVEMENT

The Antigonish movement is our second case study, named not so much for the town of Antigonish as the diocese of Antigonish, which encompasses the northeastern counties of Nova Scotia—Pictou, Antigonish, Guysborough, and the four counties of Cape Breton Island. A diocese is an administrative unit of the Catholic Church under the authority of a bishop. The fact that a diocese defines the geographic extent of the movement reflects

the sanction and support of Church leaders for organizing co-operatives in the region.

This is also a case where the state got involved, actively in this instance, with "fieldmen" of the provincial Department of Agriculture helping to organize farmers and organizers for the federal Department of Fisheries mobilizing the fishermen (Sacouman 111). As in the case with Quebec, the impetus to organize working people into co-operative associations—in this case, farmers, fishermen, miners, and steelworkers—came largely from "above." This is not to say that the conditions of people's lives in this region did not give them good cause for dissatisfaction. Nor did all of them suffer in silence waiting to be organized—militant trade unionists had already made headway among the industrial workers and miners of Cape Breton when the Antigonish movement began in the early 1930s.

The Class Basis for Resistance

Cape Breton industrial workers were classic examples of Marx's proletariat. They did not own the steel plants and mines in which they worked and had no other means of support besides their wage. Their work brought them together in large numbers, and they lived in the same neighbourhoods in coal towns or steel towns like Sydney. They worked in often brutal conditions. Where today we use diesel engines and hydraulics to move heavy rock and steel, companies used and abused men's muscle.

Injury and death were common through massive trauma from rock falls and explosions. Lives were shortened by more insidious assaults on the body from "black lung" acquired through breathing coal dust or cancer from steel plant fumes. You can see old photos of Cape Breton miners equipped with little more than a candle to light their way, a lunchbox, and a pickaxe ready to go as far as a mile underground to hack at a coal-face in cramped, watery, rat-infested seams.

Like men in many dangerous and desperate enterprises (think of war, for example), they developed intense bonds of camaraderie and a pride in their ability to survive their heroic daily battles. What they resented most was their inability to adequately feed, clothe, and house their families. Their wages were meagre. In addition, they often had to buy from company-owned stores, or rent company-owned housing at prices set by the company. They were utterly dependent on the company for their subsistence and directed all of their resentment toward this obvious local representative of "capital."

Farmers and fishermen faced great physical hardships as well. For many, these must have seemed rooted in unchangeable features of nature—thin, rocky soils with poor drainage and low fertility, or the moody, foggy, often violent waters of the North Atlantic. The social organization of their industries was also more complex than for industrial workers. There were many different ways of going to sea to catch fish. One could be captain or crew on boats owned by others—the schooners or the new trawlers that operated well offshore, or on the smaller inshore boats using hook and line or lobster traps.

Most, however, were owner-operators of small inshore boats—the least lucrative of the fisheries. In 1933 the average annual income of independent fishermen in the northeastern counties ranged from $75 to $175 (Sacouman 118–119). Think about it—many individuals would have been making less than $75 *in a year*. How would they have survived? They were losing out because of competition from large firms that owned trawlers, fish-processing and marketing operations—firms that could flood the market with cheap seafood.

The "independents" also suffered because of their reliance on others to process and market their fish. The initial buyer was typically a local merchant. Like the grain merchants in western Canada, these buyers had monopolies in the small ports where they operated and could dictate prices. Like the company stores in Cape Breton, they were often the exclusive supplier of the fishermens' retail needs and were in a position to exploit them a second time on prices for supplies.

The monopoly relationship was clinched by debt. Fishermen often had to borrow to buy rope, hooks, lumber, or other supplies in preparation for the fishing season. Instead of advancing money, the merchant would open a debit account that the fisherman would have to pay back in fish, valued as the merchant saw fit. This was called the "truck" or "credit system." You might recall Desjardins' romanticization of the way in which local, face-to-face community was supposed to temper the exploitive relations of capitalism, with the local lender taking to heart the needs of the local borrower. Evidently, this sort of *noblesse oblige* did not work in the case of the exploitive credit system in small coastal communities in the Maritimes.

Farming was also a poor source of income in northeastern Nova Scotia, in part because it was *not* sufficiently integrated into capitalist markets. Recall that prairie farmers had specialized in grain production for a global market. They produced little else and could never have survived without market income to buy the rest of their food and to amass "capital" to spend on ever more sophisticated machinery and larger tracts of land. Regions such as the Prairies with better soils, climate, and transportation infrastructure were out-competing northeastern Nova Scotia in all field crops. There were only a handful of commodities like beef and dairy for which farmers could find significant market demand beyond the

region. The kinds of capital investment demanded of prairie and Quebec farmers, the
acquisition of which created so much strain
and social dissatisfaction, would not have
paid off in northeastern Nova Scotia.

Farms remained small, and relied on
horses, oxen, and simple tools. Farmers produced a wide range of products that could
supply a family's needs on a non-cash basis—they had field and forage crops, animals,
large gardens and root cellars, orchards,
woodlots (for fuel and timber), as much for
their own use as for sale. In other words,
they farmed on a subsistence basis. As late
as 1940, 73 percent of farms in northeastern
Nova Scotia were classified this way in the
census (Sacouman 116). The physical and
economic hardships of these farm families
were steady and unrelenting, unlike others'
struggles to adapt to dynamic capitalist markets. They were more likely to address their
predicament by focusing on themselves and
their physical environment rather than on
capitalist merchants or corporations.

Subsistence strategies provide part of the
answer to the puzzle of how Maritimers were
able to survive at all on the meagre amounts
of cash they were able scrape together. (When
you hear today about the close to a billion
people worldwide who live on less than U.S.
$1 a day, you could look to similar strategies
to understand it.) The fisherman earning
less than $75 per year would probably have
eaten a lot of fish, but he might also have had
a small farm and woodlot, and owned a rifle
to bring deer or small game to the table. In
addition, various members of the household
might work for extra cash in forestry or in
the fish plant. The same applied to farmers.
In fact, many farmers of Scottish descent
earned most of their livelihood from fishing,
but insisted on calling themselves farmers
for the census because that status carried
with it the prestige of the "landed gentry" of
the old country.

The "Threat" of Militant Trade Unionism

This tendency to cross over between different employments also involved a crossing
over between different class locations, from
proletarian wage earners to petty-bourgeois
owner-operators (either buffered from the
market or under the thrall of the credit
system). The core unit was often a petty-
bourgeois landholding organized as a family
enterprise (a "family farm" in plain terms).
Husbands, wives, and children would all engage in these crossovers. Parents and young
people would travel as far as Boston for wage
work, but send money back to support the
Nova Scotia household. Certainly it would
not be uncommon for a fisherman or farmer
to have a son or a nephew in the Cape Breton
mines. The experience of exploitation, but
also the culture of resistance, could easily
cross these class and industry divides within
the region. It was for this reason that the
militant trade unionism of Cape Breton was
perceived as such a general threat.

Miners and steelworkers were aware
of Marx's analysis of the growing conflict
between two fundamental classes—the industrial proletariat and the bourgeoisie. The
theory corresponded to the simple structure
of exploitation that they saw in their own
company towns, so it was not surprising
that their leaders were typically socialists
or communists who adhered not only to a
Marxian vision of a society without "private
property" or a capitalist "cash nexus," but
also saw the road to a better world marked
by revolutionary violence. The state helped
to reinforce that expectation by opposing
worker strikes and demonstrations with violence. Six times between 1882 and 1925 the
government sent troops in to Cape Breton to
put down labour unrest (Jamieson 61).

In the 1930s when the Antigonish movement began, the Great Depression had further

weakened the legitimacy of capitalism. It was precisely the sort of crisis that Marx had predicted in which capitalist overproduction had led to business failure, massive unemployment, and ultimately to the bizarre situation where idle factories capable of producing goods stood side by side with millions of people in desperate need of those goods. One such crisis, predicted Marx, would spark the final revolution. The state clearly had an interest in finding a less inflammatory response to worker dissent, one that would rechannel worker resistance in more peaceful directions. Priests shared this interest. Their concern was not just for the political, but also the spiritual risks of their parishioners taking the militant socialist path.

Co-ops offered a legal, non-violent alternative to militant unions, an alternative that might even be educative of "capitalist" values. Co-ops were also well suited to solving some of the workers' problems. Industrial workers established co-op stores and co-op housing associations to break the control of the companies in Cape Breton coal and steel towns. Fishermen could use co-operative loan associations, the credit unions, and co-operative retail outlets to escape from the merchant-controlled credit system. They were also able to use co-ops to benefit from what we now call "value-added" aspects of their industry by setting up, for example, co-op lobster-canning plants. Like prairie farmers, fishermen and some Nova Scotia farmers created co-operatives to market their products (Sacouman 110–111).

Social Activist Priests

Priests were often the catalysts for these efforts. Activist priests in the Antigonish diocese, like J.J. "Father Jimmy" Tompkins, knew through Church networks what was going on in the co-operative movements in Europe and the rest of Canada from study, but also from meeting other activists and academics and first-hand observation. In addition, the diocese had its own university, St. Francis Xavier, which provided an institutional space for priests like Tompkins to work as professors or administrators. As vice-president of the university in the 1910s and 1920s, he advocated greater university outreach and initiated special programs of study for working people that brought academic knowledge to bear on the social and economic circumstances of their own lives. He found himself in a more activist role after 1922 in the tiny outport of Little Dover as its parish priest (he got banished there by the bishop, but that is an unrelated story) (Alexander 70).

Here he worked through a process of meeting and study and organization with his semi-literate parishioners, leading ultimately to their forming successful co-ops. Others, notably priest and professor Moses Coady, continued to mobilize in Antigonish and succeeded in establishing an extension department at the university in 1928. With extension, the model of outreach was to have university fieldworkers and occasionally faculty go out to surrounding communities and educate and organize on the Little Dover model. With Church and community leaders onside, the diocese had significant political clout and was able to muster additional state resources: fieldworkers from the Department of Agriculture and a salary from the Department of Fisheries for Moses Coady to organize the fishermen in 1929.

Coady was a charismatic presence at mass meetings and study groups he attended in rural and coastal communities. He also was able to define the movement more broadly for organizers and observers through his direction of the extension department and through his published writings. Coady emphasized that the movement was primarily educational, giving people the skills to think for themselves and come up with their own solutions to their problems. Co-operative organization was just one of the options that he would offer them.

This is not to say that he and other field-workers did not frame or pre-structure the outcome of people's thinking. One of his tenets was that the movement must remain nonpartisan, which implied being non-CCF and non-socialist. By and large, the movement conformed to this social-Catholic conception. There were exceptions. Some of the fieldworkers in the Sydney area had "moderate" socialist leanings (MacPherson 187). One Father "Mickey" MacDonald actually supported industrial unionism in 1936. In the end, the Antigonish movement, unlike the co-operative movement in western Canada, did not join the unions in bringing popular support to the CCF.

Antigonish Catholics were doing more, however, than simply acting out Church doctrine. The Church had sanctioned social justice work within a given set of parameters. The priests had to choose to act and create a program that worked in practice. Elsewhere priests took a different and opposite path. In Newfoundland in the 1910s they supported the merchants and the credit system against organized opposition from the fishermen (Brym and Neis 212–214). True, the fishermen's organization, the Fishermen's Protective Union, was class-based and not under Church guidance. Still Newfoundland priests presumably could have, but did not, mobilize a Catholic alternative. There was play here for what sociologists call "agency"—the capacity of people to alter the course of events through the creative choices they make.

There were also "structural" limits to agency. Coady and the Antigonish team campaigned with equal fervour throughout the northeastern counties of Nova Scotia. But, as sociologist James Sacouman has shown, their success varied depending on the type of capitalist exploitation the people suffered in different districts. Co-operatives did not take hold as well in census subdivisions where farming predominated, because of the prevalence of subsistence farming. (Remember that subsistence farmers were more likely to attribute their troubles to the weather or to their own efforts rather than economic exploitation.) Within farming subdivisions it was those dominated by mid-sized capitalist farms rather than the large capitalist or small subsistence farms that had higher numbers of co-ops and credit unions. Co-operative organizations were most prevalent, however, in subdivisions where the credit system dominated the fishery or the company town dominated the lives of industrial workers.

We have a bit more evidence now to answer one of the questions that I posed earlier, which was: Were co-ops used to co-opt workers into supporting capitalism? I do not think that the answer is a simple "yes," but I will let you ponder that for a while longer. The next case of the co-operative movement in Saskatchewan will complicate the answer further. Other questions have arisen along the way and I should perhaps make them explicit now. One is: Why did the co-operative movement succeed better in some places than others? The evidence so far points to a relationship with the type of capitalist exploitation.

Co-ops flourish as a response to forms of monopoly capitalist exploitation. In particular, the theme of petty-bourgeois class resistance to the dominance of monopoly capital applies to all three cases: small business people in Quebec, farmers and fishers in Antigonish, and farmers in Saskatchewan. Leadership also makes a difference. One of my interests is in how the state often supports these leaders or takes on the leadership role itself. The question again is why in some cases and not in others. My hypothesis, for you to consider, is that the state actively supports co-operatives where there is a perceived threat that working people would otherwise organize their own, much more radical anti-capitalist movements.

THE "CO-OPERATIVE COMMONWEALTH" IN SASKATCHEWAN

The Saskatchewan case reinforces this idea. The place gained provincial status only in 1905 at a time when its agricultural population was being defined by massive immigration. It had few political traditions, and there was great suspicion among legislators of the traditions that young settlers were bringing with them, particularly from eastern Europe but also from England, where many had been trade unionists before deciding to try their luck in Canada's "last best west." That unease is reflected in a report in the *Canadian Annual Review of Public Affairs* of the 1909 meeting of farmers' organization, the Saskatchewan Grain Growers' Association (SGGA). The members had passed a motion advocating government ownership of grain elevators, and the reporter warned that "[t]he discussion of the motion was notable for the expression of some decidedly Socialistic and Radical opinions."

State, Class, and the Politics of Co-operation

These young immigrants were radical and probably still smouldering with the same anger that Bob McNair had expressed in 1901. The government responded to this agitation

with (can you guess?) a royal commission. The Elevator Commission, set up in 1910, recommended against state ownership in favour of co-operative ownership supported by government grants. From this point onwards the Saskatchewan government's promotion of co-operatives only increased. In 1914 a special "Co-operative Organization Branch" of the Department of Agriculture was established to encourage and help set the agenda of co-operative development.

The SGGA proved able, without government assistance, to organize its members into grain-marketing co-ops and retail co-ops for farm supplies. The Co-operative Organization Branch focused its efforts on marketing co-ops in beef, dairy, honey, and other products that they hoped to encourage farmers to diversify into. The idea here was to make farmers less dependent on the single commodity of wheat and in this way to protect them from the volatile market somewhat like the way that Maritime subsistence farmers were buffered from global capitalism and its radicalizing effects.

In the realms of grain marketing and farm retail, co-operative organizations were formed genuinely from the "ground up" rather than being dependent on the state or some other social class of organizers, such as the small-town bourgeoisie or the priesthood. Petty-bourgeois farmers, perhaps for this reason, also retained control of the meaning of the co-operative movement. Co-operative ventures like the Wheat Pool were radical, at least in intent. The Pool was meant not merely to compete with the corporate players in the wheat-marketing industry, but to replace the market principle of organizing wheat buying and selling with the principle of democratic planning through an overarching co-operative venture.

Many understood the Pool and other co-ops to be helping to establish the values and institutions that would form the basis for a socialist society, a "co-operative com-monwealth" to replace capitalism. As one farm leader put it in 1944:

> It's really all one movement that we have here. We are building socialism through the Wheat Pool, through our co-op store, through our UFC [United Farmers of Canada, heir to the SGGA] local, as well as through the CCF [Co-operative Common-wealth Federation].... We feel that we are building the CCF when we build our co-op store, and we are building co-operation and destroy-ing the profit system when we build the CCF. (Lipset 253–254)

For many adherents to the movement, the co-op promised not just a better price, but a better world, and their commitment to it had an almost religious fervency. As the actors in a famous play about the movement put it, some were ready to "drag their ass across a field of broken glass just to buy a can of co-op peas" (Tahn, National Film Board, and Twenty-Fifth Street House Theatre). The socialist interpretation of the movement did not go unchallenged. Many, including of-ficials and fieldworkers for the Department of Agriculture, and the Extension Division of the University of Saskatchewan, preferred to represent it as simply another business strategy practical within and consistent with capitalism. However, state-supported fieldworkers had tremendous difficulty getting out into the country, meeting with farmers, and putting their message across.

Independence from State Influence

In Nova Scotia, Coady had used a car on his organizing junkets through the coastal villages. He might never have succeeded if people along the way had not been ready to haul his car out of the bog when it skidded off the icy, rock track that passed for a road, to welcome him, put him up for the night, and call the community out to hear him speak. Road conditions were, if anything, worse in Saskatchewan. Rural roads were not paved or cleared of snow in the winter. Government experts who set out on them to connect with the farmers did not get the same respect and welcome that a priest such as Coady would have done in Catholic Nova Scotia.

To make things worse, prairie farmers did not live in villages like fishermen. They lived on their farms, huge by comparison to Maritime farms. In fact, in wheat-grow-ing districts, farmers were fewer and more spread out than in any other rural region except ranching country. Fieldmen had to travel farther. And for any meeting to take place, farmers had to be willing to gather together at some predetermined spot to receive the touring expert. If the farmers were not interested, meetings would not and often did not happen.

Farmers were shielded from state influ-ence by their dispersed pattern of residence. Representatives from "their own" orga-nizations—the SGGA and later the UFC, the Pool, and the CCF—had better success touring the rural areas to shape people's thinking and mobilize support. Relying on volunteers, they could afford to put more people in the field. More importantly, they had organizers "on the ground," local people ready to receive representatives and mobilize the districts to come out to meetings. The Pool had hundreds of local "Pool commit-tees" and was eventually able to hire a team of fieldmen with offices in smaller centres whose job it was to liaise between the locals and the central offices. Department of Ag-riculture officials dreamed of this degree of organizational capacity, but never had the money or the local support to pull it off.

Anti-capitalism and Class Alliances

Saskatchewan farmers' organizations were also removed from the influence of other social classes—they tended to be almost exclusively organizations of the agrarian petty-bourgeoisie. Unique community geography—the fact that farmers did not live in villages with small-town merchants, doctors, and notaries as they did in Nova Scotia and Quebec—contributed to this exclusivity. Sociologist Robert Brym has argued, based on a comparison between Alberta, Saskatchewan, and New Brunswick, that what he calls "inter-class ties" between farmers and these small urban classes tended to make agrarian protest movements more right wing. Absence of such ties or greater ties with proletarian workers tends to produce left-wing movements (Brym 348).

Does his hypothesis apply to our other two cases? The Quebec case, where the caisse populaire movement was dominated by the small-town petty-bourgeoisie rather than farmers, seems to fit. Movement leaders, including Desjardins, were, like Coady, strongly nonpartisan and anti-CCF. The Antigonish case is more complex. The movement was more left-leaning in Cape Breton where interclass ties with industrial workers were strongest. But generally the priesthood, not of the working class, had a conservative influence. In the larger towns like Antigonish itself, many local luminaries were on side not because of any dissatisfaction with capitalism, but because they thought that co-ops could provide local economic stability and stem the out-migration of young people from the region. Their concern, like that of the Quebec petty-bourgeoisie, was for the economic survival of a region and a "people" defined in ethnic terms (i.e., Scottish Catholics), not for a social class in its struggle against capitalism. An important question that Brym does not fully answer

is why Alberta farmers made common cause with small-town people, while Saskatchewan farmers continued to see them, particularly small-town businesspeople, as part of the capitalist enemy.

Whatever the answer, the situation in Saskatchewan was unique. Under these conditions of class exclusivity, many co-ops did, as the Canadian senator had feared in 1906, become "schools" for "socialistic doctrines." People read and discussed politics in the Pool committees and union locals. There was no TV, no films, and not much to do over the long winter months. People would combine political meetings with socializing and dancing. Movement involvement could be "educative" in this sense. But people also learned how to *act* politically.

Co-ops and other farm organizations had executives and boards of directors that had to be filled by local people. Participants learned how to chair meetings, how to speak in public, how to manage funds, and run elections. In order to meet on a regular basis, these people had to be drawn from a fairly small radius. Since the population was spread so thinly in the wheat-growing regions, there were very few people to draw from. That meant that an unusually large proportion of the population was called upon and forced to learn these skills.

Here is a personal account of how this sort of education worked:

> My father was elected vice-president of the SGGA local early in the twenties. He hadn't wanted the job, but he was a leading farmer in the district and had been a member for a long time, so some of the other officials prevailed upon him to take the post.
>
> Shortly after he was elected, the local sponsored a meeting by a Progressive M.P. The chairman of the lodge took sick and my father was

told that he would have to preside over the meeting. He tried to get out of it, for he had never made a speech in his life. He couldn't, however, and had to preside. For days before the meeting he stopped all work and went around the house reciting a five-minute speech which he had memorized. The family almost went crazy listening to it.

On the day of the meeting, he delivered the speech and afterward was complimented on his ability by the M.P. After that, he lost his fear. He would chair meetings and gradually began to make speeches for the organization. By the time the CCF was organized he had no fear in facing a meeting of hundreds and speaking for hours. Before he died he must have delivered hundreds of speeches at CCF meetings, co-operative meetings and other farmers' gatherings. (qtd. in Lipset 247–248)

Farmers developed a socialist analysis and a set of skills that enabled them to act on their beliefs. Seymour Martin Lipset, who interviewed the farmer in the preceding quote, argued that the broad base of political awareness and skill kept the movement from becoming co-opted. The "grassroots" were committed socialists and were not willing to defer to authorities—politicians from the traditional parties, agricultural experts, professors, or even their own leaders—who told them otherwise. Part of the key for Lipset was that the "densely" organized movement supplied a pool of people with leadership skills ready to replace leaders who "sold out" or became too moderate in their thinking.

People were energized and confident in their ability to make a better world. They knew they could do it themselves without experts to tell them how. The Wheat Pool

committee in Salvador, Saskatchewan, typified this spirit in its report of 1933:

> We, the Co-operators, have at least the satisfaction of knowing that we have created an economic machine that works, and if the economists of today are not alive to its significance, they will shortly be compelled to construct their economic structure out of its accomplished results. The solution of the present difficulties can only be effectively accomplished by service to the community instead of profit to the individual. (qtd. in Bantjes 110)

Despite the fact that Church and state had promoted the co-operative movement to check the spread of socialism among working people, here the movement helped to mobilize popular support for socialism, or at least the CCF version of it. The CCF came to power in Saskatchewan in 1944 largely on the strength of the movement culture of which the co-ops were a part. But its program reflected a compromise of the values and interests of the other partners in the national party, including the labour movement and urban socialist intellectuals.

The Farm-Labour Coalition and Political Tensions

Many labour leaders were wary of the role of co-operatives in the socialist project. Some saw in them the potential to recruit workers to the "capitalist frame of mind," just as many state officials had (Gurney 156). Also, experience with co-operatives in England had shown that they often did not treat their own workers any better than capitalist firms did. Co-operative stores and banks typically hired managers and employees who were not members of the co-operative. Not only were these employees sometimes given low wages, but they were also sometimes discouraged from joining unions (Gurney 155). Other labour leaders were suspicious of the class basis of marketing co-ops. As they rightly pointed out, these were associations of small capitalists trying to better their position vis-à-vis larger capitalist firms.

Could capitalists who, whether large or small, were nonetheless invested in private property ever really break free of capitalism? In answering this question they often followed Lenin, who argued that the petty-bourgeoisie were "Janus-faced" or exhibited two contradictory personas. They could, like prairie farmers, join with workers' struggles against capitalist exploitation, but only for a time. In the end, because of their investment in property, their capitalist face would always reveal itself and they would side with the capitalist system.

For their part, co-operators were often wary of urban socialists. Those who supported the parliamentary route to socialism often gave a prominent role to the central government in reforming capitalism. They advocated state ownership of major industries and resources. Many in the co-operative movement valued their relative independence from government and the principle of small-scale democracy that they saw in community-based, community-governed co-ops. They warned that even if central governments were formally democratic, their scale, distance from the electorate, and their rigid bureaucratic structures gave them anti-democratic tendencies. If the powers of the state were expanded to cover all of economic life, it risked becoming totalitarian.

Many CCF intellectuals attempted to balance the two positions by arguing that while state ownership was necessary in large industries such as the transportation infrastructure (e.g., railways), it should be counterbalanced by a large co-operative sector controlled by thousands of democratic governing bodies independent of the state. The co-operatives would keep alive the democratic movement culture that could also, just as Lipset later argued, challenge and revitalize governmental democracy at the federal, provincial, and local levels. This is an important approach to solving the "problem of bureaucratization" mentioned in the previous chapter.

We can see the CCF as one of the fruits of the prairie co-operative movement. Over time the CCF toned down its socialist rhetoric, but that is a story of parliamentary politics, not of social movements. If by co-optation we mean accommodation to capitalism, then the CCF did become co-opted, but not before transforming Canada's political culture and initiating "social democratic" reforms that we enjoy today, including recognition and sanction for collective bargaining and the establishment of medicare. The co-operatives that once formed a movement of social transformation have, in the latter half of the 20th century, adapted very pragmatically to their niches within the capitalist economy.

Saskatchewan's petty-bourgeois farmers, invested in capital—land and machinery—on a scale that would be difficult to imagine for earlier generations, now vote Conservative, so perhaps Lenin was right about the petty-bourgeoisie—their capitalist face always eventually manifests itself. But after how long, and how much social transformation can they effect in the meantime? This remains an important question since small farmers and artisans continue to be key players in developing countries' transition to capitalism.

BOX 2.2:

CO-OPERATIVES AND FAIR TRADE

Co-operatives are taking part in new forms of global solidarity. Consider, for example, "Kuapa," a cocoa farmers' co-operative in Ghana. Its tremendous success in the 1990s, growing as it did from 200 to 50,000 members, was in part due to partnerships with "fair trade" organizations in Europe (Akosah). The idea behind the fair trade movement is that "free trade" benefits large traders—like multinational agribusiness firms and the Western consumers they sell to—only by exploiting global competition between desperate small producers in the developing world. Fair trade firms are willing to pay higher prices to suppliers who give a just return to their agricultural workers. Democratic farmer-owned co-operatives are ideal partners for fair trade importers. Often fair trade firms, like Canada's "Just-Us" coffee importers, are themselves co-operatives (www.justuscoffee.com/).

Kuapa's success can also be attributed to its broader vision of local economic development. It has used capital generated by the co-op to build small corn mills and palm extractors that local women use to create "value-added" products. It also lends money under a "microcredit" scheme that women can use to diversify into small-scale vegetable and poultry operations.

Support for this co-op has not come from the Ghanaian government. In fact, Ghanaian people are very suspicious of government sponsorship because of heavy-handed attempts in the past to use co-operatives as instruments of the ruling party. Similar schemes, in particular the partnerships between North and South, are sponsored by organizations like Oxfam, the International Co-operative Alliance (ICA; www.coop.org/ica/ica/coopday/enmessage2004. html), the International Confederation of Free Trade Unions (ICFTU; www.icftu.org/), and the International Labour Organization (ILO). Why would non-governmental organizations, rather than states, be players here? Do you suppose that their motivations are similar to the motivations of states as discussed in this chapter?

Source: Kwabena Sarpong Akosah, " Killing Distrust," *New Internationalist* 368 (2004), August 31, 2004, www.newint.org/issue368/distrust.htm.

What about the workers' co-operatives, which many socialists had much greater confidence in? Marx went so far as to say that in worker co-ops "the antagonism between capital and labour is overcome" (Lévesque 134). More recently management theorists have promoted various forms of worker investment as a means of getting workers to identify with the company and its interest in making a profit. Many workers' co-ops were created in Canada, particularly in Quebec, in the 1980s. However, there is little in the way of sociological analysis of them.

There is, however, a vast literature on the highly successful system of workers co-ops in the town of Mondragón in the Basque country of Spain. Mondragón co-ops are involved in industrial manufacture of such things as kitchen appliances, machine tools, and electrical components. The co-op complex includes co-ops that support this activity through technical training, research and development (of such things as robotic assemblers), and credit institutions to provide capital.

All of the workers in the industrial co-ops have shares in the enterprise and can vote at shareholders' meetings on a one-person, one-vote basis. The shareholders elect a board of directors, which in turn appoints a management team, so the workers indirectly hire their bosses. This in itself would not be enough to eliminate class antagonism and worker alienation. Two additional features help to minimize (but apparently never eliminate) these tensions (Kasmir 35–37).

First, workers are organized into cells of 10 people, each of which elects a representative to a "social council," which acts as a liaison between labour and management. Second, both workers and management are paid, not by a wage, but on a formula linked to the profits of the enterprise, so they have equal interests in the profitability of the firm. But the differentials in pay, which are determined by set criteria of skill, etc., are kept to a minimum, so that one worker's contribution is less likely to be seen as unfairly valued relative to another's. The ratio between the least skilled worker and the senior management was kept at a 1:3 ratio in the 1970 and revised to a 1:5 ratio in the 1980s. Compare this to the ratio between the salaries of the average CEO and average worker in the 365 largest U.S. firms: 42:1 in 1982 and 301:1 in 2003 (Leondar-Wright).

CONCLUSION

In many social movements people organize in order to influence the powers that be. At the beginning of this chapter I suggested that the co-op movement represented a different approach in which people organized independently of corporate or state powers to solve problems on their own. However, a more complex story has emerged through our three case studies. In Canada the state (as well as the Catholic Church) has both facilitated and in some instances promoted the co-operative movement. Judging from their own words in debate, the thinking of state legislators seems to have been that co-operatives could support a state interest in reinforcing "capitalist" values.

Our discussion of the contexts in which Canadian governments promoted co-operation suggests that legislators and bureaucrats were most keen on co-operatives where the threat from more radical forms of organization was greatest. Departments of agriculture, fisheries, and even special departments of co-operative development were using funds and fieldworkers in an effort to channel popular activism away from socialism and toward forms of economic reform more compatible with capitalism. In these instances are co-ops merely being enlisted in a state project of "governance"? If so, the independence of the co-operative movement from the "powers that be" is not as clear-cut as it at first appears.

A more general point worth remembering is that the ways in which states (or corporations, for that matter) respond to popular unrest can profoundly shape the direction that that protest takes. What might have happened in Cape Breton, for instance, if the government had continued with a one-dimensional policy of repression against the miners' unrest? Marx appears to have assumed that the state response to worker militancy would be unrelenting antagonism. But the history of the 20th century has shown a much more complex set of state responses, including compromise, accommodation, and subtle co-optation.

Another surprise for Marx would have been the extent to which anti-capitalist movements in the 20th century have gained mass support from farmers and other "petty-commodity producers" whose preferred form of organization was the co-operative. You cannot understand the way 19th-century "laissez faire" capitalism was reformed and restrained in the Canadian context without reference to the role of socialist farmers fighting for their "co-operative common-wealth." Just how "progressive" you think these reforms were will depend on how far you go with Marx and Engels in the belief that "progress" can be measured only relative to the aim of eliminating capitalism.

I did promise that we would use Marx and Engels' model of class formation as an "exemplar" against which to compare other instances of social movement organization. What would the comparison look like in the case of co-operative movement organization in Canada? Farmers and fishermen, since they are petty-bourgeois and not members of the industrial proletariat, are, from Marx and Engels' perspective, the "wrong" class for anti-capitalist struggles. Capitalist development certainly gave them cause for dissent—it was principally those threatened by exploitation by or competition from monopoly capital who resorted to co-operative organization. Did it increase their numbers and organization? Marx was right insofar as capitalist development tended to reduce the numbers of petty-bourgeois farmers and fishermen in Canada in the 20th century. (However, the co-operative movement helped to slow this decline.)

The large and expanding size of capitalist farms in western Canada did not concentrate farmers in urban locales; quite the opposite, it spread them out across huge expanses of space. However, the fact that farmers did not live in towns or villages meant that their "neighbourhoods" included only farms and ensured that their social networks were class exclusive very like the networks of shoemakers in Lynn. In addition, their inaccessibility ensured that they were relatively immune from outside influences and were able to nurture their socialist culture much as Lynn workers had nurtured their culture of working-class militancy.

Globally the co-operative movement is huge. Some 600 million people are members of co-ops (Ransom). People's involvement cannot be understood simply in class terms. Consumer co-ops, always a large component of the movement, have no clear class base. Many co-ops serve the needs of women and indigenous peoples, although typically by supporting their efforts as petty commodity producers. They play an important role in the transition to capitalism of developing countries.

Where common property traditions still thrive there is a cultural fit with the idea of co-operative organization. Do you suppose that in these contexts, the co-op movement would have an anti-capitalist and anarchist dimension as it did in Europe and western Canada? There is often an interest on the part of states and international donor institutions and development NGOs in spreading capitalist skills/resources to the poor. Would the influence of these organizations frame the meaning of co-operation in terms of integration into global capitalism?

REFERENCES

Akosah, Kwabena Sarpong. "Killing Distrust." *New Internationalist* 368 (2004), August 31, 2004, www.newint.org/issue368/distrust.htm.

Alexander, Anne McDonald. *The Antigonish Movement: Moses Coady and Adult Education Today.* Toronto: Thompson Educational Publishing, 1997.

Bantjes, Rod. *Improved Earth: Prairie Space as Modern Artefact, 1869-1944.* Toronto: University of Toronto Press, 2005.

Birchall, Johnston. *The International Co-operative Movement.* Manchester; New York: Manchester University Press. Distributed exclusively in the U.S. by St. Martin's Press, 1997.

Brym, Robert J. "Regional Social Structure and Agrarian Radicalism in Canada: Alberta Saskatchewan and New Brunswick." *Canadian Review of Sociology and Anthropology* 15, no. 3 (1978): 339-351.

Brym, Robert J., and Barbara Neis. "Regional Factors in the Formation of the Fisherman's Protective Union of Newfoundland." *Underdevelopment and Social Movements in Atlantic Canada*, edited by Robert J. Brym and R. James Sacouman. Toronto: New Hogtown Press, 1979.

Canada. "Report of the Special Committee of the House of Commons to Whom Was Referred Bill No. 2, an Act Respecting Industrial and Co-operative Societies." *Sessional Papers, Appendix No. 3*, 7 Edward VII, A. (1901).

The Canadian Annual Review of Public Affairs, 1909. Toronto: The Annual Review Publishing Co., 1909.

Gurney, Peter. *Co-operative Culture and the Politics of Consumption in England, 1870-1930.* Manchester; New York: Manchester University Press. Distributed exclusively in the U.S. by St. Martin's Press, 1996.

Jamieson, Patrick. "Antigonish, the Two-Sided Legacy." *Toward a New Maritimes*, edited by I. McKay and S. Milsom. Charlottetown: Ragweed, 1992.

Kasmir, Sharryn. *The Myth of Mondragón: Cooperatives, Politics, and Working-Class Life in a Basque Town.* SUNY Series in the Anthropology of Work. Albany: State University of New York Press, 1996.

Kropotkin, Peter. *Mutual Aid.* London: Heinemann, 1902. August 30, 2004, www.spunk.org/library/writers/kropotki/sp001503/.

Leondar-Wright, Betsy. "CEO Pay/Worker Pay Ratio Reaches 301-to-1." *Common Dreams Progressive Newswire* (April 14, 2004), August 30, 2004, www.commondreams.org/news2004/0414-10.htm.

Lévesque, Benoît. "State Intervention and the Development of Cooperatives (Old and New) in Quebec 1968-88." *Studies in Political Economy* 31 (1990): 107-139.

Lipset, Seymour M. *Agrarian Socialism: The Co-operative Commonwealth Federation in Saskatchewan, a Study in Political Sociology,* 1950. Berkeley: California Paperback Edition, 1971.

MacPherson, Ian. *Each for All: A History of the Cooperative Movement in English Canada, 1900-1945.* Toronto: Macmillan, 1979.

Moorhouse, Herbert Joseph. *Deep Furrows: Which Tells of Pioneer Trails along Which the Farmers of Western Canada Fought Their Way to Great Achievements in Co-operation.* Toronto: G.J. McLeod, 1918.

Ransom, David. "Tales of the Unexpected." *New Internationalist* 368 (2004), August 31, 2004, www.newint.org/issue368/keynote.htm.

Rudin, Ronald. *In Whose Interest? Quebec's Caisses Populaires, 1900-1945.* Montreal: McGill-Queen's University Press, 1990.

Sacouman, R. James. "Underdevelopment and the Structural Origins of Antigonish Movement Co-operatives in Eastern Nova Scotia." *Underdevelopment and Social Movements in Atlantic Canada*, edited by R. James Sacouman and Robert J. Brym. Toronto: New Hogtown Press, 1979.

Tahn, Andras, National Film Board of Canada, and Twenty-fifth Street House Theatre. *Paper Wheat.* National Film Board of Canada, 1979.

CRITICAL THINKING QUESTIONS

1. How effective do you think co-ops were in co-opting workers into supporting capitalism?
2. Explain why the co-operative movement succeeded better in some places than others.
3. How different are the interests of the proletariat and the petty-bourgeois? Was Marx right to distrust the petty-bourgeois as agents of his communist revolution? Were officials of the Canadian state right to distrust the loyalty of the proletariat to capitalism?
4. In what ways did petty-bourgeois organization follow the model of class formation outlined by Marx and Engels? In what way(s) did it differ?
5. If you were concerned about economic globalization increasing exploitation and alienation in Third World countries, would you promote the co-operative movement there? Why or why not?

FURTHER READING

Brym, Robert J., and R. James Sacouman. *Underdevelopment and Social Movements in Atlantic Canada*. Toronto: New Hogtown Press, 1979.
This is a collection of essays that employ Marxist theory to explain co-operative and union movement activity of primary producers (farmers and fishers). The approach is comparative, looking at differences in the strength or radicalism of these movements in different places in order to identify features of the social context that explain such differences.

Kropotkin, Peter. *Fields, Factories and Workshops*, 1898. Montreal: Black Rose, 1994.
Anarchist Peter Kropotkin outlines his vision of a decentralized economic and political system that inspired many in the Canadian co-operative movement.

Levesque, Benoit. "State Intervention and the Development of Cooperatives (Old and New) in Quebec 1968–88." *Studies in Political Economy* 31 (1990): 107–139.
This is an excellent study that focuses on the relationship between the state and the co-operative movement in Quebec since the 1960s.

Lipset, Seymour M. *Agrarian Socialism: The Co-operative Commonwealth Federation in Saskatchewan, a Study in Political Sociology*, 1950. Berkeley: California Paperback Edition, 1971.
This is the classic sociological study of the political success of the farmers' anti-capitalist co-operative movement in western Canada.

Rudin, Ronald. *In Whose Interest? Quebec's Caisses Populaires, 1900-1945*. Montreal: McGill-Queen's University Press, 1990.
This is the best English-language analysis of the co-operative movement in early 20th-century Quebec. Rudin shows how this apparently popular movement was implicated in projects of Church, state, and economic elites.

RELEVANT WEB SITES

Canadian Co-operative Association

http://www.coopscanada.coop/

> The national "industry association" for Canadian co-operatives maintains this Web site. Find out how they are attempting to promote co-operatives in Canada and the world. Check out their well-organized links. See especially the links on international development resources: This is a good portal for exploring the ways in which the UN and other aid organizations promote co-operatives as tools for international development.

Centre for the Study of Co-operatives

http://coop-studies.usask.ca

> This Canadian site is a must if you are interested in the role of co-operatives in agriculture in the 21st century. (See also the BC Institute for Co-operative Studies; http://web.uvic.ca/bcics/)

International Co-operative Alliance

www.coop.org

> This "co-operative information superhighway" is provided by the main international lobbying organization for co-operatives. Check out their current issues section and see what they are doing with regard to gender equality, fair trade (see also what OXFAM is doing on this issue www.maketradefair.com/), HIV/AIDS, and youth, among other topics.

La Siembra Co-op

www.lasiembra.com

> Canada-based retail co-operative and trading venture with producer co-operatives in Latin America.

Mondragón Corporación Cooperativa

www.mondragon.mcc.es/ing/index.asp

> This is the official Web site of the Mondragon complex of co-operatives. See what insights it gives you into one of the most successful and long-lasting co-operative ventures in history. The FAQ is especially worth looking at for answers to questions such as: Do you consider co-operativism to be an alternative to the capitalist production system? How do the Mondragon co-operatives contribute to a fairer distribution of wealth? Does Mondragon continue to maintain its co-operative identity even after all these years and despite the effects of globalization and a predominance of individualistic values?

TransFair Canada

www.transfair.ca

> The organization hosting this site is working to establish alternative systems of international trade in which exploitation of workers and the environment in the South is minimized.

Chapter 3

MOVEMENT INNOVATIONS IN THE 1960S: RESOURCE MOBILIZATION?

INTRODUCTION: CIVIL RIGHTS AND THE NEW VOCABULARY OF ACTIVISM

In 1963 Martin Luther King was in a Birmingham, Alabama, jail for breaking the law. The city of Birmingham had recently declared all "racial" demonstrations illegal and King had responded by organizing a demonstration. He had also been supporting and encouraging illegal "sit-ins" staged by Blacks in Birmingham. A sit-in involved taking seats at a "Whites-only" lunch counter and politely asking to be served. If you were Black, this resulted in being dragged off to jail and often attracted mobs of jeering and taunting White racists doing "demonstrations" like tying a hangman's noose to remind you of what White mobs were capable of in the South.

King and the courageous men and women who sat in at the lunch counters were practising "civil disobedience," a tradition of protest that had been defined by the American non-conformist Henry David Thoreau and perfected by Mahatma Gandhi as an effective collective-action tactic for disempowered people. The idea was to break an unjust law with the intention of being arrested, jailed, perhaps even beaten, in order to draw public attention to the injustice. The harsher and more excessive the reaction from police and authorities, the better the advertisement for injustice. From his cell King wrote: "We should never forget that everything Adolf Hitler did in Germany was 'legal,' and everything the Hungarian freedom fighters did in Hungary was 'illegal'" (King 87). (The Hungarians he refers to had risen up in 1956 against a repressive Soviet-backed communist regime only to be defeated by Soviet tanks.)

King's example of principled defiance inspired the youth of Birmingham to take up where he had left off. On May 2 1,000 jubilant, singing youth asserted their right to assemble on the streets of their town and gather at a Baptist church, one of the few sites commonly claimed as public space by southern Blacks. On the second day of demonstrations the authorities responded. For days, police, under the command of Eugene "Bull" Connor, battled protesters using batons, attack dogs, and fire hoses. These fire hoses packed enough pressure to "rip the bark off of trees, knock bricks loose from walls" and scatter bodies as though they were rag dolls (Socialist Worker).

The dogs shredded people's clothing and baton-wielding police bloodied heads and faces. Bull Connor instructed his men to allow White spectators to get a close-up look, saying, "I want them to see the dogs work" (Kaplan). All the while television news cameras were rolling. The violence made for gripping TV, but distant audiences in the rest of the United States, in Canada, and around the world did not "read" it with anything like Connor's cruel intent. Instead they were shocked, and became in increasing numbers sympathetic both to the demonstrators' aims and their non-violent tactics of resistance.

The televised drama spoke to a global public but also to the older generation of Blacks and their leadership in Birmingham, many of whom had initially opposed King and his confrontational tactics. Faced with the growing resolve of Blacks within their own city, and public and political pressure from beyond its borders, Birmingham authorities backed down and promised to rescind the city's segregationist laws and discriminatory hiring practices. Over the next three months, in hundreds of cities and towns across the southern United States, Blacks staged "Little Birminghams" where they organized demonstrations, sit-ins, and boycotts inspired by the scenes in Birmingham.

No doubt there were thousands of personal channels that linked activists and organizations between these separate locales. At the same time television had begun to act as a new channel of communication linking people unknown to one another in common action. During the arrests in one Little Birmingham, Danville, Virginia, police, apparently worried about the influence of TV on the spread of demonstrations, interviewed the Black youths in custody and learned that 70 percent had television at home (Thomas)

The global reach of news media had helped the U.S. civil rights movement throughout the 1950s and early 1960s. Civil rights activists watched what was going on in the rest of the world and took lessons from such events as the struggles against colonial domination in India, Africa, and Soviet-dominated Europe. And the rest of the world watched with intense interest the struggles of Blacks in the U.S. The U.S. claimed to be a power for good in the world, intervening in foreign affairs only to spread freedom and democracy. But how could it make this claim, many asked, when it denied its own people basic democratic or "civil rights": equality before the law, the right to free speech and public assembly, the unhampered right to vote and hold public office?

Exposure of conditions in the southern United States weakened the superpower's moral authority both with its enemies—the Soviet Union and its communist "satellites"—and also with its allies. A French commentator echoed the sentiments of so many around the world when he wrote, "If the U.S. wanted to appear as the champion of democracy throughout the world, [it] would do well to see first all [its] coloured population enjoys the benefits of democracy." (qtd. in Layton 7). The U.S. role in world affairs provided an opportunity, some social movement theorists would say a political opportunity "structure," that could be exploited by civil rights movement activists in their local struggles.

The civil rights movement was pioneering a new vocabulary of social dissent that, over the next decade, would be taken up, expanded, and transformed by young activists in the "New Left," peace, women's liberation, anti-poverty, environmental, gay rights, and Red Power movements. In this chapter we will trace this emerging vocabulary, in particular the novel uses of the electronic media to dramatize issues and to coordinate the efforts of activists. As we will see from our three main examples—civil rights, the New Left, and the peace movement—the motives, style, and participants of these new movements all confounded the expectations of existing social movement theories, including those of Marx and Engels. Social scientists scrambled to make sense of the changing reality. We will examine one of the more influential theories they came up with—resource mobilization theory—to see how well it explains the emergence and decline of the 1960s social movements.

The Electronic Sensorium

When we talk about the mass media helping civil rights activists to expose injustice globally, we are talking about more than just television. Newspapers in the 19th century and radio in the early 20th century had global reach. Television was still a popular novelty in the 1950s (although most middle-class White American youth grew up watching it). Not until the 1960s in North America did it become the essential, obligatory feature of people's everyday lives that we know it as today. People in the 1960s believed that there was something qualitatively different about this medium. Canadian theorist Marshall McLuhan became the media guru of the decade with his theory that media are cybernetic extensions of our ability to perceive the world—an "electronic sensorium." The technical characteristics of the medium shape both how we perceive the world and how we think about it.

He characterized television as a "tactile" medium, not, perversely, as a visual one. To understand what he means, think of how a blind person senses her world through touch. Her impressions are experienced sequentially, concretely, and up close—that is, within arm's reach. And they are ordered in relation to how she moves her arm as much as how things are arranged "objectively" in space. TV is like this: a sequential series of dots on the screen, making up a sequential series of images brought from different times and places and juxtaposed in your living room, close enough to touch.

Consider the TV coverage of another civil rights event, "Bloody Sunday" in Selma, Alabama, in 1965. The Student Nonviolent Coordinating Committee (SNCC) had organized a silent march to "witness" against Alabama policies that disenfranchised Black voters. The Alabama police went on a rampage of bloody violence in front of the TV cameras. The ABC network interrupted its broadcast of a documentary on Nazi war criminals, "Judgement at Nuremberg," to report the news of Selma along with the images of terrified people running from helmeted, uniformed police wielding clubs and bullwhips and firing tear gas (Africanamericans).

No one needed to make a logical argument to link these two times and places in people's minds, to suggest that Nazism was alive in Alabama or to point out that the oppression of U.S. Blacks was similar to the persecution of the German Jews. The media juxtaposition encouraged people to make the connection "laterally," analogically. The medium of TV, argued McLuhan, in this way makes its own messages, but also favours non-rational, intuitive thought. It also gives our experience of the world the closeness of face-to-face contact. Undescribed, unanalyzed representations of others' fear, distress, and cruelty seem to enter people's intimate space in the same way that everything the blind person senses with her hands is up close and personal. It is this feature of the medium that helps make distant others seem local, inhabitants of a single "global village."

This feature of television helped to mobilize public support independently of how "close" sympathizers were physically to the action or consequentially to the injustice. In other words, White supporters in Boston, Saskatoon, or Munich were not likely to be hit by police batons, or to be excluded from a lunch counter or a public park because of their skin colour. Still many felt compelled to become engaged in some way by speaking out, writing to their member of Parliament or Congress, attending a rally or "teach-in," sending money to an organization like SNCC, or perhaps just buying an LP of the folksinger Pete Seeger and singing along to the civil rights anthem, "We Shall Overcome."

In Canada, the main student activist group, Student Union for Peace Action (SUPA), on hearing the news from Selma, organized a "sit-in" at the U.S. consulate in Toronto. Media coverage attracted hundreds more demonstrators as well as donations of food, blankets, and money. SUPA was overwhelmed. This was "their" demonstration, but most of the participants were not members of their organization, and had been mobilized not by SUPA but for it. So the organization found itself struggling to catch up with its followers: "They sat down with them, explained the philosophy, described the tactics; they took them by the carloads to the Student Christian Movement (SCM) office and ran them through a 'quick session on how to do a non-violent demonstration' and returned them to the sit-in, and picked up another carload" (Kostash 10).

This phenomenon of "self-mobilizing" crowds was to become a feature of 1960s movements. Anthony Oberschall, a theorist of 1960s movements, called them "transitory teams." Increasingly they came already armed with knowledge of the culture of protest. They already knew what sit-ins and demonstrations looked like: the repertoire of dress, behaviour, slogans, and songs. As Oberschall pointed out, these transitory teams were to become important "resources" for social movement organizations. But in their media-driven understanding of movement activity and their relative independence from organizational influence, they also became a potential liability.

A New Repertoire of Contention

Within the civil rights movement we can see some of the features that were to distinguish 1960s social movements from those we have already discussed in this textbook: the labour and co-operative movements. Here we start to see a looser connection between organizations and movement supporters and participants. We begin to see how the mass media create opportunities for self-mobilizing constituencies—people outside of the organizations who either show up for political actions (the transitory teams) or offer support in less direct ways. Oberschall calls the latter "conscience constituencies."

Civil rights also helped to define the repertoire of protest tactics for the decades to follow. There was a shift away from discussion and negotiation to "direct action." Civil disobedience was direct action. Civil disobedience techniques like the sit-in were also constantly being reinvented. Sit-ins more often became occupations of the buildings of target institutions. Student radicals would camp out in the offices of university administration buildings. While they were breaking the law, their aim was not to bring attention to the injustice of laws of trespass; it was to bring the institution to a halt. In the words of student leader Mario Savio, "There's a time when the operation of the machine becomes so odious, makes you so sick at heart ... you've got to put your bodies upon the gears and upon the wheels, upon the levers, upon all the apparatus and you've got to make it stop" (Bloom and Breines 112). Sit-ins became "teach-ins," love-ins, be-ins, even "shit-ins" (I might explain this later if you keep reading). Direct action was about making change rather than asking for it. Sixties movements were unusually inventive in their use of this strategy.

The civil rights experience demonstrated that this approach was effective. Martin Luther King's "project confrontation" in Birmingham led to segregationist laws in southern cities being overturned and convinced then U.S. President Kennedy to support federal civil rights legislation (the law, the Civil Rights Act, was passed in 1964 under his successor, Lyndon Johnson). The Voting Rights Act of 1965 guaranteed the types of protections that marchers in Selma had been fighting for, and made a difference in succeeding years in the numbers of Blacks who actually registered to vote.

While the civil rights struggle was fought by and for Black Americans, it attracted an unusually large following of non-Americans and non-Blacks. This phenomenon of people acting in the name of others became another defining feature of 1960s movements. Whites marched in solidarity with Blacks. Middle-class activists became "community organizers" for the poor and dispossessed. Affluent citizens of the industrialized West denounced the "colonial" policies of their own governments and stood in solidarity with peasant revolutionaries in the "Third World."

None of this was entirely new in the history of social movements. Nor could one give too much credit to privileged radicals for making much of a difference in or even clearly understanding others' struggles. Still, to many there appeared to be a shift in the "centre of gravity" of protest from the oppressed to the privileged. This was a "problem" that needed to be explained. Why would so much protest activity erupt in the privileged centres of the world from among the very people who seemed to enjoy unprecedented affluence and political freedom?

AFFLUENCE AND ITS DISCONTENTS: THE NEW LEFT

Little boxes on the hill side, little boxes made of ticky-tacky.
Little boxes, little boxes, little boxes all the same.
There's a green one and a pink one and a blue one and a yellow one,
And they're all made out of ticky-tacky, and they all look just the same.

And the people in the houses all go to the university
Where they all get put in boxes, little boxes, all the same.
And there's doctors and there's lawyers, and there's business executives
And they're all made out of ticky-tacky and they all look just the same.
(Malvina Reynolds)

You know that the 1950s was an era of affluence and suburban conformity that has now become an easy target for parody. Even at the time the suburban dream had its critics. Radical professors like Marshall McLuhan, C. Wright Mills, and Paul Goodman, along with New York beatniks, French Situationists, and other bohemians, treated it with varying degrees of distain and revulsion.

In a groundbreaking book, *The Mechanical Bride*, McLuhan in 1951 applied his professorial skills of literary analysis to the commodified images of mass culture found in comic books, newspapers, and most of all in the advertisements—for everything from pills and Coca-Cola to coffins and engine lubricants—that saturate everyday life.

The Commodity Spectacle

In two ads for different commodities he observes how women's bodies are marketed like automobiles. They are presented "in an X-ray method familiar in motorcar engine displays of 'working models.'" One ad carries the caption: "What's the trick that makes her click?" A "girl," her clothing in cutaway view, is on the phone getting all the calls because she uses Ivory Flakes to keep her "undies *so* nice and dainty." Others are lined up to show how "Nature's Rival" girdles enforce a uniformly desirable waist on women with different figures. Reading "laterally," McLuhan sees a connection with the "chorus line," popular in Hollywood at the time, and more generally the mechanization of desire: "There is nothing very erotic about twenty painted dolls rehearsing a series of clockwork taps, kicks and swings" (McLuhan 94). These and other ads invoke genuine human desires: here for love and acceptance, in other cases for freedom and meaningful accomplishment. These were desires, argued McLuhan, that could never be satisfied by the world of standardized commodities on offer. In fact, by diverting people's longings into the sterile world of material consumption, mass culture repressed and perverted real needs.

Previous social movements representing workers and petty-bourgeois farmers and fishers had taken part in the struggle for material affluence, but that had not been

their only aspiration. True, organized farmers had created co-operatives and lobbied
for marketing boards like the Canadian
Wheat Board that limited the free play of
market forces and materially improved their
lives. They could not, however, prevent the
concentration and centralization of capital
within agriculture. Farmers with larger
operations bought out smaller ones and
tens of thousands were forced to migrate
to the cities, leaving a shrinking minority
clinging to the dream of personal autonomy
through land ownership. (To the point that
by the 1960s, there were fewer farmers than
university students in North America.)

Through their unions, blue-collar workers had fought for better wages and improved
physical safety on the shop floor. But they
had mostly failed in their struggles for "self-
management" and against the management
experts and engineers busy designing out
the thought, creativity, and discretion that
had once made manual work fulfilling. Uni-
versity-trained experts were convinced that
the best way to increase productivity was
to treat workers like machines. Employers
would rather pay higher wages than allow
more autonomy. This was the compromise
that most unions, the organized representatives of the labour movement, had accepted
by the 1950s.

For many workers who in previous decades could never have dreamed of owning
their own car, TV, or house, it was a seductive one. Outside of your demeaning work
you could construct a lifestyle that looked
"middle class." You could drink the same
scotch or go for a Sunday drive just like the
guys in power, the guys who called the shots
and were in command of their own lives.
The French Situationists called this "the
spectacle," the consumption of the outward
signs of self-fulfillment and autonomy in
ways that were passive, conformist, and
mind-numbing.

State-Subsidized
Collective Consumption

So prolific had mechanized industrial production become that the defining challenge
was now to find ways to guarantee that the
flood of commodities would be consumed.
The blandishments of the ad-man were
only part of the solution. Increasingly it was
states rather than private firms that intervened to bring about fundamental societal
changes to support "consumer economies."
In Canada, where the "old" labour and farm
movements were better organized and more
powerful than in the U.S., the state did
more to subsidize workers' spending power.
"Social welfare" programs like pensions,
unemployment insurance, social assistance,
family allowance, and subsidized education
enabled families to spend their limited
incomes on other things like modern home
appliances.

In 1962 Saskatchewan's CCF, brought to
office by the farmers' co-operative movement, was fighting to institute medicare.
Once the program was adopted federally,
the state was managing and subsidizing far
more spending on health care services than
individual Canadians could have afforded
on their own. The result was more health
care professionals and managers with good
salaries buying consumer durables and more
spending money available to families who
paid less for their own health care. Postwar
affluence was based largely on this shift
from privately funded to publicly funded
consumption or "collective consumption."
Government efforts to efficiently manage
these new services resulted in bloated bureaucracies staffed by "experts." Farmers'
original vision had been more along the lines
of the co-operative movement—decentralized
institutions under direct popular control.
In Saskatchewan there was some bitterness
about the way that the NDP had "sold out"

the locally controlled "community clinic" model in favour of a more bureaucratic approach to public health care (Kostash 23).

Similar developments occurred in the United States, but industry voices were more powerful there and had a greater effect in shaping collective consumption priorities. The state subsidized private home ownership for working-class families. New residential developments were built on the outskirts of cities where real estate was cheapest. Here houses could be widely spaced on big lots. Governments spent unprecedented amounts to service the sprawling suburbs with sewer, water, electricity, and endless miles of roads, freeways, interchanges, and parking lots that consumed more space and forced residences even further apart. Sprawl benefited the real estate and construction industries and created a "built environment" in which it was obligatory to consume—the station wagon, the lawnmower, the gallons of fuel to keep them going. Cities became physical consumption machines managed by states.

Political struggles developed around how the state would manage consumption in the cities, struggles that favoured suburbanization and sprawl more in the U.S. than Canada. Women in Canada and the U.S. had had other ideas about how to manage their household consumption. They dreamed of organizing housework efficiently so as to cut down on labour and free at least some of women's time from the kitchen and laundry and nursery. Their plans involved women pooling their labour in common facilities—exactly the model that had made industrial production more efficient. Instead, suburbanization isolated women from one another and required that each buy all of the household conveniences—the fridge, stove, washer, dryer, vacuum, ironing board, mixer, slicer, dicer, swing set, sandbox, toys—that still seemed to take up all of their time.

Consumer Alienation

The Situationists saw in this the kind of irony that Marx had warned was typical of the capitalist organization of society:

> The organization controlling the material equipment of our everyday life is such that what in itself would enable us to construct it richly plunges us instead into a poverty of abundance, making alienation all the more intolerable as each convenience promises liberation and turns out to be only one more burden. We are condemned to slavery to the means of liberation. (Vaneigem, "Basic Banalities" 30)

The structure of consumption in the suburbs reshaped social relationships. People physically separated off from one another and in their private bubbles spent three to six hours a day glued to the cathode ray tube. In the televised spectacle, distant commodities, things that are bought and sold in the capitalist market, masqueraded as real human qualities promising the purchaser youth, power, love, community. Situationist politics sought to disrupt this consumer alienation in which human qualities became invested in things, or mere images of things, while human beings were unable to realize these qualities in their own lives.

Situationists advocated the concept of the potlatch as a kind of anti-commodity, anti-capitalist practice. The potlatch was a North American Aboriginal ritual in which wealthy individuals gave away their most prized material possessions in order to create ties of obligation from the recipients. In this way, instead of social bonds being dissolved in the possession of material goods, material goods were dissolved in order to create and strengthen social bonds. (Canadian authorities had thought the Aboriginal potlatch so threatening to capitalist values that they had outlawed it.)

Situationists promoted similar practices to nullify the power of commodities:

> ... new human relationships must be built on the principle of pure giving. We must rediscover the pleasure of giving: giving because you have so much. What beautiful and priceless potlatches the affluent society will see—whether it likes it or not!—when the exuberance of the younger generation discovers the pure gift. The growing passion for stealing books, clothes, food, weapons or jewelry simply for the pleasure of giving them away gives us a glimpse of what the will to live has in store for consumer society. (Vaneigem, *Revolution*)

In Holland the "Provos" also sought in playful and provocative action to challenge the grip of commodity culture. Instead of guarding private ownership with threats of violence, city police, they argued, should be required to repair broken bicycles and deliver to the people "upon request, chicken drumsticks, oranges, contraceptives and matches." Practising what they preached, the Provos themselves repaired and distributed 50,000 white bicycles in Amsterdam (Marwick 481).

> White, anarchic, collectivized bicycles offered free for the use of the citizens to combat the antisocial behavior of gangs of aggressive psychopaths enclosed in noisy, smelly sheet-metal boxes, gangs that run rampant, undisturbed, damaging the environment and the social fabric, protected by big business and the police. (Guarnaccia)

The idea, of course, was to heal at multiple levels the privatization and atomization of social relations that commodities introduced in the consumption-intensive city.

New Left Politics of Everyday Life

Situationists, Provos, and their followers in countries throughout the industrialized West were anti-capitalist and in this sense left-wing in their politics. However, theirs was a "New Left," different in a number of ways from anti-capitalist struggles of the previous 100 years. In order to attack alienation in the sphere of consumption, they had to confront the routines, habits, and choices of everyday life. Whether you cycled to work or drove became political. Whether you ate TV dinners or homemade granola, whether you smoked a pipe or home-grown pot, whether you forced your body into "Nature's Rival" girdles or went "natural" without girdle, bra, or shaving—simple choices like these became contentious political acts.

People who flouted consumer conventions were harassed and called "freaks" and many adopted this epithet and took pleasure in "freaking people out." One could engage in this sort of politics without joining any organization. Many were suspicious of all forms of organization, which they saw as subordinating the individual to a collective identity or common program when the point was to provide the conditions for people to "do their own thing." Even the "politicos" who understood the need for coordinated action rejected the discipline and hierarchy that had come to characterize unions and oppositional parties of the old left. In this sense their vision was closer to anarchism or the co-operative commonwealth with its emphasis on decentralized, direct democracy.

They also rejected the old left interest in state power and lingering admiration for communist regimes. The state in the West had taken an integral part in organizing the alienation of everyday life. In the communist East it had become a totalitarian bureaucracy. The point for anti-capitalists was not to run the state but to "smash" it. Situationist graffiti in Paris, 1968, declared, "Humanity will not be happy until the last capitalist is hung with the entrails of the last bureaucrat." They sent the same message in a telegram to the Soviet authorities.

The New Left drew inspiration from Marx for their project, but realized that his theory of the leadership role of the proletariat no longer applied. They were confused and conflicted about what class or classes they themselves represented. The "Provos" facetiously called themselves the "provotariat," who had superseded the proletariat:

> The proletariat is the slave of the politicians ... it has joined its old enemy the bourgeoisie, and now constitutes with the bourgeoisie a huge grey mass.... We live in a monopolistic, sick society in which the creative individual is the exception. Big boss, capitalism, communists impose on us, tell us what we should do, what we should consume.... But the provotariat wants to be itself. (Marwick 481)

Radicals of the New Left tended to be young (some argued that youth itself had become a class), university educated, and either from the professional and managerial middle classes or, as university students, destined for them. Class privilege and culture separated them from wage earners.

Demonstration as Prefigurative Performance

New Left action against the alienating world of bureaucracy and the commodity spectacle was very often expressive rather than instrumental. In other words, it was more about communicating ideas and changing people's world view than about getting things done. In the mid-1960s New Left activists staged increasing numbers of sit-ins, strikes, and occupations, all of which, at least on the face of it, had instrumental goals of changing some specific institutional policy. Universities were favourite targets. Students protested funding for chemical weapons research, campus bans on political tables and booths, campus military recruiting, and any policy or regulation in the classroom, residences, or the public spaces of campus that seemed designed to force students into becoming bureaucratic clones of "the system."

However, for many who took part, the experience of occupying university and government buildings was more meaningful and valuable than any outcome in the form of actual policy concessions. Activist Dotson Rader recounts the experience of occupying the mathematics building at Columbia University in 1968. None of the consequences mattered, "... not the bust to come, nor the degrees and careers in jeopardy, nor the liberal faculty insulted and lost. All that counted was the two hundred of us in solidarity for the first time together, together in our place and in our time against the cops outside and the jocks outside." The occupiers felt that they had had a taste of what their lives would be like without alienation; it was "... the first event in most of our lives where we felt effective, where what we were doing belonged to us. Never before had I felt as effective as during the Liberation" (qtd. Breines 32).

Within imposing buildings designed to dramatize permanence and impersonal authority, new forms of spontaneous order sprang into being, without leaders and without hierarchy. This amazed and elated people. An unplanned storming of the Pentagon during an anti-war demonstration in 1967 led to the creation of "a dynamic spirit of community" among a crowd of 3,000. As people occupied the Pentagon steps, "organization grew, communication systems were set up, water and food brigades brought in supplies. Political discussions and news broadcasts from other fronts were conducted through bull horns." In the hours that followed, "a real festival atmosphere was in the air. People laughed and hugged. And they began to talk to the soldiers." Young protestors faced with rifles pointed directly at them placed flowers in the barrels. When the soldiers were eventually ordered to move in to arrest, "everyone chanted 'Join us! Join us!' And they really meant it. That was why it was important. It wasn't just empty rhetoric ... we knew we had something to offer, something good" (Breines 34).

These actions "prefigured" a possible world without alienation. They also exposed the fragile and "performative" character of the institutions that they challenged. Power depends upon the willingness of people to believe in its effectiveness. Even totalitarian states like Nazi Germany have recognized that the military and police are not enough to maintain social order. Day-to-day conformity of people is perpetuated by a "collective illusion" that the existing order is both right and unassailable. The Nazis were more aware than most regimes of how this illusion could be reinforced though "dramaturgic" means of ritual and spectacle. The "counter-performances" of the 1960s occupations threatened that illusion in the industrial democracies. If enough people exposed, mocked, and rejected the spectacle

of an alienating system, New Left theorists hoped, that system would lose legitimacy and any ability to command assent. Corporate and state bureaucracies would simply dissolve when faced with a "great refusal."

Paris, 1968: The Great Refusal

While the great refusal may sound wildly idealistic and naïve, it nearly happened in May 1968 in France. Agitating among French students were groups calling themselves the "Enragés" and the "Movement of March 22" in reference to struggles to democratize the Nanterre campus of the University of Paris. Both were inspired by the Situationists. They staged a protest at the Sorbonne on May 3 against disciplinary actions at Nanterre. The authorities responded by calling out the police, who surrounded the demonstrators and began making arrests in what many thought to be a humiliating manner. Onlookers became outraged and the protest escalated. Over the next few days, clashes with authorities broadened the sympathy and support for the demonstrators, first from students, then from French citizens, and, finally and most remarkably, from French factory workers.

Many actions were expressive. Posters and graffiti went up around the city: "The more I make love, the more I want to make revolution," "Distrust sad people, the revolution is joy" (Goodman 108). In the Latin Quarter people "in a spontaneous and playful manner" invoked images of France's revolutionary past by barricading the streets. When the police charged these fortifications, they helped to create a powerful media event, the "Night of the Barricades" (Gilcher-Holtey 261). French labour federations first called for a one-day sympathy strike, and then rapidly lost control as workers staged spontaneous strikes and factory occupations around the country. At one point 10 million workers had joined the "great refusal," many of them, inspired by the New Left, "demanding the impossible," an end to alienating conditions in work, greater worker autonomy, and self-government. Economic conditions for French workers were good in the spring of 1968; material dissatisfactions were not the issue. Nonetheless, union leaders sought to redirect worker protest back into the conventional framework of collective bargaining for better wages and material conditions.

News of the May events in France electrified student radicals here in Canada and around the world. Actions and demonstrations were staged in other countries and the images circulated back to the French, creating what to many seemed like a single global event that resonated within the McLuhanesque "electronic sensorium."

> One truly amazing aspect of May '68 was the way the protest encircled the globe: Saturday May 11, 50,000 students and workers marched on Bonn, and 3,000 protesters in Rome; on May 14, students occupied the University of Milan; a sit-in at the University of Miami on May 15; scuffles at a college in Florence on May 16; a red flag flew for three hours at the University of Madrid on the 17th; and the same day, 200 black students occupied the administration buildings of Dower University; on May 18 protests flared up in Rome, and more in Madrid where barricades and clashes with the police occurred; on May 19, students in Berkeley were arrested; a student protest in New York; an attack on an ROTC center in Baltimore—the old world seemed to be on the ropes. (Bracken)

What is surprising in retrospect is not so much that the "old world" did not fall, but that the New Left challenge to its legitimacy was so palpable that authorities were ready to revert to violence to defend it—more on this theme in the following section.

VIOLENCE AND THE PEACE MOVEMENT

In summary, the New Left of the 1960s mobilized against new forms of alienation in consumer societies: the buying-off of the working class and the loss of creativity and autonomy to impersonal bureaucracies and to the seductions of the commodity spectacle. They had diagnosed the costs *to the affluent* of the affluent society. They had also begun to expose the contradiction between local affluence and global military domination and exploitation. At the same time that Western democracies managed collective consumption to create utopias of peace and prosperity in the suburbs, they also funded, supported, and (depending on the country) actually carried out lethal violence against the poor and oppressed beyond the white picket fences of "middle-class" privilege. Certainly, being alienated amid abundance could be pretty comfortable, but not, activists felt sure, after one knew the hidden costs.

Colonialism and Military Oppression

French students had first become enraged by their own government's attempt to suppress independence struggles in one of its last colonies, Algeria. French military actions and reports of brutal torture of Algerian prisoners in French custody aroused student activists from 1957 to 1960. Cheap raw materials from colonies in Africa and southeast Asia had helped to subsidize the industrialization of European countries, but only because states in the West had used political and military coercion to ensure continuous supply at low prices. This is what "colonialism" was about.

Throughout the world former colonies were fighting for or had already won political, if not economic, independence. In 1954 the Vietnamese had defeated the French, and a temporary line had been drawn between the French-controlled south and the liberated north. The international community, through the United Nations (UN), set up a commission of three countries, including Canada, to oversee democratic elections and the reunification of the country under whichever government the Vietnamese chose.

This is where the United States stepped in with a move that was to typify a new era and a new style of colonialism. The U.S. used its military and political influence to install an authoritarian government in South Vietnam. This regime ignored the mandate of the international commission and proceeded, brutally, to repress all opposition in the country. How could the U.S., claiming to "sell" democracy abroad, block democratic self-determination in a foreign country? American officials believed they had to save capitalism. You see, the Vietnamese rebels opposed not only political domination by the French, but also the economic domination by foreign firms and the international market. Like many anti-colonial movements, theirs was also anti-capitalist.

From the American point of view, loss of a foreign country to socialism or communism meant a loss of opportunities for American companies, and ultimately a challenge to American prosperity. More importantly, socialist countries were likely to trade instead with, and receive military support from, America's arch-enemy, the Union of Soviet Socialist Republics (the USSR or Soviet Union). It did not matter if the majority voted for it or popular movements fought for it, the U.S. would do anything in its power (preferably behind the scenes, but upfront if necessary) to prevent countries from choosing socialism.

What the U.S. State Department liked to see as a war against communism, the old and New Left worldwide saw as violence against democratic choice. In Vietnam the anti-colonial resistance fighters, calling themselves the Viet Cong, went back to war. The U.S. began by giving military hardware and "advice" to its client government, which clearly could not cope unassisted against a guerrilla-style war backed by widespread popular support. U.S. involvement then escalated to the point that it could no longer pretend that it was not engaged in full-blown, high-tech, chemical, and ballistic warfare in the jungles and rice fields of a pre-industrial nation.

Closer to home, U.S. advisers were busy propping up authoritarian regimes in Latin America. President Kennedy provided covert support for an invasion of Cuba that came to be known for its defeat by the Cuban forces under Fidel Castro at the "Bay of Pigs." All of this was justified in the name of fighting communism. Interestingly, White racists also accused civil rights activists of being "communists." The beatings and murders of civil rights activists by police and vigilantes added to the conviction of many social movement activists that they were part of a worldwide struggle against a system of irrational and repressive violence endemic to the Western "democracies."

But over all the conventional war and face-to-face violence loomed the unimaginable threat of "the Bomb." The likelihood of nuclear war with the USSR became a terrifying reality in the minds of Canadian and American kids who were taught to rehearse for it.

> Every so often, out of the blue, a teacher would pause in the middle of class and call out, "Take cover!" We knew then, to scramble under our miniature desks and stay there, cramped, heads folded under our arms, until the teacher called out, "All clear!" (Gitlin, *The Sixties*, 22)

Aimed at every major city in the industrialized world was at least one nuclear missile, packing as much explosive power as all of the bombs of the Second World War.

The atomic bomb that the Americans had dropped on the Japanese city of Hiroshima was tiny by comparison, but had vaporized human bodies and baked their shadows into concrete. U.S. and Soviet leaders had at their fingertips instant, global apocalypse. "Mutual assured destruction" (MAD) in the event of nuclear conflict was official policy. This was the "Cold War." When U.S. and Soviet warships faced off in the "Cuban missile crisis" of 1962, it seemed to many that the military and political elites were poised to actually end the world.

Canadian Complicity with the Military Industrial Complex

Peace became one of the central social movement issues of the 1960s. The iconic peace symbol was created by a British peace group in 1958 based on the combined semaphore signals for "N" and "D" standing for "nuclear disarmament." It was for nuclear disarmament and Canadian non-alignment in the Cold War that Canadian students first demonstrated. The slogan for the 1959 march of the Combined Universities Campaign for Nuclear Disarmament (CUCND) was "Let Canada Lead the Peace Race!" The truth, as CUCND and its successor the Students Union for Peace Action (SUPA) were to uncover, was that Canada, despite its international image as an independent peacekeeping nation, was deeply implicated in U.S. policy in the Cold War and the Vietnam War. While we were on the UN commission supposedly to oversee elections and reunification in Vietnam, our officials were giving tacit support to U.S. efforts to undermine this agreed-upon process. We were already deeply interdependent with the Americans in our defence systems and military industries.

Soviet missiles headed for the U.S. would travel over the Canadian Arctic, so as part of Cold War preparedness, we ran the Distant Early Warning radar system or DEW Line. Our military command was integrated with the U.S. through the North American Air Defense System (NORAD), and the Defence Production Sharing Agreement of 1959 instituted a kind of "free trade" between Canadian and U.S. military industries. Canadian industries benefited from supplying Cold War hardware and experienced an economic boom as the Vietnam War escalated. We made weapons systems for U.S. aircraft used in Vietnam (Litton Systems, Canada); we even knitted the famous U.S. "green berets" (Dorothea Knitting Mills, Canada). Canada's Department of National Defence funded research at Canadian universities on military technologies, including biological weapons and nerve gas (Kostash 41–43).

"End Canadian Complicity!" came the cry from Canadian peace activists. Successive governments paid little heed. Even an embargo on military shipments to the U.S. would, according to then Justice Minister Pierre Trudeau, have "far-reaching consequences" that no government would willingly face. It became increasingly clear to peace activists that one of the limits of their influence in Canada was the weakness of Canadian sovereignty vis-à-vis the United

States. Peace activism became linked to a new Canadian nationalism.

In its formative meeting in 1965 SUPA activists recognized that they had only a foggy idea of how power worked within Canada. As part of their peace activism, they embarked upon an analysis and critique of the structures of power in Canadian society, which led them inevitably toward many of the causes and campaigns of the New Left. They organized opposition to the violence against the civil rights movement. They saw the U.S. Students for a Democratic Society (SDS) working to empower marginalized and oppressed groups through "community organizing." The idea was to help give a voice to those who were the worst victims of a sick system and thereby help to transform that system. SUPA volunteers spent summers in poor urban neighbourhoods, on reserves, and in Doukhobor communities in the B.C. interior trying to kick-start community action for change (Kostash 15–17).

Peace was an issue through which many campaigns and constituencies intersected. The Voice of Women, formed in 1960, was spearheaded by middle-class, middle-aged women, many of whom, as mothers, were motivated by concern for the future and safety of their children. They had close ties with the Quakers, a religious group that emphasizes personal conscience, non-violence, and consensus decision making. Their members also tended to be feminists. Feminists made a connection between militarism and male violence in institutions from the state to the private home. Peace marches and vigils could bring together broad coalitions of organizations.

Mobilizing Transitory Teams

But there was also a huge unaffiliated constituency "tuned-in" through various chan-

nels, including the media. Images of the Vietnam War proliferated in newspapers, magazines, and television. Some of them resonate even now: the casual gesture of the Saigon officer blowing a captive's brains out by the side of the road; the naked girl, crying, her arms outstretched, running from a bombing raid. Campus activists brought these images into public spaces with their tables, booths, posters, and traced the connections back to everyday life at home. A human face looking like something from a Hollywood horror movie is shown melted by burning napalm. "Don't buy war-maker products!" is the slogan. Napalm is manufactured by Dow Chemical, which also makes the convenient Styrofoam coffee cup that you hold in your hand. Often very small organizations of dedicated people were able to give to a much wider public the tools to act on their own.

The peace movement consisted of this unaffiliated public plus loosely orchestrated action between diverse constituencies only partially represented by groups or organizations. In the United States there was a main coordinating body called Mobe or the Mobilization Committee to End the War in Vietnam, which sponsored the big national demonstrations like the one in 1967 that brought 100,000 to Washington during "anti-draft week." Organizing a peace demonstration was a bit like promoting a rock concert or festival. Mobe set a place and time, liaised with city officials about march routes and so on, and publicized the event.

In a more organized movement such as the labour movement, people would be contacted for rallies through union membership lists. Mobe had no membership lists, just as a rock promoter has no lists of potential fans. Instead people were contacted through networks of organizations, individuals, and through the media. "From within," observed one participant,

The movement seems disorganized to the point of chaos, with literally hundreds of ad hoc groups springing up in response to specific issues, with endless formation and disbanding of coalitions ... the peace movement does have some broad continuities and tendencies well understood by the most prominent leaders, but ... its loosely participating, unstructured aspect can scarcely be overestimated. (qtd. in Oberschall 262)

While this disorderly movement had a powerful influence on public opinion and was a factor in hastening the eventual U.S. withdrawal from Vietnam, activists were tremendously frustrated by what they saw as their lack of progress. This frustration was brought to a head in August 1968 at the Democratic Convention in Chicago. Remember this was 1968 and globally, a sense of revolution was in the air. In addition to the uprising in France, the Viet Cong had intensified its resistance to U.S. forces in the "Tet Offensive." Many thought the popular army of a colonized people were poised to defeat the mighty U.S. empire in Vietnam.

Chicago, 1968: The New Imagery of Revolutionary Violence

The idea in Chicago was to influence the Democratic Party's official position on the war or at least to expose the bankruptcy of party politics and the official structures of parliamentary democracy. "Liberals" believed in parliamentary democracy; the New Left radicals did not. Liberals who supported the anti-war movement and the civil rights movement tended to vote for the Democrats. While liberals supported many New Left causes, they had become the

enemy for most activists because liberals still believed in "the system": free-market capitalism and parliamentary democracy. For many the Democratic Convention was to be a final test for liberalism, and indeed for non-violent tactics of protest.

Authorities at many levels must have felt that their grip on legitimacy was tenuous. The Chicago police force was overprepared and belligerent. Despite Mobe's efforts to ensure non-violent demonstrations, a significant contingent of demonstrators, notably the "Yippies," was in a confrontational mood. When provoked by demonstrators, the police went berserk, screaming, "Kill 'em!" They gassed, clubbed, jackbooted, and hospitalized hundreds of protestors, reporters, and bystanders (Brinkley 226). "The police were making sounds that I never heard a human being make before," one victim reported. "They sounded like angry animals growling" (Chiarito). In the convention itself, anti-war presidential candidates were defeated. In the election that followed, the Democrats lost to the pro-war, anti-hippie Republicans led by Richard Nixon.

The Democratic Convention, indeed the accumulated events of that very intense year of 1968, marked a turning point for U.S. radicals and a growing acceptance of the idea that violence must be opposed by violence. Blacks had already begun to fight back, or at least this is how many "read" a series of urban riots that began in the Los Angeles Black ghetto of Watts in 1965. Watts rioters looted, set buildings aflame, and repelled thousands of police and troops for four days. Thirty-two people, including 27 Blacks, were left dead, and 800 were wounded. Civil rights legislation had certainly not freed these people from police brutality (which had sparked the violence) or economic inequality.

The Black Panthers, formed in 1966, emblemized a shift toward greater militancy in the Black liberation movement. The Panthers advocated self-governed Black communities and armed self-defence. Malcolm X, spokesman for Black autonomy, was assassinated in 1965. On April 4, 1968 the moderate civil rights leader Martin Luther King was assassinated. Two days later Bobby Hutton became one of the first of many Black Panthers to be shot dead by police. In February 1968 in the "Orangeburg Massacre," three Black students taking part in a demonstration were shot dead by police. In June, Robert F. Kennedy, whom many Blacks regarded as the most progressive White liberal in the Democratic Party and one of the anti-war candidates for president, was assassinated. His brother, President John F. Kennedy, had been shot in 1963 before he could pass the Civil Rights Act.

Students in the occupations of Columbia University in April 1968 picked up the images of barricades from televised coverage of the Sorbonne occupation. Barricades as a military tactic against the police were rather futile, but symbolized a shift "from protest to resistance" (Gitlin 194). The "liberal" tactics of non-violent protest, civil disobedience, and parliamentary process seemed to have failed; in France the great refusal had evaporated by the end of the summer; that fall the Prague Spring, a Czech popular movement against communist oppression, was crushed by Soviet tanks. White radicals began to turn to guerrilla leaders like Che Guevara and Mao Zedong for inspiration.

By this point they did not consider Robert F. Kennedy to be one of their own. It was not until four White student demonstrators were shot and killed by National Guardsmen at Kent State University in May of the following year that White U.S. radicals had their own martyrs to the struggle. Neil Young's song "Ohio" is about this event. It is really a war anthem, a call to arms.

Many actually took up arms. The defining tactic of the new "urban guerrillas" was the bombing of symbolic targets—typically institutions rather than human beings (although in practice it is difficult to separate the two). Their idea was similar to the old anarchist idea of the "propaganda of the deed" where bold destructive acts would dramatize the fragility of the institutions of power and ignite chain reactions of popular resistance. This turn toward armed resistance was international. In the U.S. the urban guerrillas called themselves "Weathermen"; in Germany it was Baader-Meinhof; in Italy the Red Brigades; and in Canada it was the primarily nationalist (but also anti-capitalist) FLQ or Front de Libération du Québec. Of that I will say more in another chapter.

In summary, the peace movement led to an analysis of the system that produced violence; many called it the "military-industrial complex." Peace activists discovered that that system in its efforts to resist change was ready and willing to unleash violence on its own people. A radical minority in the movement concluded that the only way to overcome that violence was with violent resistance.

STUDENTS/YOUTH AND THE RESOURCES TO PARTICIPATE

So far, I have been describing some of the major threads of the 1960s social movements. (There are many others, including the women's movement, the environmental movement, the gay rights movement, and the Red Power movement, which I will pick up on later in this book.) I have been trying to give you enough context of what was going on in the world at that time, and how people interpreted these events so that you can understand their motivations and reasons for responding in the ways that they did. However, I have not been explaining these movements in the way that many social scientists understand what it means to explain.

As we saw in the cases of the labour and co-operative movements, people with very similar reasons for protest do not always respond in the same way, or at all. People in Fall River probably had more reason to organize than people in Lynn, but structural conditions prevented them from doing so. If you think about it, the reasons for protest today are very similar to those of the 1960s: alienated consumption and the commodity spectacle; Western affluence based on Third World exploitation; the U.S. defying the international community and going to war over its imperial interests (the threat of communism having now been replaced by the threat of "Islamic terrorism") while civil liberties are being challenged at "home." But there is nowhere near the same degree of activism among students. How do we explain the difference? How do we explain the rise and, perhaps more interestingly, the decline of the 1960s social movements?

Relative Deprivation Theory

Up until this time American academics had explained social movements using "deprivation theory." It was based on the simplistic assumption that mobilization was always based on pre-existing grievances. The theory did give insights into how *relative*—to others or to some socially defined standard—this sense of grievance could be. The idea of "relative deprivation" was originally Durkheim's, but it had been given a boost in the 1940s by a study of American soldiers that was designed to discover what made soldiers more or less satisfied with life in the military. Looking at promotion, the researchers observed a surprising result. Those soldiers in the air force, where most people ascended the ranks swiftly, were the most dissatisfied with their rank and prospects. In other services, where promotion was rare, soldiers were more satisfied.

Durkheim had seen a similar thing in France in the 19th-century Industrial Revolution. He found that dissatisfaction, which he measured by rates of suicide, increased in times of rapid economic growth. In these settings people measured their achievement relative to a generalized belief in unlimited success. Nothing could suffice as an enduring and satisfying accomplishment; it was always diminished by the possibility of going one better. Even though they were privileged, people suffered from "relative deprivation."

On the face of it relative deprivation seemed to fit the case of the privileged protesters of the postwar economic boom. However a new generation of academics, many of whom had taken part in social movements, found the assumptions of the relative deprivation approach both inaccurate and insulting. First, it assumed that social movement participants were irrational in the sense that they misperceived the real reasons for their activism. If they were responding to rapidly rising material expectations, then they were not really motivated by injustice toward Blacks or colonized peoples or concern for alienation. The corollary was that as soon as the system re-established equilibrium and integrated students and youth into its material reward structures, dissent would vanish.

Second, in defining "collective behaviour" relative deprivation theorists emphasized its "uninstitutionalized" character. In their sociology, bureaucracies were implicitly "normal" and rational and social movements were lumped in with "the panic, the craze, the hostile outburst" (Smelser 383). The new academics, in an approach that came to be known as "resource mobilization," emphasized the ways in which activists built social movement organizations (SMOs), set explicit goals, and devised rational strategies to achieve them.

Resource Mobilization Theory

Resource mobilization theorists borrowed from Marxist sociologists the idea that there were enduring injustices in capitalist societies that always could provide a rationale for protest action. Some went further and claimed that social movement organizations did not need to respond to *pre-existing* grievances, but could actively define and promote grievances. Just like firms can manufacture consumer demand for their products, SMOs could "manufacture dissent." The new perspective focused on SMO techniques for exploiting resources like money, public opinion, members, and staff.

It also directed attention to how SMOs handled relations with other political players within the environment: the media, the state, other SMOs competing for resources, and "counter-movements" seeking to oppose them. A new emphasis was placed on the role of human choice, effort, and creativity in

making the best of resources, opportunities, and weaknesses (like the vulnerability of the U.S.'s democratic reputation internationally) in this environment. As actors themselves, many of these theorists knew that they had not just responded to impersonal social forces but, in those moments when it had seemed like they had transcended alienation, actively made history (McCarthy and Zald).

Taking the perspective of resource mobilization, affluence could both be the cause of 1960s protests and provide the resources that SMOs could employ to build protest movements. "Conscience constituencies" in North America had money that they could and did devote to social justice causes. The new electronic media helped to advertise those causes and the key organizations that one could contribute to if one approved of their work. When actions like SUPA's occupation of the U.S. consulate captured people's imagination in an affluent city, donations of food, blankets, and supplies were easy to come by.

People were also treated as "resources" from the resource mobilization perspective. In the 1960s there were more people available, having the time and the inclination, to work on social movement causes. All of the Western democracies, in response to changing labour demands, expanded university education in the postwar period. States increasingly subsidized tuition through grants to universities or bursaries to individual students. In many European countries university education was completely subsidized—students paid no tuition at all!

Job prospects for graduates were good; student debt was minimal. Students did not feel the same pressure they do today to ensure that their studies were career directed. University was a time to experiment with ideas, with life. Campuses supported exchanges of ideas and thinkers from around the world as part of their mandate to fund research and education. Canadian campuses brought in the intellectual leaders of the New Left, like Herbert Marcuse and Paul Goodman, as well as student radicals from Europe, the United States, and Latin America. Students' relatively flexible schedules and summers off gave them ample time to participate in movement politics. Time was a resource. In the summers it was possible to take to the road, along with a great movement of itinerant youth, and get by with little or no formal employment.

Affluent societies create a tremendous amount of surfeit and waste. Youth learned to exploit myriad opportunities for living, travelling, and having fun for free. As disaffection with "the system" grew, increasing numbers found it was possible to "drop out" of school and the career path and live quite happily in the interstices of the affluent society. Hitchhiking was the main mode of transport. "Panhandling" (begging) became an acceptable means of raising cash. Much of what they did involved finding, stealing, and sharing goods and services on a non-commodified basis.

Counterculture: Subverting the Commodity Spectacle

In San Francisco the "Diggers" attempted to mobilize free services in a fairly systematic way. For example, for physical space in the "free city" they advocated,

> ... rent or work deals with the urban gov't to take over spaces that have been abandoned for use as carpentry shops, garages, theatres, etc.; rent whole houses, but don't let them turn into crash pads.... Big warehouses can be worked on by environmental artists and turned into giant free dance-fiesta-feast palaces. (Diggers 104)

"*Every brother should have what he needs to do his own thing,*" they declared. Abbie Hoffman wrote a how-to manual called *Steal This Book*, outlining more informal strategies of self-provisioning. Here he has suggestions for free food. To prepare for this one, you have to put on the correct "uniform" first:

> In every major city there are usually bars that cater to the New Generation type riff-raff, trying to hustle their way up the escalator of Big Business. Many of these bars have a buffet or hors-d'oeuvres served free as a come-on to drink more mindless booze. Take a half-empty glass from a table and use it as a prop to ward off the anxious waitress. Walk around sampling the free food until you've had enough. Often, there are five or six such bars in close proximity, so moving around can produce a delightful "street smorgasbord." Dinner usually begins at 5:00 PM. (Hoffman, *Steal this Book*)

Like the Provos and Situationists, Diggers and Yippies (like Abbie Hoffman) were attempting to subvert the commodity spectacle. Most practitioners of what came to be known as the "counterculture" were tuning in to a structure of feeling fabricated through music, camaraderie, sensuality, spontaneous action, and mind-altering drugs. In the U.S. and Canada practitioners were called "hippies," "freaks," "long-hairs," and "heads."

While politically engaged youth (the "politicos") and counterculture youth were often at odds over the issue of fighting versus dropping out of the system, there was no clear dividing line and many of the full- or part-time dropouts were casual participants in movement activities. In resource mobilization terms, they, along with students, were resources for "transitory teams." According to Oberschall, what made this "instant" membership available to SMOs as never before was the ubiquity of mass media. Television, the "tactile" medium, was able to take viewers beyond the dry issues and personalize social movement politics. When people made the move from bystander public to participant, their television experiences had already schooled them in the culture of protest—the vocabulary of radical speech, dress, and action.

Transitory Teams as Instant Solidarity

Media coverage also helped to coordinate action by informing the public of the times and places of key movement events. The media of the commodity spectacle were exploited subversively as free resources by SMOs. The "self-mobilizing" character of the transitory teams meant that SMOs could get by with far fewer resources than membership organizations like unions or co-ops. There was not the same need to keep membership lists, set up telephone trees and mail-outs, organize meetings, conduct training seminars, and maintain the files, filing cabinets, office space, and staff that all these activities demand.

Similarly for participants, movement activism could be casual, intermittent, and issue-specific. You could show up for a SUPA demonstration without signing on to the whole philosophy of the organization and without making a long-term commitment to going to meetings or doing volunteer work for an organization. By drawing on a pool of less committed supporters, SMOs that depended on transitory teams could muster larger crowds. SMOs could maintain flexible ties with the "movement" so long as the media provided information links for free. The media offered small SMOs the tools for

rapid, inexpensive, and flexible mobilization of large numbers of supporters.

The resource mobilization concept of a transitory team is an ingenious way of understanding the links between SMOs and the more fluid elements of social movements.

The concept also contains an implicit recognition that the way people were brought together was new. In the labour and co-op movements people of similar interests were sorted by geography. People in the working-class neighbourhoods of Lynn lived next to one another; farmers in open-country neighbourhoods were all of the same class in one region. Ongoing interaction in these local places helped to create bonds of community and solidarity that formed the basis for common action.

Transitory teams represented a kind of "instant solidarity." Through them people assembled in one physical locale when and only when they acted together in political solidarity. The paths that connected "team" participants were not the physical ones of daily interaction, but rather the virtual pathways of the electronic media that could draw people together from different neighbourhoods and cities. Demonstrations could even draw participants from across borders.

Recall that one of the dissatisfactions with the society of the spectacle and the design of cities as consumption machines was the way that people became atomized and focused on privatized consumption. The ways that systems eroded social bonds was an important dimension of the 1960s concept of alienation. The search for community was a central preoccupation of the counterculture. Would-be hippies fled the suburbs and took to the road to become part of a strange sort of translocal community-in-motion. They flocked to the great transitory "happenings" of the counterculture: the "be-in" in Golden Gate Park in San Francisco in the Summer of Love (1967); the

Woodstock festival in the summer of 1969. They tarried for a time in the fabled urban Meccas of the counterculture: Yorkville in Toronto, Gastown in Vancouver, Haight-Ashbury in San Francisco, or on the steps of the piazza de Spagna in Rome.

On the road they found instant camaraderie with other members of their international "tribal" culture. The outward signs of this culture were bold and instantly recognizable—you know, long hair, headbands, sandals or bare feet, bell-bottoms. But there were subtleties in style, tastes, the use of language, even the lilt in the way you walked. These evolved quickly over time in ways that only insiders could "read" accurately, so it was easier to spot phoneys and "tripsters" who were out to exploit the counterculture for free stuff and easy sex but who were not genuinely committed to its ideals.

I want you to think about the parallels between the fleeting, translocal character of the transitory teams of political activists and these spatially fluid constructions of "community" in the counterculture. One of the underlying themes that is interesting from a resource mobilization perspective is speed. Relative to the old forms of place-based communities and political solidarity that might develop over generations, these forms were almost instantaneous. Instant mobilization was a valuable "resource."

In summary, the 1960s movements arose because the capitalist democracies rested upon inherent injustices, and the spread of affluence gave people the resources to act in an attempt to remedy these injustices. The resources included money to fund SMO activity; a floating population of students and youth with enough material support to free them from work commitments and career compromises; and electronic media with global reach that were more immediate in their impact and more total in their saturation of everyday life. SMOs competed with one another and learned from one another creative ways to exploit these resources to mobilize huge followings for New Left causes. This, at any rate, was how this explosion of movement activity was explained using the resource mobilization perspective.

RESOURCE MOBILIZATION AND THE DECLINE OF THE 1960S SOCIAL MOVEMENTS

One of my favourite examples of the use of resource mobilization perspective is Anthony Oberschall's explanation of the decline of the 1960s social movements in the United States. He systematically lays out three possible explanations of the decline: (1) internal weaknesses in the movements, (2) repression by the state, and (3) sufficient success in bringing about changes in U.S. society that the movements became redundant. He weighs evidence for all three and argues in favour of the first. In his analysis, one of the key internal weaknesses was the reliance of SMOs on the mainstream media. He acknowledges the power of the media as a low-cost tool for rapid, widespread mobilization, but then goes on to outline the risks and show how, by losing control over media representations of their activity, the 1960s SMOs got channelled onto self-destructive paths.

The Medium Is the Movement

The interests of the media were very different from those of the radical anti-capitalist SMOs attempting to use them to advance their cause. Most of the large newspapers and radio and television networks were corporations driven by profit. The U.S. does not have a publicly funded broadcaster on the scale of the CBC in Canada. Editors and reporters working for corporate media understand that they are beholden to owners and advertisers whose taken-for-granted world view is business oriented. Sympathetic representations of New Left causes would be viewed by those who hold the purse strings as irrational and "biased." Furthermore, networks that must survive by competing for advertising revenue are forced to evaluate all content in terms of its capacity to attract audiences for the advertisers. Even in news coverage a premium gets placed on sensationalism.

The media's interest dramatically affected the types of messages that SMOs could communicate. So, for instance, in the Columbia University occupation of 1968, students willing to pose as "wild militants" got more coverage. As one leader, whose more reasoned message was eclipsed complained,

> The people who tended to become noticed were people who were the most activist and ... flamboyant, the ones who called for action, the ones whose rhetoric was "Tear down the walls, Seize the buildings." That was what the cameramen liked to hear. They weren't interested in what I had to say about Columbia's ties with IDA [the Institute for Defence Analysis, funding military research on campus] for instance. (Mark Rudd, qtd. in Gitlin, *The Whole World*, 193)

Here the media are getting copy that will "sell" and at the same time are distorting the representation of the movement in ways that are likely to undermine its credibility by making it appear less "rational" than it actually is. But note also how media attention promotes certain leaders over others and, since media is how SMOs speak to their broader constituency, potentially alters the direction that the organization takes.

Some of the shocking TV coverage that led to strong public sympathy for civil rights demonstrators in the early 1960s was broadcast live and uncut. Raw events "spoke" in unscripted ways and meanings "broke out" of images and sounds before the reporter's voice-over could make sense of them. As TV reporting became more sophisticated, there was greater reliance on taped broadcasts where firmer editorial control could be asserted. CBS news coverage of a half-million strong anti-war demonstration in 1969 highlighted footage of a handful of people who split off from the peaceful rally and "threw projectiles and broke windows and hurled back police tear gas." The CBS rationale was that "there were terrific pictures and sometimes—sometimes and not very often—that does determine what's on" (qtd. in Gitlin, *The Whole World*, 227). So much can be said through editing. Consider the choice of whether to show an image of police firing tear gas or protestors lobbing the canisters back (or even the order in which you show both images). What are the differences in meaning that the editor can convey?

BOX 3.1:

MEDIA CONCENTRATION IN CANADA

Journalists and thousands of readers were outraged in 2002 when the owners of CanWest Global fired the publisher of the *Ottawa Citizen* for printing an editorial that they disagreed with. CanWest had bought the Southam newspaper chain, of which the *Ottawa Citizen* was one, and tightened corporate control over editorial content. The Asper family, owners of CanWest, were unrepentant about their unsubtle approach to influencing the media. After all, it was their paper. Indeed, historically newspapers have been unapologetically partisan in their political views. However, in every city there were likely to be numerous papers offering diverse perspectives or "voices" in political debate. Workers, like those in Lynn who distrusted the news from "moneyed men or capitalists," often relied on socialist or union-based publications. What has changed is the cost of running an economically viable newspaper. Small publications taking a critical perspective on the mainstream find it harder to survive. Large media conglomerates buy up smaller media firms in an effort to compete in an increasingly global market. For instance, CanWest, along with Quebecor and Torstar Corp, owned 63 percent of all daily newspapers in Canada in 2003 (Lorimer and Gasher 201). The result, according to many analysts, is that there are fewer news sources available to the public and these respond to the interests of the huge corporate conglomerates that own them.

Part of this trend of corporate concentration is "cross-media" ownership. For example, CanWest also owns television stations (conventional and pay-TV), radio, and Internet portals. In Vancouver in 2002 it controlled 71 percent of the market share of all daily newscasts (TV and newspaper). In other cities single conglomerates control in the range of 30 percent of market share in news. In Canada corporate dominance of news is balanced by the government-subsidized CBC (radio and TV). But the CBC has undergone extensive cuts in the 1990s and CBC TV has always been dependent on corporate sponsorship in the form of advertising.

Canadians are increasingly turning to the Internet as a news source. According to the most recent figures (2003), 64 percent of Canadian households used the Internet regularly. Of these close to one-third used it as one of their news sources. However, despite the vast range of alternative news sites on the net, most Canadians are still accessing large corporate news sources. The top three Internet news sources for Anglophone Canadians in 2002 were MSNBC (Joint venture of Microsoft and NBC News), CBC, and CNN (owned by media conglomerate Time-Warner). Convenience is probably a factor here as MSN is set as the default portal for Microsoft-related software. There are, however, literally thousands of alternative Internet sites offering news and analysis of current events. A directory of about 50 Canadian alternative media sites is available at Independentmedia.ca (www.independentmedia.ca/). Have a look at some of these sites and see if you can find news about current social movements. Do they report on social movement activities that you do not hear about in the mainstream media (check the top three Internet sites listed above)? Or do they offer a significantly different interpretation of these events? If you like one of these sites, why not set it as the default start-up page on your web browser for the duration of this course? Impress your prof by bringing social movement news to class for her to comment on.

Source: Senate of Canada, *Interim Report on the Canadian News Media* (Ottawa, 2004), June 14, 2005, www.parl.gc.ca/37/3/parlbus/commbus/senate/com-e/tran-e/rep-e/rep04apr04-e.htm.

A small faction of the New Left, the Youth in Politics or Yippies, attempted in inventive ways to "freak" (subvert) the media by embracing its affinity for the non-linear, the "tactile." Here Abbie Hoffman describes his appearance with other Yippies on a television talk show.

We taped a thing for the David Susskind show. As he said the word hippie, a live duck came out with "HIPPIE" painted on it. The duck flew up in the air and shat on the floor and ran all around the room. The only hippie in the room, there he is. And David went crazy. 'Cause David, see, he's *New York Times* head, he's not *Daily News* freak. And he said the duck is out and blew it. We said, we'll see you David, goodnight. He says, oh no no. We'll leave the duck in. And we watched the show later when it came on, and the fuckin' duck was all gone. He done never existed. And I called up Susskind and went quack quack quack you motherfucker, *that* was the best piece of information: that was a hippie. And everything we did, see non-verbally, he cut out. Like he said, "How do you eat?" and we fed all the people, you know. But he cut that out. He wants to deal with the words. You know, let's play word games, let's analyze it. Soon as you analyze it, it's dead, it's over. You read a book and say well now I understand it, and go back to sleep. (Hoffman, "Media Freaking" 362)

You can see here how the talk show needed the Yippies because they were becoming celebrities and would attract viewers. At the same time the show's producers wanted and were able to control the Yippie message, in this case favouring, ironically, linear rationality.

Activists understood that media coverage had become crucial to mobilizing SMO support. They also discovered that seeing themselves and their organizations on the evening news was an adrenaline rush, an affirmation that they were important. In making the news it seemed like they were making history. It became evident that the media were not just reporting on what was "objectively" important, but making it

important by reporting on it—movement events, tactics, issues, and leaders all in this sense took form on the national and international stages through the eye of the camera. Movement leaders learned to play to the expectations of the media, hoping their messages could get through without too much distortion. In this self-referential, "reflexive" fashion, both media and SMOs were collaborating in constituting what the movement was and what it meant.

This idea of self-constitution through representation was taken furthest by the Yippies. They saw what movement activists did on the streets as theatre, but that the performance that mattered took place as much on the electronic stage of the media as in the physical streets of the city. They prepared for the demonstrations at the Democratic convention in Chicago in 1968 on this basis, promising "Free chickens and ice cream in the streets. Thousands of kazoos, drums, tambourines, triangles, pots and pans, trumpets, street fairs, firecrackers—a symphony of life on a day of death. LSD in the drinking water" (Yippies 324). Through skilful provocation they also hoped to manage the authorities' role in the drama on the streets. Against their "Festival of Life" they hoped that the police would act out a part that would dramatize militarism, brutality, and death.

In this they were largely successful. They also managed to turn what was initially a disappointingly small turnout of protesters into a media event of mythic proportions. Yippie leader Jerry Rubin argued that the media event had, as they had intended, helped similar actions to proliferate, pointing out that "the year after Chicago there were more demonstrations on college and high school campuses than any other year" (qtd. in Gitlin, *The Whole World*, 175). While it may have inspired already committed radicals, it turned off much of the bystander public to the New Left cause. It did not set off the kind of widespread "great refusal" that had been ignited in France only months before. This was a strategic attempt and failure to manufacture dissent.

After Chicago, divisions deepened within movement SMOs over leadership style and tactics. The New Left SMOs began to lose sympathy from liberals within the conscience constituency who had contributed resources. The problem was that for many New Left SMOs neither the membership nor the loosely affiliated adherents had much control over the leadership who, after all, drew much of their power from their relationship to the media. The media helped to select dramatic and outrageous spokespeople.

Internal Organizational Weaknesses

Oberschall uses the concept of "cadre" to highlight the separate status of leaders from their organizations. He estimates that there were only about 50 media stars who formed the New Left cadre in the U.S. Like other resource mobilization theorists, he also uses the rather cynical term "political entrepreneur" to describe them. There is some justification for seeing them in this way less as democratically elected spokespeople for a popular movement and more as individual hustlers drumming up media hype and popular demand for their brand of dissent.

After 1968 the storyline that the U.S. media was interested in was the shift toward revolution and violence. Even large, non-violent demonstrations found it hard to get good coverage. The cadre who collaborated with this script came to believe in their own rhetoric amplified as it was on the nightly news. They genuinely believed that

the country was on the verge of revolution. But they were making revolution by making news of revolution. They were caught in a temporal illusion in which history seemed to be moving much faster for them than for their followers and potential followers.

They enraged the Americans who Nixon, with some accuracy, called the "silent majority." They increasingly made themselves targets for arrest, lengthy trials, and imprisonment. Oberschall argues that as leaders were taken out of commission and as the media lost interest, the movements fell apart.

> ... neglect of grass roots organization and of an internally controlled communications system for information transfers and political education left the 1960s movements in a vulnerable position when media attention shifted to other issues.... The "generals" were left without means of communicating with their "soldiers" and the directionless "soldiers" drifted off. (Oberschall 273)

This is what he means by "internal weaknesses" that led to movement decline.

Limitations of Oberschall's Analysis

Even though Oberschall's is one of my favourite examples of the resource mobilization perspective applied to the 1960s social movements, I do have some criticisms of it. "Transitory team" is a clever and useful concept. I have highlighted, as Oberschall does, the idea that the teams were called into being by the SMOs and bound together by nothing more than the electronic media "nexus." But I suspect that we are overstating the case. Demonstrations were not simply anonymous crowds brought together in the eye of the media. Todd Gitlin recounts how San José peace activists became convinced that their demonstration in 1970 was sabotaged by police undercover agents or "agents provocateurs." He was later "told by a student who was present on the scene that night that the handful of stone-throwers were strangers unknown in San José's antiwar circles before or afterward" (Gitlin, *The Whole World*, 188). These "circles" are apparently pre-existing personal networks whose members think that they should know, at least by sight, casual movement participants. You can imagine how these networks might extend well beyond the boundaries of formal SMOs.

The counterculture also provided an ongoing base for movement activity independent of SMOs and the media. I have emphasized the fluid, translocal character of the counterculture. While I do not want to retract that, I want also to point out that the itinerant youth did eventually congregate and settle in particular places. Some went "back to the land" and set up communes. Most of these experiments failed, but many of the participants stayed on and established farms and businesses. They became important community builders and leaders in a new rural environmentalism.

Many settled in urban neighbourhoods where they built institutions to support countercultural values and lifestyles: alternative book and clothing stores, health food shops, and "underground" newspapers. Often these enterprises were organized as co-operatives. An effort was made to revive the values of decentralized, democratic control that the older co-operative movement had lost sight of. In Quebec this new wave of the co-operative movement was particularly strong. In addition to the types of enterprises we have just mentioned, people set up theatre and radio co-ops, co-op youth, medical and day care centres, housing co-ops, and

worker co-ops. Quebec workers' co-ops responded to the same aspirations for worker autonomy and "self-management" that had been expressed by French strikers, but rather than simply rejecting structure in a "great refusal," they were building alternative structures (Levesque 121–125).

Oberschall's analysis downplays these "resources" that helped sustain movement culture independently of the SMOs and mainstream media. The fact that there were literally hundreds of "underground" newspapers and magazines reporting on, analyzing, and supporting movement politics should make us more cautious in assessing the reliance of the movement on the mainstream media. How effective do you suppose these independent media (or "indymedia," to use a contemporary term) could be in mobilizing social movements? Your answer will depend in part on how important you think television was. There was no movement-run TV.

Also, this is less a criticism of Oberschall than a reminder that his work is very U.S.-specific; the Canadian case differed in a number of ways. In Canada there was more continuity between the New Left and old left institutions like the co-operative movement and the CCF/NDP. Here there was less of a tradition of charity donations, and movements could not rely to the same degree on money from "conscience constituencies." SUPA, for example, was starved for funds. Canadian movements were and still are more likely to turn to, of all institutions, the government for funding.

The Canadian state has used funding to co-opt social movements and channel their activities in more "acceptably" moderate directions. For example, federal officials, fearing the agitation of the Black Panthers in Nova Scotia, made funds available in 1969 to the "constructive and moderate" Black United Front. SUPA was largely undercut by the government-sponsored Company of Young Canadians, which provided funds for youth to do various community development projects (Kostash 160). While the 1960s movements were an international phenomenon, each national experience was significantly different.

Resource Mobilization as Economistic

Finally I have some reservations about the resource mobilization approach itself independent of the way it is applied in this case study of 1960s decline. Resource mobilization theorists delighted in the irony of using the language of capitalist firms to explain SMO activity. (Remember the "political entrepreneur" metaphor.) They treat SMOs as though they were firms creating "demand" for their social dissent "product." They use the term "industry" to describe the environment in which SMOs promoting similar social change agendas compete for "resources" (another economic term).

This "economistic" conceptual language both helps us to see parallels that we might not otherwise, but also tends to obscure fundamental differences between the worlds of human action for profit and human action for social change. The emphasis on "resources" imputes an overly materialistic logic to social movement activity. One could expand the definition of "resources" to include the worlds of ethics and meaning that preoccupy social movement actors. But then why choose the "economistic" term in the first place?

Finally, at the core of the resource mobilization perspective is an economistic assumption about human rationality that says that people act on the basis of rational calculations of self-interest. This was one of the ways in which young scholars attempted

to dignify social movement action to others in their own individualistic capitalist culture. They were saying in effect, "Look, it is no more crazy or incomprehensible than the behaviour of a corporate CEO." However, as we shall see in the following chapter, many examples of social movement action cannot be explained on this basis unless we so radically redefine "self-interest" as to make the term meaningless.

CONCLUSION

The 1960s social movements created a problem for social movement theorists. There were no ready explanations for an explosion of dissent among the privileged in affluent societies. In this chapter we have focused on the new "resource mobilization" approach that emerged in the United States to address this problem. Let's review the key points of the resource mobilization approach. Protest happens when resources are available and people have the skill and organization to make the best use of those resources. There is always latent dissatisfaction in capitalist societies, but social movements do not simply respond to pre-existing grievances. Rather, they actively define, promote, and in this way "manufacture" dissent. Those who run or support SMOs often take up the grievances of others. Their success or failure in mobilizing support and bringing about change must be understood by looking at their creative use of tactics. Equally important are their strategies in response to the actions of other political players: the media, competing SMOs, counter-movements, and the state. Many resource mobilization theorists employed economistic language and assumed that individuals are motivated by rational self-interest.

Resource mobilization was not the only theoretical response to the 1960s movements. European theorists developed a number of variants of "new social movement" theory, all of which were more deeply rooted in the Marxist tradition of social thought. Many Canadian social scientists prefer European to American approaches. But there is no single "new social movement" approach. Each variant has its own complex vocabulary, so I thought I would postpone introducing you to this realm of theory until later chapters.

What I would recommend now is that you do what all the new social movement theorists began by doing. That is to compare and contrast the type of anti-capitalist protest that actually happened in the 1960s with what Marx and Engels thought would happen. Consider the following points in your comparison:

- The role of class as the basis for organized dissent
- The types of "community" that people identified with or gained a sense of solidarity from
- The nature of the complaints about capitalism
- The role of lifestyle and consumption versus work in defining the issues of protest
- The nature of movement organizations and their relationship with those they (purport to) represent
- The targets of protest (employers versus the state versus the culture of everyday life)

I would also like you to think about the 1960s social movements in relation to another problem that we raised in Chapter 1. There we considered the difficulty for the labour movement of the increasing speed at which capitalist societies were changing. The rapid turnover of workers and the rapid mobility of capital disrupted workers' attempts to organize in the traditional locales of workplace and neighbourhood. Do you think that some variant of the 1960s "transitory team" with its promise of "instant solidarity" might allow for the kind of rapid, flexible mobilization that could respond to 21st-century dynamism? Of course, the main weakness of the transitory teams, according to Oberschall, was reliance on the mainstream media. Can this problem be overcome by using new forms of low-cost, wide-distribution indymedia supported by the Internet?

REFERENCES

Africanamericans. "Selma to Montgomery March." *Africanamericans.com*, July 16, 2005, www.africanamericans. com/SelmaMarch.htm.

Bloom, Alexander, and Wini Breines. *"Takin' It to the Streets": A Sixties Reader*, 2nd. ed New York: Oxford University Press, 2003.

Bracken, Len. "Remembering May 1968's 'Days of the Barricades'." *Jay's Leftist and "Progressive" Internet Resources Directory (Northeast Research Associates)*, June 16, 2005, www.neravt. com/left/may1968.htm.

Breines, Wini. *Community and Organization in the New Left, 1962-1968: The Great Refusal*. New York; South Hadley: Praeger, J.F. Bergin, 1982.

Brinkley, Alan. "1968 and the Unraveling of Liberal America." *1968, the World Transformed*, edited by Carole Fink et al. Cambridge, New York: Cambridge University Press, 1998.

Chiarito, Bob. "Chicago 1968: While the Whole World Watched, Chaos Stole Convention Spotlight." *The Columbia Chronicle*, March 11, 1996, June 18, 2005, http://homepage.interaccess.com/~chron96/back/mar1196/article1.html.

Diggers. "The Post Competitive Comparative Game of a Free City." *The Movement Toward a New America: The Beginnings of a Long Revolution*, edited by Mitchel Goodman. Philadelphia: Pilgrim Press, 1971.

Gilcher-Holtey, Ingrid. "May 1968 in France: The Rise and Fall of a New Social Movement." *1968, the World Transformed*, edited by Carole Fink et al. Cambridge, New York: Cambridge University Press, 1998.

Gitlin, Todd. *The Sixties: Years of Hope, Days of Rage*. Toronto, New York: Bantam Books, 1987.

———. *The Whole World Is Watching: Mass Media in the Making & Unmaking of the New Left*. Berkeley: University of California Press, 2003.

Goodman, Mitchel. *The Movement Toward a New America: The Beginnings of a Long Revolution*. Philadelphia: Pilgrim Press, 1971.

Guarnaccia, Matteo. "No Hands! Provos and White Bicycles." *Antonio Colombo Arte Contemporenea*, June 14, 2005, www.colomboarte.com/en/artists/mani/cataloghi-mani_eng.htm.

Hoffman, Abbie. *Steal This Book*. New York: Pirate Editions. Distributed by Grove Press, 1971. June 14, 2005, www.tenant.net/Community/steal/steal.html.

———. "Media Freaking." *The Movement Toward a New America: The Beginnings of a Long Revolution*, edited by Mitchel Goodman. Philadelphia: Pilgrim Press, 1971.

Kaplan, John. "Powerful Days." May 17, 2004. *Inthefray Magazine*, June 15, 2005, http://inthefray.com/html/article.php?sid=434&mode=thread&order=0.

King, Martin Luther. "Letter from Birmingham Jail." *Why We Can't Wait*. New York: Harper & Row, 1964.

Kostash, Myrna. *Long Way from Home: The Story of the Sixties Generation in Canada*. Toronto: Lorimer, 1980.

Layton, Azza Salama. *International Politics and Civil Rights Policies in the United States, 1941–1960*. Cambridge, New York: Cambridge University Press, 2000.

Lévesque, Benoît. "State Intervention and the Development of Cooperatives (Old and New) in Quebec 1968–88." *Studies in Political Economy* 31 (1990): 107–139.

Lorimer, Rowland, and Mike Gasher. *Mass Communication in Canada*, 5th ed. Don Mills: Oxford University Press, 2005.

Marwick, Arthur. *The Sixties Cultural Revolution in Britain, France, Italy, and the United States, c. 1958–c. 1974*. Oxford; New York: Oxford University Press, 1998.

McCarthy, John D., and Mayer N. Zald. "Resource Mobilization and Social Movements: A Partial Theory." *American Journal of Sociology* 82, no. 6 (1977): 1212–1241.

McLuhan, Marshall. *The Mechanical Bride: Folklore of Industrial Man*. New York: Vanguard Press, 1951.

Oberschall, Anthony R. "The Decline of the 1960s Social Movements." *Research in Social Movements, Conflicts and Change* 1 (1978): 257–289.

Reynolds, Malvina, composer. "Little Boxes." Pete Seeger. Schroder Music Company, 1962.

Smelser, Neil J. *Theory of Collective Behavior*. London: Routledge & Kegan Paul, 1962.

Socialist Worker. "Spring 1963: The Battle for Civil Rights in Birmingham Freedom Now!" May 16, 2003. *Socialist Worker Online*, June 14, 2005, www.socialistworker.org/2003-1/453/453_08_Birmingham.shtml.

Thomas, William G. "Television News and the Civil Rights Struggle: The Views in Virginia and Mississippi." *Southern Spaces: An Internet Journal and Scholarly Forum* (2004), June 15, 2005, www.southernspaces.org/contents/2004/thomas/4e.htm.

Vaneigem, Raoul. *The Revolution of Everyday Life: Impossible Communication or Power as Universal Mediation*. Red and

Black, 1967. June 14, 2005, http://library.nothingness.org/articles/SI/en/pub_contents/5.

————. "Basic Banalities (II)." *An Endless Adventure … an Endless Passion … an Endless Banquet: A Situationist Scrapbook*, edited by Iwona Blazwick. London: Verso/ICA, 1989.

Yippies. "Yippie Manifesto." *"Takin' It to the Streets": A Sixties Reader*, 2nd ed., edited by Alexander Bloom and Wini Breines. New York: Oxford University Press, 2003.

Young, Neil. "Ohio." *4 Way Street*. Crosby, Stills, Nash, and Young, 1970.

CRITICAL THINKING QUESTIONS

1. Why did so much protest activity erupt in the privileged centres of the world from among the very people who seemed to enjoy unprecedented affluence and political freedom?
2. How can we explain the decline of the 1960s social movements?
3. How did the 1960s movements differ from the predictions of Marx and Engels? Consider the following points in your comparison:
   a) The role of class as the basis for organized dissent
   b) The types of "community" that people identified with or gained a sense of solidarity from
   c) The nature of the complaints about capitalism
   d) The role of lifestyle and consumption versus work in defining the issues of protest
   e) The nature of movement organizations and their relationship with those they (purport to) represent
   f) The targets of protest (employers versus the state versus the culture of everyday life)
4. Do you think that some variant of the 1960s "transitory team" with its promise of "instant solidarity" might allow for the kind of rapid, flexible mobilization that could respond to 21st-century dynamism?
5. Can the problem for social movements of reliance on the mainstream media be overcome by using new forms of low-cost, wide-distribution indymedia supported by the Internet?
6. What is (or should be) the role of class as the basis for organized dissent?
7. How are political "collective actors" constituted? To what extent can we appeal to the "logic of capital" to make sense of this dynamic?

8. How is "representation" of social constituencies accomplished by the bodies that purport to speak for them?

FURTHER READING

Fink, Carole, et al. *1968, the World Transformed*. Publications of the German Historical Institute. Cambridge; New York: Cambridge University Press, 1998.
 The 1960s social movements were an international media-linked phenomenon. This collection of essays is an admirable corrective to U.S.-centric analyses. Contributors look at what was happening not only in the Americas and western Europe, but also eastern Europe and the developing world.

Kostash, Myrna. *Long Way from Home: The Story of the Sixties Generation in Canada*. Toronto: Lorimer, 1980.
 There is no better book for bringing to life the experience of the 1960s social movements in Canada.

McAdam, Doug. *Freedom Summer*. Oxford Paperbacks. New York: Oxford University Press, 1990.
 Why did privileged young White people become involved in organizing poor Black voters in the southern United States in the summer of 1964 even though they faced tremendous personal risk of racist violence and even murder? McAdam addresses this question by listening to the voices of those involved and charting how their biographies and personal networks intersected with the social and political conditions of the time.

Morris, Aldon D., and Carol McClurg Mueller. *Frontiers in Social Movement Theory*. New Haven: Yale University Press, 1992.
 This collection of essays offers samples of American work in the resource mobilization tradition. In response to the limitations of the crudely economistic approach of some early resource mobilization theorists, authors here attempt to integrate themes of culture, social networks, identity, and meaning.

Tarrow, Sidney. "Cycles of Collective Action: Between Moments of Madness and the Repertoire of Contention." *Social Science History* 17 (1993): 281–307.
 This is an influential article that applies quantitative techniques to the analysis of patterns of social movement culture, in particular the choice of tactics in Italy during the 1960s and 1970s. Despite his reliance on numbers and graphs, the author writes lyrically and seductively.

RELEVANT WEB SITES

"Act UP" Civil Disobedience page
www.actupny.org/documents/CDdocuments/CDindex.html
 Learn about the contemporary practice of non-violent civil disobedience and what to do if and when you are arrested for breaking the law over an issue of conscience.

The ACTivist Magazine
www.activistmagazine.com
> News, resources, and strategy for activists sponsored by the Toronto-based peace organization, Act for the Earth.

CampusActivism.org
www.campusactivism.org
> If you want to get plugged in to student activism in North America, this is a good place to start. The site is U.S.-based, but has good links to Canadian organizations, campaigns, and events. It contains a wealth of "how to" guides and resources.

Indymedia
http://maritimes.indymedia.org
> Activists have new tools unavailable in the 1960s for making their own news. Check out the "open publishing" model at one of Canada's indymedia sites. I have listed the site for my region (the Maritimes). Other regions are listed at www.independentmedia.ca/. This independent media (as distinct from indymedia) site also has an excellent list of sources of Canadian "non-corporate" news and analysis on- and off-line. Indispensable for activists.

The Situationist International Text Library
http://library.nothingness.org/articles/SI/all/
> Sample the brilliant, irreverent, and creative thinking of the Situationists. Look at the classics, *The Society of the Spectacle* and *The Revolution of Everyday Life*. Explore!

Weblogs
> "Blogs" are the latest phenomenon in democratic political exchange that evades the constraints of mainstream media. They are meant to be (entertainingly) biased, but are open to comment, criticism, and debate from readers. Blogs Canada (www.blogscanada.ca/directory/Default.asp) indexes political blogs according to the categories "left," "right," and "general." Some have great titles like *Canukistan* and *Cold, Bitter Canadian Truth*. Sample randomly and find your favourites.

Chapter 4

RESISTANCE TO STATE TERROR

INTRODUCTION

Victor Jara was a folk hero in Latin America in the 1960s. He was a key figure in the "Nueva Cancion" (new song) movement in which musicians decried the stark inequalities within Latin American societies and gave voice to the emotional lives and aspirations of workers and the poor. For this he was arrested in 1973 by the military government in Chile under General Augusto Pinochet. Along with others he was led to the Santiago boxing stadium where for four days he was "tortured, beaten, electrocuted" (Coles). Finally, they taunted him to play his guitar after they had shattered the bones in his hands and wrists. Bravely, he sang one of his songs of hope and justice before the bullets ripped through his chest. In his last days in the boxing stadium he had scribbled a few lines of a poem, including: "Silence and screams are the end of my song."

Amazingly, despite risking a fate like Jara's, people in Chile continued to resist the Pinochet dictatorship. They eventually prevailed, winning democracy for their country, and were recently nearly successful in bringing Pinochet to justice in international courts. Our question for this chapter is: How is resistance possible against extreme forms of state repression? We answer it through a comparison of three cases of resistance to state terror in Argentina, Uruguay, and Chile. First, though, we discuss repression as a state response to social dissent. This is a much uglier approach to social movements than the co-optation that we discussed in Chapter 2. Often states employ both as complementary strategies. In the following section we will see how in the U.S. the state used police repression against the New Left, and how in Latin America, states, with U.S. sanction, employed outright terror. While state terror is our theme, our focus is on how it influences social movements and how social movements can mobilize to resist it.

STATE REPRESSION IN PERSPECTIVE

In the previous chapter we saw how Oberschall explained the decline of the 1960s movements in terms of "internal weaknesses," in particular, organizations' reliance on the media. One of the other explanations that Oberschall considered was state repression. It is quite eye opening to learn both the scale of the secret operations against activists as well as the extent to which state agencies were willing to act illegally in their zeal to crush legitimate dissent.

Oberschall, of course, looked only at the United States and not Canada. The legal tools that could justify state action against 1960s radicals were limited. In most countries it is illegal to act to overthrow the government by non-parliamentary means. This is generally called "sedition." It is also illegal to destroy property, to riot, or to incite a riot. But laws against sedition and rioting are usually balanced by laws protecting the rights of free speech and assembly. These protections for dissent were particularly strong in the United States. It is legal to advocate "smashing the state" so long as you are not actually smashing it or causing it to be smashed.

In specific cases it is the judges, not police or politicians, who decide where to draw the line between free speech and sedition or inciting a riot. Oberschall shows that U.S. federal judges (he does not consider state or county cases) viewed most 1960s activism as perfectly legal dissent. Even Abbie Hoffman, whose role in provoking the "police riot" in Chicago you read about earlier, was tried but in the end not indicted for inciting a riot.

Police, on the other hand (and this was true in both the U.S. and Canada), seem to have acted on the assumption that almost any form of dissent was or should be illegal. The FBI alone conducted 500,000 investigations of activists and organizations suspected of "subversion" or sedition. Under the Nixon administration there were 2,000 agents devoted full-time to investigating the New Left (Oberschall 275-276). These officers would tail subjects, open their mail, record their telephone conversations, and break into their offices and homes to seize documents and other evidence.

Covert Police Operations against the American New Left

Much of this activity involved invasion of privacy and to do it legally, police had to convince a judge that there was good reason to believe that their target was engaged in criminal activity. Since this was often difficult to do, police routinely acted on their own through burglary, illegally tapping people's phones, or gaining access to their income tax records. We know most about the FBI's actions undertaken through its "counter-intelligence program" or COIN-TELPRO, since it came under scrutiny from a U.S. Senate committee in 1976.

COINTELPRO was set up in the 1950s to gather information on "communist"-influenced groups in the United States. By the 1960s it was deployed against a wide range of political dissent, including the New Left. Since the New Left was international, the CIA (responsible for foreign intelligence) had its own parallel program amassing files on 13,000 people between 1967 and 1972 (Brandt). Many city police departments contributed their own staff, organized into "Red Squads," and resources to this massive surveillance operation.

The frustrating truth for the police was

that the courts viewed the vast majority of this activity under surveillance as legal, legitimate dissent, so they employed an additional strategy that involved infiltrating New Left organizations and events and using the infiltrators to incite illegal activities such as bombings and the destruction of property. This is an old strategy. Its name, "agent provocateur," comes from its use by the French police in the 19th century. Its aim was summarized by a police director in Tsarist Russia: "We shall provoke you to acts of terror and then crush you" (Marx 402). It is a way of legitimating police repression. When protestors are seen to go "too far," not only does this furnish legal grounds for police action, but it outrages the public and provides support for the police and for tougher legislation against the "terrorist" threat.

Of course the irony, as we now know, is that not only were undercover agents responsible for inciting violence in the 1960s, but they were often the ones committing it using explosives and arms supplied by the police and paid for by taxpayers. There are numerous documented examples. Here are a couple. An agent posing as a student demonstrator at the University of Alabama tossed firebombs at police and set fire to a university building. Police were able to use his actions to declare the demonstration "unlawful" and make 150 arrests. A Seattle agent was commissioned by police to stage a bombing. Unable to get a Black Panther to do it, he hired a Black youth for $75, supplied him with explosives, and drove him to the site where he ended up being shot by waiting police (Marx 406-408).

What impresses Oberschall is that despite this massive and often unscrupulous police effort, there were remarkably few arrests and convictions. In fact, on the charge of sedition, there was not a single conviction. This is the main thrust of his argument—that it was not repression but internal weaknesses that led to the decline of the 1960s social movements.

However, obtaining convictions was not the only aim of police operations. Oberschall himself points out that even without convictions, criminal prosecution could be an effective way of tying up movement leaders' time and resources. In some instances the limited funds of SMOs were used to pay for leaders' legal fees, compromising their effectiveness and causing resentments to build within the organizations.

Many activists also recall how obvious it sometimes was that they were under surveillance. The stakeout car would be in clear view of their apartment. Their mail delivery would start to follow an abnormal pattern, arriving erratically in bundles. Mysterious clicks on their phone lines would give them the impression that they were being listened to or taped. The apparent intent here was to let people know that they were being watched in order to intimidate them or make them paranoid.

COINTELPRO documents show that the FBI fuelled paranoia and distrust within and between New Left organizations with all the devious spy-thriller techniques they could dream up. Spreading false accusations was a favourite. Activists would receive anonymous letters telling them that a fellow activist was a police informant, or that their partner was being unfaithful, or that someone in the movement was out to kill them. Here, for instance, is a letter that the FBI sent to Black Panther Fred Hampton:

> Brother Hampton:
> Just a word of warning. A Stone friend tells me [name deleted] wants the Panthers and is looking for somebody to get you out of the way. Brother Jeff is supposed to be interested. I'm just a black man looking for blacks working together, not more of this gang banging. (United States Senate)

The FBI often went to great lengths to discredit leaders with their followers. FBI agents hid microphones in Martin Luther King's hotel rooms to collect evidence of sexual infidelity (not, note, a crime and therefore not something that they could have got a legal warrant to investigate in this way). They attempted to use the tapes they made to break up his marriage and/or drive him to suicide. They also circulated unsubstantiated personal attacks, and placed pressure on universities not to grant him honorary degrees and on the Pope not to grant him an audience (United States Senate).

FBI efforts to discredit King were spectacularly unsuccessful. He went on to win the Nobel Prize and stands alongside figures like Gandhi and Nelson Mandela as one of the great heroes of struggles for human justice. However, police were successful in spreading paranoia within the New Left about surveillance and infiltration. The key here is that this tactic weakened trust between activists. We have seen how important trust is for successful collective action. At least some of the internal weaknesses that plagued New Left organizations in the 1970s—divisiveness and waning commitment—should be attributed to police repression.

Extra-legal killings played a minor role in state repression in the United States. (In Canada police killed no civil rights or New Left activists.) In 1964 local Mississippi police conspired with the Ku Klux Klan to murder three civil rights activists, James Chaney, Andrew Goodman, and Michael Schwerner. In at least one instance police staged "shootouts" that were to provide apparent legitimacy for assassinations of Black Panther leaders. Fred Hampton and Mark Clark died and a number of other Panthers were wounded when Chicago police raided their apartment at 4:30 a.m. Ballistic evidence later showed that police shot all but one of the rounds fired that morning

(Lindsey). The various shootings of students at Kent State and Orangeburg might have seemed like premeditated acts of state terror to paranoid activists. Subsequent evidence points instead to poor policing gone disastrously wrong.

State Terror against the New Left in Latin America

The record on state terror was quite different in Latin America, however. Consider the case of Mexico, a formally democratic country. In 1968 it was hosting the Olympics. As in every other Western democracy that year, its youth and many of its workers were caught up in the revolutionary fervour of the New Left. Both the activists and the authorities recognized that the Olympics would transform Mexico City into a global stage. Along with international New Left issues, students wanted to dramatize U.S. imperialism within Latin America and their own government's increasingly repressive reactions to their movement. The government wanted to show the world that Mexico was an attractive and stable site for international investment.

By September 1968 the government had already killed students in demonstrations. That month troops occupied the National Autonomous University of Mexico and tens of thousands of students marched in Mexico City in protest. Government representatives invited students to talk at the Plaza de las Tres Culturas in Tlatelolco. By nightfall there were 5,000 people in this square—workers, students, citizens, and children—chanting "México, Libertad." Police and troops surrounded the square with tanks and armoured vehicles. They opened fire on the crowd, slaughtering hundreds of people.

The official story was that "communist" snipers had started shooting at police, who had no choice but to defend themselves. Only recently has evidence finally confirmed what many have suspected. The snipers were plainclothes police, agents provocateurs, armed with machine guns and with instructions, probably from the president's office, to fire on both troops and protestors (Dillon). The troops no doubt thought they were being attacked by "communists" and responded in kind.

In the "Tlatelolco Massacre" we have a very clear case of state terror used as a weapon against legitimate dissent. The intent here is to paralyze dissent, not through prosecutions or court battles or through creating suspicion and distrust among activists, but by creating an environment of mortal fear. How would you respond in these circumstances? If you knew that you could be shot dead by authorities with impunity for expressing your opinion, would you remain silent? The surprising thing is that many people speak out nonetheless. This is one of the questions that we take up in the following section. How and under what conditions do people still engage in social dissent despite state terror? A corollary to this question is: What conditions make state terror more or less effective?

One of the best studies attempting to answer these questions is "High-Risk Collective Action: Defending Human Rights in Chile, Uruguay, and Argentina" by Mara Loveman. She compares the responses to state terror in three Latin American countries in the 1970s: Chile, Uruguay, and Argentina. All three were responding, like Mexico, the United States, and Canada, to the "threat" of New Left revolutionary activism, but they murdered and tortured not hundreds but tens of thousands of their own citizens to combat it. You already understand some of the global context and have an appreciation for what New Left activism in these countries probably meant for those engaged in it.

You will probably also want to understand why some governments' response was so much more brutal and excessive than others. This question cannot be our main focus since our purpose in this textbook is to understand social movements. Still, I can make some suggestions about how to answer that question.

Understanding State Terror

First, we need to recognize that the impulse toward repression was present within the U.S. and Canadian states. In some ways the Canadian state went further than its U.S. counterpart, enacting martial law in the form of the War Measures Act (more on this in a later chapter). The important point is that there were institutionalized limits to state powers. The "state" is not a single power but is comprised of different institutional bases of power that do (or ideally should) constrain one another. For these constraints to work, there should be a framework of human rights and civil rights that governments recognize as legitimate and inviolable. There must be a body of law reflecting these rights and protecting citizens against arbitrary state action. The judiciary must be sufficiently independent from government to uphold that law. States' resources of naked force—the police and the military—must be clearly subordinated to the judiciary and elected government.

To further guarantee that states "play by the rules," their actions have to be subjected to public scrutiny. The Mexican government was ready to slaughter hundreds of its citizens because it calculated, rightly, that it could cover up its role and deny responsibility. To this day it has denied access to all records of this event on the grounds of "national security." The Mexican media failed to challenge the government's version of events. While in the United States there were many desperate to keep COINTEL-

PRO secrets, there were relatively powerful tools—a Senate investigation, freedom of information laws, a press that still took seriously its watchdog role—available to those who wanted to make these secrets public. This quality of institutions, where citizens are enabled to "see into" their hidden workings, is referred to as "transparency."

In order for states in Chile, Uruguay, and Argentina to engage in the extreme repression that they did, governing factions, in collaboration with the military, had to dismantle or neutralize these countervailing powers. In Argentina, a history of military coups and corrupt "strongman" politics meant that these checks on state power were relatively weak to begin with, but that was not the case with Chile and Uruguay. Before the coups of 1973, these were by any measure healthy democracies. The fact that they could so quickly descend into brutal dictatorships continues to raise disturbing questions for any democracy.

STATE TERROR IN CHILE, URUGUAY, AND ARGENTINA

Silence and Screams: Terror as a Governmental Strategy

> First, we will kill all the subversives; then we will kill their collaborators; then their sympathizers; then the indifferent and finally, the timid (Argentine Brigadier-General Ibérico Manuel Saint-Jean, qtd. in Loveman 477).

Patricia Marchak, in her study of the military repression in Argentina, describes the nature of torture in that country:

Torture often involved electric prods being applied to the genitals, nipples, gums, ears.... Many persons were put in the "pits," deep holes in the ground, where they were buried, naked, their heads above ground, for several days. When they were extracted, they were covered with insect bites, worms, infections, and their own excrement.... Often, women were raped, repeatedly raped, and mutilated. Not infrequently prisoners would be told that their loved ones were also being held and that a spouse, child, or parent had died. Occasionally a prisoner was brought face to face with an almost dead or raped and tortured loved one. (153–154)

The torturers were both inflictors of pain and witnesses to the victims' humiliation and depersonalization. They extracted confessions and denunciations of others, and drove home a deep sense of shame and guilt in order to destroy the victims' very sense of who they were. Victims and potential victims were forced to witness the destruction of their friends and comrades. Those already in prison could hear the screams. Outside they would hear the rumours or periodically learn of a corpse bearing the marks of torture being dumped by the side of a roadway. The Argentine regime regularly murdered victims after torture, often by throwing them from cargo planes into the sea. In this way between 10,000 and 20,000 political captives were murdered during the tenure of the generals (Falcoff 3).

The military regimes in all three countries shared information and collaborated on practices of state terror, but in Uruguay they preferred more subtle approaches that emphasized the outcome of the destruction of the victim's identity. They reserved most of the brutal infliction of pain for pre-trial extraction of confessions from detainees. They murdered relatively few. There are 20 documented cases, although the Uruguayan human rights organization SERPAJ estimates that 109 were killed. (Uruguayan dissidents who fled to the neighbouring countries were often "disappeared" by these more brutal regimes at the behest of the Uruguayan authorities. Perhaps 200 died in this way (Corradi, Fagen, and Garretón Merino 98).

In Uruguay, far more people went to jail than in the other countries. As many as one in every 50 Uruguayan citizens found themselves at some point in the infamous "La Liberdad" (Liberty) prison for political crimes and misdemeanours (Neild 357). This Orwellian institution was in a clean, modern building designed as a "panopticon." In other words, it was designed to keep prisoners under surveillance at all times. When prisoners were admitted, they had a friendly chat with a psychologist who was apparently interested in how to heal their psychological scars, anxieties, and weaknesses. Prison officials would then design a regime calculated to exploit these weaknesses. Harassments that were invasive, relentless, and arbitrary in an environment pervaded by the threat of violence or total annihilation were enough to destroy many personalities (Weschler 123–132).

Anti-imperialist Revolutionaries

The Latin American New Left, among the principle targets of this repression, were similar in many ways to the New Left in other countries. Typically they were young, drawn from the middle classes, educated, and idealistic. Imperialism had a special significance in their analysis of injustice. They counted their countries as among the Algerias and Vietnams of the world—economically dependent upon and subject to political meddling from the great powers, chiefly the United States. They were enamoured not only by the success, but also by the revolutionary élan of their fellow Latin American, Che Guevara.

One woman recalled the mood of young people in Argentina just before the coup. It was 1972, and she was 17.

> A that time being an activist was normal. We all believed that Argentina was going through the same process as that of May, 1968, in France, and the revolution of 1959 in Cuba. The role of Che Guevara gave us a sense of belonging. For us teenagers it was very important that he was an Argentine. We felt that we were part of the revolutionary history of Argentina. There was no possibility of being young and not being an activist; it was like a destiny. (qtd. in Marchak 248)

Che Guevara, Fidel Castro, and a relatively small group of guerrillas based in the mountains of Cuba had succeeded in mobilizing popular support for the overthrow of a corrupt, U.S.-backed regime in that country in 1959. Their revolution had not followed the Marxist model. It was not led by an organized urban proletariat. This feature of the Cuban revolution gave hope to middle-class revolutionaries that they, too, could initiate armed struggle in the name of the oppressed. To use a Cuban metaphor, they aspired to start the "small motor" that would set in motion the "large motor" of popular revolution.

As was the case in the U.S., Europe, and Canada, a minority of the young radicals turned to violence in the early 1970s. Canadians and Americans had an abstract appreciation of the violence of the "military-industrial complex," but mostly saw its effects at a distance. Latin Americans had

already experienced egregious examples of state violence against peaceful protestors in their own countries. For them it was easier to lose faith in non-violent tactics. Their guerrilla groups were larger, more effective, and, at least initially, attracted far more public sympathy than their counterparts in Europe and North America.

The Tupamaros in Uruguay were able in their early actions to combine revolutionary violence and public theatre, rather like Yippies with guns. They enforced "potlatches," stealing food and distributing it among the poor. They carried out armed exposés, raiding money-laundering operations and publishing the records they discovered there, implicating government officials and prominent businesspeople in corruption. They attacked exclusive clubs of the rich, leaving behind graffiti such as "O Bailan Todos o No Bailan Nadie" ("Either everybody dances or nobody dances") in one nightclub. So well did they reputedly treat their kidnap victims that Uruguayans took to joking, "Hey, Tupamaros! Kidnap me!" (Weschler 103–105).

The most successful guerrilla group in Argentina, the Montoneros, was able to raise millions of dollars through their kidnappings. They also carried out assassinations of symbolic victims like General Aramburu, responsible for a 1959 coup. Subsequent guerrilla groups refer to them as "the pure ones" for their youthful idealism (Marchak and Marchak 122), but there was an ugly logic to the kind of warfare that they and the Tupamaros engaged in with authorities that bred brutality on all sides. The playful, pranksterish debut of the Tupamaros did not last long. The Montoneros even went so far as to torture captives (Marchak and Marchak 295). In Chile, the idea of armed struggle had few followers because there the parliamentary route to change had so much more promise. In 1970 a socialist coalition party, headed by Salvador Allende, came to power through a democratic election. As in Canada, Chilean governments can be elected without a majority of the popular vote. This was the case with Allende. His new government's policies only broadened existing opposition from capitalists and petty-bourgeois segments of the electorate. At the same time it was unable to satisfy the rising expectations of change from the unions and the radical left.

Its program of nationalizing major industries (not uncommon for the period, notably in Canada) aroused powerful enemies outside the country from the multinational companies who lost assets and from the U.S. State Department interested in protecting the interests of those companies and stopping the spread of "communism," which many of the ideologues could not distinguish from socialism. This was the political "crisis" that served as the rationale for General Pinochet's coup in 1973. In Uruguay and Argentina, the rationale was the threat of left-wing terrorism in the form of the Tupamaros and Montoneros.

Coup d'État: Suppression of Parliament, Civil Rights, and an Independent Judiciary

What is a coup d'état? The key defining feature is the suspension of Parliament and imposition of direct rule by unelected military hierarchy. This happened in Chile and Uruguay in 1973, Argentina in 1976. However, coups also involve the dismantling of civil rights and any legal or social guarantees that preserve them. This clearing of the political landscape to make way for the exercise of authoritarian power is often a slow, incremental process that can begin long before the generals dissolve Parliament. All of the "countervailing powers" within the state are first restricted, then eliminated.

In Uruguay, years before the coup, state protection of freedom of speech and freedom of assembly were revoked on the basis of "emergency security measures" that applied only to certain individuals and organizations. Left-wing political parties were "temporarily" banned, union members arrested, left-wing presses were shut down, and others were prohibited from reporting "subversive news." Repeatedly, people's individual rights were suspended under "emergency" law. These would include the right to privacy, the right to remain silent if arrested, the right to receive legal counsel, the protection against being detained without being charged with an offence. In all three countries these protections against police abuses were eventually suspended.

In democracies judges should have authority independent of the government and police that they can use to rein in excessive policing, guard the rights of the accused, and apply discretion in the interpretation of the law. All three countries undermined this "judicial independence" by eliminating judges' immunity from dismissal or retribution or by simply replacing them with military tribunals. Without a critical judiciary, it actually became possible to indict people charged under ludicrous new laws such as the one in Argentina (1976), which made "offending 'dignity' of military personnel" illegal.

Military governments were able to flout Western legal tradition by inventing laws that criminalized thoughts and types of persons rather than acts. Uruguay's "State of Dangerousness" law (1975) made it illegal to have "inclinations" to communist views or to have inclinations to commit crimes, even if one had never actually done anything wrong (Loveman, unpublished appendices C1–3). (This is morally problematic, but the legal difficulty has to do with evidence. You have to throw out the high standard of proof "beyond a shadow of a doubt" to argue that someone has an inclination to commit a crime if they have never committed one.)

The criminalization of belief justified the purges of judges, professors, and civil servants working in state bureaucracies. In Uruguay people who were employed or sought to be employed in these positions were officially classified according to ideology as "A," "B," or "C." If you were in category "C" (left-leaning), you were in deep trouble. Universities were seen as particularly troublesome sites

of "subversion," so they came under surveillance, harassment, and eventually direct military control. All three regimes were obsessed with controlling not just what people did, but what they thought. The net of control extended far beyond the revolutionaries who practised violence to include trade unionists who believed in the rights of workers and pro-capitalist liberals who just wanted to see that people's civil rights were protected.

BOX 4.1:

INTERNATIONAL STATE TERROR NETWORK?

Imagine that you were flying home to Canada from overseas. The only flight you could get with your air miles has you stopping over in Switzerland, then landing at JFK Airport in New York at 2:00 p.m. and waiting a few hours for your connecting flight to Montreal. You get pulled aside at immigration and taken to a separate area. You are made to wait for two hours. There are no other passengers in this special area. Finally, officials show up and your story unfolds as follows:

They took my fingerprints and photographs. Then some police came and searched my bags and copied my Canadian passport. I was getting worried, and I asked what was going on, and they would not answer. I asked to make a phone call, and they would not let me.

Then a team of people came and told me they wanted to ask me some questions. One man was from the FBI, and another was from the New York Police Department. I was scared and did not know what was going on. I told them I wanted a lawyer. They told me I had no right to a lawyer, because I was not an American citizen.

They asked me where I worked and how much money I made. They swore at me, and insulted me. It was very humiliating. They wanted me to answer every question quickly. They were consulting a report while they were questioning me, and the information they had was so private I thought this must be from Canada.

I told them everything I knew. They asked me about my travel in the United States. I told them about my work permits, and my business there. They asked about information on my computer and whether I was willing to share it. I welcomed the idea, but I don't know if they did.

They asked me about different people, some I know, and most I do not. They asked me about [Mr. A.], and I told them I worked with his brother at high-tech firms in Ottawa, and that the [A.] family had come from [S—] about the same time as mine. I told them I did not know [Mr. A.] well, but had seen him a few times and I described the times I could remember. I told them I had a casual relationship with him.

They were so rude with me, yelling at me that I had a selective memory. Then they pulled out a copy of my rental lease from 1997. I could not believe they had this. I was completely shocked. They pointed out that [A.] had signed the lease as a witness. I had completely forgotten that he had signed it for me when we moved to Ottawa in 1997, we needed someone to witness our lease, and I phoned [A.'s] brother, and he could not come, so he sent [A.].

But they thought I was hiding this. I told them the truth. I had nothing to hide. I had never had problems in the United States before, and I could not believe what was happening to me. This interrogation continued until midnight. I was very, very worried, and asked for a lawyer again and again. They just ignored me. Then they put me in chains, on my wrists and ankles, and took me in a van to a place where many people were being held in another building by the airport. They would not tell me what was happening. At 1:00 in the morning they put me in a room with metal benches in it. I could not sleep. I was very, very scared and disoriented. The next morning they started questioning me again. They asked me about [my views on politics]. They also asked me about the [places] I pray in, my bank accounts, my e-mail addresses, my relatives, about everything.

This continued on and off for eight hours. Then a man from the INS came in and told me they wanted me to volunteer to go to [S—], a country where torture is common practice]. I said no way. I said I wanted to go home to Canada or sent back to Switzerland. He said to me "you are a special interest." They asked me to sign a form. They would not let me read it, but I just signed it. I was exhausted and confused and disoriented. I had not slept or eaten since I was in the plane. At about 6:00 in the evening they brought me some cold McDonald's meal to eat. This was the first food I had eaten since the last meal I had on the plane.

At about 8:00 they put all the shackles and chains back on, and put me in a van, and drove me to a prison. I later learned this was the Metropolitan Detention Center. They would not tell me what was happening, or where I was going. They strip searched me. It was humiliating. They put me in an orange suit, and took me to a doctor, where they made me sign forms, and gave me a vaccination. I asked what it was, and they would not tell me. My arm was red for almost two weeks from that.

They took me to a cell. I had never seen a prison before in my life, and I was terrified. I asked again for a phone call, and a lawyer. They just ignored me. They treated me differently than the other prisoners. They would not give me a toothbrush or toothpaste, or reading material. I did get a copy of the [Holy Book] about two days later.

After five days, they let me make a phone call. I called [my wife]'s mother, who was here in Ottawa, and told her I was scared they might send me to [S—], and asked her to help find me a lawyer. They would only let me talk for two minutes.

On the seventh or eighth day they brought me a document, saying they had decided to deport me, and I had a choice of where to be deported. I wrote that I wanted to go to Canada. It asked if I had concerns about going to Canada. I wrote no, and signed it. The Canadian consul came on October 4, and I told her I was scared of being deported to [S—]. She told me that would not happen. She told me that a lawyer was being arranged. I was very upset, and scared. I could barely talk.

The next day, a lawyer came. She told me not to sign any document unless she was present. We could only talk for 30 minutes. She said she would try to help me. That was a Saturday. On Sunday night at about 9:00 p.m., the guards came to my cell and told me my lawyer was there to see me. I thought it was a strange time, and they took me into a room with seven or eight people in it. I asked where my lawyer was. They told me he had refused to come and started questioning me again. They said they wanted to know why I did not want to go back to [S—]. I told them I would be tortured there. I told them I had not done my military service; I am a [religious affiliation]; my mother's cousin had been accused of being a member of the [a religious organization] and was put in prison for nine years.

They asked me to sign a document and I refused. I told them they could not send me to [S—] or I would be tortured. I asked again for a lawyer. At three in the morning they took me back to my cell. At 3:00 in the morning on Tuesday, October 8th, a prison guard woke me up and told me I was leaving. They took me to another room and stripped and searched me again. Then they again chained and shackled me. Then two officials took me inside a room and read me what they said was a decision by the INS Director.

They told me that based on classified information that they could not reveal to me, I would be deported to [S—]. I said again that I would be tortured there. Then they read part of the document where it explained that INS was not the body that deals with Geneva Conventions regarding torture.

Then they took me outside into a car and drove me to an airport in New Jersey. Then they put me on a small private jet. I was the only person on the plane with them. I was still chained and shackled. We flew first to Washington. A new team of people got on the plane and the others left. I overheard them talking on the phone, saying that [S—] was refusing to take me directly, but [J—] would take me.

Then we flew to Portland, to Rome, and then to Amman, Jordan. All the time I was on the plane I was thinking how to avoid being tortured. I was very scared. We landed in Amman at 3:00 in the morning local time on October 9th.

They took me out of [the] plane and there were six or seven Jordanian men waiting for us. They blindfolded and chained me, and put me in a van. They made me bend my head down in the back seat. Then, these men started beating me. Every time I tried to talk they beat me. For the first few minutes it was very intense. (Arar)

As you have probably guessed by now, this is Maher Arar's story. I have replaced a few specific details with general ones to allow you better to "get inside his skin" and to see his experience from the perspective of someone, like yourself, who is innocent (at least of crimes of terrorism). From Jordan, he was taken to Syria, where he was tortured, just as he feared he would be. He was thrown into a windowless cell, "the grave," he called it: 3 feet by 6 feet, with no light, sink, or toilet. Here he stayed for 10 months and 10 days with no idea when or how he would be released. He was beaten, usually with an electrical cable, and continually threatened with more and worse punishment. His captors made sure he heard the screams of other prisoners to let him imagine what he could expect.

Almost as shocking was his treatment in New York. He was held without being told what crime he was charged with. He was denied access to a lawyer of his choice. For eight days he was not allowed to contact anyone in the outside world. Neither he nor any lawyer representing him was allowed to see the evidence being used against him. These are all rights that Canadian and American citizens are supposed to have to protect them against police abuses that can lead to wrongful detention and wrongful convictions. U.S. authorities did not notify the Canadian consulate before deporting him, thereby violating the Vienna Convention on Consular Relations. Deporting him without a fair hearing to a country where he might reasonably be expected to be tortured is a violation of the UN Convention against Torture and Other Cruel, Inhuman or Degrading Treatment or Punishment.

Public outcry in Canada eventually forced the government to set up a commission of inquiry into the case. Judge O'Connor, the author of the Commission report, concluded that the RCMP had wrongly linked Arar to al Qaeda on the basis of poor evidence, like the rental agreement witnessed by "A—" (Abdullah Almalki), whom the CIA suspected of al Qaeda involvement. The RCMP also broke its own rules in the way that it shared this information with U.S. authorities. O'Connor absolved Canadian officials of direct involvement in the decision to send Arar to Syria, although doubts remain. We do not know exactly what American officials knew or the rationale for their decisions since they refused to co-operate with the inquiry. However, it is probable that they sent Arar to Syria in the hope that the Syrians would be able to extract useful information under torture. Increasingly, after the al Qaeda attack of 9/11, the U.S. has engaged in what officials call "extraordinary rendition" where they send non-U.S. citizens suspected of terrorist activity to countries that engage in torture. The "open secret" is that not only do they expect suspects to be tortured, they also expect to use information obtained by this means. As one U.S. official (anonymously) reported to the *Washington Post*, "We don't kick the shit out of them, we send them to other countries so they can kick the shit out of them" (Priest and Babington A01).

The U.S. has also alleged that the information they used to detain Arar was obtained from Canada. No doubt the RCMP and Canada's spy agency CSIS share information on terrorist suspects with their U.S. counterparts. The more worrying question for Canadians is to what extent are Canadian security services complicit in the "extraordinary rendition" program? If they co-operated in the Arar case in the knowledge that he risked deportation to a third country for torture, they would be complicit in "rendering" their fellow citizens.

Canada possibly, but the United States most probably, is engaged in depriving people of legal rights and delivering them to "torture by proxy" in the name of their "war on terror." What is the difference between this and the use of torture by terrorist states like Uruguay and Argentina in the 1970s? After all, they, too, had the excuse of wars against terrorists—the Tupamaros and Montoneros. One difference is that the U.S. relies primarily on a network of foreign states willing to engage in terror on its behalf. Another is that it applies these techniques to non-citizens. Does this absolve it? What are the risks of its actions encouraging the spread of state terror?

Political struggles over the use of state terror and the human rights abuses that that involves are very much alive, and uncomfortably "close to home." If you are interested in becoming engaged in some way, you could start by visiting the Web sites of some of the Canadian human rights organizations involved: Amnesty International Canada (www.amnesty.ca/canada/), Canadian Civil Liberties Association (www.ccla.org/news/), Maher Arar's Web site (www.maherarar.ca/get%20involved.php).

Source: Maher Arar, "Statement," November 4, 2003. CBC News Online, July 29, 2005, www.cbc.ca/news/background/arar/arar_statement.html.

A great deal of the oppression of the citizens of Chile, Uruguay, and Argentina was done under the facade of "legal" legitimacy. Many people in these countries accepted this claim to legitimacy. But the destruction of countervailing powers gave the police and military the freedom to engage in "extra-legal" arrests, torture, and killings with impunity. However, there are institutions outside of the state that in normal democracies take an independent, critical perspective on state activities, call its actions to account, and in this way limit abuses. Universities often play this role. This is one of the reasons that repression was directed against them. However, they are typically state-funded and state-sponsored organizations and in this way are more, like the judiciary, an element of the state system.

Coup d'État:
Suppression of Civil Society

What I am more interested in here is the realm of "civil society," which I will define for now as "public, political activity organized independently of the state." Non-governmental organizations (NGOs) that have a political or social agenda fall into this category. That includes all social movement organizations and unions. Political parties, which, even when in power, are distinct from the government, are part of civil society. In Latin America the churches, engaged in social justice work, were an important element of civil society. The press, though organized on a for-profit basis (unlike NGOs), when it plays its public advocacy role, is sometimes also conceived as a part of civil society.

Authoritarian power depends on the elimination of countervailing powers within the state and civil society as well. In Chile, Uruguay, and Argentina, unions and political parties were harassed, constricted in their activities, then outlawed entirely. The newspapers that were not banned outright were censored in order to prevent them from playing their critical role. For example, the Argentine regime declared it illegal to publish "... all news referring to terrorist activity, themes related to subversion, kidnappings, discovery of cadavers, or related to security force personnel ... unless it is announced by an official source" (Loveman, unpublished Appendix C). This was to ensure that illegal police abductions and "disappearances" would not be subject to critical scrutiny.

In these societies the state could arbitrarily—depending on what you thought, or what they suspected that you thought, or even how you looked (it was dangerous for young people to have long hair or wear green, the colour of revolutionaries)—break into your house at night and drag you to the torture chambers. No due process would protect you; no one would dare speak out for you or even admit publicly what had happened to you. What this accomplished was the psychological elimination of the barrier between prison and society. The terror of the screams, the mutilations, and the humiliation radiated out from the torture cell and permeated everyday life. State terror, like 21st-century al Qaeda terror, amplifies its intimidating force by demonstrating that no one is immune. In these three countries state terror became a system of total societal control rather than a technique for dealing with urban guerrillas. Long after the Tupamaros and Montoneros had been crushed, these states widened the powers and intended targets of repression.

RESISTANCE TO STATE TERROR IN CHILE, URUGUAY, AND ARGENTINA

Mara Loveman's research attempts to show what enabled people to create new forms of resistance after military rulers had put in place reigns of terror. Initial resistance involved the defence of human rights. The mere formation of human rights organizations (HROs) took courage enough. These organizations began carefully to take steps to assist victims of state brutality. Loveman's approach to understanding them is comparative. She observes that HROs emerged earliest in Chile where they made the boldest moves in support of human rights. They emerged latest and had the least force in Uruguay. Argentina was an intermediate case. She asks what was different about the conditions in the three countries or in the mobilization of opposition that can account for relative success in Chile and failure in Uruguay.

Perhaps you can already think of some possible explanations. Loveman conceptualizes her answer using resource-mobilization language. She argues on the one hand that the "political opportunity structure" was least favourable in Uruguay. There the project of governance through the deployment of terror was more complete and total than in the other two countries. On the other hand, she argues, the resources available to HROs were more extensive in Chile. There some remnants of civil society, particularly under the auspices of the Catholic Church, were left standing. In addition to civil society organizations, strong personal networks of those engaged in social justice issues had survived the repression. Her third category of resources, in addition to civil society NGOs and personal networks, is "external links." Human rights activists in Chile had the strongest links to international civil society organizations, in particular human rights organizations such as Amnesty International. These links brought them symbolic as well as financial "resources."

Variations in the Strength and Timing of Resistance

Chile

Let us consider her argument in detail, beginning with the comparison of the relative success of human rights activism. In Chile, surprisingly, two human rights organizations formed the very year of the coup when the Pinochet regime murdered and "disappeared" the largest number of victims and was most active in legislating away the rights of civil society organizations. The socialist government of Allende had welcomed thousands of left-wing refugees fleeing from oppressive regimes in other countries. It had also ratified a UN treaty on the treatment of refugees. After the coup, UN officials, Chilean representatives of the World Council of Churches, and other religious leaders persuaded the junta to honour this treaty and allow the refugees, who would otherwise certainly have been targets of the repression, to leave the country. Hoping no doubt to avoid adverse international attention, the Pinochet regime tolerated the formation and activities of the first HRO, the Comité Nacional de Ayuda a los Refugiados (CONAR) or National Committee for Aid of Refugees. CONAR succeeded in arranging safe passage for about 4,000 people.

Church leaders of different denominations established a second group that year to assist Chilean nationals. The Comité de Cooperación para la Paz en Chile (COPACHI) began cautiously to assist individuals subjected to repression and their families. The organization represented its work in terms of religious charity rather than political action. In other words, it avoided overtly criticizing the regime's systematic human rights abuses. Many of the regime's supporters in Chile were social conservatives and devout Catholics. Strategists within the regime understood that they could lose legitimacy with this constituency by directly attacking an organization such as COPACHI that had the blessing of the Church. Still, within a year COPACHI volunteers were being subject to harassment and intimidation.

When a group of priests and nuns allegedly helped members of a banned left-wing revolutionary group obtain asylum in foreign embassies, Pinochet accused COPACHI of harbouring "Marxist-Leninist agitators" (Loveman 494). This gave him sufficient moral leverage with his right-wing supporters to demand that Church leaders shut down the organization. They complied, but the archbishop of Santiago replaced it that year (1975) with a new organization, the Vicaría de la Solidaridad (Vicariate of Solidarity), which continued its work under the direct auspices of the Catholic Church.

When the regime moved against the Vicariate, Chilean bishops, with the support of the international Church, courageously stood their ground. The sanctity, at least in Chile, of Catholic Church authority saved them. The regime backed down. The Vicariate continued to provide victims of repression with legal advice and humanitarian assistance, wrote petitions to international human rights organizations on behalf of close to 2,000 individuals, and also provided safe haven for the growth of covert civil society activity in Chile (Hawkins 56). They were joined in this work by the newly formed Fundación de Ayuda Social de las Iglesias Cristianas (FASIC, Social Aid Foundation of the Christian Churches).

The Vicariate was able to use this "moral shield" that the bishops' stance had established to begin the implicitly political work of documenting the abuses. Toward the end of the decade and increasingly throughout the 1980s, independent research institutes contributed also to the work of documentation. Remember that Chile, along with the two other regimes, imposed restrictions on the press and the universities to prevent them from exposing the states' ugly secrets. Many social scientists purged from the universities found positions in independent research institutes that had been set up with funding and assistance from various international bodies: The United Nations, international donor foundations, foreign governments, and the Catholic Church.

The prestige of their international sponsors afforded these institutes some immunity to overt repression. Their premises and staff, confined within the borders of a terrorist state, were illuminated by a spotlight of international attention. Arbitrary arrest, disappearance, or torture carried out within this circle would invite precisely the kind of scrutiny the regime sought to avoid. Regime officials opted to tolerate these organizations, but could not avoid scrutiny. The documentary work of the Vicariate and the research NGOs was used first to embarrass the regime and, much later, it was used in efforts to bring the perpetrators of state terror to justice (see the box in this chapter,"Will Pinochet Answer for His Crimes?").

By the 1980s in Chile there were two sorts of "political space" that had become relatively immune from the grip of state terror. These became the staging grounds for a slow rebuilding of a civil society independent of state control. Here people could meet, create networks, discuss ideas. Previously banned organizations of civil society, including unions, political parties, local self-help groups, and critical media, became active again. Governments, labour unions, and political foundations in Europe and North

America funnelled millions of dollars into the country to support the establishment of these groups. The new Chilean groups helped to mobilize popular opposition to Pinochet in an upcoming plebiscite. Their foreign supporters organized international monitoring to ensure that the plebiscite would be free of corruption. Pinochet lost the referendum in 1988, a defeat that signalled the beginning of the end of his regime.

Uruguay

In Uruguay HROs were fewer and less effective than in either Chile or Argentina. The first and only HRO, Servicio Paz y Justicia (SERPAJ), was not formed until 1981, eight years after the coup and long after the worst of the state repression. For that period the state had completely colonized everyday life and prevented the re-formation of an independent civil society. It was international pressure, coming in part from the Carter administration in the U.S., that forced the regime to begin reintroducing democratic institutions. Their first move was to hold a referendum on a new constitution designed to affirm the military's hold on political power.

With no safe forums in which to discuss the issue publicly, most Uruguayans believed the constitution would pass. When it was defeated, the psychological grip of terror was weakened. "Already the next morning," one woman later explained, "everything had clearly changed. People in the street regarded each other differently" (qtd. in Weschler 151). Those who had wondered in isolation about how to resist the regime now knew that the majority were with them. No doubt this is what emboldened them to form SERPAJ.

Still, SERPAJ's range of action remained far more constrained than that of COPACHI in Chile. Its director was repeatedly impris-

oned only to be released under international pressure. It was too dangerous for SERPAJ to receive the kind of international financial support that Chilean NGOs had enjoyed. A former member of the organization recalled: "There wasn't a single person who dared to receive a check, to give to a family member of a political prisoner, for fear of being sent to La Liberdad prison" (qtd. in Loveman 506–507).

Argentina

Argentineans created an impressive array of HROs, but, as in Uruguay, these organizations proved to be limited in what they could accomplish. Argentina had a long history of military coups and the abuses of law that come with them. As early as 1937, the Liga Argentina por los Derechos Humanos, with links to the Communist Party, formed to defend against these attacks on individual and political rights. Before the 1976 coup there were warning signs that the state was willing again to dismantle human rights protections in the name of its war on Montonero "terrorism." Three new organizations formed in response to this threat.

An Argentine division of SERPAJ (Servicio Paz y Justicia) became active in 1974. Some religious leaders involved in SERPAJ found its approach to be too timid. In 1976 they created an ecumenical HRO, Movimiento Ecuménico por los Derechos Humanos (MEDH), that perhaps, they hoped, might enjoy some of the "religious immunity" of COPACHI in Chile. Secular human rights activists, recognizing the liability of the old Liga's communist connections, formed a parallel HRO in 1975 Asamblea Permanente por los Derechos Humanos (APDH).

All three terrorist regimes learned from one another, including each other's "mistakes." In an effort to avoid the public scrutiny suffered by Pinochet, the Argentine generals attempted to keep all of their dirty work "off the books." Even the "legal" imprisonment of the Uruguayans left a paper trail and living witnesses. The Argentines relied instead on "disappearance." This involved abducting people, usually from their homes in the dead of night, torturing them, murdering them, and disposing of the bodies, typically at sea. Sometimes if the intended targets were not at home, other potential witnesses to the abduction were disappeared: family members or innocent guests. Disappearance created tremendous anxiety for the families left behind. They needed to know if their loved ones were alive or dead. Maybe they had escaped the country; maybe they had died, but perhaps not through unspeakable torture at the hands of the military.

Quite unexpectedly, and very inconveniently for the regime, relatives of the disappeared, typically mothers, began in 1977 to gather in a major public square in the capital—the Plaza de Mayo—with pictures and descriptions of their missing loved ones in mute protest against the government's unwillingness to assist them in their search. The Madres (Mothers) de la Plaza de Mayo, as they came to be known, gained international attention. The government's silence spoke eloquently of its complicity in the disappearances. The regime's attempts to intimidate the Madres by arresting them and "disappearing" their leaders only added to their prestige as martyrs. Mothers were joined by grandmothers, "abuelas," in a parallel organization, Abuelas de la Plaza de Mayo.

The regime's response to all of these efforts was to continue the repression and extend it to human rights activists.

> Repression of the human rights movement touched every organization, affecting both the leadership and grass-roots members. Many members of the original leadership

of Las Madres "disappeared" while the Movimiento Ecumenico lost two nuns, several priests and a Protestant minister. The co-founder of the Asamblea ... was kidnapped, tortured and imprisoned for several years.... Several Liga lawyers disappeared and a secretary of the Familiaries was kidnapped, tortured, and forced to give false statements to the press denying her disappearance and alleging connections to guerrilla forces. Rank-and-file members of Las Madres were arrested repeatedly following demonstrations.... The offices of Asamblea, CELS, La Liga and Movimiento Ecumenico were raided. (Brysk, qtd. in Loveman 511)

There are two points that must be made here. The first is that HROs did not, to the same extent as their counterparts in Chile, create safe political "spaces" for the re-emergence of civil society and eventual resumption of democracy. The second is that people nonetheless acted independently of the state. They fought against the regime for abstract principles of "rights" that might benefit others in the future, but in ways that certainly put themselves at immediate and grave risk.

HROs emerged early and with relative strength in Chile, late with minimal effectiveness in Uruguay, and early with numeric strength but minimal effectiveness in Argentina. To explain these differences in outcome, Loveman compares: (1) the strength of surviving civil society, particularly church organizations; (2) the strength of personal networks of activists; and (3) the strengths of the HROs' international links. When she discusses civil society, she focuses almost entirely on religious organizations, not because these are normally the most important players, but because these were among the few NGOs that the regimes did not attempt to wipe out in their efforts at total societal domination.

Variations in Church and Civil Society

Throughout Latin America, Catholicism is the dominant religious tradition, but each country's history has shaped that tradition in different ways. Everywhere other denominations (Protestant and, particularly in Argentina, Jewish) have had an influence. However, Loveman argues that it was the differences in Catholicism between the three countries that were decisive for the survival of HROs. Uruguay's democratic traditions had to be fought for against the opposition of the Church. Its institutions of civil society and the state, including its universities, were built on a principled rejection of religious and clerical influence.

Uruguayan generals had a free hand to attack those churches that dared to oppose them. Methodists and members of Jesuit and Dominican orders were arrested, tortured, and in some cases murdered. General Forteza charged that "international communism" had "reached the Church itself, violating in this institution the rights and obligations that the State has granted to the different religions" (Forteza, qtd. in Loveman 500). Only in Uruguay could a general insist in this way on the Church's subordinate status in matters of political authority. In both Chile and Argentina it remained a powerful moral force. In Chile, as we have seen, the HROs benefited from that authority, but in Argentina the Church gave its blessing to the regime.

In our chapter on co-operatives we tried to make sense of why the Catholic Church sometimes supports social movements and sometimes joins in efforts to repress them. Remember, it is an institution slow to change and burdened with an undemocratic structure. It has had difficulty accepting the growth of liberal democracy and has been adamantly opposed to socialism, communism, and even militant trade unionism. Its effort to deal with the modern world in its 1891 statement *Rerum Novarum* showed that it also had strong objections to capitalism and the social inequalities that it generated. The world changed in the 1960s and the Church responded with one of its most dramatic revisions of doctrine, Vatican II. Vatican II softened resistance to democracy within the Church and opened the door for greater popular and local input into Church practice. Bishops were invited to "evaluate and restructure ... pastoral ministry in light of the context in which it is carried out" (Kater).

For the Latin American bishops who met in 1968 in Medellin, Colombia, this meant addressing the needs of the poor in the "developing" economies of the region, not just offering comfort but recognizing the human causes for their suffering and giving them the tools for change. Under this "preferential option for the poor," priests listened to their parishioners' concerns, then, often drawing on the writings of neo-Marxists, helped them to identify the economic and political causes of their oppression, and encouraged them to organize "Christian base communities" to work for change. This form of Catholicism, also known as "liberation theology," proved tremendously relevant to congregations among the poor and working classes. In Argentina and Chile it inspired middle-class revolutionaries as well. Many of the Montoneros, for example, had been members of Catholic youth organizations introduced to liberation theology by their priests.

Of course, for many in Latin America the "preferential option for the poor" spoke neither to their experience nor their political interests. There were struggles within the hierarchies of national churches between right-wing and left-wing factions. In Argentina the right wing prevailed, in Chile the left. The Argentinean Church was a powerful moral force in politics, but it used that power to support the military regime in its war on "terrorism" and "communism." It drew on the authoritarian, anti-democratic elements within the Catholic tradition to justify its stance. Church authorities turned a blind eye to the torture and murder, even tolerating the disappearance of left-wing priests and nuns. Churches turned away victims and their families who appealed to them for help. The Church might have been able, but did not provide a safe political space for the development of HROs and other civil society organizations.

The moral shield of Church blessing worked for HROs in Chile because, even though the generals hated the Church's position, they could not afford to appear anti-Church. Key to understanding these regimes and their eventual fate is that they all needed some form of legitimacy. Rule by pure violence, as sociologist Max Weber has shown, is a costly and unstable form of governance. Some of the population, the more the better, must comply willingly and actively because they see the state as justified in its course of action. (Perhaps you remember our discussion in earlier chapters of the "autonomization" of power.) Argentinean and Chilean generals drew on religious language because their people understood the use of Catholicism to support authoritarian power. They tried to convince their publics that they were heroically defending "western Christian civilization" (Hawkins 66; Loveman 513) from the evils of "terrorism" and "communist subversion."

In summary, Loveman concludes that the remnants of civil society were strongest in Chile because of the authority of a left-leaning Church and weakest in Uruguay because there the Church had no public legitimacy as a voice in politics. The next factor she looks at is the strength of face-to-face networks among human rights activists. Her central point is that there had to be deep trust among these people in order for them to risk working together in such dangerous conditions. The great fear was of surveillance, infiltration, and betrayal.

Variations in the Strength of Network Connections

The Madres de la Plaza de Mayo exposed themselves to these risks to a greater degree than most, first because they demonstrated out in the open, but also because they worked with people with whom they had no history in common. It was easy for police to pose as bereaved mothers. Even if no one had seen them before, who was to say that their son or daughter had not been disappeared? Nine of the Madres' organizing members lost their lives as a result of a military informant infiltrating their meetings.

People preferred to work with those that they had known for a long time and who had proved themselves in terms of their personal and political loyalties: a comrade from a New Left student organization, a professor or priest who had been a former mentor, a close personal friend, or even a family member. Working with such people reduced risks, but face-to-face relationships with "significant others" also helped to sustain for people their sense of identity and encourage them in courses of action that confirmed that sense of self, no matter how dangerous.

Loveman argues that these networks were stronger and more extensive in Chile than in the other two countries. During the most dangerous initial period, human rights activists, according to a former member of

FASIC, were "clearly made up of a network of persons who, if they didn't all know each other personally, had faith in the friends of those they did. Nobody came in off the street" (Loveman 492). For trust to have developed, these networks had to have a history. They were formed prior to the coups and mostly through the unions, political parties, churches, and social movements that were active in the 1960s and early 1970s. Most observers agree that this sort of civil society activity was strong in all three countries, Uruguay in particular. So how can Loveman say that all of a sudden after the coups there was such a significant difference?

She argues that only in Chile did members of the Church figure prominently in these networks. This had two important consequences. First, Church connections linked otherwise loosely affiliated networks. The country's most prestigious universities were Catholic affiliated and many people destined for politics, law, and the "social justice professions" would have come into contact here. Many were involved in political parties, such as the centre-left Christian Democrats, which were explicitly Catholic in orientation. Liberation theology was popular among priests and nuns. Their political work in communities, in political parties, and through the Catholic universities put them in a position to act as "network nodes" through whom numerous personal ties came together. The second consequence was that after the coup, the Church's relative immunity to repression ensured that its networks remained somewhat intact and had places to operate.

Variations in International Ties

The third type of "resource" that, according to Loveman, contributed to HRO success consisted of ties to international organiza-tions. International organizations could funnel money to the HROs. More importantly, the light of international public attention made it more difficult to silence the HROs or threaten their staff and volunteers. Remember that in the 1960s there was already an international consciousness among social movement activists. The students of 1968 in Paris looked to the example of the civil rights activists in the southern United States and the Algerian anti-colonialists; civil rights leaders looked to Gandhi; the Montoneros admired the Parisian students of 1968 and Che Guevara in Cuba. When a democratically elected socialist government came to power in Chile in 1970, people from a broad spectrum on the left watched with sympathy and anticipation to see how this new experiment would unfold.

While global awareness was one of the New Left's great strengths, its organizational capacity, as we saw in the previous chapter, was weak locally and even weaker internationally. Churches and, to a lesser extent, labour unions had much better international organizational capacity. International church organizations like the World Council of Churches and the Catholic Church itself learned of the first abuses of the coup in Chile not from the media but from their own people "on the ground" in that country. Church leaders from a variety of denominations in Canada responded quickly, forming the Inter-Church Committee on Chile, and, days after the coup, met with Canada's minister of Foreign Affairs to persuade the government to refuse recognition of the new military regime and to grant asylum to Chilean refugees.

Church leaders were surprised to discover that the minister (Mitchell Sharp) and his aides were not very sympathetic to their concerns, insisting that this "was just another Latin American coup of no great importance" (Inter-Church Committee on Human Rights in Latin America). Sharp may not have known this, but it was in fact a coup partly made in the U.S.A. When Allende was elected, President Nixon and his advisers met and agreed to do everything in their power to "bring him down" while retaining "an outward posture that is correct" (Memorandum of Conversation, NSC Meeting—Chile [NSSM 97], November 6, 1970). Henry Kissinger, as national security adviser, oversaw secret operations to destabilize Allende's government, offering advice and assistance through the CIA to Chileans plotting sedition—i.e., the violent overthrow of a democratically elected government. The CIA likely took an active role in some of the dirty work, like the assassination of a general loyal to Allende.

The U.S. administration also offered CIA assistance to Uruguay's terrorist regime. The CIA provided instruction on "modern" torture, supplying a manual pointing out "35 nerve points" on the human body where electrical shocks could be applied. The CIA allegedly advised the Uruguayans to murder rather than incarcerate their victims once they had finished torturing them (McSherry 148). When the Argentine military began "disappearing" their opponents in 1976, Kissinger told the admiral acting as Argentine foreign minister, "Look, our basic attitude is that we would like you to succeed." Get the dirty work over quickly before the U.S. Congress resumes, he advised, then, "Whatever freedoms you could restore would help" (Osorio).

The generals could perhaps be forgiven for believing that international pressure was not going to be a big problem for them. After all, the most powerful country in the world had apparently given them the wink and nod. What they failed to understand, which is not surprising for military dictators, is how democracy works in the United States, or the new ways that democracy was beginning to work internationally. For instance, in Canada, Church leaders were undeterred by the government's cool response. They con-tinued to lobby and document stories from the increasing number of refugees as well as contacts remaining in the affected countries.

International Civil Society in Action

By 1976 they had raised sufficient funds to take a delegation, including Canadian members of Parliament, to observe conditions for themselves. They were denied access to Chile, but were able to gather first-hand evidence from Argentina and Uruguay. For the first time, they systematically documented the lesser known conditions in Uruguay in a report titled *One Gigantic Prison* (Inter-Church Committee on Human Rights in Latin America) This information was shared and the efforts of different groups worldwide—such as Amnesty International, Oxfam, and the World Council of Churches—reinforced one another. Lobbying by international and American groups on American-elected officials led to Congress voting in favour of sanctions against the Pinochet regime in 1974. Sanctions were later followed by cuts to military and economic aid, in direct contradiction to what Nixon and his senior advisers like Kissinger would have preferred.

Coordinated international action among civil society organizations nudged governments, but also quasi-state organizations to take action. What I mean by "quasi-state" are those human rights bodies set up by states through intergovernmental treaties. These include the United Nations Human Rights Commission and, in the Americas, the Inter-American Commission on Human Rights (IACHR). In the 1970s the U.S. was a powerful influence in both of these bodies. South American dictatorships no doubt hoped that the U.S. would use this influence to minimize the scrutiny and downplay criticisms of their human rights abuses from these organizations.

In 1975 Pinochet appealed to the U.S. for support in his country's refusal to allow the UN Human Rights Commission to conduct an investigation. He asked the U.S. to oppose, by veto if necessary, any effort within the UN to have Chile expelled for non-compliance. Still, largely because of pressure from international civil society, the UN took unprecedented steps against the military regime. The UN General Assembly passed resolutions condemning it, and the UN Human Rights Commission called for an investigation of alleged abuses. Previously the UN had acted on human rights abuses only within a member country only if these posed a threat to international peace (Hawkins 54).

Chile, desperate for international legitimacy, gambled on allowing the IACHR to enter the country and investigate the human rights situation. Most of the American countries that were party to the IACHR had waged covert wars against the left and many also had blood on their hands. Perhaps the generals imagined that they would get some sympathy here. They were wrong. The IACHR report in 1974 honestly recorded the abuses and condemned the regime.

Thereafter Chile closed its borders to human rights investigators. Uruguay refused to allow an IACHR delegation to enter the country. The Argentine military allowed IACHR observers in, perhaps confident that their more clandestine approach to terror would be difficult to document or that they could intimidate witnesses from coming forward to speak with the delegation (Marchak and Marchak 229). They, too, were mistaken. People bravely came forth and furnished enough evidence for the IACHR to issue a damning report in 1979.

Precisely when the generals were attempting to extinguish civil society within their own borders, a new form of civil society was beginning to demonstrate its power to mobilize across borders. Internationally linked Church, human rights, and labour organizations showed that they could provide the kind of critical scrutiny that could hold not merely national governments, but also international bodies to account. If agencies like the UN or the IACHR did not act forthrightly when called upon to investigate human rights, there were hundreds of independent non-governmental organizations, like Canada's Inter-Church Committee on Human Rights in Latin America, prepared to do the work themselves. International agencies could not afford the embarrassment of being undercut and exposed in this way and began to act to a higher standard on human rights issues. This new role for NGOs showed the promise of what has come to be referred to as "global civil society."

BOX 4.2:

WILL PINOCHET ANSWER FOR HIS CRIMES?

General Pinochet, many of his victims, and their relatives are still alive, and the fight for justice continues. Human rights organizations (HROs) have been working to strengthen international law and to see that Pinochet is tried and convicted for his role in torture and murder during the worst years of his rule in Chile, 1973–1976. They recently helped to win two extraordinary legal decisions that have set the stage for a new era in international justice. In 1996 a Spanish court ruled that Pinochet could be tried in Spain for his crimes, even though these crimes did not take place on Spanish soil and the victims and perpetrators were not Spanish citizens. Human rights lawyers successfully argued that the link that gave Spain jurisdiction was based not on the fact that the parties were citizens of the same country, but rather "that we are all human beings" (Human Rights Watch). This "universal jurisdiction" also crosses borders. The crime does not have to take place in the prosecuting country, but anywhere on the planet that humans share. The principle of universal jurisdiction can be applied to torture, genocide, crimes against humanity, and war crimes.

Pinochet was not in Spain in 1996. The second legal decision, this time from a British court, established in principle that another country could extradite him to Spain. Pinochet had flown to England in 1998 for medical treatment. On the request of a Spanish judge, he was arrested for extradition on charges of murder and torture. Pinochet's lawyers argued that he had immunity from extradition since the alleged acts had been committed as part of his function as head of state. The British judges ruled first that torture could never be considered a "function" of a head of state. Their final, more limited, ruling was that immunity was forfeited when Chile ratified the United Nations Convention against Torture (Human Rights Watch). With this judgment, the tools were in place that might one day make it impossible for state terrorists to find safe haven anywhere in the world or escape accountability for their crimes. At the very least, it now means that terror suspects, such as the U.S.'s Henry Kissinger, must consult their lawyers before travelling abroad.

There have been many legal twists and turns in the Pinochet case since 1998. For an update, you should visit the Web sites of some of the HROs involved in prosecuting it: Human Rights Watch (www.hrw.org), Amnesty International (www.amnesty.org), Memoria y Justicia (www.memoriayjusticia.cl/english/en_home.html), Redress Trust (www.redress.org), the Medical Foundation for the Care of Victims of Torture (www.torturecare.org.uk), and the International Rehabilitation Council for Torture Victims (IRTC; www.irct.org). A number of Chilean HROs have been involved, some of which you will recognize from this chapter. With the exception of SERPAJ, their Web sites are in Spanish only: Agrupación de Familiares de los Detenidos Desaparecidos, (AFDD; www.afdd.cl), Comité de Defensa de Los Derechos Del Pueblo (CODEPU; www.codepu.cl), Centro de Salud Mental y Derechos Humanos (CINTRAS; www.cintras.tie.cl), Fundación de Ayuda Social de Iglesias Cristianas (FASIC; www.fasic.org), and Servicio Paz y Justicia (SERPAJ-Chile; www.serpajchile.cl/english/index.html).

As you can see, many HROs, both at the domestic and international level, are involved in this effort. These are only a tiny fraction of the growing number of HROs worldwide that have sprung up in the last three decades as part of a growing "global civil society." Whether or not they succeed in bringing Pinochet to justice (he is getting old and may die or be declared unfit to stand trial because of dementia), they are strengthening the international institutional basis for human rights accountability. What we are seeing is the increasing power of global civil society acting through HROs to put in place a new kind of "independent judiciary" that has legal tools that are immune from influence from any particular government or military. However, I want you to realize that this is very much a "work in progress" that is likely to encounter continued opposition. Consider the fact that even democratic states sometimes find it convenient to draw upon international state terrorist networks, as Canada and the U.S. appear to have done in the Maher Arar case.

Note: On Decemeber 10, 2006, just prior to the publication of this text, Pinochet died and thereby evaded facing justice for his crimes.

Source: Human Rights Watch, "The Pinochet Case: A Wake-up Call to Tyrants and Victims Alike," March 2000, Human Rights Watch Web site, August 17, 2005, www.hrw.org/campaigns/chile98/precedent.htm.

Links with international NGOs were valuable "resources" for the work of HROs in Chile, Uruguay, and Argentina. They provided a "moral shield" of international public attention, assisted in HRO work by lobbying for international investigations, and also supplied them with funds. Why were the links stronger to Chilean HROs than to those in Uruguay or Argentina? To explain this, Loveman appeals again to the role of the churches. Only in Chile did the Catholic Church have the strength to protect and foster anti-regime networks within the country and, as an international organization, to maintain active ties to the outside world. International action brought pressure to bear on the other two countries. In Argentina there were HROs that could benefit from international assistance, but in the case of Uruguay, action had to be taken on behalf of the Uruguayans with minimal collaboration with people or organizations "on the ground."

Variations in Political Opportunity Structure

Loveman rounds out her explanation by pointing out that there were also differences in the "political opportunity structure" between the three cases. What she means is that the states in Uruguay and Argentina deployed more powerful means for controlling their populations. Both were able to lay groundwork in advance of the coups, mobilizing public support for increasingly drastic anti-terror legislation and anti-terror tactics against the Tupamaros and Montoneros. (There is an interesting, and some would say very worrying, parallel here with the advance of anti-terror legislation, particularly in Britain and the United States, but also in Canada and other Western countries.) They had time to expand their military forces

and put in place the kinds of systems and training that would prepare them for the systematic coercion of civilian populations.

Uruguay also benefited from geography. Its people were concentrated within a tiny land area, and most lived in one urban centre. Surveillance, as Jeremy Bentham once observed, is easiest when the population is concentrated and most difficult when it is thinly scattered over a large area. It was easier in Uruguay to keep the entire society under Orwellian surveillance and to erase that line in people's minds between the torture cell and the security of their private lives.

Recall from the previous chapter that resource-mobilization theorists predict that social movements are more likely to emerge when more resources are available. They used this insight to explain the paradox of the 1960s explosion of social dissent in the midst of affluence. Loveman is satisfied that this principle applied to Chile once the Church had called upon its Catholic and ecumenical contacts abroad, stood up to Pinochet, and established the Vicariate's immunity to overt repression. HROs then had at their disposal the "resources" of political space, international funding, and legitimacy. These resources attracted more participants and emboldened their efforts and so the human rights movement grew. So far this makes sense.

The Remaining Problem of Explaining Self-Sacrifice

However, resource-mobilization theorists assume that people are acting here on the basis of rational calculations of self-interest. Potential activists see that the costs to themselves in terms of risks to personal safety have been lowered and benefits, in terms of tools to get the work done, are available. They act on the basis of weighing these costs and benefits. Loveman is not happy with this assumption of what she terms "rational choice." What about those who act first before anyone can be sure that the state will back down to the Church or that international organizations will be willing or able to offer meaningful support?

In this context, no matter how rational you are, it is almost impossible to calculate how likely it is, if you take action against the state, that you will be murdered or tortured. Sometimes people seem to act on the basis of what Max Weber called "value rationality" rather than "instrumental rationality." In other words, instead of weighing personal costs and benefits, they often do what they think is right no matter what the consequences to themselves.

Consider the case of the Madres de la Plaza de Mayo. In Chile a similar group formed under the protection of the Vicariate, which gave them an office to operate from on Church property. However, the Argentinean Madres acted without the "protective shield" of the Church, secure "political spaces," or the support of long-time networks of trusted associates. They knowingly exposed themselves to deadly risks by carrying their photos and petitions in the open under the direct gaze of the death squads. How would you prepare yourself mentally to set out as they did for the Plaza de Mayo? Surely you would have to convince yourself that what you were doing was more important than your own life. You would have to be willing to accept torture and death as a likely outcome of your action.

Choosing death is irrational in terms of "calculations of self-interest." The selfish rationalist would choose to be what rational choice theorists call a "free rider." In other words, it takes only a handful of mothers to show up at the Plaza to embarrass and place pressure on the regime. If you are not among them, you get the same benefit, but with no personal cost. You "ride" for free, pulled along by the brave actions of others.

Loveman concludes: "If the likely result of action is death, rational choice models would predict inaction, unless they determined ex post facto, with reference to the individual's behaviour that the first order preference is a certain 'value' that requires a sacrifice. This of course, is tautological" (Loveman 481). In other words, the rational choice theorist could look at a case of self-sacrificing behaviour and assume, after the fact, that there must have been a rational cost-benefit analysis going on in this person's mind. In addition, they would have to assume that this was an unusual person who gives greater weight to intangible "benefits" like a clear conscience than to her own life.

By making these assumptions, Loveman says, the theorist would be cheating. If the theorist is prepared always to "make things up" in this way just to save the theory, then there could never be a case that could contradict the theory. It could be used to "predict" *any* behaviour after the fact, but nothing specific in advance.

If resource mobilization cannot explain the self-sacrifice of the Madres de la Plaza de Mayo, or the actions of those who are the first to brave incalculable risks, then how do we explain it? Some have attempted to understand the Madres' political strategy in terms of their invocation of social myths and meanings that surround the status of motherhood. Motherhood evokes the values of unquestioning familial duty and tradition that all three authoritarian regimes appealed to for their own legitimacy. The fact that mothers and grandmothers, concerned only for their children and grandchildren, stood up to the authorities and faced assassination was very bad PR for a regime that pretended it was protecting "family values." While their deployment of the status of motherhood was effective in terms of attracting international public sympathy and undermining the legitimacy of the regime, it did not afford the Madres personal protection. They still were targets for harassment and murder. To understand the personal motivation, Loveman turns to the work of Craig Calhoun, who relies for his understanding on the concept of identity.

Human beings are not just about physical survival and advancement. We also live in a shared world of ideas. That is where our experience of what is meaningful in the world, who we are, and how what we do fits into the world take shape. The close personal networks of human rights activists had helped to define for them during their formative years as students, as campus activists, as young professionals, an identity as someone who recognizes and fights for social justice. Since they were little girls, the Madres would have learned, through gendered practices of socialization typical in most societies, that motherhood means nurturing, protecting, and advocating for their children at whatever cost. They acted against great personal risk, perhaps even fatalistically, because of who they were as much as for any calculated outcome.

As Calhoun puts it, high risks were accepted "not because of the likelihood of success in manifest goals but because participation in a course of action has over time committed one to an identity that would be irretrievably violated by pulling back from risk" (Calhoun, qtd. in Loveman 492). Loveman finds confirmation of this idea in the personal accounts of activists. She quotes a psychologist who had worked for FASIC in Chile: "In my view, motivations to participate were ethical, political, and very personal. For me, the suffering of the people I was helping was intolerable, the persecution of my students, their disappearance and death still cause me pain today. I believe that one commits oneself to things because of who one is. I believe that

I would have lost my own dignity and self-respect if I hadn't done the work that I did" (qtd. in Loveman 492).

Understanding dissent against state terror may require that we use tools other than a resource-mobilization perspective or rational choice theory. The Madres case makes more sense if we abandon the language of "resources" and instrumental rationality for concepts of "identity" and "symbolic systems" or "culture." This choice requires a different approach to study. We would have to spend more time listening to what people say to get a better understanding of their world of meaning as they see it. We might also have to revise some unspoken expectations about what scientific study can achieve.

Loveman seems to be concerned with the ability of rational choice theorists to predict social movement activity. If people respond in the same "logical" way to certain external resources and societal conditions, perhaps we could predict what they were likely to do. Social science explanation would be much more like causal explanation in physics or chemistry. Once we can predict outcomes, of course, it is then possible to come up with ways to control outcomes. We might learn how, by changing societal conditions or available resources, to eradicate dissent.

However, even if we could, would we really want to give regimes like Uruguay's, which already relied upon "scientific" forms of repression, the tools to make them even more effective? Marx was happy with the idea of causal models of dissent because he thought he had proven that the victory of the workers' revolution was inevitable, and that the bourgeoisie were doomed to contribute to their own downfall. Suppose that the bourgeoisie learned from reading Marx's predictions, and changed history to avert their downfall? What would this tell us about causal explanations in the social sciences that purport to predict human behaviour?

I admit I am just raising questions that I am not going to answer for you here. My point is that it is important always to think about *how* social scientists explain or understand as much as what they are trying to explain or understand. In Loveman's case, you have to think about why HROs emerged under one terrorist regime and not another. You also have to ask what tools she is using to answer her question, and if these are the right tools. Using a different set of theoretical tools can often lead to very different insights about the case under study. You need to do that with Loveman, and you also need to do that with me as author of this text. I often have a theoretical agenda. You want to learn how to spot it and name it.

In this chapter, at the same time as presenting the resource-mobilization approach, I have been surreptitiously highlighting the value of a more interpretive approach. When I discussed the physical means of torture and terror, I emphasized the ways in which regimes attempt to amplify the reverberations of terror throughout the culture. Physical violence becomes in this way a means for the creation of the generalized *perception* of the possibility of violence. It also becomes like a theatrical performance whose audience, outside the prisons, must read and interpret its social control message. (This notion of violence as theatre will be useful in later chapters.) Conversely, the decisive weapons against the regimes were symbolic in character. The Chilean generals hesitated when faced with Church defiance because they were worried about the cultural meanings that would be generated by overt repression of the Church and the ways in which others' interpretation of their actions would undermine their legitimacy.

Legitimacy is an intangible, intersubjective construct. It is something created by thousands of people "reading" the actions of others, talking about them, thinking about them, forming judgments of them. To treat this dynamic process as a "symbolic resource" out there in the environment that can be discovered and exploited like iron ore seems to me crude at best.

CONCLUSION

In the chapter on co-operative movements we saw how states can at times promote social movements in order to channel their activities in less radical, more "acceptable" directions. We called that strategy "co-optation." In this chapter we have seen how states can also act viciously to repress social movements. These two state responses to social movements may seem contradictory, but they can be used as complementary strategies. On the one hand, the state attempts to channel dissent away from fundamental challenges to capitalism and state authority. On the other hand, it seeks to push toward illegality and violence those who refuse to be co-opted. When it succeeds, it has licence for formal repression. This is the "agent provocateur" strategy. The state divides the movement and turns its benevolent face toward the docile stream and its ugly face toward the defiant remainder.

The United States and Canada took this dual approach to the 1960s protests, placing greater weight on the co-optive rather than the repressive strategy. That was not true of many Latin American countries. There coercion predominated, with the blessing and encouragement of the United States, which was anxious to stamp out left-wing activism within its "neighbourhood," and less concerned about doing it legally and democratically in foreign countries. We looked at three examples of states that attempted the total repression of dissent. They used terror generated through violence, torture, and assassination as a means of governance. The precondition for the spread of this terror throughout society was the eradication, or at least the attempted eradication, of all institutions within the state or civil society that could intercede on behalf of citizens against the state's coercive apparatus (the police and military).

Loveman's study demonstrated first that totalitarian regimes are fallible. They do not actually succeed in eradication dissent. People continue knowingly to put themselves at great personal risk to stand up for what they believe is right. By comparing the three regimes of Chile, Uruguay, and Argentina, she was able to identify what conditions made social dissent more likely under conditions of extreme repression. The first is rather obvious. The better a state can eradicate countervailing powers within the judicial system, the media, and civil society, as Uruguay did, the greater its success in preventing the emergence of opposition.

Powers that the state has or does not have at its disposal she calls the "political opportunity structure" for the movements. Political tools that are available to the movements she calls "resources." She identifies three types of resources that explain the early formation of strong human rights organizations in Chile and the late formation of weak HROs in Uruguay. These are: (1) the survival of civil society organizations and "spaces"; (2) personal networks that people could trust; and (3) external links to supportive networks and organizations and funding from outside the country.

To simplify, you can think of all three as dimensions of civil society (public political activity independent of the state). Civil society organizations are very often the formal face of underlying networks. External links were to civil society networks and organizations, most of which were part of what we now call "global civil society." Despite limited efforts, the generals discovered that their coercive reach did not extend beyond their borders. The power of global civil society to cast light on their misdeeds, undermine their legitimacy, and support opposition within their borders was something they had not calculated on. In Chile, the Catholic Church, because it had legitimacy in the eyes of junta supporters, remained as a political force after the rest of civil society had been swept away. It provided safe spaces for civil society activity within the country and maintained external links to international civil society.

Still, explaining the emergence of opposition when it was most risky and where, as in Argentina, there was no protection from the Church, would have been difficult if Loveman relied upon the resource-mobilization perspective alone. Self-sacrificing behaviour like that of the Madres de la Plaza de Mayo does not fit assumptions of "rational choice" derived from economics. She made a case that we must develop new theoretical tools that refer to "identity" and "culture." I concurred and suggested that we might also have to rethink our aims in explaining social movements, giving up the interest in finding causes or being able to predict social movement activity. Identity and culture are themes we take up in the following chapter.

REFERENCES

Arar, Maher. "Statement," November 4, 2003. CBC News Online, July 29, 2005, www.cbc.ca/news/background/arar/arar_statement.html.

Brandt, Daniel. "The 1960s and COINTELPRO: In Defense of Paranoia." *NameBase NewsLine* 10 (95), August 16, 2005, www.namebase.org/news10.html.

Brysk, Alison. *The Politics of Human Rights in Argentina: Protest, Change, and Democratization*. Stanford: Stanford University Press, 1994.

Calhoun, Craig. "The Problem of Identity in Collective Action." *Macro-Micro Linkages in Sociology*, edited by Joan Huber. Newbury Park: Sage Publications, 1991.

Coles, Mark. "They Couldn't Kill His Songs." September 5, 1998. BBC News, August 12, 2005, http://news.bbc.co.uk/1/hi/world/americas/165363.stm.

Corradi, Juan E., Patricia Weiss Fagen, and Manuel A. Garretón Merino. *Fear at the Edge: State Terror and Resistance in Latin America*. Berkeley: University of California Press, 1992.

Dillon, Sam. "General Illuminates '68 Massacre in Mexico." The *New York Times* on the Web, June 29, 1999; July 23, 2005, www.nytimes.com/library/would/Americas/062999mexicosniper.html.

Falcoff, Mark. "Between Two Fires: Terrorism and Counterterrorism in Argentina, 1970–1983." *The Politics of Terrorism: Terror as a State and Revolutionary Strategy*, edited by Barry M. Rubin. Washington: Foreign Policy Institute, School of Advanced International Studies, Johns Hopkins University Press, 1989.

Hawkins, Darren. "Human Rights Norms and Networks in Authoritarian Chile." *Restructuring World Politics: Transnational Social Movements, Networks, and Norms*, edited by Sanjeev Khagram, James V. Riker, and Kathryn Sikkink. Minneapolis; London: University of Minnesota Press, 2002.

Human Rights Watch. "The Pinochet Case: A Wake-up Call to Tyrants and Victims Alike." March 2000, Human Rights Watch Web site, August 17, 2005, www.hrw.org/campaigns/chile98/precedent.htm.

Inter-Church Committee on Human Rights in Latin America. "Chile Overview," June 8, 2005. Inter-Church Committee on Human Rights in Latin America Web site, August 17, 2005, www.web.net/~icchrla/Chile/chile-b.htm.

Kater, John L., Jr. "Whatever Happened to Liberation Theology? New Directions for Theological Reflection in Latin America." *Anglican Theological Review* (Fall 2001). August 17, 2005, www.findarticles.com/p/articles/mi_qa3818/is_200110/ai_n8984675.

Lindsey, Jessica. "'All Power to All People': Visions of the Black Panther Party." *Journal of Ethnic Studies* 1, no. 2 (2005). July 23, 2005, http://isis.csueastbay.edu/dbsw/ethnicstudies/jes2/jes-2-toc.htm.

Loveman, Mara. "High-Risk Collective Action: Defending Human Rights in Chile, Uruguay, and Argentina." *The American Journal of Sociology* 104, no. 2 (1998): 477–525.

Marchak, M. Patricia. *Reigns of Terror*. Montreal: McGill-Queen's University Press, 2003.

Marchak, M. Patricia, and William Marchak. *God's Assassins: State Terrorism in Argentina in the 1970s*. Montreal: McGill-Queen's University Press, 1999.

Marx, Gary T. "Thoughts on a Neglected Category of Social Movement Participant: The Agent Provocateur and the Informant." *American Journal of Sociology* 80, no. 2 (1974): 402–442.

McSherry, J. Patrice. "Operation Condor: Clandestine Inter-American System." *Social Justice* 26, no. 4 (1999): 144.

"Memorandum of Conversation, NSC Meeting—Chile (NSSM 97), November 6, 1970." National Security Archive, Chile Documentation Project.

Washington: George Washington University, 2000. August 17, 2005, www.gwu.edu/~nsarchiv/news/20001113/.

Neild, Rachel. "Report from Uruguay: Forgive & Forget?" *Commonweal* 116, no. 12 (89): 358–360. ABI/INFORM Proquest, Angus L. Macdonald Library, Antigonish, July 20, 2005, http://libmain.stfx.ca/newlib/electronic/databases/.

Oberschall, Anthony R. "The Decline of the 1960s Social Movements." *Research in Social Movements, Conflicts and Change* 1 (1978): 257–289.

Osorio, Carlos. "Kissinger to Argentines on Dirty War: 'The Quicker You Succeed, the Better.'" *National Security Archive Electronic Briefing Book*, no. 104. Washington: National Security Archive, George Washington University, 2003. August 17, 2005, www.gwu.edu/~nsarchiv/NSAEBB/NSAEBB104/.

Priest, Dana, and Charles Babington. "Plan Would Let U.S. Deport Suspects to Nations that Might Torture Them." Washington Post 30 Sep. 2004: A01. November 16, 2006, www.washingtonpost.com/wp-dyn/articles/A60779-2004Sep29.html.

United States Senate. "Final Report of the Select Committee to Study Governmental Operations with Respect to Intelligence Activities, Book III." 1976, www.icdc.com/~paulwolf/cointelpro/churchfinalreportIIIc.htm.

Weschler, Lawrence. *A Miracle, a Universe: Settling Accounts with Torturers*. New York: Pantheon Books, 1990.

CRITICAL THINKING QUESTIONS

1. What was different about the conditions in the three countries or in the mobilization of opposition that can account for relative success in Chile and failure in Uruguay?
2. If resource mobilization cannot explain the self-sacrifice of the Madres de la Plaza de Mayo, or the actions of those who are the first to brave incalculable risks, then how do we explain it?
3. Are truly predictive theories possible in the social sciences? Are they desirable?
4. Would it be possible for the bourgeoisie to learn from reading Marx's predictions and change history to avert their downfall? What would this tell us about causal explanations in the social sciences that purport to predict human behaviour?
5. Do people always act out of self-interest or is genuine altruism possible? Is altruism common?

FURTHER READING

Corradi, Juan E., Patricia Weiss Fagen, and Manuel A. Garretón Merino. *Fear at the Edge: State Terror and Resistance in Latin America*. Berkeley: University of California Press, 1992. There are many good books that attempt to explain the state's deployment of terror, such as Cecilia Menjívar and Néstor Rodriguez, *When States Kill: Latin America, the U.S., and Technologies of Terror* (Austin: University of Texas Press, 2005); M. Patricia Marchak, *Reigns of Terror* (Montreal: McGill-Queen's University Press, 2003); Alexander George, *Western State Terrorism* (Cambridge: Polity Press in association with Basil Blackwell, 1991). This is one of the few that also addresses our mandate in this chapter, which is to understand the resistance to state terror.

Cunningham, David. *There's Something Happening Here: The New Left, the Klan, and FBI Counterintelligence.* Berkeley: University of California Press, 2004.

Undercover police have been actively involved in protest activity with the aim of driving social movement activists to illegal extremes or sowing confusion among them. Cunningham documents this sort of "counterintelligence" carried out against the New Left and the KKK in the United States in the 1960s and 1970s. He explains counterintelligence excesses, not in terms of the magnitude of the social movement "threat," but the structure of the FBI itself.

Ekiert, Grzegorz, and Jan Kubik. *Rebellious Civil Society: Popular Protest and Democratic Consolidation in Poland, 1989–1993.* Ann Arbor: University of Michigan Press, 1999.

There is a growing literature on the transition to democracy of authoritarian regimes in eastern Europe. Here is an example that focuses on the role of popular movements and civil society.

Loveman, Mara. "High-Risk Collective Action: Defending Human Rights in Chile, Uruguay, and Argentina." *The American Journal of Sociology* 104, no. 2 (1998): 477–525.

This award-winning paper is one of the best analyses of resistance to state terror available. Its great strength is Loveman's systematic use of comparative method to answer her question concerning the conditions that favour resistance.

Seidman, G. *Manufacturing Militance: Workers' Movements in Brazil and South Africa, 1970–1985.* Berkeley: University of California Press, 1994.

Seidman shows how and why unions played a role in opposing authoritarian regimes in Brazil and South Africa. This is an interesting contribution to debates about the continuing relevance of unions in militant social movement politics.

RELEVANT WEB SITES

Amnesty International Canada and Amnesty International
www.amnesty.ca/canada/; www.amnesty.org

Amnesty International is one of the most effective popular organizations opposing abuses of state power. At their sites you can join close to 2 million members worldwide who engage directly in efforts to stop individual human rights abuses. The Canadian organization focuses on human rights issues within Canada: the Anti-Terrorism Act, the Maher Arar case, and abuses of indigenous rights within Canada.

Campaign for Labor Rights
www.clrlabor.org

This is a dynamic and effective example for North-South solidarity involving citizens and workers. I have included it here because they are particularly vocal against violent repression of union activists. If you want to stay informed, sign up for their e-mail labour alerts.

Canadian Civil Liberties Association
www.ccla.org/news/
> Here is where you can get into the legal details of the defence of civil rights in Canada.

Human Rights Watch
www.hrw.org
> When Amnesty was focused mainly on the abuse and torture of individual prisoners, Human Rights Watch formed to address a broader range of human rights abuses. It relies less on individual appeals of its members and instead mobilizes media attention, influential states, and NGOs to bring pressure to bear on repressive states. They have taken up the important issue of state abuses in the name of the new "war on terror"—see their pages on counterterrorism.

Polaris Institute
www.polarisinstitute.org/polaris_project/corp_security_state/corp_security_state_
> index.html
> The Polaris Institute devotes a section of their Web site to the risks to democracy and legitimate dissent of the "corporate security state."

Redress Trust
www.redress.org
> Here is where you can learn more about the concept of universal jurisdiction from an organization that is seeking to put it into practice by bringing torturers to justice.

Chapter 5

CULTURE AND THE POLITICS OF IDENTITY

INTRODUCTION:
THE PERSONAL IS POLITICAL

Playing with Barbies can be political. This is something Susan Stern realized when her daughter invented a game called "Jealous Barbie."

> In Jealous Barbie, Nora insisted we play that her Barbie had everything better than mine—better hair, better boyfriend, better imaginary car—and my Barbie was jealous. My Barbie was jealous for hours on end. Amused and intrigued, I gave Nora what I have come to call "Feminist Lecture #205: Women Don't Have to Be Jealous of Other Women." Nora listened to me patiently. "Okay, Mom," she finally said. "How about we first play Jealous Barbie—and then we can play what you want to play?" (Stern and Kolmar 189–192)

Stern became fascinated with the ways that people acted out cultural scripts using this iconic toy as a medium.

She decided to document other people's stories in a film titled *Barbie Nation: An Un-authorized Tour* (1998). She is critical of the way that gender gets constructed in Barbie culture. As a plastic realization of female desire, Barbie's body is impossibly (and ethnocentrically) "perfect" and her interests altogether too focused on accessorizing. But Stern treats culture not as something created for people and imposed on them by corporations like Mattel and their advertising industries. After all, Mattel does not make a "Jealous Barbie"; it is her daughter's invention. In fact, in response to feminist criticisms, Mattel has attempted to create a broader range of feminine ideals by making Barbies who have serious careers that would

enable them to compete with men for power, rather than compete with other women for powerful men.

By playing "Jealous Barbie," she and her daughter were making, or perhaps remaking, in their private, everyday lives a culture that, to Stern's mind, pits women against one another and thereby disempowers them. Stern's response was to make culture in the public sphere—a documentary film—that helped others to see and think critically about the ways that they collaborate in playing out often debilitating cultural scripts. She also documents the creative ways in which people attempt to subvert cultural scripts: the demonstration against breast implants outside the Barbie Hall of Fame in California, the rock video in which Barbie gets barbequed.

Stern's anecdote illustrates how culture, identity (i.e., what it means to be a contemporary woman), and the politics of liberation can all intersect. It also shows how, at this intersection, resistance or political opposition can take place in both the public and the private spheres of everyday life. This was what feminists of the early 1970s meant by the slogan "The personal is political." In this chapter we will explore the creative ways in which the women's liberation and gay liberation movements attempted to challenge personal and public culture in order to refashion, in more positive and empowering ways, what it means to be women or gay.

The new "identity politics" that feminists, gays, and lesbians pioneered in the late 1960s posed challenges for both Marxist and resource mobilization theories. Resource mobilization theory lacked a good conceptual language for analyzing the cultural practices that were so central to identity politics. Many turned to "frame analysis" to amend this shortcoming. We, too, will equip ourselves with the concepts of frame analysis, which we will use to understand social movement culture here and in later chapters. Identity politics also added to the "newness" that convinced many Marxists that a "new social movement theory" was required. In this chapter we will add another layer to our understanding of that complex tradition in social movement theory. We begin by stating more clearly the unique aim of the liberation sought by identity politics activists, and the unique problem that it poses.

INTERNAL COLONIZATION

Frantz Fanon, a Black writer from Martinique, a former French colony with a history of slavery, was discussing the intersection of culture, identity, and politics even before the women's liberationists. In *The Wretched of the Earth*, he wrote about revolutionary struggles against European colonialism in ways that inspired the New Left. He distinguished between the colonizers, mostly European and white-skinned, and the "colonized," mostly Black or what we now refer to as "people of colour." What troubled him was not simply the physical regimes of surveillance, repression, and terror that many colonial administrations used to dominate the colonized.

In a later book, *Black Skins, White Masks*, he explores, in part from bitter experience, the ways that the subordinate status of the colonized becomes inscribed upon their bodies ("Mama, see the Negro! I'm frightened!" 112) and in their psyches. In Martinique, he writes:

> There is a constellation of postulates, a series of propositions that slowly and subtly—with the help of books, newspapers, schools and their texts, advertisements, films, radio—work

their way into one's mind and shape one's view of the world of the group to which one belongs. In the Antilles [the Caribbean, where Martinique is located], that view of the world is white because no black voice exists. (152–153)

Young Blacks of his generation grew up thinking "White" and speaking "White" and had no vocabulary or concepts for making sense of their black skin, for integrating it into a whole sense of self that was culturally validated and valued.

> In the collective unconscious, black = ugliness, sin, darkness, immorality. In other words, he is Negro who is immoral. If I order my life like that of a moral man, I am simply not a Negro. Whence the Martinican custom of saying of a worthless white man that he has "a nigger soul." (Fanon, *Black Skins*, 192)

The colonized self suffers a debilitating internal injury:

> A feeling of inferiority? No, a feeling of non-existence. Sin is Negro as virtue is white. All those white men in a group, with guns in their hands, cannot be wrong. I am guilty. I do not know of what, but I know that I am no good. (Fanon, *Black Skins*, 139)

This concept, which we will call "internal colonization," struck a chord with the Black Power and Red Power movements of the late sixties in North America. At that time "women's liberation" and "gay liberation" movements also forged their own versions of the idea. It made sense to those who were made to feel inferior, worthless, even "sick" for being who they were or rather for being who others saw them to be. Like Stern, Fanon is aware of the subtle ways in which the colonized can become complicit in their own colonization. Black people find they judge themselves and other Blacks with racist categories. Women find they have internalized sexist categories that they perpetuate in their interactions with other women and men.

However, Fanon is careful not to blame the victim here. The colonized struggles with self-doubt and self-blame not because there is something wrong with *him*, but rather with the cultural categories he inherits from the colonizers. Still, internal colonization is a personal problem; it affects one's sense of self-worth and limits one's potential. It is also

a problem of political mobilization, for how can one oppose, as Fanon puts it, "all those white men in a group" when one has a nagging suspicion that they "cannot be wrong?"

Finally, overcoming it becomes a political objective in its own right. The defining problem for what we will call "identity politics" became how to combat internal colonization. What sorts of "new" social movement practices would be suited to this struggle that takes place on the boundaries between the public and private, the political and the personal? We will explore this question by focusing on tactics developed by radical feminists—in particular "consciousness raising"—and gay liberationists—"coming out" and laying claim to public space.

BOX 5.1:

"IT'S NOT SEXIST IF 'GIRLS' DO IT"

The female residents of Burke House on St. Francis Xavier University campus woke up one morning in January 2005 to find condoms filled with fake "semen" taped to their doors. In their common room they discovered a poster of a "trophy" that rival MacIsaac House had created, featuring a large penis directed toward a spread-eagled effigy and the words "We f***ed your mother." Downstairs the dryers had been turned on with sardines and women's panties thrown inside.

Students were divided over how to interpret these events. One woman was quoted as saying, "I was on the floor that was apparently sexually harassed [and] I wasn't offended whatsoever. It wasn't offensive to me at all and I don't think anyone should have been offended." Others did not agree. Another woman, who had been taking women's studies courses, read it as an assault on female sexuality and a threat to women that had to be publicly opposed. She contacted others, including professors, who in turn sparked a discussion on the faculty listserv.

Most of the professors who spoke publicly were loud in their condemnation and lobbied the administration for strong sanctions against the perpetrators, in particular the cancellation of "BurMac," a wildly popular hockey game that was a grudge match between Burke and MacIsaac Houses. One Jewish professor wrote, "A verbal assault (also one on a poster) is an assault. It harms the dignity, the reputation, and the well-being of the victim.... My parents and their siblings were verbally and also physically assaulted in school, under the enthusiastic support of their teachers, just because of who they were. Thus I, especially, would not want to be part of any educational enterprise in which such assaults were tolerated."

The university president responded quickly with a public statement condemning the incident. His words gave an official stamp to the interpretation of events as "acts of misogyny [woman-hating], harassment and vandalism." In addition to calling for sanctions against individual perpetrators under the campus "Community Code," he cancelled BurMac. I teach a social movements course at this university and we happened to be talking about identity politics that week. When the incident came up for discussion in the class, I was amazed to learn that for many—perhaps most—students, the "problem" was not sexism or misogyny, but that "the profs" were trying to shut down BurMac. As for sexism or misogyny, their slam-dunk argument was that "the girls had done it." In other words, women in MacIsaac house had put up the poster and taped the condoms to doors; therefore, these demonstrations could not be seen as anti-women.

After the cancellation of BurMac there was an angry, rearguard action in the interpretive struggle over this event. Banners went up: "We [heart] BurMac. Thank you. We are proud of U." People vented on an unmoderated Web site popular with students: "Title: Why We Hate Feminists. You f**kin whores ... why the hell are you so concerned about a healthy rivalry ... you f**ked everything up ... we should kill you all."

There are a number of things I find interesting about this incident. The first is the deeply entrenched nature of sexist culture 30-some years after the second wave of feminists mobilized to eradicate it. Do you think that you would see the same cultural assumptions at your university? Is St. Francis Xavier different because its reputation for small-town (Antigonish has a population of 5,000) and Catholic conservatism attracts a certain type of student?

The second is the reversal of roles from what we saw on campuses in the late 1980s and early 1990s. "Old White males" like the president, the Jewish professor, and myself joined with feminist faculty to take the "identity politics" line, while young *female* students saw us as imposing "political correctness" upon them. They seemed to see some new form of empowerment in taking part side by side with men in a formerly exclusive frat house culture of hazing rituals, macho group bonding, and brutal sports rivalries.

What do you think? Do they have a point, or are they collaborating in misogynist rituals that reinforce their "internal colonization?"

Source: Faculty Listserv, St. Francis Xavier University, http://listproc.stfx.ca/scripts/lyris.p/?enter=faculty & text_mode=&lang=english, February 1, 2006.

FEMINIST CONSCIOUSNESS RAISING

The young women who defined what we now call the "second wave" of the feminist movement gained their political experience and political perspective mostly from their involvement in the New Left. Consider the New Left concern for the alienation of human potential, here expressed in the 1960 manifesto of the Students for a Democratic Society, "The Port Huron Statement":

We regard *men* as infinitely precious and possessed of unfulfilled capacities for reason, freedom, and love. In affirming these principles we are aware of countering perhaps the dominant conceptions of man in the twentieth century: that he is a thing to be manipulated, and that he is inherently incapable of directing his own affairs. We oppose the depersonalization that reduces human beings to the status of things. (Students for a Democratic Society 65)

140   SOCIAL MOVEMENTS IN A GLOBAL CONTEXT

Sexism in the New Left

The gendered language is telling. However if you re-read this passage, substituting "women" for "men"/"human beings" and "she"/"hers" for "he"/"his," the principle remains the same, but a surprising new set of connotations arises. This is in effect what happened when women applied New Left principles to their situations and experience. What perhaps shocked them most was what they began to see in their relations with their male comrades in the New Left. For example, when the women in the Student Union for Peace Activism (SUPA) held a women-only caucus in 1967, they found that the men ridiculed them. They sniggered that maybe the women would organize a bake sale to support the Viet Cong (Kostash 168). As they talked among themselves, the women became aware of patterns of behaviour within the organization that reflected assumptions about their incompetence as political activists.

> We talked about how it was the men who did the writing and women the Gestetnering,[1] about how our political influence was directly related to how "heavy"[2] the guy was that we were coupled with. (Kostash 168).

Men dominated the political discussions. A woman in the American draft-resistance movement remembers that if a woman tried to contribute, there would be "a silence in which the men looked embarrassedly away from her before picking up just where they had been" (DuPlessis and Snitow 73). Men's idea of women's support for draft resistance was to "refuse to sleep with anyone who still carried a draft card" (Kostash 184). Their slogan was "Girls say yes to boys who say no" (Dunbar 92). Women's ideas were not welcome, but their bodies could be used as a kind of medium of exchange.

When women tried to put sexism on the agenda of New Left organizations, they were often met with open hostility from the men. "Their faces," recalls Dana Densmore, "would get red, veins would stand out on their necks, chest and arm muscles would tighten and lift, and in tones of anger and agitation they would talk irrationally and in complete *non sequitur* of our having made men the 'enemy,' talk of our castrating them (a shocking and disturbing image of physical mutilation), talk of our wishing to 'kill all men'" (Densmore 76). New Left men were probably no more sexist than other men at the time, but their rhetoric of social justice, rights, and liberation made their participation in oppression that much more transparent.

Densmore underlines how difficult it was in the 1960s for women to challenge men.

> A thorough-going, smirking disrespect for women permeated every aspect of society. I despair of conveying to young women of the nineties the chilling and depressing effect of this: they can't imagine how we could have been such low-self-esteem wimps to put up with it ("I would have smacked him one!"). I try to explain how it feels when it seems that all men, including the men one respects, sneer and ridicule or, at their best, condescendingly take for granted the inferiority of women. And how it feels when it seems that all the *women* around one take that supposed inferiority for granted. The most self-respecting women did little better than to try to deny, each in her embattled isolation, that she was herself that contemptible thing: "I'm different!" (72)

Densmore is describing internal colonization, reinforced by the way others, employing the restrictive cultural categories of the "colonizers," perceived women. Just as Fanon knows that he is "different," his being cannot be encompassed by the "ugliness, sin, darkness, immorality" of blackness, so Densmore and others like her knew their potential could not be circumscribed by the passivity, dependency, frivolity, and irrationality encoded in prevailing conceptions of "femininity." Young feminists discovered that the key to freeing themselves from internal colonization was to get out of their "embattled isolation" to talk to one another without men around to judge, correct, or trivialize what they had to say. Women in the New Left began doing this spontaneously.

Consciousness-Raising Groups

The world of shared experience that had until then gone unspoken was a revelation: "You feel like that? My God, I thought only I felt like that" (Keating 91). In New York a new group calling themselves the Radical Feminists recognized the potential of these sorts of women-only exchanges as a way to politicize women. They gave them a name—consciousness-raising or C-R groups—and some ground rules. In 1968 they promoted the idea at the First National Women's Liberation Conference in the U.S. C-R caught on widely and almost instantaneously since it gave form and political legitimacy to something women had already begun to do on their own initiative.

The process was for some both exciting and risky. "At first we feared disclosing personal information. We each thought we might be ridiculed, rejected, misunderstood, gossiped about by the others" (Boston Women's Health Book Collective 5-6). Ground rules helped to guarantee trust: "No one in the group should ever repeat what the other women say—not in bed, not at the table, not on the phone" (Piercy and Freeman). They also helped to ensure acceptance: "never challenge or judge anyone else's experience, try not to give advice" (Brooke 18). Women were consciously remaking the ways that they related to one another. "After being taught to expect nothing but bitchiness and backstabbing from other females," wrote one C-R advocate, "it is a delight to immerse oneself in a world of deliberately kind, deliberately sympathetic sisters" (Brooke 18).

In private living rooms, in women's centres, women were trying to create "safe spaces" in which to explore new possibilities of how to engage with one another and with the world as women. They also tried to ensure that these were inclusive spaces. Having experienced how male "heavies" dominated discussions and took up "space" at the centre of attention, they tried to guarantee that everyone would have an opportunity to speak and be heard. C-R groups were kept small. They would "go around in a circle," giving everyone a chance to contribute. People were not supposed to interrupt. Sometimes, if particular women did dominate, the group would resort to issuing tokens: "Every time anyone talks, she has to spend a token."

The formula worked and became tremendously popular. Myrna Kostash describes the spirit of C-R groups based on her own experience and her interviews with other Canadian women.

> Women read together *The Feminine Mystique, The Second Sex* by Simone de Beauvoir, *The Golden Notebook* by Doris Lessing and giggled and chitchatted over a bottle of wine, debating the pros and cons of using deodorant and shaving your legs and wearing make-up—the hilarity of it as the ribald and preposterous

confessions came out: "I remember a lot of times feeling uncomfortable because we should be more *serious* but another part of my mind realized this was the first time I'd spend a whole evening with a bunch of women and just had *fun* with them." Women learned how to be articulate and get the ear of others for the first time, discovered that, like a cork out of a bottle of champagne, women, pulled out from the confines of male-dominated groups, gushed with literacy and eloquence and intellect and prefigured, here in the sisterly circle, a politics of their own, a politics of absolute commitment, of unqualified support, of innovation. (Kostash 170–171)

Topics of discussion were open, but tended to focus on those areas of intimate, domestic, and sexual relations that until then had been ignored as irrelevant to politics, but which women recognized as central to their own experience of oppression. They talked about the expectations placed upon them growing up.

> In my home I got a complicated message. On the one hand I was told I was as important and as competent as men. In other ways I was told this was not true. Money was set aside for my brother to go to college but not for me. (Boston Women's Health Book Collective 6–7)

They examined the patterns of housework or "domestic labour" and even the arrangements of domestic space.

> I look at the way we have divided up the space in our house. My husband has a little space that is considered

his own, and I have no space that is mine. It is as if I exist everywhere and nowhere. (Boston Women's Health Book Collective 7)

They discussed their emotions—what they felt and what they were socially "permitted" to feel: "We did fight a lot at home, but I never made a public display of anger or aggression. That was unladylike" (Boston Women's Health Book Collective 10).

They discussed their feelings about sex, menstruation, their own bodies.

> I remember coming home from high school every day and going over my body from head to toe. My forehead was too high, my hair too straight, my body too short, my teeth too yellow, and so on. (Boston Women's Health Book Collective 7)

Cultural Politics of the Body

They recognized that their place in society and indeed in movement politics was defined in terms of their bodies. (How else should they interpret the "Girls say yes" campaign?) They sought greater understanding of how their bodies worked—knowledge that the male-dominated medical profession either lacked or thought "unnecessary" to divulge. They realized that simple choices about how they presented themselves in public could begin to challenge constraining cultural expectations. It was a kind of "do-it-yourself" cultural politics of the body. While it sounds simple, it was explosive and perilous.

> ... we talked about cosmetics. Suddenly it was no longer an imperative of nature that we paint our faces and squeeze our breasts into little cones. Some of us decided to give

up makeup and brassieres. It was a brave thing to do. I remember the feeling I had the first time I went out without my eyeliner. It was like wearing a big day-glo sandwich sign saying "HATE ME. I NO LONGER CARE WHETHER I'M PRETTY." (Kesselman et al. 40)

Even at a feminist conference, such body politics could shock and outrage. As part of a presentation on the political implications of stereotypical body image, one woman with Barbie-blond hair agreed to have it cut on stage "to a more practical chin length." "There was pandemonium in the hall, with women shouting 'Don't do it!' One woman shrieked, 'Men like my breasts too; do you want me to cut them off?'"(Densmore 85) This incident illustrates not just that North American culture has changed since 1969 (women can *shave* their heads with fewer repercussions), but that changing it is not merely about simple personal choices.

The judgmental gaze of others is real in its effects on us. This is what gives culture the qualities of "externality" and "constraint" and makes it appear, as Durkheim would put it, like a "social fact." C-R groups, as alternative *social* spaces, helped to counteract the censure of others. They offered a "supportive and non-judgmental" refuge "... there to help when we come back battered or ridiculed from trying to change our worlds" (Keating 93).

The territory that women explored in their C-R groups was either uncharted or had been analyzed and written about only from a male perspective. Like Fanon, whose "... view of the world [was] white because no black voice exist[ed]," women confronted a male world where women's voices were silent. They felt they were on their own, since "... so little existing theory and knowledge about women could be trusted" (Keating

87). That in itself was exciting.

> We challenged everything that was male, their rationality, their logic, their intellectualism, I mean we saw that even the way buildings are built and streets are laid out is masculine; we felt that in the entire culture there was nothing that had anything to do with us because we had not made it, we had no history, no art, all we had was ourselves, our sisterhood. (Kostash 171)

Like the natural philosophers who cleared the way for the "scientific revolution," they fell back on their own observations and experience. Women in C-R groups were supposed to speak from their own particular experience. For example, on the question of the differences between men's and women's intelligence, they did not want to get into a review of the existing academic literature: "For every scientific study we quote, the opposition can find their scientific studies to quote." Instead, they argued, "we know from our own experience that women play dumb for men because, if we're too smart, men won't like us. I know, because I've done it. We've all done it. Therefore, we can simply deduce that women are smarter than men are aware of, and that there are a lot of women around who are a lot smarter than they look and smarter than anybody but themselves and maybe a few of their friends know" (Sarachild).

Politics of Public Culture

New knowledge was to emerge through a process that C. Wright Mills called linking "personal troubles with public issues." As a Cape Cod C-R group explained:

... when we go around the room talking about how each of us feels about her appearance, and we hear every single woman expressing the same dissatisfaction with her body or her personality (my breasts are too small, too big, too flabby, my stomach is too round, my legs are too thick, I'm too loud, too quiet, etc.), we begin to realize we are dealing with something larger than a personal hang-up. (Piercy and Freeman)

The "public issue" here is the cultural construction of impossible ideals of female beauty that makes most women's bodies seem to them to be woefully inadequate. Women were learning how to create feminist knowledge and theory in a "participatory, collective manner." This, of course, was another means of making culture. "From our consciousness-raising meetings," writes Sarachild, "was coming the writing which was formulating basic theory for the women's liberation movement [such as Shulamith Firestone's *The Dialectic of Sex*, Anne Koedt's 'The Myth of the Vaginal Orgasm,' and Pat Mainardi's 'The Politics of Housework']" (Sarachild, qtd. in Keating 87–88).

The original intent was always that C-R groups be sites for the creation of a feminist "counterculture" and stepping-off points for action to challenge sexist categories in the culture at large. "Radical" means literally "of the root." The idea of being a "radical feminist" was to go to the root cause of women's problems. Since many of the "personal problems" with women's sense of self that arose in C-R sessions could be traced to "public issues," radical solutions had to be sought in public action. The actions they chose targeted institutional realms that most affect the shaping of women's sense of themselves and their bodies: mass media,

educational curriculum, the health professions, and language.

Feminist cultural provocations or "zaps" were sixties-inspired ways of making news. One of the most influential was a 1968 demonstration against the Miss America Pageant featuring a "huge Freedom Trash Can" into which women threw "bras, girdles, curlers, false eyelashes, wigs, and representative issues of *Cosmopolitan*, *Ladies Home Journal*, *Family Circle*, etc.," as well as a boycott of "all of those commercial products related to the pageant." "Male reporters," declared the organizers, "will be refused interviews. We reject patronizing reportage. *Only newswomen will be recognized*" (Radical Women 482).

They identified media representation of women, and cultural representation more generally, as a key "public issue." Women critiqued and parodied the sexist content of films, advertisements, TV series, and lobbied the institutions responsible for creating and distributing them. They scrutinized the ways in which gender roles were represented in children's readers. They drew attention to the absence of women as significant players in history textbooks. They lobbied for better and more inclusive representations of women in school curricula, but they also went ahead and started creating those representations themselves.

They set up women's studies programs at the graduate level at universities. They wrote non-sexist stories for children. In 1973 a women's collective in Saskatoon put together the first Canadian "herstory" calendar profiling women who had made contributions to Canadian society unrecognized in the standard histories. Their first entry featured Violet McNaughton, now recognized as an important figure in the prairie co-operative movement, a pioneer of socialized medicine, and a strong advocate for feminist causes. Before they did the research for the calendar, none of them had even heard of her.

Women questioned the often-sexist knowledge and advice of medical and psychiatric professionals. They put together their own medical self-help manuals such as the widely read *Our Bodies, Ourselves* by the Boston Women's Health Book Collective. They established women's clinics, rape crisis centres, and shelters for battered women. Shocked by the evidence that MDs and psychiatrists were overprescribing "mood-modifying drugs" to women for conditions they saw as social in origin, they provided alternative counselling and other resources for women dealing with depression.

They recognized that language structures our categories for understanding the world. When the words for most professions and positions of power—fireman, chairman, etc.—or the general pronoun for describing human character and achievement—"man the tool maker," "a small step for Man; a giant leap for Mankind"—were coded as male, these words became subtle signals to young girls to exclude themselves from these realms of endeavour. By insisting on greater awareness of the implications of language, they have been able to change the way that we speak and write.

Consciousness raising—starting from the personal, the domestic, the subjective—was supposed to lead to action in the public sphere. The personal was not meant to remain personal; it had to become political. This is what separated C-R from personal therapy. There was a pervasive "therapy culture" in the 1970s in Canada, and even more so in the U.S. People got into "gestalt therapy," "transactional analysis," and a whole variety of "touchy-feely" approaches to healing damaged psyches and identities. Women took "assertiveness training" in which they learned to express anger and say "no" without guilt and to build self-esteem. These were practices aimed at transforming the self primarily.

While C-R groups could help women achieve "personal self-help" objectives, their primary aim was to transform the culture. Public action that emanated from C-R was action in the name of others—women in general. For political feminists, anything less would have been seen as individualistic and self-indulgent. As a politics of identity, C-R was about creating what we will call "collective identity." As one New York radical feminist explained, "our aim ... was to start a *mass movement of women*" (Sarachild).

The new sense of empowerment in being a woman was connected to a politicized sense of unity with other women that we have elsewhere referred to as "solidarity." Just as (male) workers had in earlier decades used a familial metaphor to represent their solidarity, referring to their comrades as "brothers" and their organizations as "brotherhoods," women's liberationists invoked the idea of "sisterhood." "Sisterhood is Powerful!" was their slogan.

C-R was to be a staging ground for a larger political project with more than just "cultural" objectives. Some groups engaged in solidarity actions for low-paid women workers; some worked in anti-poverty actions; others lobbied for law reform to legalize contraception education and abortion, to get date rape recognized as a legal category, to reform policing in domestic abuse and rape cases. However, C-R was a very decentralized, non-authoritarian approach to creating a mass movement. There was nothing stopping women from modifying it and reinterpreting it to suit their own needs and understandings.

In an individualistic "me first" cultural context like that in North America, inevitably, therapeutic, self-help variants emerged. No doubt many women used the improved self-esteem and public confidence that they gained here to pursue conventional routes to personal success in the masculine "public sphere." The pioneers of C-R would have seen this as a betrayal. "What is now called 'making it' was called 'selling out' then. The possibility of women doing that and rising in the corporate world tickled our fancy in 1970—it was so absurd. No real feminist would dare hold such a job" (Leonard 17).

FRAME ANALYSIS

Young women in the 1970s identified sexist culture and its damaging effects on women's sense of self as one of the main causes of women's oppression. By focusing their new movement for women's liberation on this problem of "internal colonization," they helped to redefine the possibilities for movement politics. Unlike previous movements, they defined as central political tasks the creation of [non-sexist] culture and new social identities [for women and men]. The two main theoretical perspectives that we have discussed so far, Marxism and resource mobilization, were ill equipped to deal with identity construction and cultural innovation.

Many social scientists have turned to "frame analysis" to fill this theoretical gap. Using the conceptual tools of frame analysis has helped them to discover how important the construction of movement culture and movement identities is in many, if not all, social movements. (Women's liberation did something more than this by setting as its goal the transformation of culture and identity in the society beyond the movement.)

Frames and Culture

We should consider for a moment these conceptual tools of frame analysis that some social scientists have found so help-ful, beginning with the idea of a "frame." The Canadian sociologist Erving Goffman brought attention in the 1960s to the ways that we "accomplish" our day-to-day encounters with others smoothly with no explicit planning but minimal confusion or awkwardness. We give verbal and non-verbal cues; we "read" these cues from others and from the situation and we ad-lib or "make stuff up" as we go along.

So, for instance, you are walking to class in conversation with someone and you come to a closed door. There are an infinite number of ways that one or both of you could open the door and walk through—one could move to be the first; one could defer to the other, etc. These choices could be signalled and agreed upon in myriad different ways. Goffman was fascinated by the inventiveness of people on the spot, particularly in situations where there was a miscue and interaction stumbled. However, he also recognized that people bring formulaic expectations to encounters that allow them to act without thinking. These are interpretive frameworks or "frames" for making sense of encounters and the situations they take place in.

For example, in the 1960s there was a gendered frame for the doorway encounter. The "chivalrous" man always deferred to the woman and held the door open in such a way as to allow her to go through first. Women's liberationists redefined this frame, re-reading the chivalry as patronizing and implying that women were helpless and in need of male assistance. The new feminist frame created interactional uncertainties for a period, but also provided feminist women with a useful way of "reading" male behaviour. How a man finessed the doorway situation "said" a lot about his political awareness and attitudes toward women.

You can see here how the "frame" allows one to interpret events and others' actions within the social world. Social scientists studying social movements were interested in not just the "framing" of face-to-face encounters, but also of larger world events. A frame could orient how people made sense of U.S. foreign policy or the Miss America pageant. Two of the people who introduced the concept to social movement studies, David Snow and Robert Benford, define it in this way: "... it refers to an interpretive schemata that simplifies and condenses the 'world out there' by selectively punctuating and encoding objects, situations, events, experiences and sequences of actions within one's present or past environment" (Snow 137).

They are using "punctuate" in the sense of "to point out." Frames help to point out what is relevant in the social environment. For example, the feminist interpretive frame helped to point out, in ways that had rarely been noticed before, details of domestic and intimate environments: Who did the dishes or the "Gestetnering"? Who interrupted whom in conversations? Who habitually took the floor in discussions? It "encoded" these practices as instances of "male domination."

Frame Alignment and Identity

Snow and his colleagues (1986) were originally interested in the ways in which people who joined social movements learned new interpretive frameworks. They call the process "frame alignment." Through it, activists learn "to articulate and align a vast array of events and experiences so that they hang together in a relatively unified and meaningful fashion" (Snow 137–138). Think about consciousness raising in these terms. It was itself an encounter guided by an interpretive frame. "Going to my first consciousness-raising meeting," Vicky Leonard recalled, "I knew I was supposed to learn about the ways our society had wronged women by looking

at the ways it had wronged me" (Leonard 17).

But more importantly, within that circle of women she would have observed the kinds of personal confessions that other women made. This would have provided her with hints as to where to look in her own experience for details "significant" in terms of gender oppression. She would also have learned how to put these experiences into words in ways that would be consistent with the feminist frame. She would have learned not only a new intellectual understanding of the world, but an appropriate emotional response to it.

Verta Taylor and Nancy Whittier emphasize how the second wave feminist movement helped women to restructure their emotional responses to their experience and redefine "acceptable" expressions of emotions for women. For example, they helped one another overcome the taboo against women expressing anger in public. (The lingering power of that taboo was so great, however, that the image of the "angry feminist" was and still is used against them.) Women who had very good reason to be angry, who had been raped, suffered incest or physical abuse, tended instead to feel shame, self-loathing, and fear.

Feminists helped women reframe these experiences in different terms that carried new connotations. "Victims" of abuse became "survivors." The understanding was that a survivor had not just suffered and lost, but had actively, bravely overcome adversity. With this conceptual reframing came an emotional reframing: instead of shame and fear, one should feel pride and anger. Here, of course, we see how "framing" and the construction of identity can intersect. Using the feminist "frame," "survivors" are constructing a new sense of self.

Meaning Work and Agency

"Frame alignment" happens when women learn to reinterpret themselves and their experiences in terms of a feminist analysis or world view. Snow and Benford recognize that this process within social movements is more dynamic than that. There is no clear-cut division between a "frame" on the one hand and a new recruit on the other. The new recruit does not simply "learn" the frame. As women explored together in their C-R groups, the "frame" changed and developed and they all contributed to the making of it. Frameworks of meaning are, as Snow and Benford put it, "social productions that arise through the course of interactive processes" (136).

This insight is central to Goffman's work, and no doubt this is one of the reasons that Snow and Benford appeal to Goffman for their theoretical language. They do not like the way that many resource-mobilization theorists treat culture and meaning as "symbolic resources." Movement participants do not simply find and exploit ready-made social meanings, but engage in "meaning work," which Snow and Benford define as the "struggle over the production of ideas and meanings," or the "politics of signification" (136). "Struggle" is an important word here. You can see it in feminists' efforts to define public expressions of anger as empowering as against anti-feminists' insistence that it is ridiculous and discrediting.

Still, Snow and Benford, along with Goffman himself, recognize that "ready-made" social meanings and interpretive frameworks do exist. What is so interesting about social movements is the ways in which they adapt, transform, and sometimes subvert these pre-existing or conventional understandings of the world. Consider the way in which women's liberation adapted New Left principles concerning the libera-

tion of human potential by applying them to women's situation. As participants in the New Left, women activists already took for granted neo-Marxist concepts of alienation and liberation as part of their interpretive frameworks. They merely extended them to new territory.

Frame Extension/Transformation and Social Movement Innovation

Snow and Benford call this "frame extension." Women met with resistance from male radicals who drew on sexist categories from the larger culture to discredit them. "Our meetings were called coffee klatches, hen parties or bitch sessions," recalls Kathie Sarachild. "We responded by saying, 'Yes, bitch, sisters, bitch,' and calling coffee klatches a historic form of women's resistance to oppression" (Sarachild). Here women were turning sexist categories on their heads, subverting their original meanings. This example, along with much of second wave feminist "politics of signification," involved transforming pre-existing frames, or "frame transformation."

At the individual level there is always what Marx would have called a "dialectic" between learning and creating interpretive frameworks. At the collective level, social movements both borrow "ready-made" cultural frameworks and extend, transform, and sometimes create entirely new frameworks. When people are acting creatively, doing things in innovative ways, or imagining novel perspectives on the world, sociologists call this "agency." People are acting as free agents rather than conforming to some conventional script or ready-made "frame" (no matter how radical).

The opposite of agency—the ready-made patterns of action or cultural frameworks—they refer to as "structure." One of the most difficult skills in analyzing any form of social action is getting the balance right. Part of the skill is knowing how to "call" it, knowing when people are conforming to convention and when they are playing around with or transforming convention. Part of the skill, though, is recognizing the "dialectic" quality of agency and structure—that is, recognizing that the two are merely aspects ("moments," Marx would say) of the same dynamic process that cannot be easily separated.

Dialectic of Agency and Structure

Resource-mobilization theorists liked frame analysis because it gave them a way of bridging between a subtle understanding of culture and the sorts of structural conditions that they used to explain social movement activity. They were able to make the bridge to structure by emphasizing the structural "moment" in frame analysis. The frames that social movement actors construct become part of a cultural repertoire that other movements can borrow from. As that repertoire grows and changes through time, the possibilities for innovation also change. In resource-mobilization language, the possibilities for innovation are conditioned by the cultural resources available at a given place and time in history.

Also, individuals, depending on their social class, gender, race, language, and life experiences, will differ in their knowledge of and ability to draw from this repertoire. So, for example, it was mostly White, middle-class women with college education and experience in New Left organizations who were able to innovatively construct the women's liberation frame incorporating elements of the culture of the New Left. These women had access to different cultural resources or "cultural capital" from other women.

Frame analysis can nonetheless be used crudely in ways that neglect the dialectical quality of culture or that forget that a "frame" is only a metaphor. "Frames" are not actual "things" in the social world. Most people do not know what they are. Those of us who do would probably have difficulty deciding where our own interpretive frames begin and end. A "frame" is simply a tool to help social scientists visualize what goes on when people, individually and together, make sense of their worlds. When we treat our concepts as "things" in the world, this is called "reification." Reification is something to avoid.

In the following section, I discuss the culture of the gay liberation movement. I have based this section on work by Taylor and Whittier and Elizabeth Armstrong, authors who I think are skilled at avoiding reification but at the same time showing the ways in which culture is concretely realized in the social world. I want you to think about where, concretely, we actually find interpretive frameworks (or find expressions of what we call interpretive frameworks) in the social world.

An obvious answer is that they are recorded in people's memories. The interpretive frameworks that social movements employ are also written on paper in manifestoes and political pamphlets. For Goffman, frames are also inscribed as readable codes in the interactional practice of face-to-face groups (e.g., the C-R group) and in the "readable" body (consider, for example, the valuation of the "natural" in hippies' unshaven body hair). Taylor and Whittier also look at ritual and spatial arrangements (consider the household described earlier where the woman recognized she had no personal space, while her husband did).

"COMING OUT" AND THE POLITICS OF PUBLIC SPACE

In 1966 Everett Klippert was in a Saskatchewan jail for "gross indecency." That year, in compliance with federal law, he was declared a "dangerous sexual offender" and his sentence extended to "indefinite preventive detention." His "crime" was simply that he was a homosexual. He had had sex with other men, but it was always consensual and took place in the privacy of their homes. His case sparked public debate not so much about the taboo subject of homosexuality as the appropriateness of the law.

Member of Parliament Robert Kaplan epitomized the attitude at the time when he argued that homosexuality was "a form of sexual perversion which arouses a sense of horror in most people. But many Canadians feel an equal sense of horror about the present treatment of homosexuals in this country" (Kaplan, qtd. in Kinsman 168). Following the lead of Britain, Canada enacted new legislation that made a sharp distinction between "public" and "private" sexual behaviour. The state was no longer to apply the sanctions of the criminal justice system to consensual acts in private. "There's no place for the state," declared Justice Minister Pierre Trudeau, "in the bedrooms of the nation."

Public Repression of Gay Sexuality

This change did not signal official acceptance of homosexuality. Legislators were following the advice of medical experts who saw homosexuality as a sickness best "treated" by psychiatry rather than criminal prosecution. Socially homosexuals were still expected to deny their sexuality in public and privately to seek help overcoming it. Police

and the courts still played an enormous role in punishing public displays of gay sexuality. Spaces in which we normally expect some privacy, such as a stall in a washroom, were legally designated "public." Performing fellatio in a stall was considered a public display of "gross indecency." Gay bars were similarly designated "public" even though gays went there to avoid homophobic public scrutiny. In 1964 two men dancing together in a gay bar could be charged with gross indecency (Kinsman 158).

A lot of policing effort, much of it excessive and often brutal, was directed toward the repression of gay sexuality. Undercover agents were paid to frequent gay pickup spots and entrap men into acts of "indecency." Gay bars and bathhouses were repeatedly raided. In one 1977 bust, 50 officers were deployed with machine guns and bulletproof vests (Warner 108). Police would follow up these actions by publishing the names of those arrested. As late as the 1980s the social stigma attached to their alleged behaviour was so powerful that men would be fired from their jobs (particularly if they were teachers) and in some cases resort to suicide.

In the 1960s most homosexuals lived in constant fear of exposure. The main strategy for avoiding damaging public censure, not just from a few bigots, but from their doctors, police, and political representatives, was to attempt to "pass" in public as heterosexual. Passing was a practice that fascinated Goffman for what it revealed about how we dramatize "normalcy" in everyday encounters. It involves the minute self-examination of gesture and word and a heightened ability to shift between an "acceptable" and a "stigmatized" self-presentation according to context.

It also involves one in complicity in stigmatizing one's own "discredited" identity. "When jokes were made about 'queers,'" one man recalled, "I had to laugh with the rest, and when talk was about women I had to invent conquests of my own. I hated myself at such moments, but there seemed to be nothing else I could do. My whole life became a lie" (qtd. in Goffman 87). Such encounters were ritual dramatizations of self-loathing.

Coming out: Public Politics of Self

Even organizations for gay rights, part of what was then called the "homophile" movement, saw little alternative to passing. Changing laws was one thing, but changing such powerfully entrenched public attitudes seemed an insurmountable task. Most homosexuals wanted to get on with their lives in the here and now, relatively free from harassment. Perhaps you can understand then how bold the strategy of "coming out" must have seemed when gay revolutionaries, "gay-revs," and gay liberationists promoted it in the late 1960s. "Coming out" was more than just admitting to friends, family, co-workers, or fellow students that one was gay. It also involved embracing the stigma—the physical marks and signs—of a formerly discredited identity. Young gay men adopted in public the effeminate or "fey" mannerisms of speech and gesture that former generations had so studiously suppressed.

As if to underline the diverse and theatrical nature of their new public personas, many also constructed a sexually inflected hypermasculine style:

> First of all, the clothes are worn differently in the gay subculture from the way they are worn by "real men." They are much tighter fitting, especially tailored to be as erotic and sensual as possible. Parts of the body will be purposely left exposed in an attempt to attract others.... These subtle changes and transformations

of objects infuse the style with a new meaning of eroticism and overt sexuality—that is, they are used explicitly to make one appear sexy and attractive to other men. This can be seen as distinct from any celebration of masculinity as such. Instead it may be an attempt to show that masculine or "ordinary" men can be homosexual too.... It forces the wider culture to question its stereotypes and question the legitimacy of linking femininity and homosexuality. (qtd. in Kinsman, 187)

They also "reinvented" aspects of marginal male subcultures like bodybuilding and outlaw bike gangs. The style choices were quite different, but the principle was similar to the "body politics" of women's liberationists whom gay liberationists initially saw as comrades in a struggle against gender oppression.

Like women radicals, the new gay activists were "alumni" of the political and countercultural New Left. They placed the same value on fighting for personal authenticity and self-fulfillment in the face of an alienating "system." They understood that the "political" was also "personal" and how political battles could be fought in the realm of everyday practices. They recognized in the struggles of women and Blacks the same need to overcome the debilitating effects of internal colonization or "self-oppression."

The call for "gay pride" was modelled on "Black pride."

> The Negroes are saying "I'm black and I'm proud" and saying it loud. Also they say "Black is Beautiful" and it is beauty! Well, what are our people saying? Inside I know I am saying, "I'm a homosexual and I'm Proud." And for me "Male is

beautiful." What is the rest of the community saying? (Charles Thorp, qtd. in Armstrong 70)

Gay activists borrowed from the feminist repertoire of tactics, engaging (at least in the early 1970s) in consciousness raising and "zaps." (Lesbians were able to carve out a positive space for the idea of women loving women within feminist C-R groups.)

Gay consciousness raising devolved more readily into support groups that gave recognition and encouragement to those taking the traumatic step of becoming openly gay in a hostile public milieu. Taking place in private locales, they were nonetheless social spaces where it was "safe" to try out one's gay identity. Zaps were used to protest anti-gay reporting or to overturn anti-gay definitions within psychiatric manuals. However, lobbying for changes to homophobic assumptions within the wider culture did not become as much a preoccupation for gay activists as overcoming mainstream sexism had done for feminists.

Gay men (and lesbians) "came out" or stepped beyond the bounds of the private in increasing numbers and with increasing confidence over a very short period in the early 1970s. They discovered that it was not necessary to wait for prevailing homophobic attitudes among heterosexuals to change. Activists were able to "reframe," *for gays and lesbians*, a once terrifying experience into one that was both liberating and psychologically rewarding. Lois Hart's 1969 testimony typified this new understanding.

There is no question that you will feel more whole and happier when you can be who you are all of the time. This is no easy thing, I know. It took me until age 32 to finally give in to myself and though it felt at the time that I was losing

everything (the good opinion and sanction of this society from my family right on up to any career dreams I have ever had), I have in truth gained the whole world. I feel at a loss to convey to you right now what that means. I can just say that I have never felt better in my life. I know now in retrospect that I only began to be really alive when I was able to take that step. (Hart, qtd. in Armstrong 69)

Not only did this reframing construct a new emotional logic for being "out," it inverted the former "risk calculus." The risks of psychological harm inflicted on oneself by denial were represented as more damaging than the risks of harassment or the potential loss of friends, family, or work opportunities. "Understand this," warned Martha Shelly in 1973,

... that the worst part of being a homosexual is keeping it a *secret*. Not the occasional murders by police or teenage queer-beaters, not the loss of jobs or expulsion from schools or dishonourable discharge—but the daily knowledge that what you are is so awful that it cannot be revealed. (qtd. in Armstrong 70)

The stigma had been reversed. "Closet queenery" was now understood as self-destructive, a psychological "problem," and an act of betrayal not only of one's own identity and self-worth but also of the collective pride of one's "gay brothers and sisters" (Armstrong 70). "Closet queenery must end. Come out." declared a 1972 Gay Manifesto. The promise that coming out would be self-affirming was not merely abstract. As more people responded to the call, a critical mass developed. Social support networks for openly gay men and women grew and extended well beyond the private spaces of C-R groups and into the public sphere.

Claiming Gay Spaces

It became increasingly "safe" to be "who you are all of the time" and while perhaps not in every place, certainly in the new urban spaces where gays congregated and began to build supportive institutions. In rural areas, small towns, and cities throughout North America, one did (and still does) risk social death and physical injury by being openly gay. However, in major cities like Toronto, Vancouver, New York, and San Francisco, enclaves of gay culture developed and became Meccas to which gays from across the continent migrated.

Spatial concentration as a means of reinforcing identity construction was not available in the same way to heterosexual feminist women. A kind of "erotic logic" worked against it. Heterosexual women who gravitated to "separatist" feminist communities diminished their chances of erotic fulfillment. Gay women, by contrast, increased them. The seductions were more intense for gay men whose public culture was more explicitly sexualized. Gay spaces, like the Castro district in San Francisco, became not just sites of social acceptance, but erotic Utopias.

Activists promoted "gay pride parades" as a ritual means of laying claim to public space. Pride parades suspend business as usual and transform city streets into a festival stage for the celebration of gay identities. Like the New Left occupations of buildings, they briefly "prefigure" alternative possibilities of social relationships. By taking possession of the physical embodiments of our social world—streets and buildings—they "demonstrate" that what we often take as permanent and alien can be reimagined and remade.

Marching, dancing, singing, and chanting are all ritual elements of the demonstration. Ritual involves embodying and acting out meanings. Repetitive and rhythmic elements in ritual engage participants physically, sensually. Durkheim thought that ritual was the way that people in all societies imbued abstract social ideas with tangible presence and emotional power (Durkheim). Note that ideas and emotions are here situated not just within individuals' heads, but also out in the public world "embedded" in observable practices.

It was not possible to make even these temporary, symbolic claims to public acceptance without a struggle. In Toronto the parades were initially confined to marginal locales and shunned by the media. The city in the 1970s denied permission to march on the main thoroughfare, Yonge Street, and elsewhere residents objected to the parade in their neighbourhoods. By the late 1980s participants in the event had grown to the tens of thousands, and while it now had gained access to major streets, the city refused to issue any official proclamation of "Pride Day."

By the 1990s gays had become well enough organized to influence municipal politics in the city. Also, interestingly, city politicians and businesses began to wake up to the economic implications of the event, which was beginning to attract thousands of gay tourists. The organizing committee in 1996 estimated that "pride tourists" spent $46 million in the city. The city began to embrace and promote the event, with the mayor in 1998 taking part for the first time, riding on one of the floats.

Spatial Logic of Gay Community

A pride parade is a temporary, mobile possession of public space and the "built environment." Gay men and women also made more permanent claims to urban space as part of their construction of gay culture and community. They "hung out" in certain areas, frequenting certain coffee shops, restaurants, bars, parks, or beaches. In the 1970s they began buying businesses in these areas, laying legal claim to the built environment. Sometimes ownership was co-operative. This collective model was favoured by feminist ventures such as women's bookstores. If private, they clearly identified as part of a gay community building project—catering to gay clientele, assisting other gay businesses, or donating to gay causes.

In 1978 gay businesses in Toronto formed their own association. Nearly 90 businesses were part of it by 1986, including "bars and baths ... architects, florists, travel agents, real estate agents and lawyers" (Kinsman 182). In addition to commercial gay districts, gay men in particular began buying residential property in adjacent neighbourhoods. Ownership, Marx reminds us, gives control. This is not total control. Gay-owned bars and theatres, for example, are still legally "public" places subject to police intervention. Still, owners were better positioned than non-owners to define the "look and feel" as well as the uses of gay urban space.

Gay urban places and institutions provided a physical setting for the supportive networks of community. In the streets of gay neighbourhoods, one could be "out" and feel welcomed. One could make a living and have a respected place in the (gay) community regardless of how intolerant the larger culture remained. This was a powerful solution to the problem of forging gay identities and overcoming the problem of "internal colonization." It was not a tactic that made sense for heterosexual feminists. Nor was it as easy for lesbian feminists as for gay men. Like all women, lesbians earned less than men on average. They were handicapped in

raising capital and buying property. Sexism in the world of work contributed to their disadvantage relative to gay men. Women had to rely more on mobilizing human rather than economic resources.

This is not to say that mobilizing people was unimportant to male gay liberationists. Many understood gay pride as one step in the formation of a mass movement to challenge sexism and capitalism. Allan Young, in 1971, wrote:

> Gay liberation, on the surface, is a struggle for homosexuals for dignity and respect—a struggle for civil rights. Of course, we want to "come out," ... to forbid such terms as "faggot," "dyke," and "queer," to hold down jobs without having to play straight, and to change or abolish those laws which restrict or denigrate us.
>
> But the movement for a new definition of sexuality does not, and cannot end there.... The revolutionary goals of gay liberation, including the elimination of capitalism, imperialism and racism, are premised on the termination of male supremacy. (qtd. in Armstrong 56)

The Canadian theorist Gary Kinsman still embraced a similarly broad vision in 1987. He called upon gay liberationists to become "part of a broad alliance for sex-positive, anti-sexist, and fundamental change" to "capitalist patriarchal society" (Kinsman 230).

"Pure" Identity Politics

However, it proved possible to go a long way toward achieving much of the gay pride agenda without challenging either capitalism or sexism. A cynic might argue that the (male) gay pride agenda actually benefited from both capitalism and sexism. While it remained important for gays to mobilize people for political lobbying to change laws, police practices, and media representations, this was never as important as it was for feminists. In these ways, gay (male) liberation remained more purely an "identity politics." In other words, the construction of gay identity was not primarily a means of creating a political "fighting force" to achieve broader societal objectives. Instead, as Armstrong emphasizes, "gay liberationists ... saw the visible display of gay identity as an end in and of itself" (Armstrong 62).

In summary, Black power, women's liberation, gay liberation—movements representing people marked as culturally inferior—developed new social movement strategies to overcome "internal colonization." Their example helped social movement theorists recognize the importance of constructing identity and transforming culture in all social movements. Gay liberation's body politics and struggles to create gay urban spaces remind us that culture, something that is often conceived abstractly, can also be embedded in the concrete.

"The concrete" includes physical spaces and structures of the "built environment," the acting out of ritual, the display of body adornment, and the performance of identity through what Goffman would call "interactional practice." Feminists were leaders in defining these realms of cultural struggle. They also helped to identify and develop strategies for challenging the more impersonal, institutional realms of cultural production such as the media, curriculum, the medical professions, and language.

Neither identity nor the problem of internal colonization was the primary focus of feminism. However, the tools that they helped to develop were adopted by those for whom these were primary concerns.

Self-described "identity politics," popular on university campuses in the late 1980s and early 1990s, was both more inclusive in its sympathies and narrower in its selection of tactics. The "I.D. warriors" on campuses acted in the name not just of the self, but of a range of identities marginalized by the "old White males" in control of cultural production: women, gays, lesbians, bisexuals, transgendered people, "people of colour," and people of minority faiths such as Muslims in North America.

However, they tended to narrow their tactics to struggles over representation in the media, curriculum, and language. As Naomi Klein, a Canadian activist, explains:

> ... representation was no longer one tool among many, it was the key. In the absence of a clear legal or political strategy, we traced back almost all of society's problems to the media and the curriculum, either through their perpetuation of negative stereotypes or simply by omission. Asians and lesbians were made to feel "invisible," gays were stereotyped as deviants, blacks as criminals and women as weak and inferior: a self-fulfilling prophecy responsible for almost all real-world inequalities. (108)

Klein is critical not of identity politics' aims but of the narrowness of its tactics. She argues that for her generation, all social movement politics collapsed into cultural politics or what Snow and Benford call the "politics of signification." Even their cultural politics was excessively abstract or idealistic. Criticism of identity politics, notably from other "progressive" social movements, has been surprisingly common. This is something we will attempt to understand better in the next section.

IDENTITY POLITICS AND THE "REVOLUTIONARY SUBJECT"

Remember Densmore's account of how feminism sent some men in the New Left into red-faced hysteria? They found it difficult to be challenged on their taken-for-granted everyday practices. Patterns of speech and behaviour that they themselves had barely noticed were being stigmatized as "sexist" and they were being pressured to change. Similarly, "old White males" on campuses became enraged at being labelled "sexist," "homophobic," or "racist" and being asked to change what they taught, the language that they used, or the ways in which they related to their female students.

Many joined the opponents of identity politics, labelling its tactics "political correctness" and hinting that its proponents were similar in their thinking to fascist book-burners. These reactions can be understood as defensiveness against personal criticism, but also reluctance to change when change involves giving up privilege. Change would mean that male activists would have to cede the floor more often in discussions; it would mean that male academics would lose the benefits of preferential hiring and promotion; and it would mean losing, as Densmore put it, the "privilege of feeling superior" (Densmore 76).

Challenge for Marxism

Problem of Class Unity

New Left activists also saw the increasing demands being made from a variety of oppressed identities as divisive. Of course they were anti-racist because racism could be understood as a part of colonialism and capitalist exploitation. They were surely opposed to the exploitation of women as workers because these women's struggles could be linked to the struggle against capitalism. But the drift of identity politics seemed to be away from such collaborative anti-capitalist struggles.

First Black organizations, then women's organizations and gay organizations, insisted on excluding Whites, men, and heterosexuals respectively. The personal problems that some White male activists had, particularly with feminist demands, contributed to growing friction. These were yet additional strains widening the "internal divisions" that Oberschall believed led to the decline of the 1960s social movements.

The emergence of identity politics also posed new problems for conceptualizing social movement unity. Academics in Canada, Europe, and Latin America were more sympathetic than their U.S. counterparts to socialism, anti-capitalism, and the New Left. They tended to turn to Marx and Engels for theoretical inspiration and were wary of the economistic language of the American resource-mobilization perspective.

Marx and Engels did not, however, give them much guidance for understanding the ways that either the New Left or the gay and feminist movements mobilized "collective identities." Feminist and gay activists were better than the New Left at creating enduring networks sustained by institutions and embedded in physical places. The New Left, as you will remember from the last chapter, relied more on "transitory teams" linked up through the mass media. Neither pattern looked particularly like what Marx and Engels had envisioned.

BOX 5.2:

SOLIDARITY OR "FLUIDARITY"?

Kevin McDonald believes that young anti-capitalist activists are developing a new model of collective action that involves neither class consciousness nor collective identity. Like New Left activists, they are wary of organization and bureaucracy. They rely instead on personal networks, often mediated through the Web, and will work together only in small "affinity groups" of like-minded friends. They see their groups as fleeting responses to specific needs, such as mutual aid in a large and potentially dangerous demonstration, or issues, such as the WTO's stand on patenting genes. As though to underline the idea that these groups are not to be taken seriously as permanent social entities, they are either not named or else named only playfully. For example, a group planning to dress as Santa Claus to protest the global biotechnology giant Monsanto, as part of a larger anti-free trade demonstration, called itself "Monsanto Claus." Others had names like "AWOL" (Autonomous Web of Liberation) and "Revolutionary Valley Girls." Unlike, for example, unions, which, when they march in anti-free trade demonstrations, carry banners, insignia, even wear group colours, affinity groups do not publicly declare a group identity in any way. The group is not something that participants identify with or see as "representing" them. Conversely, no one can claim to represent the group. This is often explicit policy. So, for example, if interviewed by the press, no one could speak for the group or say what "Monsanto Claus" stood for. They could only speak personally. Nor is it possible for anyone in the name of the group to delegate tasks to others. McDonald contrasts this refusal to grant independent existence to the group or organization to what happens in unions.

Union membership implies obligations to the organization. One votes for leaders or policies, but once these are in place, one obeys the leaders or acts in accordance with policy, behaving in a sense as an "instrument" of the organization. One also identifies with a "we," the steelworkers' "brotherhood," let's say, that encompasses the "I." One is often ready to sacrifice one's self or personal interests in the interests of the larger collectivity. With the affinity group there is neither organization nor "collective identity," invested with independence from, or greater importance than, the individual. One activist reported to McDonald her irritation at being asked at a demonstration to join a traditional membership organization: "... don't ask me to join an acronym!" (117).

In place of obligation to an abstract collective identity there is friendship and personal obligation to specific, concrete others. "The affinity group," explains one activist, "is a group of people that you know and who you can trust. Before things happen you talk about what you are going to do, if you are going to get arrested or not. You help each other, you watch out for each other. Each person knows what the other can do and is prepared to do. If one person intends to get arrested and another doesn't, you help each other in this" (116). It is important, according to McDonald, that participants *experience* their involvement as a set of personal choices rather than as the social requirements of an organizational role. This is not to say, however, that affinity group involvement is individualistic. One indicator of this is the way in which activists often use multiple aliases, for example, when posting to discussion lists, or else share invented names with other activists. In this way they downplay the ideas of individuality and authorship. First wave feminists did a similar thing by refusing to sign or take individual credit for many of their pamphlets and collective publications. "The relationship between person and identity," writes McDonald, "is fluid, not fixed and transparent" (118).

Many of the public actions of affinity groups are like anonymously co-authored "publications." They are expressive—communicating a political meaning such as a criticism of Monsanto's policies. McDonald sees them as also ritualistic embodiments of new ways of relating personal and public "selves." McDonald illustrates what he means by looking at two examples of collaborative action: puppet making and video activism. Larger-than-life puppets, representing everything from evil capitalists to huge gossamer-winged "butterflies" threatened by genetically modified crops, have become a part of the visual culture of "anti-globalization" street demonstrations. McDonald is interested not so much in the way they are paraded through the streets as the collaborative process through which they are designed and assembled. As many as 50 people are involved over a period of weeks. There is no overall plan or blueprint. People make design choices that express an idea. Others are free to come along and reinterpret that idea and alter the creative direction. McDonald sees the process as like a conversation that becomes embodied in the puppet as a "narrative." The outcome is a public "text" that is not individual but still contains traces of each personal contribution. In addition to communicating a political statement about genetically modified foods or capitalism, the puppet communicates something about the way that individuals can relate to common endeavour without subordinating themselves to the dictates of an organization or collective identity.

Video activism is perhaps a more obvious way of weaving one's personal contribution into a larger, "public" story. High-quality video cameras have become relatively cheap and lightweight so that activists find it increasingly easy to bring them along to document demonstrations and other public actions. Digital cameras can easily be linked to the Internet through direct streaming or their images archived on indymedia Web sites. They also offer a low-cost medium for "activist films" such as *This Is What Democracy Looks Like* for distribution through alternative channels (see www.thisisdemocracy.org/). Activists of the 1960s record feeling a kind of media "rush" at seeing their actions reported on the evening news. It meant that they had been recognized and thereby validated as players on the national or international public stage. McDonald is interested in the way that 21st-century media activists are able themselves to create a similar sort of affirmation of their public existence. Activists film each other in action and in interview, then get together and watch and discuss the results. As one explained, "I use video activism so that people will see themselves, *so that they will know that they exist*" (McDonald's emphasis, 122) Like puppet making, video activism is a set of practices engaged in collectively. The outcome is also a narrative that places the self, and thereby helps to define the self, in some meaningful relation to public events. McDonald sees in both puppet making and video activism a means to construct a "public experience of the self" that is both personal and shared with others. These "public experiences of self and other" are situational, embodied in the moment. They are neither as abstract nor as permanent as the collective "we" of solidarity. "We are not creating solidarity," declared one activist, "we are creating fluidarity!"

If McDonald is right, then this new development (which probably has it roots in the "anti-structure" ethic of the New Left) poses a challenge to all of the social movement theory we have so far discussed. We would not only have to rethink the Marxist paradigm, which places such strong emphasis on working-class solidarity and class consciousness, but also most of new social movement and resource-mobilization theory, which relies on the concept of "collective identity." It would not be the case, as some theorists have claimed, that "collective action cannot occur in the absence of a 'we' characterized by common traits and specific solidarity.... A collective actor cannot exist without reference to experiences, symbols and myths which form the basis of its individuality" (Della Porta and Diani, qtd. in McDonald 92). It is also interesting that the people who embrace fluidarity are struggling against capitalist globalization. One of the sources of power of global capitalism is its own "fluidarity"—in other words, the mobility of capital and the use of "labour flexibility" to undermine working-class solidarity. Could fluidarity provide a more nimble, flexible model of mobilization for capitalism's opponents, one that does not require that people already share some common identity or attempt to forge one where it does not already exist?

Source: Kevin McDonald, "From Solidarity to Fluidarity: Social Movements Beyond 'Collective Identity': The Case of Globalisation Conflicts," *Social Movement Studies* 1, no. 2 (2002): 109–128.

To begin with, neither mobilized on the basis of Marxist classes. Women and gays did not constitute classes that could be defined in terms of any one "relationship to the means of production." New Left students training to become managers and professionals were often categorized as members of the "new middle classes" between owners of the means of production (capitalists) and those who had only their labour to sell (the proletariat). But for Marx and Engels, these were the "wrong" classes to carry forward the revolution against capitalism. Like the petty-bourgeoisie (workers, but also small-scale owners of their means of production), they had too much invested in "the system" to act when it came down to the crunch—the final destruction of capitalism.

The beauty of Marx and Engels' analysis of the proletariat was not only the economic guarantee of their commitment to revolution, but the dialectical way that capitalism itself would empower them. Remember the irony that this tremendously powerful system would, in spite of itself, help to increase the numbers and organization of its enemies—the alienated and emiserated working class.

For neo-Marxists, the last 30-odd years have posed in bolder terms than ever the problem that Marx and Engels thought they had solved with their "dialectic." That is, how do powerless people successfully oppose the most powerful system on earth—global capitalism? Since 1970 transnational corporations have invested and traded more freely around the world. This "mobility of capital" has given firms tremendous new powers over workers' organizations—wherever unionization is too strong, they close down the factories and move the jobs elsewhere.

The threat to move capital across borders has also weakened elected governments and made states much more ready to concede to the demands of capitalist firms and investors. Neo-Marxists have been reluctant in the face of these developments to give up the promise of a dialectically generated *class unity*. The splintering of anti-capitalist movements into groupings with no class basis has seemed to many to be a betrayal of any hope for real change.

The Marxist dialectic of "class formation" also had a necessary, inevitable character. Compare how Marx and Engels understood the formation of working-class community to the way in which gay communities formed. Both involve geographic concentration—migration from the country to residential neighbourhoods in large cities. In the Marxist model, economic forces drive people against their wills (capitalist development in agriculture destroys rural jobs). Gays' migration is more intentional, or chosen, indeed often driven, by desire.

The urge to build their own culture is a motivating force for gays. Marx and Engels thought workers would be swept along by forces not of their making. Once in the cities, workers do begin to fashion a new "socialist" culture based on equality and mutual aid, but only because their common circumstances of impoverishment and exploitation leave them with few other options. Culture for Marx and Engels arises as an expression of more "real" economic and physical conditions. It is, to use their terminology, an "epiphenomenon."

Problem of Political Identity

If, as the successes of the gay and feminist movements suggest, cultural innovation can shape history, and if the character of this innovation is chosen rather than conditioned by historical "laws," then historical outcomes are arbitrary and unpredictable. Since culture construction and identity construction are intertwined, then the making of collective identities is similarly arbitrary. This second consequence was particularly troubling for Marxists. Accepting it meant giving up the idea that there was a real and true path of class formation.

It had once been taken for granted by Marxists that workers who bought into capitalism and failed to develop a socialist culture and working-class solidarity were victims of "false consciousness." Theorists could argue, for example, that the blandishments of the capitalist "culture industry" had obscured *temporarily* the "real" relations and "real" interests of class. In this formulation they were able to link what was theoretically true with what was morally and politically right.

It is only fair to recognize that even some gays and feminists were uncomfortable with the idea that individual and collective identities are purely cultural constructions. Some gays want to believe that "coming out" represents the embrace of a true identity "real" in the sense of being biologically based. Some feminists want to believe that features of feminine identity that they value—nurturance, pacifism, egalitarianism—are based in "nature." This position is called "essentialism." The idea is that we all have an inner "essence" that seeks expression despite the ways in which our culture represses or distorts it.

The opposing, "constructionist" perspective on identity dismisses biological and economic "necessity" in the formation of the self. In so doing it also abandons one sort of moral justification for mobilizing particular identities. It is not possible to argue that closeted gays or pro-capitalist workers or anti-feminist women are denying their "true" selves or their "true interests" in common with others. One socially constructed individual or collective identity is as "true" as another.

New Social Movement Theory

The emergence in the 1960s of the civil rights movement, the New Left, the peace movement, and, in the 1970s, of second wave feminism, gay liberation, and the environmental movement eroded faith in Marxist certainties about class formation. Europeans and Latin Americans such as Alain Touraine, Claus Offe, Juergen Habermas, Alberto Melucci, Ernesto Laclau and Chantal Mouffe proposed "new social movement" theories.

These people were still sympathetic to Marxist and New Left political objectives, but were willing to give up Marxist theoretical assumptions about the unique revolutionary role of the proletariat and the dialectic of class formation. It is helpful to think of "new" here as referring to new theory, not new movements. There had been feminist, peace, anti-slavery, and environmental movements as far back as the 19th century, but Marxists had been able for theoretical reasons to dismiss them as irrelevant to the revolutionary project or else subsumable under the logic of class struggle.

New social movement theorists accepted that the working class was not the only possible "revolutionary subject." In this they were merely catching up to what the Situationists and Provos had realized in the early 1960s. There were other "political subjects" capable of challenging capitalism. The use of the term "collective identity" to replace "class consciousness" signalled this more inclusive conceptualization. They also accepted that there were routes to the formation of collective identity quite unlike the one that Marx and Engels predicted. Some were unwilling to give up the idea that these collective identities were generated dialectically by the "logic" of capitalist development. They argued, for example, that the capitalist state's efforts to buy off workers through collective consumption created new middle classes responsible for administering collective consumption and expanding it in ways that served the interests of the working class against those of capitalists.

German theorists Offe and Habermas saw the New Left celebration of spontaneity and cultural provocation as a defence of the "lifeworld" against what Provos called the "huge grey mass" of state and union bureaucratization. While this was not a class-based form of resistance to capitalism, Offe and Habermas insisted on seeing it as dialectically conditioned by the logic of capitalist "modernity." Others, like Melucci, were

more willing to concede that the cultural provocations of the New Left or the cultural innovations of identity politics did not have to arise out of some underlying dialectic of struggle built into the logic of capitalism.

New social movement theorists recognized that the formation of collective identity did not have to take place at the sites where concentrations of people were subjected to capitalist economic exploitation: the workplace and factory neighbourhoods. Women, for instance, created the collective "feminist" identity in geographically dispersed private sites: homes and women's centres where they arranged C-R sessions. Theorists accepted that the sites, as well as the targets of struggle, had changed. Instead of mobilizing to attack capitalist firms or the state exclusively, movement activists engaged in struggles over everyday cultural practices in what German theorists like to call the "lifeworld." Finally, some theorists were willing to concede that the formation of legitimate collective identities within social movements did not always have to be directed toward an anti-capitalist project. Indeed, identity formation could, as was evident in identity politics, become an end in and of itself.

CONCLUSION

In this chapter we have considered women's liberation and gay liberation as examples of identity politics. Activists in both movements responded to the problem of internal colonization or the internalization of debilitating self-images derived from cultural categories created by one's oppressors. In so doing they created new social movement tactics and helped to redefine our conception of political action. They showed how the "personal is political." In other words, oppression is often acted out in our day-today dealings with others and can be opposed through struggles over how we act and express meaning in everyday life.

They showed how social movement politics can be about the making of culture, through "do-it-yourself" reforms of everyday practices, but also through challenging cultural institutions such as the mass media, educational curricula, the medical professions, and language. These projects of remaking culture were directed toward remaking identity. Feminists and gay activists sought to create positive and empowering cultural frameworks for understanding what it means to be female or gay. These were simultaneously conceptual, emotional, and psychological reframings of identity.

The two cases in this chapter were chosen for their similarities but also for their differences. Women's liberationists tended to see the construction of a feminist identity as a means to broader political ends. The feminist ideal of "sisterhood" was meant to create solidarity and inspire women to fight collectively for societal change. In other words, it was what social scientists call a "collective identity." Women were to use their collective power to lobby for changes in cultural representations of women, but also to fight more traditionally "political" battles like pressuring governments for better legislation or services for women or helping working women to demand better labour rights.

Gay liberationists also hoped to unify gays to fight for institutional changes within society at large. They have had notable success in changing societal attitudes and legislation, particularly in Canada. However, they discovered that they could more readily create cultural institutions for themselves within geographically defined gay communities. The aim of gay politics tended to be to create cultural conditions in which it was safe for individuals publicly to construct gay identities.

Here "identity" takes on a slightly different political meaning. The validation of identity *for the individual* becomes a movement end in itself. It is not primarily a means to mobilize a "mass movement" for broader political objectives. This is the feature that, for many, defines identity politics. However, you can think of identity politics more broadly as a political response to the problem of internal colonization.

Providing you with an introduction to identity politics has not been my main objective in this chapter. Movements that give such priority to cultural change as an objective raise questions about how best theoretically to understand culture and how best to study cultural practices. The case studies are intended to help you think about these questions. How do we make sense of the fact that culture seems at times external and constraining—in the way that public condemnation of their sexuality seemed so concrete and unassailable to homosexuals in the 1950s—and at times so like a fiction that we can simply "rewrite" it as gays did when they made "coming out" a joyful reality?

As a first step toward understanding, we invoked the notion of a dialectic between agency and structure. There are moments when culture seems part of the taken-for-granted furniture of the social world, and moments when the taken-for-granted is questioned, its constructedness revealed, and people feel invited to reconstruct it. The notion of a "dialectic" suggests that there is a dance between moments of agency and structure and that culture itself is neither one nor the other. A second step toward understanding is to recognize that while culture as sets of social meanings—"symbol systems," some anthropologists say—is abstract, it also can be embedded in concrete artifacts and practices.

We saw how the making of culture in gay communities involved ritual practices, body adornment, and making spatial claims to the built environment of cities. In these physical instantiations, culture can take on a more permanent character. It is not just in the head, but takes form in the external world of physical "things." Finally, it is important to remember that the reproduction of taken-for-granted culture, as well as cultural innovation, takes place both within daily face-to-face interaction and within "impersonal" institutions that produce culture such as the mass media and the education system.

To help deal with the subtleties of cultural analysis, many social movement theorists have turned to "frame analysis." Frame analysis is not so much a theory as a set of conceptual tools for analyzing culture within social movements: "interpretive frame," "frame alignment," "frame extension," the "politics of signification," etc. The concept of "frame transformation" recognizes the moment of agency or culture construction that is so important to many social movements. Frame analysts recognize that movements also work within pre-existing interpretive frames. These pre-existing frames might be from the larger culture—like the conceptual linking of femininity and nurturance and pacifism.

Over time social movements themselves create a cultural legacy of "frames"—like the New Left valuation of personal authenticity in opposition to alienating systems—that other movements can draw upon. The concept of a "frame" emphasizes the structural moment of culture. Resource-mobilization theorists like it because they can treat frames as one type of "resource" that social movements attempt to mobilize. There is a danger in this use of reifying culture—that is, treating it as a "thing" only and forgetting its constructed quality.

Identity politics raises questions about how to analyze culture. It also brings into focus problems with theories of political identity, particularly the Marxist theory that the working class was the only true "revolutionary subject." Marx and Engels thought that the numbers and organization of the workers would grow as a necessary consequence of the development of capitalism. Workers' sense of unity and common purpose, their political identity or "class consciousness," would emerge in opposition to capitalism and would be guaranteed by the very success of capitalism. The New Left and movements inspired by it like women's and gay liberation confounded Marxist expectations in two ways. First, the political identities of participants seemed more intentional and constructed. Their formation was not obviously linked to any "logic of capitalism." Second, the political consciousness was not based on the "right" sort or indeed any sort of class-based experiences.

"New social movement" theorists sought in various ways to make theoretical sense of these developments. Some proposed the notion of "collective identity" to replace the more narrow "class consciousness." Some attempted to link the emergence of the New Left to a new logic of capitalism. The background concern driving this intense and often complex theoretical effort was Marx's problem of identifying a force equal to and able to challenge the tremendous power of global capitalism. It remains an important one for critics of capitalism and an interesting one for students of social movements.

What do you think? Do people have to identify with one another to fight together for the same cause? Can people with very different political identities work effectively in coalitions (we will consider this possibility in Chapter 11)? Many people in the contemporary anti-capitalist movement reject the ideas of collective identity and any kind of subordination to organization (see the box "Solidarity or 'Fluidarity'?" above).

Do they have any hope of making change on the basis of radical personal autonomy or "fluidarity"? Or are they destined to wander off in different directions and lose the power of concerted action?

NOTES

1. A Gestetner was like a small hand-cranked printing press. Creating masters to be copied was fussy work; cranking out copies was tedious.
2. Politically important.

REFERENCES

Armstrong, Elizabeth A. *Forging Gay Identities: Organizing Sexuality in San Francisco, 1950–1994.* Chicago: University of Chicago Press, 2002.

Boston Women's Health Book Collective. *Our Bodies, Ourselves.* New York: Simon and Schuster, 1973.

Brooke. Review of *Woman's Fate: Raps from a Feminist Consciousness-Raising Group,* by Claudia Dreifus. *Off Our Backs* 5, no. 1 (1975): 18.

Densmore, Dana. "A Year of Living Dangerously: 1968." *The Feminist Memoir Project: Voices from Women's Liberation,* edited by Rachel Blau DuPlessis and Ann Barr Snitow. New York: Three Rivers Press, 1998.

Dunbar, Roxanne. "Outlaw Woman: Chapters from a Feminist Memoir-in-Progress." *The Feminist Memoir Project: Voices from Women's Liberation,* edited by Rachel Blau DuPlessis and Ann Barr Snitow. New York: Three Rivers Press, 1998.

DuPlessis, Rachel Blau, and Ann Barr Snitow. *The Feminist Memoir Project: Voices from Women's Liberation.* New York: Three Rivers Press, 1998.

Durkheim, Emile. *The Elementary Forms of the Religious Life.* 1915. Free Press Paperbacks. New York: Free Press, 1965.

Fanon, Frantz. *The Wretched of the Earth.* New York: Grove Press, 1963.

———. *Black Skin, White Masks.* New York: Grove Press, 1967.

Goffman, Erving. *Stigma: Notes on the Management of Spoiled Identity.* New York: Simon & Schuster, 1986.

Habermas, Juergen. "New Social Movements/Social Movements—Theory." *Telos* 49 (1981): 34.

Keating, Cricket. "Building Coalitional Consciousness." *NWSA Journal* 17, no. 2 (2005): 86.

Kesselman, Amy, et al. "Our Gang of Four: Friendship and Women's Liberation." *The Feminist Memoir Project: Voices from Women's Liberation,* edited by Rachel Blau DuPlessis and Ann Barr Snitow. New York: Three Rivers Press, 1998.

Kinsman, Gary. *The Regulation of Desire: Sexuality in Canada.* Montreal: Black Rose Books, 1987.

Klein, Naomi. *No Logo: Taking Aim at the Brand Bullies.* Toronto: Random House, 2000.

Kostash, Myrna. *Long Way from Home: The Story of the Sixties Generation in Canada.* Toronto: Lorimer, 1980.

Laclau, Ernesto, and Chantal Mouffe. *Hegemony and Socialist Strategy: Toward a Radical Democratic Politics.* London: Verso, 1985.

Leonard, Vickie. "C-R: It Ain't What It Used to Be." *Off Our Backs* 10, no. 2 (1980): 17.

McDonald, Kevin. "From Solidarity to Fluidarity: Social Movements beyond

'Collective Identity': The Case of Globalisation Conflicts." *Social Movement Studies* 1, no. 2 (2002): 109–128.

Melucci, Alberto. "On Social Movements, Democracy, and the Reinvention of Codes of Meaning as a Mode of Resistance and Transformation." *Nomads of the Present: Social Movements and Individual Needs in Contemporary Society*, edited by Alberto Melucci. Philadelphia: Temple University Press, 1989.

Offe, Claus. "New Social Movements/Social Movements—Theory: Challenging the Boundaries of Institutional Politics." *Social Research* 52, no. 4 (1985): 817–868.

Piercy, Marge, and Jane Freeman. "Getting Together: How to Start a Consciousness-Raising Group." 1972. WMST-L. October 5, 2006, http://research.umbc.edu/~korenman/wmst-crguide2.html.

Radical Women. "No More Miss America." *"Takin' It to the Streets": A Sixties Reader*, edited by Alexander Bloom and Wini Breines. New York: Oxford University Press, 2003.

Sarachild, Kathie. "Consciousness-Raising: A Radical Weapon." *Feminist Revolution*. Sarachild and Redstockings, Inc. New York: Random House, 78. 144–150. October, 5, 2006, http://scriptorium.lib.duke.edu/wlm/fem/sarachild.html.

Snow, David A., and Robert D. Benford. "Master Frames and Cycles of Protest." *Frontiers in Social Movement Theory*, edited by Aldon D. Morris and Carol McClurg Mueller. New Haven: Yale University Press, 1992.

Snow, David, E.B. Rochford, S.K. Worden, and R.D. Benford. "Frame Alignment Processes, Micromobilization, and Movement Participation." *American Sociological Review* 51 (1986): 464–481.

Stern, Susan, and Wendy Kolmar. "Remembering Barbie Nation: An interview with Susan Stern." *Women's Studies Quarterly* 30.1/2 (2002): 189–196. ABI/INFORM Proquest. Angus L. Macdonald Library, Antogonish. November 16, 2006, http://libmain.stfx.ca/newlibelectronic/databases/.

Students for a Democratic Society. "The Port Huron Statement." *"Takin' It to the Streets": A Sixties Reader*, edited by Alexander Bloom and Wini Breines. New York: Oxford University Press, 2003.

Taylor, Verta, and Nancy Whittier. "Analytical Approaches to Social Movement Culture: The Culture of the Women's Movement." *Social Movements and Culture*, edited by Hank Johnston and Bert Klandermans. Minneapolis: University of Minnesota Press, 1995.

Touraine, Alain, ed. *Return of the Actor: Social Theory in Postindustrial Society*. Minneapolis: University of Minnesota Press, 1988.

Warner, Tom. *Never Going Back: A History of Queer Activism in Canada*. Toronto: University of Toronto Press, 2002.

CRITICAL THINKING QUESTIONS

1. Are young anti-feminists the victims of internal colonization?
2. Is the unity of "collective identity" arbitrary or conditioned by history?
3. Does dissent arise dialectically through the "logic of capital"?
4. How do we analyze culture in such a way as to recognize both its external and constraining as well as its freely "constructed" moments?
5. Do people have to identify with one another to fight together for the same cause?
6. Do young activists have any hope of making change on the basis of radical personal autonomy or "fluidarity"? Or are they destined to wander off in different directions and lose the power of concerted action?
7. Review your answers to the question from Chapter 3 ("How did the 1960s movements differ from the predictions of Marx and Engels?") in light of what you have learned in this chapter.

FURTHER READING

Jasper, James M. *The Art of Moral Protest: Culture, Biography, and Creativity in Social Movements*. Chicago: University of Chicago Press, 1997.

Using case studies from the antinuclear and animal rights movements, Jasper attempts to understand the place of culture, identity, and creativity in mobilization. The choice of tactics, he argues, can be explained as much in terms of culturally conditioned "tastes" as the sort of instrumental utility or available material resources invoked in resource-mobilization theory.

Melucci, Alberto. "On Social Movements, Democracy, and the Reinvention of Codes of Meaning as a Mode of Resistance and Transformation." *Nomads of the Present: Social Movements and Individual Needs in Contemporary Society*, edited by Alberto Melucci. Philadelphia: Temple University Press, 1989.

Learn more about Melucci's take on new social movement theory in his own words. What does he actually say about the role of culture and agency versus the inevitable historical forces of capitalist development?

Offe, Claus. "New Social Movements/Social Movements—Theory: Challenging the Boundaries of Institutional Politics." *Social Research* 52, no. 4 (1985): 817–868.

To make sense of the much-disputed "new social movement theory," one must return to its original formulations, such as this article by Offe. See how Offe characterizes this new anti-institutional politics of the lifeworld. Pay particular attention to his treatment of class.

Snow, David A., and Robert D. Benford. "Master Frames and Cycles of Protest." *Frontiers in Social Movement Theory*, edited by Aldon D. Morris and Carol McClurg Mueller. New Haven: Yale University Press, 1992.

Snow and Benford offer a condensed discussion of frame analysis. They provide a reference list for those who want to read further.

Taylor, Verta, and Nancy Whittier. "Analytical Approaches to Social Movement Culture: The Culture of the Women's Movement." *Social Movements and Culture*, edited By Hank Johnston and Bert Klandermans. Minneapolis: University of Minnesota Press, 1995.

Taylor and Whittier provide an excellent example of how to analyze the cultural (ritual and discursive) elements of social movements. They begin with an excellent overview of recent theory, including new social movement theory.

RELEVANT WEB SITES

DisAbled Women's Network Canada
www.dawncanada.net
Explore the intersection of feminism and the disability movement in Canada.

Gay & Lesbian Alliance against Defamation
www.glaad.org
This is the site of an organization dedicated to changing the language and imagery we use to represent gender identities and sexual orientation. You may be interested in learning about their achievements, which they list in detail.

The Guerrilla Girls
www.guerrillagirls.org
The Guerrilla Girls Web site is dedicated to "reinventing the 'f'-word—feminism" for a new generation.

Media Watch
www.mediawatch.com
Media Watch seeks to challenge media constructions of race, gender, and violence. You can join debates over the offensiveness of specific images in their "hall of shame." Canada's Media Watch (www.mediawatch.ca/) deals mostly with gender issues.

PAR-L—Feminist Policy, Action, Research List
www.unb.ca/PAR-L/
Here you can join a network of Canadian feminists in discussions related to gender and justice. This is where most of Canada's feminist academics, as well as many activists, hang out online.

Chapter 6

BUREAUCRATIZATION AND ANARCHIST RESISTANCE

INTRODUCTION: BUREAUCRATIZATION AND LIBERATION MOVEMENTS

In his book *Political Parties*, published in 1915, Robert Michels came to a pessimistic conclusion about democracy in social movements. At one time he had been inspired by socialism's promise of a society based on human freedom and equality. Marx and Engels had actually observed new forms of social organization emerging spontaneously within working-class neighbourhoods. These seemed to them to be based not only on equality of material conditions—everyone was equally impoverished—but also equality of contribution. Without being required to by anyone, people gave generously of their time and labour to help one another. Without formal education or instructors, the poorest workers educated themselves and confidently gave voice to their own opinions on society and the world. Recall Engels' description from Chapter 1 of self-educated workers "... whose fustian jackets scarcely held together, speak[ing] upon geological, astronomical, and other subjects, with more knowledge than the most 'cultivated' bourgeois in Germany possess" (Engels 265).

Between 1844, when Engels wrote, and 1915, European workers had organized large union federations and political parties. Michels observed how self-education had become replaced by formal training institutes for union and party officials. These people had become bureaucrats whose specialized knowledge set them apart from the workers whose collective affairs they administered. A new cadre of paid officials and elected representatives had emerged. Largely on the basis of their monopolization of knowledge and daily information about the goings-on in their large organizations, these people were able to monopolize power. They controlled the organizations' monetary resources, formulated policy, publicly spoke for the thousands of members, and mobilized them, when necessary, into action.

Socialist organizations had become bureaucracies ruled by a few. In other words, they had become oligarchies. The irony, of course, is that the very purpose of working-class organization had been to eliminate inequalities of power. The very process of organization had apparently resulted in a kind of alienation that Marx and Engels had not foreseen. Egalitarian workers invest their collective will and intelligence in an organization that takes on a life of its own, undermining equality and robbing them individually of knowledge and the power to influence the direction of their own action. For Michels, the lesson in this tragic irony was that we should give up hope for true democracy not just in social movements but for societies in general. For if those whose fundamental value and aim is democratic equality cannot achieve it, then who can?

This idea that our institutions are doomed to become oligarchical is popularly held. It is the theme of The Who's old song, "Won't Get Fooled Again." You have probably heard the words:

> Take a bow for the new revolution
> Smile and grin at the change all around
> Pick up my guitar and play
> ... Meet the new boss
> Same as the old boss

The questions it raises form the basis of this chapter. How democratic can groups and organizations be? Is it inevitable that organizations eventually become undemocratic?

Many refuse to accept Michels' pessimism. They are convinced that there is some way around the process that he saw play out in European labour organizations. Many social movements of the 20th century have made democratization a central aim of their efforts to change society. This has been true of anarchists. It was also true of western Canadian farmers in the co-operative movement that you learned about in Chapter 2. They believed that they could avoid oligarchy in their large co-ops like the Wheat Pool by building in decentralized decision-making structures, tinkering with its organizational form to make it as "... delicately sensitive to the control of its individual members as human conceptions of democratic control can make it" (qtd. in Bantjes 103).

Democratization was also an aim of the New Left and the counterculture, but the sixties approach was to reject structure altogether. Many second wave feminists saw oligarchy as a feature of the "male" institutional world that women, with different values and ways of relating to one another, could avoid in their organizations. One of the case studies that we will look at in this chapter is of women's organizations: women's centres in Britain. The other is online communities of computer programmers, which are often taken as inspiration for the modern anarchist movement. We will ask whether the "network society" of the 21st century holds new hope for the anarchist dream.

MICHELS-WEBER THESIS

If we want to understand how a group or organization could escape the tendency toward oligarchy, we need to understand what causes oligarchy to develop in the first place. The great sociologist Max Weber, who was one of Michels' teachers, helped to lay bare the mechanism by which Michels' "iron law of oligarchy" operates. Michels' and Weber's contributions together are referred to as the "Michels-Weber thesis."

Michels and Weber do not argue that people by nature need leaders or are psychologically programmed to follow them. In fact, Weber was inclined to agree with Marx that for most of human history, people lived in small face-to-face groupings that were relatively egalitarian and where the exercise of individual leadership was limited and occasional. Marx thought these hunting and gathering societies were examples of "primitive communism." Both Marx and Weber saw a kind of tragedy in the drift away from this simple organization of life.

Modern societies organize anonymous millions across vast territories. It is the technical requirements of coordination on this scale that demand the delegation of enormous power to a few within bureaucracies. People submit to oligarchy often against their wills and possibly even against their "natures." The Michels-Weber thesis is quintessentially sociological in explaining oligarchy not by nature or psychology but as a feature of social systems created by humans.

Weber stressed that organizations compete for power with other organizations. Workers' parties, like the ones observed by Michels, compete with other social movement organizations, such as the anarchists, for influence over workers. They also compete with other political parties for influence over the state. Modern states and parties have to coordinate the actions of millions of people dispersed across immense distances. These people, the citizens of a nation, the working class of a country, are too numerous and far-flung to all know one another personally; they could never in principle meet face to face.

So they have to be coordinated through impersonal structures. These structures have to be lasting to perform predictably over time. History shows us, according to Weber, that bureaucratic structures are the most efficient at coordinating the actions of many people across great distances in reliable and predictable ways. Therefore, any organization that mobilizes large numbers of people and aims to wrest power from existing political bureaucracies must either itself become bureaucratic or fail to take power.

Two key features of bureaucracies are meant to ensure their efficiency. First is the division of labour. As Adam Smith observed, when people specialize in one set of tasks, they learn to complete them more swiftly and often more effectively. The division of labour in bureaucracies involves defining what each administrative position or "office" is and is not responsible for. It also involves giving each office-holder specialized knowledge and training in his or her own sphere, but not letting the person know more than necessary.

The second efficient feature is a clear line of command. Offices are organized in a hierarchy—a pyramid with fewer, more powerful offices as you ascend to the top. Decisions can be made quickly at the top and carried out by those who have unambiguous responsibility for them in the relevant offices below. All offices keep written records. Lower offices compile records on the organization's clients or members. This is why bureaucracies have long been associated with filling out forms—in triplicate.

Summary data culled from these forms travel upwards in the hierarchy and help to inform decision making at the top. However, knowledge does not necessarily travel back down. Offices often jealously guard knowledge that can be used in decision making. Knowledge equals power. The compartmentalization and control of knowledge is one of the key sources of power in bureaucracies.

The division of labour and the chain of command are supposed to make bureaucracy efficient. Three additional, interrelated features are meant to make this efficiency reliable and stable over time. All three have to do with making the exercise of power impersonal, or less reliant on the whims or vulnerabilities of specific individuals. Rules governing the division of labour and chain of command are written down. Even those who sit in the most powerful offices must follow them. Similarly, the data on all of those forms—along with records of meetings, decisions, justifications of those decisions, appeals, etc.—all go on paper and are stored in files or, more recently, are recorded electronically and stored in data banks.

In this way, when powerful individuals quit, get fired, or die, the valuable knowledge on which they based their power is not lost but is retained by the institution as a kind of "institutional memory." The institution need not falter. Finally, and this is already implied in the emphasis on institutional rules and institutional memory, individual office-holders do not "own" the knowledge or power that comes with their position. Mechanisms are in place to discipline them if they abuse the powers of office. Weber calls this the "separation of office and incumbent."

"Impersonality," "record keeping," "rules"—this all sounds very dull and oppressive, I am sure, but sometimes it is quite useful. Think of your professor. It is great if she treats you as a person, but you would not want her grading your work on the basis of her personal likes, dislikes, or desires respecting you. It is helpful to have bureaucratic rules that she must follow and bureaucratic procedures of appeal that you can call on if you think she is abusing her power over you for personal reasons.

Michels and Weber thought that bureaucracies were supremely efficient at coordinating human activity across distances and reliably over time. They were so efficient that even people who sought to organize others to bring about social change would, at least in modern bureaucratic societies, find themselves either giving in to bureaucracy and oligarchy or giving up on social change. Is this really true?

WOMEN'S ORGANIZATIONS AND DISTRIBUTED LEADERSHIP

Helen Brown is interested in women's efforts to follow a different path from that preordained by the iron law of oligarchy. She begins her paper with a striking image of large-scale human organization without leaders. Women peace activists in 1982 camped out in protest around the U.S. air base at Greenham Common in England. They assembled in numbers worthy of an occupying army, but their principles of organization could not have been further from military hierarchy.

One journalist marvelled:

> Faced with a demonstration, the first thing a policeman or journalist is trained to look for is a leader. Any organization begins with a committee, and that provides leaders and, therefore, someone to interview, and if the situation requires it, someone to arrest. When the peace movement grew, mushroom-like, from the group of dedicated women camped outside the Greenham Common air base, the press began to look for leaders and to create personalities. But the peace camp movement, as distinct from the Campaign for Nuclear Disarmament, appears to have no organization and no leaders. [....] Every woman at Greenham Common starts an interview by making clear she speaks only for herself, and she is not a leader. [...] The potential strength of this system cannot be underestimated. (qtd. in Brown 225)

The journalist represents leaderlessness as not merely a form that allows 30,000 people to act together, but also as an asset vis-à-vis hostile authorities. We will look at the latter theme again in Chapter 7, but right now let us look at what most interests Brown, which is how women's organizations can get things done without relying on hierarchical chains of command.

Her case study is a number of women's centres in Britain that she examined systematically. However, as her reference to Greenham Common suggests, she thinks that the achievements of these women's centres reflect a value placed on non-hierarchical organization that is widely held among second wave feminists. Strongly held cultural values are important in Brown's explanation. However, to be fair, we have to remember that others, like Michels' German workers, placed strong value on equality. Brown implies that reluctance to assert power over others is much more deeply embedded in women's culture.

Non-hierarchical Feminist Culture

Women's experience in institutions from the family to the workplace to social movement organizations is more likely to be one of subordination. Through their socialization they are more likely to internalize skills of listening, facilitating, and accommodating others. In addition, the experience of feminists within the consciousness-raising phase of the women's movement taught them to observe, analyze, and thereby challenge the "micro-politics of power" more subtly than perhaps had ever been done before within social and organizational settings.

This experience helped them to realize that the New Left dream of eliminating power inequality could not be accomplished by doing away with structure altogether.

Women like Jo Freeman were able to recognize how in supposedly "structureless" women's groups, informal power structures re-emerged. These were all the more insidious for being unstated, even wilfully overlooked, and therefore difficult to challenge. What Brown observes within women's centres is an effort to explicitly recognize the problem and design, not so much formally written rules, but rather clearly understood norms meant to prevent the emergence of patterns of unequal power. In other words, they are creating anti-hierarchical structures.

Women's centres, like co-ops, attempt to bring about social change not by fighting corporations or state bureaucracies, but by simply doing it themselves. They provide a range of community services to women. They respond to whatever local needs are, but typically help women with education, counselling, and referral regarding issues such as domestic violence, women's health, and the special challenges of poverty for women, particularly single parents. They do engage in advocacy—lobbying for better state policy and services in these areas—but that is not their central mission.

Women's centres can be found in most major cities in Britain, but also in most industrialized countries. They are often long lasting, and do effectively get things done. Brown emphasizes that despite the time and effort devoted to their internal objective of remaining anti-hierarchical, women in the centres that she studied continued to meet their external objectives of providing services to other women.

Brown lets the women explain their organizational strategies in their own words. The Tyneside Rape Crisis Centre outlines how decisions are made.

> We are nonhierarchical—that is we don't have an executive committee or elected officers, as these functions are shared among members. [...] The tasks arising out of business meetings [are] undertaken by a member or members volunteering to carry them out. [...] We also try to pay as much attention to the form and process of our meetings and interactions as we do to content, ensuring that all women are involved in decision making, and the tasks of the group. Often, those more used to formal structures and hierarchical organizations will query whether feminist principles are compatible with getting things done—but we can say to them that we managed to set up a rape crisis centre after only a few months of work. (qtd. in Brown 228–229)

So all of the members of the organization take part in making decisions. This is referred to as "direct democracy." That is, members do not elect representatives—to committees, boards of directors, or parliaments—to make decisions in their name. Instead they make the decisions themselves directly.

Consensus Decision Making

Decision making takes place in face-to-face meetings of all members. This is admittedly difficult to accomplish. The constraints of space can prevent it if the group is very large. Small women's centres did also find timing to be problematic. Decisions often need to be made on an ongoing basis and it is difficult to wait to call a meeting. Timing could exclude people from decisions: "If you weren't there, you wouldn't be part of it" (Brown 233). Decisions are meant to be arrived at through consensus.

Through consensus we are working not only to achieve better solutions, but also to promote the growth of community and trust. [...] Consensus does not mean that everyone thinks the decision made is the best one possible, or even that all are sure it will work. What it does mean is that in coming to that decision, no one has felt that her/his position on the matter was misunderstood or that it wasn't given a proper hearing. Hopefully, everyone will think that it is the best decision; this often happens because when it works, collective intelligence does come up with better solutions than could individuals. (qtd. in Brown 233)

Consensus is different from majority vote. Where there is disagreement, majority vote can be quicker since debate can be terminated by putting a question to a vote. However, the minority is more likely to feel that the decision is something external, imposed upon them from without. The consensus process is meant to make people feel more fully included in the outcome and therefore more willing to act in support of it. Some women in the peace movement use a kind of voting that reflects this internal commitment to the outcome. Once they have discussed a course of action, each woman takes one of four positions: (1) "I support it and am willing to work toward it"; (2) "I support it"; (3) "I oppose it"; (4) "I oppose it and am willing to work against it." If even one woman votes for the fourth position, the group will not act against her.

Consensus decision making can very easily cloak informal power structures. Women with more knowledge, experience, and/or better verbal skills can subtly lead the consensus. A network of informal "insiders" can confer prior to meetings and decide how they want the discussion to go. Women's centres dealt with this problem by developing ways to share knowledge and skills and minimize the differences between insiders and outsiders or new and more experienced members.

Distributing Leadership Tasks and Skills

Their key strategy was to minimize the effects of the division of labour. People were encouraged to focus their energy on specific tasks such as doing the financial accounts, fundraising, or talking to the media, but only on a short-term basis. They were expected to try their hand at and become familiar with most of the organizational tasks. This sort of "temporary task allocation" was challenging.

We had to learn to criticize each other's work constructively, not to moan behind backs or secretly correct errors when the person who'd made the mistake had left for the day. Oldtimers had to face their responsibility to teach newcomers, something we all found hard at first as it seemed like giving orders. As time went on some women did specialize; we had only one woman doing the accounts at one time. Other specialisms weren't so necessary and change involved the specialist letting go her hold and communicating her skill and the others having confidence and willingness enough to learn. *In the end*, the necessity to do things made us all able to do them. (qtd. in Brown 229)

The intentional sharing of knowledge and skill enables all women to share equally not just in the day-to-day running of the centre, but also to be equally informed and therefore to participate with more authority and confidence in the decision-making meetings. But as this quote makes clear, sharing skills and knowledge is itself skilled work and takes extra time. This is "inefficient" only if the objectives of the centre are viewed narrowly in terms of delivering community programs and accomplishing the background administration to keep the centre afloat. However, with the extra time they are also accomplishing a very elusive and challenging social change objective—putting direct democracy into practice.

Temporary task allocation ensures that each woman develops a pretty good idea of what everyone needs to do to accomplish the centre's objectives. Consensus decision making helps people commit to working for centre objectives, so much of the time people can be expected to volunteer to do things without being asked and without having to be instructed. Still, these contributions often had to be coordinated or directed or else people needed to be encouraged to take on some task. These Brown refers to as "leadership acts."

Someone has to do this, but women recognized that it did not always have to be the same person or group of people. The woman whose temporary task allocation was to complete a new fundraising drive might for that period only ask others to collaborate and assist in various ways. For other projects or tasks, others would perform leadership acts. In this way leadership exists and is recognized as important to organization, but it is "distributed" among many.

Accomplishing "distributed leadership" becomes an ongoing task for all members of the centre. It involves rotating tasks in the day-to-day running of the centre and taking time to communicate and share skills so that those tasks get done effectively. It also involves ensuring that knowledge and skill is distributed in decision-making meetings.

> The less verbally facile can be assured that the group [...] is willing to put up with stumbling or help them with longwindedness, and most important, actually listens to and understands what they are saying. [...] The more potentially influential can themselves curb impulses to speak or try to influence the group. (qtd. in Brown 230)

You will recall that similar efforts were made in women's consciousness-raising groups and often supplemented by conventions like "going around the circle" to give everyone a chance to speak, or issuing tokens that women spend every time they take the floor.

Distributed Leadership Versus Bureaucracy

Note the differences between Brown's "distributed leadership" and Weberian bureaucracy. There is no chain of command. While there is division of labour, no one is permanently assigned an "office" or limited to a single sphere of competence. Rules are not written down; however, they do exist and are explained and discussed on an ongoing basis as part of the culture of the organization. Brown does not tell us much about practices of record keeping. However, it is clear that information is widely shared. It flows horizontally rather than vertically as in a bureaucracy. There is little opportunity for monopolizing information and therefore power. The women's centres endure over time. (Brown is not specific on this, but perhaps for a decade at the time that she did her research). They get things done. So, does the feminist practice of "distributed leadership" refute the Michels-Weber thesis?

Some of you will point out that women's centres are based on small face-to-face groups. They do not attempt to coordinate the actions of large numbers of people across great distances. The participants can all still meet in the same room. It is primarily large-scale organizations, according to Michels and Weber, that will demand bureaucratization and oligarchization. True, but consider this. Women's centres exist throughout Britain and much of the Western world. There is no central body that coordinates them, sets policy, or defines core values for them. Still, they operate with remarkable similarity of structure and purpose. They hold very similar democratic values and respond to very similar women's needs in their communities. What we see here is a large-scale, transnational pattern and order without any organizational command structure of any kind. Perhaps these centres are linked by networks of women's movement activists. Perhaps the women involved read the same feminist texts, or follow the same international news of feminist activism. Nonetheless, whatever is behind this large-scale form of social order, it is not bureaucracy.

Others of you will point out that women's centres are not mobilizing to fight the bureaucratic structures of the state or large corporations. Therefore, they do not have to organize as efficiently as their opponents. (Remember that this sort of "competition" with other organizations was the principle force behind bureaucratization for Weber.) True again. However, could Michels and Weber be overlooking an alternative model of social change, one that aims less at attacking the centres of power and more on building alternative structures from the ground up?

This turning away from the traditional targets of social movement struggle is another feature that new social movement theorists believe has become much more typical of popular activism since the 1960s. So is the aim of democratization, not necessarily of the increasingly powerful institutions of "the system," but of the immediate sphere of the "lifeworld" or "civil society" over which individuals feel they have more direct control.

NETWORK SOCIETY AND TECHNO-ANARCHISM

Governments of the Industrial World, you weary giants of flesh and steel, I come from Cyberspace, the new home of Mind. On behalf of the future, I ask you of the past to leave us alone. You are not welcome among us. You have no sovereignty where we gather.

We have no elected government, nor are we likely to have one, so I address you with no greater authority than that with which liberty itself always speaks. I declare the global social space we are building to be naturally independent of the tyrannies you seek to impose on us. You have no moral right to rule us nor do you possess any methods of enforcement we have true reason to fear. (Barlow)

The dawn of the 21st century may be a pivotal moment for social movement challenges to oligarchy. On the one hand, we can see a drift toward unprecedented centralization of power. Democratically elected governments are losing sovereignty to transnational institutions like corporations, global financial markets, trade treaties such as NAFTA and the World Trade Organization, and financial institutions such as the International Monetary Fund and the World Bank.

On the other hand, new ways of organizing large-scale endeavours have begun to favour the horizontal relationships characteristic of networks rather than the vertical, hierarchical relationships characteristic of bureaucracies. Many see new opportunities here, not only to hack into existing power structures, but also to create large-scale alternative structures immune to centralized control and therefore resistant to oligarchization.

Networks and Horizontal Information/Power Flow

Manuel Castells believes that we are in the midst of a fundamental shift in the way power is organized, from industrial capitalism to the "network society." Information and knowledge have always been resources of power for capitalist firms and state bureaucracies. However, new information technologies have exponentially increased the volume and availability of information at minimal cost. As data collection becomes increasingly automated, there is less need to fill out forms in triplicate. When the cashier swipes the bar code on your purchase, information gets automatically recorded. If you hand over your customer loyalty or similar points or benefits card for the cashier to swipe, it will automatically add your purchases to a digital profile of your consumer behaviour, which, along with millions of other such profiles, helps the corporation target its marketing efforts.

Not only is this data easily collected, digital technologies make it easier to store (no more steel filing cabinets or flesh-and-blood filing clerks), reproduce (as many copies as you like before a clerk could even begin to make a paper duplicate), and dis-

tribute (globally to thousands of recipients in seconds, if you desire). Satellite and fibre-optic networks make instantaneous global distribution possible. Corporations construct global information networks linking data on you and millions like you at the cash register to relevant data on the various players in their supply chain—ordering and shipping departments, design and marketing departments, overseas manufacturing sources, sources of credit and capital. These networks are "reflexive"—that is, they offer instant feedback on trends, problems, and opportunities. They allow firms to be much more nimble and flexible in how they respond to challenges and opportunities.

Castells argues that when firms do respond to shifting global trends, they no longer attempt to do everything and organize everything themselves from a centralized head office. The most successful achieve flexibility and adaptability by subcontracting manufacture and supply to subordinate firms and entering into strategic partnerships with specialist firms on the more entrepreneurial aspects of project development. These partnerships engender fluid networks of firms.

Through them, corporate executives, engineers, and marketing gurus develop inter-firm personal networks based on sharing knowledge and expertise. What is important here is that, for these networks to be productive, knowledge must flow freely and "horizontally." Of course new information technologies facilitate that free flow of information through e-mail discussion and file sharing, teleconferencing, and similar forms of instant "connectivity" typical of the early 21st century.

"A network," writes Castells, "is a set of interconnected nodes" (15). A node could be a firm in a partnership, or it could be a person in an inter-firm project team. If you imagine connections as lines, you can picture the most important nodes in a network as those in which numerous lines intersect. Many come to the person or firm at that node for the quality of their ideas or information. Notice here how importance is defined, in a sense democratically, by everyone else in the network. Regardless of what "office" a network participant might hold in a formal bureaucracy, he or she will effectively be sidelined or dropped from the active network if the participant does not have good-quality information and is not open to sharing it.

Castells argues that network-based forms of organizing complex enterprises across vast distances are supplanting Weberian bureaucracy for Weberian reasons—because they are more powerful and will out-compete traditional hierarchies, which attempt to restrict the flow of information and command from a single point. If he is right, then the "network society" will irrevocably alter the mechanisms that once guaranteed the iron law of oligarchy.

BOX 6.1:

WIKIPEDIA ON ANARCHISM

The entry on anarchism in the Internet encyclopedia "Wikipedia" begins with the following warning:

> **The neutrality and factual accuracy of this article are disputed.**
> Please see the relevant discussion on the **talk page**.

It is not a bad warning to keep in mind for most things that you read (including this textbook).

In Wikipedia it is interesting for two additional reasons. First, it reflects the anarchist process by which the entry was written. If you click on the tab marked "Edit this page," you or anyone else with an Internet connection can add to or rewrite the article. You do not have to have credentials, just ideas. Your ideas will, however, be subject to comment and criticism from the whole community of writers interested in anarchism, and may eventually be deleted or modified beyond recognition. However, your contribution and the rationale for changes will be recorded on two additional pages, one that records editing history and one that records discussions (the "Talk page" in the above warning).

Much of the contention on the page has to do with an old dispute within anarchism between right-wing tendencies common in the United States, where anarchism gets conflated with individualistic libertarianism, and left-wing tendencies more common in Canada and Europe. The following exchange from the discussion gives you a taste of the debate.

> All I can say is this article is total waste now, totally inaccurate, and full of shit. Might as well just vandalize the whole page to be the sentence "anarchism cannot be defined correctly on wikipedia."

What do you regard as inaccuracies? [MrVoluntarist] 01:16, August 22, 2005 (UTC)

I'm pretty confident that this user is referring to the inclusion of "anarcho-capitalism" and "national anarchism" as forms of anarchism. I know that I personally find this article hard and even quite a bit depressing to look at with their inclusion. It effectively hijacks the furthest left-wing attitude and folds it back onto the right. Ironically, I'm a former anarcho-capitalist myself and at the time would have said I was "anarchist," but only because I had such a poor grasp of the subject to know otherwise. In fact, I was so confused I thought anarcho-capitalism was the only "true" anarchism because I considered anarchism to only oppose the state when in effect it opposes all means of oppression. As it happens, I now consider capitalist structures much more powerful than a simple state.

In fact, if you think about it, anarcho-capitalists are no more "anarchist" than communists, who are insistent on destroying capitalism albeit preserving the state, after you consider that they consider capitalism the more potent threat. To a right libertarian, such an idea is apparently beyond any sort of comprehension. The only peace of mind I'm left with is my confidence that these topics will be removed from the article in some fashion or another. [Sarge Baldy] 02:15, August 22, 2005 (UTC)

This collaborative editing process, along with the software developed specifically to facilitate, it is referred to as "wiki" (pronounced either *wee-kee* or *wick-ey*). Hence the "Wikipedia" is an encyclopedia based on it (see http://en.wikipedia.org/wiki/Wiki). Despite the anarchist approach, or perhaps because of it, the results are often quite impressive. The page on anarchism is one of the best introductions to this topic on the net. Have a look. See how they deal with the basic issues, including the common misconception that anarchism implies chaos and/or violence.

The intense debate generated by readers (this is the second reason I think the warning is interesting) is an index of a 21st-century revival of interest in anarchism. It is not merely an academic topic but a philosophy that many of the contributors to the page hope to live by. Their section on "Anarchism Today" consequently is particularly strong.

Incidentally, there is a suggestion on the "discussion" page: "We don't have an article called 'Anarchist Movement in Canada' ... but you can write it!" This could be your term project for the course.

Source: http://en.wikipedia.org/wiki/Anarchism#Anarchism_today.

Anarchists of the 21st century place great faith in the democratic potential of network organization. They point to historical precedents in the Spanish anarchist tradition. In the late 19th century people would meet regularly in the cafés of Barcelona to discuss ideas and plan political action. These "tertulias" networked with one another and plugged into a larger anarchist culture through a popular anarchist press. In the 1930s similar small groups of friends and comrades called "grupos de afinidad" or affinity groups formed the grassroots of the Spanish anarchist federation (FAI), which briefly came to power in Spain in 1936 (Dolgoff xxvi-xxvii).

Affinity groups come together freely. Action is personal and voluntary; no one "represents" the group or delegates tasks to its members. However, when the Spanish anarchists in 1936 were faced with the myriad tasks involved in running a country, they supplemented affinity groups with a variety of decentralized structures. Industry was reorganized on the basis of workers' collectives that elected managers from among themselves. Some effort was made to do away with all "external" incentives like money, but these did not last.

"Open Source" Programming Networks: Self-Organization through Reflexivity

Our own era, the turn of the 21st century, offers much better examples of true network organization of work on anarchist principles. Software design has become one of the most essential and lucrative sectors in the "new economy." One of the remarkable achievements in software design, a computer-operating system superior in many ways to Microsoft Windows called "Linux," was created by an online community of programmers working for free. The person who initiated and coordinated this effort, Linus Torvald, did not delegate tasks or issue directives. He had no means of enforcing his will, since he wasn't paying anyone (nor was he being paid). He simply made an open offer to anyone and everyone linked to the Net with some understanding of programming to contribute. Hundreds of talented people from around the world took part simply because the work and the virtual community engaged in it were stimulating (see the box "Free Labour").

Like all networks, the productivity of this one depended on open information sharing. Documentation on the Web ensured transparency. The underlying "code" (written instructions governing how the software

behaves) of commercial software is a jealously guarded secret. Linux, by contrast, was "open-source," meaning not only that the code could be downloaded and modified, but also that anyone could go to the Web site and read discussions of and rationales for design decisions made along the way. "The Linux community," Eric Steven Raymond observes,

> ... seemed to resemble a great babbling bazaar of differing agendas and approaches (aptly symbolized by the Linux archive sites, who'd take submissions from *anyone*) out of which a coherent and stable system could seemingly emerge only by a succession of miracles. (Raymond)

The astonishing thing was that instead of producing confusion and inconsistency, the process resulted in a product that was simple, "coherent and stable." Torvald's main contribution to maintaining coherence was not telling people what to do but showing them what they had done. As contributions were added, he would publish new versions so that everyone could see how the overall product was taking shape. In this way he ensured "reflexivity"—feedback between collective actions and results.

The Linux process demonstrated that anarchist forms of order could be effective in getting complex tasks accomplished. The network that did it was large, translocal, indeed global in scale, and motivated by no "external" incentives—no money, no chain of command, not even one established by majority vote. Raymond points out that in a similar project that he was involved in (the design of "fetchmail") the number of collaborators—up to 800—was far more than most firms could afford to hire. "Perhaps in the end," he writes,

... the open-source culture will triumph not because cooperation is morally right or software "hoarding" is morally wrong (assuming you believe the latter, which neither Linus nor I do), but simply because the closed-source world cannot win an evolutionary arms race with open-source communities that can put orders of magnitude more skilled time into a problem.

The process can engage large numbers over great distances and stably over time. "The development of the GNU Emacs editor," Raymond points out:

... is an extreme and instructive example; it has absorbed the efforts of hundreds of contributors over 15 years into a unified architectural vision, despite high turnover and the fact that only one person (its author) has been continuously active during all that time. No closed-source editor has ever matched this longevity record.

Not only can the network anarchist approach be as effective against the kinds of obstacles that Michels and Weber thought insurmountable without bureaucracy, but it might be more effective than traditional forms of management in commercial enterprises.

BOX 6.2:

FREE LABOUR: THE LINUX PROJECT

Karl Marx shared with anarchists a faith that people, under the right conditions, would work together willingly and without any need for coercion or "external" incentives like money. They would offer their services "freely"—both in the sense of without constraint and also without recompense—to the community. Marx saw work as a public project through which we transform the world and define who we are to ourselves and others. Work contains its own intrinsic rewards.

Something akin to this is apparently what motivates computer programmers to collaborate in designing "free" software. DiBona, Ockman, and Stone, in their online text *Open Sources: Voices from the Open Source Revolution*, ask, "Why do people write free software? Why do they give away freely what they could charge hundreds of dollars an hour for? What do they get out of it?" Their answer is worth quoting at length:

The motivation is not just altruism. The contributors here may not be loaded down with Microsoft stock options, but each has achieved a reputation that should assure him opportunities that pay the rent and feeds the kids. From the outside this can seem like a paradox; you can't eat free software after all. The answer lies, in part, in thinking beyond conventional notions of work and compensation. We are witnessing a new economic model take shape, not just a new culture.

Eric Raymond has become a kind of self-appointed participant anthropologist to the Open Source community, and in his writings he touches on the reasons why the people develop software only to give it away.

Keep in mind that these people have been, for the most part, coding for years, and don't see programming itself as burdensome, or as work. A very complex project like Apache or the Linux kernel brings the satisfaction of the ultimate in intellectual exercise. Much like the rush a runner feels while running a race, a true programmer will feel this same rush after writing a perfect routine or tight piece of code. It is difficult to describe the joy felt after completing or debugging a hideously tricky piece of recursive code that has been a source of trouble for days.

The point is that many programmers code because it is what they love to do, and in fact it is how they define their intellect. Without coding, a programmer feels less of a person, much like an athlete deprived of an opportunity to compete. Discipline can be a problem with programmers as much as with athletes; many programmers really don't enjoy maintaining a piece of code after having mastered it.

Still, other programmers don't take this "macho" view of their craft, and take a more scholarly view. Many programmers consider themselves, rightly, to be scientists. Scientists aren't supposed to hoard profits from their inventions, they are supposed to publish and share their inventions for all to benefit from. A scientist isn't supposed to let profits come at the expense of the pursuit of knowledge.

What all these introspections on programming have in common is an emphasis on reputation. Programming is a gift culture: the value of a programmer's work can only come from sharing it with others. That value is enhanced when the work is more widely shared, and that value is enhanced when the work is more completely shared by showing the source, not just the results from a pre-compiled binary.

Programming is also about empowerment, what Eric Raymond calls "scratching an itch." Most Open Source projects began with frustration: looking for a tool to do a job and finding none, or finding one that was broken or poorly maintained. Eric Raymond began fetchmail this way; Larry Wall began Perl this way; Linus Torvalds began Linux this way. Empowerment, in many ways, is the most important concept underlying Stallman's motivation for starting the GNU project.

Source: Chris DiBona, Sam Ockman, and Mark Stone, *Open Sources: Voices from the Open Source Revolution,* O'Reilly & Associates, Inc, 1999, October 23, 2005, www.oreilly.com/catalog/opensources/book/toc.html.

Reflexivity is clearly important to network self-organization. Consider the example of "video Pong," demonstrated by Loren Carpenter at a meeting of computer graphics specialists. Carpenter gave his audience hand-held paddles with contrasting colours on each side and hooked up a video feedback so that everyone in the audience had a bird's-eye view of the audience. He asked one half of the audience to flip the paddle to one side and the other to flip to the opposites side to create a "court" on screen. He then asked someone to create a "ball" by flipping over her paddle and two small groups to create "paddles" in the same way.

After some initial coaching, the audience was able to coordinate their actions independently of Carpenter by simply responding to one another's actions as relayed back to them on the video screen. They "began to play a giant game of self-organized video Pong, finally creating a graphic representation of an airplane and flying it around the screen" (Rheingold 177). In this case, the network linked by video feedback is also physically assembled in one place. However, information technology has the potential to extend the scale and geographic range of the reflexive feedback, and therefore of self-organization, well beyond the local.

Reflexivity and Self-Mobilizing Demonstrations

Rheingold documents how a similar mechanism helped over a million people rapidly to self-organize a mass demonstration powerful enough to bring down a government. In 2001 the Philippines' corrupt president, Joseph Estrada, was facing impeachment proceedings. (Impeachment—that is, removal from office—is one way of disciplining office-holders in bureaucracies who abuse their power.) When it became evident that the system was about to fail—that insiders loyal to Estrada had suspended the proceedings—people began distributing text messages, which read "Go 2EDSA, Wear blck." Text messages can be sent in batches to all or some of the people in one's address book. Those with lots of contacts, particularly if they are respected and trusted by those contacts, become important "nodes" in cellphone-linked networks.

From node to node, the message spread quickly and widely. Within 75 minutes, 20,000 people had responded to the call. They assembled in the capital, Manila, on Epifanio de los Santos Avenue (a.k.a. EDSA), many of them, as instructed, wearing black. Over the next four days, more than a million joined the demonstration. Governments cannot act against crowds of this scale without sabotaging their own legitimacy. The military withdrew its support and the government collapsed.

As text messages moved throughout the cellphone network, duplications and cross-postings multiplied. People separated from one another in their homes, on the streets,

in offices, could gauge the scale of the mobilization as it was taking shape by the number of text messages in their in-box. This was the reflexive element of the mobilization, allowing each to see how many others were filled with the same anger and intent and were ready to move in the same direction.

Attending a demonstration is a bit like attending a party; you are more likely to go if you have some idea of who else is going to be there. If there are going to be 20,000 rather than 20, there will be greater safety in numbers and more of a political impact. You and others like you are more willing to take part. As you signal your intent, the self-referential loop continues. Collective self-knowledge lowers in this way what Granovetter calls the "action threshold" of crowds.

Text messaging has a number of advantages as a tool of popular resistance. It is cheap. In some developing countries where conventional infrastructure is lacking, it is the only reliable way to bridge distance. Telephone networks are also instances of "peer-to-peer" communication. E-mail, by contrast, is not. When you send an e-mail, it goes first to a large computer called a "server" owned by an Internet service provider, such as AOL or Sympatico, before being sent out to the recipient's computer. Spurred by post-9/11 fears of terrorism, governments have extended their powers to seize and search records of e-mails and Web transactions stored on these servers. Peer-to-peer communications are not routed through or recorded at central hubs and are therefore not as easily subject to surveillance or control.

Text messaging is also an example of mobile peer-to-peer. In other words, users are not stuck at their desks; they can remain connected while moving through the city or around the globe. When members of a connected network can move about, they can self-organize in real time in the way that we saw in the video Pong example. This is what happened in Manila. It also happened in Seattle in 1999, except here reflexivity did more than merely lower the action threshold of the demonstrators.

Anti-WTO protesters in Seattle had at their disposal a wide variety of media. In addition to cellphones they used hand-held digital video and audio that they could either upload or directly stream to the World Wide Web at "indymedia" sites and download to the streets again with wireless Palm Pilots. Street anarchists, in particular the Direct Action Network (DAN), employed radios and police scanners so that they could adapt to police tactics. The protests went on for days and eventually police "successfully squashed DAN's communication system," prompting an alternative described here by Paul de Armond.

> The solution to the infrastructure attack was quickly resolved by purchasing new Nextel cell phones. According to Han Shan, the Ruckus Society's WTO coordinator, his organization and other protest groups that formed the Direct Action Network used the Nextel system to create a cellular grid over the city. They broke into talk groups of eight people each. One of the eight overlapped with another talk group, helping to quickly communicate through the ranks.

Armond invokes a memorable image of all of this real-time information exchange "floating above the tear gas [as] a pulsing infosphere of enormous bandwidth, reaching around the planet via the internet" (qtd. in Rheingold 161). The point is that the "pulsing infosphere," like the video feedback in video Pong, was a means by which dispersed demonstrators could self-organize on the ground in response to events as they

unfolded. Rheingold calls groups that physically self-organize through mobile communications "smart mobs."

New information technologies were also important in the mobilization leading up to the demonstrations in Seattle. The Internet was a central medium of information exchange. Organizations like the Global Exchange, Third World Network, and Rainforest Action Network published their analyses of the issues on their Web sites. People exchanged ideas more interactively on sites like Indymedia where readers can post news and commentary, or through listservs and other forms of online discussion. Organizations, most of which were by no means anarchistic in structure, were merely nodes in an online network that included many who neither needed nor sought any organizational affiliation—individuals and affinity groups.

Think of the parallel with the transitory teams of the 1960s. Most activists who showed up for demonstrations were not members of the SDS or Mobe or SUPA. They simply "plugged in" to movement culture and news through "underground" and corporate forms of mass media. Oberschall thought the reliance on corporate media undermined the movements' ability to shape their own culture and set their own priorities. The "pulsing infosphere" of the late 20th century is far more under the control of the activists themselves.

Just as important, with the Internet and phone systems as distribution networks, these are not mass media. They are not one-way media distributing messages from one sender to many recipients. These are two-way media in which recipients themselves become broadcasters. In addition to the shift in power from corporate media to movement media, there is a corresponding shift in power from movement organizations to unaffiliated movement participants.

Remember from the previous chapter how members of affinity groups resist the ideas of solidarity and collective identity. They do not want organizations to "represent" them, speak for them, or define who they are. They want to contribute to action with others from a standpoint of radical personal autonomy. Networks, self-organized through the "pulsing infosphere" of new media, may be one of the only ways that their action could ever take shape on a large scale or have significant political effect.

Individuals and groups could sign on and off to projects flexibly according to tastes and interests, just as the collaborators to Linux did, without ever subordinating their will or identity to something larger than themselves. Perhaps affinity groups plugged in to communications networks will become the 21st century's "transitory teams on steroids."

CONCLUSION

We began this chapter with two questions. How democratic can groups and organizations be? Is it inevitable that organizations eventually become undemocratic? The cases that we looked at—British women's centres and open-source programming communities—demonstrate that sometimes, under some conditions, groups can be very democratic. These examples undermine the assumption that many people make that human beings have a fixed, inherent tendency to follow and take orders from leaders.

However, the sociological argument advanced by Michels and Weber is much more difficult to challenge even with these cases. The Michels-Weber thesis states that bureaucratic organization, which is hierarchical and oligarchic, is technically superior to other forms. It is the most efficient way of coordinating the activities of large numbers of people dispersed over large territories. While anarchist organization might briefly be possible, it can never withstand competition from or head-on confrontation with the large-scale bureaucracies that organize states and corporations and carry out the ongoing business of complex modern societies.

The efficiency of bureaucracy derives from its strict division of labour and chain of command. Its predictability and reliability from its impersonality—the way in which it separates people from their offices or administrative functions and inscribes all administrative rules, procedures, and ongoing transactions in external written form. Information flows vertically in the hierarchy and accumulates in the higher offices where it is monopolized along with technical knowledge and skill as a resource of power.

In both the cases that we examined, conscious efforts were made to ensure that knowledge, skill, and information are distributed horizontally and are difficult to monopolize. Women's centres attempted to minimize the division of labour by rotating tasks, but programming communities leave specialization up to contributors. Likely people do choose to focus on areas of the project in which they feel they have the greatest competence. In both cases people did away with chains of command. The two differ in the emphasis placed on documentation. Written documentation is crucial to programming communities. It contributes to reflexivity, but also ensures the horizontal accessibility of knowledge across the Net and available to *anyone*. This generic, perhaps impersonal, feature enables these network communities to coordinate large numbers across great distances—something that bureaucracies also do, although not in quite the same way.

A final, but quite striking contrast between the women's centres and programming communities has to do with the form of decision making. Women's centres have put into practice well-known alternatives to representative democracy: direct democracy, or decision making by everyone concerned, and resolution of disagreement through consensus rather than voting. They are still, like bureaucracies, employing a deliberative process that results in collective resolutions. Programming communities, like "smart mobs," rely on quasi-automatic "self-organization" accomplished by reflecting back to participants rich information about their action in relation to one another and their environment, and allowing participants individually to decide what to do next.

Social movement actors like the women's centres, New Left anti-structure advocates, or present-day techno-anarchists do want to democratize society. They begin with the "lifeworld," their immediate interactions with others, but envision a democratic transformation throughout the social order. It is this vision over which the Michels-Weber thesis casts its most sombre shadow. The promise that techno-anarchism holds out against it is largely theoretical and speculative. It depends first on the idea that societies in the 21st century are increasingly network based as suggested by Castells and others. As the Wikipedia people would say, "the neutrality and factual accuracy" of this claim is disputed.

Second, it depends on the claim, made by people like Leonard, that truly "open-source" networks are technically superior to ones in which information is jealously guarded. Furthermore, the model of self-organizing networks may be technically superior only in certain contexts. Indeed, it may work only for certain types of human tasks like programming, writing online encyclopedias, or doing research. Until we

know more, how you evaluate the Michels-Weber thesis will depend as much on what might be possible as what has actually been proven in practice.

REFERENCES

Bantjes, Rod. *Improved Earth: Prairie Space as Modern Artefact, 1869-1944.* Toronto: University of Toronto Press, 2005.

Barlow, John Perry. "A Declaration of the Independence of Cyberspace," February 8, 1996. Electronic Frontier Foundation, October 23, 2005, http://homes.eff.org/~barlow/Declaration-Final.html.

Brown, M. Helen. "Organizing Activity in the Women's Movement: An Example of Distributed Leadership." *International Social Movement Research* 2 (1989): 225-240.

Castells, Manuel. "Materials for an Exploratory Theory of the Network Society." *British Journal of Sociology* 51, no. 1 (2000): 5-24.

de Armond, Paul. "Black Flag Over Seattle," February 29, 2000. *Albion Monitor*, November 16, 2006, www.monitor.net/monitor/seattlewto/index.html.

Dolgoff, Sam. *The Anarchist Collectives: Workers' Self-Management in the Spanish Revolution, 1936-1939.* Edited by and introductory essay by Murray Bookchin. New York: Free Life Editions, 1974.

Engels, Friedrich. *The Condition of the Working Class in England: From Personal Observation and Authentic Sources.* 1844. Introduction by E.J. Hobsbawm. London: Granada, 1982.

Freeman, Jo. "The Tyranny of Structure-lessness." *Berkeley Journal of Sociology* 17 (1972–1973): 151–164.

Michels, Robert. *Political Parties: A Sociological Study of the Oligarchical Tendencies of Modern Democracy.* 1915. Translated by Eden and Cedar Paul. Glencoe: Free Press, 1949.

Raymond, Eric Steven. *The Cathedral and the Bazaar.* Thyrsus Enterprises, 2000. October 23, 2005, www.catb.org/~esr/writings/cathedral-bazaar/cathedral-bazaar/index.html.

Rheingold, Howard. *Smart Mobs: The Next Social Revolution.* Cambridge: Perseus Publishing, 2002.

Weber, Max. "Bureaucracy." *From Max Weber: Essays in Sociology,* edited by H.H. Gerth and C.W. Mills. New York: Oxford University Press, 1946.

CRITICAL THINKING QUESTIONS

1. How democratic can groups and organizations be?
2. Is it inevitable that organizations eventually become undemocratic?
3. Are there new social conditions now that Michels and Weber did not take into account in their pessimistic assessment of the potential for genuine democracy? To what extent should any of the following make us revise their assessment: (a) new information technologies; (b) network capitalism; (c) the fact that many radical social movements do not go head to head with states or corporations?
4. How widely could the wiki model of self-organizing human collaboration extend into other realms of human endeavour, particularly off-line realms?

FURTHER READING

Axelrod, Robert M. *The Evolution of Cooperation.* New York: Basic Books, 1984.
  Anarchists have faith that humans tend to self-organize without external coercion. This book documents and explains some remarkable examples of spontaneous mutual aid that add credibility to anarchist claims.

Castells, Manuel. "Materials for an Exploratory Theory of the Network Society." *British Journal of Sociology* 51, no. 1 (2000): 5–24.
  This is a good place to begin if you want to explore the idea that modern structural changes might provide new openings for anarchist models of social organization.

Kasmir, Sharryn. *The Myth of Mondragon: Cooperatives, Politics, and Working-Class Life in a Basque Town.* SUNY Series in the Anthropology of Work. Albany: State University of New York Press, 1996.
  This is a critical look at the world's most famous complex of worker co-operatives from the perspective of workers. One of the myths that the author questions is the idea that worker co-operatives reconcile workers and management in a way that makes unions unnecessary.

Vickers, Jill. "Bending the Iron Law of Oligarchy: Debates on the Feminization of Organization and Political Process in the English Canadian Women's Movement, 1970–1988." *Women and Social Change*, edited by J.D. Wine and J. Ristock. Toronto: James Lorimer and Co., 1991.

Vickers evaluates the limited success of the National Action Committee on the Status of Women's efforts to remain decentralized and democratic despite the challenges of coordinating activities across great distances and cultural divides.

Zald, Mayer N., and Roberta Ash. "Social Movement Organizations: Growth, Decay and Change." *Collective Behaviour and Social Movements*, edited by Louis E. Genevie. Itasca: F.E. Peacock, 1971.

Zald and Ash argue that social movements do not always succumb to oligarchy and conservatism. They offer a good summary of the Michels-Weber hypothesis and give a list of counter-hypotheses that anyone serious about this topic should be familiar with.

RELEVANT WEB SITES

ACT UP Guide to Affinity Groups
www.actupny.org/documents/CDdocuments/Affinity.html
ACT UP's how-to guide on affinity groups.

Anarchist Action Network
www.zpub.com/notes/aadl.html
More anarchist resources with a youth culture edge.

Flag.Blackened.net.–The Pierre J. Prudhon Memorial Computer
http://flag.blackened.net
The best site for resources on the history and modern practice of anarchism.

Mobilization for Global Justice (Washington, DC)
www.globalizethis.org
The link on this site to "Affinity Group Information and Resources" gives an overview of affinity groups from an activist point of view. The history section makes the connection between affinity groups, Spanish anarchism, and worker self-management.

Wikipedia on consensus decision making
http://en.wikipedia.org/wiki/Consensus_decision-making
Wikipedia is generally good on anarchist-related issues. The entry on consensus decision making is an excellent guide to the principles and practice of non-hierarchical democracy.

Chapter 7

TERRORISM AND THE "WAR ON TERROR"

INTRODUCTION:
THE FLQ MANIFESTO

In October 1970 Francis Simard and his fellow members of the Chenier cell of the Front de Libération du Québec (FLQ) are on the road driving north out of New York toward Quebec, listening to the car radio. This is how they learn, to their surprise, that the "Liberation" cell back in Montreal has kidnapped James Cross, British commercial attaché to Canada.

The CBC announcer, complying with one of the hostage takers' demands, reads the FLQ manifesto.

> We pulled over to the side of the road to listen.... "The Front de Libération du Québec ... is a group of québécois, we're fed up with our spineless government bending over backwards to seduce American millionaires...." We knew the manifesto by heart. We'd helped write it. We'd fought over every word, for hours at a time, every comma, every sentence. It was our manifesto. But when we heard it read on the radio, it stopped belonging to us.... Nobody talked. Nobody could have. (Simard 13–14)

They arrive back in Montreal in a state of paranoia, knowing that the police will be on high alert, perhaps already waiting for them. They cannot contact other FLQ cells, but they are desperate to know how the Liberation cell will handle the kidnapping, and, more importantly, how the government will respond. "We read the papers. We listened to the radio. We talked" (Simard 15).

The cellular structure of the organization is designed to protect them at times like these. It was borrowed from the model of anti-Nazi resistance movements in occupied France. Resistance cells were relatively autonomous and each member knew as little as possible about the names, locations, and operations of members in other cells. If a cell was infiltrated or a member captured, tortured, and forced to talk, the damage to the rest of the network would be limited.

The FLQ are a target for police repression because their organization is, just as the French Resistance was, willing to use violence as a tactic of resistance. They had already been engaged in the theft of arms and explosives; had robbed banks to raise funds, and had blown things up to make political points. How could this all make sense to them? Our first task in this chapter is to try to understand the internal logic of violent political activism. Through cases studies of the FLQ and al Qaeda, we will learn how "terrorist" networks are structured. We will also investigate the meaning, for perpetrators, of the decision to kill for a social movement cause.

In addition to understanding, we need to explain why activists resort to terror in some contexts and not in others. We will consider a structural explanation that helps to explain the appeal of terror to al Qaeda and the FLQ as well as the decline of that appeal within the Quebec independence movement. In the process we will discover how terror initiates a "dialogue" with and about the state and a "discursive struggle" over the meanings of state versus insurgent violence. The course that violence takes depends crucially on how the state answers the provocation. We will use what we learn to question the wisdom of the current War on Terror.

FLQ PROPAGANDA OF THE DEED

Context: Revolutionary Action as a Moral Obligation

Simard and his comrades proceed to carry out their own hostage taking, one that plays out toward a tragic and brutal conclusion. In order to understand what was going on in their heads, you need to remember the over-heated context of 1970 as the radicals experienced it. The Great Refusal had brought France to a standstill for a few weeks in the spring of 1968. A worker/student revolution had almost been ignited.

The U.S. military machine was pound-ing away at the anti-colonial resistance of the Vietnamese, defoliating the land with deadly chemicals, carpet-bombing civilians, and melting flesh with burning napalm. In April 1970 the war escalated as a new U.S. president (Nixon) announced that troops were being deployed to Cambodia as well. Outraged students demonstrated across the U.S. and Canada. At Kent State University, four of them were shot dead by National Guardsmen.

One Canadian peace activist recalled, "I remember being in tears about Cambodia and the Kent State events, and then phoning people, saying, 'We've got to do something.' I mean, when were they going to turn their rifles on us?" (qtd. in Kostash 224). On May 11, an anti-war demonstration in To-ronto erupted into violence when charged by police on horseback. Demonstrators "... scattered and ran over to city hall square where a hundred motorcycle cops charged them again. Swooped down with batons. 'I was standing beside a kid whose head was split open, he was gushing blood, I was yell-ing, "Somebody help! This boy is dying" and a cop came after me, flailing away. It was positively American'" (qtd. in Kostash 225).

Simard and his comrades felt that world events placed an inescapable moral obliga-tion upon them. As Pierre Vallières, an FLQ-ist and theorist, put it in 1968:

> Sartrian responsibility, like Chris-tian responsibility, was only an ideology that served as a façade, an ideology required by the daily spectacle of millions of innocent people throughout the world being massacred by the imperialist West. "Lucidity," verbal protests, peti-tions, scathing essays, denuncia-tions that earn you the Nobel Prize, etc.—"refined" and artful ways of washing one's hands! And to think that after twenty years, in the era of the atomic bomb, the war in Vietnam, famine in India, and the bloody repression of the revolutions in Santo Domingo [Dominican Republic], the Congo, and Watts, this "respectable" comedy still goes on in Saint-Germian-des-Prés [hangout of the philosopher Sartre in Paris] and elsewhere. (153)

This awful sense of responsibility weighed heavily upon them in October 1970 as they awaited the government's response to the Liberation cell's demands.

To their disgust, they see that the kidnap-ping is not being taken seriously enough. The Quebec premier, Robert Bourassa, does not even cancel his trip to talk to U.S. financiers.

> FLQ demands were called "futile" and "far-fetched." The manifesto was a collection of nonsense. Of course, people were living or trying to live in the slums of East End Mon-treal, across town from the wealth of Westmount, but what could be done about it? Of course, you can't

often work in French in Quebec, but
we're living in North America, don't
forget that. Of course there's social
injustice, but the government's trying to correct it and that takes time!
(Simard 16–17)

The government takes a hard line in
negotiations and the Liberation cell starts
to compromise on its demands. It no longer
demands the reinstatement of the Lapalme
workers. Four hundred and fifty unionized
mail truck drivers had lost their jobs when
the federal postal service reorganized mail
distribution in Montreal. A violent strike,
characterized by bombings and attacks on
post office property, had ensued, which
FLQists interpreted as incipient working-
class revolution. The only remaining condition for James Cross' release was the freeing
of "political prisoners"—FLQists jailed for
a variety of crimes associated with their
violent resistance.

Public broadcast media become the
unwitting channel through which the Liberation cell communicates with the rest of
the FLQ. The Chenier cell can communicate
with no one. Simard and his four comrades
must decide independently what they are
going to do if the negotiations fail and
Liberation wins no concessions. They share
with the others an interpretive framework
that comes from their common experiences,
cultural backgrounds, reading, and past discussions together. All of this gives shape to
their thinking about tactics.

Unlike many North American radicals,
most of them come from genuinely working-class backgrounds. This is not surprising as the Québécois in 1960s Canada are
overrepresented among the working class,
the unemployed, and the poor. This is an artifact of the English Protestant domination
of capital in Quebec (the same condition
that stimulated the rise of the co-operative

movement discussed in Chapter 2). One
of the most painful memories for young
FLQists, from their experience growing up
working class and poor, is watching how
alienation crushes the dreams and aspirations of their parents.

It is not so much physical deprivations
(although there are many of these to remember) as injuries to the psyche, what
Richard Sennett calls the "hidden injuries
of class" that hurt the most. Vallières, in his
book, *White Niggers of America*, describes
confronting his mother and "through her,
the entire [Québécois] population":

> "For God's sake, why do you go on
> existing?"
> [...]
> "You're not living any more
> ... you're just running on the last
> momentum of ... I don't really know
> what. You're going to die of old age
> the way a watch wears out in the
> end, inevitably. Why don't you even
> protest? Why?"
> "We don't have the means to
> protest. And besides, even if we
> did ..."
> [...]
> "We don't have the money, we
> don't have the education, we don't
> have any experience in all those
> things that you call politics. What
> do you want us to do? With whom?
> We don't even know each other in
> this damn town...." (137)

Vallières has read Marx; in fact, he
describes "discovering" him as a kind of
revelation.

> When I discovered Marxism, I felt
> as if I had found what I had always
> been seeking, what my father too
> had sought confusedly ... (201). I felt

as if I were at last beginning to live in open air. I came back to social reality, no longer seeing it as a weight to drag me down or as an obstacle to freedom but as the locus of that freedom; no longer seeing it as a "spectacle" but as a responsibility to be assumed *together with other men.* Truth and freedom no longer stood outside history, outside our past, present, and future. I was coming to understand that they are born, live, and die with us; that we affirm their reality and power through action, through practice, through continual transformation of the world.

I was coming to understand that to agree to live is to take responsibility for a collective history that is being made at the same time always remains to be made, that is ceaselessly made, unmade, and remade, according to our knowledge and abilities, to our struggles, passions, hopes, interests, needs, and choices. (200)

However, he does not see the solution to his parents' problem in classical Marxist strategy. He is enamoured by the idea of transformative action, but not necessarily of building working-class community and organization. Simard, in his moment of indecision, considers backing down from confrontation and working on "building an organization," but he and his cell, without even discussing why, do neither. Instead they prepare for a second kidnapping—this time of Pierre Laporte, Quebec minister of Labour.

They wait for a final press conference to hear if any of the Liberation cell's demands will be met. The enormity of their choice of how they will act if the answer is "no" preys upon their minds. They know that the path they are about to embark upon may involve

murder, but they do not speak about this; they do not have to.

> We had to react. And quickly too, to show them we were serious and sincere. The way I'm putting it, the way I state the logic, might sound shitty. What we did and what we wanted to do in the FLQ didn't have anything to do with adventure. It wasn't action for action's sake. We weren't looking for an outlet for our need to revolt, it wasn't some kind of personal assertion thing. We were trying to get hold of our lives, our situation as workers, our poverty. For us, the words in the manifesto weren't abstract theory. They weren't some kind of text, a bunch of pleasing words strung together in the comfort of an Outremont salon. We weren't mamma's boys with guilty consciences. *We* were the manifesto. It was our lives, our daily grind in Ville Jacques-Cartier, Saint-Henri, Gaspé, in our daily work. It was our lives, my father's life, Paul and Jacques and Bernard's father too. It was our life, our daily bread.... (Simard 20)

Violence as Communicative Action

The words of the manifesto, Simard claims, arise out of action, the hard experiences of working-class lives. But they also demand action as a way of embodying the words, giving them weight, making them real. He sees both words and actions as a genuine assertion of identity, but a collective, rather than personal, identity.

He and his fellow revolutionaries understand their contemplated violence as a communicative act, amplified by global media.

The first order of business was to keep October from getting away from us. It was the first time the FLQ undertook an action like that, an action that went beyond Quebec's borders. Media all over the world talked about it, breaking the illusion of a democratic Canada. It was the first time the FLQ published a manifesto. A text that attempted to describe what the FLQ was, what its objectives were, a manifesto distributed throughout the population. October was a kind of act of communication, not just because we published a manifesto; it was action talking too. Unveiling the force of people who'd never had the right to speak before. Showing that we'd had it with the society of profit-takers. Making other people want to speak out and take charge of their lives by taking a step forward. Showing that progress is possible. That nothing's immutable and set down for ever. Taking our exploitation and pain and poverty away from those who profited from it, triumphing over it … by wiping it out. (Simard 21)

Their "speech" is directed at different "audiences." One is the international community. The FLQ hope to take their place alongside the notorious urban terrorist organizations of the day—the Palestine Liberation Organization (PLO), the IRA, and the Tupamaros—and to highlight to the world the injustices suffered by those in whose name they act. They are speaking to the Quebec and federal governments. Most importantly, they are speaking to their fellow Québécois, burdened, like their parents, by centuries of silence and acquiescence.

For Simard, *refraining* from action would also be a kind of "speech."

It would be like saying to the guys at Lapalme, to the cheap labour, to the workers getting laid off, the ones caught in the minimum wage trap, on unemployment or welfare, "Don't even think about trying to take power, getting a hold of your destiny, running your own life, because the guys who have the power and know how to use it, they'll never let you." (Simard 19)

Simard implies that there are two ways to assist the strikers and working-class people of his parents' generation. One is to act/speak for them, in this case to coerce the federal government to reinstate the striking workers. The other is to "demonstrate" that they can act/speak for themselves in a way that the authorities will have to take notice. This is the main point: to actively prove to working-class Québécois people that they can step up and take control of the forces that shape their world. They must act, as Simard puts it, in order to "build and structure the will to struggle" in others (Simard 20).

FLQists understand the colonization of the Québécois to be in part an internal colonization. Vallières' treatise, *White Niggers of America*, draws the parallel between the debilitating sense of social and cultural inferiority of the Québécois and Blacks in North America and former European colonies. This is a problem not even identified by Marx. For the FLQ, public violence, amplified by the media, becomes a kind of moral "shock treatment" intended to jar people into new ways of thinking about themselves and their potential to transform themselves and their world. This was a version of the Cuban idea that a dedicated band of revolutionaries could be the "small motor that would activate the large motor of people's action" (Fournier 72).

There were two important differences. The Cuban revolutionaries began with more traditionally military actions and objectives—capturing territory, attacking, and weakening the state's military forces. The FLQ actions were designed to play out first in the realms of "demonstration," signification, and the construction of identity. Secondly, Cuban revolutionaries' violence was directed first and foremost at military targets—people to be sure, but those who had enlisted in the ugly business of war. FLQ violence was directed first at property, then, with the kidnappings, at civilians. The latter is one of the defining features of modern "terrorism."

FLQ Terrorism: Violence against Civilians

The moral implications of targeting a person for violence weigh heavily on Simard and his comrades.

> From a human point of view, you can't accept a kidnapping. You can't be "for" a kidnapping. There's something odious about bargaining with human life. Even if I could justify it politically by saying it was already going on day in and day out, that every day they were bargaining with the lives of the unemployed, with welfare recipients, with the chronically ill in hospitals. That the people in power were doing the bargaining. The ones "administering" life and health as if it was a big shipping warehouse outfit. Sickness was another piece of merchandise, a profit centre like the others. (18)

He seems to be aware that the political justification cannot carry the weight that it would need to in order to clear his con-

science. They never speak about this, but they all know that if they act on their plan, they will threaten to kill their hostage and may have to carry through with that threat. How does a "moral" person murder someone in cold blood?

> But the whole time, every second, there was a kind of reticence ... a fear ... a refusal to go through with it. You feel you are preparing for a kind of suicide action. A leap into the unknown. You get the feeling that afterwards things will be different, life will never be the same again, you won't be the same person you were before.
>
> On the human level the moment is very strong. A sudden feeling that one life has ended and a new and totally unknown one is about to begin. It's a lot more than just waking up in the morning and starting a new day! It was like everything I'd experienced up until then (I was 23 years old) came to a halt. As if the 23 years I had lived were coming to an end. A total transformation that starts in your guts and flows out of your skin. Like a total break ... with everything that went before.
>
> I've said I'm against violence. I've never felt aggressive towards other human beings. I don't have a grudge against anyone. Everything I did was for and with other people. But here was a concrete action that went against all that. You're going to kidnap somebody, another human being. His name is Pierre Laporte, he's the Minister of Labour and Immigration and one of the people most responsible for the situation that turned you into an FLQ member in the first place, one

of the people responsible for the situation that makes action necessary. But he's still a human being. And the kind of contact you're going to have is human contact, because you're going to kidnap and sequester him. (24)

As the moment draws near, he feels strangely alone, and aware of the personal, individual nature of the choice and its consequences.

Everything was finished around four or five in the afternoon. We were ready; our deadline was Jérôme Choquette's press conference that was supposed to reply to the final demands of the Libération Cell. It was set for six o'clock. Everything was ready. All that remained was time ... time spent waiting with your fears ... your anxiety ... your uncertainties.

When you get ready to do a thing like that, you feel very much alone.... You wouldn't do it if the others weren't with you, but that doesn't mean you're in it any less. You're still a whole human being. And you feel it in your own way, in your guts....

You wait. You pace. You sit down. You get up. You look at the others and know they're going through the same thing, with the same feelings, anxiety, tensions.

You talk to yourself to try and forget the silence and the time ticking down. It's almost too much. You talk to yourself. You ask yourself questions to keep from breaking. Indecision and uncertainty have a hold on you and won't let go. "Okay, we have to do it ... but are we *going* to

do it?" It's great to say we're ready, but we haven't done anything yet. It's not six o'clock yet.... Maybe the government's answer will be positive.... And even if Choquette says no and refuses to negotiate, does that really mean we have to get up, leave the house, get in to the car and go ... ? Is it really necessary? It's not too late to call it off. All you'd have to say is, "Sorry, I'm not up to it ... I can't go through with it." Then everything stops. We'll go on building an organization the way we intended. The manifesto was broadcast throughout Quebec, there's always that. A lot of people supported it. (Simard 26–27)

At the press conference, Choquette does not say what they want to hear. They are offended as much by the tone as the content of the message: "it was full of condescension, full of the contemptful [sic] smugness of the ruling class whose feathers we'd ruffled" (Simard 29).

The only possible answer to that was to carry out another kidnapping.
... We weren't wearing smiles on our faces. We didn't drive off shouting. "Hurray, we're on our way! They refused to negotiate, all right! Into the breach, forward comrades!" We went to the door, not exactly depressed, but on the other hand ... there's a whole distorted image around it, you act, but not without reticence. You count the steps from the house to the car. You're walking on air, you're not going to some kind of party. You feel strange. Humanly, it's very heavy. As if your body weighed more than before....

When I remember that day, I can't picture myself or the others.

I recall the atmosphere but I don't see anybody. I can't remember much about the inside of the house, just the general shape. As if the tension of the moment had devoured everything. The physical environment disappears completely when you experience a moment like that. (Simard 30–31)

French-speaking radicals were more likely than the English to have read Sartre and to be immersed in the "structure of feeling" of existentialism. There is something distinctly existentialist about this lonely commitment to action, experienced as a kind of tragic destiny and a "leap into the unknown." Existentialists understood freely chosen action as self-creation, writing the narrative of self *for* oneself rather than knuckling under, following a conventional script, and thereby becoming an "inauthentic" instrument of the powers that be. Perhaps this was the FLQ's answer to the question Vallières poses to his mother: "Why do you exist?"

The story of the kidnapping is a gripping one. Perhaps you don't remember how it ends. Simard and his comrades do end up murdering Laporte and stuffing his body into the trunk of a car that they abandon for the police to find. You may want to read the rest of Simard's account for yourself. I have led you through it this far so that you can start to comprehend, if not sympathize with, the logic of a Canadian terrorist. For all the existential angst and Marxist revolutionary fervour, the stark reality of the murder cannot be diminished.

They extinguished the life of a frightened, depressed, utterly dependent person who posed no threat to them. They reduced Laporte to a political means, a symbol for something larger than himself, denying his particular humanity in order to provide a rationale for taking his life. Most Cana-

dians do not believe that death is a just penalty for any crime. How could Simard argue that someone should die for "crimes" that he has been made to *symbolize*? What would happen to individual rights in a new social order founded by people who could justify such a thing?

THE "REPLY" OF THE CANADIAN STATE

CBC reporter: ... My choice is to live in a society which is free and democratic which means you don't have people with guns running around in it....

Trudeau: ... Yes, well there's a lot of bleeding hearts around who just don't like to see people with helmets and guns. All I can say is, go on and bleed. But it is more important to keep law and order in the society than to worry about weak-kneed people who don't like the looks of—

CBC reporter (interrupting): At any cost? How far would you go with that? How far would you extend that?

Trudeau: Well, just watch me. (Ottawa, October 13, 1970)

The FLQ terrorist acts were conceived of as "demonstrations," whose intended effects were as much discursive—aimed at changing people's minds—as coercive—forcing the government to act on the terrorists' demands. To use the old anarchist phrase, the kidnappings were meant to be a kind of "propaganda of the deed." A crucial element was not only what the act "said" but also what the response of the state "said" in reply. The hope was that the truly coercive nature of the state would be unmasked and its legitimacy undermined. This is presumably what Simard means when he refers to the media coverage "breaking the illusion of a democratic Canada." In the FLQ case, the "propaganda of the deed" failed. However, other cases, such as the Tupamaros and 9/11, show that it can succeed.

As Simard points out, there was sympathy in Quebec for the FLQ manifesto. Thousands of students demonstrated in support while the FLQ was holding its hostages, but before the murder of Laporte became known on October 17, 1970. Quebec students also demonstrated when the first wave of troops was sent into Montreal, accompanied by "Hercules C-130 troop and vehicle transport aircraft, helicopters, jeeps, truck convoys, supply vehicles, ambulances" (Kostash 227). Pierre Vallières exhorted the students to stand in solidarity: "We cannot afford to encourage the police to take reprisals against us." "FLQ! FLQ! FLQ!" chanted the crowd. On October 16, at 4:00 in the morning, the federal government invoked the War Measures Act, and began immediately rounding up suspects. Like Argentine death squads, police came in the night, roused people from bed, ransacked homes and offices. By dawn they had 242 people in custody.

The Theatre of State Violence and Failure of the Propaganda of the Deed

The War Measures Act, passed at the outbreak of the First World War, was designed as a tool to suppress internal dissent in times of war. It was aimed in part at those who *might* be sympathetic to the enemy powers. It was used on these grounds to expropriate the property of Japanese Canadians and send them to internment camps during the Second World War. War can provide a political opportunity for other kinds of challenges to the state as the Bolsheviks demonstrated

in Russia in 1917. The War Measures Act was broad enough to apply to socialists or communists; indeed, there were no restrictions at all on whom the Act could be applied to.

It suspended normal legal rights of suspects. Police were empowered to search without warrant (i.e., the right of privacy was revoked). Suspects could be held without being charged for as long as six months. Neither the person nor his or her lawyer would have any power to challenge the grounds upon which the person was imprisoned, since the state was under no obligation to state what those grounds were. In 1970 police simply went through the files on left-wing and *indépendantiste* "subversives" that they had been collecting throughout the 1960s and imprisoned whomever they wanted to.

Most people did not see this unfettered police power. What they did see was the massive deployment of troops and military hardware in city streets. You may have seen a famous image of little kids, sitting on their bikes, marvelling at a soldier on the steps of a public building with a machine gun in his hands and a military helicopter behind him. What was the point this display? Military helicopters and fighter jets (they had a squadron up from Bagotville) are not good tools for neutralizing terrorists in dense urban areas. The justification was that the troops were there to free up the police to do their anti-terrorist work. But then, helicopters and fighter jets are even worse tools for day-to-day urban policing unless they are understood primarily as symbols of power—a kind of theatre of state violence.

This was the state "speaking" in answer to the FLQ provocation. Perhaps as intended, it polarized people. One radical later recalled, "Machine guns pointed at you in the streets *are* intimidating" (Kostash 237). Most Canadians preferred to believe that the guns were pointed only at dangerous and threatening "others."

They felt comforted. Even in Quebec, opinion polls showed that an overwhelming majority approved of the War Measures Act and the deployment of troops. Three major Quebec unions spoke out about the dangers of suspending civil liberties. NDP Leader Tommy Douglas spoke out against it in the House of Commons ("The government, I submit, is using a sledgehammer to crack a peanut"). But that was all; there was no popular uprising. Even the students remained relatively quiet.

People identified with and collaborated with state power. Fernand Dumont remembers the mood in Quebec.

> Men who had still been lucid the day before welcomed unconditional authority. Parents denounced teachers. Unionists called the police to break up arguments. Priests formed a coalition against their bishop. Editorial writers blamed defrocked priests.... If you showed the slightest hesitation, even if only to show a personal appraisal of the tragedy, people replied that the time for philosophy was over, that it was the time now for the police: and that it was too late to chat about "the sex of freedom." (94)

This was the measure of the failure of the FLQ's propaganda of the deed.

Legalized State Repression

In November the state expanded its powers even further by passing the Public Order Temporary Measures Act, which made it illegal to belong to the FLQ or "any group of persons or association that advocates the use of force or the commission of crime as a means of or as an aid in accomplishing the

same or substantially the same governmental change within Canada as that advocated by the said Le Front de Libération du Québec...." If you belonged to a group that was for an independent, socialist Quebec, and supported the use of civil disobedience of the kind practised by Rosa Parks, you could, even if you never engaged in civil disobedience yourself, face up to five years in jail under this new law.

The law disregards the legal principle that says "guilt by association" should never be a basis for indictment. By further making it illegal to "communicate [...] statements on behalf of [or] ... advocate [...] or promote [...] the unlawful acts of, or the use of the unlawful means advocated by, the unlawful association," the law undermines free speech. Vallières' speech to the student crowd or publication of the FLQ manifesto (read it for yourself: http://english.republiquelibre.org/manifesto-flq.html) had become indictable offences.

Canada had taken the first steps down the road of "legalized" repression that the Uruguayan state had taken around this time in response to its own terrorist threat from the Tupamaros. The Canadian government went much further down this road than the U.S. government (notwithstanding U.S. police "riots," shootings, and covert operations) ever did in this period. This episode raised a number of questions. First, were the actions of the state effective in quelling dissent in Canada? The FLQ did not last much longer. The independence movement in Quebec suffered, at least briefly. October 1970 also sent a chill throughout the 1960s movements across Canada.

Activists were shocked and intimidated by how easily the state could suspend civil rights, and how ready most Canadians appeared to allow that to happen.

It was like a nightmare, as if it wasn't real. Repression had always been something that happened somewhere else and didn't immediately affect us. Now, as it sank in, it crystallized my feelings about Canadian politics. Horror at the lack of accountability. Then I began to feel very isolated, from my own family even. A very lonely feeling. In incredible loneliness and isolation I began to question my whole politics. (qtd. in Kostash 238)

Oberschall rules out state repression as an important cause of the decline of the 1960s movements in the United States. Kostash argues that it had a much bigger impact in Canada. In fact, she and others have suggested that the intent of the government was to use the October Crisis as an opportunity to target dissent generally—the New Left, the unions, the peace activists.

Terrorism: Manufactured by the State?

She and others go even further and raise the related question: Did the state help to manufacture the "terrorist threat" in order to justify state repression? Similar suspicions have been raised about repression in Latin American countries, and more recently about the U.S. response to the al Qaeda threat. There are two ways in which states are alleged to manufacture a terrorist threat. The first is by covertly encouraging or facilitating activists' use of violence. This is the "agent provocateur" strategy discussed in Chapter 3. The second is by magnifying the perception of danger.

The Canadian government certainly overstated the threat posed by the FLQ. A commission of inquiry (the Keable Com-

mission) later concluded that the government perception "was without relation to the reality." It was not true that the FLQ had a plan to overthrow the government, despite Trudeau's announcement on October 30 that he had "solid information" that *indépendantistes* were making ready to form a "provisional government." Simard and his comrades had little knowledge of what other cells were doing and barely knew what they themselves were going to do from one moment to the next. In the two cells that took hostages, there were no more than 10 people and no more than 35 active FLQists in the whole of Quebec.

The government certainly dramatized their inflated estimation of the threat by deploying troops and military hardware in the streets. Canadians could hardly avoid "reading" this as a powerful sign of the danger that the country was facing. Importantly, though, the Keable Commission concluded that the government was unaware of how inaccurate its information and its message to the public was.

The more difficult allegation is that the state was somehow complicit in the FLQ violence. Those who take this line point out that the police had informers close to FLQ networks, that they knew of and had under surveillance many of the key FLQ activists prior to the October Crisis, but failed to prevent the kidnappings from taking place. Potential targets of kidnapping were not put under police protection. Simard and his accomplices were amazed at how they found Laporte.

When we got there we saw Pierre Laporte right in the middle of the street! He was playing ball with somebody. We never imagined it would be like that. A diplomat had been kidnapped a few days earlier. The acting premier of Quebec when Robert Bourassa was away

was relaxing in front of his house.
Like there was nothing going on,
with nobody standing guard. We
couldn't believe it…. There wasn't a
cop in sight. The street was practi-
cally deserted. (Simard 33)

Difficult to believe, perhaps, but probably more difficult to believe is the idea that the acting premier was being set up by the police. Simple oversight, naiveté, or incompetence can never be ruled out.

The police did manage to get agents provocateurs active in FLQ cells advocating and engaging in violence. The Keable Commission later recommended that officers be charged for their actions in undercover operations, including the following.

… the 1973 theft of the list of the
Parti Québécois (Operation Ham),
the 1972 break-in into the offices of
L'Agence de Presse Libre du Québec,
the issuance of a forged communi-
qué, ostensibly by the FLQ, by the
RCMP, the theft of dynamite by the
RCMP, the burning of a barn by the
RCMP, and the illegal detention of
two alleged FLQ members by the
RCMP. (Tetley 13)

However, these actions all happened after the October kidnappings and could not have contributed to the FLQ's turn toward terrorism, which the state used to justify repression. Still, the scale of the RCMP's belated infiltration of the FLQ was impressive. The Keable Commission concluded that by 1973 "… we [the police] were the FLQ."

There is one final point that many of you may already have wondered about. How could the government justify invoking the War Measures Act when the country was not at war? The Act contained an additional clause that said that its powers could be used if there was an insurrection "real or apprehended." The government claimed that they had apprehended an FLQ insurrection (i.e., plot to overthrow the government). Did they, to use the words of the Act, have "conclusive evidence that war, invasion, or insurrection, real or apprehended, exist[ed]?" (See http://home.cc.umanitoba. ca/~sprague/wma.htm.) You decide.

GLOBAL TERRORISM: 9/11

Who of your generation can ever forget September 11, 2001? The replayed images are invariably of the stricken twin towers of the World Trade Center, belching smoke or unbelievably collapsing inward upon themselves. One hijacked jet also slammed through the walls of the Pentagon, the military nerve centre of the most powerful state on the planet. Another was headed for the White House. This was a military operation of breathtaking originality and devastating effect.

It was also a media provocation—the 1960s formula magnified beyond the Yippies' most psychedelic dreams. It flooded news channels instantly, globally, non-stop for days: Internet, TV, radio, newspaper. You could not escape it. During this period, al Qaeda remained silent, not claiming responsibility nor stating a motive nor in any way articulating a "meaning" for the attack. They allowed their provocation to hang like a huge blank canvas that anyone who ever had reason to want to strike against U.S. economic, military, or political power could fill in for themselves.

The Politics of Representing Terrorism

All media outlets went into overdrive to perform what Elliott, Murdock, and Schlesinger call "ideological labour" in order to reframe the al Qaeda canvas within a fairly narrow range of interpretation and acceptable discussion. Elliott and his colleagues use this term to describe how English television covered IRA terrorism in the 1980s. They put "terrorism" in quotation marks to highlight the idea that the term itself is ideological and has built into it assumptions about "good" violence against people versus "bad" violence against people. When states themselves engage in such violence through war or counter-insurgency, this is often not considered terrorism. When social movements resort to violence against people, they are more likely to be labelled "terrorist."

However, where there is little sympathy for the regimes that they target, erstwhile "terrorists" often become "insurgents," "guerrillas," or even "freedom fighters." This is how the U.S. administration, for example, has tended to view terrorist attacks against Cuba or other left-wing regimes in Latin America. This is also how people tend to view the resistance movements against Nazi occupation in Europe.

Elliott et al. observed how television news coverage tended to channel interpretations of IRA terrorism according to rigid and pejorative scripts. This "official discourse" insists that terrorism be understood as irrational and criminal rather than political behaviour. In the FLQ crisis, for example, the Liberation cell was demanding the release of FLQ "political prisoners" imprisoned for various violent acts. The government insisted that these people were common criminals. The focus of reporting and discussion in "official discourse" is on understanding the victims of terror and their families—their suffering and personal losses. The official discourse encourages the viewer to identify with the victims against the perpetrators whose "story" is suppressed, rendering them unintelligible, pathological, outside of normal human motivation. (Even separatist René Lévesque dismissed the FLQ kidnappers as non-human, "sewer rats.")

Elliott and his colleagues also found that in other formats—for example, documentaries and in-depth analyses—more critical "alternative" perspectives were voiced. While discussions here emphasized the condemnation of violence and sought ways to prevent it, they also raised the question of the legitimacy of state violence. Tommy Douglas expressing concerns about the War Measures Act threatening civil liberties would be an example of this sort of "discourse." The alternative discourse also explores the rational, political motivations of terrorism and seeks to understand the "root causes" in terms of real or perceived social and political injustices.

Finally, Elliott et al. found rare instances of an "oppositional discourse" in which the case *for* IRA violence from the perspective of the terrorists was at least represented, if not validated. These tended to be made-for-TV dramas, aired outside of prime time, where the "fictional" nature of the narrative gave the authors a certain licence to explore controversial ideas. Here a common theme was exposing the illegal, covert violence of state security forces against which the insurgents had to contend. Examples from the FLQ era would include *alternative* press or publications justifying terrorism as the "democratization of violence" that would otherwise be monopolized by the state.

BOX 7.1:

"HATE CRIMES" IN CANADA

Almost a month after the terrorist attacks of 9/11, Sunera Thobani, a women's studies professor at the University of British Columbia, addressed a conference on "Women's Resistance: From Victimization to Criminalization." On the events of 9/11 she said she felt the pain of the victims "every day," but nonetheless warned women to be skeptical of the post 9/11 rhetoric and not to support blindly whatever "security" or military course of action the U.S. administration responded with.

The most dangerous threat to global security, she argued, was not international terrorists, but the U.S. administration itself, responsible for "unleashing prolific levels of violence all over the world." "From Chile to El Salvador, to Nicaragua to Iraq," she went on, "the path of U.S. foreign policy is soaked in blood." Her audience, sympathetic to the theme of "women's resistance" and probably better able than most people to see the question of global "security" from the perspective of victimized "others" in developing nations, gave Thobani a standing ovation. Many others could not see it this way.

Her phrase about U.S. foreign policy being soaked in blood received headline coverage throughout Canada and she was loudly condemned for it on both sides of the border. "Outrageous," cried Foreign Affairs Minister John Manley. Thobani's speech was "hateful," according to B.C. Premier Gordon Campbell, and those who applauded it were propagators of hate. Joe Clark, leader of the Progressive Conservatives, accused Secretary of State Hedy Fry, who had merely sat at the same table as Thobani, of embarrassing the government.

Stockwell Day, of the Canadian Alliance, thought the government should make an official statement of condemnation to the U.S. administration. The University of British Columbia was forced to call a press conference, "to declare that its reputation as an academic institution had not been compromised by what she had said." On the basis of a complaint from a citizen, the RCMP placed her under investigation for a hate crime under section 319 of the Criminal Code. Other citizens in Canada and the U.S. attacked her with anonymous threats, phone calls, and e-mails. She had to be provided with security outside her classes. "It is just unbelievable what it is like," she is quoted as saying. "I am getting all of this porn and hate mail."

Now that more than 2,000 Americans and tens of thousands of Iraqis are dead from the U.S.-led invasion of Iraq, more Canadians and Americans are aware that there is some truth to the "drenched in blood" imagery. More people would likely agree that Thobani's warning against uncritical responses should have been more widely heeded, since the U.S. subsequently went to war on the basis of false, and probably fabricated, information on the terrorist threat posed by the Iraqi regime. However, at the time people were widely caught up in the "ideological work" of suppressing any "alternative discourse."

What is interesting is how, not just the mainstream media, but official spokespeople and the public at large collaborated in this project of narrowing the acceptable range of discourse on "terrorism." What does this incident say about the political culture in Canada, in particular our tolerance of free speech? What does it say about our capacity, in public and policy forums, to openly discuss and therefore fully understand the issues of state and social movement uses of terror?

Voltaire's famous line, "I disapprove of what you say, but I will defend to the death your right to say it," reminds us that there is a difference between defending free speech and defending what gets said under the protection of free speech. Conversely, there is a difference between disagreeing vehemently and in strong language with what someone says and denying them the right to say it.

While the police investigated Thobani on a hate crimes complaint, they did not charge her. Under the law, a hate crime must be directed against an "identifiable group," which is defined as "any section of the public distinguished by colour, race, religion or ethnic origin." Furthermore, for the law to apply, a "public incitement of hatred" against an identifiable group must lead to a "breach of the peace." Still, would you say that the Canadian outcry against Thobani was nonetheless coercive?

Sources: Glenn Bohn and Kim Bolan, "Thobani Accused of Hate Crime against Americans," *Vancouver Sun* (October 10, 2001); Brian Laghi, "Reaction to Thobani Threatening, Women Say," *The Globe and Mail* (October 5, 2005): A9; Michael Valpy, "Thobani Is Not Alone," *The Globe and Mail* (October 6, 2001): F9.

In the weeks after 9/11, the major American networks kept coverage almost exclusively within the bounds of "official" discourse, focusing on the experience of the victims, the rescue efforts at the Trade Center site, and the security response to terrorist attacks. Americans did raise other issues through other channels, such as Internet discussion groups and weblogs. For example, a former director of the CIA's Office of Regional and Political Analysis in an online interview on WashingtonPost.com argued, "I think we need to understand the root causes behind the terrorism and do something about them."

In a clear illustration of what Elliott would call "alternative discourse," he elaborated:

> I have six root causes on my list, four are major issues in the Middle East, and two are more global in scope. On the Middle East, I'd include the Israel-Palestine issue, the continued bombings of and sanctions on Iraq, the U.S. military presence in Saudi Arabia, and the anger of many Arabs and Muslims with their own authoritarian and often corrupt governments. My two global issues are the U.S. drive to spread its own hegemony and its own version of unregulated, freemarket globalization worldwide, and (2) the very kind of war the U.S. now wages. On the globalization issue, poverty is THE main factor. (Christison)

There has yet to be a systematic study of this, but it appeared that this sort of alternative perspective was almost entirely absent from mainstream media coverage in the U.S.

Pierre Trudeau, during the FLQ crisis, and Margaret Thatcher, prime minister during the IRA violence of the 1980s, both stressed the "responsibility" of the media not to give free publicity to the terrorists. The terrorists' political issues were not to be placed on the agenda for discussion or analysis. George Bush did not need to make such demands; the major networks censored themselves in this regard. Bush was able to go further, belligerently insisting that people had to be either "with us or with the terrorists." "The time for philosophy was over," as Dumont put it in the Canadian context of 1971, "it was the time now for the police."

Alternative Readings of 9/11

However, in 2001, U.S. networks, for all their global reach, could not "spin" the story how they pleased for networks in other countries and for other media channels. Television networks (like the CBC in Canada) and newspapers (like the *Guardian* in the U.K.) did begin to explore "root causes." Alternative media superstars like Noam Chomsky and Michael Moore in the U.S. argued that there were good reasons for Arab resentment against U.S. foreign policy in the Middle East.

However, no matter how the story was pitched, it played very differently to audiences in Muslim and Arab countries. Once al Qaeda was typecast as Arab and Muslim, Muslims and even those who merely looked Arab living in European and North American countries began to fear reprisals directed against them. Most Muslims were revolted by al Qaeda violence in the same way that Quebeckers had been appalled by the FLQ. Few, however, would have failed to appreciate at least some part of the resentments and aspirations that motivated al Qaeda and its followers.

For a significant minority, predominantly young men, al Qaeda's "propaganda of the deed" was a glorious inspiration. Think of it—Simard and his band had carried machine guns, but the 9/11 terrorists were armed only with everyday objects—plane tickets and box cutters. Not only were they taken seriously, they threw the world into a panic. Global systems that to alienated youth seem untouchable and immutable came unstuck. Stock prices tumbled; the world's greatest military power lurched into war, defying the United Nations and many of the allies that it had relied upon for most of the 20th century.

The strategy of "propaganda of the deed" is meant to provoke a reaction that exposes state violence and strips it of its legitimacy.

In invading Iraq, the Bush administration defied international law, and deceived its own public with false stories of "weapons of mass destruction" and implied links between the Iraqi regime and al Qaeda terrorists. Covert military intervention that the U.S. had been carrying out for years in the Middle East became overt and so devoid of justification that U.S. allies, never mind alienated Muslim youth, could not bring themselves to support it. Here was the measure of success of al Qaeda's propaganda of the deed.

Al Qaeda Networks

The global, satellite-borne telecommunications infrastructure of the 21st century was the medium that enabled this propaganda of the deed. This same infrastructure provides the medium of communication for the al Qaeda network itself. Al Qaeda relies on media in ways that are similar to the ways that 1960s movement organizations relied upon media. However, al Qaeda's use of it is more systematic and sophisticated. There is a formal organizational kernel to al Qaeda. This kernel is hierarchical and operates from a physical locale—for a time in Afghanistan where it ran its infamous training camps. As such, it is something that might be bombed or otherwise attacked through the physical arsenal of conventional war.

Al Qaeda's core organization also relies on material resources such as arms and money. It has developed a transnational network for raising and distributing funds. This network requires experienced financiers to manage the flow of funds through a tangle of NGOs, investments, and bank accounts. Like any transnational firm, the network relies on computer-based transactions and (encrypted) e-mail to do its business and co-ordinate its affairs. While al Qaeda designs these links and transactions in such a way as to be difficult to trace, they are, in principle, traceable. Exposing these communications is one of the aims of anti-terrorism legislation that expands police powers of surveillance over new media of communications.

However, many of those who act in the name of al Qaeda are not formally members of this core organization or its transnational network. They are not on any membership list; they do not take direct orders from bin Laden. One of the authorities on al Qaeda, Jason Burke, goes so far as to say that al Qaeda "does not exist." What he means is that it does not exist as an organization in the usual sense of the word. "Al Qaeda" is often translated as "base," which might mean a physical locale, but, Burke points out, it has further connotations in Arabic, including the more abstract notions of "precept, rule, principle, maxim, formula, method, model or pattern."

Self-organizing al Qaeda cells tap into this way of thinking and model for action in very much the same way that "transitory teams" tapped into the culture and protest style of the New Left, or that anti-globalization "affinity groups" now tap into anti-globalization culture and tactics. When CBS covers the latest terror attack or al Jazeera airs the latest videotape of Osama Bin Laden, the al Qaeda network "speaks" to its "transitory teams." What is important to recognize is that these communications links are untraceable, or rather they are traceable to everyone who watches CBS or al Jazeera and therefore to no one in particular.

Also, al Qaeda as principle is abstract and unlocateable; it becomes part of a generalized culture that can continue to exist whether or not the formal organization of al Qaeda is destroyed or all of it members are in prison or dead. It evades the reach of the kinds of policing or military strategies invoked in the current "War on Terror." Like the principles that

motivated 1960s activism, it is embedded in a broader culture of which violent organizations or violent tactics are merely one expression. In the next section we will try to understand the nature of that broader political and cultural context in the Muslim world.

ISLAMIC ANTI-GLOBALIZATION

On March 22, 2004, Israeli fighter jets flew low over a mosque from which worshipers had just emerged from morning prayers. The deafening noise masked the sound of a helicopter gunship rising above a nearby building, giving it enough time to lock on to its target, an old man in a wheelchair, and fire three missiles. Muslim religious leader Sheikh Ahmed Yassin died along with a handful of people who stood near him.

Israeli officials represented Yassin as a military commander, others as a "spiritual leader" of the terrorist organization Hamas, which had been conducting suicide bombings in Israel since the early 1990s. His assassination raised questions about the legitimate use of state violence even from the United States, itself guilty of excesses under its new "War on Terror." Obituaries of Yassin also revealed how the players in this drama had shifted since the 1970s.

From Secular to Religious Resistance to Colonialism

In the 1970s, popular movements that resorted to "armed struggle" were likely to be inspired by Marxist and anti-colonial writers like Frantz Fanon (who wrote the influential book *Wretched of the Earth*). While they were often also nationalistic—fighting not just in the name of a universal working class or exploited peasantry but for a particular linguistic and cultural "identity" like the Québécois or the Palestinians—they did not frame this identity in religious terms. In Palestine the lead organization was the Palestine Liberation Organization (PLO).

Sheik Yassin and the religious organization he was associated with, the international Muslim Brotherhood, was marginal to the politics of resistance to Israeli occupation. He advocated religious revival against Western secular morality, including its ideologies of "liberation" and the doctrine of armed struggle. He embodied religious virtues of selflessness, devotion to service, and renunciation of material reward.

By the 1990s his legitimacy and following rivalled that of the PLO. When he shifted to the advocacy of violence, he was able to frame it within terms of the kind of religious self-sacrifice that could make suicide a meaningful strategy. The heavy reliance on suicide attacks is one feature that distinguishes the "armed struggles" of the 1970s from those since the 1990s.

This shift from a secular to a religious framing of anti-colonial, anti-capitalist, and, more recently, anti-globalization struggles is what we will try to understand in this section. Although the shift takes place in the Arab and Muslim world, there is nothing in the religion of Islam that uniquely encourages it. Nor is there anything about the nature of Islam as opposed to any other religion that lends it especially to the advocacy of violence characteristic of some Islamist organizations like Hamas and al Qaeda.

The Islamic tradition, like the Catholic tradition, is complex, layered, and can be interpreted in a variety of different ways and adapted to changing social contexts. Recall that Catholicism provided an interpretive framework for resistance to the social and economic transformations being wrought by capitalist "modernization" in early 20th-century Canada. Religious leaders in Rome and in the rural parishes of Nova Scotia and Quebec, like Marx, abhorred Adam Smith's "liberal" notion of the "cash nexus" where human relations were reduced to impersonal contracts between individuals and value reduced to measures of money. They were also aware of how capitalism could create new inequalities of power and feared that the formation of organized class-based resistance to that power would divide "Christian communities" and undermine traditional authority.

They promoted the formation of co-operatives—secular organizations within civil society—as an alternative to militant trade unions. In Quebec, the caisse populaire (credit union) movement was also conceived by religious leaders as part of a nationalist project of "decolonization." The capital needed to transform the Quebec economy was controlled "impersonally," at a distance by Montreal anglophones who were largely Protestant or, in many cases, Jewish. Control of credit through local community-based co-ops was a means of asserting "national" control over capital for a "nation" defined in very particular religious, cultural, and linguistic terms.

The Church-sponsored caisse populaire movement also helped to habituate French Catholic borrowers, lenders, and administrators of the co-ops in capitalist skills and a capitalist ethos while attempting to frame these "modern" skills within the bounds of traditional Catholic morality. Muslim leaders today are similarly seeking to sponsor and direct some form of "Islamic modernization" not dominated by Western interests and free of Western religious, cultural, and linguistic influences as well as what they see as the worst features of Western "liberal" values.

State-Sponsored Nationalisms

In Quebec after the Second World War the state became a more powerful vehicle than the co-operative movement for the promotion of nationalist modernization. In what was called a "Quiet Revolution," francophone Québécois began to dominate positions of power within their own state bureaucracies and legal system. Around the world similar revolutions, some not so quiet, were taking place as Third World nations took control of their own governments and state bureaucracies from former colonial rulers. This was the process of "decolonization." For a time at least, these states were effective instruments for promoting capitalist development and directing it toward "national" objectives.

Economic Development

States could invest in infrastructure—roads, power grids, communications systems—providing these assets "free" to local business. Through tariffs and subsidies they could promote "import substitution." In other words, instead of relying on foreign multinationals for manufactured goods, technology, and the research and development that goes into producing them, they could nurture such industries within their own borders, controlled by their own people. The state itself could play "capitalist" by investing directly in "development" megaprojects. In Quebec hydro power was one such area of state investment.

Capitalist development succeeds only at the cost of social dislocation and the creation of new inequalities that have no legitimacy within pre-capitalist world views. It creates jobs, wage work, but not without the social trauma of expropriation and uprooting from traditional land-based employments. Wage work, as Marx and Engels warned, creates new dependencies and new opportunities for exploitation. It also creates new social formations as workers organize to defend themselves.

In Quebec, state-sponsored modernization helped to expand a working class whose aspirations could not be satisfied through Church-sponsored co-operatives. Quebec workers built an increasingly militant trade union movement without the sanction of the Church. In other words, modernization stimulated the growth of secular organization within civil society. The Quebec government initially retained Church sanction during the reign of Premier Duplessis, and opposed the unions. This was an unsustainable strategy.

Legal Inclusion

Everywhere the experience of industrializing societies, beginning with England in the 19th century, has been that the way to deal with the social dislocations of capitalist development is to use the state to promote new forms of social inclusion. The law is an important tool that it can use to this end. Legal inclusion is one of the positive features of liberalism. The liberal idea here is that we are, first and foremost, *individuals* and that our collective and social statuses (gender, race, belief, sexuality, etc.) should be irrelevant in the eyes of the law. This principle has been a powerful tool in struggles to extend legal rights to powerless groups—to include them within the rights of what is often called "bourgeois" citizenship.

Workers have gradually been able to win rights of equality before the law, the right to vote, the right to organize, rights of free speech, the right to strike. In legislating these rights, the state helps workers to organize independently and thereby create their own forms of social inclusion and also fight for greater economic inclusion. Once the process of expansion of rights begins, there is little *rational* ground for liberals to defend other exclusions: to women, Aboriginal peoples, gays, or minority religious groups.

Even something as apparently simple as extending the right of equality before the law to, say, women, can be socially explosive in traditional societies. It can involve extending the legal understanding of "rape" to include rape in marriage and "date rape" as well as expanding the powers of police to intervene in domestic violence. Such changes undermine patriarchal authority and the inviolability of "the family." This has been one of the great objections of the Catholic Church as well as of contemporary Muslim clerics to the cultural accompaniments of capitalist "modernization."

Social Inclusion: Social Welfare

In order for the Quebec state to assume the project of expanding liberal rights, it had to disassociate itself from the Church. After the defeat of Duplessis, the *state*'s role in the nationalist project became increasingly secular. In addition to law, states have also used social programs as a means of social inclusion. To overcome the disparities in income created by capitalist development, the state can offer free or heavily subsidized services open to all: education, health care, unemployment insurance, pensions, various forms of income assistance. If you recall Marx and Engels' analysis and the case study of Lynn and Fall River from Chapter 1, you will remember that these were the types of services that working-class communities provided for their own members either informally through mutual aid or, increasingly, through mutual aid organizations and cooperatives.

These forms of mutual aid create powerful bonds of solidarity—people commit to groups that embrace and take care of them. Working-class solidarity was, of course, often defined in opposition to the larger national society. States can provide social services more systematically, across the board, and more generously and for this reason working-class people often fight for state provision. When states do provide it, they reduce the need for working-class self-help and redirect allegiance toward "community" defined in national terms. This strategy of state inclusion goes beyond liberal precepts. It is referred to as social welfare and states that rely on it as "welfare states."

Legal inclusion and social welfare were used in varying degrees in Quebec and newly independent states in the Third World as ways to minimize the social tensions generated by capitalist modernization. As Pierre Vallières attests, these strategies do not eliminate those tensions, nor do they satisfy everyone. (Marxists insist that capitalism can never be anything but exploitive and alienating; anarchists abhor the centralized power of welfare states.)

Still, in many Muslim countries, women in particular remember this period of the 1960s and 1970s as one of unprecedented freedoms and opportunities for education, for choice concerning issues of marriage and family, for participation in the public sphere. As in Quebec, Muslim countries, both state and civil society, were becoming increasingly secular; some were run by secular, left-wing parties. This trend has continued in Quebec, but reversed in Muslim countries where there has been a shift toward religious, clerical control, particularly within civil society, and nationalism has come to be understood in increasingly religious terms. What accounts for the difference?

Neoliberalism and the Assault on Third World States

Global Mobility of Capital

The short answer, according to political economist Mustapha Pasha and sociologist Paul Lubeck, is that globalization has undercut all nations' ability to continue funding social welfare. Third World states have been hardest hit. The mechanism should be familiar to you now. Corporations exploit the opportunities for global mobility made possible by new means of transportation, communication, and computerized systems of coordination at a distance. They seek out countries or regions where taxes are lowest, where raw materials can be extracted the most cheaply and with the fewest regulations, where labour is inexpensive, and where workers are least likely to strike because they are unprotected by a "safety net" of social welfare.

The "nationality" of firms makes little difference. Even companies nurtured by states with subsidies and tariffs can threaten to invest elsewhere if governments do not reduce taxes, reduce social spending, and clamp down on strikes. Countries and regions are forced to compete with one another to attract investment. One way that they do this is by cutting taxes, offering special tax incentives, tax holidays, and the like to those who have the greatest capacity to pay—large corporations.

States and the people they represent are coerced but also cajoled into dismantling their social welfare programs. A new "fundamentalist" liberalism, "neoliberalism," preaches that the minimum of state spending and state regulation is good for all citizens, rich and poor alike. States must uphold basic legal order, but beyond that, the cash nexus can provide all the social regulation that a society needs. Neoliberal-

ism was developed and promoted primarily by American economists and policy analysts and, as packaged and exported to the Third World, has become known as the "Washington Consensus."

The Debt Crisis

The "consensus" has had to be imposed on the developing world, and the opportunity to do that came with the debt crisis of the 1980s. The World Bank's mission is to enable countries to borrow money to rebuild economies shattered by war or crippled by chronic underdevelopment. It is an international institution supported by the major industrial countries, but led and largely controlled by the United States. It lent generously to newly independent Third World states that invested the money in infrastructure and large-scale development projects.

Interest on the loans was relatively low and developing countries could afford to pay it, since their exports commanded good prices on world markets. Despite efforts at import substitution, they were still primarily exporting "staples," raw materials that could be harvested from the land or sea or mined from beneath the surface (oil was especially important for Arab countries). Oil-producing nations, many of them Muslim, were able to co-operate with one another and force oil prices up to unprecedented highs in the late 1970s. They were soon awash in "petro-dollars," which they deposited in Western banks.

Banks lend at interest—this is how they make money—so they encouraged more, often excessive, Third World borrowing to employ their surfeit of petro-dollars. Capitalism, Marx had warned, is crisis-ridden: overinvestment inevitably precipitates economic recession. This is what happened in the early 1980s to bring about the debt crisis. First, oil prices collapsed, then prices for most commodities on the world market. Many heavily indebted countries found they no longer had the cash to pay the interest on their loans. They borrowed more money—typically from the International Monetary Fund (IMF), another international financial institution like the World Bank but with a mandate more suited to short-term cash flow problems.

Mexico defaulted (i.e., the government declared it could not and would not pay its debts) in 1982, and the threat that other countries would follow suit panicked lenders. Private banks, the World Bank, and the IMF used their power as creditors to impose new financial "discipline" on indebted countries. They were able to tell countries that their capacity to finance their loans and to borrow in the future depended on adopting neoliberal policies.

Structural Adjustment Programs (SAPs)

The neoliberal policy "package" imposed by the IMF/World Bank was called "structural adjustment programs" or "SAPs." Governments were required to give up all subsidies and tariffs that promoted local import substitution, to "privatize" or sell off all state-owned enterprises, and to relax any laws that favoured local over transnational firms. The idea was to shift control over the economy from governments to private firms, expose local firms to competition from transnational firms, and gradually to reshape the economy to suit the needs of global markets. The "payoff" was meant to be increased tax dollars through increased international trade and therefore increased ability to pay down the debt.

The costs have been social since the neoliberal package accelerates the social dislocations of capitalist modernization. Subsistence-based forms of livelihood are swept away, wage-earners lose their jobs with the collapse of state-supported industries, local markets are flooded with foreign commodities—McDonald's and Mickey Mouse—bearing with them foreign tastes, languages, and values.

Further stipulations of the SAPs prevent governments from cushioning people from these shocks of modernization. SAPs required that any new tax dollars raised be spent first toward debt reduction. Debtor nations were required to cut spending on social welfare, including core services like education and health care. Even spending on infrastructure has suffered so that many "developing" nations can no longer provide conditions for economic investment, never mind social inclusion.

Loss of State Legitimacy

The legitimacy of these regimes to their own people is undermined in two ways. First, they are clearly taking orders from Western financial institutions, led by the United States. By opening the economy to transnational firms, they are giving up any hope of a non-Western model of capitalist modernization. Second, they can no longer build allegiance by "taking care" of the population through social welfare spending.

Having so recently gained their independence from former colonial masters, they now found themselves subject to a new type of colonialism that many refer to as "neocolonialism." The realities of neocolonialism take some of the appeal out of Western promises of "democracy." People realize that even if they are allowed to vote against neoliberal policy, neoliberal policy is what they will get.

Regimes in Third World countries cannot be viewed simply as victims in this new global situation. They must bear a large share of responsibility for their lack of legitimacy with their own people. Many, like the Saudi Arabian royal family or the Iraqi Ba'athist Party, ruled without free elections. Much of the state-directed investment in development megaprojects was ill conceived from economic, environmental, and social perspectives. Some of it was not even for economic, but rather for state military projects, including the violent repression of the countries' own citizens.

Even though this sort of "investment" could hardly be expected to generate direct economic returns, Western lenders assumed that it could guarantee the "security" and economic stability needed for capitalist development. For this same reason, the U.S. State Department had offered, and these regimes had willingly accepted, U.S. military support as well. The appearance of U.S. influence, increasingly damaging to these regimes' legitimacy, was often of their own making.

Power to Co-opt Civil Society

Neoliberal globalization has also been a challenge to legitimacy of states in the West, including Canada. They, too, have had to justify cutbacks in government spending. The most difficult to sell to Canadians have been changes in support to medicare and education. As a student, you will know that governments have nonetheless been successful in forcing universities to charge higher tuitions and rely increasingly on corporate donations and research partnerships to finance operations.

In general, states have sought to shift the delivery of programs to citizens and organizations in civil society. Charity-based food banks and shelters take up the slack from underfunded social assistance programs. Governments may regulate these services

or encourage citizens to support them by giving tax breaks for charitable donations. To use a neoliberal metaphor popular in the 1990s, states may help to launch and steer these civil society "boats," but they leave citizens to pick up the oars and row them. This is a version of the strategy (familiar from Chapter 2) of the "autonomization" of state power. We saw how in Quebec in the 1970s, co-ops became vehicles for 1960s political aspirations. The legacy of this citizen action included housing co-ops, which in the neoliberal era could be called upon to alleviate homelessness, and workers' co-ops, which became a means for workers to resist plant closures caused by global "free trade" competition. However, the Quebec government "took its hands off the oars" of these co-ops and revoked direct funding.

Still, Quebec, a province in a developed country with a diversified economy and control over its own hydroelectric power, has enjoyed far more resources than Third World states. Quebec governments have generally spent more on "social inclusion" than other provincial governments in Canada. Quebec university students pay far less for tuition than other Canadians and have access to generous government bursaries. The fact that hundreds of thousands went on strike in 2004 when these bursaries were threatened says much about the different expectations of Quebeckers about what the state should provide.

Quebec has never been constrained by SAPs and is better able than developing nations to use legislation to protect culture, demanding that multinationals operate in French in Quebec and protecting "culture industries" from foreign, U.S., and anglo-Canadian competition. Broadly based secular parties like the PQ (provincially) and the Bloc Québécois (federally) still consider the state to be a vehicle for protecting Québécois "national" interests, culture, and identity.

The risk for all states in pursuing "autonomization" as a strategy is that they will help to organize and empower civil society groups that will oppose the government in power or its projects—the promotion, for instance, of neoliberal modernization, or the construction of a secular national identity. In Quebec there is a secular "anti-globalization" movement organized independently of the nationalist parties. Groups affiliated with it demonstrated in force at the Quebec summit of the Free Trade Area of the Americas (FTAA) in 2001. They are opposed to the neoliberal project and the Quebec state's complicity with it; still, they hardly dominate Quebec civil society.

In Muslim countries, states have had to abandon too many government services to civil society and have too few resources to monitor or steer the independent civil society "boats" that are beginning to carry the political aspirations of their people. As in most societies, a diverse range of charity and social movement organizations and resistance movements are active within Muslim countries. Some are Western-backed, some are supported by international Muslim charities, some are secular, and others are sponsored by religious groups of various doctrinal persuasions.

Islamist Domination of Civil Society

Muslim fundamentalist religious organizations, like the Muslim Brotherhood, have slowly been gaining predominance. Lubeck outlines the scope of their penetration of civil society.

> [Islamic movements] construct dense webs of Muslim associations connecting mosques, schools, welfare associations, pilgrimage associations, clinics, missionary activity, com-

> munity development associations, student associations, and Islamic versions of most kinds of organizations found in the West. (162)

States are increasingly unable to compete with these dense organizational networks. In some cases, state schooling is so underfunded that even middle-class families turn to the Islamic schools for their children's education. By actually taking care of people's needs and shielding them from some of the shocks of neoliberal "market governance," Islamic organizations win people's emotional allegiance to their movement. In addition to framing conceptions of "community," "identity," and "nation" in Islamic religious terms, they also frame them in opposition to neoliberalism and the secular, neocolonial state. (Imagine if anti-globalization activists ran the schools in Canada!)

Lubeck elaborates on this oppositional discourse.

> [Islamist] actions include: organizing demonstrations, mobilizing civil society against structural adjustment, ... protesting American military adventures in the Muslim world, demanding charity (zakkat) for the poor, denouncing repression and torture, and, most importantly, constructing parallel institutions to dispense material, social and emotional support for those marginalized by the relentless march of global neo-liberalism. (Lubeck 163)

The discursive framing is remarkably similar in outline to secular anti-globalization movements in the West. The same contrast is made between a humane ethic of care for the most powerless in society versus a purely materialistic promotion of markets and profits in the interests of foreign multinationals and guaranteed by the military might of the global superpower, the United States. Why then does a secular anti-globalization, anti-colonial movement not capture this discourse in Muslim countries?

Muslim organizations enjoy a number of advantages over secular organizations in providing social services and mobilizing popular resistance. Their religious credentials allow them to attract more charitable donations. Osama bin Laden, in his early work, for instance, used his family's considerable fortune to promote and fund Muslim social welfare projects. By building an ideology of resistance on the principles of Islam, they can draw upon a "ready-made" framework that most people understand without having first to acquire a grounding in economic or Marxist theory. The strict morality of fundamentalist Islam helps to ensure that their organizations are self-regulating. In practice they are less prone to corruption and inefficiency than the state bureaucracies and secular organizations that they compete against.

Where they oppose authoritarian regimes, they can, just like Catholic organizations were able to in Chile, benefit from the "moral shield" of religious sanctity.

> The [... Islamists] can operate within
> and behind a network of mosques,
> welfare organizations, foundations,
> and other Muslim institutions,
> which the government feels it can-
> not suppress. Liberal democrats
> have no such cover and hence are
> more easily controlled or eliminated
> by the government. (Huntington,
> qtd. in Lubeck 161)

Finally, they have a shining example of the effectiveness of the religious path of resistance in the Iranian revolution of 1979 that overthrew an undemocratic regime backed by the U.S. military. The "political opportunity" offered by the Islamic path is so promising that many Marxist anti-colonialists of the 1970s shifted allegiance. For example, 60 percent of the members of the militant religious organization Hamas are reported to be former Marxists.

Islamism and Globalism

"Islam" encompasses a concept of collective identity and "nation" that transcends existing national borders. The Ayatollah Khomeini, first leader of the Islamic revolution in Iran, embraces ethnic diversity within much of the Middle East.

> As far as Islam is concerned there is
> no question of Kurds, Turks, Fars,
> Balachi, Arab, or Lor or Turcomen.
> Islam embraces everyone and the
> Islamic Republic observes the right
> of all such groups under Islamic
> justice.... Everyone shall enjoy the
> protection of Islam. (Kaldor and
> Muro 165)

Al Qaeda, by embracing Indonesian and African Muslims, makes it clear that "race" should not divide Islam. Islamists maintain international links and emphasize solidarity between Muslims in anti-colonial struggles around the world, in particular with Palestinians in their struggle with Israel for expanded territory and political autonomy. "Islamism," Lubeck concludes, "has become the world's most extensive and militant anti-systemic social movement" (Lubeck 163).

Like the secular anti-globalization movement, while its leaders speak in the name of the marginalized, poor, and oppressed, they themselves are often relatively privileged. Many have university degrees, often from

Western institutions; they have professional skills, have travelled and lived abroad. They understand the modern world and, again like anti-globalization activists, are happy to use the infrastructure of globalization—satellite-mediated communications, Internet, and jet travel—to mobilize global resistance to neoliberal globalization. Despite similarities in the structure and "target" of mobilization, this "anti-systemic movement" is fundamentally at odds with other anti-systemic movements within "global civil society" (both secular and religiously inspired) over the principle of universality.

Islamism and Universalism

The principles of the philosophical enlightenment inform Western ideas of human "liberation" within both the individualistic liberal tradition and the socialist tradition. One of these principles is that all human beings—regardless of social, cultural, or religious background—are equal in their capacities for reason, love, and suffering. Therefore, if any rights were to be extended—guaranteeing that people can govern their own affairs, or be protected from certain harms or abuses of power—these should be extended to all "universally" (assuming the "universe" here to be all human beings). People have had to fight to ensure that women and Blacks were included in this "universe," but they have done so by reference to this enduring principle.

Most ideologies that divide the world into good and evil, the righteous and the damned, are at least in tension with, if not openly hostile to, universalism. It is hard to extend equal rights to the damned. The *Western* religions that emerged from the ancient civilizations of the Middle East—Judaism, Christianity, *and* Islam—all have this dualism built into them. The

same structure of thought can also inform Western ideologies of liberation, like Marxism. So, for the Chenier cell of the FLQ, Pierre Laporte, as an agent of the (evil) capitalist system, is already condemned and is easier to cast out of the sphere within which their ethic of humane care applies. Modern nationalisms, too, have frequently demonized "enemies" to the nation and its aspirations—think of Nazi Germany's "final solution" against "non-Aryan races" or, more recently, the "ethnic cleansing" in Bosnia or Rwanda.

The fundamentalist interpretation of Islam favoured by Islamists is similarly based on an exclusive understanding of the people who matter and to whom rights should be extended. Not everyone has a right to social welfare; only those who are Muslim of a particular doctrinal stripe. Women continue to be denied the same rights in principle as men. "Infidels" are unwelcome within the territory claimed for Islam and would be denied the same citizenship rights to participate in Islamic government.

Islamist Framing of Violence

Violence or armed struggle is only one thread in Islamist tactics of resistance to neocolonialism. Most of the efforts of Islamist organizations are devoted to education, community self-help, and public demonstration. The turn to violence should not be understood by reference to the religious doctrine that they draw upon. There is a much clearer justification of violence in the secular anti-colonial tradition. European colonies were built on the slaughter of the colonized and maintained often through state terror. Fanon believed that the colonized come to frame their very identity as subjects of violence. There is a violent resonance to internal colonization: "All those white men in a group, with guns in their hands cannot be wrong. I am guilty" (Fanon 139). Violence is necessary because the colonizer will not relinquish power without a struggle. The experience of taking up arms—thereby becoming the subject rather than the object of violence—is necessary for the psychological liberation of the colonized. Finally, violent resistance is justified by the prior violence of domination.

This frame could easily fit the Middle Eastern situation without recourse to Islamic doctrine. Repression and torture are ongoing realities in Western-backed regimes. Tens of thousands of citizens have been killed in recent wars by the former Soviet Union and the United States vying for control of the region and its vital resource of oil. Islam can, in fact, be an impediment to the use of violence. For example, it takes a good deal of sophistry for terrorist organizations like al Qaeda to get around very clear religious prohibitions against attacks on non-combatants (i.e., innocent civilians) in Jihad or holy war.

Still, a successful framing in fundamentalist religious terms may shape and perhaps intensify violence in two ways. First, a religious framing can more readily make sense of the kind of self-sacrifice required for suicide bombings. (Suicide bombings are undoubtedly the most devastating tactic of popular violence against states.) Second, a religious, nationalist framing that rejects the principle of universality lends itself better to radically "othering" the godless enemies, placing them beyond the reach of normal human regard.

In summary, the roots of resistance in Muslim countries can be traced to social conditions: the social dislocations of capitalist modernization that states are unable to shield their citizens from, the political humiliation and cultural threat of neo-colonialism. The Islamist movement has emerged as the popular voice of that resis-

tance by successfully occupying the vacuum within civil society left by neoliberal states. While religious sanction may facilitate a particularly deadly turn in the form of suicide attacks, violence is still framed in terms of the "prior violence" of colonial and neocolonial domination.

If this analysis is correct, then the "War on Terror" and its excesses—the invasion of Iraq, U.S. torture at Abu Ghraib prison, the U.S. and Canada's "rendering" of Muslim suspects to torture under repressive regimes, extra-legal assassinations like that carried out by the Israelis against Sheik Yassin—surely only add to the prestige of violent resistance among young Muslims, organized and radicalized by the Islamist movement. The discourse of the War on Terror has its own dark, anti-Enlightenment elements. The division between "us" and the "terrorists" mirrors and reinforces the Islamists' own religious dualism. "Terrorism" becomes a category of absolute evil that can be used to radically "other" a category of people and to justify revoking normal human rights, sanctioning torture and extra-legal assassination.

DISSENT AND THE WAR ON TERROR

Anti-terrorism Legislation

After 9/11 governments have rushed to create new "anti-terrorism" laws. Why? Was it not already illegal to hijack planes, murder people, and destroy property before September 11, 2001? The intent has been to create more powerful "tools" for law-enforcement agencies to monitor, detain, and prosecute *suspected* terrorists before they commit violent acts. These laws define "terrorism" as a legal category and allow normal legal rights to be relaxed for people suspected of terrorism. They give police greater powers of surveillance, for instance, to tap into communications by mail, phone, and Internet with less judicial oversight. They weaken suspects' legal rights by limiting access to the evidence being used against them.

The rights of foreign citizens are even further circumscribed. The extreme case is the U.S. treatment of terrorist suspects captured mostly during the Afghan war and detained at Guantanamo Bay, Cuba. Many of these people have been held indefinitely without trial and minimal access to legal counsel. Commenting on what appear to be clear cases of detainees innocent of terrorist involvement, a U.S. official asked, "What if this is a truly bad individual, the next World Trade Center bomber, and you let him go? What do you say to the families?" (Rupert). Clearly, in his mind the detainees' status is "guilty until proven innocent." Not only are these prisoners stripped of normal legal rights, but the U.S. also refuses to grant them status as prisoners of war and therefore to recognize the protections required by the Geneva Convention.

A key difficulty with anti-terrorism legislation is that it allows police to make judgments about who can be treated as a terrorist before due process of law. We have experience from the 1960s with the concepts

of "subversion" and "sedition" and the astonishingly broad misapplication of these terms by police. Many fear that the category of "terrorist" will be similarly misapplied to people engaged in legitimate dissent or else to people whose Muslim faith or Arab appearance put them under suspicion by association. Cases like that of Maher Arar, the Canadian who was "rendered" to Syrian police to be tortured because he was suspected by Canadian and U.S. intelligence agencies as having links to terrorists, fall into the latter category. What about the former?

A War on Dissent?

Many were concerned that Canada's anti-terrorism law, Bill C-36 enacted in 2001, would be a kind of peacetime version of the War Measures Act, unnecessarily curtailing citizens' rights and allowing police to cast a broad net, criminalizing or, at the very least, intimidating legitimate dissent. Just as in the 1970s many thought that the target was not only the FLQ, but the whole of the radical New Left, so many now wondered if the target were not merely al Qaeda-style "terrorists," but the new anti-globalization movement that had shown its considerable strength for the first time in Seattle in 1999 and again in April 2001 in Quebec City.

BOX 7.2:

"TERRORISM" OR LEGITIMATE DISSENT?

Perhaps the best way to determine whether anti-terrorism legislation criminalizes legitimate dissent is to evaluate how broadly it defines terrorism. I have given you two examples (below): one from the USA PATRIOT Act and one from Canada's Bill C-36. As you read the definitions, try applying them to cases that you know: the FLQ kidnapping; the 1843 labour protest described by Engels in which locked-out brickmakers advanced on their factory "... in military order, the first rank armed with guns"; the 1971 Lapalme strike in Quebec where post office property was vandalized and destroyed, occasionally with explosives; the erection of barricades in the streets of Paris in 1968. Also, do you think these definitions would provide a legal basis for charging police with acts of terrorism, as in the case, for example, of the Chicago "police riot" of 1968 where police "screaming 'Kill 'em!' ... clubbed, jackbooted, and hospitalized hundreds of protestors, reporters, and bystanders" (Chapter 3)?

Here is how the USA PATRIOT Act (2001—HR.3162.ENR) defines "domestic terrorism." (The PATRIOT Act actually amends the "U.S. Code Title 18, Section 2331"—this is where the final wording is most clearly recorded.)

> ... the term "domestic terrorism" means activities that
>
> (A) involve acts dangerous to human life that are a violation of the criminal laws of the United States or of any State;
>
> (B) appear to be intended—
>
> > (i) to intimidate or coerce a civilian population;
> >
> > (ii) to influence the policy of a government by intimidation or coercion; or
> >
> > (iii) to affect the conduct of a government by mass destruction, assassination, or kidnapping; and
>
> (C) occur primarily within the territorial jurisdiction of the United States.

The Canadian legislation encountered a lot of critical attention when it was first drafted and had to be amended in an effort to ensure that it did not cast too wide a net. Here is how Canada's Bill C-36 (2001) defines "terrorist activity." How well do you think it distinguishes between legitimate dissent and terrorism?

> "Terrorist activity" means,
>
> (a) [this section simply lists international laws that define acts like hijacking that are typically considered to be terrorist]
>
> (b) an act or omission, in or outside Canada,
>
> > (i) that is committed
> >
> > > (A) in whole or in part for a political, religious or ideological purpose, objective or cause, and
> > >
> > > (B) in whole or in part with the intention of intimidating the public, or a segment of the public, with regard to its security, including its economic security, or compelling a person, a government or a domestic or an international organization to do or to refrain from doing any act, whether the public or the person, government or organization is inside or outside Canada, and
> >
> > (ii) that intentionally
> >
> > > (A) causes death or serious bodily harm to a person by the use of violence,
> > >
> > > (B) endangers a person's life,
> > >
> > > (C) causes a serious risk to the health or safety of the public or any segment of the public, causes substantial property damage, whether to public or private property, if causing such damage is likely to result in the conduct or harm referred to in any of clauses (A) to (C), or
> > >
> > > (D) causes serious interference with or serious disruption of an essential service, facility or system, whether public or private, other than as a result of advocacy, protest,

dissent or stoppage of work that is not intended to result in the conduct or harm referred to in any of clauses (A) to (C), and includes a conspiracy, attempt or threat to commit any such act or omission, or being an accessory after the fact or counselling in relation to any such act or omission, but, for greater certainty, does not include an act or omission that is committed during an armed conflict and that, at the time and in the place of its commission, is in accordance with customary international law or conventional international law applicable to the conflict, or the activities undertaken by military forces of a state in the exercise of their official duties, to the extent that those activities are governed by other rules of international law.

Source: United States, "Uniting and Strengthening America by Providing Appropriate Tools Required to Intercept and Obstruct Terrorism" (USA PATRIOT ACT) Act of 107th Congress, 2001 (HR.3162.ENR), Library of Congress, Legislative Information, http://thomas.loc.gov/; Canada, Bill C-36, 37th Parliament, 1st Session, "An Act to amend the Criminal Code, the Official Secrets Act, the Canada Evidence Act, the Proceeds of Crime (Money Laundering) Act and other Acts, and to enact measures respecting the registration of charities in order to combat terrorism," www.parl.gc.ca/LEGISINFO/index.asp?Lang=E&Chamber=N&StartList=A&EndList=Z&Session=9&Type=0&Scope=I&query=2981&List=toc-1

To assess whether these new laws could criminalize dissent, it is important to look not only at the wording of the law (see the box on "'Terrorism' or Legitimate Dissent?" above) and how that wording gets interpreted in court, but also how it gets interpreted by police and informs their everyday policing activities. Does the new climate of tolerance for limiting civil rights encourage police to abuse their new anti-terrorism powers and extend them into areas for which they were not intended? We will consider this question again in Chapter 12 when we look again at the "anti-globalization" or, as some prefer, the "global justice" movement.

Is Anti-state Violence Justifiable?

One final and difficult issue should be acknowledged in any discussion of the legitimacy of armed or violent dissent. Two of the first bourgeois democracies whose founders defined many of the principles and values upon which democratic theory is based were established through violent revolutions. I am referring, of course, to France and the United States. Many of the revolutionaries of this era considered it their right, and a right of all people, to violently oppose any government that they considered to be oppressive and tyrannical.

The main tools of popular opposition were civil rights: the right to vote, the right to criticize (i.e., free speech), the right to organize. However, for cases where the arts of debate and assembly failed, the American founding fathers (they were all men) reserved the right to take up arms. "The strongest reason for the people to retain the right to keep and bear arms," wrote Thomas Jefferson, "is, as a last resort, to protect themselves against tyranny in Government." It was the justification that the Black Panthers used for arming themselves.

Canadians, of course, tend to view this idea as foreign, and our rejection of it as one of our definitive differences from the United States. Perhaps in a stable and effective democracy it makes little sense to acknowledge the right of popular violence. At the same time, it is well to keep in mind the experience of Uruguay, which was a stable and effective democracy before descending into legalized state terror in the 1970s.

CONCLUSION

"Terrorism" is a contested term used to characterize political uses of violence, not against property but against other human beings. It is frequently applied in a pejorative sense. So to describe state "counter-insurgency" or popular "armed struggle" as "terrorist" is to de-legitimate these uses of violence. Concerted "ideological labour" is often required by state spokespeople, media, and academics in order to represent movement uses of violence as unquestionably evil without at the same time de-legitimating state deployments of violence. Movement activists and apologists counter with their own ideological labour.

Acts of terror themselves are often conceived by their perpetrators as in part "discursive" contributions to this ideological struggle. Violence as "propaganda of the deed" aims to awaken oppressed people's will to act, but also to provoke the state into acts of violence that it cannot legitimate. The more desperate the state's response to the "terrorist threat," the less it justifies its response in terms of democracy or the rule of law, the greater the propaganda's success.

When revolutionary cadres target civilian populations, however, their propaganda of the deed can easily backfire. The very people whom they are attempting to liberate with violence are likely to see themselves as potential victims of that violence. The FLQ, for example, succeeded only in creating sympathy for the Trudeau government's use of repressive powers under the War Measures Act.

Al Qaeda's use of the propaganda of the deed has been far more successful, at least in its effect on its target audience in the Muslim world. It provoked the excesses of the U.S.-led War on Terror. The deaths of tens of thousands of Muslims in the Iraq war; the disregard of international law; the denial of

legal rights to Muslim "terror suspects"; the torture of prisoners; the continued Western support for undemocratic regimes and for the Israelis, counter-insurgency war against the Palestinians; the revelations that the U.S. used chemical weapons in Iraq, have all created a public relations nightmare for the U.S. and its client states in the Middle East.

All of this can be "spun" in the West in terms of the greater good of bringing democracy to the Middle East and containing terrorism. However, despite their global reach, U.S.-based media are not the only voice in the Middle East and cannot frame the issues with the kind of unanimity that they do within the U.S. Whatever the source of news, it gets read within a framework defined by Islamist organizations that increasingly dominate civil society in the Muslim world. Here the promise of Western democracy is seen as a sham, and the main "story" remains the "prior violence" of state terror, which can be used to legitimate "armed resistance."

In this sense, the War on Terror collaborated in promoting al Qaeda's propaganda of the deed. Also, the military and policing thrust of this war is designed for a physical, locatable target. However, as Jason Burke points out, the key to understanding al Qaeda (and this probably applies to other forms of "global" terrorism) is that it is not a conventional organization with identifiable members and a physical "address." It is also an abstraction—a framework for understanding Muslim oppression and a model for action that "cells" of activists can undertake more or less independently. The provocation of 9/11 advertised both with spectacular effectiveness.

The real problem for an effective response to Islamic terrorism is understanding the attraction of the al Qaeda model. The answer lies in the changing culture of resistance in the Muslim world, in particular the spread of the Islamist movement. Most Islamist organizations do not collaborate with al Qaeda or even advocate suicide bombings, but they do support a very similar analysis of Muslim oppression and vision of Islamic rule within the Muslim world. They frame Muslim resistance in the language of war, a holy war or Jihad, divide the world between the righteous and the damned, and grant full human citizenship only to the righteous. For those who adopt this frame, it is but a small step to the embrace of "armed resistance," even against "infidel" civilians.

Throughout this chapter we have attempted to understand both the social basis for Muslim resistance, its religious framing and resort to violence by comparison with Quebec. The initial similarities are clear. In both cases, societies have had to deal with the social strains of capitalist modernization—social uprooting and new forms of inequality. This was not capitalist development from within as England experienced it in the 19th century, but capitalism imposed from without by foreign colonial powers that additionally threatened political autonomy and linguistic and cultural identity.

Newly independent colonies in the 1960s and 1970s were able to ease the trauma of social upheaval with new forms of inclusion: legal rights and social welfare. They also became the *secular* vehicles for nationalist aspirations: the desires of their people to prevent their linguistic and cultural distinctiveness from being swallowed up in the global sameness of modernization. Globalization, driven by a new mobility of capital, has now intensified the social trauma and has everywhere reduced states' capacity to alleviate it. In Quebec the secular state has managed to remain a credible voice for nationalist aspirations and social inclusion; in Muslim countries, states have lost these roles to religious fundamentalist organizations within civil society.

The differences have to do with states' ability to maintain legitimacy under pressures from globalization. Quebec did not have to suffer the humiliation of neocolonialism experienced by most developing countries. It avoided the debt crisis of the 1980s, and therefore did not have the "neoliberal package" of deregulation and spending cutbacks dictated to it by international financial institutions like the IMF and the World Bank. In developing countries that have had to take orders from the West, secular states have lost legitimacy. Indeed, the very promise of Western democracy, supposed to be part of the modernization package, has lost credibility. These states have also had to give up their projects of protecting national identity and promoting social inclusion through social welfare.

Both of these projects have been taken up by organizations within civil society. In the Muslim world, Islamist organizations have captured popular aspirations and framed resistance to neoliberalism and neocolonialism in intolerant religious terms. The failure of terrorism in Quebec has in part to do with the draconian response of the federal government under the War Measures Act. In other words, it has to do with state repression (which the propaganda of the deed failed to discredit). However, it also has to do with the Quebec state's capacity to co-opt anti-colonial and anti-capitalist sentiment among the Québécois in a way that states in Muslim countries have not been able to.

The primary response of Western states to the threat of terrorism in the 21st century has been to increase their coercive powers at the expense of civil liberties. Even if we dismiss the conspiracy theorists who say that this was one of the aims, we have to ask whether the domestic wars on terror will have the same chilling effect on the anti-globalization movement as the War Measures Act had on New Left activism in Canada.

REFERENCES

Bohn, Glenn, and Kim Bolan. "Thobani Accused of Hate Crime against Americans." *Vancouver Sun* (October 10, 2001).

Burke, Jason. *Al-Qaeda Casting a Shadow of Terror.* London: I.B. Tauris, 2003.

Christison, William. "Globalization and the Root Causes of Terrorism," April 10, 2002. WashingtonPost.com, reprinted by the Freedom of Information Center. November 19, 2006, http://foi.missouri.edu/terrorbkgd/rootcauses.html.

Dumont, Fernand. *The Vigil of Quebec.* Toronto; Buffalo: University of Toronto Press, 1974.

Elliott, Philip, Graham Murdock, and Philip Schlesinger. "'Terrorism' and the State: A Case Study of the Discourses of Television." *Media, Culture and Society* 5, no. 2 (1983): 155–177.

Fanon, Frantz. *Black Skin, White Masks.* New York: Grove Press, 1967.

Fournier, Louis. *F.L.Q.: The Anatomy of an Underground Movement.* Toronto: NC Press, 1984.

Kaldor, Mary, and Diego Muro. "Religious and Nationalist Militant Groups." *Global Civil Society Yearbook.* September 1, 2004, http://www.lse.ac.uk/depts/global/yearbook/outline2003.htm.

Kostash, Myrna. *Long Way from Home: The Story of the Sixties Generation in Canada.* Toronto: Lorimer, 1980.

Laghi, Brian. "Reaction to Thobani Threatening, Women Say." *The Globe and Mail* (October 5, 2005): A9.

Lubeck, Paul M. "The Islamic Revival: Antinomies of Islamic Movements under Globalization." *Global Social Movements*, edited by Robin Cohen and Shirin Rai. London, New Brunswick: Athlone Press, 2000.

Pasha, Mustapha Kamal. "Globalization, Islam and Resistance." *Globalization and the Politics of Resistance*, edited by Barry K. Gills. New York: St. Martin's Press, 2000.

Rupert, James. "Writers Jailed in 2002 for Political Satire." Newsday.com, October 31, 2005. November 20, 2005, www.newsday.com/news/nation-world/world/nywobadr0944924470ct31,0.

Sennett, Richard. *The Hidden Injuries of Class.* New York: Vintage Books, 1973.

Simard, Francis. *Talking It out: The October Crisis from the Inside.* Prose Series 4. Montreal: Guernica, 1987.

Tetley, William. "Appendix E: The Aftermath to the Crisis (in chronological order—1 January 1971 to 2002). *The October Crisis, 1970: An Insider's View.* Montreal: McGill-Queen's University Press, 2006. December 7, 2006, www.mcgill.ca/maritimelaw/crisis/.

Vallières, Pierre. *White Niggers of America.* Toronto: McClelland & Stewart, 1971.

Valpy, Michael. "Thobani Is Not Alone." *The Globe and Mail* (October 6, 2001): F9.

CRITICAL THINKING QUESTIONS

1. How important a factor was state repression in the decline of the 1960s social movements in Canada?

2. Did the state help to manufacture the "terrorist threat" in order to justify state repression?
3. Was the government justified in invoking the War Measures Act when the country was not at war? On what grounds?
4. How would you define "terrorism"? Can you define it in such as way that your definition does not contain biases about what is and is not a legitimate use of violence?
5. Is the War on Terror also a war on legitimate dissent?
6. Is the structural explanation offered by Pasha and Lubeck sufficient to explain why activists resort to terror?

FURTHER READING

Burke, Jason. *Al-Qaeda: Casting a Shadow of Terror.* London: I.B. Tauris, 2003.
Much of the writing about al Qaeda is sensationalist or blinkered by presuppositions. Burke avoids these pitfalls. He is a journalist, not an academic, but was one of the first to understand the loose network structure of al Qaeda.

Elliott, Philip, Graham Murdock, and Philip Schlesinger. "'Terrorism' and the State: A Case Study of the Discourses of Television." *Media, Culture and Society* 5, no. 2 (1983): 155–177.
Elliott et al. have developed a sophisticated and critical model for analyzing representations of "terrorism." They argue that complex "ideological labour" is involved in representing state violence in one light and insurgent violence in another. However, their case study of English television representations of IRA violence show surprising ways in which alternative analyses can be heard.

Gills, Barry K. *Globalization and the Politics of Resistance.* New York: St. Martin's Press, 2000.
This collection contains the essay by Pasha that we used to explain the roots of contemporary Muslim social movements. Check out the other essays for more on the international context as well as analyses of other social movements in the developing world understood within the context of neoliberal globalization.

Sidel, Mark. *More Secure Less Free? Antiterrorism Policy & Civil Liberties after September 11.* Ann Arbor: University of Michigan Press, 2004.
This book will give you an idea of the full extent of the domestic "War on Terror" in the United States and its implications for restrictions on freedom and the independence of civil society. Sidel compares the U.S. situation with that in the U.K., Australia, and India, but, unfortunately, neglects Canada.

Vallières, Pierre. *White Niggers of America.* Toronto: McClelland & Stewart, 1971.
Vallières makes a case for revolution in Quebec. In addition to documenting the social and economic oppression of the Québécois, he takes you on his own personal and intellectual journey toward the FLQ. His account burns with the intensity of youthful passion.

RELEVANT WEB SITES

Al Jazeera
http://english.aljazeera.net/HomePage
> Here is where you get the Arab perspective on world events. It is particularly useful to provide balance to the U.S. media treatment of Muslim resistance movements and "terrorism."

Electronic Intifada
http://electronicintifada.net/new.shtml
> U.K.-based Net activism in support of the Palestinian cause. Their take on Palestinian "terrorism" will be different from that of the Institute for Counter-Terrorism.

Institute for Counter-Terrorism
www.ict.org.il
> This research institute provides insight into contemporary terrorism from the standpoint of protecting the security of Israeli and other citizens. You may find their discussion of female suicide bombers particularly interesting (http://www.ict.org.il/articles/articledet.cfm?articleid=470).

Muslim Wake Up!
www.muslimwakeup.com
> Muslims and non-Muslims come here to discuss the faith and social justice in a post-9/11 world. Shortly after the arrest of 17 Canadians on suspicion of plotting a terror attack, Shujaat Wasty asks, "Why is it that when a Canadian Christian or Canadian Jew or Canadian Hindu or Canadian Sikh commits a crime, their fellow members in faith are not asked to apologize for him or her, but when a Canadian Muslim commits a crime, all Muslims are expected to do so?"

Third World Network
www.twnside.org.sg
> The Third World Network is a research organization based in Malaysia. From their Web site you can learn more about the effects of neocolonialism and the neoliberal revolution seen from the vantage point of the "developing" world.

Chapter 8

CONSUMER-CITIZEN:
THE MARKET AS A SOCIAL
MOVEMENT TOOL

Introduction:
The Good Corporate Citizen

In 1997 the transnational corporation Stora Kopparberg stopped spraying herbicides on forests in Nova Scotia. Local environmentalists were pleased but perplexed. Most had given up fighting Stora on this issue back in 1984 when they were defeated in the infamous Herbicide Trial. So unfair had the judgment in that trial seemed that they were convinced that not only the corporation, but the province and judicial system would go to any lengths to oppose them. Provincial ministers had labelled them "subversive elements" out to destroy the modern way of life.

In their favour, a Swedish expert had presented to the court a methodologically sophisticated study on the long-term health effects of the chemicals in the herbicide—2,4-D and 2,4,5-T. Comparing a large number of people who had been exposed to the chemical to a "control" group who had not, his team concluded that chemical exposure led to a significantly higher risk of cancer. The judge, however, was much more impressed by the testimony of Dow Chemical's "hired gun," who assured everyone that so long as they didn't drink the herbicide, they would be safe. The environmentalists had been seeking a court injunction to stop the spray.

The judge ruled against them and, implying that they had frivolously attacked the poor corporation, demanded that they pay Stora's legal costs. Not only did they have to endure 2,4-D and 2,4,5-T being sprayed close to their lands, but they also faced losing their property and homes. The intent was to discourage "in their infancy" these sorts of legal challenges to corporate environmental practices.

So what had happened between 1984 and 1997 to awaken the corporation's conscience? The provincial government's attitude had not changed. Officials in the Department of Natural Resources opposed the phasing out of herbicides. They thought there was no better way to kill hardwoods and promote the kind of softwood monoculture that the provincial pulp and paper industry demanded.

The 1984 herbicide decision had been very unpopular in Sweden, Stora's home country. After all, 2,4-D and 2,4,5-T had already been banned in Sweden due to health concerns. Swedes, like many Europeans, also had a romantic (and inaccurate) notion of Canadian wilderness as untouched "nature" lost long ago in Europe. The fact that Mi'kmaq Indians were among the environmental challengers to Stora only added to the romance. The European environmental movement is in many ways stronger than that in North America. It has been much more successful in politicizing a broad-based consumer movement against genetically modified foods, beef raised using growth hormones, and forest products obtained through cutting old growth, clear-cutting, or other "unsustainable" practices.

As a multinational, Stora must develop products, but also a corporate "brand" that appeals across all markets. Corporate strategists decided that the best way to appease European consumers was to apply for independent environmental certification through the International Standards Organization (ISO). Phasing out herbicides was just one of a number of voluntary commitments that Stora made in its plan of improvement mandated by the ISO 14001 series of environmental standards.

Admittedly Stora's "conscience" was awakened by external pressure, but it is nonetheless acting as a better "corporate citizen." Social movement actors are key to this transformation. The irony is that it was not local people who had a direct, material interest in the health consequences of the spray, but distant players whose interest was much more abstract—the preservation of an imagined natural integrity—who had the decisive power here. A further irony is that the medium of their influence over a transnational firm was the capitalist market itself. How far could social movements go in reforming capitalist firms by using the capitalist market?

There have been some remarkable successes in the use of market activism. In this chapter I will describe one in detail—the campaign to stop clear-cutting in Clayoquot Sound. Together we will explore the idea that consumer activism exploits features of neoliberalism and the "new economy." Here we will draw upon Naomi Klein's hugely popular book on anti-corporate activism, *No Logo*. Klein's analysis raises the question of whether the new market activists' identities are so deeply embedded in the commodity culture of capitalism that they could never fundamentally challenge it.

NEOLIBERAL MARKET GOVERNANCE

As power shifts, so do the strategies and tactics of social movements. In the 1990s, as you know, power shifted from states to markets. The new mobility of capital was the coercive force behind this realignment. The shift was also actively promoted by international lending institutions, governments responding to business interests, and international treaty organizations like the World Trade Organization and the North American Free Trade Agreement. In order to compete for investment, governments reduced corporate taxes and where they could, they reduced government spending, including in such sensitive areas as health care, education, and the environment. Budgets for federal and provincial departments of the environment were slashed.

The neoliberal faith was that environmental health could still be protected with less direct government regulation and reduced government spending. You remember from the previous chapter that the idea was to find new ways of "autonomizing" state power. Corporations and individuals within civil society were encouraged to "row their own boats" with the government at most helping to steer or, better still, setting out buoys to mark the course and only occasionally checking in to see how well corporate and other citizens were following it.

"Environmental citizenship" was the theme of Canada's Green Plan for environmental governance in 1991. Neoliberal legislators assumed that corporations could be trusted to "govern themselves" because they all, like Stora, had a growing interest in their reputations as good corporate citizens. Civil society organizations were encouraged to inform corporate citizenship through voluntary participation on government-sponsored panels and round tables. Individuals were called upon to expand their conception of citizenship by extending it into the realm of consumer behaviour. The new consumer-citizen was meant to help "govern" corporations by sending them "messages" through their purchasing decisions.

Product Certification

The Canadian government hoped to frame and channel this market nexus between corporate and individual citizens by setting up its own environmental certification scheme—more comprehensive than the ISO's 14001 standard. Canada's Environmental Choice certification was developed in consultation with environmental organizations, and set high standards for compliance. Perhaps this was one of the reasons for its failure. Compliance for many firms would have meant substantial changes to their production processes. Few applied and fewer got products with the Environmental Choice logo on them on to the shelves. Consumers remained largely unaware of the program's existence and consequently there never was an Environmental Choice "bandwagon" that other corporations felt the need to climb on to.

Corporations found that it was much easier to conform to their own environmental standards and "codes of conduct." The ISO is an industry-controlled organization that initiated its 14001 series of environmental management standards to head off numerous and competing standards-setting initiatives being developed by governments (Nash and Ehrenfeld 37–38). Unlike Canada's Environmental Choice program, ISO 14001 sets no specific requirements for how products must be harvested, manufactured, or distributed in order to be considered environmentally sustainable. Instead it mandates a plan for improvement.

Firms must commit to environmental principles, set goals, and monitor their own efforts to comply with these goals. The ISO 14001 is better than other "corporate codes of conduct" in recognizing that companies themselves should not be evaluating how well they are following the environmental path, but should periodically submit to audits from independent third parties. Still, if they choose, they can keep embarrassing lapses secret since there is no requirement for the public to have access to the audits.

Finally, a company certified by ISO 14001 does not have to demand that its suppliers or distributors follow environmentally responsible practices. Transnational firms have often been able to outsource "dirty work" involving poor environmental or labour practices. While Nike may not engage in hiring sweatshop labour, the shoes they sell you might still be made by sweatshop work-

ers. The Canadian Pulp and Paper Association supported an ISO-style Environmental Management System through the Canadian Standards Association.

Critics argue that this standard tells consumers little about the environmental practices followed in making the products that they buy (Von Mirbach). Paper could be made with no recycled content from trees grown using herbicides and pesticides and clear-cut harvested. Lumber could come from clear-cutting old-growth forests. Even more damaging practices might be involved in producing the raw materials bought from suppliers.

Greenwash: Selling a Simulacrum of Environmental Virtue

Critics of "market governance" point out that corporations have numerous ways of evading pressures from politicized consumers. When faced with negative public perceptions of their product or production process, the first impulse of many firms is to try and change public perception. Selling idealized images of themselves is, after all, part of their main business—many spend far more on marketing than on actually making the things that they sell. It is cheaper and easier to sell what cultural theorists call a "simulacrum" of environmental virtue to the public instead of the real thing.

Cost efficiency, not ethics, is still key to capitalist survival. Sometimes firms simply make false claims about the environmental virtues of their products. Mobil Chemical claimed, for example, that their "Hefty" plastic garbage bags were biodegradable. The truth was that while sunlight would eventually make the bags crumble into small plastic fragments, these fragments would add no usable nutrients to the soil. This is not really what "biodegradable" means. Mobil failed to point out that even this much degradation would not happen if the bags were buried in a landfill—the normal fate of garbage bags.

In order to provide room to fudge their claims, corporations have lobbied against legal definitions of terms like "biodegradable" and "recycled" (Beder 191). Or they have lobbied for lax definitions. Agribusiness firms, for instance, would like to see the United States Department of Agriculture's definition of "organic" foods include genetically modified foods.

The most common form of corporate "greenwash" involves taking credit for small environmental initiatives in order to divert attention from an overall record of environmental harm, or active anti-environmental campaigns—weakening environmental legislation, taking legal action against community groups, and attacking the legitimacy of environmental NGOs. The 2005 Awards for "America's 10 worst greenwashers" gave the number eight spot to TruGreen ChemLawn for its *Project EverGreen,* which "teaches consumers about the environmental benefits of well-maintained landscapes."

> At the same time, through lies of omission, the awareness campaign hides the environment costs of chemically-dependent lawn care. Along with other members of the self-styled Green Industry, TruGreen ChemLawn has fostered an American obsession with "the perfect lawn." Each year, more than 70 million pounds of pesticides are used on America's 30 million acres of lawn. Of the 32 pesticide products available through TruGreen ChemLawn's residential services, 17 contain possible carcinogens, 11 contain known or suspected reproductive toxins, and all 32 threaten non-targeted species and

> ecosystems. Despite the growing popularity of organic lawn care, TruGreen ChemLawn does not offer customers an organic option. (Greenlife)

The top spot went to Ford for attempting to bask in the "green" glow of its new hybrid SUV (which produces less CO_2, the major greenhouse gas, than regular gas-powered SUVs) and factory at River Rouge that incorporates state-of-the-art technologies for energy efficiency and wastewater treatment. In part due to its heavy marketing of SUVs, Ford's overall fleet of vehicles had (for the fifth year running) the worst fuel economy of all major automakers. Only one half of one percent of this fleet has hybrid engines. The company continues to lobby against U.S. initiatives to legislate lower CO_2 emissions. In balance its actions are speeding the rate of climate change—the 21st century's most ominous environmental threat.

CORPORATE DECEPTION: FRONT GROUPS

When companies have serious "image problems"—chemical leaks that kill people outright, oil spills that devastate natural habitat, or products (like cigarettes) that lead to untimely death, they can turn to public relations specialists like Burson-Marsteller. Apparently no challenge is too great for this firm. It accepted the Argentine military junta as a client and helped it improve its international image while it continued its "dirty war" against dissent in the late 1970s (Rowell 116).

One of the options big PR firms offer clients with environmental problems is to attack their environmentalist critics. Instead of trying, like Ford or Stora, to speak the language of environmentalism, they can subvert and undermine that language. One of Burson-Marsteller's specialties is mobilizing anti-environmental lobbying campaigns that appear to come from "citizens' groups." PR firms advise their clients to "put your words in someone else's mouth" for the appearance of greater legitimacy (Porter/Novelli spokesperson, qtd. in Beder 27).

The American Petroleum Institute (API) and the oil giants it represents have pursued this strategy. They set up the Global Climate Coalition to fight the Kyoto Protocol and have spent millions to spread disinformation about climate change. Debate always exists within science, but climate change debates are now about the details, not about whether or not human-induced climate change is occurring. Climate-change deniers cannot get published in peer-reviewed journals and depend upon industry-funded "think tanks" like the Competitive Enterprise Institute and industry-sponsored media outlets like Tech CentralStation.com to get their message out (Mooney). Uncritical media attention to this corporate-generated "controversy" has helped to make the United States one of the few countries in the world where people actually believe that climate change is not "real" (Dispensa and Brulle).

BOX 8.1:

"DON'T BUY SFI"

The following image is from a recent campaign of the Rainforest Action Network (RAN). It is an example of "culture jamming." RAN activists have taken a corporate eco-label (the tree with the leaf-like circle) and sabotaged it. The RAN slogans are also interesting. The one that they have highlighted "Don't Buy SFI" has dual meaning. Literally it is asking consumers not to purchase wood with this eco-label. However, perhaps more importantly, it is telling consumers not to buy into the hype.

Many anti-corporate "market" campaigns of the 21st century are as much about what Snow and Benford (in Chapter 5) called the "politics of signification" as they are about literal boycotts of products. Undermining corporate hype could be a step toward the type of boycott that RAN has shown itself capable of organizing. However, RAN would be targeting corporate buyers in addition to individual consumers. When this Web campaign was active (December 2005), that did not seem to be their main thrust.

In fact, a boycott might have been difficult to bring off since it would be necessary to boycott all of the members of the American Forest & Paper Association (AF&PA), including "... the largest loggers in the United States and Canada and the largest wholesale distributors of global wood products." All AF&PA members were required to participate in the certification program when the SFI label was created in 2002.

 The second slogan, "Same-old Forest Industry"—elsewhere on the site it appears as "SFI = Same-old Forest Industry"—is catchy, particularly if you have never heard of the corporate "Sustainable Forestry Initiative ®." This "anti-logo" is designed to be downloaded and made into 3-inch by 4-inch stickers that "hactivists" can put wherever their fancy strikes them—presumably on wood products sporting the corporate eco-label.

This is a low-cost way of broadcasting from the Net to the world of physical encounter. Volunteer hactivists, not even members of RAN, distribute the stickers out of concern for the forest or for the sheer pleasure of "sticking it" to a hypocritical corporate initiative. People looking for wood see the sticker, and, because there is a Web address, can go to the Web site and see what the fuss is about.

The Web site gives a point-form overview of RAN's argument that SFI is corporate greenwash. It also provides reports from a number of NGOs who assess in detail the SFI scheme and its inadequacies from an environmental point of view. Sympathetic people are invited to take part in the culture jamming, but also to engage in a very traditional letter-writing campaign to protest the weak standards of the SFI certification. Check out the Web site as an example of 21st-century social movement strategy. You may also want to read some of the reports and see if RAN is justified in its attack on SFI.

Source: Rainforest Action Network, www.RAN.org.

By misrepresenting their environmental credentials or misrepresenting environmental science, corporations engage in a kind of "communications jamming" that makes it difficult for consumers to make informed decisions. In so doing, they undermine the mechanism that is supposed to make market governance work. They also undermine confidence in the discourse of "corporate citizenship," the idea that corporations can govern themselves and follow socially and environmentally responsible codes of conduct without stringently enforced government regulation.

Market governance as conceived by neoliberals involves consumers acting as individuals, watching the ads and cruising the aisles in isolation from one another. Citizens who are organized through churches, unions, and environmental groups have taken different, some might say subversive, approaches to the idea of using the market to govern corporations: shareholder activism and consumer boycotts. Neoliberal governments and corporations have tended to be hostile to these forms of "market governance."

Shareholder Activism: Petty Capitalists with Social Consciences

The ownership structure of capitalist firms has changed since Marx and Engels' time. Instead of being owned by individual capitalists, most large firms are now owned by a multitude of shareholders. Here many individuals act legally as one "body"—this is what the term "corporation" refers to. Corporations are similar in this way to co-operatives except that they do not follow the principle of one person, one vote. Individuals or other firms that own numerous shares have more votes and a greater say in the affairs of the corporation. Small investors tend not to show up or vote at shareholders' meetings, so corporations normally operate as though owned by a small handful of capitalists.

Some activists are attempting to change this. They point out that workers and other civil society actors are actually part owners of corporations. Workers invest through union pension funds; churches and large NGOs through investments designed to generate income for their activities. Coalitions like the Interfaith Center on Corporate Responsibility (ICCR; see their Web site at www.iccr.org) hope that by pooling their combined votes, civil society investors can challenge business as usual, advance meaningful codes of conduct, and ensure that they are followed (Hutchinson). In Canada activist shareholders have had to overcome serious legal hurdles. Despite government rhetoric about citizen involvement in corporate governance, it was illegal throughout the 1990s for shareholders to propose corporate policy that would promote "... general economic, political, racial, religious, social or similar causes." In 2001 after nine years of lobbying led by the Taskforce on the Churches and Social Responsibility, this line was struck from the Canada Business Corporations Act, but the law remains ill suited to genuine shareholder democracy (Yaron 16–17).

Nonetheless, shareholder activists can claim some part in convincing companies to boycott South Africa in the 1980s. These company boycotts were an essential component of the international pressure that brought an end to apartheid. The tactic they used was not to vote on proposals at shareholder meetings, but simply to sell off their shares in protest. This is a form of investor boycott. Movements have found investor and consumer boycotts to be powerful tools, and this strategy is what we turn to in the following section.

MOVEMENT SUBVERSION OF MARKET GOVERNANCE: CLAYOQUOT CASE

The Problem with Clear-cutting

The planet's forest cover is dwindling in the face of relentless global demand for timber and paper. This is a global concern since, as you probably know, forests draw CO_2 out of the atmosphere and thereby slow the rate of climate change. They also harbour biodiversity, an ecological value that will increasingly be threatened by climate change in the 21st century. Many people have also become alarmed at the local effects of industrial forest practices designed to maximize the rate of extraction.

In Canada, practices like herbicide and pesticide spraying, clear-cutting, and the deployment of massive machines that can harvest and process trees day and night are all of relatively recent origin. People who live in forestry-dependent areas have concerns about the effects on "non-target" species (including humans) of poisonous spraying, the loss of jobs to mechanization, and whether the rate of regrowth will keep up with the rate of harvesting. In British Columbia local concern has focused on clear-cutting of "old-growth" forests.

A mature forest is a vertical, multi-storeyed habitat. Some species of lichens and insects exist only at the upper level, near the canopy. Clear-cutting eliminates much of this habitat, at least temporarily. Critics argue that the regrowth is never as biologically diverse and may take many generations to become so. Without the canopy, the forest floor is exposed to erosion, the loss of soil and nutrients to the streams, dramatically so on the steep slopes characteristic of the B.C. coast. Silt and nutrient overload degrade stream habitat. Streams alternately dry up and flood in the hotter, drier microclimate and no longer can support the same diversity of life. Local people and outfitters find the fishing is worse. Most dramatic, however, are the aesthetic effects. Clear-cutting turns a green, mossy world that many experience as like a living cathedral into an apocalyptic "moonscape."

State Co-optation of Local Activism

Local efforts to oppose clear-cutting in Clayoquot Sound began in 1979. People from the town of Tofino formed the Friends of Clayoquot Sound (FOCS) to stop MacMillan Bloedel from logging Meares Island, which dominated the town's "viewscape" and was the source of its drinking water. The local Tla-o-qui-aht band of the Nuu-chah-nulth First Nation joined with FOCS in a blockade in 1984. West Coast First Nations never signed the treaties that had elsewhere "extinguished" Aboriginal legal title to their lands. In the case of Meares Island, the Tla-o-qui-aht were able to convince the courts to halt all logging until their claims to title had been resolved.

MacMillan Bloedel's ambitions, however, extended throughout Clayoquot Sound—a glacier-carved valley and coastal inlet—and social movement opposition was to continue and grow. For the first decade conflicts were largely state-mediated. Until 1993 the provincial government struggled to contain them within the bounds of the "local" and state-managed "due process."

After another blockade in 1988, FOCS helped set up the Clayoquot Sound Sustainable Development Steering Committee to build community-based consensus on the future of the region. They sought broad representation, and participants included "a village alderman; a logger; a fisheries technician; the owners of a construction business; and a member of the Chamber of Commerce" (Shaw 31). Karena Shaw, who has written about Clayoquot politics, represents this locally based, democratic search for solutions as the ideal approach.

However, it is not the local community but the province that has jurisdiction over natural resources. Provincial ministers have no obligation to heed self-appointed local committees. Acknowledging this limitation, the Steering Committee decided to invite the province to participate in the hope of gaining some official support and recognition. In so doing, it handed over the power to define the process and frame the agenda. The province began by changing the representation of the committee.

Its new Clayoquot Sound Sustainable Development Task Force encompassed a larger administrative unit—the Alberni-Clayoquot Regional District—which included the communities of Port Alberni and Ucluelet, where pro-logging support was greater than in Tofino. Provincial officials also invited on board two multinational companies interested in logging in the area (Fletcher Challenge [Canada] and MacMillan Bloedel), the province's largest forestry workers' union (the IWA), government departments, and, not the local Tla-o-qui-aht band, but the broader Nuu-chah-nulth tribal council. Who was to say that these were not all members of the real "community" of interested parties?

Needless to say, this was a more difficult group in which to reach consensus. The first issue that they failed to agree on was whether logging should continue before the task force had come up with its recommendations. Negotiations were difficult and drawn out. Environmentalists began to feel that "representation" was stacked in favour of pro-logging interests. The big players—the union, corporations, and government departments—could afford to send paid representatives to meetings whereas Friends of Clayoquot were all volunteers who struggled to find the time to meet and do the research to build their case. In order to deal with the impasse, the government referred the question of short-term harvesting policy to the B.C. Cabinet. It restructured the task force (which now became the Clayoquot Sound Sustainable Development Strategy Steering Committee or CSSDSSC) and refocused its mandate on long-term planning.

The B.C. Cabinet disappointed local opponents to clear-cut logging when it decided neither to stop nor significantly limit clear-cutting while the new CSSDSSC did its work. The whole exercise started to seem like a deliberate strategy to keep the opposition engaged in futile debate while clear-cutting went ahead unchecked. Representatives of the Friends of Clayoquot decided in 1991 that they would no longer help legitimate this "talk-and-log" strategy, so withdrew from the committee, which they now labelled the Clayoquot Sound Sustainable *Destruction* Strategy Steering Committee. The government-sponsored forum had proved unable to contain the opposing forces and still maintain legitimacy. Conflict again spilled beyond its boundaries. It exploded first in acts of personal frustration: a logging bridge was sabotaged, and "shouting matches" erupted in local parking lots (Shaw 33–34). However, that frustration developed quickly into organized civil disobedience.

Global Environmental Actors

At the same time, national and international environmental organizations, along with a global "bystander public," began to take notice of the conflict. The "community of interest" was again expanding, but this time in a way that would shift the balance in favour of the Friends of Clayoquot. Global actors were already implicated. Actual people recognized themselves behind the anonymous "global market" for wood products that drives intensified harvesting in distant places. 1992 was also the year of the United Nations' Earth Summit in Rio, which raised public consciousness about environmental issues and established the principle of international collective responsibility for finding solutions.

It was at this conference that the framework agreements on limiting greenhouse gasses (later called Kyoto) and preserving

biodiversity were signed. In the Convention on Biodiversity, negotiators from countries in the North made claims on "hotspots" of biodiversity that needed protection in the South. The Brazilian rainforest, under assault from state-sponsored road building, logging, and ranching, was the poster child of hotspots. Already the most influential international conservation organizations—the IUCN and the World Wildlife Fund (WWF)—had been seeking alliances with indigenous users of the forests against corrupt governments at work in liquidating them.

In B.C. an NGO called Ecotrust began documenting indigenous knowledge of the Clayoquot rainforest and discovering the astonishing diversity of plant and animal species for which the Nuu-chah-nulth had cultural uses. The Victoria-based Western Canada Wilderness Committee began building walking trails that would allow outsiders to experience and learn about Clayoquot. Journalists from as far away as Japan began to arrive with television crews to capture for their viewers the drama of a battle to save the wilderness. The Sierra Club organized a solidarity caravan from Atlantic Canada under the slogan "From the Oceans without Fish to the Forest without Trees." All of this traffic in Tofino created demand for more spaces at bed and breakfasts, more restaurants, more gas and groceries. Local infrastructure, a physical "platform," was required to accommodate this growing international solidarity. A new local industry based on "conflict tourism" developed, driven (like forestry) by global market demand (Shaw 36–37).

Clayoquot Summer: Peaceful Direct Action

Friends of Clayoquot led a dedicated band of "forest protectors" in a blockade of the Clayoquot Arm Bridge in the "Rainforest

Summer" of 1992. Activists were willing to put themselves in harm's way by locking their bodies to the bridge or to logging trucks. One young woman put her life at risk by perching on a log suspended in such a way that if a logging truck crossed, she would be pitched into the ravine below. As direct action, these tactics were meant to slow "business as usual" for the logging companies.

There was also an element of "witnessing" to injustice. Many waited passively for the RCMP to haul them away—there were 65 arrests that summer. There was also, as Dan Lewis explains, an experiential element of personal self-affirmation:

> So was it all worth it? We didn't succeed in stopping the logging, but we certainly put Clayoquot Sound back in the news. So often we hear of invasions into wild country by multinational logging companies. It's easy to become overwhelmed, and filled with despair. But taking direct action with other people to create positive social change is an antidote to despair. People become empowered when they stand up for their beliefs and this empowerment sends ripples through society. This was perhaps the greatest benefit of Rainforest Summer. (Lewis)

The following year hundreds came from the rest of Canada and around the world in search of this "antidote to despair." "Clayoquot Summer" attracted a broad cross-section of people. In addition to the environmental counterculture, young and old, there were forestry workers, Anglican ministers, members of Parliament, businesspeople, retirees. The "Raging Grannies," dressed outrageously and sang their signature protest songs. Greenpeace was able to convince the rock band Midnight Oil to play simultaneously for the protesters at the "Peace Camp" and to the world through Much Music. Robert F. Kennedy Jr. made a highly publicized appearance.

Many would-be eco-warriors were also drawn to Clayoquot Sound that summer. However, as one of them complained, the blockade was run by "peace Nazis," and "... Earth First! was definitely not welcome at that point, nor were tree-sitters, or lock-ons, or elves [members of the Earth Liberation Front dedicated to inflicting 'economic sabotage on Earth-rapers'] (Expatriated Biocentric Turtle Island Earth First!er)." The position of Friends of Clayoquot and the general feeling of activists gathered at the "Peace Camp" was that any appearance of "eco-extremism" would be a public relations liability.

Instead, each morning at dawn, they engaged in a ritual confrontation. Demonstrators would gather. A handful who were prepared to go to jail would stand in the path of the logging trucks. The RCMP would read the court injunction against the blockade, then make their arrests. One of the Raging Grannies felt that the RCMP officer who had arrested her "pried her off the pavement" so gingerly and politely that she knit him a pair of socks. She went to jail nonetheless (Delaney).

Clayoquot Trials: SLAPPed by the Law

Nine hundred people allowed themselves to be arrested for these acts of conscientious defiance. The aim of civil disobedience is to bring attention to an injustice by taking a principled stand against an unjust law. Those who publicly defy the law have to face the possibility of imprisonment—this is the measure of their strength of conscience. Still, many of the 860 who were eventually tried for their part in the blockade were not prepared for the severity of the court's retribution.

They were not given the opportunity to defend their actions in terms that they understood—altruistic motive and the compelling nature of their cause. The judges were simply interested in evidence of contrition and respect, and where they did not find it, they sentenced people to over a month in jail with fines up to $3,000. A convicted car thief laughed when an imprisoned protestor told him his sentence: "'This is my third time and I'm getting less time than you.' 'Yes' came the reply, 'but you didn't steal a car from MacMillan Bloedel. Try that next time and see what you get'" (qtd. in Hatch 128).

The harsh sentences reflected the nature of a legal injunction. Court injunctions are often used in domestic abuse cases. There is already a law against domestic abuse. But where there is good reason to believe that an abusive spouse is likely to break that law, the court intervenes between the two parties, saying in effect, "Try to mess with her and you will have to deal with me first." The deterrent effect depends upon the authority of the court and defying that authority is treated as an insult to, or "contempt of," court—in this case, "criminal" contempt. What is at stake is the very credibility of state power, something much more grave than simply the breaking of a law.

Injunctions have been used in Canada against striking unions in ways that many argue undermine civil rights: the right to strike and the right of public assembly. Some legal scholars argue that it should be used (as in the domestic abuse case) only where there is a credible threat of violence. However, there was no violence from protestors in the Clayoquot case. There were also existing laws—against mischief and trespass—that could be used to keep people from blocking a logging road.

In granting the injunction at MacMillan Bloedel's request, the B.C. court invoked extraordinary powers in the suppression of dissent. Furthermore, it took the onus off the multinational corporation. The "offence" was not against MacMillan Bloedel, as it would have been under a charge of trespass, but against the state. While the judiciary operates independently of the government, that was not the perception of the public in this case. Both the government and the courts appeared to be acting together in the interests of a multinational corporation. The fact that the government had recently bought a large block of shares in MacMillan Bloedel only added to the perception of collusion (Hatch 132–133).

While MacMillan Bloedel's own record before the courts had no legal bearing on the case, people were also outraged that no corporate executives had been held legally responsible for the company's numerous convictions for illegal logging practices, while peaceful protestors were being found criminally liable for acts of conscience. Civil disobedience succeeded, to this extent, in bringing attention to injustice in the law.

However, the apparent arbitrariness of the use of state power also had a chilling effect, just as it had in Nova Scotia after the Herbicide Trial. Many activists had begun to see a pattern in corporate uses of the law against dissent and had come up with a term for it: SLAPPs or "strategic lawsuits against public participation." The idea of a SLAPP is to harass activists, particularly leaders and organizers, with lawsuits, regardless of the likelihood of gaining a conviction. Environmental NGOs, particularly the popular grassroots groups, have limited financial resources and rely mostly on people's volunteer time. Lawsuits are financially intimidating for people who must defend themselves or, for people represented by organizations, put strain on these organizations' finances.

More importantly, they absorb time and can take leaders out of action at strategic moments in a struggle. Tzeporah Berman, a talented organizer at the Peace Camp, became the target of a SLAPP in the Clayoquot case. MacMillan Bloedel, hoping to disable people like Berman, had applied for an extension of the injunction to those "aiding and abetting" the civil disobedience, but was rejected on the grounds that this would unduly infringe upon people's freedom of speech. Somehow the RCMP arrested Berman in any case. Despite the fact that she had not, nor was there any evidence to suggest that she had, engaged in civil disobedience herself, the case went to trial and it took the judge more than a year to decide that it should be dismissed (Hatch 147; Shaw 44).

In the end, the Clayoquot trials failed in terms of legitimating state authority and channelling the conflict toward state-managed "due process." Activists redirected strategy. Instead of trying to convince the state to better regulate forest harvesting, they turned to the corporations themselves. Instead of using legal tools, they turned to the global market.

Brazil of the North: The Market Campaign

Colleen McCrory, of Canada's Future Forest Alliance, had already demonstrated the power of rebranding with her "Brazil of the North" campaign. In part sober comparison (the Forest Alliance showed in 1992 that while Canada clear-cut and burned a similar area of trees annually, it protected less than a third of what Brazil had) the idea resonated, like any powerful brand imagery, and invited multiple readings. It repositioned Canada, idealized in the European mind as a vast repository of unspoiled nature, in troubling relation to a globally understood symbol of environmental pillage. It played upon northern complacency rooted in the assumption that only "Third World" states were incapable of governing responsibly.

While the slogan was meant to apply to Canadian forestry generally, the rainforest connection (the West Coast is considered "temperate rainforest") made it adhere most tenaciously to B.C. where it interfered with the province's own efforts to brand itself as "super-natural," "Beautiful British Columbia." Provincial officials, like corporate marketing executives, were beginning to understand the economic value of branding. Global "brand recognition" of B.C. that conveyed the right "meanings" was crucial to its tourism industry, but also increasingly to the ability of other industries like forestry to access international markets.

The B.C. government was spending millions of dollars on a public relations campaign, which was increasingly focused on countering the damaging "Brazil of the North" imagery. Money went to advertisements, publicity tours to Europe, and also to an NGO, confusingly named the "Forest Alliance." The Forest Alliance had been set up by the forestry industry on the advice of Burson-Marsteller, and was attempting to undermine the credibility of McCrory's Future Forest Alliance claims. The premier of B.C. led a delegation to Europe in 1994 to defend the province's forest-harvesting standards. Greenpeace led an environmentalist counter-tour that staged press conferences and demonstrations challenging the government's message wherever the premier went.

Greenpeace, now a global player, had actually started out in 1970 in B.C. By 1994 it had established independent chapters in countries throughout the world, and had carefully positioned itself as global "brand" signifying "no compromise," but also integrity in ecological campaigning. Its global reputation, and also the infrastructure of support that its international networks provided, suited it to counter-PR on this scale. No local or provincial environmental organization would have been able to pull this off without the help of an international player.

Greenpeace had begun to work in concert with the Friends of Clayoquot in 1993 and had become frustrated with the intransigence of the B.C. government. Organizers also began to rethink the Clayoquot strategy of trying to protect "special places" while clear-cutting went on unopposed in the rest of the province. Their new strategy had two parts. The first was to convince corporate buyers with large contracts to boycott MacMillan Bloedel and in this way to coerce the company to negotiate in the Clayoquot case. The second was to persuade major purchasers to stop buying *any* wood or paper products made with old-growth wood. Greenpeace collaborated with the U.S.-based Rainforest Action Network (RAN), which had influence in the American market. Greenpeace led where it already had influence in Japan and Europe. Together they mobilized environmental movement support, bringing on board national and regional organizations like the European Rainforest Alliance.

They and their partners lobbied corporate buyers of wood products with remarkable success. It may seem a bit uncharacteristic for corporations to sign on to an environmentalist-led boycott. The persuasiveness of Greenpeace, RAN, and the Rainforest Alliance lay in the credibility of their claims to "represent" and/or to be able to mobilize the sentiments of a broad buying public. This is a curious form of representation because these NGOs are speaking for people, most of whom are not members and do not vote on the organizations' policies. Greenpeace and its allies were claiming to tap into and, through their own sophisticated public relations capacity, to shape the cultural *zeitgeist*

more effectively than corporate or government spin doctors.

Both prongs of the strategy were effective. Europe's largest home-improvement retailer, B&Q, agreed to phase out products derived from old-growth wood. By the end of 1998, 27 corporations in North America—including computer giants IBM and Dell, Kinko's copy centre, 3M, Mitsubishi, and clothing retailers Nike and Levi-Strauss—made similar commitments. The Rainforest Action Network's main target was Home Depot, the continent's largest lumber retailer. "We tried to go with the strategy that a swarm of wasps can drive even an elephant crazy," explained Chris Hatch, one of RAN's campaign organizers (qtd. in Johnson).

The "wasps" included a coalition of environmental organizations able to mobilize anti-Home Depot demonstrations in hundreds of locations: Greenpeace, Sierra Club, Natural Resources Defense Council, Forest Action Network, Rainforest Relief, Student Environmental Action Coalition, Free the Planet, Sierra Student Coalition, Action Resource Center, American Lands Alliance, Earth Culture, and scores of others. In addition to public demonstrations, they lobbied large shareholders such as unions and churches to place pressure on Home Depot to change its policy. In 1999 Home Depot joined the other corporations in agreeing to remove old-growth products from its shelves. This was a major victory for environmentalists.

Greenpeace had some success in getting buyers to boycott MacMillan Bloedel over its Clayoquot practices. However, the growing threat of the broader market campaign was enough to make the company realize that it had better seek some sort of compromise. It entered into a new set of negotiations over the future of Clayoquot, negotiations that this time completely bypassed the state. There were no federal, provincial, or local government representatives. Decisive power had shifted to players able to control the international market campaign. Across the table from MacMillan Bloedel were two transnational NGOs, Greenpeace and the U.S.-based Natural Resources Defence Council, along with their local affiliates: Greenpeace Canada, the Sierra Club of B.C., and the Western Canada Wilderness Committee. The Nuu-chah-nulth were also represented (Shaw 55).

Compromise: Ecological Harvesting

From the time that they had intervened to save Meares Island from clear-cutting, Aboriginal peoples had played a pivotal role in Clayoquot politics. While they had collaborated with non-Native locals in this instance, they were conscious of undercurrents of racism in the community. They, perhaps more than others, were committed to this place where their people had lived for generations. However, they did not and could not subsist on traditional low-impact hunting and gathering. They needed to expand local employment for their people. Locals had opposed one of their tourism developments as potentially "unsightly." Nuu-chah-nulth interest in forest-based resource industry was potentially at odds with local environmentalists' preference for wilderness protection.

Like all B.C. First Nations, they had a growing interest in negotiating with the provincial government over unresolved land claims, a strategy that could eclipse all others in terms of potential gains for their people. Courts had recently recognized that, in the absence of treaties, legal claims to Aboriginal title had standing. The provincial government had promised to begin dealing with these claims. In 1993 the province

saw here an opportunity to widen the split between Natives and non-Natives over Clayoquot. At the same time that it was punishing Clayoquot Summer demonstrators, it favoured the Nuu-chah-nulth and put it first in line to have its land claims settled. While negotiations were taking place, the Nuu-chah-nulth were to have significant powers over development within disputed lands in Clayoquot Sound (Shaw 42).

Environmental protection of Clayoquot Sound would not be possible without First Nations co-operation, in part because of their growing local power. Also the idea of Aboriginal peoples as "natural" stewards of the environment had enduring symbolic resonance for the global public to which international environmental organizations pitched their message of wilderness protection. The truth that Europeans and distant urbanites often failed to grasp was that "wilderness" is never "untouched." It has always been inhabited and exploited by human beings in ways that transform it. International NGOs could not be seen to be opposing Aboriginal peoples.

However, in order to keep First Nations on side, environmental organizations were learning, they would have to address their ongoing and changing need to exploit natural resources. The Nuu-chah-nulth were interested in logging in Clayoquot Sound. In order to develop necessary skills and knowledge and to benefit from existing tree-harvesting licences, they had formed a joint venture with MacMillan Bloedel called Iisaak (pronounced "E-sock") Forestry. They were also interested in what they could learn about ecological approaches to harvesting and marketing from the environmental organizations, and saw them as a potential counterweight to their powerful corporate partner (Shaw 55).

In 1998–1999 these three parties were able relatively quickly to work out an agreement, a "Memorandum of Understanding" (MOU), on "conservation-based" forestry practices for Iisaak Forestry in Clayoquot Sound. Women, interestingly, were the chief negotiators for all organizations except the Nuu-chah-nulth. Karena Shaw sees this as part of the reason that compromise was reached so quickly.

Iisaak means "respect" in the language of the Nuu-chah-nulth and its forestry philosophy is based on the principles of respect for cultural integrity and ecological sustainability. In the MOU, Iisaak Forestry agrees to refrain from logging in "pristine watersheds" and to ensure that wildlife corridors link these protected areas in the Clayoquot region. Here non-timber uses, including scientific research, ecotourism, and sustainable harvesting of other forest resources (such as mushrooms, herbs, berries, and the like) will be developed.

In harvested areas, Iisaak agrees to practise "variable retention logging." In other words, it will attempt to keep the canopy intact, leaving behind many trees with high economic value in order to preserve an environment that favours regrowth with old-growth characteristics (under the canopy, trees struggle to reach the light, growing thin and tall, with few knots and tightly spaced rings—this is what makes old growth such desirable wood). If Iisaak fulfills these promises, the environmental groups agree to share their scientific, economic, and marketing expertise as well as to help the Nuu-chah-nulth build independent capacity in these areas.

Perhaps ironically, Greenpeace and its partners found themselves committing to helping a logging company finance its operations and market products from old-growth forestry. There may have been some public relations benefit for them here. In the 1990s forestry campaigners had become the target of a powerful anti-environmentalist movement known as "wise-use" (or "Share" in Canada). One of the environmentalists' great weaknesses in the "symbolic struggle" of the period was the charge that they showed no regard for people in their zeal to protect wilderness.

They stood to lose potential allies among working people and Aboriginals who were learning to associate "preservationism" with disregard for human welfare. For its part, MacMillan Bloedel, as part owner of Iisaak, stood to benefit from continued logging in Clayoquot Sound. While variable retention logging would be less lucrative than clear-cutting, following ecological practices in this high-profile region would give the firm bragging rights as a model "corporate citizen."

Ironies of Market Governance

There are a number of ironies in this story. The central one is how the state was able to manoeuvre itself into irrelevance. All levels of government were left out of the final negotiations. Here the key players were civil society organizations with the power to mobilize "consumer citizens." The irony is that it was governments, embracing the neoliberal philosophy, that had promoted consumer citizenship and other forms of "market governance" in the first place. Neoliberal advocates of market governance had not really envisioned how their individualistic model of consumer citizenship would be "subverted" by organized consumer boycotts.

However, this "subversive market governance" has proved to be a powerful tool in the hands of social movement organizations. Governments and corporations in the Clayoquot dispute felt they could safely crush the largest demonstration of civil disobedience in Canadian history that took place during Clayoquot Summer. However, both stood up and took notice when contracts with European, Japanese, and American buyers were threatened. In the end, the corporate players capitulated and promised major changes in corporate policy.

This is only one story of "market victory" and an incomplete one at that. How reliable is a corporate promise, and who is monitoring such promises? They have no legal force, so governments and the courts will not be policing them. Has Home Depot succeeded in getting all old-growth wood off its shelves? Now that the heat of the Rainforest Action Network campaign is off, will firms be tempted to bask in the green glow of past commitments and find loopholes that allow them to revert to business as usual?

In the case of Iisaak (now co-owned by Weyerhaeuser, which bought out MacMillan Bloedel), it obtained Forest Stewardship Council certification for its forestry operations in 2002. This standard of certification requires independent third party audits that will help to keep the company honest. Also, when the MOU was signed, Friends of Clayoquot volunteered to act as an independent (they did not themselves sign the MOU) civil society monitor to see that all parties were living up to their commitments. Civil society actors like the Friends and the FSC can play an effective role in non-state governance.

But their efforts tend to be piecemeal and leave huge gaps in the regulatory net. Iisaak was not the only firm with licences to cut in Clayoquot Sound. Another company, Interfor, was still happily clear-cutting after the MOU was signed. Clayoquot Sound was not the only "pristine" watershed threatened by clear-cutting. Despite the commitments of some major firms, there were still lots of buyers eager for old-growth wood harvested by any means possible. Government regulation has the advantage of universality. If the B.C. government were to legislate against the clear-cutting of old growth, the prohibition would apply across the board to all places and players.

A final question that Karena Shaw poses has to do with how democratic it is to sideline the state. She is critical of the fact that there were no elected representatives of the people of British Columbia at the talks that led to the MOU. The key players are unelected international NGOs whose claim to "represent" was based on the power to influence consumer behaviour. With the exception of the Nuu-chah-nulth representatives of Iisaak, there were no "locals" involved. What do you think? Is this undemocratic, or simply a different way for popular voices to be heard?

DISSENT IN THE ECONOMY OF SIGNS

Consumers of FSC-certified wood products are not simply buying what Marx would call a "use-value," like a table valued for its beauty or functionality. If they buy them *because* they are FSC certified, they are also consuming an idea. The purchase says something about their commitment to environmental sustainability, how they relate to their world, and, by extension, what sort of person they are. They are engaging in the kind of everyday "politics of signification" pioneered by feminists, gays, and the counterculture in the 1960s, except the difference is that they are buying their cultural statement as an off-the-shelf commodity rather than a "do-it-yourself" construction like a tie-dye shirt (the original ones that people dyed themselves), a homemade peace sign, or an afro.

Not only have cultural artifacts become increasingly commodified, but more of the lucrative commodities in 21st-century capitalism have, like the FSC-certified table, taken on the abstract ideational quality of cultural symbols. In the global economy the largest economic transactions, worth trillions daily, are for various forms of "investments," little more than digitally recorded numbers whose value reflects constructions of meaning—of corporate reputation and imagined future trends. Tourism, one of the largest modern industries, is about the consumption of often idealized place images. The new information-based economy depends upon purely intellectual "properties" in software development, biotechnology "inventions," and the like. Some see a changing capitalist paradigm toward what British sociologist John Urry calls the "economy of signs" (Urry and Lash). Canadian writer and theorist Naomi Klein has argued that features of this new capitalism favour the sort of market-based politics that we saw illustrated in the previous section.

Abstract Commodities: Brand Equity

According to Klein, corporate trendsetters began thinking differently about production during the 1990s. They had an epiphany of sorts when in 1988 Philip Morris bought a brand-name corporation, Kraft, for six times the value of its actual physical assets. Over and above the cost of physical plant, offices, machinery, cheese slices, and other warehoused food products, Philip Morris paid some $10 *billion* for the purely abstract asset of the widely recognized Kraft name. Attaching an economic value to the brand made it "real" in the corporate mind, a new type of commodity that could be bought, sold, and manufactured—"brand equity."

The new mobility of capital made it possible to refocus production priorities on the marketing and promotion that builds brand equity. Global players found that they could subcontract the less profitable aspects of production, including the actual making of physical things, to subordinate companies that were often located in low-wage economies around the world. Subcontractors competed with one another to sell indistinguishable products to the brand-name companies at the lowest price and therefore the lowest possible profit margin.

By persuading consumers to buy into the unique magic of the brand identity, corporations like Nike and Calvin Klein were able to resell these products for astronomical markups and huge profits. The new philosophy was to "dematerialize" production in two ways. The first was by manufacturing and selling brand images. The second was by divesting themselves of physical assets in the form of factories and assembly plants, along with the commitments to real flesh-and-blood workers that went with them.

Even companies that sold real physical things—like sneakers, polo shirts, or coffee—inverted the relationship between marketing and the thing marketed. Instead of the brand being a way to sell the main commodity—the sneaker—the sneaker becomes merely a medium for the sale of the brand idea. Nike's main commodity becomes "the magic of sports" and the purchase of the sneaker is merely a way for the consumer ritually to participate in this brand vision. For Starbucks, coffee becomes one of a number of stage props for the brand essence, which is "the romance of the coffee experience, the feeling of warmth and community people get in Starbucks stores" (CEO Howard Shultz, qtd. in Klein 20) or "immersion in a politically correct, cultured refuge ..." (qtd. in Klein 112). Someone else makes the lowly physical thing.

The transcendent corporation produces "conceptual value added," or "brain ware." "Tom Peters," writes Klein:

... who has long coddled the inner flake in many a hard-nosed CEO, latched on to the branding craze as the secret to financial success, separating the transcendental logos and the earthbound products into two distinct categories of companies. "The top half—Coca Cola, Microsoft, Disney, and so on—are pure "players" in brainware. The bottom half [Ford and GM] are still lumpy-object purveyors...." (Klein 22)

Brand transcendence, this ability of the brand idea to rise above any particular physical instanciation, can be used to extend the brand to new commodities in the way that Caterpillar extended from bulldozers to backpacks or Virgin from records to airlines. But that is not its main thrust. The ideal is better articulated by a Diesel Jeans spokesperson: "We don't sell a product, we sell a style of life. I think we have created a movement.... The Diesel concept is everything. It's the way to live, it's the way to wear, it's the way to do something" (Renzo Rosso, qtd. in Klein 23).

The ideal is for brand meanings to become instantiated in everyday practices that define intimate qualities of human interaction, aspiration, and identity. It is, in short, to create cultural values and identities. Starbucks is about hip urban community. Nike is about the will ("just do it") to realize personal dreams. Body Shop stores "... aren't about what they sell," founder Anita Roddick tells Klein, "they are the conveyers of a grand idea—a political philosophy about women, the environment and ethical business" (Klein 24). Polaroid is about sharing the instant replay of social interaction. Polaroid's brand consultant explains how their "vision process" helped the company realize that "Polaroid is not a camera. It's a social lubricant" (qtd. in Klein 23).

Commodities and the Construction of Postmodern Identity

These are all wonderful human values/capacities that ordinarily people can realize on their own. Here corporations are offering to package and sell them back to people. In other words, they are commodifying human qualities. Is this the same consumer alienation that the Situationists' were so critical of in the 1960s? Recall how these cultural critics thought that in consumer societies people lost themselves in a world of prepackaged illusion that they called the "commodity spectacle."

The Situationists' exemplar, though, was of the consumer passively watching a remote spectacle on the TV screen. The 21st-century situation is far more complex, participatory, and reflexive. Consider a couple of recent examples of consumer relationships to marketing and the commodity. University campuses have become attractive sites for trying out innovative marketing strategies. "There is simply nowhere else," explains Dale Buss of the "BrandChannel," where marketers "... can find a nearly captive audience of Generation Y-ers away from home and wide open to a flood of new influences on brand choices that they'll be making ... for years to come." The emphasis, Buss argues, should be on engaging students actively.

Zila Pharmaceuticals got American students in 2002, for a $500 donation, to organize their own "Stressbuster Olympics." The event coincided with exams and "... included a yoga demonstrator, free massages—and samples of Zilactin [Zila's cold-sore medication targeted at young women]." "Finals are a big reason for stress and therefore cold-sore outbreaks on campus," explained one of Zila's consultants. "This was a chance to wrap the brand in an experience that helped associate a good emotion with it." Playboy, too, was able to co-opt volunteer marketers.

Student "reps" (15 percent of them women) in 2002 did things like organize online gaming tournaments, mostly for the excitement of being "part of" the brand.

> The reps usually work an average of one or two hours a week for little recompense other than Playboy-branded apparel, says Lisa Natale, senior vice president and marketing director for Playboy Publishing. During a big on-campus campaign, each rep might be working several hours a week and also collect, say, U.S. $200 for their efforts. "They don't get compensated much monetarily," Natale says. "Just being part of the Playboy brand is exciting for them." (Buss)

This used to be called "selling out." But if the ad executives are to be believed, for this generation of young people, "Selling out is not only accepted, it's considered hip" (Jensen, qtd. in Klein 65). In the early 1990s people began inscribing logos onto their bodies, shaving them into their hair, or offering to rent themselves out for this purpose. In so doing they blurred the line between corporate commodity and self. Some also gained notoriety in the process and saw their identities briefly amplified on the public stage.

The great personalities in the public pantheon—sports heroes, pop stars, celebrities—sell out as a matter of course, and in ways that can establish or enhance their celebrity. Klein points out, for example, that when Rufus Wainwright appeared in a Gap ad in 1998, "... his record sales soared, so much so that his record company began promoting him as 'the guy in the Gap ads'" (Klein 46). "Selling out" becomes instead "cross-promotion." Considering the relationship between basketball superstar Michael Jordan and Nike, Klein concludes:

> In an era in which people are brands and brands are culture, what Nike and Michael Jordan do is more akin to co-branding than straight-up shilling, and while the Spice Girls may be doing Pepsi today, they could easily launch their own Spice Cola tomorrow. (61)

Individuals, both at the personal and celebrity levels, are able to see themselves as in partnership with corporate sponsors in the construction of their public selves.

Their choices might be in terms of sports or sexual politics—Body Shop feminism or the cheesy retro-charm of Playboy—or the "social movement" that Diesel styles itself to be. However, it is not from these off-the-shelf political identities that the interesting postmodern politics emerges for Klein. In fact, she is hugely critical of the way in which her own "identity politics" was co-opted by some of the most hip "attitude brands" of the 1990s.

It did not take marketers long to figure out that Generation X, the notoriously media-savvy and cynical "demographic" of which Klein was a part, could be seduced by the language of "diversity."

> Abercrombie & Fitch ads featured guys in their underwear making goo-goo eyes at each other; Diesel went further, showing two sailors kissing ... ; and a U.S. television spot for Virgin Cola depicted "the first ever Gay wedding featured in a commercial," as the press release proudly announced. There were also gay-targeted brands like Pride Beer and Wave Water, whose slogan is "We label bottles not people," and the gay community got its very own cool hunters—market researchers who scoured gay bars with hidden cameras.

The Gap, meanwhile, filled its ads with racially mixed rainbows of skinny, childlike models. Diesel harnessed frustration at the unattainable beauty ideal with ironic ads that showed women being served up for dinner to a table of pigs. The Body Shop harnessed the backlash against both of them by refusing to advertise and instead filled its windows with red ribbons and posters condemning violence against women. (Klein 112)

Politics of the Postmodern Self

There is a reflexive loop at work here. Klein's media-bred generation learn to believe that liberation—of gays, women, people of colour—is reducible to a politics of cultural visibility and "representation." Around this received illusion, they nonetheless construct their own unique social movement culture in the form of campus identity politics. Marketers commodify this social movement culture and sell it back to young people. "[T]he radical critics of the media clamouring to be 'represented' in the early nineties," Klein writes, "virtually handed over their colourful identities to the brandmasters to be shrink-wrapped" (Klein 115).

In a completion of the loop, young people who buy prepackaged diversity imagine that they are buying into radical social protest. So, for example, of the "Girl Power" movement, one observer commented, "at this intersection between the conventional feminine and the evolving Girl, what's springing up is not a revolution but a mall.... Thus, a genuine movement devolves into a giant shopping spree, where girls are encouraged to purchase whatever identity

fits them best off the rack" (Powers, qtd. in Klein 114).

The real political critique emerges, not as it did for the Situationists, from a revolt of an "authentic" self against its alienated expression in branded, commodified form. Culture and identity are, in the 21st century, too deeply entwined with commercial consumption choices. It is far more difficult now to imagine, as the hippies once did, that you could separate an authentic self from the influences of consumer culture. Young people have increasingly organized to attack the corporate players in their branded world precisely because their own identities are irrevocably bound up within it.

It is precisely because North American kids at some level feel "part of" the brand that they get outraged when they learn that Coke has, for example, racist hiring practices. The more that people feel seduced by the "politically correct" Starbucks experience, the more ready they are to act when they learn that the coffee beans are supplied by exploited farmers in the developing world or that the chain aggressively undermines community-based competitors at home. The more that they buy into the Nike's motivational hype for girls, the more shocked they will be to hear of the ways the Nike subcontractors select young women workers for their passivity and powerlessness to challenge low-wage work and dehumanizing conditions.

When anti-globalization protestors began smashing windows in Seattle in 1999, it was retail outlets of the hippest brands—Nike and Starbucks—that bore the brunt of the rage, not big banks or corporate headquarters. The hip brands, by promising a simulacrum of the politics of social justice, find themselves increasingly called upon to deliver the "real thing."

Global Commodities as Free Communications Infrastructure

Brands of global corporations have the potential to link activists across the world. This is what happens when anti-sweatshop campaigners on North American campuses work with labour organizers in the Philippines or Singapore to publicize poor working conditions, and to pressure brand-name buyers to demand better conditions from their Third World subcontractors. Klein's analysis offers insight into a question that arose in Chapter 1 concerning the motivation for such cross-border solidarity. Part of what makes young affluent consumers in the West care about what happens to distant workers, is their *identification with* the brands implicated in exploiting those workers.

As young consumers learn more about working conditions overseas, they find more to identify with. In order to buy brand-name commodities, they, too, must work, typically in the retail and service industries. Here they make better money, but experience similar low-skilled jobs designed to make individual workers temporary, expendable, and their time "flexible" in order to bend to the rhythms of corporate advantage. The anti-sweatshop movement of the 1990s, characterized by consumer boycotts in support of labour rights, focused on a handful of lifestyle brands targeted at youth. If Klein's analysis is right, then the scope of this style of anti-corporate activism is likely to spread—to encompass different issues and corporate targets—as the generation that pioneered it begins to age.

Like the Clayoquot market campaign, anti-sweatshop activism depends upon exposure. Activists must be able to make consumers aware of what really goes on in the production and distribution of the products that they buy, even if these corporate activities take place on the other side of the globe.

To do this, Clayoquot campaigners relied upon international organizational infrastructure. Greenpeace had the contacts and resources to organize tours through Europe and to bring journalists and policy makers back to B.C. to witness forestry operations first-hand.

Successful anti-sweatshop campaigns also rely on some international organizational capacity to bring off similar face-to-face exchanges. You may recall from Chapter 1 that the campaign to support Guatemalan Coca-Cola workers fighting for union recognition received help from transnational NGOs: the Interfaith Centre on Corporate Responsibility; the International Union of Food, Agricultural, Hotel, Restaurant, Catering, Tobacco, and Allied Workers' Associations. Canada's main anti-sweatshop coalition, the Maquila Solidarity Network (www.maquila-solidarity.org), includes national union federations and Oxfam Canada, both of which have international links. Once companies finally agree to sign "codes of conduct," they require ongoing independent monitoring to ensure that the conditions of the agreement are being honoured. NGOs need the capacity to conduct or commission site inspections in foreign countries.

Klein, however, argues that the high-profile brands also offer activists free communications infrastructure. Many had no idea what MacMillan Bloedel was about or even what it produced, but few around the globe could say the same about Nike or Coke. Low-budget activists can "hitch on" to high-profile brands in a kind of "hostile co-sponsorship." Collaborating with a high-profile brand can raise a celebrity's profile. So, similarly, can cleverly, inventively critiquing it raise an anti-corporate campaign's profile.

This is another reason why brands like Nike take the brunt of consumer activism. It is not that Nike's labour or environmental record is the worst; in fact, after a decade or more of responding to consumer pressure, the firm's practices are probably better than most. Instead it is that catchy slogans like "Justice: Do it!" or images of workers impaled on the Swoosh logo so readily capture popular attention and consumer imagination. "Culture jamming," postering city streets with subverted corporate logos, "sculling" emaciated models on billboards, or posting spoof Web sites online are all low-cost, do-it-yourself points of entry into anti-corporate campaigns. However, they can powerfully undermine the carefully nurtured "street cred" of brands that are worth billions of dollars to their corporate makers. The more invested corporations are in "brand equity," the more vulnerable they become to this form of attack.

In her introduction to *No Logo*, Klein captures in an image this idea of the logo as free global communication device:

> I came across an American student group that focuses on multinationals in Burma, pressuring them to pull out because of the regime's violations of human rights. In their communiqués, the student activists identified themselves as "Spiders" and the image strikes me as a fitting one for this Web-age global activism. Logos, by the force of ubiquity, have become the closest thing we have to an international language, recognized and understood in many more places than English. Activists are now free to swing off this web of logos like spy/spiders—trading information about labour practices, chemical spills, animal cruelty and unethical marketing around the world. (xx)

Like Marx, Klein has attempted to expose the ways in which capitalism itself creates the tools for its opponents. The shift to an economy of signs, in which the creation of profit involves the construction of cultural meanings and identities, places at risk billions of dollars worth of "brand equity" in a game of cultural construction that anyone can play. People want to play because they feel compromised by their very identification with corporate culture and therefore all the more easily aroused to action over its hypocrisies. Global brand recognition gives activists a free communications channel for their critiques.

Culture Jamming: Anti-capitalist?

Other theorists, neo-Marxists in particular, are deeply suspicious about how this model could ever genuinely be anti-capitalist. Commodity consumption sustains capitalism, and any strategy of "resistance" organized around it might reform the practices of this or that corporation, but could never fundamentally challenge capitalism. In Klein's model of consumer activism, the motivation for protest comes out of identification with the brand; it is an identification with a commodity form, not, as with the Situationists, a rejection of commodification.

Even if you buy only FSC-certified wood products, say the skeptics, you are still accumulating "stuff." Trees are still falling in the forest, and fossil fuels are being burned to make them into commodities and deliver them to your door. Worse, you are still defining your environmental identity to yourself and others through the commodities you purchase. Old New Leftists also shiver with horror at the implicit abandonment of any "subject position" or "authentic" political identity that is independent of the commodifying reach of the cash nexus.

The issue here has in part to do with what different theorists think the "proper" aim of social movements should be. Klein's hope for "logo-forged global links" is that through them "Global citizens will eventually find sustainable solutions for this sold planet" (xx). Hers is a call for the reform, not the overthrow, of capitalism.

BOX 8.2:

CAMPUS ANTI-SWEATSHOP CAMPAIGNS— WHAT HAPPENED?

Do you identify with your university, cheer for its sports teams, and cherish its totemic colours, logo, or special ring? Increasingly universities are learning to exploit the economic potential of the emotionally charged constellation of meanings that grow up around their institutions. On its Web site, the university where I teach promotes itself as Canada's Premier Undergraduate Experience. Here it is marketing itself to potential students whose tuition furnishes an ever-greater proportion of its revenue. Universities also compete for donations from alumni and corporate funders.

They have to because governments, as part of the neoliberal agenda, have steadily eroded funding for higher education. They have had to learn to commodify their identity, to sell their "brand," in an effort to distinguish themselves from their competitors for new sources of funding. They have also been able to boost revenue by selling the rights to use the brand, or else subcontracting suppliers of branded merchandise—everything from key rings and ball caps to backpacks and clothing. Or else they have entered co-branding agreements where brands like Coke or Nike become exclusive suppliers on campus or for campus teams or events. Students find that their allegiance to their school becomes inextricably bound up with an allegiance to one or more corporate sponsors.

In the late 1990s students at Duke University began to question both the commodification of university culture as well as the corporate practices of some of the firms their school had become associated with. Students throughout North America had begun investigating where the merchandise that bore their school logo was manufactured. What they found were classic sweatshop conditions in export-processing zones.

While they paid close to $20 for a ball cap, they learned, the worker who assembled it received 8¢. These workers were young people, not unlike themselves, as they discovered when union organizations helped sponsor worker tours to campuses. The price of their privilege became hard to ignore. Naïve pride in the badges and insignia of that privilege became harder to support. "While the workers are making our clothes thousands of miles away," explained one Princeton student, "in other ways we're close to it—we're wearing these clothes every day" (qtd. in Klein 408).

Duke students led the way. Perhaps the fact that their university sold around $25 million of branded clothing each year made them recognize that they had more potential market clout than others. Student activists were able in 1998 to convince the university to enact a code of labour standards for clothing suppliers using the Duke brand. Manufacturers had to respect minimum wage and health and safety laws—surprisingly difficult conditions to guarantee—and genuinely support the right of workers to unionize. The code insisted on independent third-party audits to ensure compliance, something that many firms adamantly opposed.

The success of Duke University students inspired activists on other campuses. They helped one another pass similar codes. They networked, exchanged information and strategy, and formed a coalition called Students against Sweatshops. A Canadian chapter based at UofT was active for a while. However, when I wrote this in 2006, their Web site had vanished—a fairly good sign in this era of Web activism that the organization was at least dormant, if not defunct. Has commitment to this issue waned since the late 1990s? Was there an anti-sweatshop movement on your campus? Does it still exist? If not, what happened? Does your university's experience suggest problems with Klein's theory discussed in the previous section?

Source: Naomi Klein, *No Logo: Taking Aim at the Brand Bullies* (Toronto: Random House, 2000).

Neo-Marxists' concern is about the ineffectiveness of market strategies as a challenge to the power of capital. Others, who see these strategies as a new source of power for social movements, raise questions about the responsible exercise of that power. As we saw, Karena Shaw questioned the way in which they transfer power from the local to the translocal following the route of global market influence. Global actors "speak" on local matters without nuance or compromise. European and American buyers concerned with the global issues of climate change and biodiversity loss are not as constrained as those in Tofino, Nova Scotia, or the Brazilian rainforest who have to face the potential strains on local economies, the loss of tax revenue, or the social conflicts between locals who hold very different ideas about the value of the forests.

How much right should global players have to speak on local issues? Conversely, how "local" are these issues really if they affect the global community? Shaw questions not only the way in which market strategies can transfer power out of the hands of local actors, but also out of the hands of elected bodies. Recall how all three levels of government were left out of the negotiations that led to the MOU on logging in Clayoquot Sound.

Local Foreign Policy

Klein, on the other hand, makes a case that market strategies can in surprising ways be used to return power to local democratically elected bodies through what she calls "local foreign policy." In the 1980s governments joined with civil society organizations to impose economic sanctions on South Africa in protest of its system of apartheid, a legalized system of exclusion of Blacks from civil rights and economic opportunities. Both were expressing a growing popular sentiment that holds that an offence to human rights anywhere in the world is an offence to a global "human community."

However, in the 1990s this feature of "ethical globalization" came increasingly in conflict with the demands of economic globalization. Klein argues that nation-states, in increased competition for corporate investment within their own borders, but also for market opportunities for their companies overseas, have been much more willing to turn a blind eye to human rights abuses. Currently, for instance, no state is willing to jeopardize its chances in the emerging Chinese economy despite ongoing anti-democratic and repressive governance within that country. In the 1990s campaign against the brutal dictatorship in Burma, civil society organizations were largely on their own until 1995 when the *local* government in Berkeley, California, passed a "selective purchasing" law targeted at Burma.

The interests of local governments are not tied to international trade and investment in the same way that the interests of national governments are. Municipal voters in the U.S. are not as ready to compromise their ethics for the benefit of U.S. multinationals abroad. Just as global actors are uncompromising when speaking on local issues distant to them, so local actors can be equally uncompromising when speaking on distant global issues. By the time *No Logo* was published in 2000, 22 cities, one county, and two states had followed Berkeley's example. These jurisdictions do not have the power of embargo. They cannot ban imports of goods from any country.

They do, however, purchase in volume, everything from paperclips to police uniforms to fleets of vehicles. If they refuse to buy from corporations that have dealings with Burma, they can have the force of a powerful boycott. In a sense, "selective purchasing agreements" are ways for people to vote democratically on their participation in a boycott. They also make a clear statement to national legislators of popular sentiment. Largely because of democratic expressions of popular support at the local level, the U.S. government has become the only national government that has responded to citizen pressure, not with an embargo (which it does have the power to enact) but with a more limited ban on investment in Burma.

CONCLUSION

We began this chapter with two illustrations of the power of market strategies for achieving social movement objectives. In Nova Scotia and B.C., activists fighting for better state regulation of forestry companies suffered defeat in the courts, but ultimately saw their objectives realized through some form of consumer pressure aimed directly at corporations. In the second half of the chapter we considered theoretical arguments that link the rise of market strategies to recent changes in capitalism.

States have responded to the increased mobility of capital by reducing corporate taxes, cutting back many areas of government spending, and, in the 1990s, embracing neoliberal theories of minimal state governance. Accordingly, states have encouraged "self-government" by individuals, civil society organizations, and corporations, all supposedly made responsible by the disciplines of the market.

This new effort at "autonomizing" power has not always worked as intended. Activists have become increasingly successful in "subverting" consumer citizenship through organized consumer boycotts that achieve governance objectives while excluding the state from any meaningful input. Corporations that lobbied for the "self-government" model and states that acquiesced to it have ironically helped to invite this new form of resistance.

Economic globalization has involved a shift in the focus of power from states to global markets and the firms that dominate them. As the focus of power shifts, so must the focus of social movement challenges to that power. Not only have dominant firms extended their global reach, many have invested more heavily than ever in "brand equity." Brand equity is an expensive but abstract commodity that consists of a fragile constellation of meanings that corporations attempt to propagate like viruses in the everyday practices through which people create culture and identity. By inviting people to identify with corporate myths, corporations, despite themselves, invite people to hold them accountable to those myths. They cement the emotional attachments that turn to outrage when these myths are exposed.

The fact that corporations invest so much capital in the field of meaning and identity makes them economically vulnerable to do-it-yourself meaning construction on the part of activists. Low-cost culture jamming, often associated with but not reducible to brand boycotts, becomes a threat of greater magnitude than ever before, and a point of leverage for activists who want to influence corporate policy, if not to undermine capitalism per se. That, at any rate, is the theory.

REFERENCES

Beder, Sharon. *Global Spin: The Corporate Assault on Environmentalism*, rev. ed. Totnes; White River Junction: Chelsea Green Publishing, 2002.

Buss, Dale. "Big Brand on Campus," January 27, 2003. BrandChannel.com, January 10, 2006, www.brandchannel.com/more.

Delaney, Rachelle. "Coming of Age." *Nature Canada* 34, no. 1 (2005). January 10, 2006, www.cnf.ca/magazine/spring05/grannies.html.

Dispensa, Jaclyn Marisa, and Robert J. Brulle. "Media's Social Construction of Environmental Issues: Focus on Global Warming—a Comparative Study." *The International Journal of Sociology and Social Policy* 23, no. 10 (2003): 74. ABI/INFORM Proquest, Angus L. Macdonald Library, Antigonish. August 28, 2004, http://libmain.stfx.ca/newlib/electronic/databases/.

Expatriated Biocentric Turtle Island Earth First!*er. "Wilderness & Resistance: Bears, Blockades & Burning Bridges." *Do or Die* 6, no. 97: 87–92. January 21, 2007, www.eco-action.org/dod/no6/canada.htm.

Greenlife. *Dont Be Fooled: America's Top 10 Greenwashers*. 2005. January 10, 2006, www.thegreenlife.org/dontbe-fooled.html.

Hatch, Ronald B. "The Clayoquot Show Trials." *Clayoquot and Dissent*, edited by Ronald B. Hatch. Vancouver: Ronsdale Press, 1994.

Hutchinson, Moira. "The Promotion of Active Shareholdership for Corporate Social Responsibility in Canada." 1996. Share (Shareholder Association for Research and Education). December 12, 2005, www.share.ca/files/pdfs/SHAREholdership%20REPORT.pdf.

Johnson, Erica et al. "The Push for Eco-Friendly Lumber," January 2, 2001. CBC Marketplace, January 10, 2006, www.cbc.ca/consumers/market/files/environ/goodwood/.

Klein, Naomi. *No Logo: Taking Aim at the Brand Bullies*. Toronto: Random House, 2000.

Lewis, Dan. "Clayoquot Arm Bridge Blockade 1992," 1992. B.C. Environmental Network, January 10, 2006, www.bcen.bc.ca/bcerart/Vol2-4/clayoqua.htm.

Mooney, Chris. "Some Like It Hot." *Mother Jones* (May/June 2005). January 10, 2006, www.motherjones.com/news/feature/2005/05/some_like_it_hot.html.

Nash, Jennifer, and John Ehrenfeld. "Code Green." *Environment* 38, no. 1 (1996): 16–20, 36–45.

Rainforest Action Network. *Don't Buy SFI*, 2005. January 10, 2006, www.dontbuysfi.com/home/

Rowell, Andrew. *Green Backlash: Global Subversion of the Environmental Movement*. London, New York: Routledge, 1996.

Shaw, Karena. "Encountering Clayoquot." *A Political Space: Reading the Global through Clayoquot Sound*, edited by Warren Magnusson and Karena Shaw. Minneapolis; London: University of Minnesota Press, 2003.

Urry, John, and S. Lash. *Economies of Signs and Spaces*. London: Sage, 1994.

Von Mirbach, M. "Demanding Good Wood." *Alternatives Journal* 23, no. 3 (1997): 10–17.

Yaron, Gil. "Canadian Institutional Shareholder Activism in an Era of Global Deregulation." 2002. Share (Shareholder Association for Research and Education). December 12, 2005, www.share.ca/files/pdfs/02_02_11_final2.pdf.

CRITICAL THINKING QUESTIONS

1. How far could social movements go in reforming capitalist firms by using the capitalist market?
2. When we speak of what "the community" wants in an environmental (or any other) issue, how should the boundaries of community be defined?
3. Is the growing power of NGOs like Greenpeace and the Natural Resources Defence Council undemocratic, or simply a new way for popular voices to be heard?
4. Has commitment to anti-sweatshop activism waned since the late 1990s? Was there an anti-sweatshop movement on your campus? Does it still exist? If not, what happened? Does your university's experience suggest problems with Klein's theory discussed in the previous section?
5. How much right should global players have to speak on local issues? Conversely, how "local" are these issues really if they affect the global community?

FURTHER READING

Borowy, Jan, Shelly Gordon, and Gayle Lebans. "Are These Clothes Clean? The Campaign for Fair Wages and Working Conditions for Homeworkers." *And Still We Rise: Feminist Political Mobilizing in Contemporary Canada*, edited by Linda E. Carty. Toronto: Women's Press, 1993.
This article gives a good example of how market campaigns can be used as part of the new social unionism as well as feminist politics. You should also look other essays in the collection to learn more about contemporary and third wave feminism in Canada.

Klein, Naomi. *No Logo: Taking Aim at the Brand Bullies*. Toronto: Random House, 2000.
No Logo, by Canadian Naomi Klein, has become one of the essential texts for anti-corporate activists. It is a call to arms about the corporate domination of popular culture.

It is also one of the best analyses of the structural basis and social change potential of consumer activism.

Magnusson, Warren, and Karena Shaw. *A Political Space: Reading the Global through Clayoquot Sound*. Globalization and Community v. 11. Minneapolis; London: University of Minnesota Press, 2003.
Market-based campaigns were only one aspect of West Coast anti-clear-cut politics. This is the best place to start to learn more about this important chapter in Canadian social movement history.

Micheletti, Michele, Andreas Follesdal, and Dietlind Stolle. *Politics, Products, and Markets: Exploring Political Consumerism Past and Present*. New Brunswick: Transaction Publishers, 2004.
As one of the very few, as well as the most recent, academic treatments of the phenomenon of consumer activism, this text is worth reading for anyone interested in the topic.

Nash, Jennifer, and John Ehrenfeld. "Code Green." *Environment* 38, no. 1 (1996): 16–20, 36–45.
Nash and Ehrenfeld survey and critique of product certification schemes supposedly designed to allow consumers to make environmentally responsible purchases. Are such schemes merely marketing exercises that benefit corporations?

RELEVANT WEB SITES

Ethical Consumer (U.K.)
www.ethicalconsumer.org/boycotts/boycotts_list.htm
Boycotts are the most subversive forms of "market activism." Here is where you can find out who is boycotting what and why.

Friends of the Earth
www.foe.org/international/shareholder/links.html
This links page posted by the Friends of the Earth is the best place to start to learn the latest on shareholder activism and ethical investing.

Maquila Solidarity Network
www.maquilasolidarity.org
The Maquila Solidarity Network is a Canadian-based organization concerned with international labour and women's issues. At their Web site you can plug into international labour solidarity and anti-sweatshop activism.

Oxfam Canada
www.oxfam.ca
The Oxfam Canada site is very participation oriented. Check out their anti-sweatshop and fair trade campaigns.

Sweatshop Watch
www.sweatshopwatch.org

This is the site of one of many U.S.-based anti-sweatshop organizations. Check out their resources page for others.

Chapter 9

DISCOURSE AND THE POWER
OF CONSTITUTION:
"SPEAKING FOR" THE ENVIRONMENT

INTRODUCTION:
CORPORATE UNDERDOGS

"The big corporations, our clients," explained a PR executive in 1991, "are scared shitless of the environmental movement.... They sense that there's a majority out there and that the emotions are all on the other side—if they can be heard. They think the politicians are going to yield up to the emotions" (qtd. in Beder 22). Of course he believes his public relations firm, Hill & Knowlton, can offer embattled clients effective solutions to their perceived problems. We saw examples in the previous chapter of the sorts of strategies that public relations firms recommend.

Corporate "greenwash" is one. Instead of challenging popular support for environmentalism, the firm attempts to camouflage its own environmentally destructive practices through selective and/or misleading advertising. The very fact that many firms attempt to simulate a green colour says something about the cultural background that they are attempting to blend into. A second type of strategy involves promoting and funding "front groups" whose aim is to transform that cultural background. Front groups mimic existing NGOs devoted to environmental protection, consumer rights, product safety, and the like in order to oppose and undermine them.

You might think that the Global Climate Coalition was concerned with finding solutions to the most pressing environmental issue currently facing humanity—climate change. Instead, what we found in the previous chapter was that it was a coalition of some of the most powerful corporations in the world fighting, perversely, *against* efforts to solve the problem. Not only did it oppose the Kyoto Protocol to limit greenhouse gasses, but it sought also to undermine the

public credibility of the science of global warming. In the United States it has been instrumental in changing the cultural environment, minimizing understanding of climate science, and reducing public support for efforts to solve the problem of climate change. Perhaps, as the Hill & Knowlton executive goes on to reassure them, there was not such a need for corporations, in the early 1990s, to be scared shitless.

The National Wetlands Coalition, with a logo (a duck flying over a marsh) that brings to mind Ducks Unlimited, is another coalition of oil and gas companies. It does not, like Ducks Unlimited, want to protect vanishing wetlands in the U.S.; rather, it wants to protect the corporate right to drill for oil on them. Consumer Alert is a corporate front group that opposes consumer safety legislation. Keep America Beautiful lobbies against recycling programs in the U.S.

In Canada, you may remember the B.C. Forest Alliance set up on the advice of the public relations firm Burson-Marsteller to advocate in favour of industrial forestry during the Clayoquot Sound disputes. Its name echoed that of the Future Forest Alliance, a genuine environmental group, responsible for the Brazil of the North campaign. The B.C. Forest Alliance billed itself as a "... group of concerned British Columbians" dedicated to providing a "... voice of reason and information between the hard rhetoric of the preservationists and the tough talk of the forest industry" (Rowell 195–196). Its claim to be an uncompromised voice was belied by the industry ties of many on its board of directors and the fact that all of its $1 million initial budget was paid for by forestry companies.

One part of that story that I did not tell you was that in 1994, nearly a year after the mass demonstrations of Clayoquot Summer, 15,000–20,000 *pro*-logging protesters assembled on the lawn of the British Columbia Legislature. The crowd included union people, independent contractors, forestry workers, their families, and supporters from forestry-dependent communities in British Columbia. Many had donned their work clothes to mark their class status and wore yellow ribbons to signal their affinity for something called the Wise Use movement.

The Wise Use, or Share movement as it was called in Canada, was clearly corporate sponsored. The B.C. Forest Alliance helped to mobilize it. However, the 20,000 working people on the Legislature lawn were not out there as paid advocates. They were speaking out for the corporations against the environmentalists, but there is little doubt that they believed in what they were saying. They looked awfully like a pro-corporate popular movement. In this chapter we will analyze this example of a pro-capitalist, anti-environmentalist working-class movement. I am going to ask you to consider parallels between pro-corporate and New Left models of mobilization, parallels that I think profoundly challenge assumptions within existing social movement theory.

Workers speaking for corporations on the one hand, and on the other environmentalists purporting to speak for the environment in Clayoquot Sound, invite a more general question. How are groups able legitimately to speak for or represent the interests of others? In the second half of the chapter we will look at the very subtle ways in which the state in Canada attempts to construct the "voice of the public" through public hearings. The case study of hearings into the environmental impacts of the Alpac pulpmill in Alberta illustrates both the state's strategy to co-opt public discourse and activists' efforts to assert an independent popular voice.

CORPORATIONS AND THE POWER OF CONSTITUTION

Corporate Voices against Environmental Concern

Corporations have resorted to front groups in response to growing public skepticism. Corporate spin doctors recognize that the informed public discount the claims that corporations make on their own behalf. In the words of critics Megalli and Friedman:

> ... if Burger King were to report that the Whopper were nutritious, informed consumers would probably shrug in disbelief.... And if the Nutrasweet Company were to insist that the artificial sweetener aspartame has no side effects, consumers might not be inclined to believe them either.... But if the "American Council on Science and Health" and its panel of 200 "expert" scientists reported that Whoppers were not so bad, consumers might actually listen.... And if the "Calorie Control Council" reported that aspartame is not really dangerous, weight-conscious consumers might continue dumping the artificial sweetener in their coffee every morning without concern. (qtd. in Beder 28)

Consumers would have to do a bit of digging to discover that neither of these "councils" were independent of the corporate interests that they defend and that the expert scientists are essentially paid advocates whose research is neither published nor peer reviewed in independent journals.

"Any institution," warned PR executive Merrill Ross in 1991, "with a vested commercial interest in the outcome of an issue has a natural credibility barrier to overcome with the public, and often with the media" (qtd. in Beder 27). His advice, which corporations have increasingly heeded, was to "put your words in someone else's mouth." Think of it as a kind of "corporate ventriloquism." Front groups pose as independent third parties and pretend to speak in the public interest when in fact they speak from corporate scripts and defend private corporate interests.

The National Wetlands Coalition, the Global Climate Coalition, and the B.C. Forest Alliance were all NGOs with paid staff, offices, and budgets, like the environmental NGOs that they mimicked. While formidable, the institutionalized sector of the environmental movement was not the only perceived threat for the corporate clients of the PR industry in the late 1980s. Ads from one consultant reminded customers of an additional worry. They depicted an old woman with a sign reading "Not in my backyard." She was meant to represent the dreaded "NIMBY"—a pejorative label for a new form of neighbourhood-based "anti-toxics movement" that had won a string of victories in the U.S. in the 1980s. "Don't leave your future in her hands," the ad read. It went on to sell a new strategy that went beyond simple front groups. "Traditional lobbying is no longer enough. Today numbers count. To win in the hearing room, you must reach out to create grassroots support. To outnumber your opponents, call the leading grassroots public affairs communications specialists" (qtd. in Beder 34).

Grassroots Voices: The Anti-toxics Movement

The term "grassroots" is an appropriation here. Anti-toxics activists used it and the term "local" to underscore the idea that, at least initially, members of their movement had to organize and educate themselves. No paid consultants or staff of any organizations—including government departments of the environment and mainstream environmental organizations—took them seriously or gave them assistance when they first began to raise the alarm about toxic waste in their neighbourhoods.

One of the first and best-known anti-toxics struggles was over Love Canal in the state of New York. Here the Hooker Chemical Company had abandoned an old chemical dump and sold the land for residential development. Women, led by then housewife Lois Gibbs, learned of the risks of living in the new neighbourhood only by observing patterns of health problems in their children. To their amazement, despite mounting evidence of leaking toxic chemicals and damaging health effects, including 239 families with instances of birth defects and miscarriages, they had to fight local, state, and federal officials to get them to take action. Faced with threats to their children's physical well-being, they understandably got "emotional," resorting at one point to taking two federal Environmental Protection Agency (EPA) officials hostage.

Officials for their part were terrified of the precedent that would be set by paying for the cleanup of 20,000 tons of toxic waste and relocation of a whole residential neighbourhood. The EPA was aware that there were between 30,000 and 50,000 similar sites within the United States. Gibbs' local organization eventually prevailed and the final cost to state and federal agencies was U.S.$60 million, which they were later able to recoup by suing Occidental Chemical. Not wanting others to struggle in isolation as her group had done, Gibbs formed the Citizens Clearinghouse for Hazardous Waste in 1980 to provide information and organizing assistance to the thousands of other communities facing similar legacies of industrial pollution.

The Clearinghouse and similar organizations helped local groups to network and build what was to become known as the anti-toxics movement. Throughout the 1980s the movement inspired opposition not only to existing and abandoned toxic waste sites, but to proposed hazardous facilities in the chemical, nuclear, and waste-incineration industries as well as disposal sites for the wastes that these generated. In some jurisdictions in the U.S. it began to seem like it would become next to impossible to locate hazardous facilities. At almost every target site citizens would organize "not in my backyard" campaigns.

Corporations and permitting agencies insisted that economic development required that these things had to be in *someone's* backyard. Movement spokespeople responded by demanding "toxics use reduction"—that is, requiring firms to re-engineer their production processes to minimize hazards to workers and communities. In addition to demanding that polluters pay for cleaning up the toxic by-products of hazardous production, many called for greater corporate liability for end-of-life solutions for the commodities they spew out. If firms had to pay the full costs of recycling or safely storing their products once they were discarded, they would have a genuine incentive to design them so that they were not so disposable. And of course there would be less need for waste incinerators or waste dumps located in people's "backyards."

The truth that the growing backlash against "selfish" NIMBYism obscured was that there had always been those who could rest assured that unpleasant and dangerous developments would remain out of their backyards. Prior to the 1980s these had tended to be people of privilege. They tended to be White, well off, politically influential, and to live in urban areas—except where the wealthier among them maintained summer homes in rural retreats.

Members of the U.S. East Coast establishment, for example, kept summer homes in places like Kennebunkport, Maine, where they could appreciate the "unspoiled" coast, and subscribe to a certain style of environmentalism. They might belong to the Audubon Society or their family foundation might help fund the Nature Conservancy, which buys choice tracts of land to protect them from development. If there had to be unsightly or dangerous development, it was convenient that there were people living in trailers or subsidized housing in the Maine woods somewhere without political connections or organizational savvy.

Love Canal was a blue-collar neighbourhood. This was no accident. The tens of thousands of hazardous sites in the U.S. and Canada tended disproportionately to be in rural areas close to working-class, low-income, Black, Hispanic, and Aboriginal communities. The political and economic logic favoured this association. Property values tended to be lower, political clout tended to be less. Likely, too, there was a presumption on the part of developers that these people "didn't matter" as much as others. The real threat, when these people began, contrary to all expectations, to organize and resist, was the spectre of a genuinely popular environmentalism that crossed class and racial lines.

Established environmental NGOs in the U.S. initially ignored the anti-toxics movement. Many like the Audubon Society and the Nature Conservancy continued to do so. But others like the Natural Resources Council, the Sierra Club, and, of course, Greenpeace hired community liaison people or anti-toxics coordinators committed, to varying degrees, to working with the new movement. This kind of coalition building across class and race during the 1980s no doubt fuelled the anxiety that had many corporate executives "scared shitless" by

1990. As we will see in the next section, the corporate-sponsored anti-environmental movement of the 1990s helped to head off this collaboration by framing environmental issues in adversarial class terms.

Astroturf: Corporate-Sponsored "Grassroots"

The corporate antidote to NIMBY was to hire "grassroots public affairs communications specialists" whose job was to create at least the appearance of citizen support for corporate initiatives. By 1992 most major U.S. firms also had senior staff dedicated to "grassroots organizing" (Beder 23). Their simplest strategies for mobilizing the voices of citizens evolved out of direct mailing campaigns that had been used extensively to raise funds for right-wing causes in the United States. Their techniques blended social movement and direct marketing strategies.

Market research techniques helped them target mailing and telephone lists toward likely supporters. Lists from successful campaigns would be purchased, combined, tested, and refined. The pitch to potential supporters would similarly be "market tested" and reworked, just as ads are, to improve "response rates." Different messages could be tailored to different market demographics. The first trick was to get a positive response. The second was to translate that response immediately into action. A direct mailing might be accompanied by a prepaid postcard that respondents could mail to their political representative, or a form letter that they could sign or copy out as though it were their own.

Some marketers went to great lengths to make these canned responses appear authentic, as though the senders had fashioned the words themselves.

If they're close by we hand-deliver it. We hand-write it out on "little kitty cat stationery" if it's a little old lady. If it's a business we take it over to be photocopied on someone's letterhead. [We] use different stamps, different envelopes.... Getting a pile of personalized letters that have a different look to them is what you want to strive for. (qtd. in Beder 36)

To get an immediate response to telephone appeals, some firms would persuade people to speak to their political representative directly and transfer their calls before they had time to change their minds. The idea is that no matter how few people respond to the message—say, that a waste incinerator will be good because it will provide tax revenue and local employment—if most of them actually speak out, the appearance will be of a much more powerful voice of support. Not unlike a demonstration, a flood of letters or phone calls stands for and is read as representing a much larger body of the concerned public.

Within the public relations industry this sort of "grassroots activism" is known as "Astroturf"—a tacit acknowledgement that, like Astroturf, it is a synthetic product that can be mass-produced. Marx, you will remember, thought that the political advantage that workers had over capital was their numbers and organization. Astroturf offers capital the possibility of instantly mobilizing the appearance of numbers without actual organization. Or, more accurately, the organization comes not from those mobilized but from largely automated systems paid for by private firms—corporate databases, telemarketing staff, and telecommunications infrastructure.

However, there is a more interesting and ambiguous form of corporate-led mobilization that only begins with these sorts of resources, but eventually results in social organization. Consider the efforts of Trans Mountain Pipe Line to get citizen support for its proposed tanker terminal and pipeline in Washington state. The company commissioned a survey, which revealed that the majority, 65 percent of the population, opposed the plan for environmental reasons. However, a significant minority were also sympathetic to the idea of oil and gas projects as part of economic development in the region. The company used direct mail to encourage these people to form their own organization, Citizens for Full Evaluation (CFE).

> More than 200,000 issue-oriented brochures and letters were mailed to registered voters along the proposed route, sounding themes developed from the poll. Supporters were quickly and cost-effectively identified where no organized support had existed before.... CFE's mailing list grew to more than 5,000 in six largely rural counties. Entered into a computer database, the list could be broken down geographically, by level of support or by what members were willing to do. (qtd. in Beder 42)

Many would be tempted to call CFE a corporate front group. However, cases like these are not as clear-cut as the National Wetlands Coalition or the American Council on Science and Health. CFE was made up of genuine citizens, and 5,000 is a very respectable number for a local single-issue citizens' organization. They were not paid advocates or corporate employees. Many volunteered their time and took a public and potentially controversial stand in their communities. While they no doubt sang to the corporation's tune, that tune resonated with ideas that they held prior to Trans-Mountain Pipeline's arrival on the scene.

To help distinguish this sort of sponsored citizen organization from simple front groups, I will borrow a term from sociologist Pierre Bourdieu: the "power of constitution." He defines this as the "power to conserve or transform current classifications in matters of gender, nation, region, age and social status, and this through the words used to designate or describe individuals, groups or institutions." It is "a power to make a new group, through mobilizations, or to make it exist by proxy, by speaking on its behalf as an authorized spokesperson" (Bourdieu 332).

One of the questions that we will be taking up in this chapter is whether and on what grounds we could dismiss corporate-sponsored popular movements as not "genuine" social movements. In the case study that we will be looking at—the anti-environmental Wise Use movement and its Canadian counterpart, the Share movement—the issue is made more poignant by the fact that the main groups that appear to speak in the voice of capital are workers and small owners.

In previous chapters we have seen how these two groups have historically and should have theoretically (at least according to Marxists) raised their voices in opposition to capitalism or, at least in the case of small owners, in opposition to its large corporate players. What I have called the "corporate ventriloquism" of front groups and the curious case of workers speaking for capital raise an additional set of questions concerning this phenomenon within social movements of spokespeople speaking on behalf of other people or in the name of some interest or issue.

Vested Interests and the Legitimacy of Voice

The public relations executive is quite right, spokespeople lose public credibility if they can be shown to speak "with a vested commercial interest in the outcome of an issue." Anti-toxics activists like Lois Gibbs spoke from an emotional interest in their children's welfare, which they were willing to defend at considerable cost to themselves. However, theirs was hardly a commercial interest. The immediate financial impact of speaking out about chemical leaks in their neighbourhood was that their own property values plummeted.

In previous chapters we saw how "conscience constituencies" often speak out on issues that do not directly influence them. For example, White liberals supported the Black struggles for civil rights often at great cost to themselves. Church groups in other countries spoke out against the torture and disappearances in Chile, Argentina, and Uruguay. The legitimacy of these voices is strengthened by the fact that they are raised in the general interests of "humanity" rather than any selfish, personal, or commercial interest.

Environmentalists tend to be similarly motivated by conscience. This is one of the public relations challenges to anti-environmentalist corporations. The effects of climate change will emerge slowly in the 21st century. Most of those who advocated passionately for action on this issue in the 20th century know that they will die of old age before being personally affected by the catastrophe that they are trying to avert. They are fighting for future generations. A Canadian who campaigns to preserve biodiversity in the Brazilian rainforest cannot expect any direct personal or financial benefit other than the satisfaction of "doing good." Nor can a European who refuses to buy furniture made from old-growth B.C. wood.

Lois Gibbs' environmentalism was "anthropocentric" or human-centred. The environment for her was primarily a place where humans dwell. Her main concern was

not the environment in and of itself, but its impacts on human health and well-being. Many environmentalists, by contrast, take an "ecocentric" perspective. Humans, they argue, are one species among millions. We are a newcomer to the planet, not necessarily "better" than other species, but certainly very troublesome for them. Some of us, they insist, must take the perspective of and speak for the interests of other species and ecosystems as a whole.

Environmentalism, particularly ecocentric environmentalism, raises two questions about the legitimacy of spokesmanship. First, how can environmentalists claim to speak for others who cannot in principle speak for themselves in human debates—non-human others or future generations? Second, how can anti-environmentalists undermine the legitimacy of those who claim to speak so disinterestedly?

CORPORATIONS AND THE POWER OF CONSTITUTION: THE WISE USE/SHARE MOVEMENT

Anti-environmentalist Loggers

I introduced one of the central problems of this chapter with the example of the 1994 Share demonstration at the B.C. Legislature. Unfortunately, we do not have a detailed study that looks into how this event was organized or the more subtle meanings that participants attached to their involvement. We know that Wise Use philosophy and tactics were being promoted in British Columbia and Ontario under the guise of the Share movement, and we can look at how this likely shaped people's understandings of the issues. Anthropologist Thomas Dunk has also done an excellent study of the culture of loggers in a resource-dependent community in northern Ontario, which may give us insight into the culture of B.C. loggers. What Dunk discovered, interestingly, was that while Ontario loggers had "no use" for environmentalists, they actually agreed with many of environmentalists' criticisms of industrial forestry practices.

As recreational hunters and fishers, they were conscious of the impacts on fish and wildlife of clear-cuts, single-species regrowth, and the use of herbicides and pesticides. As one cutter explained to Dunk:

> The machinery today is more damaging. It harms the smaller growth which is all flattened out.... Also now they plant only one species of tree. The forest doesn't seem to regenerate back the way it used to. With the old way [of harvesting] with horses the forest seemed to grow back almost naturally the way it was. With clear cutting ... nothing seems natural. Where I cut 30 years ago that's grown up, looks natural, but in clear cut areas only one species of tree is planted and grows. There will never be wildlife. (21)

They were also concerned with the rate of cutting and realized that unrestricted harvesting would compromise the long-term viability of the communities that depend upon the forest industry. "Without protecting the environment on a long term basis," one logger warned, "we're left with nothing" (Dunk 23). "[T]oo many people," complained another, "just look for today and don't worry about tomorrow.... One day there won't be anything left ... (because) right now they're highgrading [i.e., cutting only the largest, best-quality trees]" (Dunk 24). They recognize that big firms have other places in the world

to go, while local people have a greater investment in place. Their commitment to place is one of the ways in which they understand their identities as well as their resentments of "outsiders," including city-based environmentalists who "meddle" in local affairs.

Dunk's respondents were also aware that it was not just overcutting, but changes in harvesting technology that were threatening their jobs. Environmentalists involved in forestry issues have long tried to make common cause with forestry workers on this issue. The evidence, they argue, all shows that the real threat to workers' jobs is not the creation of parks and wilderness protected areas, but industry's drive to mechanize harvesting. For example, of the 27,000 forestry jobs lost in B.C. in the 1980s, only 2 percent were lost to parks, the rest to mechanization (Rowell 194).

The sort of selective harvesting favoured by environmentalists creates more jobs than clear-cutting. International forestry companies, they claim, also export jobs by shipping raw logs rather than manufacturing wood products in forestry-dependent communities or provinces. Ecological approaches to forestry like that of the First Nations company, Iisaak (mentioned in Chapter 8), encourage a diversity of economic uses from an ecologically diverse forest. The result should be stable employment for forestry communities.

Class and Discursive Constructions of Environmentalism

This message apparently was not getting through to Dunk's respondents. When asked about the type of person they imagined an environmental activist to be, Dunk got quite heated responses, like this one from logger "R" and his wife "L":

L: I would say [they live in] Toronto, well, the real answer to this is ... [Do you mean a] Greenpeace type?

R: Extremist type? Is that what you're talking about? Or just ...

TD: Well, it's interesting that you make that distinction.

R: Like, the thing that bothers me about this is when you say environmental activist ... I sort of look at myself, sort of as an environmentalist. I do, yes. For the simple fact that a lot of the stuff that goes on irritates me and I don't think it's right, so therefore, I think I'm going to have to call myself one. But, I've seen a lot of them on TV that carry it way, way out of line. Like ...

L: Greenpeace.

R: ... sure, maybe that's, that's how they feel about it, and they really are serious about it and that's how they show it. Like you've got animal rights lovers, you've got greenpeacers. I don't think that they are looking at the whole picture.... The people I see on TV are going way overboard over it, hugging trees and all this other crap. (26)

Dunk quotes this couple at length. One of their themes is the supposed one-sidedness of environmentalists and their inability to compromise. The other is that environmentalists fail to understand the hard realities of how they themselves derive their needs from nature. Living in cities, they are divorced from these realities, and make easy judgments about those who do their dirty work for them. The theme of different ways of knowing runs throughout the interviews and, Dunk believes, relates to cultural constructions of class.

Working-class people recognize the power of, but at the same time resent, "expert knowledge." They know how their own un-derstandings of their immediate world, based on their practical experience and "common sense," can be overruled by government bureaucrats, corporate engineers, or other often distant experts who make claim to abstract "universal" knowledge. They "invert" these cultural categories, insisting on the value of knowledge that is locally based and practical as against "book learning."

Somewhat oddly, the "environmental activist" gets fused with the bureaucrat and corporate executive, who is "Somebody in Toronto with a great big suit on and doesn't have a clue of what's going on. They seem to be the ones raising the most stink and that but they don't really know what the area is like up here" (qtd. in Dunk 26). Borrowing a term from Ernesto Laclau, Dunk argues that these workers are constructing discursive "chains of equivalence": "southerner, city-dweller, middle class, abstract (or perhaps ignorant), environmentalist—which is juxtaposed to another chain—northerner, local, worker, practical (common-sensical)" (Dunk 28). These binary oppositions help to define for them who they are in opposition to distant actors who seek to control their lives.

What is interesting is that the "subject position" of the "other" here could equally be occupied by the environmentalist, the government regulatory official, or the corporate executive. Indeed the "great big suit" seems a better fit for the latter. The thrust of the Wise Use movement's discursive strategy has been to ensure that the environmentalist and the government conservation officer, not the corporate executive, occupy this subject position. When workers' lives are in crisis because of genuine threats to their jobs, they lash out at the environmentalists, not, as one journalist put it, "... economic decisions in air-conditioned boardrooms by distant executives determined to rationalize costs, and the introduction of new technology" (Hume, qtd. in Rowell 194).

Wise Use Discourse

Wise Use discourse also speaks to a central value of woods workers, farmers, and others who work in resource industries. Humans have a place within nature as *users* of natural resources—this unavoidably involves killing animals, cutting down trees, and digging up the earth. The idea that these resources should be used responsibly and wisely has almost universal appeal within the target constituency. It is hard not to step into the "subject position" of a Wise Use advocate. The next discursive move of Wise Use activists is to demonize what Wise Use is not and manoeuvre environmentalists into this position of "other."

Binary Opposition: Wise Use/Preservationism

The antithesis of Wise Use is the "preservationist," who, for naïve or nefarious motives, wants to protect nature by prohibiting all human uses of it. As Chuck Cushman, a Wise Use "field organizer," explains:

> The preservationists have become like a new religion, a new paganism that worships trees and sacrifices people.... They say that they want to be reasonable, they want 50 percent. So you agree and go on with your life. Five years later they're back. And what do they want? Fifty percent. Understand that these guys have a gun at your head and they want to take what you've got. (Helvarg 142)

Through a chain of equivalences, the simple wise use–preservationist binary opposition is further used to situate "commonsensical" people in complicity with extreme right-wing views.

Wise Use ideologues, like Americans Alan Gottlieb and Ron Arnold, teach that the individual owner, unfettered by any government regulation, is the wisest user of his or her own property. The idea has broad appeal among small-business owners—trucking entrepreneurs, pulp contractors, and small woodlot owners in the forestry sector, and farmers and ranchers in agriculture. It also resonates with working-class constructions of the value of local, practical knowledge. The man who has worked all of his life on the land knows as much or more about land stewardship as the government biologist peering into a computer screen at a GIS map or the UN scientist worried about the abstractions of climate modelling.

The idea has been used in the United States to attack the right of the state to own land—what is in the U.S. called "public land" and in Canada "Crown land"—as well as the right to regulate. For example, as wetlands disappear in North America and scientific awareness of their ecological value has increased, governments have restricted property-owners' right to fill in marshes in order to build houses, shopping malls, or other developments.

Right-Wing Libertarianism

American Wise Use advocates want these sorts of restrictions to be viewed as legally equivalent to land expropriation and for the state to compensate landowners for the value of foregone economic opportunities. While superficially this sounds "fair" to the development-minded landowner, the net effect would be to make environmental regulation prohibitively expensive for the state (Beder 61). Landowners large and small would be largely free from environmental regulation.

Extreme liberals can represent this as "freedom" only by conveniently bracketing out the ways in which landowners are in fact regulated by global market pressures that often force them to exploit resources in the most damaging ways in order to compete. (This is, after all, why many firms feel they have to clear-cut or ecologically minded farmers feel that they have no choice but to use pesticides.) Still, it is an anti-state libertarian message that plays well, particularly to an American context.

Blue-Collar Yippies

Wise Use organizers were also skilled in adapting 1960s social movement tactics of public theatre and direct action to a working-class idiom. Chuck Cushman inspired local groups with emblematic "war stories" that highlighted colourful and effective tactics. In order to send a message to Democratic Congressman Ron Wyden about job retraining for redundant loggers, Cushman explained how he

> ... called up this friend of mine and said, "I need to know the name of the biggest logger you know." And he said, "There's Nils Madson, about 6'6" and 320." I talked to Nils and said, "Come dressed for work and bring the biggest chainsaw you can find," and he came down in front of Wyden's office with that chainsaw on his back and we put a sign on him saying "Congressman Wyden, I want to be retrained. I want to be your brain surgeon." (qtd. in Helvarg 144)

Shocking, perhaps, but also fun in a kind of redneck, Yippie fashion.

Madson, with his physical prowess and apparent bad-ass attitude, is like a character out of the World Wrestling Federation.

Another story of Cushman's, this time highlighting direct action, appeals to rural know-how. In order to disrupt a "preservationist" public meeting,

> ... we brought with us two logging trucks and two cattle trucks and we pulled the cattle trucks on either side [of the hall] and we put the mama cows in one truck and the baby cows in the other truck and for the next three hours we had stereophonic cow.... They couldn't hear themselves think." (qtd. in Helvarg 144)

It was effective, legal, and a kind of "in-joke" that only people with practical knowledge of cattle raising could have thought of.

Physical imagery of power—big guys with intimidating power equipment—makes sense to blue-collar men who want to demonstrate their strength publicly. This is a tacit recognition that they have few other ways to assert social power. It is not surprising that loggers' demonstrations would feature big guys with chainsaws or truckers and farmers' demonstrations would involve convoys of massive tractors or tractor-trailers. Wise Use organizers exploited this sort of working-class idiom in ways that were popular with many workers but a potential liability with broader publics.

Wise Use and Share groups tended to favour violent rhetoric. Share supporters showed up at B.C. demonstrations bearing slogans like:

> "Save a logger, Bugger a Hugger"
> "Save a Logger: Spike a Preservationist" (Rowell 193)

The "inversions" of environmentalist rhetoric here are clever. This motif of the logger as an "endangered species" threatened by anti-human preservationists runs throughout Wise Use literature. The allusion to tree spiking, a tactic attributed to Earth First!, and alleged to result in injuries to millworkers when spiked trees passed through saws, became an icon for anti-environmentalists of environmental extremism in the 1990s.

However, efforts to position "preservationists" as "eco-terrorists" were constantly undermined by Share and Wise Use groups' own resort to the "theatre" as well as the crude practice of violence. On the ground in B.C., the Clayoquot "peace camp" was much better at keeping in check the militant "elves" and Earth First!ers than the Share groups were at preventing their members from intimidating and beating up their opponents.

Demonization of the "preservationist" was part of an effort discursively to reposition Wise Use and its affiliates as moderate. Publications of B.C. Share groups "promoted theirs as the voice of reason, balance and sincerity against extreme 'preservationist' propaganda" (Beder 189). Such efforts to claim the middle ground were destabilized by the persistent appeal of Wise Use to the right-wing fringe in the U.S. The National Rifle Association supported Wise Use, whose anti-state rhetoric appealed to those gun lobbyists who believe that the state is trying to "take their guns away" so that they cannot rise up in armed rebellion. Prior to the 1995 Oklahoma City bombing, where a libertarian terrorist blew up a government building, Ron Arnold encouraged the support of right-wing "militias."

The Wise Use "Sahara Club"—its name a parody of the Sierra Club—defended the right of dirt bikers to tear up ecologically sensitive desert habitat on public lands. Sahara Club organizers advocated an excessive "theatre of violence." Rick Seiman boasted that club members were armed with "baseball bats and bad attitudes." His organization's publications listed lo- cal environmentalists' names, addresses, licence plates, and phone numbers along with the arch recommendation, "Now you know who they are and where they are. Just do the right thing and let your conscience be your guide" (Helvarg 248). After hearing a Rick Sieman "dirty tricks" workshop described as "harmless stuff that added humour to the summer [of 1990]," a logger with the Wise Use group WE CARE "tossed a box wrapped in duct tape and containing a stack of Sahara Club newsletters into the Arcata Action Center, the local environmental storefront, shouting a warning as he ducked out the door" (Helvarg 250).

The Wise Use movement also attracted support from a right-wing religious cult known as the "Moonies" (after their spiritual leader Sun Myung Moon). Connections to Moonies, who had been vilified by the press in the 1980s for their bizarre views and questionable recruiting practices, became a public relations liability for Wise Use. The movement's own key spokespeople, such as Ron Arnold, were also prone to undermining their own claims to be moderate.

Extreme Right-Wing Rhetoric

In 1984, the year of the Nova Scotia Herbicide Trials, he addressed a pro-spray group in Halifax, suggesting that environmentalists were the tools of a Soviet conspiracy.

> ... the Soviet Union would never allow such a thing as a wilderness area in which valuable resources of petroleum or timber or nonfuel minerals could be extracted, yet they encourage the Free World to voluntarily lock up more and more of their natural resources from economic production.... Environmentalism is an already existing vehicle by which

the Soviet Union can encourage the Free World to voluntarily cripple its own economy. (qtd. in Helvarg 139)

This "watermelon theme" was a Wise Use staple. Environmentalists were alleged to be "green on the outside, but red on the inside" (Switzer 209). Many distanced themselves from Wise Use's key spokesperson, Ron Arnold. Arnold himself had constantly to distance himself from the Moonies and other of his extremist admirers.

However, Arnold argued that no one person or organization represented the whole movement. Using resource-mobilization language, he pointed out that late 20th-century movements are "segmentary, polycephalous, ideological networks" (qtd. in Helvarg 120). Wise Use, like the anti-war movement of the 1960s, was made up not of one but many voices. Key organizations attempted to mobilize others. There were numerous personal networks that linked organizations that were formally independent of one another. Ultimately what provided coherence to the movement was political culture—interpretive "frames" that anyone could sign on to.

Working-Class Signifiers

Along with efforts to reposition Wise Use as moderate, organizers attempted to position the movement in class terms as representing ordinary "working people." The wearing of work clothes and hard hats at rallies became an important "signifier" of class. As one U.S. reporter observed, "the working-class getup proved to be far more effective than the pin stripes of most industry lobbyists" (qtd. in Beder 56). However, as Sharon Beder points out, much of the stage-managing of these events was facilitated by very un-working-class players. Interested corporations frequently gave their employees time off work to attend these

events or bussed them to the demonstration site. They helped to fund seminars where public relations experts of the "pinstripe" set taught loggers how to perfect their "salt of the earth" voice for the media.

Wise Use class discourse also involved positioning the "preservationist" opposition in class terms. We have already seen how Ontario loggers were inclined to see environmentalists as Torontonians in "great big suits." Wise Use spokespeople like Arnold simply amplified this kind of (mis-)perception:

> When you are talking about environmentalists, you have people who, in my experience, are divided into two classes, the upper class and the upper class. One of the upper class is academics. There are an awful lot of people in either academia, or from academia in nice posts such as mathematicians in large aerospace companies who have tenure and therefore the ability to say or think anything they want, are comfortably off, but not particularly wealthy. And then there's the coupon-clippers that are living on daddy's money. I've had any number of those on the hiking trails. (qtd. in Beder 51)

The aim of this elite is, in this version, not to aid the Soviets but, somewhat more plausibly, to "preserve ... public lands as their summer playground." Environmental organizations, according to this theme, are represented as large bureaucracies with professional staff and ample foundation funding, which collectively constitute "the most powerful superlobby on Capitol Hill" (Beder 51). Working-class people often feel they are the victims of those in more powerful positions. Wise Use activists give shape to this feeling: "The environmental movement is the establishment now, and we are the rebels coming to tear them down. Now they're the Goliath and we're David, and we intend to put the stone in their head" (Arnold, qtd. in Switzer 197).

Wise Use "class discourse" obscures the degree to which the movement was conceived as a vehicle for corporate interests and has relied upon corporate funding and support for its survival. Ron Arnold began with a genuine commitment to anti-environmentalism and a conviction, based on reading sociological theory, that the "only way to defeat a social movement is with another social movement," or what some sociologists call a "counter-movement" (Helvarg 137). He also understood the extent to which dissent can be manufactured and mobilized given the right resources and strategies. He was taking his cue from the innovations of 1960s left-wing activists. However, what he had additionally in his favour was the knowledge that anyone mobilizing for right-wing causes would have potentially greater economic resources at their disposal.

Commercial Mobilizing Strategies

In 1984 he hooked up with Alan Gottlieb, who had developed a commercial model for how to finance political organizing. Gottlieb ran a direct-mail organization called the Center for the Defense of Free Enterprise (CFDFE). The core idea was to use computer technology to manage targeted mailing lists. In the late 1990s the Center's database contained some 5 million names drawn from a variety of sources—such as membership lists of right-wing organizations, lists of people with grazing permits or timber licences on public lands—plus information on their responsiveness to past appeals. Using mail, fax, and e-mail, Gottlieb would send out political alerts and request funding for action. In true free

enterprise fashion, he skimmed a profit from the donations the organization received.

Before Arnold approached him with the Wise Use idea, Gottlieb had been focusing on promoting Reagan conservatives and pro-gun lobbies. Unapologetic about his commercial motives, Gottlieb recalled:

> I've never seen anything pay out as quickly as this whole Wise Use thing has done. What's really good about it is it touches the same kind of anger as the gun stuff, and not only generates a higher rate of return but also a higher average dollar donation. My gun stuff runs about $18. The Wise Use stuff breaks $40. (Gottlieb, qtd. in Helvarg 137)

Arnold, with a good political "product" to sell, hired himself out as a consultant to businesses and business associations.

In addition to the general outline of Wise Use discourse, he advised corporate clients on a strategy of covert promotion. Give anti-environmental groups the money, he told them, and "get the hell out of the way" (Helvarg 139).

> The public is completely convinced that when you speak as an industry, you are speaking out of nothing but self-interest. The pro-industry citizen activist group is the answer to these problems. It can be an effective and convincing advocate for your industry. It can utilize powerful archetypes such as the sanctity of the family, the virtue of the close-knit community, the natural wisdom of the rural dweller … And it can turn the public against your enemies…. I think you'll find it one of your wisest investments over time. (Arnold, qtd. in Beder 44)

Corporate-Sponsored
Popular Movement

Arnold aspired to more than just assisting individual corporations deal with localized opposition. His aim, as he told the *Toronto Star* in 1991, was no less than "... to destroy, to eradicate the environmental movement ..." (qtd. in Rowell 14). For this he needed to inspire a concerted corporate effort to promote anti-environmentalism from multiple points of origin. In 1988 he organized the first Wise Use conference, which attracted over 200 corporations, industry associations, and right-wing NGOs. DuPont and Exxon were there, as well as forestry giants MacMillan Bloedel, Louisiana-Pacific, Georgia-Pacific, and Weyerhaeuser (Beder 45).

While the conference took place in Reno, Nevada, a number of representatives of Canadian corporations, including MacMillan Bloedel, were present and signed the resultant *Wise Use Agenda* (Rowell 189). Arnold had also been selling the message in Canada. Mindful of Canadian sensibilities, he advised that, "whatever you do must be completely Canadian, in name, form and operation" (qtd. in Simon 19). Canadian "citizen groups" were encouraged to use the term "share" and "multiple use" rather than "wise use."

He also recommended that firms help set up a Canadian equivalent of the Center for the Defence of Free Enterprise to promote movement culture in three ways.

> First, ... such an institute must help local groups gain access to politicians and the national media, and coordinate whatever information resources may be needed to deal with developing issues.
>
> Second, it must publish books, articles and other media features designed to gradually shift the intellectual climate towards the approval of the forest products industry in Canada. It must take every opportunity to recruit opinion leaders to write and speak in favor of permanent multiple use policies and find outlets for their messages.
>
> Third, it must create a long-term unfinishable agenda and train interns to carry the multiple use philosophy into every corner of Canadian society. (Simon 19)

MacMillan Bloedel, in the early 1990s, became one of the industry leaders in funding local Share groups as well as the B.C. Forest Alliance, the provincial answer to Arnold's recommendation of a "general purpose non-profit ... institute" (Rowell 191).

Wise Use and its Canadian variant, Share, are good examples of what we earlier called "corporate-sponsored popular movements." We asked whether there were grounds for ruling them out as genuine social movements. Certainly their corporate roots expose putative citizens' groups to public criticism and loss of legitimacy when revealed. An investigation into B.C. Share groups commissioned by two Canadian MPs concluded that:

> Although grass-roots movements, advocacy and lobbying are considered normal, legitimate and desirable in a democratic society, such activity is open to criticism if it deliberately misrepresents, deceives, or conceals the identity of the interests involved and their desired objectives and goals. With respect to B.C. Share groups, the forestry companies have provided these "local citizens coalitions" with much of their organizational and financial backing. Their apparent objective has been to

pit labor against environmentalists and environmentally-oriented persons. Their effect has been to divide communities and create animosity in the very places where honest communication and consensus should be encouraged. While the rank-and-file membership of the Share movement may not be aware of its connection with the Wise use movement, the tactics and language of the two movements indicate a common source of counselling and training, namely, Ron Arnold and his associates. (qtd. in Simon 20)

Deception is certainly unethical in politics, but hardly unknown. We probably should not use our ethical qualms as a basis for sociological definitions. The issue is whether this particular deception misleads us into confusing popular and corporate political action. If we want to claim that Wise Use is corporate politics in disguise, we have to look carefully at its differences from, but also its similarities to, other examples that we have already accepted as popular social movement action.

The line separating corporations and members of powerful elites from the organizations involved in social movements is not always very clear. Consider the Natural Resources Defense Council (NRDC), which helped organize the U.S. boycott of old-growth wood and was one of the negotiators with Greenpeace to come up with the memorandum of understanding on sustainable forestry in Clayoquot Sound. It is a "membership organization" in the sense that some 650,000 people support the organization's work by contributing money.

However, these members did not organize themselves to lobby on environmental issues, nor do they speak for themselves on environmental issues. Rather, NRDC's

250 paid staff of scientific, legal, and media experts speak for them. In order to do this work, the organization requires a huge budget, in the range of U.S. $50 million per year, which comes largely from individual donations. In order to generate those donations, NRDC and other NGOs like it make targeted appeals using techniques similar to those developed by Gottlieb's Center for Free Enterprise.

NRDC also relies on money from "foundations" that ultimately comes from charitable donations from corporations and wealthy individuals. Foundations are, however, designed to operate at arm's-length from their donors. NRDC does not accept direct corporate donations, although some environmental NGOs of its size do. It does nonetheless have a few corporate executives on its board of trustees. The contacts of someone like Alan Horn, vice chair, president, and COO of Warner Brothers, surely help in drumming up private donations.

Genuine Versus "Fake" Voices of the People?

Some would like to categorize such bureaucratic NGOs as part of civil society, part of an institutionalized world of politics as usual, but not genuinely part of social movements. They would like to think that social movement organizations are "people's organizations," "grassroots" groups whose members are self-organized, speak for themselves, and rely only on their own volunteer labour. People do organize spontaneously with little or no capital or institutional support, but these pure "grassroots moments" are often fleeting.

Take the example of the anti-toxics movement. Very early in her struggle, Lois Gibbs was put into contact with Cora Tucker, a community organizer working with an organization called the National Toxics Campaign. Tucker herself had gained her experience and political analysis from working with civil rights organizations. The National Toxics Campaign provided local groups like Gibbs' not only with tools for organizing, but a framework for understanding the toxics issue in terms of gender, class, and racial oppression.

It worked to construct a coalition consciousness and common program. It was one of the promoters of the "toxics use reduction" idea. Gibbs herself paralleled these efforts with her Citizens Clearinghouse for Hazardous Waste. In order to keep that organization afloat she received grants from two foundations with multi-million-dollar budgets: the Beldon Fund and the Arca Foundation. The Arca Foundation was created in the 1950s by a young heiress, Nancy Reynolds Bagley, with money from her father's tobacco company, R.J. Reynolds.

Arca money, derived from big tobacco, has, ironically, supported civil rights and women's liberation organizations in the 1960s, the anti-toxics movement in the 1980s, and even anti-corporate activist groups like the Ruckus Society in the 1990s. The difference between this and MacMillan Bloedel's funding of Share groups is that no corporation controls the spending and that spending does not support any discernable corporate agenda.

Still, the Arca Foundation and others like it that specialize in left-wing causes are not working-class organizations, nor are they run by working-class people. They do help to mobilize working-class people at the "grassroots" through funding organizations like the National Clearinghouse or the Worker Rights Consortium. In so doing, such foundations and the NGOs they support are (rather like Marx and Engels themselves) not working class but acting in the name of the working class. They help to define for working people the nature of their oppression in environmentalist terms, a coalition consciousness, and a common program.

In mobilizing workers around environmentalist, anti-corporate causes, are they representing workers' interests better or more genuinely than Wise Use NGOs attempting to mobilize workers around anti-environmentalist, pro-free enterprise causes? "Genuine" working-class voices came down on both sides. Many loggers in B.C. stood with the demonstrators in the peace camp. Conversely, even in successful anti-toxics struggles, there were local people who thought that their interests were better served by keeping their mouths shut, and actively opposing their neighbours who spoke out.

Who has the right to speak on behalf of a collectivity like the "working class," the "local community," or "the people"? Or, more to the point, when competing players attempt to exercise this "power of constitution," as they inevitably do, how do we know which is the correct or accurate version? Marxists had a coherent answer to this question. The history of class relationships under capitalism demonstrates that the "real" interests of workers are always anti-capitalist, even though the capitalist press, government propaganda, and the commodity spectacle sometimes lull them into "false consciousness" about these interests. While workers are the preferred spokespeople for their own interests, it may take some time and some assistance (from bourgeois intellectuals like Marx and Engels) before they perceive those interests clearly. Social movement activists and social movement theorists have increasingly turned away from this sort of answer.

From an activist perspective, it is a bit condescending to tell people that they do not know what is in their "real" interests. Resource mobilization theorists, observing how political identities and causes were promoted in the United States in the 1960s, developed the idea that dissent could be "manufactured" by "issue-entrepreneurs." While they sympathized with the left, they provided little theoretical grounds for distinguishing between issue-entrepreneurs like Martin Luther King, Abbie Hoffman, or Ron Arnold.

Their frank appreciation of the theatrical elements of popular politics was an implicit challenge for those who had tended to associate radical opposition and truth. Like many of the activists they studied, they understood the extent to which popular politics was a game of appearances and how the "simulacrum" of popular insurrection could have the same social effect as actual popular insurrection. They provided little ammunition to those who would criticize the Wise Use simulacrum of a popular insurrection against environmentalism.

In Europe and Latin America New Social Movement theorists also felt forced by the experience of the 1960s to rethink Marxist assumptions about class interests and class identity. Marxism had reduced all interests in popular struggle to class interests. This reduction did not seem to fit the new politics of the women's movement, gay liberation, and the environmental movement. Identity politics in particular seemed to be less about articulating pre-existing "real" interests and "authentic" political identities than the cultural construction of novel ones.

Not all New Social Movement theorists took a constructivist approach to this question. However, those who did disconnected interests and identities from any underlying historical necessity or "truth." In so doing they made our question unanswerable. In other words, when competing voices attempt to speak for an oppressed group or exercise the "power of constitution" in the name of that group, there is no way to say that one is more accurate or authentic than the other.

STATES AND THE POWER OF CONSTITUTION

States are well placed to exercise the "power of constitution." We have seen examples of the exercise of this power in previous chapters. Legislators promoted co-operatives as a means of channelling working-class and petty-bourgeois radicalism in more moderate directions. Co-operatives were meant to displace adversarial unions as collective expressions of working-class aspirations. The hope was that this would reframe working-class identity. Instead of defining themselves in opposition to capitalists, workers would engage in an enterprise in which they would have to acquire some of the skills and outlook of capitalists. Governments had the power to define the legal framework that made co-operative enterprise possible, as well as the power to allocate funds, which they used to hire organizers and offer technical assistance to co-ops.

We also saw how the B.C. government was able to define the community of interest, at least for a time, in the debate over the fate of Clayoquot Sound. Here the government was attempting to define who gets to speak for "the community" and also in the name of the environment of Clayoquot Sound. Recall how the province expanded the geographic extent of this "community" and added players such as government departments and multinational corporations that had stakes in the issue, but were not in any commonsense way residents of any geographic community. This reorganized body diluted the strength of the environmentalist voice and in this way prejudiced the outcome of discussions. Here the state's power of constitution derived from its near monopoly on legislative power, as well as its (contested) legitimacy as a voice of the people. The environmental group, Friends of Clayoquot, was unhappy with the restructuring, but felt that it had to go along with it, otherwise its own deliberative process would simply be ignored by the government.

In this section we will look at a "discursive" approach to understanding the state's power to constitute the voices that speak legitimately and authoritatively on environmental issues. Mary Richardson, Joan Sherman, and Michael Gismondi have taken this approach in their analysis of a dispute over the building of a pulpmill on the Athabasca River in northern Alberta. In this case the state attempted to mediate the dispute through a public hearings process. The public hearing, including royal commissions and public inquiries, is a very common device employed by states when faced with making decisions on highly contentious issues.

Public Hearings: Co-optation of the Voice of the Public

The government—that is, the governing political party—sets up the hearing as a process that is, or is meant to appear to be, independent and acting at arm's-length. (It is a state, not a government forum.) It consists of a panel of commissioners acting like judges, who collect facts, listen to testimony, and at the end of the hearing process, write a report in which they summarize the facts, adjudicate between competing value interests, and make recommendations. Public hearings and commissions never have the power to legislate; governments can choose to ignore or implement their recommendations as they see fit.

Social movement activists have tended to be highly skeptical of the public hearings' claims to impartiality. For example, prior to the 1984 Herbicide Trial in Nova Scotia, there had been a growing and increasingly successful popular movement against in-

dustrial forestry practices in the province. The province responded in 1982 with a Royal Commission on Forestry designed to "take the heat" off the politicians. The commission's final report contained no serious criticisms of the industrial forestry model; the public debate had "cooled" and the government felt empowered to do nothing.

As the environmentalists understood it, the commission was a means of channelling public action into talk and containing that talk within a forum that it could control. The faint promise of influencing government policy gets the activists busily researching and writing their briefs or in the room talking, instead of out in the streets or on logging roads, demonstrating and engaging in direct action. By offering this forum for input, the state hopes to represent those who remain on the street as the illegitimate voice of the public: messy, emotional, "extreme." The hearing is meant to counter with the sober, balanced voice of broad public input, as summarized in the commission report.

Social scientists, too, have argued that commissions of inquiry often serve to co-opt public voices in support of state agendas. Richardson, Sherman, and Gismondi accept that co-optation may be the purpose of commissions, but are interested in the ways that citizens can subvert that purpose. Their theoretical approach derives from "discourse analysis." According to this approach, there is no "objective" way to measure "true" public opinion on any issue. Even opinion polls, despite their pretence of objectivity, sample people's most superficial, "off the shelf" responses, which are sometimes merely made up to satisfy the interviewer.

Discourse Analysis

People come to know only by entering into some form of dialogue, through reading and writing texts (the kind of thing that your professor gets you to do in this class), or through discussions with others. Through this dialogic or discursive process, they do not discover, but rather they construct their knowledge of and their views on issues. Public opinion is always in this way a "discursive construct." It does not exist, and therefore cannot be "measured" before we talk about it. (The poll results merely reflect the most superficial of dialogues—perhaps with what the respondent has heard through the media, or from the pollster.)

"Discourse" refers to various forms of expression through words, both spoken and written. It also includes non-verbal ways of dramatizing meaning, including "… spectacle, gesture, costume, edifice, icon, musical performance and the like" (Lincoln, qtd. in Gismondi and Richardson 47). Those who use discourse analysis pay particular attention to non-verbal meaning as well as to the meanings that words convey that are not explicitly stated. We have already seen examples in feminist analyses of language and interaction. Their "reading" of the choice of the word "girl" to refer to adult women was that it infantilized and disempowered women. Their reading of the patterns of interruption in discussions involving men and women revealed a hidden "discourse" on the relative value of what men versus what women had to say.

Not only were they "reading" discourse in new ways, but 1960s feminists were also uncovering the subtle ways that power operates through it. Different social actors have different discursive resources at their disposal. Some are able to control what can be talked about and how, some are able to claim greater authority for their own voices or confer that authority to others. These are the sorts of dynamics that Richardson, Sherman, and Gismondi are looking for in the Athabasca pulpmill hearings. They see

it play out between those who claim "lay" versus "expert" knowledge, on the basis of class, on the basis of race (Aboriginal peoples were important players), and, to a lesser degree, on the basis of gender. Perhaps, most importantly, the state plays a role in the "stage setting" that happens prior to the "performances" in the hearing rooms.

Public Hearings: Framing Discourse

The state can influence what gets said by defining "the question" and the "terms of reference" of the debate. The proposal of the multinational company Alberta-Pacific (Alpac) to build a pulpmill on the Athabasca River raised a whole series of issues that people wanted to discuss. Some dealt with air and water pollution. However, others had to do with impacts on the boreal mixed forest. Alpac proposed to use new technology that could process a wider range of species than previous mills. This meant that the company could use local aspen and clear-cut large areas to supply its mill. The terms of reference of the hearings excluded discussion of forestry impacts. This was defined as a separate issue that could be abstracted from the impacts of the mill itself. This exclusion, many thought, narrowed the grounds of opposition and thereby prejudiced the outcome.

Many participants in the Alpac hearings felt that the government was consulting them for appearance's sake only after the real decision to approve the mill had been made. It is true that by the time most hearings are announced, the planning and approval process between industry proponents and government is already well underway. Proponents often come prepared with years of corporate-funded study, all tending toward the same conclusion, while citizens who want to raise critical objections are left with very little time or resources to play catch-up. One "discursive strategy" available to them is to expose this dynamic, drawing into question the impartiality of the process. One woman challenged the Alpac panel, noting:

> I can see the level of confidence over there and I understand where it comes from … the bids were out on road construction three weeks ago for this mill. There are ads in the Athabasca local paper for workers for roadbuilding. I guess the government hasn't told them yet but this is not a sure thing. (qtd. in Richardson, Sherman, and Gismondi 33)

She and others also commented on the physical stage setting of the hearings. Hearings took place in different venues in different locations, but typically the Alpac proponents, "the 14 business suits," sat, like the review board members, behind a table facing the audience and armed with microphones, technical documents, and audiovisual equipment. Citizen presenters lined up to speak from a lectern facing the head tables of board members and proponents. Many read this arrangement as conferring special authority on the proponents, but also associating their voice with the official voice of the review board. "I envisaged a more neutral body," one man complained. "That's what a panel would be … then, to see the pulp mill representatives there and fielding questions and smoothing over things [that surprised me a little bit]" (qtd. in Richardson, Sherman, and Gismondi 29).

By determining who will be able to appear at the public hearings, the state can pre-define the "interested public" in ways that can prejudice outcomes. Presenters to the Alpac hearings recognized the politics of defining "the public." A local farmer made a bid to grant special priority to narrowly "local" representatives.

I'd like to talk about involvement, it seems to me that everybody wants to call themselves "the public." I would like to know who the public is. Is it me here, is it that gentleman sitting there, is it the Friends of the Athabasca [an environmental group opposed to the project], or is it the 1500 people that came out to the mill rally [in support of the project] last summer? (qtd. in Richardson, Sherman, and Gismondi 34)

He was answered by an environmentalist who argued for a more universal definition. As we saw in the Clayoquot case, people furthest from the immediate economic costs and benefits are more likely to speak purely on the basis of environmental values.

> Well, it's neither you or me right? It's not only the people of Alberta, it's the people of Canada. Not only that, it's the people of the world and everybody that is concerned about this issue. Is that true? (qtd. in Richardson, Sherman, and Gismondi 34)

The government had no intention of including "the people of the world" concerned about this issue. It did seriously have to consider how far downstream on the Athabasca the community of interest should extend (downstream people can expect fewer benefits and more costs from a polluting mill), and whether it should encompass the city of Edmonton. Governments have the power to include or exclude explicitly, but also covertly and perhaps unintentionally, through the design of the hearings' itinerary and schedule. Aboriginal peoples in far-flung northern communities are unlikely to be well represented unless the review board is willing to fly to many small locations to take the hearings to them.

In terms of timing, citizens in public hearings frequently complain of bias in favour of proponents. Governments like to guarantee that these deliberations will be swift, so as not to add unpredictable delays to already bureaucratic approvals processes. Those called upon to represent "the public" feel they rarely have enough advance warning, insufficient time to prepare, and, unlike proponents, no benefit of staff paid to attend on an ongoing basis. An exasperated presenter, in pointing out this handicap, also contested the impartiality of the Alpac panel.

> [I] question how seriously the government, Alpac and this panel takes this public input. How in the name of all that is good and holy am I, employed in a different occupation, supposed to read the EIA [environmental impact assessment], understand it—remember we are talking leading edge technology here—and make intelligent responses to it in the 14 days between 16 October and 30 October? All this, as well as make a living ... pretend I'm married, and pay some attention to my children. (qtd. in Richardson, Sherman, and Gismondi 40–41)

Public Hearings as Dramatic Performance

A curious feature of all public hearings is their emphasis on oral presentation. Many have commented on the "time-wasting clumsiness of the oral hearing process and its inefficiency in delivering hard facts" (Ashforth 7). It makes sense if we understand it not as instrumental, but as performative. The hearing process puts speech on display in a ritual demonstration. Who spoke, *that*

they spoke and were heard, as well as how they spoke becomes as important as the content of what the participants said. Participants feel that something has happened. Visible representatives of "the state" have heard, seriously considered, and responded to their words.

The formal staging of speech subtly privileges certain types of self-presentation over others. Review board members adopt the demeanour of court judges, speaking in a tone and grammar consistent with their claims to impartiality and objectivity. Participants are not supposed to chant, shout, sing protest songs, or recite poetry. Such demonstrations would, by contrast, speak of "emotionalism" and "irrationality." Some citizen presenters did nonetheless claim the right to speak personally and passionately. However, they did so knowing they were challenging the prevailing norms of the hearing process.

> Some of the presentations that are pro the development have talked about, you know, they want to hear the hard, cold facts and not to be emotional. I would say that the cold, hard facts I have seen suggest that if you aren't emotional, perhaps you don't have any business making these decisions. (Judy Evaski-McLean, qtd. in Richardson, Sherman, and Gismondi 37)

The face-to-face exchange of the hearing room allows all of the usual ways of authorizing identities. Physical self-presentation marks distinctions of social prestige and authority. For instance, women activists in a 1980s Royal Commission on Uranium mining in Nova Scotia, recognizing that the testimony of men on technical issues carried more weight, recruited men to speak for them on such issues. In Alberta, some presenters marked their "localness" in terms of class, race, and/or social connections.

> I have owned and operated my own business in the area for the last ten years. My father was Frank Lafferty from Lafferty Bouvier family, a well-known native family throughout the north. My mother was Beatrice Rose Lepine ... born and raised in the north. My father was a much respected riverboat pilot on the Athabasca River.... My parents were married at Athabasca Landing in 1913.... As a native person, I will always remember what Billy Mills said one time ... we must learn to walk with one spirit in both worlds. I think it's time that our native people and other people in the community of Athabasca take advantage of opportunities.... I believe that I represent the majority of the ordinary citizens of this town Athabasca when I say that we are enthusiastic about the prospect of having work for our people, and we believe that the mill can be brought into this community and the environment can remain safe for us to continue to live here. (qtd. in Richardson, Sherman, and Gismondi 38)

Here the claim is to representativeness and a certain kind of knowledge—of the truly "local" people.

Claims to Authority of Voice

While such claims carried weight, Richardson, Sherman, and Gismondi argue that the privileged knowledge claims in this and other public hearings derived from scientific and bureaucratic expertise. Scientists mark their status in these contexts, not by actually wearing lab coats, but by announcing their credentials and speaking in "value-neutral" language. So, for example, instead of saying that pulpmill effluent is "harmful" to fish or ecologically "damaging," he or she might say that the effluent is associated with a measurable increase in the mortality of fish, and provide numbers. This careful wording implies that others, not the scientist, should add the judgment as to whether this rate of mortality is "harmful" or "bad."

Unlike the authority of the local person, the scientist's authority derives from removing himself or herself personally from the things that he or she says. Figures of speech dramatize this distancing. Constructions like "the data show ..." suggest that the person is not speaking; rather, the facts are somehow "speaking for themselves." Instead of using the first person pronoun, "I," the speaker might use "we" to invoke the generalized scientific community. They can go further and substitute the active ("I [or we] concluded that ...") for the passive voice ("it was concluded that"). Here, we are meant to understand that it is not a person, but objective science talking.

Challenging Official Discourse

In summary, Richardson, Sherman, and Gismondi are arguing that public hearings are state forums designed to pre-structure public debate, privilege certain types of discourse, and bias outcomes. The hearing ritually invokes the voice of the public with the aim of co-opting popular assent for state agendas. The authors use discourse analysis to reveal this dynamic, but also to analyze the discursive strategies that citizens can use to undermine it.

Value-Neutral Language

The first is to demystify the conventions of objectivity in expert testimony. Citizens were able to expose the value assumptions in supposedly value-neutral language. Scientists referred to effluents (a.k.a. water pollution) as "contributions," a vague term with positive connotations. Forestry experts described poplar trees as "weed species," invoking valuation in terms of human use. Scientists reported that standard laboratory tests showed that pulpmill effluent was "non-toxic." The standard test is the "LC50" in which fish are exposed to undiluted pulpmill effluent for 96 hours. If 50 percent or more of the fish survive, then the effluent passes the test. In other words, if it kills only 49 percent of the fish, it is still "non-toxic."

It required another scientist, Dr. Ian Birtwell, to expose and question the assumptions behind this "objective" measure.

> My main area of research is on the sub-lethal effects of contaminants, that is, levels that don't inherently kill fish outright, but perhaps may have an effect at a level below that, that would have killed them.... Many times an animal may be debilitated and essentially ecologically dead by conditions far below those which kill it in four days.... In regulatory bioassays where effluents are exposed to fish, typically one may consider the effluent as being acceptable if it does not kill fifty percent of the fish within four days. Well, from my perspective, it's those zero to fifty percent which are equally important. For biological purposes, we've typically used the fifty percent response level, but I think we also have to consider response at the one percent, the five percent, and

the ten percent level. Those fish, or whatever animal we are studying and testing, is also of relevance in the environmental context. (qtd. in Gismondi and Richardson 51–52)

Gismondi and Richardson make much of Birtwell's use of language that links him personally to his knowledge claims ("I think ...," "from my perspective ...") and reveals a "love of fish." Note how he also chooses his words to establish his scientific credentials ("My main area of research is ..."), and signals competency by invoking technical jargon ("In regulatory bioassays ...").

Ethnocentric Assumptions

Richardson, Sherman, and Gismondi discuss a number of examples where non-scientists familiar with the land as farmers or trappers were able to use their local knowledge to question and correct scientific testimony. They highlight a case where Alpac scientists attempting to apply "universal" standards for toxicity failed to account for local particulars. Again, it required another scientist to make the case. Alpac experts accepted that the mill would "contribute" small amounts of dioxin to the Athabasca River, and that dioxin does "bioaccumulate"—that is, it persists in animal tissue and becomes more concentrated in animals, like humans, higher in the food chain. Company toxicologists assured the review board that dioxin would affect only people who ate fish, but even so would remain below "acceptable thresholds."

A scientist, Dr. Swain, speaking for the government of the Northwest Territories, challenged the use of this standard that assumed a "normal" human diet of perhaps one meal of fish per week. Aboriginal peoples downstream from the Alberta mill still relied on "country food" for much of their diet, including large amounts of fish. Their weekly consumption of fish could be as much as 10 times that of the "average Canadian." Unlike the average Canadian, they ate many of the organs, and considered the liver of the burbot, where toxins concentrate, to be a special delicacy.

A member of the panel from the Northwest Territories summarized the problem.

> ... the kind of studies that you are talking about are very ethnocentric as far as standards are concerned.... We were in Fort Resolution when we were told the man eats fish five times a week. That's a father. And the mother also eats five fish a week. That's 10 fish, one week, in one family's life. Considering what you told us this morning, we are not only talking about 10 parts of dioxin, but taking into consideration PCB and all the other compounds, when you look at its long-term or cumulative impact, what would you say to the people of the Northwest Territories? What do they have to look forward to? (qtd. in Gismondi and Richardson 60)

The supposedly objective scientific standard was shown to have an "ethnocentric" bias in favour of non-Native culinary culture, treating it as though it were "universal." Gismondi and Richardson see this as a demystification of scientific claims to objectivity. The idea that science might have an ethnic/racial bias opens it further to political readings. They write:

> Once the ethnocentrism of dioxin standards is established, Dr. Swain's evidence of the intergenerational impact of toxins (i.e., behavior disorder; decreased IQ by four points

every generation; decreasing sperm counts) links the issue to a more profound and powerful discourse which speaks to the possibility of the slow, invisible genocide of native people. (61)

Objectivity of the Market

Participants at the hearings also challenged the idea that "the market" was objective and apolitical. Mill proponents argued that the chlorine bleaching process that produced dioxin was unavoidable because of market demand for white paper. "By our own nature," as one mill supporter put it, "we demand a white paper." Consumer demand and the market forces they put into play are, according to this discourse, "natural" and unchanging like laws of gravity.

A woman, Ms. Peruniak, who presented to the panel, was told by one of the Alpac spokespeople, Mr. Fenner, that not only could the company not avoid using chlorine, but they could not mix in recycled fibre to the pulp because this would affect the paper's colour and its marketability.

> Ms. Peruniak (a housewife): What do you base your market research on?
> Mr. Fenner (Alpac): ... the market itself.
> Ms. Peruniak: ... I put it to you that within the next decade, you're going to see major changes in the bleached kraft pulp market. And I think my estimations are probably as good as yours....
> Dr. Schindler (board member): Mr. Fenner, to what extent does the pulp and paper industry determine these markets or try to drive them? It is my experience from soap and detergent companies and the power

industry that these markets can be driven rather than predicted. They push the markets in the directions they want them to go. I once over-heard one, admittedly drunken, de-tergent executive brag to one of his colleagues that they could package horseshit in a yellow and orange box and housewives would still buy it.

Ms. Peruniak: Not this housewife.

(qtd. in Gismondi and Richardson 51)

Fenner, in a few words, invokes powerful social myths of the market as a quasi-natural force, external and constraining.

The interventions both of Peruniak and Schindler expose key assumptions of this myth—that consumer desire is natural and that it drives market forces. Consumer desires, they point out, are social constructs. Large corporations have tremendous power, through advertising and marketing strategies, to shape consumer demand. Consumers themselves are agents. They are capable of critically re-evaluating and changing their consumption habits. Peruniak, write Gismondi and Richardson, "announces the presence in the 1990s of environmentally conscious persons who refuse to be victims of the market or cor-porate decision makers" (52).

The simple words "the market" are powerful because they carry with them a whole constellation of meanings that are deeply embedded in our culture and that we rarely examine. Richardson et al. call such complexes of meaning "sacred truths," and identify a number of them at play in the hearings: "the impersonal authority of science and technology; the wisdom of the market; the need for job creation to keep the traditional rural family together; the superiority of humans over nature; the abil-ity of technology to solve social problems" (Richardson, Sherman, and Gismondi 17).

They also point out how certain tropes of language can similarly pre-structure our thinking on issues. For example, "binary oppositions" are simple and entrenched ways of organizing our understanding of the world into contrasting categories: "good versus evil," "the powerful versus the pow-erless," "local people versus outsiders."

Jobs Versus the Environment

We saw how the Wise Use movement em-ployed all of these, plus the potent "jobs versus environment" opposition in order to mobilize anti-environmentalism. Northern Alberta rates of unemployment were higher than those for the rest of the province. Partly as a result, northern communities had been suffering declines in population, so Alpac's promises of job creation, both in the mill and in forestry, were seductive. Supporters of the project regularly invoked "jobs versus environment" discourse to undermine en-vironmentalist opposition.

A number of presenters attempted to deconstruct this binary opposition. Meri-lyn Peruniak insisted that it was a false dichotomy.

With this bleached kraft pulp mill proposal we are being given a choice between jobs and environment. What kind of choice is that? Cer-tainly, not a fair one. It's like tell-ing someone they can either have a pair of lungs or heart, but they can't have both. We need both to survive, lungs and heart, environ-ment and jobs. (qtd. in Gismondi and Richardson 129)

Two unions, the Canadian Paperwork-ers and the Pulp, Paper & Woodworkers of Canada, insisted that organized workers demanded both. Chlorine-based bleaching processes are dangerous not just to the environment outside the mill, but to the work environment within its walls. Chlorine spills can kill workers outright, but also, as the Canadian Paperworkers Union representative argued, "... many toxic chemicals are used in the process and hundreds of others are produced as byproducts ... the harmful effects of these chemicals range from allergic reactions to the incidence of cancer higher than that of the general population" (qtd. in Richardson, Sherman, and Gismondi 135). Both unions opposed the mill on health and environmental grounds.

Other presenters questioned the presumption that the Alpac mill stood unequivocally on the "jobs" side of the dichotomy. The mill, as they pointed out, threatened existing forms of employment. The mill site and roads were to be located on farmland and would have taken much of this land out of production. Many farmers argued that the mill's air emissions would hurt the viability of their livestock operations. Downstream it would threaten trapping, fishing, and tourism industries.

Similarly, people challenged the assumption that jobs could not be placed on the "environment" side of the dichotomy.

> [We] believe this whole project has been sold to the public in an inappropriate way. The basic misconception is that there are only two alternatives for northern Alberta: a bleached kraft pulp mill or no development.... [W]hat are the other ways we could develop the north beside a kraft pulp mill ... we should be looking at the economic alternatives as well as the environmental impact.... [W]e thought that the Board should consider the impact of the mill on

> alternative, existing and future economic developments when assessing the total pros and cons of the Alpac mill. In other words, we wanted the Board to look at opportunity costs. (qtd. in Richardson, Sherman, and Gismondi 144)

Anthropocentric Assumptions

I want to consider one final example of the "discursive strategies" that the authors discuss in this environmental debate. This was an effort by some to shift the discourse away from the very powerful "anthropocentric" paradigm toward an "ecocentric" one. Alpac was arguing that a new process that they had developed allowed them to offer for human benefit a formerly useless "weed tree." A local sawmill operator seconded the company's line in these terms.

> This poplar forest has been around as long as I've been around, and a lot longer probably. It is rotting; it is dying; it is giving off gases; it is tipping over; it is causing a breeding ground for insects of all types. It is old; it is overmatured.... You can't do nothing with it because it is too old and it is too rotten.... The only thing that can use it is the pulp mill.... It would create a lot of employment for a lot of children. (qtd. in Gismondi and Richardson 56)

In the following example of environmentalist counter-discourse, the speaker first locates human need within a larger ecosystem context, then references the needs of non-human species and questions the separability of humans (and human needs) from biological and physical processes in the environment.

Forests are not just trees or cellulose factories. They are home to thousands of kinds of living things with their own lives to live in their own evolutionary destinies. The way we view the land, whether or not we see ourselves as part of the land and partner with a living community, determines in large measure what the land can and will get us. Once our air and water are fouled and the old-growth forests are gone, the potential for sustainable and environmentally sound development will have been taken away. And with that potential, gone will be the wood warblers, the woodland caribou, rare orchids, epithetic lichens, marten, and countless other creatures. To maintain that trees that grow old and die of natural causes are "wasted" is a mercenary view at best. One might also argue that old people who die of natural causes are wasted. This is nonsense. Old trees and old people enrich the lives of all living things dependent upon them, be they chickadees, caribou or children. You and I and every living thing here is composed of recycled carbon that was once part of living, breathing plants and animals. The water in our bodies was once rain, snow and river water. We are the ash of a supernova and a universe filled with everyday miracles. Let us hope we can work towards greater dignity and humility and viewpoints that befit our critical role in the history of our planet. (qtd. in Gismondi and Richardson 56–57)

This is a clear example of someone attempting to "speak for" the environment rather than any particular human interest group.

By exposing and challenging the preconceptions built into language, taken-for-granted constellations of meaning, and the structure and terms of reference of the hearings process, citizen activists were able to open up the hearings to a more genuine debate about alternatives. They were able to influence the review board members sufficiently that in their report they recommended a halt to the mill until a number of environmental concerns were addressed. The citizens "won" or, as Richardson, Sherman, and Gismondi put it, they "won back the words." What they mean is that the victory was not just over this particular proposal to build a mill; rather, people won back some control from the state over the construction of their voice as "the public."

CONCLUSION

In this chapter we have highlighted two case studies: the Wise Use movement and an environmental public hearing process. Both illustrate ways in which the "power of constitution" can be exercised. In one case corporations, with the help of public relations firms and issue entrepreneurs like Ron Arnold, attempted to constitute in class terms a new political identity of the anti-environmentalist, pro-industry "ordinary person." In the other case a state, through the institution of the public hearing, attempted to constitute "the" public and prompt that public to speak in sober, "rational," pro-development terms.

These are cases in which two of the most powerful actors in modern societies, corporations and governments, attempt to co-opt relatively powerless actors to speak in the interests of the powerful. To the extent to which such efforts are successful, they raise questions about how we draw the line between politics of the powerful and popular politics. Examples of corporate front groups and "astroturf" are easy to dismiss as political activism of powerful institutions masquerading as activism of "the people." Front groups are paid advocates engaging in blatant deception both about their political aims and social support. Astroturf has no social coherence other than what is provided by corporate-owned databases and mailing lists.

However, in cases like the Wise Use movement, where corporations actually set in motion volunteer associations whose members embrace, reproduce, and adapt corporate-inspired interpretive "frames" that define their political identities and values, it becomes difficult to separate corporate-sponsored mobilization from the many other examples of sponsored mobilization that have increasingly characterized popular politics since the 1960s.

There are numerous ways in which states attempt to co-opt social movements or undercut them by authorizing more "moderate" voices of "the people." The Alpac case study allowed us to examine a particularly subtle state strategy. It also features a theoretical approach, "discourse analysis," particularly suited to exposing the subtle ways in which debate and its outcomes can be pre-structured in public hearings. Discourse analysis directs our attention to unspoken meanings and to the form as well as the content of speech and interaction. It exposes the non-linear, non-rational dimensions of communication and persuasion—the theatrical and rhetorical dimensions.

Discourse analysis is compelling when it uncovers ways in which those claiming to speak rationally and objectively are in fact relying on rhetoric and drama. However, I would like you to consider some questions about the approach and how it is applied in the Alpac case study. In order to understand the success of the citizen activists, Richard-

son, Sherman, and Gismondi clearly want to focus on the form of their discursive interventions. However, is it the form or the content that is persuasive in the above examples? Presenters certainly attempted to expose the rhetorical devices of their opponents. How much, though, did the force of their own arguments rely on rhetoric rather than reasoning and evidence?

Many who use discourse analysis turn their demystifying gaze with particular delight upon science, in particular the natural sciences. Are Richardson, Sherman, and Gismondi demystifying the authority of particular practitioners of science, such as the Alpac toxicologists, or of scientific rationality in general? They write, "Part of the reason science enjoys a high status in western society is its purported reliance on a rational methodology, which is thought to place it above personality, prejudice, and ethnocentrism" (Richardson 87). They certainly celebrate challenges to this belief. Are they saying, though, that no one can claim to rely on a rational and objective methodology because there is no such thing? If this is what they mean, what would the implications be for social movements?

Everyone would be relying on rhetoric, and their appeals to science, reason, and evidence would be no more than rhetorical devices. Many social movement activists appeal to truths verifiable through rational methodology. Some believe that truth, objective truth that applies to and must be accepted by all, is one of the greatest weapons against arbitrary power. Environmentalists in particular rely heavily on scientific theory and evidence for their claims. Climate science is the most powerful tool against the inaction of legislators over climate change.

The kind of understanding that environmentalists use to make claims to speak for the environment are based almost exclusively on science. Re-read the ecocentric testimony we quoted from the Alpac hearings. It is informed by biology, geology, and astrophysics. Consider the fact that advertising and PR firms are really in the business of producing rhetoric (with or without appeal to reason or evidence) for a price. As the U.S. case of corporate climate change deniers shows, with enough financial backing the authority of PR can outweigh the authority of science. If scientific rationality is a myth and rhetoric is for sale, what are the prospects of the powerless winning discursive struggles?

REFERENCES

Ashforth, Adam. "Reckoning Schemes of Legitimation: On Commissions of Inquiry as Power/Knowledge Forms." *Journal of Historical Sociology* 3, no. 1 (1990): 1–22.

Beder, Sharon. *Global Spin: The Corporate Assault on Environmentalism*, rev. ed. Totnes; White River Junction: Chelsea Green Publishing, 2002.

Bourdieu, Pierre. "Social Space and the Genesis of Groups." *Theory and Society* 14 (1985): 723–744.

Dunk, Thomas. "Talking about Trees: Environment and Society in Forest Workers' Culture." *Canadian Review of Sociology and Anthropology* 31, no. 1 (1994): 14–34.

Gismondi, Michael, and Mary Richardson. "Discourse and Power in Environmental Politics: Public Hearings on a Bleached Kraft Pulp Mill in Alberta, Canada." *Capitalism Nature Socialism* 2, no. 8 (1991): 43–66.

Helvarg, David. *The War against the Greens: The Wise-Use Movement, the New Right and Anti-environmental Violence*. San Francisco: Sierra Club Books, 1994.

Richardson, Mary, Joan Sherman, and Michael Gismondi. *Winning Back the Words: Confronting Experts in an Environmental Public Hearing*. Toronto: Garamond Press, 1993.

Rowell, Andrew. *Green Backlash: Global Subversion of the Environmental Movement*. London, New York: Routledge, 1996.

Simon, Alexander. "Backlash! Corporate Front Groups and the Struggle for Sustainable Forestry in British Columbia." *Capitalism, Nature, Socialism* 9, no. 4 (1998): 3.

Switzer, Jacqueline Vaughn. *Green Backlash: The History and Politics of Environmental Opposition in the U.S.* Boulder: L. Rienner Publishers, 1997.

CRITICAL THINKING QUESTIONS

1. How would you define genuine "popular" or grassroots movements? Would your definition include the Wise Use movement? Why or why not?
2. Is there such a thing as false consciousness? Can we ever say that a person or group of people who think that they are speaking in their own interests are mistaken? If so, then on what grounds?
3. Who has the right to speak on behalf of a collectivity like the "working class," the "local community," or "the people"? Or, more to the point, when competing players attempt to exercise this "power of constitution," as they inevitably do, how do we know which is the correct or accurate version?

4. Are Richardson, Sherman, and Gismondi saying that no one can claim to rely on a rational and objective methodology because there is no such thing? If this is what they mean, what would the implications be for social movements?
5. If scientific rationality is a myth and rhetoric is for sale, what are the prospects of the powerless winning discursive struggles?

FURTHER READING

Beder, Sharon. *Global Spin: The Corporate Assault on Environmentalism*, rev. ed. Totnes, White River Junction: Chelsea Green Publishing, 2002.
Beder documents corporate campaigns to influence public discourse and popular political action. She argues that corporate front groups, industry-funded researchers, think tanks, and PR firms traffic in deception and disinformation.

Dunk, Thomas. "Talking about Trees: Environment and Society in Forest Workers' Culture." *Canadian Review of Sociology and Anthropology* 31, no. 1 (1994): 14–34.
Dunk analyses the discourse of Ontario forestry workers and discovers a language of environmental concern. However, workers embed their environmentalism in working-class understandings that make it difficult to identify with what they see as an urban, middle-class environmental movement.

Gismondi, Michael, and Mary Richardson. "Discourse and Power in Environmental Politics: Public Hearings on a Bleached Kraft Pulp Mill in Alberta, Canada." *Capitalism Nature Socialism* 2, no. 8 (1991): 43–66.
Gismondi and Richardson illustrate how state efforts to use the public hearing process to construct a compliant "voice of the public" can be subverted.

Szasz, Andrew. *EcoPopulism: Toxic Waste and the Movement for Environmental Justice.* Minneapolis: University of Minnesota, 1994.
Szasz represents the "ecopopulism" of the anti-toxics movement as a genuine voice of the dispossessed raised in defence of the environment. This is one of the better analyses of a very important movement.

RELEVANT WEB SITES

Clary-Meuser Research Network
www.mapcruzin.com/greenwash/
This site includes an excellent page dedicated to exposing greenwash. In addition to a list of front groups, it includes discussions of the abuses of science in aid of anti-environmentalism. See also the Corpwatch greenwash awards (www.corpwatch.org/article.php?list=type&type=102).

The Green Life
www.thegreenlife.org/draft/dontbefooled.html
> Check out the top 10 greenwashers according to the U.S.-based organization The Green Life.

Multinational Monitor
http://multinationalmonitor.org/links/scat.php?scat_id=12
> On this page the Multinational Monitor publishes a list of corporate front groups.

Sourcewatch
www.sourcewatch.org
> Sourcewatch is a project of the U.S.-based Center for Media and Democracy. On their site you will find case studies of deceptive PR campaigns, the activities of front groups, think tanks, industry-funded organizations, and industry-friendly experts.

Spinwatch
www.spinwatch.org
> This U.K.-based organization is dedicated to exposing government and corporate propaganda in the U.K. and E.U.

Chapter 10

BEYOND NATION-STATE SOVEREIGNTY: INDIGENOUS PEOPLES' INTERNATIONALISM

INTRODUCTION: TRANSLOCAL LOCAL POLITICS

In the summer of 1994 I was travelling the back roads of Maine interviewing environmental activists. I was interested in the question of how it is that people speak up in the name of the environment. I was finding answers in terms of people's immediate relationships to the places that they lived. The anti-toxics movement was still going strong in the state. Many people had become active around local threats of toxic pollution—things that could cause them direct bodily harm. Unions in Maine were concerned about toxic pollution in workplaces and were forming alliances with the anti-toxics groups to lobby the state government for "toxics use reduction" legislation.

So when I learned of this person, Conrad Heeschen, living in northern Maine who had formed a group called No Thank-Q Hydro Quebec, I did not quite "get it." People I interviewed would frequently recommend others whom they thought were important. In this way I heard that Heeschen was a very bright and forward-looking thinker concerned with big, long-term issues like energy policy. I, however, could not quite picture how he was going to generate a popular movement on this issue, based as he was in rural Maine and focused on a Quebec hydro project. Consequently I did not make a special trip up to see him, and I missed one of the most important developments in environmental politics in the 1990s.

I learned later that No Thank-Q Hydro Quebec was part of a larger network of international environmental NGOs and local organizations throughout New England that had formed an alliance with the James Bay Cree and was eventually successful in opposing the Great Whale hydroelectric project of the Quebec government. In the

first part of this chapter we will explore how the Grand Council of the Crees, representing communities of primarily hunter-gatherer people, was able to construct a transnational coalition in order to defend its local interests. I also want to investigate what I failed to understand in 1994, which was the complex motivations of New Englanders who engaged in popular resistance alongside a Canadian indigenous group.

More generally, in this chapter I want to understand the move toward an international and global indigenous politics. In the second part of the chapter we will look at how the Grand Council of the Crees, along with indigenous organizations from around the world, have used the United Nations as a global "platform," a physical and discursive space within which to advance indigenous rights. They have both used, but also transformed this platform in ways that have called into question notions of national sovereignty and self-determination. At the same time they have begun to transform what it means to be "indigenous" in interesting and paradoxical ways. First, we must consider some background on the Cree and their opposition to hydroelectric development in northern Quebec.

CREE OPPOSITION TO HYDRO-QUÉBEC: BACKGROUND

Picture the map of North America with the huge bowl that is Hudson's Bay carved out of the top. Another bay protrudes from the base of this bowl into northern Ontario and Quebec echoing the way Florida protrudes from the continent into the Caribbean. This is James Bay, drainage basin for much of northern Ontario and Quebec. In the 1970s the Quebec government became interested, not in the bay, but the catchment area where water collects on the Precambrian shield and is channelled north to the bay. This was the period of the first energy crisis when it looked like global oil supplies might be running out. To Quebec policy makers and engineers, the North was an undeveloped and relatively "uninhabited" resource. If northern rivers could be dammed and diverted through electric turbines, Quebec would benefit from a perpetual, clean, cheap source of power.

Crees' Local Lifeworld

To the James Bay Cree and, north of the Arctic Circle, the Inuit, this catchment area was their entire world. Apart from a few mining and logging operations, the region was inaccessible by road in the 1970s. People still obtained at least part of their living off the land. They fished, migrated to follow game, and trapped in the winter using a mix of modern and ancient techniques. Their cultural understandings of the world and their place within it were intimately tied to their experiences travelling through and using the land. Young Crees learn from excursions with their parents and elders that the landscape is not just a resource for physical livelihood but also a kind of cultural map.

Anthropologist Harvey Feit describes the understanding as follows:

> ... the land is layered with histories both personal and far-reaching. Place names known to and used by hunters who live on a particular hunting territory over many years cover nearly every feature of the landscape, and many are tied to stories of how the name came to be given—stories that recall past persons, events and associations. They also record past ties to Europe

through the fur trade, as at "Dress-up Creek," where hunters prepared to descend the last stretch of the Rupert river to enter the fur-trade post and meet the European traders. The presence of other Indigenous peoples is recorded, for example, by the Cree places named for Iroquois, or Haudenosaunee, who raided the area in the late seventeenth century by travelling along particular rivers that now carry their Cree names. Connections to Canada and the United States occur through the names of the first places where an early American sport hunter, known in Cree as a "long-knife," did something memorable. They record corporate connections and histories of commercial fisheries, mines, sawmills and trading posts, now closed.

Cree society was neither static nor unconnected with the broader world. Photographs of the people from 1972 show a layering of cultural influences taken from across time and space. In one shot they are building a teepee. In another, young men adopt the then universal idiom of counterculture rebellion: hip-hugger jeans, long hair and headband, a patch with the words "Keep on Trucking" (www.mat.ucsb.edu/˜g.legrady/glWeb/Projects/jb/james_bay.html). These young men were constructing their Cree identities from diverse sources. However, they were still learning to map their identities to the place where they lived in ways that relied upon not just the preservation of the landscape, but also the traditional economy that required them to make intimate journeys through it with their elders. According to Cree leader Matthew Coon Come, "the land is part of us.... I guess we can say that we are the land."

State/Corporate Land Claims

The Cree had little knowledge of and until this point no reason to contest non-Native attempts to inscribe this land with legal notions of "sovereignty" and "title." As Matthew Coon Come put it, the Cree had no idea that the first European traders had come:

> ... because a king across the sea had scratched on a piece of paper saying that he "gave" our lands to his cousin Prince Rupert. Similarly, in 1873 when the same lands, our lands, were ceded to Canada by the Hudson's Bay Company, this was not of significance to us. We were not asked or told, and we continued to live as usual. Once again in 1898 and 1912, when our lands were transferred by Canada to the Province of Quebec, we did not know about this. We continued to pursue our way of life, and also we fed and clothed the small number of Wemistigoosheeyiwits [Europeans] who were living among us.

Quebec's plan for hydroelectric development, however, was to have wide-reaching impacts on the land through road building, construction, and flooding. The Cree recognized immediately the threat to their land-based way of life and the culture that depended upon it. In 1972 they went to court to try and establish some legal basis for their traditional claims to the land. Initially the courts recognized that the Cree had certain "undefined" rights to land and on this basis granted a temporary injunction against the project.

In 1973 the Quebec Court of Appeals overturned this ruling, arguing instead that the Cree were essentially "squatters" on their ancestral lands. "The judges," writes Coon

Come, "said our rights in and to our lands had all been extinguished, because in 1670 King Charles II had 'given' the Hudson's Bay watershed to his cousin Prince Rupert and the Hudson's Bay Company." The James Bay Cree had never signed treaties.

Over the next decades the Cree were to become much more adept in the game of legal abstractions, creating those powerful lines scratched on pieces of paper in distant places. In the mean time, bulldozers had already begun carving lines out of the rock in their territory. A 650 km road had been completed and work was underway on the 20-storey dam that was to contain the La Grande River. The Cree felt compelled to accept whatever concessions they could get from the Quebec government. In an out-of-court settlement they, along with the Inuit, signed the James Bay and Northern Quebec Agreement in 1975.

The First Hydro Agreement

In exchange for approving Phase I of hydroelectric development, the Cree obtained a number of commitments from the Quebec government and the Crown corporation in charge of the project that were meant to help the Cree adapt to and benefit from development in their territory. Traditional land use was to be protected, but new opportunities were to be found for Aboriginal business ventures and wage work. The Cree were to get greater resources for community development as well as more control through expanded self-government. All of this came with a cash settlement of $130 million as compensation for what they saw as an incursion into their territory and disruption of their culture.

Quebec was ready in 1989 to initiate Phase II, the so-called Great Whale megaproject involving wholesale diversion of rivers and massive flooding. This time circumstances had changed for the Cree. They had had experience with a hydroelectric project as well as a government treaty and were unhappy with both. In addition to the loss of land through flooding, the Cree had discovered that mercury leached out of the rock, contaminating the fish and making it dangerous for human consumption. Many government commitments to social services had not been fulfilled. The Cree had received almost no benefit through employment and business opportunities. They had, however, increased their governmental capacity and now had economic resources that they could use for political action.

MAKING A TRANSNATIONAL ALLIANCE

The political strategy of the Cree was to shift their sights from the Quebec state toward international allies. Many of the issues they raised were environmental: the large-scale destruction of habitat and contamination of river systems. International environmental organizations had increasingly made claims on "local" issues as being of global concern and had intervened on behalf of indigenous peoples against their development-minded governments. The Cree were already predisposed to view the Quebec government's sovereignty claims over Cree land with some skepticism. They had no qualms about circumventing the province and were beginning to recognize how powerful this strategy could be.

Market Strategy

Their initial international contacts followed the flows of commodities in the internation-

al market. Electricity is a mobile commodity that can be sold and distributed throughout the North American power grid. In order to be financially viable, the Great Whale megaproject had to get commitments from buyers on this grid. The fact that the New England states, including New York, Maine, and Vermont, were negotiating contracts with Hydro-Québec for James Bay power was what alerted many Americans to the project and its implications for the Cree.

There was also a significant tourism market that linked New England and northern Quebec. Jim Higgins, a Vermonter, knew of the James Bay region from having canoed many of its "wilderness" rivers. In 1989 he contacted the Grand Council of the Crees and invited delegates to Vermont to talk about ways to prevent their destruction. Later the Cree collaborated with an American outfitter to organize whitewater-rafting tours down the Great Whale River for American policy makers (McRae).

In Maine, Conrad Heeschen was concerned about a New England energy policy focused on buying new power from environmentally damaging sources instead of promoting energy conservation. He invited Matthew Coon Come to speak at the Maine Legislature, address the media, and meet activists in the group No Thank-Q Hydro Quebec (Craik). In these ways market ties were being translated into personal ties that were to become the basis of a political coalition.

New Englanders recognized that their stake in the issue, as well as their point of leverage, lay in their role as potential buyers of Quebec hydro power. They began organizing consumer boycotts. The difference between these and the consumer boycotts in the Clayoquot Sound case was that the prospective buyers of power were state and municipal governments. At the state level, in addition to No Thank-Q Hydro Quebec, Vermonters formed the New England Coalition for Energy Efficiency. New Yorkers formed two organizations, the James Bay Defense Coalition and PROTECT. All of them lobbied their legislators to cancel energy contracts with Hydro-Québec in the hope that the Quebec government would deny approval to the Great Whale project.

Translocal Demonstrations

The Cree worked with their American allies to raise awareness of the issues within New England. In 1991 they collaborated with the Inuit to build an *odeyak*, a hybrid between a canoe (*owut* in Cree) and a *kayak* (the Inuit word for kayak), which together they paddled to New York City. In a bid for maximum publicity, they timed their arrival for Earth Day celebrations and were able to exhibit their *odeyak* in Times Square, one of the great global information hubs.

Their American hosts helped to provide a platform in New York, finding them places to stay and venues to speak. The Cree and Inuit toured university campuses and inspired student activists. Among other things, students lobbied their universities to sell off their investments in Hydro-Québec bonds in protest (Craik). New Englanders organized bicycle tours of their states, encouraging people to vote against buying Quebec power in local referenda.

The Cree cause got sympathetic coverage in the mainstream American press. *Time* and the *Boston Globe Magazine* carried features critical of the Great Whale project. The Grand Council of the Crees commissioned its own media representation, including the film *The Land of Our Children*, a slide show, co-produced with the Sierra Club, as well as posters and T-shirts that thousands of New Englanders distributed through a politics of everyday interaction. The pop-culture marketing also included celebrity endorsement

and a series of three benefit concerts. The "Ban the Dam Jam for James Bay," which raised nearly U.S. $300,000 for the Grand Council, featured Canadian musician Bruce Cockburn plus Jackson Browne, James Taylor, Roseanne Cash, and Dan Fogelberg (Morrison and Nitsch 9).

Major environmental organizations raised the issue with their members and went on record publicly in support of the Cree. In Quebec, these included Greenpeace Quebec and Les Amis de la Terre (Friends of the Earth). In the U.S. the National Audubon Society, the Natural Resources Defense Council, the Sierra Club, and the Humane Society were all on board. Many joined with Greenpeace in the James Bay Coalition, which paid for a full-page ad in the *New York Times*. They were demonstrating their power to mobilize public opinion, but also alerting U.S. legislators like New York Governor Mario Cuomo that hydro contracts could become an important election issue (Morrison and Nitsch 9).

Localist Interests in New England

The Cree and Inuit welcomed and clearly benefited from these efforts of their coalition partners. It is easy to understand where the Cree interest in this international collaboration lay, but less so the thousands of New Englanders who committed their voices, time, and effort. As with any coalition, motivations and interests no doubt varied. International environmental organizations and their supporters were already committed to the notion that the natural environment was a common human heritage and that local threats to environmental integrity were of global concern. However, anthropologist Glenn McRae shows in his study of Vermont that popular participation was driven, ironically, by far more localist concerns.

Vermont, like Maine and some other New England states, has a strong ethic of land stewardship. There is broad popular support for legislation that protects rural landscapes from damaging practices in industrial forestry, farming, and commercial developments. Vermonters were able to identify with what they saw as similar efforts on the part of the Cree. Vermonters' attachment to land and commitment to place is also expressed in terms of local self-sufficiency.

They understand this economically, preferring, for example, to buy locally grown, especially organically grown, foods. They also understand it in political terms. Local government has historically claimed and exercised an unusual degree of autonomy in New England. New Englanders like to think of themselves as taking charge of, but also taking responsibility for their own affairs locally (McRae).

In truth, this ideal of self-sufficiency has always been more myth than reality. Issues like the proposal to buy Canadian hydroelectric power simply highlighted their global dependencies in ways that made Vermonters uncomfortable as well as guilty. Promoting energy efficiency was seen by many as both a more ethically responsible as well as a more self-reliant path to follow. They were acting in a global coalition in order to reinforce local self-sufficiency. Their collaboration with the Cree, according to McRae, helped them to reconfirm their own commitments to localism as well as to reassess its limits.

The Cree: Balancing Global Influences and Local Culture

For their part, the Cree were wary of being swept up in the agendas and priorities of their American and environmentalist partners. Collaboration with Greenpeace was viewed with special caution since Greenpeace was well known for its opposition to the kinds of hunting and trapping that the Cree still relied upon (Craik). The Grand Council had its own resources and was careful to mandate its program of action with its own people. They used a referendum to demonstrate that the James Bay Cree were nearly unanimous in favour of halting the Great Whale project (Craik). The people were happy to volunteer when called upon, but the day-to-day running of the campaign was carried out by a small cadre in the Grand Council. They used council funds to hire experts, including the public relations firm Hill & Knowlton, which coached Cree spokespeople in techniques for addressing the media (Morrison and Nitsch 8). However, despite maintaining control of their political engagement, the Cree could hardly escape being shaped and changed by it.

The very idea of a central body like the Grand Council that could speak for all Crees in the region was a relatively recent and somewhat alien convention to the Cree. Local communities had been relatively autonomous and required little in the way of formal leadership structures. It was only in response to the first wave of hydroelectric development that they formed what they called the Winnebegoweeyouch Notchimeeweeyouch Enadimadoch (Coastal and Inland Cree Working for One Another's Interests) or Grand Council.

While they did not endorse discourses of animal rights or "wilderness protection" they did learn to speak the language of Western environmentalism. For example, in their presentations they stressed the value of energy conservation (not an indigenous Cree concept) as an alternative to hydroelectric development. More importantly, they were learning the language and practice of the law through their ongoing battles in the courts, as well as bureaucratic practice and media savvy. Notably, it was the universal language of rights—rights to self-determination and rights to land—that they would incorporate most thoroughly into their cultural repertoire.

Parallel with its international campaign the Grand Council was pursuing legal challenges, slowly enough to allow public pressure to build in their favour. In 1991 they won the right to have a joint federal-provincial environmental assessment on the Great Whale proposal. The U.S. campaign was also instrumental in getting key contracts cancelled, although spokespeople for the New York City decision insisted that they were withdrawing for purely financial reasons. The Quebec government ultimately was forced to shelve the Great Whale project.

The key to the Cree's successful political strategy was moving the struggle to a terrain on which the Quebec state had no pre-determined advantage. In the U.S., Quebec had no sovereignty, no legislative authority, and no greater capacity than its opponents to set the terms of debate. Hydro-Québec attempted to shape public debate with a Burson-Marsteller-sponsored front group, Coalition for Clean and Renewable Energy. However, they were completely outclassed in their capacity to mobilize popular support by the Grand Council and its environmental NGO allies.

INDIGENOUS POLITICS ON THE GLOBAL STAGE

The James Bay Cree were able to gain political advantage by appealing to an international community beyond the borders of the provincial and federal states in a way that implicitly challenged the sovereignty of those states. This was not the first indigenous appeal to an international community. In 1923 Levi General Deskaheh travelled to Geneva on behalf of the Iroquois Six Nations to ask the League of Nations to intervene on their behalf in a dispute with the Canadian government.

Many countries' representatives were willing to give them a hearing, but Canada, with the support of Britain, which still wielded the power of empire, refused to give any credibility to the Iroquois claim to the status of self-governing nations. The Iroquois insisted not only that they were nations that had entered into treaties with the British and Canadian governments on an equal footing, but that their own "state of the Six Nations, that is to say, the Mohawk, the Oneida, the Onondaga, the Cayuga, the Seneca and the Tuscarora," was a league of nations that predated the one meeting in Geneva (Niezen, "Recognizing Indigenism," 125).

Deskaheh came away disappointed. As one sympathetic observer noted, "The representative of the world's first League of Peace received no welcome from the world's newest" (qtd. in Niezen, "Recognizing Indigenism," 125). However, the project that he initiated of using the League of Nations and its successor, the United Nations, as a platform for the indigenous struggle for "nation" status was revived in the 1970s and now has the backing of an international coalition of indigenous representatives. The insistence of many Canadian indigenous peoples on the title "First Nations" signals their commitment to this project. In this part of the chapter we will explore how indigenous peoples have been able to "go global" and construct an international UN-based coalition. We are also going to look at how indigenous activists have helped to transform and complicate what it means to be a "nation" or to have sovereignty over a territory.

Red Power:
Against Liberal Civil Rights

The young Cree men photographed in 1970 in counterculture dress, one of them holding a rifle, invoke the cultural signifiers of a political awakening and resistance that was known as "Red Power." Red Power, like so many movements of the 1960s and 1970s, was inspired by the example of Black resistance in the United States. Indian activists, however, felt greater affinity for the Black Power contingent (including the Black Panthers), which was critical of the civil rights movement for being too "liberal." Civil rights—the right to vote, to own property, to equality before the law, and so on—are all individual rights. Indians in Canada still enjoyed rights—notably rights to land and to harvest certain resources—obtained through treaties with the Crown. These are collective rights claimed by people not on the basis of their individuality but their inclusion within a larger collective identity. Liberal theory is hostile to notions of collective rights.

The Canadian state has tended to share this hostility. One of Canada's aims in extending civil rights to Native peoples has been to displace collective rights. For example, before 1960 full enfranchisement (i.e., the right to vote) often meant giving up some part of one's treaty rights. The more subtle reality, which Canadian Indian people knew from bitter experience, was that in order to fully act on these rights, to avoid discrimination and exclusion based on race, one had to be culturally enfranchised—that is, to give up one's Indian-ness.

As you no doubt are aware, the Canadian state systematically and coercively promoted this cultural enfranchisement or "assimilation." Stories that emerged in the 1990s of physical and sexual abuse of Native children in residential schools have brought attention not only to the suffering of the abused but also to the pain and confusion of the whole generation of children who were re-educated in non-Native culture. While many acquired skills valuable in non-Native society, they lost their Aboriginal language and connectedness to their own people and traditions, which they later recognized as crucial to finding one's place in the world and giving meaning to one's life.

BOX 10.1:

IDENTITY AND VIRTUAL CULTURE

In a New Delhi slum there is an Internet portal set up and paid for by a computer services company in 2000 as a social experiment. They wanted to see how illiterate slum residents with little or no formal education would respond to the new technology. They discovered that young people between the ages of six and 12 became hooked almost instantly and were incredibly innovative in the ways they used the machine and developed skills to do so.

They also witnessed a fascinating interplay between the global culture available on the World Wide Web and the local culture of the children's own experience. PC and Internet conventions are defined by a foreign, mostly English-language, U.S.-based culture. Much of the content of the World Wide Web is also of North American and European origin. One of the children's favourite sites was www.Disney.com. However, they did not just soak up cartoons as they might have with a TV.

Instead they played an interactive game featuring Mickey Mouse. To this they provided their own names and narrative in Hindi. They knew Mickey, affectionately, as "the rat." They loved the two-way, interactive resources of the machine, such as Microsoft Paint, which allowed them to be creative.

Once they worked out how to download and play MP3s, it was not international pop, but local Hindi music that they played incessantly. They could not read English. While many computer icons are meant to be cross-cultural, they have no referents in Hindu culture.

The hourglass, meant to indicate that the computer is busy for a few moments, was never a Hindu artifact. The children see it as Shiva's drum. "The god Shiva has a drum that he shakes—the drum is called damru in Hindi—and it's shaped like an hourglass. So that's the word they came up with" (Cohen). The cursor arrow they call the "needle" or "sui." "... when the computer is busy," explains one of the engineers who observed the project, "the sui turns into the damru" (Cohen).

What is happening here is that the children are using the computer and the Internet not simply to absorb global culture, but to make their own culture. While what they come up with is a hybrid between local and global culture, their preference and emphasis is on the local.

Other Internet users have much more systematically employed the technology to represent and promote local cultures, including indigenous cultures. Organizations representing the Sami (of northern Scandinavia; www.sapmi.net) the Maori (of New Zealand; www.maori.org. nz/papa_panui/), the Innu of Labrador (www.innu.ca), the James Bay Cree (www.creeculture. ca/e/institute/index.html), and many other indigenous groups have created their own Web portals.

These provide content—stories, histories, genealogical research, music, and dialogue—that are a globally available resource for anyone wanting to strengthen their connections with their indigenous traditions. These sites provide virtual cultural memory independent of place.

Much of this content is provided in indigenous languages. Many sites offer language learning for tongues that are threatened with extinction. The Cree have developed ways to modify computers to accommodate Cree syllabics. This is a form of writing developed by early missionaries that more faithfully represents the sound and structure of the Cree language. You can download software that reprograms your keyboard, as well as stickers that relabel your keys so that you can work on the computer in Cree. Like the Hindu children, they are refiguring the syntax of the new technology in their own cultural terms.

These are all creative uses of a "global" technology to reassert local cultures and identities. Some use the term "localization" to describe this sort of resistance to the global march of cultural homogeneity. The threat of globalization arouses it, and the technologies of globalization empower it. What do you think; does globalization invoke localization as an equal and opposing cultural force?

Source: David Cohen, "slums.surfing.com," *Guardian Unlimited* (October 17, 2000). <http://www.guardian. co.uk/Archive/Article/0,4273,4077471,00.html>.

Cultural hybridity, having a foot in the Native and non-Native traditions, no doubt helped 1970s Red Power activists to acquire and critique the language of civil rights. It also helped them deploy the tactics of social movements against policies of the state. The Canadian government proposed a new approach to Indian affairs in its 1969 White Paper, which advocated eliminating treaty rights. The idea was to promote equal rights alongside the respect for diversity. Cultural identity would be a private thing, tolerated and even promoted by the state, so long as it was not attached to any legal or political rights that were not shared by all Canadians.

Aboriginal leaders and activists were convinced that without treaty rights, Aboriginal culture could not genuinely be protected, and that the proposal was little more than covert assimilation or, as they put it, "cultural genocide." In response to this threat, they organized and networked within Canada and beyond its borders. This new organizational base was the initial platform that was to enable indigenous peoples eventually to step on to the global stage. Through contacts with other indigenous organizations, they became aware of common issues of cultural survival, state repression, and an emerging insistence on collective rights.

The UN Platform

Networking is powerful for sharing ideas about issues and strategies, but as we have seen in previous chapters, networking across borders is costly and logistically difficult, especially for people with limited resources, as indigenous peoples tend to be. There has to be a compelling reason, such as the need that contemporary workers see for a global reach of organized labour to mirror the global reach of capital. Aboriginal

organizers perceived not so much a global threat as an opportunity in the UN.

They discovered that discussion had already been taking place without them on "the Indian problem," and that the UN, more so than the League of Nations that Deskaheh had visited, was developing an interest in and language for the protection of minority rights. The promise of discourse at UN forums is that once consensus forms, its principles can become universal norms, and ultimately can be written into international law. The UN provides the framework for the making of agreements or treaties between nations that have the force of law.

UN Principles: Minority Rights/Self-Determination

Shortly after the Second World War, UN member states had ratified two treaties relevant to minority rights: the Convention on the Prevention and Punishment of the Crime of Genocide, and the Universal Declaration of Human Rights. Fresh on their minds was the Nazi program of genocide against the Jews. This was not the only, but certainly the clearest reminder that even highly "civilized" nations could not always be relied upon to protect their own people. It also established the principle that the internal affairs of one nation could be the common affair of all.

The international community could be called upon to speak for and protect a people against the state that supposedly represented it. This was an attractive principle to indigenous peoples, many of whom felt that their own governments threatened their survival and some of whom had been subject to outright campaigns of genocide. Indigenous peoples also saw potential in another UN concept, that of "self-determination"—the idea that a distinct "people" could claim the right to represent and govern themselves.

Existing NGOs with international experience and capacity, like the World Council of Churches, helped the new indigenous NGOs prepare for entry into the UN system. The UN accredits NGOs to speak on behalf of various popular constituencies such as labour, women, and so on. Since there were at the time no international indigenous bodies, the Canadian National Indian Brotherhood sought and achieved accreditation first in 1972. Uncomfortable with speaking for indigenous peoples worldwide, it collaborated with others through a series of international meetings with the aim of forming a common body.

The Port Alberni (B.C.) meeting of 1975 featured a mix of Western and indigenous languages and styles of dress from the equator to the Arctic Circle. Despite a diversity that was "hard to absorb," delegates succeeded amidst "great euphoria" in writing a common statement of interest and establishing the World Council of Indigenous Peoples to act as their UN representative.

UN Reliance on Civil Society

The main focus of the UN is getting states together to write and enact treaties—the making of international law. This is the exclusive realm of states. However, a huge amount of investigation, discussion, and consultation takes place often years or decades in advance of treaty signing. Once treaties are signed, they rely upon accountability—ongoing monitoring and reporting of compliance—as their only means of enforcement.

So, for these ongoing functions the UN provides a physical platform: budgets, offices and meeting rooms, permanent staff who provide logistical support, translation, documentation, and record keeping. These are situated in cities—mainly Geneva and New York—that are capable of hosting tens of thousands of international delegates. They are the complex and expensive tools of global political action.

They are made available not only to states and governmental bodies, but to non-governmental organizations as well. NGOs have been given permanent space on the platform because they serve a purpose both in the preparation for treaty signing as well as the monitoring of compliance once treaties have been signed.

States are less likely to flout their obligations to environmental or human rights treaties if they know that environmental or human rights NGOs within their country have visibility and a voice in UN forums. Thousands of NGOs and their members worldwide act as the UN's eyes and ears on the ground, providing a channel of information at little cost to the UN system. The effectiveness of treaties has to do both with what states do or fail to do as well as with what people within those states do or fail to do. The UN has implicitly adopted the view that states can govern best if they include their own people in the process of governing.

People are more likely to comply with a law that they feel they have had some input in creating. States (and by extension intergovernmental bodies like the UN) can strengthen their governmental authority by at least consulting their own people on what legislation is needed and can work. So even though some member states do not have working parliamentary democracies or are hostile to civil society input, the UN invites civil society participation at the international level in the consultations over international law. However, NGOs are never meant to have voting rights or decision-making power, just consultative status.

Enlarging the UN Platform

Initially, indigenous peoples were making use of an opportunity that already existed. They rode the UN platform, but they also lobbied for its expansion, often against resistance from the states sponsoring the whole enterprise. The story initially was one of quantitative expansion. They represented indigenous perspectives to the Sub-committee on Racism, Racial Discrimination, Apartheid, and Decolonization active in the late 1970s and succeeded in 1977 in getting a special conference dedicated to their issues, the UN NGO Conference on Discrimination against Indigenous Populations. Many states went to great lengths to intimidate their indigenous delegates: some were denied passports, some were "disappeared," and many had to seek political asylum for fear of reprisals if they returned to their home countries (Niezen, "Recognizing Indigenism," 127).

New Forums

Indigenous activists persuaded UN officials that their concerns merited an ongoing forum. In 1982 a Working Group on Indigenous Populations was set up and began meeting annually. In 2000 that became a Permanent Forum. The UN General Assembly often creates temporal signposts to mark the importance of an issue. Indigenous peoples got a decade, a year, and a special day dedicated to the indigenous cause. These provide ritual reminders for UN personnel to note and assess progress on an issue.

The Working Group made meeting rooms, offices, and staff available to indigenous delegates on a semi-permanent basis. Its legitimacy and global import also made it a media platform. Delegates offering testimony on human rights abuses got press

attention that their own governments could no longer suppress or ignore. The Working Group also became a social nexus through which indigenous peoples from around the world met, socialized, and developed a common language and set of understandings (Feldman, "Making Space," 37–38). While it was not made up exclusively of indigenous delegates, one of the group's main tasks became the drafting of a Universal Declaration of the Rights of Indigenous Peoples, which indigenous representatives came to see as an authentic expression of their common voice.

New Principles:
The Universal Declaration of the Rights of Indigenous Peoples

Once the Universal Declaration had been drafted, which was no small feat for such a culturally and politically diverse group, the next task was to advance it slowly through the UN system toward eventual ratification. The first step, in 1994, was to transfer the document to a body made up of state representatives, the Inter-sessional Working Group. This was a UN forum at which NGOs could observe, but not take part in decision making. In other words, indigenous NGOs could not make motions or vote. At this point indigenous activists intervened to challenge state privilege.

They knew that many states were hostile to the idea of Aboriginal rights and would likely try to gut many of the declaration's provisions, notably those referring to land rights, self-determination, and self-government. They insisted that the Inter-sessional Working Group "immediately adopt the Declaration as a minimum standard and then hold general debates about the legal and political implications underpinning it" (Feldman, "Making Space," 40). The chair ignored them on the grounds that as NGO representatives they had no right to make motions and that the mandate of the Working Group was not to adopt, but to "elaborate" the draft.

The consensus among indigenous groups at the UN was that they represented more than just minorities or interest groups within nations, but rather nations in their own right. They believed that they deserved a different kind of representation on "state" bodies like the Inter-sessional Working Group than that enjoyed by other accredited NGOs. They staged a walkout in protest. The chair was forced to suspend the meetings because many state representatives argued that an indigenous boycott compromised the Working Group's legitimacy.

Winning Quasi-State Privileges

This was a tacit recognition that state authority to govern in this area could not be exercised without indigenous support. When the Working Group reconvened, the chair had accepted that specially accredited indigenous delegates could have standing in debates and that no amendments would be approved without consensus among both state and indigenous representatives. The victory represented a major revision of UN procedure (Muehlebach 248).

The following year indigenous delegates continued to dramatize the issue of inclusion. Deskaheh's 1923 visit is recognized annually by Geneva's mayoral office. Commemoration of this exclusion was coordinated with a celebration of 20 years of continuous UN involvement. Indigenous delegates donned traditional dress and took their seats in a ritual affirmation of their resolve to take their place at, as Feldman puts it, "the nations' table."

The indigenous project has been to expand their place at this table and transform the nature of their participation—in Feldman's words,

to "refigure the architecture of state power and governmentality" (Feldman, "Making Space," 40). Parallel to these efforts to occupy and modify the global platform provided by the UN, indigenous peoples have also sought to transform the conceptual framework that the UN had developed concerning universal rights and self-determination. That is what we will consider in the following section.

SOVEREIGNTY AND INDIGENOUS SELF-DETERMINATION

"Nations" are inventions of the 19th century. Remember Adam Smith, who before the century had begun, envisioned the eclipse of village-based enterprise by the "joint labour of a great multitude"—people connected, but not personally known to one another and dispersed over vast distances. He believed that distanciated social relations of this sort would be coordinated by the impersonal market.

Marx was not the only one appalled at this idea. Some form of social governance was still required, many insisted, in order to manage people's collective affairs. These new forms of social governance had also to coordinate across great distances but, in addition, had to command the allegiance of the faceless millions. State bureaucracies, as Weber showed, had the technical capacity to coordinate huge populations at a distance. However, in themselves, they lacked the capacity to command allegiance.

States and the Construction of "Nations"

States promoted the idea that they represented "nations" in order to overcome this problem. "Nation" gave a human face to what was otherwise an abstract, impersonal form of governance. The nation was constructed as an ersatz "community" of people who shared a common history and collective identity. Unlike village communities, where the bond is based on ongoing face-to-face relationships, nations are made up of people who could not possibly meet every one of their compatriots. Their bond is abstract and must be imagined. For this reason Benedict Anderson has called them "imagined communities."

By using the term "imagined community," Anderson does not mean to say that nations are imaginary. Nations are real, since the idea of nation has powerful social and political effects. However, their self-conception has always had elements of, shall we say, myth. Hobsbawm and Ranger have shown that many of the customs, costumes, and traditions that nationalists claim reach into the distant past, are often of very recent, indeed of 19th-century origin.

Nationalists have also claimed that their identities are based in blood ties. However, modern genetics gives very little support for this idea. In the 19th-century nationalist myths of a common genetic heritage were aided by confusion as to how genetic inheritance worked. People erroneously believed that cultural traits could become "bred in the bone."

Claims to nationhood have also been promoted by questionable claims to physical territory. The history of occupations of territory tends to show that people move and intermingle much more than is convenient for nationalist myth making. All of these are efforts to embed an abstraction in tangible markers: blood, land, and history.

Since cultural, linguistic, and genetic sameness is rarely found within the boundaries of states, they have used their power in efforts to create it. They have used national education systems as well as propaganda to create linguistic and cultural homogeneity. This is what Canada was doing with the Indian residential schools. They have also resorted to violence to coerce culturally distinct populations to conform or simply to expel or eradicate them. This is what Nazi Germany was up to with its genocidal program against Jews and Gypsies (Roma). This is what recent examples of "ethnic cleansing" are about.

Where reality contradicts the myth that nation emerges from the soil, the state, or some nationalist militia violently assaults that reality. Such projects, even at the hands of single-minded totalitarian regimes, have been remarkably unsuccessful. No culturally distinct group has survived intact within the borders of a hostile state, but many, like thousands of indigenous peoples, have retained their sense of collective identity as well as a fighting spirit.

After the horrors of the Second World War, UN member states were forced to recognize the limits of this nation-making project. The concepts and principles in the first treaties designed to protect the rights of culturally distinct groups against the incursions of states contained within them a subversive thread. Aboriginal theorists grasped and drew out the implications of these threads for themselves in ways that were to challenge states' (already problematic) self-conception as "nations" and as "sovereign" over their territories.

Conflicting Nation-Building Projects

One such concept was "self-determination." It referred to the collective right of distinct "peoples" under the rule of a foreign state to form their own government. Signatories of the first treaty to use the term—the International Covenants on Civil and Political and on Economic, Social and Cultural Rights—understood it contextually. It applied only to former European colonies like India or Algeria. This was hard enough for the colonial powers to concede. You may remember from Chapter 3 that anti-colonial struggles were often bitterly opposed by states like France and Britain.

Remember also that anti-colonial movements in Algeria and India (led by Gandhi) inspired many 1960s activists. In Canada the Québécois asked, "If Algeria, has a right to self-determination, why not us?" Quebec, they asserted, was also a colony, annexed by a hostile foreign power, albeit in the past. "If the Algerians, and the Québécois," demanded Red Power activists, "why not the Cree or the Mohawk?" They, too, were peoples who had had their territories annexed by hostile foreign states.

Self-Determination and Separatist Struggles

UN member states opposed this extension of the term, fearing that it would lead to the carving up of their territories by secessionist movements. In the world of the UN, language can have powerful consequences and struggles erupt over subtleties in meaning. "Self-determination" and the related word "peoples" became contested. Some states wanted to claim that Aboriginal groups are made up of culturally distinct people, but are not "peoples." Of course you see the difference: the first is a group of individuals who may have rights to the protection of their culture; the second could claim collective rights to establish their own state.

Canada has had to deal with claims to self-determination from two directions: Quebec sovereigntists and indigenous peoples. The differences between the two approaches are instructive and can be seen

as they play out in Quebec between the James Bay Cree and sovereigntist governments. The conflict over hydro development on Cree territories pits two nation-building projects against one another.

The Quebec state has been able to use the power utility, which it owns, as a tool for its nationalist aspirations. First, it has helped to promote Quebec-based and Québécois-controlled capitalist development. As we saw in Chapter 7, nationalist identity develops in reaction to both political domination, and economic, corporate domination Hydro-Québec was going to charge New York four times as much per kilowatt-hour as it charged Quebec-based magnesium and aluminium smelters. Cheap power was being offered as a stimulus to targeted "national" industries (Morrison and Nitsch 4).

Industrial development creates taxable revenue and money for government programs. This was a prerequisite for a second and more subtle dimension of the Quebec nationalist project. Remember that the secular state was in competition with religious and class-based organizations to define Québécois collective identity. The Quebec government was able to do what most states have attempted to do, which is to encourage popular allegiance by providing mutual aid. Through social welfare programs, the "imagined community" of the nation-state behaves like "real" communities are supposed to: in an inclusive and caring way toward all of its members.

In part because of its control of cheap energy, the Quebec state succeeded where others, notably financially starved states in the Muslim world, have failed. It became the primary vehicle for the expression of nationalist aspirations. As you well know, the Parti Québécois has articulated those aspirations in terms of separatist self-determination. It requires an autonomous state with a separate territory over which it exercises full sovereignty in order to realize the distinct cultural aspirations of the Quebec people.

However, the territory claimed by the province is arguable no more culturally homogeneous than the territory claimed by Canada. Remember that the North was annexed to the province without consulting its Cree inhabitants. They have a rather strong basis for making the sorts of claims that nation-states have pretended to: linguistic and cultural integrity, connection to a definable territory "since time immemorial," even strong genetic similarities within a definable population.

Non-secessionist Self-Determination

Like the Québécois, the Cree want legal recognition as a people and as a nation. They want to claim all of the rights that flow from that legal status, including the right to "freely dispose of [their] natural wealth and resources" (Draft Declaration of the Rights of Indigenous Peoples, qtd. in Muehlebach 249). They do not, however, want to secede from Quebec, nor do they want Quebec to secede from Canada (Niezen, "Recognizing Indigenism," 137–138).

The Grand Council of the Crees was one of the earliest indigenous organizations to be accredited with the UN. Cree leaders have been party to the process of defining an international indigenous conception of self-determination that does not involve secession. The process is evolving and contested, yet appears to be moving toward a novel (some will say incoherent) concept of parallel sovereignties that can coexist within the same territory and under the same state.

Sovereignty

Sovereignty, originally the prerogative of sovereigns (i.e., kings), has historically been understood as absolute and exclusive. Only one body can exercise it over a given territory. Sovereignty differs from political autonomy and self-government. These are delegated by the sovereign power and exist only at its pleasure. A sovereign state can, for example, dissolve a self-governing body like a municipality, or set up a new one. To have sovereignty over a territory is more than to have ownership over it.

The sovereign power grants ownership as a bundle of limited rights to land to private or corporate individuals. The state typically withholds a whole series of rights from the property owner: rights to minerals beneath the ground, various rights of way, etc. Private property, like self-government, is a derivative right superseded by the collective rights of sovereignty. Indigenous peoples insist that they want more than self-government or ownership of land and resources; they want the sovereignty that comes from self-determination (Muehlbach 252).

Non-exclusive Sovereignty

As Andrea Muehlebach describes it, the interest of Aboriginal peoples is in the "legal personality" conferred by the designation of a self-determining people. However, rather than exercising that status in absolutist terms the way an 18th-century monarch or 19th-century state would, they see it as a basis for negotiation between equal partners. This is the exercise of nationhood that they see practised at the UN. Absolutist notions of sovereignty are, they argue, being overtaken by history: first by globalization, but also by the very process of international treaty making that states themselves initiated after the Second World War.

In the words of a Mohawk delegate to the Working Group on Indigenous Peoples,

> No-one has a patent over the definition of self-determination. Nobody exercises self-determination in isolation—it's shared, and surrendered, and you make treaties all the time. All governments here at the UN have given up some of their self-determination when they agreed to join the UN. You all agreed to live under the UN charter. We all need to make treaties in order to live side by side. (qtd. in Muehlebach 259)

What is so novel about their approach is the idea that these equal partners might negotiate within a single territory governed by a single state.

Many sociologists see the indigenous project as part of a larger trend toward the "decentreing of the state." States are being pushed toward genuine sharing, not just of power, but also of sovereignty with non-state entities. Some see in this the potential for the democratization of governance. The governing centre is being opened up toward realms where social movements have some greater claim: e.g., indigenous politics and UN politics. While "decentreing" is largely metaphor, it does have real spatial implications. Sovereignty becomes detached from exclusive territory. States face competing sovereignty claims from within as well as beyond their borders. While nation never has corresponded well to fixed territory, the disjuncture now claims formal acknowledgement.

First Nations share Canadian territory; some of them, like the Iroquois Six Nations, cross international borders. But also, increasingly, they disperse and inter-mingle with non-Native populations. Like so many people in the history of capitalist development, Aboriginal peoples are being uprooted from traditional places. They are migrating from the reserves and hunting grounds to which they have a collective claim to cities where they are dispersed as individuals.

Still, despite pulling on that subversive thread that has unravelled so many of the myths of nationhood, it is not at all clear that indigenous leaders are prepared to face the idea of their collective identity no longer being tied to place, to coherent, bounded territories. This question of the relationship between identity and place is what we turn to in the next section.

Paradoxes of Indigenism

Throughout its 200-year history, industrial capitalist development has threatened the identities of culturally distinct peoples. It has made old employments obsolete and new ones irresistible, driving people off their ancestral lands to cities and to other countries in search of the means of subsistence. Recall how in the 19th-century workers from across the Atlantic migrated to industrial centres like Lynn and Fall River, Massachusetts.

While initially they attempted to preserve their cultural distinctiveness, they were swept up in two competing projects. One, sponsored by the state, to enable it to govern such mobile, diverse, and far-flung populations, was the national one of creating Americans, who spoke English, learned to revere the United States' revolutionary heroes and to emulate the values of self-reliance and republicanism that they represented. The other, sponsored by the unions, to create solidarity against capitalist exploitation, was the making of a working-class identity.

Modernization

The construction of states, the building of nationhood, and even the formation of class opposition are social responses to the development of capitalism that exhibit a monolithic sameness or homogeneity. Together they form a complex that sociologists refer to as "modernity," the making of which is called "modernization." Capitalist production and exchange drives it, and capitalist commodity culture is another of its signal features.

Think global production for mass markets of Coke, McDonald's, Mickey Mouse, and the Marlboro Man. Modernity is the "huge grey mass" that the Situationists and Provos rebelled against. Islamic radicals, like most in the developing world, recognize that this is "universal" culture that comes from a particular point of origin. To them it is not so much modern as Western, principally American, "cultural imperialism."

The latest round of globalization has accelerated the cultural conquest of modernity and has exposed thousands of indigenous societies on the margins of the world economy to the full force of its destructive-creative dynamic. There are as many as 4,000 indigenous societies worldwide representing thousands languages. They are not alone in worrying about the loss of their languages to the global languages of English (for international business and science) and English, French, and Spanish (for much of international politics). Many of them still preserve, at least in remnant form, unique knowledge systems and alternative economies embedded in local traditions of land use. Each is a numerically small but extraordinarily rich repository of cultural diversity, and all face the threat of extinction in the face of modernization.

The communications infrastructure that has made 21st-century globalization possible has become a tool both to undermine but also, ironically, to reassert local cultures. Consider the questions of migration and assimilation. When my father immigrated to Canada from South Africa in the late 1950s, he travelled by steamship. There was no travelling back at Christmas holidays to visit relatives left behind. There were no opportunities in the new country to hear or speak his native Afrikaans language. Trans-Atlantic calls were prohibitively expensive. People would call on special occasions, for a few precious minutes, long enough to say, "It's so nice to hear your voice again."

Diasporic Identity

In the 1970s, jet travel became affordable, and he was able to return for the first time. In the late 1990s, long-distance telephone rates plummeted, and the people he called no longer needed to feel guilty that "This must be costing you a fortune." He got his first computer with an Internet connection and began reading Afrikaans news online, re-establishing connections with old friends and even making new "cyber-friends" from South Africa.

Within my father's lifetime there has been a shift from a modern to a "postmodern" model of migration that has new implications for cultural identity. The postmodern migrant is much better able to maintain links of community across borders and over great distances. While the same underlying forces of modernization uproot and disperse people, they are able to maintain their identities relatively independently of location.

Their place of origin remains an important marker of that identity, and their sense of connectedness to it is kept alive by frequent return. Nonetheless their collective identity is still significantly "deterritorialized," or disembedded from particular places and political jurisdictions. Cultural theorists use the term "diasporic identity" to describe this sort of common identity of geographically dispersed people.

Indigenous uses of the tools and infrastructure of globalization for the maintenance of collective identity is more complex and intriguing. As we have seen, they have exploited the emerging infrastructure of global governance—that is to say, the UN system. In cases like the boycott of the Great Whale hydro project, they have also been able to use global market relations to support local struggles of cultural survival. Modern transportation and communications technologies have become important tools for establishing and maintaining the international networks that make these sorts of initiatives possible.

Many indigenous groups and organizations now have sophisticated Web sites that they use for networking and information exchange, but also as tools for the revival of indigenous language and cultural memory (see the box "Identity and Virtual Culture"). In these ways the tools of globalization are used for the promotion and revival of threatened local cultures. Social scientists use the term "localization" to describe this process, and many see it as a dialectical opposite that globalization arouses and arms.

Indigenism as Diasporic Identity

Anthropologist Ronald Niezen exposes an additional irony in indigenous uses of globalization. In the process of defending thousands of local indigenous place-based cultures, activists have begun to create a new collective identity that embraces all indigenous peoples and is necessarily diasporic. It began with the construction of a common voice through which they could speak coherently at UN forums. Of course

they had to speak to one another through translation or in the European languages of global political dialogue.

Universal Elements

Key categories through which they framed their common understanding and common program were not derived from their particular cultural traditions but were universalistic and of recent origin. Human rights, nation, sovereignty, self-determination—these are all concepts that postdate the European Enlightenment and would not have had had equivalents in pre-contact Aboriginal languages and political understandings. The very concept of "indigenous" only came to be used to refer to peoples in the early 1980s. It is a category constructed through Aboriginal peoples' participation in the UN, and until that time did not exist with this meaning in English or any other language (Niezen, "Origins of Indigenism," 3).

Neizen sees in the construction of "indigenous peoples" the creation of a "new kind of political entity," not unlike the construction of the idea of "nation" in the 19th century. Just as nationalism is the embrace and promotion of the idea of nation, so "indigenism" is the embrace and promotion of the idea of a common indigenous identity. Indigenism faces the same problem as nationalism, that is, it must make emotionally concrete a set of distanciated connections among millions of dispersed people.

The initial point of connection was a common experience of oppression. UN forums provided a place to expose publicly and to document ongoing cultural genocide, land expropriation, and human rights abuses against indigenous peoples. While this witnessing had an external audience (the international community of nations' representatives), it defined common experiences and cemented common bonds among indigenous delegates themselves. They discovered that their common narratives of oppression also reached back in time to the beginning of European colonization. The "universal" features of that project—racism, genocidal cruelty, and economic plunder—gave a universality to indigenous historical memory.

European, Western projects of colonization and modernization have built universal categories into indigenous experience. This was the experience of post-European contact. Niezen points out that the indigenous memory of pre-contact culture may also have been influenced by these European projects. Modernization has always had its European opponents. The 19th-century Romantics worshipped nature and abhorred machine systems. Anti-indigenous racism has always had its double of European idealization in the figure of the "noble savage."

European Romantic Elements

Marx was a minor contributor to this tradition. He thought that hunting and gathering societies were examples of "primitive communism." He wanted to believe that existing Aboriginal societies were "survivals" of truly egalitarian political and economic systems that predated capitalism and feudalism. The Romantics wanted to believe that Aboriginal peoples were living examples of how humans could live in harmony with nature.

It is difficult now for Aboriginal peoples to sort out what is European myth from what were the actual practices and world views of their pre-contact ancestors. Nationalist campaigns of assimilation have damaged their cultural memory. Ironically, many have to rely on the writings of early missionaries or the work of 19th- and 20th-century European anthropologists to reconstruct their own pre-contact traditions.

Many of their current non-Aboriginal allies—environmentalists, new age spiritualists, back-to-the-landers—are heirs to the European tradition of opposition to modernization. They want to see indigenous peoples through the lens of European romanticism and political idealism. Niezen writes,

> ... there is, in popular imaginings of the inherently ecological Indian or egalitarian hunter, an element of nostalgia, a longing for things that cannot be found in conditions of modernity. Indigenous leaders must struggle against the temptation to take both libels and outrageous flattery as the truth about themselves and their peoples. (Niezen, *Origins of Indigenism*, 11)

The temptation is greater when constructing a universal indigenous identity than when reconstructing the past of a specific Aboriginal group. The European figure of the anti-modern "noble savage" ideal builds in universals to the construct of "indigenous." This allows it to appeal across borders to highly diverse cultures. Playing to the European myths also attracts potent political allies.

Collective Identity

From what Neizen and others have observed, the emerging sense of indigenous identity is not a convenient fiction (Niezen, "Recognizing Indigenism," 120; Feldman, "Transforming Peoples," 149). Nor does it represent a coalition like the Great Whale coalition, where the separate partners are kept at a distance. It is rather more like the collective identities that we have already seen being constructed by social movements like the labour movement or the gay rights movement.

Niezen describes the experience of it from the perspective of an outsider. He has been a long-time observer of indigenous meetings at the UN, but can still feel, as he enters a room, as though he is "a scarcely tolerated visitor in a remote village." Looking around, he sees

> ... a striking variety, seemingly the entire range of human appearance of costume (including tattoos and decorative scarification). Within this variety there is an attachment that all participants share to some form of subsistence economy, to a territory or homeland that predates the arrival of settlers and surveyors, to a spiritual system that predates the arrival of missionaries, and to a language that expresses everything that is important and distinct about their place in the universe. More importantly, they share the destruction or loss of these things. (Niezen, *Origins of Indigenism*, 23)

As a social movement, indigenism is an interesting hybrid. The construction of a diasporic identity is a strategy for collective action (and is as "genuine" as any other example we have considered). Also, as in identity movements like gay rights, indigenism's aim, the construction or reassertion of local identities, is an end in itself.

CONCLUSION

In this last section of the chapter we have seen how indigenous peoples have been able to use the infrastructure of globalization to revive and defend their own local cultures and identities. This infrastructure includes the spaces and resources that make the UN a physical "platform," plus the language of

universal rights, self-determination, and so on forged within UN forums, plus new or lower cost transportation and communications media: jet travel, low-cost long-distance telephoning, the Internet, global news networks, and the like. In the first section of this chapter we saw how the James Bay Cree were able to act on the global stage by exploiting opportunities provided by international flows of commodities. International connections in the market for electrical energy gave them the tools to put pressure on the Quebec government through the threat of a boycott.

In both cases, stepping on to the global stage has enabled indigenous peoples to circumvent their own "national" governments. Exposed to the eyes of the world, it has been less easy for these governments to fall back on their old practices of ignoring, silencing, or violently repressing indigenous dissent. The Cree won their initial fight to put a halt to the Great Whale project. Many nations, including Canada, have been rebuked by UN bodies for their failures to recognize rights or honour commitments to Aboriginal peoples.

One key difference between the cases is the role that coalitions have played. In the Quebec hydro case the Cree entered strategically into common cause with environmentalists and local U.S. community activists, but all parties maintained their distinctiveness and separate paths. However, the collaboration among worldwide indigenous representatives through the UN has led to ongoing solidarity and the emergence of a sense of collective identity.

Indigenism is universalistic, diasporic, and placeless. There is a double irony in indigenism being the spearhead in the fight to promote local, particular identities deeply attached to place. Remember that for the James Bay Cree, their ancestral hunting grounds were the indispensable setting for the enactment of cultural practices and the ground upon which their cultural narratives were inscribed. As Coon Come understands it, the connection between identity and place could not possibly be closer; the Cree in a sense "... are the land." This tension raises questions about the politics of the relation between place and collective identity.

Modernity is characterized by that same dynamism that Marx and Engels attributed to capitalism: "All fixed, fast-frozen relations, with their train of ancient and venerable prejudices and opinions, are swept away, all new-formed ones become antiquated before they can ossify. All that is solid melts into air ..." (Marx and Engels). The current round of globalization is an historical moment of accelerated change. States are caught up in the tide and can no longer cling to the myths of nation fixed in tangibles like ancestry and territory. The transnational power of corporations and, to a lesser extent, transnational treaties have brought into question the notion of exclusive sovereignty over territory. The Aboriginal resurgence has ridden this tide. The concepts that Aboriginal activists have championed, like self-determination without succession and parallel sovereignties, promise further to disembed the fixed realities of the last two centuries.

Some anthropologists expect that Aboriginal reframings of their own collective identities will reflect these changing circumstances. Iris Young has argued that postmodern self-determination, in order to be coherent, must be "detached from territory" (qtd. in Muehlebach 258). Indigenous activists, however, argue that they need a counterweight to the power of states and, given their small numbers, only sovereignty over territory can offer it. Furthermore, the touchstone of their cultural identity is still primarily within hunting and gathering or horticultural complexes that are tied to specific landscapes and land-based practices. It is impossible to preserve culture without preserving these pre-capitalist economic practices. And it is impossible to preserve these economic practices without securing collective rights to the territories in which they take place. Indigenous culture and thereby indigenous identity, they argue, is indissolubly linked to "territorialized practice" embedded in place. The question that lingers for many observers is how far such intensely place-based identities can challenge or survive the ongoing dynamism of modernity.

REFERENCES

Anderson, Benedict R. O'G. *Imagined Communities: Reflections on the Origin and Spread of Nationalism.* London: Verso Editions and NLB, 1983.

Cohen, David. "slums.surfing.com." *Guardian Unlimited*, October 17, 2000. March 31, 2006 www.guardian.co.uk/Archive/Article/0,4273,4077471,00.html.

Coon Come, Matthew. "Survival in the Context of Mega-Resource Development: Experiences of the James Bay Crees and First Nations of Canada." *In the Way of Development: Indigenous Peoples, Life Projects, and Globalization,* edited by Mario Blaser, Harvey A. Feit, and Glenn McRae. Zed/International Development Research Centre, 2004. March 2006, www.idrc.ca/pda/en/ev-58137-201-1-DO_TOPIC.html.

Craik, Brian. "The Importance of Working Together: Exclusions, Conflicts and Participation in James Bay, Quebec." *In the Way of Development: Indigenous Peoples, Life Projects, and Globalization,* edited by Mario Blaser, Harvey A. Feit, and Glenn McRae. Zed/International Development Research Centre, 2004. March 14, 2006, www.idrc.ca/pda/en/ev-58137-201-1-DO_TOPIC.html.

Feit, Harvey. "James Bay Crees' Life Projects and Politics: Histories of Place, Animal Partners and Enduring Relationships." *In the Way of Development: Indigenous Peoples, Life Projects, and Globalization*, edited by Mario Blaser, Harvey A. Feit, and Glenn McRae. Zed/International Development Research Centre, 2004. March 14, 2006, www.idrc.ca/pda/en/ev-58137-201-1-DO_TOPIC.html.

Feldman, Alice. "Transforming Peoples and Subverting States: Developing a Pedagogical Approach to the Study of Indigenous Peoples and Ethnocultural Movements." *Ethnicities* 1, no. 2 (2001): 147–178.

————. "Making Space at the Nations' Table: Mapping the Transformative Geographies of the International Indigenous Peoples' Movements." *Social Movement Studies* 1, no. 1 (2002): 31–46.

Hobsbawm, E.J., and T.O. Ranger. *The Invention of Tradition*. Past and Present Publications. Cambridge; New York: Cambridge University Press, 1983.

Marx, Karl, and Friedrich Engels. *Manifesto of the Communist Party*. 1848. Edited by Rick Kuhn, based on the 1888 translation by Samuel Moore. August 20, 2004, www.anu.edu.au/polsci/marx/classics/manifesto.html.

McRae, Glenn. "Grassroots Transnationalism and Life Projects of Vermonters in the Great Whale Campaign." *In the Way of Development: Indigenous Peoples, Life Projects, and Globalization*, edited by Mario Blaser, Harvey A. Feit, and Glenn McRae. Zed/International Development Research Centre, 2004. March 14, 2006, www.idrc.ca/pda/en/ev-58137-201-1-DO_TOPIC.html.

Morrison, Allen J., and Detlev Nitsch. "Hydro-Quebec and the Great Whale Project." 1993. *Thunderbird: The Garvin School of International Management*. March 15, 2006, www.thunderbird.edu/faculty_research/case_series/cases_1997/hydro_quebec_whale.htm.

Muehlebach, Andrea. "What Self in Self-Determination? Notes from the Frontiers of Transnational Indigenous Activism." *Identities: Global Studies in Culture and Power* 10, no. 2 (2003): 241–268.

Niezen, Ronald. "Recognizing Indigenism: Canadian Unity and the International Movement of Indigenous Peoples." *Comparative Studies in Society and History* 42, no. 1 (2000): 119–148.

————. *The Origins of Indigenism: Human Rights and the Politics of Identity*. Berkeley: University of California Press, 2003.

CRITICAL THINKING QUESTIONS

1. Are indigenous constructions of collective identity more (or less) authentic than those of nation-states?
2. Can you think of other contemporary "identity movements" that use the infrastructure of globalization to maintain or promote a local identity? What are the similarities and differences between their strategies and those of indigenous peoples?

3. When nations or nationalist movements compete for sovereignty over the same territory, like the Québécois and James Bay Cree, how do you think their competing claims should be resolved?

4. We have seen how globalization has led to cultural homogenization. We have also seen how it creates both the stimulus and the tools for localization, or the reassertion of cultural difference. Which trend do you think, on balance, predominates?

5. Can indigenous peoples maintain their unique cultures without self-determination and sovereignty over land?

FURTHER READING

Alfred, Taiaiake. *Peace, Power, Righteousness: An Indigenous Manifesto*. Toronto: Oxford University Press Canada, 1999.
  This book is a political manifesto—a timely and inspiring essay that calls on the indigenous peoples of North America to move beyond their 500-year history of pain, loss, and colonization and make self-determination a reality.

Blaser, Mario, Harvey A. Feit, and Glenn McRae. *In the Way of Development: Indigenous Peoples, Life Projects, and Globalization*. Zed/International Development Research Centre, 2004. March 14, 2006, www.idrc.ca/pda/en/ev-58137-201-1-DO_TOPIC.html.
  This is an excellent collection of online articles placing the James Bay Cree struggles against hydro development within the context of local Cree culture as well as similar struggles worldwide.

Holloway, John, and Eloína Peláez. *Zapatista! Reinventing Revolution in Mexico*. London; Sterling: Pluto Press, 1998.
  If you want to be informed about indigenous internationalism, you must know something about the Zapatistas of Mexico. They led the way in the use of the Net to globalize a local struggle against the effects of the neoliberal revolution. They have developed a very sophisticated politics of representation in answer to a state campaign of physical repression.

Long, David. "Culture, Ideology, and Militancy: The Movement of Native Indians in Canada, 1969–91." *Organizing Dissent: Contemporary Social Movements in Theory and Practice*, edited by William K. Carroll. Toronto: Garamond Press, 1992.
  Like so many contemporary movements, the Indian movement in Canada had its roots in the late 1960s. Here you can find out more about that history. The article is in one of the best collections of essays on social movements and social movement theory in Canada.

Maaka, Roger, and Chris Andersen. *The Indigenous Experience: Global Perspectives*. Toronto: Canadian Scholars' Press, 2006.
  In attempting to present the reader with some of the richness and heterogeneity of indigenous colonial experiences, the articles featured in this provocative new volume

constitute a broad survey of indigenous peoples from around the globe. Examples are drawn from the North American nations of Canada and the United States; the Hispanic nations of Latin America; Australia, New Zealand, Hawaii, and Rapanui from Oceania; from northern Europe and the circumpolar region, Norway; and Nigeria from the continent of Africa.

Niezen, Ronald. *The Origins of Indigenism: Human Rights and the Politics of Identity.* Berkeley: University of California Press, 2003.

You will be familiar with some of Niezen's ideas from having read this chapter. He is on the forefront of theorizing indigenous internationalism and he does so on the basis of Canadian cases.

Passy, Florence. "Supranational Political Opportunities as a Channel of Globalization of Political Conflicts: The Case of the Rights of Indigenous Peoples." *Social Movements in a Globalizing World*, edited by Donatella Della Porta, Hanspeter Kriesi, and Dieter Rucht. Houndsmills, Basingstoke, Hampshire; New York: Macmillan, St. Martin's Press, 1999.

Passy gives a slightly different perspective from Feldman's on the construction of an international platform for indigenous politics. I prefer Feldman's emphasis on the spatial, which is why I have used her work in this chapter, but you should read further afield. You will also find other good articles on the internationalization of social movements in the collection of which this is a part.

RELEVANT WEB SITES

Aanischaaukamikw (Cree Cultural Institute)
www.creeculture.ca/e/institute/index.html

See how the James Bay Cree are using the Net to revitalize their language and culture. The section on Cree syllabics is particularly interesting. (Check out the Maori site for the use of genealogy as a tool of cultural survival: www.maori.org.nz/papa_panui/.)

Canadian Aboriginal News Sources

There are two sites that claim to be Canada's national Aboriginal news source: First Perspective (www.firstperspective.ca/index.php) and *Windspeaker* (www.ammsa.com/windspeaker/). Check them out and decide which you prefer.

The Culture of Diasporas in the Post-colonial Web
www.thecore.nus.edu.sg/post/diasporas/diasporaov.html

This is an excellent place to explore further the concept of diasporic identity. Get a taste for some of the terms in post-colonial theory, and a better understanding of how textual analysis can be used to understand culture and identity.

United Nations High Commissioner for Human Rights
www.unhchr.ch/indigenous/main.html

> The UN provides an important platform for international indigenous politics. At this site you can find out what is currently happening with indigenous politics at this level. There are links to the Working Group on Indigenous Populations, the Permanent Indigenous Peoples' Forum, and the Draft United Nations Declaration on The Rights of Indigenous Peoples.

Z-Net Chiapas Watch
www.zmag.org/chiapas1/index.htm

> The Zapatistas (Ejército Zapatista de Liberación Nacional, EZLN) are leaders in the use of the Web to globalize indigenous struggles. Their official sites (www.ezln.org.mx) are in Spanish, but are beautiful and worth visiting nonetheless. The Z-Net site contains translated Zapatista communiqués and excellent links to sites dedicated to support and analysis of the EZLN struggle in Chiapas, Mexico.

Chapter 11

COALITION POLITICS

INTRODUCTION: THE PROBLEM

"The only way that you can take on global capitalism is with a global movement of people." These are the words of Ron Judd, of the King County Labor Council, trying to make sense of the coming together of organized labour and a diverse array of environmental, indigenous, women's, students', peace, anarchist, and other groups from around the world in the Battle of Seattle. In the final months of 1999, 50,000 people took to the streets in Seattle and helped to derail a WTO meeting aimed at further liberalizing world trade. To many, Seattle announced a new type of social movement politics for the 21st century and a new challenge to neoliberal globalization. Coalitions that cut across political identities and geographic boundaries were one of this event's defining features.

Judd and others, interviewed for the film *This Is What Democracy Looks Like* (www.thisisdemocracy.org), attempt to define what coalition means for the constituencies they represent. Hop Hopkins, of the Brown Collective, an affinity group formed for the demonstration, highlights the respect for difference:

> We've got to have solidarity on these things but solidarity doesn't mean that we don't talk about the issues that separate us. That's the biggest change that I see happening: not for us to buy into the whole "kumbaya—let's sit around the fucking campfire" idea and just march down the road together. That's part of it. But you've got to take it that step further: race, class, gender, sexism, heterosexism—the whole nine yards. If that's not in your analysis, then you're only half stepping; then you're really not working for the revolution.

Jeff Engels, representing the dockworker's union (ILWU/IBU), expresses humility about the role played by organized labour: "Without being liberal and fake about it, figure out how to work with groups that are in struggle and have been in struggle and not like, say 'Come follow us,' but like 'Oh, we're finally awake; gee, we're kinda late, let's get something together here.'" He is careful not to claim that labour was either an instigator or a leader in this convergence. Hopkins insists that it cannot be a convergence of sameness or of the "group hug" of emotional oneness.

How are conceptions of coalitions among social movements changing? How are convergences across groups and across borders accomplished? These are two of the questions that we will be exploring in this chapter. We will do it by tracing the long roots of the convergence that sprang into the light of public attention in Seattle in 1999. It is a story that begins decades before in numerous locales throughout the world, but notably in Canada in the late 1980s, with a left-wing nationalist movement opposed to the first U.S.–Canada free trade deal.

The Challenge to Marxism

As Judd suggests, the convergence that Seattle announced was the closest thing the world had so far seen to a popular front against global capitalism. It raises theoretical questions for the Marxist tradition, which has the most to say about what popular resistance to capitalism should look like. Organized labour is just one player alongside the new social movements that have burst into action since the 1960s. Theorists sympathetic to the Marxist tradition have had to work through their theoretical difficulties with the new social movements and deal with the orthodox Marxist assumption that the working class must define and lead any genuinely anti-capitalist coalition.

Recall from chapters 3 and 5 the objections that Marxists had to theories that placed the 1960s movements and identity politics at the forefront of "progressive" social change. These theories abandoned the dialectical promise of Marxism. The problem, as Judd reminds us, is explaining how the powerless can overcome the might of international capitalism. Its Marxist solution lay in the dialectical irony that the very success of capitalism would incite and empower its opposition.

Exploited and alienated workers would grow in number and would be brought together in factory neighborhoods where workers, through necessity, would build common culture and organization. This proletariat would become a powerful "political subject" united in organization, but also in a common identity. Only it could be entrusted with the anti-capitalist project because only its members faced daily the indignities of alienation and exploitation in capitalist workplaces. There was a built-in "historic necessity" to the formation of this political subject, and a built-in guarantee of the eventual success of its aims.

By contrast, the new political identities of gay, women's, or environmental activists were not grounded in the realities of class or in any reliable way in the logic of capitalist development. They were cultural constructions that cut across class and threatened to divide class unity. The unease for Marxists did not arise from intolerance for diversity (although there was some of this in the old New Left) but from the idea that political identities were contingent.

If a worker could redefine his primary political identity in terms of his sexual orientation, then why not in terms of Wise Use, right-wing libertarianism? The Marxist theory of class interests had ensured that while a worker could, through manipulation or propaganda, be deceived into thinking that her interests lay with the Wise Use movement, the realities of her position within capitalist society—her class location—would militate against the deception.

If the pull of affiliation to political identities defined by one's gender, race, disability, or relationship to nature is stronger for many than their identifications with class, why not accept that? Why not work in coalition with those groups whose aims overlap with, even if they are not identical to, those of the working class? The principle of collective power would be not a unitary subject but unity of purpose among separate and distinct subjects.

The problem for Marxists, and this was the same problem that Marx had with the petty-bourgeois anarchists and co-operators in the First International, is that any movement or coalition not defined and led by the working class may not lead all the way to revolution. Many of the demands of movements like the various individual rights movements might be satisfied within the framework of capitalism. Liberal feminists, for example, might succeed in promoting women's entry into the corporate hierarchy, while leaving the corporate power structures unchallenged in their ongoing exploitation of workers, both women and men.

Marx had witnessed a number of historical examples where coalition partners, as soon as they felt able to achieve their particular goals, had either dumped or turned against their working-class allies. Coalitions of convenience were to be viewed with caution. With respect to the anti-globalization coalition, we need to raise, if not answer, some further questions. Where do the interests of the various players overlap? How likely are they to part ways over the question of anti-capitalism? Does organized labour actually guarantee an anti-capitalist agenda within the coalition?

New Social Movement Theory: The New Middle Classes

Some new social movement theorists tried to rescue historical necessity by arguing that the new movements were still class-based. Many of the 1960s activists were either from the middle classes or, as university students, were training to become members of the new middle classes. These were the teachers, health care professionals, community organizers, environmental scientists, human rights lawyers, and the like who saw employment opportunities expanding, not within capitalist firms, but within the growing welfare state and not-for-profit sectors.

Consider, for example, those engaged in the early environmental movement. Their activism helped force governments to set up the first departments of the environment in the early 1970s. They also formed non-governmental environmental organizations that, particularly in the United States, amassed large budgets and supported full-time staff. Movement activism created platforms for new middle-class employment.

The new middle classes were largely professionalized; that is, they were university educated, generally well paid, and did not endure the same degree of alienation in their work as the working class. Nonetheless, they had a class interest in collaborating with workers, the poor, and marginalized people. For example, it made sense to help organize and give voice to the poor or the homeless to demand better public services from the city government. The quality of city life would improve for all, but new middle classes would also benefit as providers of expanded services.

It is not surprising, therefore, that members of the new middle classes were behind much of the urban coalition politics of the 1970s. When, for example, they fought for public daycare, they brought together social welfare and women's rights advocates. When they fought for subsidized public transit, they brought together issues of access for the poor, environmental quality (through reduced traffic emissions), and quality of urban life (through reduced traffic) that cut across class lines.

In all of these actions they were addressing the unwelcome effects of unregulated capitalist development. Their independence from direct private sector employment allowed them to stand against the advance of the principles of free market capitalism into many areas of social life. This is not to say that they were necessarily anti-capitalist. They depended upon the welfare state. Welfare state projects of social inclusion were meant to ease the social tensions caused by capitalist development in ways that were consistent with the maintenance of a capitalist economy. Still, when these projects came under threat from neoliberal programs of government cutbacks, privatization, and deregulation, members of the new middle classes, as well as their public sector unions, became important both as players and coalition builders in the opposition.

The point is that some new social movement theorists attempted to integrate class analysis into their understanding of so-called new movements. In so doing they provided an element of historic necessity to the emergence of opposition if not to capitalism per se, then to the neoliberal extension of capitalist principles to all facets of social life. They also presented the new middle classes as candidates for coalition leaders potentially able to represent their own interests as well as the interests of others.

HEGEMONY AND THE INDUSTRIAL WORKING CLASS

During the same time that the potential of the new middle classes to represent the interests of others was getting theoretical attention, the capacity of the "old" working classes was coming into question. It appeared that many workers and their organizations had begun to accept the capitalist system, buying into consumerism and supporting the growth interests of the firms that they worked for. Many theorists saw this as an example of a subordinate group granting consent to a system that continued to dominate them. They used various concepts to understand it: legitimation, ideology, co-optation, and hegemony.

Hegemony, Dominant Ideology, and Co-optation

In this textbook I have tended to use the concept of co-optation. In chapters 1 and 2 we considered state and corporate projects to repress or co-opt radical unionism. For example, in the early 20th century some governments promoted the co-operative movement as an alternative channel for realizing working-class aspirations, a channel that was meant to reshape their outlook and "make workers into capitalists." Some theorists include this sort of institutional co-optation along with propaganda, corporate-controlled media, state-run education—all under the rubric of "ideology." Together these constitute an "apparatus" that generates a "dominant ideology."

Hegemony

Others prefer the term "hegemony." It was developed by an Italian Marxist, Antonio Gramsci, meditating in prison (where he had been put by the fascists) on how radical working-class movements often get outmanoeuvred both politically, but also, importantly, culturally by other powerful players in society. Hegemony means, in part, leadership. The Church, a pro-capitalist movement, or a right-wing nationalist movement may gain leadership of popular forces within a society. In a cultural "war of position" they can hijack popular support away from radical working-class movements.

In Canada, the Catholic Church's involvement in promoting co-ops in order to frame their objective in terms of Catholic social teachings is a good example of a hegemonic strategy. The Wise Use movement's efforts to hijack working-class environmental concern toward a pro-business, anti-environmentalist agenda is another. It is not only the state, corporations, or the media that play a role in hegemony, although these all can play a part and may work in concert with other actors in civil society.

What many find attractive about Gramsci's way of conceptualizing hegemony is that the outcome of the war of position is not decided in advance. This is in contrast to many treatments of the "dominant ideology" thesis (Abercrombie, Hill, and Turner). Many of you may be familiar with the work of Noam Chomsky, for whom the power of corporate media is so great that it can seem to his readers that there is no way to challenge it (see Herman and Chomsky). Many Marxists have treated ideology in this way so that its total dominance seems like a foregone conclusion.

For Gramsci, the radical workers sometimes lose, but sometimes win in the hegemonic struggle. Consider the co-op movement in Canada. Western farmers were able to hijack it away from a pro-capitalist framing of its meaning and intent. Consider also the Wise Use movement, which in the end failed to become a credible leader for many Canadian forestry workers.

Co-optation of Working-Class Radicalism

There is also a subtle difference of emphasis between ideology on the one hand and hegemony and co-optation on the other. Co-optation works not so much by changing people's minds through direct persuasion, but rather by changing the logic of their situation in such a way as to give them real interests in making choices and engaging in practices that support the status quo.

Collective Bargaining

This may be the main sort of strategy that helped turn organized labour in industrialized countries away from their former radicalism. It hinges on the way in which the state and corporations insisted on framing collective bargaining. Unions had been fighting on the political front for a century for the basic right to have employers recognize them and bargain in good faith. It was only after the Second World War that a compromise was struck in law and in common understandings.

The state required employers to go to the bargaining table so long as they were facing, not the working class, but some duly constituted collective bargaining unit elected from among their employees. The legal game of collective bargaining favoured negotiations over a narrow range of workplace-related issues. "Capitalism" was never on the table. Nor were issues of worker control or workplace alienation. When Parisian workers took to the streets with Marxist and Situationist students in 1968, this was the last gasp of aspirations for these sorts

of freedoms. Employers were absolute in their refusal to give in to worker demands for control or the kind of autonomy in work that the Lynn shoe workers had fought for.

Workers learned to compensate for workplace alienation with demands for better wages and conditions. Aspirations for freedom had to be redirected toward the suburbs and the commodity spectacle. Protest became commodified in ways that were entirely compatible with capitalist profit making. Within this new logic of the situation it was in the workers' interests to treat the union like a bureaucracy whose purpose was to obtain material benefits for its members.

Community: From Neighbourhood to Bargaining Unit

The new arrangement also shaped the nature of working-class community. The bargaining unit, not the working-class neighbourhood, increasingly defined the working-class "brotherhoods" of solidarity. The Lynn workers had been able to resist the temptation to exclude from their unions the unskilled workers who were still part of their community.

By contrast, unions disconnected from broader communities and focused on material gains often used skill as a means to exclude less powerful workers from union benefits. Women, immigrants, and people of colour were often seen as competitors for hard-won union gains. Narrow collective bargaining, but also suburbanization, which broke up old working-class neighbourhoods, helped to redefine working-class interests.

Workers' new logic of the situation did not favour general solidarity or the "brotherhood of man" and the lofty goals of freedom from alienation and equality for all. Action was channelled in such a way that its beneficiaries were not "mankind" or even the working class, but the members of a narrowly defined bargaining unit. The achievable benefits were not simply material, but material rewards that depended for their realization on the health and profitability of specific private firms.

The pro-industry stance of forestry workers antagonistic to wilderness preservation, or construction unions that want to see a huge hydro project go ahead, is in their interests when their interests are defined in this narrow way. There is no need for corporate media to convince workers to support capital; it is already "rational" for them given the new logic of their situation.

Radical, socially conscious workers and union activists persisted throughout the postwar period, but they were losing the hegemonic war of position. It became difficult for them during the 1960s to argue that their union brothers and sisters could take a leadership role in the political activism of the period. Most did not display the capacity to look out for the interests of others like the poor, people of colour, women, gays, or Aboriginal peoples threatened by development projects, or workers in other countries suffering human rights abuses or dying in imperialist wars.

Labour's Bureaucratic Organizational Style

Established unions and union federations also had problems with the style of the 1960s movements. The "transitory team" model seemed to them to be undemocratic. Union bureaucracies based their own claims to represent on the same model used by states. In other words, leaders were voted into office by the whole membership. Leaders spoke and acted for the membership. When the membership did act when called upon to strike or demonstrate in the streets, it was a

corporate decision made by the leaders or by majority vote.

When unions act politically, as they did in Seattle, they often do so through a number of levels of representation. Judd's King County Labor Council is a county-wide federation of different unions that included Engels' International Longshore and Warehouse Union. Both are affiliated with the American Federation of Labor and Congress of Industrial Organizations (AFL-CIO), which is a national federation that is the main voice for unions when lobbying the federal government on public policy. The Canadian equivalent is the Canadian Labour Congress (CLC).

As credible representatives of millions of voters, the union federations were, at least for a time, somewhat influential voices in government. In the 1960s they certainly had more behind-the-scenes influence on parliamentarians than the radicals in the streets. Leaders of the union federations clung to what they saw as their greater legitimacy as democratic expressions of popular will and voices in government. They saw themselves as privileged spokespeople, not so much as Marxists would have wanted because they were anti-capitalist, but because they were part of the establishment. Of course from a Marxist perspective, this was an illusion of influence and yet another dimension of working-class co-optation.

From Co-optation to Confrontation

The political weight of the union federations depended upon representing large numbers. Numbers were recruited and maintained on the basis of shop floor-based collective bargaining units. Beginning in the late 1970s the narrowly defined bargaining unit proved to be an easy target for a new campaign of union busting and union bashing. Globalization was shifting the political terrain so that corporations and governments no longer needed to co-opt unions.

We have already seen how the mobility of capital allowed firms to close down union plants and relocate operations in countries where labour rights were poorly protected or in the new export processing zones set up as legal grey zones in which workers were easily exploited. The increasing dynamism of capitalist production and consequent demands for labour flexibility meant that unions found it harder to organize the new temporary, part-time workers. Governments, led by Margaret Thatcher in Britain and Ronald Reagan in the United States, undid many of the legal protections for unions and unionization drives. It became easier for firms to hire strikebreakers and for governments to legislate strikers back to work.

These were all examples of union busting, the purpose of which was to eliminate unions. There was also a parallel ideological campaign of union bashing designed to discredit them. Listen the next time you hear reporting of a strike. Is it represented as a "labour dispute"? Even if the conflict was precipitated by, say, a management demand for a cut in wages, you are not likely to hear it called a "management dispute."

Union workers tend to be represented as selfish, making demands for more than their market worth. For Thatcher they were no less than unpatriotic. However, there is some degree of truth to the claim that they have been motivated by self-interest rather than the common good. This is an artifact of the way that collective bargaining became co-opted.

Social and Community Unionism

What is important for us, in this chapter about coalitions, is that the new attack on organized workers has meant that many

have begun to shake themselves loose from the old collective bargaining paradigm. We have seen this already in the example of community unionism from Chapter 1. Recall how the International Ladies' Garment Workers' Union (ILGWU) began organizing South Asian sweatshop workers in Toronto in the early 1990s.

They did not start with the shop floor; this would have been impossible, as the workplaces were in private homes scattered throughout the city. Instead they set up a community centre. They organized a Homeworkers' Association rather than a union local and assisted with a wide range of social and work-related needs and avoided collective bargaining altogether. They built a coalition with non-union organizations—women's and church groups—and adopted NGOs' styles and tactics, including the consumer boycott. In this style of unionism, the sites, partners, and tactics in struggle shift from being workplace-centred to community-centred.

Other unions, such as the Canadian Auto Workers (CAW), have adopted what they call social unionism. Like community unionism this involves broadening the definition of union concerns beyond material benefits for members. A look at the CAW Web site in 2006 (www.caw.ca/index.asp) showed them speaking out on gay rights and the national child-care program. In the mid-1980s CAW leaders were making overtures to environmentalists.

In 1986 CAW leader Bob White argued for a reframing of worker interests:

> First, ... the real issue for us is not to choose between economic growth and the environment. We must organize society to achieve both because we must have both. The environment sustains and enriches us. Economic growth and technol-

ogy are tools for helping us to develop as individuals and as a society. Second, ... rejecting the false choice between economic progress and the environment requires putting these issues into a broader social context. It means recognizing that we don't have to take the world as given but can change it, that we don't have to be dominated by the priorities of the marketplace, but can change them and establish our own different priorities. And third, ... if we do want to address such changes in society, we can only do it by articulating our own vision of what the world can be like, building alliances, and mobilizing amongst those who are likely to share our goals. (qtd. in Adkin 256)

For autoworkers, environmental commitment can involve serious challenges. In the 1990s CAW officials were contemplating what it would take to support an environmental transport policy reliant, not on private automobiles, but on public transit. (Adkin 324).

Those promoting community and social unionism are part of a hegemonic war of position. (Some theorists use the term "counter-hegemony" to describe this, reserving the term "hegemony" for the struggles to legitimate capitalist inequalities of power.) The political opportunity for these new forms of unionism has, ironically, been created by capitalist firms and, to a lesser extent, states, which have changed the logic of the situation for organized labour.

Both strategies depend upon labour building alliances with and learning from the sorts of citizens groups that emerged from the so-called new movements of the 1960s. This need to form alliances is a reflection, in part, of weakness: organized labour

needs friends. Jeff Engels speaks for the new readiness of labour to make social partnerships when he says, "We're finally awake ... let's get something together here."

RESISTANCE TO NEOLIBERALISM: CANADIAN NATIONALIST MOMENT

The Neoliberal Revolution

Globalization did not just happen of its own accord in the 1970s; people made it happen. It was a project that could not have succeeded without co-operation among states. They had to collaborate to create an international legal framework that allowed commodities to move freely across borders, and also allowed corporations to operate unhindered within the different legal environments of countries around the globe.

States did not use the UN for the treaty making that this involved. Instead, they set up a number of parallel forums. The G7 was a conference of rich nations in which strategy was laid out. In the 1970s, states negotiated new rules through the General Agreement on Tariffs and Trade (GATT), which in 1994 became housed in a new institution called the World Trade Organization (WTO), which became the target in 1999 of the Battle of Seattle.

A number of parallel, regional treaties were also negotiated. In Europe it was the Common Market, later to become the European Union (EU). In North America, it was first the Canada–U.S. Free Trade Agreement (FTA), signed in 1988, which was expanded to include Mexico in 1994 under the North American Free Trade Agreement (NAFTA). Currently, negotiations are still underway for a Free Trade Area of the Americas (FTAA) to include much of Latin America as well.

"Free trade" was the slogan of Adam Smith and his liberal followers. In the current era it has become the slogan of a new liberalism or neoliberalism, which is a faith more radical even than Adam Smith's that the market is the best principle for all forms of social governance.

It has clearly been a threat to alternatives. The making of global free trade has simultaneously been the undoing of social governance through the welfare state. As corporations became freer to cross borders, they found they could abandon their social contracts not only with labour, but also with the state. They were no longer willing to pay the high taxes required to support welfare state programs. Their new global opportunities meant that they could play states off against one another and have them compete for corporate investment by offering lower taxes or less regulation. Free trade has also been a threat to nationalist projects that were often tied to welfare state politics of inclusion.

Canadian Economic Nationalism

In the 1970s, Canada, like many other nations, was still engaged in nurturing "national" capitalist development. The models here were countries like Japan and Sweden that had been able to use state-supported capitalist development to favour high-tech engineering and manufacturing industries. Canada's proximity to the aggressive U.S. economy was viewed as a threat to this project. So we had programs in place, like the Foreign Investment Review Agency, designed to limit U.S. investment, particularly in strategic areas of the economy like energy or steel production.

In the same way that Quebec used hydro-power as a tool for regional development, so the federal government attempted to use the oil and gas industry. Cheap energy can stimulate other forms of economic development, and Canada's National Energy Program sought to use that principle to help the regions develop equally in order to ensure that the project of national development remained inclusive.

When Conservatives came to office in 1984, they scrapped both of these programs and set up a royal commission (the Macdonald Commission) to consider options for greater economic integration with the U.S. Commissions of inquiry, as we have learned, are state efforts to invoke a public voice on contentious social issues. One of the few citizens' organizations to focus on economic issues of this kind was the Committee for an Independent Canada (CIC), which in the 1970s had raised the alarm about growing U.S. ownership in the Canadian economy.

CIC members, notably publisher Mel Hurtig, mobilized their networks and helped to form the Council of Canadians (www.canadians.org) as a way to guarantee a coherent voice of public opposition, independent of the commission. From the outset, the Council of Canadians framed the issue in terms of national sovereignty. By accepting free trade, they argued, Canadians would be surrendering the sorts of economic levers that we had for a century used to build an independent nation.

Left Nationalism

The CIC had support from Canadian business and political leaders. However, the curious thing about Canadian nationalism in this period was the extent to which the left, at least the anglophone left, also bought into it. Anglophone Canadians have long defined their sense of national identity in opposition to Americans. Our myths of nation include repelling an American invasion in 1812 and building a transcontinental railway to link the country east to west and pre-empt north-south integration with the U.S.

Our conception of what marks us off as different from the U.S. was once framed in terms of British-ness. That would no longer do after the assertion of Quebec national-ism. In the 1970s ethnicity was being dis-placed by multicultural inclusiveness as a mark of Canadian-ness. We were the ethnic mosaic; the U.S. was the melting pot (or so the story went). Parallel to the idea of ethnic inclusiveness, Canadians developed the belief that we were more committed than Americans to social inclusion. This is what attracted the left.

After all, we invented medicare. Our government offered health services for free, while Americans could be turned away from hospitals if they did not have the money to pay. Canadians donated blood; Americans had to be paid. Our social programs, like unemployment insurance, pensions, and maternity leave, were more generous and covered more people. As a consequence, levels of inequality were less extreme here than in the U.S. (Although the truth is, we were much closer to the U.S. on measures of inequality than most European countries.)

We saw ourselves as more caring and committed to a "just society." We were not afraid to use the state to guarantee this commitment. We understood Americans, by contrast, to be much more liberal in Adam Smith's sense of the word: individualists who embraced commodified, contractual relationships and were suspicious of any state intervention in their lives.

Opponents to the first free trade deal argued that these Canadian values and the institutions in which they were expressed would all be threatened by granting equal rights to U.S. corporations in Canada and promoting increased mobility of capital. What is important for us, in this chapter, is not so much the validity of their arguments as the way in which they were able to invoke nationalism as a unifying frame for an anti-free trade coalition.

Anti-free Trade Coalition

The leading actors in the opposition move-ment, alongside the Council of Canadians, were church and women's groups. The church groups' perspective was shaped by their inter-national networks. They had seen the effects of trade liberalization on congregations in the developing world, and had begun to advocate "fair trade" rather than free trade, which, as they saw it, capitalized on the weak, who sold their labour or their agricultural products at desperately low prices. The Canadian Con-ference of Catholic Bishops in 1983 published their *Ethical Reflection on the Economic Crisis*, which helped to stimulate debate about neoliberalism and called for the "building of a social movement for economic justice in Canada" (qtd. in Ayres 39).

Women's organizations, led by the Na-tional Action Committee on the Status of Women (www.nac-cca.ca), had long been fighting for the expansion of state services in child care, health, and education. Their interest was in better services for children and working mothers. They also recognized that the state sector had provided the most employment opportunities for women.

Public sector workers represented by the nurses' and teachers' unions and the Cana-dian Union of Public Employees (www.cupe. ca) were vocal in their defence of the welfare state. As early as 1984 they joined women's and anti-poverty groups in an alliance, the Working Committee for Social Solidar-ity, formed to oppose the new Conservative government's cutbacks in social spending.

Private sector unions, represented by the Canadian Labour Congress (http://ca-nadianlabour.ca), had related concerns, although their interests were shaped in slightly different ways. To them, free trade would mean that union jobs would likely be lost to regions in the United States, such as the South, where unions were scarce, laws protecting them were weaker, and the social safety net for workers was inadequate. A weak social safety net means that workers have little to fall back on and consequently are less willing to risk losing their jobs by engaging in union drives or exercising their union rights.

Both public and private sector unions had an interest in protecting the welfare state. For the public sector the risk was not that their jobs would be exported to other countries, but rather that they would simply be eliminated at a cost to union members, but also to the poor and marginalized groups that many of them served. There was a greater temptation for private sector unionists to see the threat as coming from competition from foreign low-wage workers. This perspective was entirely consistent with a nationalist opposition to free trade, but it was to become more of a liability when Canadians sought international alliances against neoliberalism.

BOX 11.1:

WHOSE LABOUR MILITANCY?

In October 2003 union president Kim Ju-Ik hung himself from a crane at Hanjin Heavy Industries where he worked. This was how he chose to end his 129-day sit-in on the crane tower in protest of repressive anti-union tactics of the company and anti-union laws enacted by the Korean government. The courts had been awarding costs and damages to companies whose workers went out on strike "illegally." Firms were able to use a recent law that allowed them to seize the assets or to garnishee the wages of individual unionists in order to pay court-awarded costs. Kim Ju-Ik had lost his home in this way (Griswold; Cook).

Since the 1980s, independent trade unions had grown in strength and militancy in Korea and had achieved significant improvements in wages and labour standards. Corporate spokespeople began to raise the alarm about international competitiveness. Korea's "traditional strengths in the low value-added, labor-intensive goods such as footwear and electronics" were, according to one economic think tank, being "lost to China and Southeast Asia" (Forcese). Pressure built in the 1990s to tame the labour movement and set up EPZs as "industrial action-free areas" (Cook).

Korean workers' resistance to these challenges is a remarkable story, largely untold in the West. Suicides like Kim Ju-Ik's were common as expressions of absolute commitment to the cause. They have apparently become part of the Korean repertoire of contention. Korean workers have also repeatedly shown their willingness, despite great personal costs and draconian police response to engage in civil disobedience, and defy what they consider to be unjust laws.

Later that year (November 12, 2003), 150,000 workers went out on strike and tens of thousands demonstrated in the streets. From an unsympathetic *Korean Times* article we learn that their issues were the support of union rights, not just for unionists but also for vulnerable casual workers, as well as a broader social agenda encompassing peace and social welfare:

> The KCTU [Korean Confederation of Trade Unions] leadership called for the demonstration in the heart of Seoul to stop employers from provisionally seizing the property of unions in damage suits against their illegally-staged labor strikes and to demand the abolition of what they claimed was discrimination against irregular workers.... They also demanded that the government refuse the U.S.-requested troop dispatch to Iraq and correct the national pension system for better benefits of wage earners.

Astonishingly, for a description of people who frequently commit suicide for their cause, the journalist goes on to assure us, "However, the basic goal of their violent action was to get more for themselves ..." (Editor).

The Korean case raises a number of questions. One has to do with media representations of workers' political action. I am thinking here not just of the *Korean Times* article. It at least covered the story. If you read the Western media, you might never know that the Korean labour movement existed. When 30,000 American trade unionists took to the streets in Seattle in 1999, this was global news. Admittedly this protest involved international coalitions and focused on a global target, the WTO. Still, acres of print were devoted to trying to understand what this meant in terms of renewed labour militancy. The labour dimension of Seattle was arguably less militant, less violent, and on a smaller scale than Seoul. Presumably it was more newsworthy because it involved largely American workers.

This raises a related question about our focus as theorists. There is a tendency among sociologists, even in the era of globalization, to assume that "society" is what happens within the borders of our country or within the countries that "matter" like the United States or those in the European Union. We have theories that explain the declining proportion of industrial workers within "the" economy and the declining radicalism of those workers because of legal and societal changes. Are we really just talking here about the "West"? How much would we have to revise our views on these questions if we took a truly global perspective?

Sources: Terry Cook, "Thousands of Workers in South Korea Strike against Repressive Labour Laws," November 19, 2003, World Socialist Web site. April 21, 2006, www.wsws.org/articles/2003/nov2003/kore-n19.shtml; Editor, "Korea Is a Law-Abiding Country—Firebombers Should Not Be Tolerated," *Korean Times*, November 10, 2003. April 23, 2006, http://times.hankooki.com/lpage/opinion/200311/kt2003111018414711300.htm; Craig Forcese, "Korean Labor Crackdown," *Multinational Monitor*, June 4, 1995. April 21, 2003, http://multinationalmonitor.org/hyper/issues/1995/06/mm0695_04.html; Deirdre Griswold, "Worker Suicides Lead to Massive Street Battles," Workers World, November 20, 2003. April 21, 2006, www.workers.org/ww/2003/skorea1120.php.

One of the most persuasive public education tools for the free trade opponents was a question-and-answer booklet, *What's the Big Deal?*, illustrated by Montreal cartoonist Aislin. The cover picture shows then Prime Minister Brian Mulroney, green and dripping under a shower of acid rain, asking, "And why shouldn't we trust the Americans on Free Trade?" It refers to the fact that American legislators had been slow to require that factories limit sulphur-dioxide emissions, which produce acidic compounds in the atmosphere. The prevailing winds were blowing the result north where it fell as acid rain and killed plant life in lakes, attacked deciduous trees, and threatened that very symbol of Canadian-ness, the sugar maple industry.

Environmentalists argued that American environmental regulation was weaker than Canadian, and that free trade would pressure us to harmonize our regulations with the lower U.S. standards. Open access to U.S. companies would also intensify pressure to overexploit our resources. Canadians, the environmentalists concluded, would lose sovereignty over natural resources and environmental protection.

Many of the letters of support that Mel Hurtig received while the Macdonald Commission hearings were underway spoke of concerns for the survival of Canadian cultural identity.

> As I look around I see a consciousness of Canadian identity that extends not much beyond the Stanley Cup, a declining awareness of our origins and founding principles that distinguish our society from that of the U.S., and the pervasive penetration of American values, via television. The political parties offer no relief from these anxieties. (qtd. in Ayres 34)

The CBC was supposed to ensure a Canadian voice in broadcasting both in radio and TV. The fact that the Conservatives had recently slashed the CBC budget raised doubts about their commitment to cultural sovereignty.

Many Canadians worried that if the free trade deal did not have special protections for Canadian publishers, as well as for television, film, and music producers, we would be more swamped than we already were by made-in-America culture. The reasoning was not that American products were necessarily better or that Canadian consumers preferred them. Rather, the market gave them an unfair advantage. American consumers far outnumbered Canadian. For American producers, U.S. sales were usually enough to cover the cost of production. From that point on it was relatively inexpensive to make additional copies of films, records, or

whatever and sell them in Canadian markets more cheaply than local products.

Organizations representing the cultural sector, the Canadian Conference of the Arts and the Alliance of Canadian Cinema, Television and Radio Artists (ACTRA), also raised their voices against the deal. Organizations representing farmers (the National Farmers Union), pensioners (One Voice, the Canadian Seniors Network), Aboriginal peoples (the Assembly of First Nations), peace activists (the Canadian Peace Pledge Campaign), and academics (Academics against Free Trade) joined the already long list of opponents to the proposed Canada–U.S. free trade deal.

Most of these players had never really worked together before. Women in the National Action Committee on the Status of Women were instrumental in getting many of their representatives together in the same room for the first time. Discussions at their first meeting in 1984 helped them to articulate a common cause.

> What happened in there was that most people started out with a narrow view and started broadening it. It was a very moving experience ... to sit around and have people suddenly look at free trade from a big perspective—how it would shape all aspects of economic and social life—people now had a sense of it being part of a larger project—a long-term project. We recognized that we had been isolated and that there was no need to be—we had a sense of us all being in the same spot and there was a transformation in consciousness in that room that night. (qtd. in Ayres 43)

The outcome of this meeting was the formation of the Coalition against Free Trade. This was followed in 1986 with the formation of the Pro-Canada Network (PCN), probably the first broadly based popular sector coalition in Canadian history.

The government was aware of the potential for popular resistance to its plans. Its strategy to pre-empt this resistance, leaked in a memo in 1985, was to "... rely less on educating the general public than on getting across the message that the trade initiative is a good idea" (Pro-Canada Network). The Pro-Canada Network's counter-strategy was to ensure that the Canadian public did become educated. Their pooled resources were still far fewer than the government's. By 1988 the government had already spent $30 million on pro-free trade advertising.

The Network's advertising spending was a little over $750,000. It relied heavily on the internal communications systems that member organizations had with their constituencies. The Pro-Canada message touched upon most of the themes that we have already raised. However, while they were opposed to granting greater rights to U.S. corporations in Canada, they were careful not to appear anti-trade. *What's the Big Deal?* argued that we should diversify trade partners. With 80 percent of our trade with the U.S., we were more reliant than any other country in the world on one powerful trading partner.

In addition to circulating a blizzard of anti-free trade pamphlets and flyers, the Network and its member organizations staged actions and demonstrations to attract media attention to the cause. When quoted, it could make credible claims to being a representative voice of the people:

> ... our main strength lies in the links we have organizationally with a diversity of grass-roots constituencies that comprise well over 10 million people across Canada. In the coming months we'll be speaking in a voice that our constituents understand— on the shop floor, on the farm, in our

congregations and conventions. In this way we hope that the vast majority of people in this country will come to know the truth about the deal and decide to reject it through a federal election. (qtd. in Ayres 78)

The Role of Organized Labour in the Coalition

However, there were tensions between member organizations within the Network. Representatives of what Ayres calls the "popular sector" were suspicious of the bureaucracy of the Canadian Labour Congress. A few years earlier, organized labour had done to its popular sector allies in British Columbia what Marx had seen done to labour in the 19th century. In 1983 the B.C. Federation of Labour had abandoned its allies in order to cut a deal with the government. The large labour federations still felt that they had a privileged position with governments. As long-standing organizations they also had more material resources than many of their coalition partners and used this to their advantage in vying for leadership of the coalitions they entered into.

At the conference that led to the formation of the Pro-Canada Network, women's and church representatives challenged the labour bureaucracy to rethink its approach to coalition building. "People stood up to the CLC," one of them recalled,

> ... and said that coalition building would have to take a different position, posture, and direction. Popular-sector groups gave a signal that things would not be able to operate along established models in the future—that new models would have to be created for working in coalition politics in the future. (qtd. in Ayres 58)

The labour hierarchy was not alone in feeling threatened by giving up control to a coalition. Many NGOs implicitly compete with one another to represent the public on given issues and to attract moral as well as financial support. The organizations risk their interests by entering into alliances. However, often the individuals who work within those organizations can distance themselves from these considerations of "organizational maintenance."

What happened through the ongoing work of mobilizing resistance to free trade was that personal ties began to develop across organizational boundaries. These ties, based on commitment to the larger issues, often superseded organizational allegiances. A network of activists developed whose members' trust in and support for one another enabled them to keep the organizations that they represented at the table and on track with the coalition.

So, for example, in organized labour, advocates of social unionism within the Canadian Auto Workers or CUPE could develop close ties with the popular sector and at the same time influence the more conservative leaders in the Canadian Labour Congress. This is a typical pattern for coalitions. Very often they are based in formal ties between NGOs, but also rely for their effectiveness on informal networks among activists. The real solidarity and sense of common purpose is focused at this network level.

Successes and Failures

Jeffrey Ayres has written the most complete analysis of popular resistance to the free trade deal. He makes much of the resource-mobilization idea that movements succeed or fail in part because of what they do but also because of the "political opportunity structure" created by their opponents. The talks

between the U.S. and Canada leading up to the deal became bogged down. The tough U.S. negotiating position alarmed some, including those in the business community. More importantly, stalled negotiations gave additional time to the Pro-Canada Network to build opposition and publicize its objections.

The U.S. was holding out for the right to unilaterally impose "trade remedies." It resisted the idea of an FTA binding arbitration panel, which might limit its sovereignty over trade decisions. In other words, it wanted to be able to slap duties on Canadian imports if the U.S., and the U.S. alone, thought that these were unfairly subsidized. (Softwood lumber was a case in point. During the negotiations in 1986 the U.S. imposed a 15 percent duty on Canadian softwood imports. It continues to reserve the right to do this 20 years later despite repeated rulings of a binding arbitration panel that it agreed to and yet selectively ignores.)

The Pro-Canada Network used the extra time effectively, and was able to sway public opinion. When the proposed deal was first announced, polls showed most Canadians in favour of the idea of greater free trade with the U.S. By 1988 support slipped to a low of 26 percent, with 50 percent opposed to the deal (Ayres 100). This was the eve of a federal election widely regarded as the final test for free trade: if the Liberals, running on an anti-free trade platform, defeated the incumbent Tories, free trade would be shelved (at least for a time).

The business community launched a counter-offensive to the Pro-Canada Network. In the previous year the Canadian Manufacturers' Association and the Business Council on National Issues had created and funded the pro-free trade Canadian Alliance for Trade and Job Opportunities (CATJO).

This Alliance did not include any popular sector organizations and relied instead upon corporate networks of influence. Their answer to popular mobilization was the Canadian Manufacturers' Association's call to member firms to lobby their own employees. The Alliance's real strength, though, was monetary. It was able to spend $2.3 million on advertising. It published a cartoon-style booklet to answer the influential *What's the Big Deal?*, and was able to distribute it far more widely.

Elections can be won on short-term mobilization of opinion in place of long-term popular organization. The last-minute blitz was enough to get the Tories re-elected. As one Pro-Canada activist reflected later, "when the business community reacted so vigorously, we just didn't have any counterpunch left after that" (Ayres 106).

The popular alliance failed to stop the free trade deal. However, it had succeeded in building a coalition network, a legacy of political experience, and a broadly popular anti-free trade discursive framework anchored in concepts of national identity, sovereignty, and anti-neoliberalism. This network, led by the Council of Canadians under Maude Barlow, and a newly formed transnational organization, Common Frontiers (www.common-frontiers.ca), was able to advance the fight against free trade in the international arena.

RESISTANCE TO NEOLIBERALISM: TRANSNATIONAL

The public response to free trade in the United States was "a collective yawn" (Aaronson 110). There was little reason to fear for the country's tremendous economic and political power in relation to a minor developed nation like Canada. U.S. unions and popular sector activists did not yet see the U.S.–Canada free trade deal in the way that their Canadian counterparts did as part of a neoliberal revolution that would increasingly be fought out on the international stage.

Canadians were to take the lead among developed nations as that fight took shape over the next decade. People in developing nations suffering under World Bank/IMF-imposed structural adjustment programs were already wide-awake to the human costs of neoliberalism. For them, joining an international common front would mean mainly overcoming problems of resources and logistics.

Prior to Seattle, two key struggles helped to mobilize popular awareness and resistance in the developed world. The first was the failed opposition to NAFTA; the second, a successful campaign against the multilateral agreement on investment (MAI), a sort of international bill of rights for transnational corporations that many feared would further compromise social and environmental regulation.

The work of coalition building is often transformative. Through seeking common ground with others, players' perspectives are broadened and their way of framing issues can change. Canadian activists discovered that their experience fighting the FTA provided valuable lessons that their counterparts in Europe and the U.S. learned from and emulated (Aaronson 111–116). However, some of their language, particularly left nationalist discourse, made little sense to their international partners.

From Left Nationalism to Popular Sovereignty

Nationalism in Germany was associated with the right, and still carried ugly associations from the Nazi era. In Australia, too, it invoked right-wing xenophobia and anti-immigrant discourse. Even in Canada during the free trade debate, the concept had both united and divided. The Québécois read it as anglophone nationalism, something for which they had no sympathy. Even the coalition name, Pro-Canada Network, which made sense as a positive spin on "anti-free trade," invoked for the Québécois Trudeau's "Pro-Canada" slogan in the 1980 referendum debate. For the Quebec left, Pro-Canada meant anti-Quebec sovereignty.

The Americans understood the concept of patriotism, but there was no such thing in their vocabulary as "left nationalism," particularly the Canadian variety that was pro-welfare state. Their left-wing tradition is rooted in a kind of populism that is equally suspicious of big business and big government.

A new common frame had to be constructed, one element of which was the idea of popular democracy. In all of the free trade debates, elites had sought to limit public involvement. The MAI was the worst. State-level negotiations were kept entirely secret. It was only through leaks by sympathetic government officials that civil society organizations learned that talks were taking place at all and later, what the text of the draft agreement was.

Whatever their positions on capitalism or international trade, all civil society organizations could agree that they should have greater involvement at the nations' table. In part, this is the principle that we introduced in the chapter on state terror—that democracy is more than parliamentary representation and must involve independent organizations that can monitor, criticize, and hold the state to account.

There was also something more, perhaps inspired by indigenous peoples' rewriting of the concept of sovereignty at the UN. One of the lead Canadian activists in the MAI struggle helped to reframe the Canadian conception of national sovereignty in terms of "popular sovereignty." Tony Clarke, of Canada's Polaris Institute (www.polarisinstitute.org), explained it this way:

When we talk about "sovereignty," we do not mean "national sovereignty" per se. Instead, we are talking, first and foremost, about the fundamental democratic rights of people.... The Universal Declaration of Human Rights—which calls for the recognition of the fundamental rights of all people to food, clothing and shelter, employment, education, and health care, clean environment, cultural integrity and quality public services, plus fair wages and working conditions—is really a declaration about "popular sovereignty." It is this "popular sovereignty" that is the foundation stone of democracy itself, which is directly threatened by the MAI as a "corporate rule" treaty. (qtd. in Johnston and Laxer 61)

Johnston and Laxer argue that this opposition between, on the one hand, the threat of corporate rule and, on the other, the promise of popular sovereignty became from this period (1998) a "master frame" for anti-globalization coalitions. The state—the welfare state as traditionally conceived by the Canadian left—is here eclipsed as a signifier of a common ideal.

TEAMSTERS AND TURTLES: TOGETHER AT LAST?

The global threads of the coalition leading up to Seattle are too numerous to list. Every country contains a similar array of constituencies to those we outlined for Canada—varying in proportions and organizational strength. In addition to hundreds of national players in hundreds of countries, there was during the 1990s a proliferation of transnational organizations and coalitions numbering in the tens of thousands. Many of these were inclined to see the WTO as yet another institution of corporate rule and its potential power and relatively closed governance structure as a threat to popular sovereignty.

Common interests in opposing neoliberalism crossed borders. So, for instance, the impacts of free trade on public sector workers were similar whether they were from Iran or Finland. However, there were important North–South differences, notably in agriculture. Industrial-scale farmers enjoy generous subsidies in the European Union, the U.S., and, to a lesser extent, in Canada. Free trade for their powerful governments—and they have insisted on this in a number of treaties, including the WTO—means greater freedom to sell heavily subsidized agricultural commodities in Third World markets. Peasants and small farmers, one of the largest constituencies in the developing world, do not have the same interests on this issue as farmers in the North.

North–South Divisions

Globally there are significant barriers of geography and culture that can prevent the formation of coalitions despite underlying common interests. We saw this at play in the efforts of North American environmentalists to form alliances with forestry workers. While workers had the same concerns about pesticide use and overharvesting, they often had a hard time overcoming their resentment of what they felt was environmentalists' class privilege expressed in so many subtle signifiers of speech, dress, and attitude. Similar tensions can emerge between privileged northerners and coalition partners in the South, especially if northerners take the attitude that their role is to "help the less fortunate."

Seattle was understood by many to be the first physical embodiment of a global civil society coalition against the neoliberal revolution. Many of the coalition players had spoken with a common voice against the MAI, but that action had been organized largely in virtual space through e-mails and teleconferencing and had involved face-to-face meetings only within a network of core activists. Seattle brought not just the network leaders, but broad swaths of their popular constituencies on to the streets in a huge three-day demonstration. It was a way of announcing to the world that a coalition crossing many borders had come into being. I want to see what we can learn by "reading" this announcement as a cultural expression of coalition.

Reading Seattle

Much of the culture of political demonstration is visual and auditory. To really understand it, you should see the film *This Is What Democracy Looks Like*, since it is one of the best visual archives of the Seattle demonstration. It is important because it is also an extension of the civil society performance. Like most demonstrations since the beginning of the television age, Seattle was an event on the physical stage—the streets of the city—but also on the virtual media stage. Activists strategize as much around how they will be represented as what they will actually do. What had changed between Abbie Hoffman's time and 1999 was the proliferation of ways for activists to make their own media. *This Is What Democracy Looks Like* draws on footage shot by hundreds of independent video activists wielding hand-held video cameras.

"The banner, 'Teamsters and Turtles together at Last!'—that was so wonderful," says one of the demonstrators. "Of course we belong together: the same people who exploit natural resources exploit human resources. We belong together." The Teamsters, of course, are a major union. The turtles were threatened by a recent WTO ruling saying that the U.S. had no right to ban imports of tuna from countries that failed to follow U.S. environmental regulations. The U.S. required that its tuna fishers use "turtle-exclusion devices" to prevent sea turtles from getting caught in the nets.

In Seattle, environmentalists dress up as turtles or as giant butterflies (threatened by genetically modified plants), dancing and swaying to the rhythmic beat of street music. Teamsters and other blue-collar unionists dress in work clothes, some with hard hats. Their signs and banners are printed in block letters. There is a lot of colour in the labour crowds, but it is typically the "team colours" of different unions rather than the artsy, creative expression of other demonstrators. Unionists march in ranks and chant "Power to the people!"

How together were they with the environmentalists and other popular sector activists? Their opening moves on Tuesday, November 30 took place in different parts of the city. Young activists, spearheaded by the Direct Action Network, the Ruckus Society, Earth First!, and others converged on the WTO conference venues downtown. Peaceful demonstrators occupy strategic intersections. They sit down and some lock themselves to iron grates or whatever urban hardware they can find. Others create a street festival atmosphere.

There is no centralized coordination, but the emergent logic is to physically claim the city centre as a kind of WTO-exclusion zone. These actions are hugely popular. Demonstrators flock to the city centre and create a delicious media spectacle. There are more cameras and electronic communications devices in the hands of demonstrators than in the hands of the official media.

The AFL-CIO sponsored a rally at a stadium half a kilometre north of the action downtown. The International Conference of Free Trade Unions (ICFTU) had invited labour leaders from around the world and many of these addressed the rally calling for international solidarity. "A Ford maquiladora worker," one witness recalled, "got a huge response ... when she shouted 'Long Live the Zapatistas!'" referring to an indigenous group in Mexico that had launched its own Net-based war on neoliberalism (Crosby). When the speeches ended, some 30,000 unionists marched toward downtown following a route pre-approved by city authorities. Union marshals formed cordons to herd the crowd, separating unionists from other groups and keeping them from breaking rank to join the direct action protesters.

Union officials turned the march away before it entered the epicentre of protest where another 20,000 were facing off with police. As one AFL-CIO official explained,

> ... the police cooperated with us; they informed us what was happening and gave us the opportunity to get our people out. And we got our people out, and our signs out and the media was pretty fair in explaining that it was clearly not an AFL-CIO protest. (qtd. in Freidberg and Rowley)

She is mindful here of her organization's positioning in the street as well as in the eye of the media. Many activists saw this as a betrayal. To some it was clear that the police waited until the column of unionists had turned back before intensifying their assault on the protesters:

> Within minutes after the last labor marchers had headed back the way they came, loud cannon-like booming was heard in several locations, followed by clouds of tear gas smoke. (Smith)

What the two contingents of demonstrators were playing out here were differences in organizational style, choice of tactics, and cultures of self-expression. The media angle on the first day's events was to raise public alarm about the direct action protests and implicitly to separate off "good" protesters from "bad." Jeff Engels, of the ILWU, complained, "there was an intentional focus to split the coalition. It wasn't just labor doing it on itself but police pressure, the news, everything wanted to do that" (Friedberg and Rowley).

Rank-and-file unionists were divided. Ron Judd, as the regional AFL-CIO representative, got calls from people telling him "that it was absolutely ridiculous that we were out there." Many unionists, who had seen the violence first-hand, did not buy the media representation of it. One labour leader, clearly shaken with emotion, addressed the young protesters:

> When I saw this morning ... I stayed out there in the rain and I watched. I watched youngsters who were peacefully demonstrating who weren't doing a damn thing to hurt anybody. I watched them jack-booted by helmeted club-holding ... you were treated shabbily. If this were my city I'd apologize to you for that happening in this city. Now I welcome ... this is where you belong: right here with the labor movement!
> (qtd. in Freidberg and Rowley)

Rituals of Action as Expressions of Coalition

There were a lot of words of solidarity such as these, but what really defines "demonstration" is rituals of action. By the following day (Wednesday, December 1), the mayor of Seattle had called in the National Guard and, on questionable legal grounds, declared the downtown core a "no-protest zone." Protesters were being arrested in the hundreds. The Steelworkers held a rally near the docks and invited the Direct Action Network for a show of solidarity. Again the emphasis was on speeches: "I would like to say from all of us in Direct Action Network who are still out of jail came down today to support you guys and show them what coalitions are!"

Activists, increasingly bored by the ensuing speeches, began to shout "Downtown! C'mon downtown!" (Highleyman). "Then the rally ended," recalled Bob Hasagawa, of the Teamsters, "and then there was no march.... There was such a sense of disappointment at that point that we weren't actually going to challenge this no-protest order ... so some of us got together and organized a follow-up march" (qtd. in Freidberg and Rowley).

Details are a little sketchy, but it appears that a group of 3,000 to 4,000 trade unionists and other demonstrators headed toward downtown, taking up the direct action chant "Whose streets? Our streets!" and adding, "WTO shut it down! Seattle is a union town!" (Sustar; Freidberg and Rowley). En route, they witnessed some of the more spectacular police violence of the week, beginning when they saw "... a group of 2,000 people ... moving from our left to our right and it was obvious they were running from something."

Union marchers were shocked by what they saw. Ron Judd received more calls:

> People got pissed. And I had trade unionists who just a matter of days before were saying we shouldn't be out there calling me up saying, 'When are we going to protest next? I wanna be there because what's going on is wrong!' And one thing that you gotta say

about the labor movement, you know, when our sisters and brothers think something is wrong they will get engaged. Sometimes it takes a while to get there, right? You know, we all have to connect the dots. But, you know, when they saw people that they had marched with on Tuesday, that they had developed relationships with on Tuesday, being beaten and being gassed right; that ... [here he just shakes his head]. (qtd. in Freidberg and Rowley)

In the days that followed, the focus of activism shifted to supporting those who had been arrested and were being held in jails. Hundreds gathered outside the King County Jail and staged a 48-hour vigil and "festival of resistance" (Highleyman). Here labour activists joined with Food Not Bombs in distributing food. "It created a sense of community," recalled Rice Baker-Yeboah, a musician and community organizer:

> ... because that was where the steel-
> workers and the other unions were
> bringing food and blankets and
> water and taking care of people;
> and people were just taking care
> of people in what seemed to be
> the most natural way for human
> beings to function, but which we
> had never really seen before. (qtd.
> in Freidberg and Rowley)

This was meaningful collaboration, reminiscent of the sort of mutual aid that forged union bonds in the 19th century, and it had an emotional impact. In addition, the Dockworkers' union (ILWU) asked Judd, "to deliver the message that if this wasn't resolved then the ILWU were going to shut down the ports in solidarity" (Freidberg and Rowley).

Hegemony on the Streets

I want you to think about these events in terms of Gramsci's concept of a hegemonic war of position. The hegemonic moves in Seattle included physical manoeuvres in the street; tactical discussions among leaders of the different groups, the police, and city authorities; and decisions made at the editorial desks of media outlets. The object in this war was to place organized labour, either within or outside the popular coalition, as radical or moderate. If you take seriously the Marxist theoretical perspective, then you must ask if labour leads in this war of position. Also important from a Marxist perspective is the related question of whether labour pulls other players in an anti-capitalist direction.

Some Marxists have retreated from the claim that labour must always lead counter-hegemonic struggles. Neo-Gramscians, Carroll and Ratner tell us, insist only that labour must be part of any coalition "if it is to be equal to the task of radical transformation" (Carroll and Ratner 11). For Carroll and Ratner, the ultimate aim of coalition building is to "challenge the immense power of transnationals in the global arena," which they still see as an anti-capitalist project. Workers, they argue, have a guaranteed place in this struggle because of the objective nature of their class interests. These interests will always make it easier to lure a steelworker out on to the streets with the activists than to convince, say, a business administration major or an investment banker. This is hard to dispute.

But the Battle of Seattle reminds us of the further tactical questions of how you lure them out and keep them at the barricades. It is still not at all clear how firmly North American workers have stepped into their guaranteed place. How fragile is the alliance that emerged from Seattle? Answering these questions is tricky. Hegemonic struggles are cultural; they have as much to do with representation and interpretation as with what is "actually" happening. They are also reflexive.

The representation of workers' actions at Seattle—whether they betrayed the other activists or whether they supported and took care of them when they were in need—will shape how both parties act toward one another in the future. Most of the evidence we have of what happened at Seattle—mainstream media reports, activist documents like *This Is What Democracy Looks Like*, eyewitness accounts by participants—are implicated in projects of building or splitting the coalition. Look again at the film; it is partly a report, but it also makes its own argument about the coalition between organized labour and other popular constituencies.

COALITIONS: CULTURE AND CONSTRUCTIONS OF IDENTITY

Some of the more helpful analyses of the "how" of coalition building are non-Marxist and are generally agnostic about the outcome, with no theoretical investment in who leads or in what direction. James Jasper, for example, has looked at an alliance between anti-nuclear protesters that was, like the alliance in Seattle, marked both by generational differences and differences over the use of direct action and civil disobedience.

Taste in Tactics

The activism of the groups that he studied, the Mothers for Peace and the Abalone Alliance, was rooted in very different identities and lifestyle choices. Full collaboration over tactics would have compromised their

sense of who they were. When asked about the Abalone people, one of the Mothers for Peace "... smiled and rolled her eyes. 'Well, they have a certain charm to them,' she said, picking her words slowly. 'We don't deal with them more than we have to, 'cause they drive us crazy'" (qtd. in Jasper 230).

The two groups worked together strategically, but acknowledged that many of their differences were insurmountable. These were not always differences over what strategies would be more effective or would best serve the coalition partners' political interests. Jasper concluded that the two groups were often exercising different "tastes in tactics" consistent with the types of people they understood themselves to be.

Activists at Seattle recognized that alliances can involve accepting and working around different tastes, choices, and identities. A young poet and anarchist, who goes by the name War Cry, explains:

> You have to kind of embrace a diversity of people as well as a diversity of tactics. If you're 45 and you're working at a factory and you've got a family of four to feed, your tactics and thinking at this protest are going to be a little bit different than if you're 17 or 18 or 19. Our differences are our strengths; I don't think anybody wants to live in a homogeneous culture. (qtd. in Freidberg and Rowley)

She does not expect to see the 45-year-old in a "lock-down position" doing civil disobedience. Perhaps in this spirit, the Direct Action Network should not have expected labour marchers to confront the police, or been disappointed when it did not happen.

Race and Style

Even when coalition partners have interests or issues in common, they must negotiate cultural divides. The markers of cultural difference around race have a singular immediacy. Although many people of colour occupied prominent positions as speakers and leaders in the Seattle demonstrations, others who found themselves in the crowd and later in the prisons felt uncomfortable in a sea of whiteness. Their unease was not simply to do with the numeric demonstration of their minority status, but also with the self-presentation of White activists.

Walking into a "convergence" space where other activists were preparing for the demonstrations, one of them recalled, "the room was filled with young whites calling themselves anarchists. There was a pungent smell; many had not showered. We just couldn't relate to the scene so our whole group left right away." "I just freaked out and left," recalled another, "... It wasn't just race, it was also culture, although race was key" (qtd. in Martinez).

These accounts are from American activists. It would be interesting to explore the impressions of activists from countries of the South for whom their coalition partners must have seemed even more exotic from across such divides of race, language, and geography. Clashes of style are real but not insurmountable impediments to coalition building. Convergences in physical space, such as in the streets of Seattle, both reveal them, as well as provide the setting to negotiate around them.

After their initial culture shock, some of those who had fled went back to the convergence space and discovered there was much for them to learn. "We realized we didn't know how to do a blockade. We had no gas masks. They made sure everybody had food and water; they took care of people. We could

have learned from them" (qtd. in Martinez). These differences also get negotiated in the virtual media space that amplifies major demonstrations. Look again at the film *This Is What Democracy Looks Like* for what it says about the role of racial difference in Seattle.

Mouffe: Multiple Subject Positions

Chantal Mouffe is a leading thinker who has tried to give theoretical expression to the idea, expressed by the War Cry spokesperson, that "our differences are our strengths." One of her insights is that we do not stake out mutually exclusive identities as workers, women, Aboriginal peoples, or what have you. Rather, we occupy "multiple subject positions." For instance, second wave feminists experienced the contradiction of simultaneously identifying as New Left socialists advocating the "liberation" of workers and as women whose own oppression was going unnoticed. This was a fertile tension that helped women push the New Left to rethink its analysis of oppression and apply more broadly the principles of freedom and equality.

Third wave feminists, who identified as feminists and Black women, or feminists and working class, similarly expanded the feminist project to deal with "multiple oppressions." This sort of thinking is echoed by Hop Hopkins when he says, "... race, class, gender, sexism, heterosexism.... If that's not in your analysis then you're only half stepping; then you're really not working for the revolution."

For Mouffe, no one "political subject" can reliably speak for the interests of others. Only by giving voice to difference can a genuinely emancipatory project emerge. These voices often clamour from within, as when, for instance, Black women or environmentalists speak out as workers from within the labour movement. Unlike traditional Marxism, her analysis offers no theoretical guarantees. The only thing she is sure of is that the project will expand genuine democracy based on freedom and equality. This is because each step involves extending the tools for political participation on an equal footing with others.

She does not embed the project in any necessary logic of capitalism. Nor does she guarantee that its outcome will be anti-capitalist. The crux is whether capitalism can be made compatible with freedom and equality. If at the end of repeated struggles, partners in a broad-based coalition learned that capitalism always defeats the project of "radical democracy," then capitalism itself might become the target of their opposition.

CONCLUSION

Coalitions are strategic collaborations among people whose social identities are distinct and whose political interests are different yet overlapping. Coalitions are one solution to Marx and Engels' problem. That is, how can the powerless challenge the power of international capitalism? Marx and Engels had placed their faith in the working class, whom they believed were capable of representing the interests of all other oppressed people, and under whose leadership all anti-capitalist struggles would be subsumed, creating a single political identity or "unitary subject." Theorists of coalition recognize that there are multiple oppressions in modern societies around which distinct political identities form. They accept that the experience of class oppression does not authorize workers to speak for others. Some nonetheless argue that the working class must lead coalitions; others, like Mouffe, do not.

Marxist reluctance to relinquish the privilege of working-class leadership points to risks that all organizations face in coalitions. Coalition partners sign on in the hope of advancing the interests that they share as well as those that they do not. They are understandably wary of how they will fare when interests diverge. So, for example, the fear of many of the partners in the Pro-Canada Network was that organized labour would do what it had earlier done in B.C. That is, labour leaders might make common cause with the coalition only to intensify public pressure on the government. When the government was ready for compromise, these leaders could negotiate separately, offering union support if the government made concessions in the free trade deal on labour rights at the exclusion of concerns of the other partners, such as environmentalists, academics, supporters of the CBC, etc.

Weak partners face the risk of betrayal; strong partners face risks from success. Many social movement organizations compete with one another for members and funding. In this competition they trade on their perceived effectiveness. Entering a coalition means that they will have to publicly support their competitors and share the glory of any victory they achieve together. In successful coalitions these sources of distrust are typically overcome through personal ties that link people across organizational boundaries. People develop allegiances to the informal network that counterbalance their commitments to the organizations that they formally represent. Their face-to-face contacts in the network help them to see the broader picture. They can help to steer their own organizations beyond narrowly conceived organizational interests. Network participants are also the first to negotiate around the cultural barriers that divide the constituencies that their organizations represent. Such networks are often the tangible core and animating force of coalitions.

The traditional Marxist faith in workers' ability to represent the interests of others has been based on two increasingly contested assumptions. One is the idea that everyone's problems stem from capitalist alienation and exploitation. The other is that workers' experiences predispose them to be anti-capitalist. The record of organized labour in the developed nations, especially in contrast to the radical social movements of the 1960s, has made the second assumption difficult to support. Theorists have used a variety of conceptual frameworks to make sense of this gap between theory and history. Some argue that workers have been duped by a dominant (capitalist) ideology pervasive throughout education, the media, and popular culture. Some focus on the ongoing work of militant working-class leaders and argue that they have lost more often than won in a hegemonic war of position.

Others maintain that workers have been influenced not so much by persuasion as by the changing logic of their situation. Collective bargaining and suburbanization helped to reshape their interests. It became more "rational" for them to focus on narrowly defined material benefits for union members to the exclusion of other workers and other oppressed groups. The advancement of these interests became for workers tied to the advancement of the particular capitalist industries that employed them. As the logic of this situation changes, so too should workers' political priorities. Organized labour is struggling to again broaden its political mandate in ways that favour coalition building.

These approaches represent differences of emphasis and could easily be, and often are, combined to explain the co-optation of worker radicalism. The theoretical difference that is more difficult to reconcile is between those Marxists who cling to the idea that ideology or co-optation distorts and somehow falsifies "real" working-class interests, and those who argue that worker politics has to be taken at face value whatever it becomes. If workers embrace consumer capitalism, according to this latter view, then that is their politics. They might change their minds, but there is no inherent "logic of capitalism" working behind the scenes to bring this change about.

We have looked at two theoretical innovations that sought a way forward out of Marxism's new uncertainties and have helped to make sense of coalition politics. One extended class analysis to the new middle classes of professionals and service workers who benefited from the growth of the welfare state and not-for-profit sectors. These people embraced the new social movements, spoke out on behalf of the socially marginalized, and formed alliances with others in ways that were consistent with their own interests. The new middle classes have remained in the forefront of efforts to oppose government cutbacks, deregulation, and the privatization of social services. In other words, they tend to support anti-neo-liberal struggles. Based on this class analysis, would you go further and argue that they are also predisposed to be anti-capitalist?

The second theoretical innovation we considered was Mouffe's "radical democracy." She abandons the idea that the working class or any other "unitary subject" should speak for or lead popular politics. She no longer expects that political interests or outcomes will be guaranteed by the logic of capitalist development. She pins her hope on the democratic promise of freedom and equality that has accompanied the expansion of capitalist relations in the west. She is aware that "freedom" and "democracy" have often been held out as ideological justification of fundamental inequalities that characterize capitalist societies.

Still, this very promise has repeatedly inspired demands for genuine freedom and equality through the anti-slavery, workers' suffrage, women's rights movements, and the like. Those who are excluded are best able to identify and give voice to that exclusion. The only thing that will make popular struggles truly universal is the inclusion of the most diverse range of voices. The final word in this democratic struggle, what it will mean in terms of a vision of social institutions or the economy, can only emerge as an end product of dialogue and popular collaboration, not as a prescription of some theoretical or political vanguard.

Our main case study in this chapter—the coalition building in Canada in opposition first to the U.S.–Canada Free Trade Agreement, then NAFTA, the MAI, and the WTO—illustrates both the nature of coalition building, but also the social basis and structure of a new transnational movement in opposition to the global neoliberal revolution. The list of players is long and their differences many, but the process of building the coalition, first within Canada, then with U.S., Mexican, and European partners, and increasingly with partners from the developing world, has helped to define commonalities. The notion of national sovereignty around which anglophone Canadians had coalesced had to give way to the more transnational and inclusive concept of popular sovereignty, an amalgam of the ideas of direct democracy and civil and social rights as broadly defined in the Universal Declaration of Human Rights. The emergent frame of this new movement defines popular sovereignty in opposition to the threat of corporate rule.

Being opposed to corporate rule is not the same as being opposed to capitalism, nor does it entail being opposed to international trade. Canadian opponents to the FTA and NAFTA were clear that what they opposed were rules of international trade that shifted power from democratically elected governments, unions, and people's organizations to transnational corporations. While it is often referred to as "anti-globalization," the emergent frame for this new movement is not so much anti-globalization as anti-neoliberal globalization. Some refer to it as the "alter-globalization" or "counter-globalization" movement to indicate that its adherents are looking for alternatives to the neoliberal model of globalization.

Others represent it as a movement to expand global civil society. This is one example of an alternative project of globalization, ensuring that NGOs and people's organizations gain a strong voice in global governance to counterbalance that of transnational corporations and states. The nature and strategies of this growing movement will be the focus of our final chapter.

REFERENCES

Aaronson, Susan A. *Taking Trade to the Streets: The Lost History of Public Efforts to Shape Globalization*. Ann Arbor: University of Michigan Press, 2001.

Abercrombie, Nicholas, Stephen Hill, and Bryan S. Turner. *The Dominant Ideology Thesis*. London: Allen and Unwin, 1980.

Adkin, Laurie Elizabeth. *The Politics of Sustainable Development: Citizens, Unions, and the Corporations*. London; New York: Black Rose Books, 1998.

Ayres, Jeffrey McKelvey. *Defying Conventional Wisdom: Political Movements and Popular Contention against North American Free Trade*. Studies in Comparative Political Economy and Public Policy. Toronto: University of Toronto Press, 1998.

Carroll, William, and R.S. Ratner. "Between Leninism and Radical Pluralism: Gramscian Reflections on Counter-Hegemony and the New Social Movements/Social Movements—Theory." *Critical Sociology* 20, no. 2 (1994): 3–26.

Cook, Terry. "Thousands of Workers in South Korea Strike against Repressive Labour Laws," November 19, 2003. World Socialist Web site, April 21, 2006, www.wsws.org/articles/2003/nov2003/kore-n19.shtml.

Crosby, Jeff. "The Kids Are Alright," *Global Action: May Our Resistance Be as TransNational as Capital*, December 6, 1999. May 25, 2006, http://flag.blackened.net/global/100kidsalright.htm.

Editor. "Korea Is a Law-Abiding Country—Firebombers Should Not Be Tolerated." *Korean Times*, November 10, 2003. April 21, 2006, http://times.hankooki.com/lpage/opinion/200311/kt2003111018414711300.htm.

Forcese, Craig. "Korean Labor Crackdown." *Multinational Monitor*, June 4, 1995. April 21, 2003, http://multinationalmonitor.org/hyper/issues/1995/06/mmo695_04.html.

Freidberg, Jill, and Rick Rowley. *This Is What Democracy Looks Like*. Prod. Seattle Independent Media Center and Big Noise Films. Dir. Jill Freidberg and Rick Rowley. Seattle Independent Media Center and Big Noise Films, 2000.

Gramsci, Antonio. *Selections from the Prison Notebooks*, edited and translated by Quintin Hoare and Geoffrey Nowell Smith. New York: International Publishers, 1979.

Griswold, Deirdre. "Worker Suicides Lead to Massive Street Battles." *Workers World*, November 20, 2003. April 21, 2006, www.workers.org/ww/2003/skorea1120.php.

Herman, Edward S., and Noam Chomsky. *Manufacturing Consent: The Political Economy of the Mass Media*. New York: Pantheon Books, 2002.

Highleyman, Liz. "Scenes from the Battle of Seattle," November 20, 1999. Black Rose Web Pages, May 25, 2006, www.black-rose.com/seattle-wto.html.

Jasper, James M. *The Art of Moral Protest: Culture, Biography, and Creativity in Social Movements*. Chicago: University of Chicago Press, 1997.

Johnston, Josee, and Gordon Laxer. "Solidarity in the Age of Globalization: Lessons from the Anti-MAI and Zapatista Struggles." *Theory and Society* 32, no. 1 (2003): 39–91.

Martinez, Elizabeth Betita. "Where Was the Color in Seattle? Looking for Reasons Why the Great Battle Was So White." *ColorLines* 3, no. 1 (2000), www.arc.org/C_Lines/CLArchive/story3_1_02.html.

Mouffe, Chantal. "Hegemony and New Political Subjects." *Marxism and the Interpretation of Culture*, edited by C. Nelson and L. Grossman. Chicago: University of Illinois Press, 1988.

Pro-Canada Network. *What's the Big Deal*. Ottawa: Pro-Canada Network, 1988.

Smith, Jim. "Labor Eyewitness to the Battle of Seattle." *L.A. Labor News* (99). May 25, 2006, www.lalabor.org/Battle_of_Seattle.html.

Sustar, Lee. "Organizing to Fight Corporate Greed: The Battle in Seattle." *Socialist Worker Online* (99). May 25, 2006, www.socialistworker.org/2004-2/500Supp/500S_19991210_Seattle.shtml.

CRITICAL THINKING QUESTIONS

1. Have the working class or its organizations led in the hegemonic struggle in the way that Gramsci hoped they would? Could they or should they?
2. Is solidarity necessary for creating or maintaining a coalition? What about a common interpretive framework or set of common cultural understandings?
3. To what extent does people's class position shape their politics? Consider the proletariat and the new middle classes. In each of these classes, are people predisposed to be anti-capitalist, anti-neoliberal, or to speak for the interests of other oppressed people?
4. If a Canadian worker supports neoliberal governance at home and neoliberal trade policies internationally, is she acting against her true interests? Are there objective social forces at play that might bring her to recognize her true interests?
5. Why do people so happily buy into the commodity spectacle? Are they duped by advertising and the mass media or is there more going on?
6. What are the difficulties that coalition partners face in making coalitions work?
7. List all of the players involved in Canada's anti-free trade coalition. Where did the interests of the various players overlap? How likely were they to part ways over the question of anti-capitalism? Did organized labour actually guarantee an anti-capitalist agenda within the coalition?
8. What potential do you think the counter-globalization movement has to challenge: (a) capitalism, (b) the global neoliberal agenda?

FURTHER READING

Ayres, Jeffrey McKelvey. *Defying Conventional Wisdom: Political Movements and Popular Contention against North American Free Trade*. Studies in Comparative Political Economy and Public Policy. Toronto: University of Toronto Press, 1998.
   Canada's anti-free trade coalition laid the groundwork for some of the transnational alliances active against the global neoliberal revolution. This excellent study is where you should start if you want to know more about this (ongoing) chapter in Canadian social movement history.

Carroll, William K. *Organizing Dissent: Contemporary Social Movements in Theory and Practice*. Toronto: Garamond Press, 1992.
   This collection of essays provides an analysis of coalition building in Canada in the 1980s from a neo-Gramscian perspective.

Conway, Janet M. *Identity, Place, Knowledge: Social Movements Contesting Globalization*. Halifax: Fernwood Publishing, 2004.
   Conway examines Canadians' entry into the counter-globalization movement through a case study of Toronto's Metro Network for Social Justice. "World cities" like Toronto

offer platforms where local struggles against neoliberal policy connect with global partners and campaigns.

Laclau, Ernesto, and Chantal Mouffe. *Hegemony and Socialist Strategy: Toward a Radical Democratic Politics*. London: Verso, 1985.
This has been a tremendously influential book in theorizing coalitions and the role of organized labour within them.

McDonald, Kevin. "From Solidarity to Fluidarity: Social Movements Beyond 'Collective Identity': The Case of Globalisation Conflicts." *Social Movement Studies* 1, no. 2 (2002): 109–128.
McDonald argues that among the new generation of anti-globalization activists, traditional notions of solidarity and coalition may no longer apply.

RELEVANT WEB SITES

After Seattle: The New Anti-Globalists
www-personal.umich.edu/~mlassite/internetdocuments467/finnegan.html
In this Web article, William Finnegan gives an insider's look at the coalition-building style of young anti-globalization activists.

Canadian Auto Workers (CAW)
www.caw.ca
See how the CAW articulates its commitment to "coalition work" and "international solidarity" in the document "We Are a Social Union" (www.caw.ca/whoweare/CAW-constitution/conventionpapers/pdfs/part_2.pdf). Check out their main site to see what they have been doing in this direction.

Common Frontiers
www.commonfrontiers.ca
Common Frontiers was one of the outcome organizations of the coalition to oppose NAFTA. Visit their Web site and see what they are up to now.

Council of Canadians
www.canadians.org
In addition to its criticisms of North American free trade deals, the Council of Canadians has become one of the more active Canadian citizens organizations addressing a wide range of issues, notably the privatization of water and health care.

National Action Committee on the Status of Women (NAC)
www.nac-cca.ca
NAC is itself a coalition of women's groups and was a leader in building Canada's anti-free trade coalition.

Chapter 12

IN SEARCH OF GLOBAL "PUBLIC SPACE"

SEATTLE/QUEBEC/QATAR: ENCLOSING PUBLIC SPACE

Seattle: Battle over Public Space

On Tuesday, November 30, 1999, when mostly young demonstrators marched from the north and south to converge on the Seattle Convention Centre, many had a mind to challenge what they saw as the WTO's democratic exclusion zone. A WTO treaty enforced, as it would be, with real economic sanctions could have more weight than UN treaties in the emerging regime of global governance. Yet it was being negotiated without UN-style consultation with civil society. NGOs were not invited to speak at the meetings. They were not even given observer status. The only show of dialogue had been a transparent public relations exercise on Monday where hand-picked NGO representatives had said nice things about the potential of trade treaties (Zoll). Activists responded by locking themselves down on Seattle streets to create their own WTO exclusion zone.

Negotiation of global treaties requires physical spaces. Delegates need hotels and restaurants and convention centres where they must meet face to face. In moving from one venue to another, they crisscross public space. Demonstrators were saying in effect, "If we are to be excluded from your 'private' spaces of discussion, we will exclude you from our public space of the streets." Seattle authorities were clearly unprepared for how effective this strategy would be. A popular chant of the days to follow was "Whose Streets? Our Streets!" Delegates felt under siege; scheduled meetings had to be cancelled. The police resorted to force to remove peaceful protesters from the streets.

In order to invoke broader powers of anti-protester coercion, the mayor declared a state of emergency. A state of emergency mandates special powers that the mayor used to create a 25-block no-protest zone around the convention centre. Police got to define what constituted "protest" and arrested people for simple acts of free speech like handing out leaflets and wearing buttons. The whole of downtown was put under dusk-to-dawn curfew, making it illegal simply to be on the street at night.

These moves refocused the demonstrations on to the issue of public space, and people's ability to exercise their rights of free speech and assembly in it. The chant of the thousands who were determined to defy the no-protest zone was "Peacefully assembled!" It invoked the words of the American constitution whose first amendment prohibits any law that would "abridge ... the right of the people peaceably to assemble...." "We have the right," as one megaphone-wielding activist shouted to the crowd, "to assemble peacefully, to gather in our streets, in our city, on our planet!" (Freidberg and Rowley).

Quebec City: Pre-emptive Closure of Public Space

Seattle authorities had clearly been playing catch-up. They had to call in reinforcements almost immediately. Their tear gas ran out and they had to scramble to find additional supplies. Elsewhere, authorities took note. The Canadian response, in preparing for the FTAA meeting in Quebec City in April 2001, was simply to close down public space in advance. Around the old walled citadel of Quebec they erected a 3-metre-high fence of steel and concrete 4 kilometres long. Only summit delegates and local residents were issued security passes to enter this exclusion zone. In addition to the city being walled against its own citizens, the borders of the country were being closed to many would-be demonstrators from the United States, Mexico, and Latin American countries affected by the FTAA.

Extra police and military personnel were assembled in Quebec City for a total force of around 6,000. In order to accommodate official personnel and displace civil society delegates, the RCMP block-booked hotel and rental accommodations in an area well beyond the security perimeter. NGOs that had reserved up to a year in advance were bumped. Alternative "accommodation" was being made available, however. The minister of Public Security of Quebec announced that the 600 inmates of Orsianville Prison were being relocated to make room for arrested protesters. To many, the ease with which Canada was willing to bracket the civil rights of its own citizens was reminiscent of the 1970 invocation of the War Measures Act.

There was much sabre rattling prior to the summit, which may have been meant to intimidate, but looked to many like provocation. Thousands responded to the challenge. The security perimeter became, just as the no-protest zone had in Seattle, a key issue and strategic focus of the demonstrations that followed. Quebec City became another battle over public space. It was one that was to involve increasing costs and dilemmas both for authorities and for the often-fragile networks and coalitions among the demonstrators.

In Canada the role of the Direct Action Network was played by CLAC (Convergence des Luttes Anti-Capitalistes—Anti-Capitalist Convergence) and Mobglob (Mobilization for Global Justice). The CLC (Canadian Labour Congress) was just as reluctant as the AFL-CIO had been to join these young radicals bent on breaching the wall. Many feminists and peace activists too were leery of the macho rhetoric of confrontation (Rebick).

Qatar: Elimination of Public Space

States risked compromising their legitimacy by having to suppress legitimate dissent within their own borders. Later that year, WTO organizers hoped to solve the dilemma by holding their meetings in Qatar, a country that had little democratic legitimacy to lose since it already repressed dissent as a matter of routine. Local civil society representatives in Qatar feared to speak out for fear of imprisonment. The country simply refused visas to all foreign activists and anti-globalization NGOs. The only NGO to get anywhere near the action of the summit was Greenpeace. It was the only one that had a ship, *The Rainbow Warrior*, which it anchored just off the coast of Qatar from which vantage point it broadcast an alternative perspective on the proceedings.

Even in Qatar the optics for negotiating states were not good. The rhetoric of free trade invoked the ideals of freedom, and even the extension of democracy, through global trade. Yet here the advocates of it had been sealing off borders and erecting exclusion zones to people. In Qatar they had finally resorted to negotiating in secret under the protection of an authoritarian state. It did appear, as the activists charged, that free trade might be more about the cross-border flow of commodities than the opening of borders to people and that the freedoms it invoked might actually be the freedoms of corporate, not individual, citizens.

For activists as well as for students of social movements, the closure of public space that Qatar represented posed new questions. How much does democracy and the dissent that invigorates it depend upon access to physical public space? For those social movements that seek to act on the global stage, and civil society organizations that want a voice in emerging global governance, how crucial is it that they have access to global public space—the cities that serve as the physical platforms for global summits? How can they adapt to the new "enclosure" movement designed to exclude them?

These will be central questions that we take up in this chapter. Along the way we will also be asking: What exactly do people mean by the term "global civil society" or "global" social movements? Throughout, we will be paying particular attention to the spatial dimensions of this abstraction known as the "global."

THEATRES OF VIOLENCE

Respect for Diversity of Tactics

As if to mirror the increasing militancy of the authorities, CLAC and Mobglob prepared for confrontation in Quebec. CLAC had inherited the spirit of working-class militancy of an earlier generation of Quebeckers. In Chapter 7 you heard it articulated by Pierre Vallières and Francis Simard. The position of the Québécois within their own province had improved since 1970. However, class inequalities persisted. Indeed, in those places on the globe touched by the neoliberal revolution, class inequalities had been growing. This was not as evident in Quebec as in many places, but with the passage of the FTAA, many believed that Quebec would join the list.

CLAC networks intersected with those of people who lived on the street or close to it, relying on food banks and evading police harassment. In these people's lives they saw, as FLQist Francis Simard had done 30 years earlier, the action of a "prior violence" of the system. "[E]very day," Simard had written, the authorities "... were bargaining with the lives of the unemployed, with welfare recipients, with the chronically ill in hospitals" (Simard 18).

Literal police violence, in their view, was a routine feature of "managing" the dispossessed. CLAC activist Tania Halle, in an NFB documentary *View from the Summit*, explains her own radicalization: "... when I saw police repression with my own eyes, it was the first step in questioning the role of the police. They're supposed to protect citizens, but they beat up my friends." Activists from CLAC did not claim to speak for the urban disposed; that would be an imposition of leadership or spokesmanship inconsistent with their anarchist principles.

However, they insisted that no one else had the authority to prevent such people from expressing their voiceless rage through violence. Better that they attack a symbol of oppression like the headquarters of a multinational corporation or the security perimeter of a global trade summit than direct their anger inwards, as so many of the poor do, in acts of self-destruction. Violence here is conceived, much as the FLQists saw it, as "... action talking.... Unveiling the force of people who'd never had the right to speak before" (Simard 21).

CLAC and Mobglob were, just as the Direct Action Network had been, firmly committed to the principle of "respect for diversity of tactics." "Respect" here was understood in anarchist terms. Halle, appealing to other activists, explained: "I see pamphlets from some groups saying things like: 'We will not tolerate the wearing of hoods.' To say 'We will not tolerate' is to impose something. It's hierarchical and goes against our principles. Let's start by respecting each other."

Elsewhere she explains the specifics of diversity for CLAC: "... we created three blocs: 'festive demonstration,' 'obstruction,' and 'disruption.' ... [These involve] different levels of action: one is joyful, creative, artistic. The second involves occupation, civil disobedience, or other defensive, non-confrontational tactics. The third aims for maximum disruption of the summit, and might include an attack on the fence, which is totally illegitimate" (qtd. in Lapointe, Ying Gee Wong, and Ménard).

One of the ways to deal with CLAC's insistence was to agree upon a geography of tactics within the city. "Green zones," like Rue St. Jean to the north of the security perimeter, and L'Îlot Fleuri, an urban waste-land located under a series of overpasses, were to be safe areas for people who did not want to engage in the types of direct action or civil disobedience likely to incite the wrath of the police. "Red zones," such as the St. Jean Baptiste neighbourhood adjacent to the security fence, were to be open to the full range of diversity of tactics.

"War Drama" in the Red Zone

Jennifer Bennett, who identifies herself as an *Anishinaabe kwe* (Ojibway woman), describes the culmination of a peaceful CLAC march from Université Laval down Boulevard René Lévesque and into the red zone. Scores of activists, clinging to the fence, rocked it back and forth until the barrier was breached and a few charged into the exclusion zone.

She writes as though describing a field of combat where military strategy is a problem of geography—the direction of the wind, positions of forces, and routes of attack and retreat. This is not the sort of "war of posi-tion" that Gramsci was talking about.

> I think this was a turning point in the police reaction to our presence. They began loading canisters into a gun, projecting the tear gas further into the crowd. I found out later that their restraint, for which they were commended by Prime Minister Chrétien, flew out the window as the weekend progressed. The police

began to aim their guns at protest-ers, sometimes at distances of only ten metres. One man suffered a broken arm when he was struck by a launched tear-gas canister. Despite police efforts, the wind still carried the gas away from us back onto the police. I watched happily as some protesters picked up canisters and threw them back at the fence. I didn't have my vinegar-soaked han-kie or any eye protection but thought that I could always retreat if things got bad, so I continued to watch the clash unfurl as the tension in the air intensified. Those who'd been on the frontlines when the first of the tear gas was released were now running back into the crowd to get treated by medics with water or a neutralizing solution. A few were treated right next to my feet, and tears welled in my eyes listening to their cries of pain—on their knees, faces flushed, noses running and eyes swollen shut.

When I decided I'd witnessed enough chaos, I began to retreat but was cut off by two police vehicles, each armed with a mechanical fire hose on its hood, like a zit with a vengeance. The crowd quickly parted as the trucks blared through the rear of the crowd. And then, in one of the most amazing acts of bravery that I witnessed that weekend, one man, completely alone, walked right up to the first truck with a white sheet tied to a tree branch that read "democra-tie," and he planted his sign in the nozzle. The crowd must have held its breath for a full sixty seconds while we digested what we saw. He stopped it. He stopped the truck. After a few eternal seconds, people nearby scurried up behind him, starting a tidal wave of people that forced the truck to retreat. The crowd chased the trucks back, but the police insisted on mowing down two dozen retreating protesters with a cannon blast of water in five-degree weather and fierce winds.

I thought the trucks marked the end of the rear attack, but the police finally figured out how to use the wind to their benefit and released the tear gas at our backs. I began to gag. My eyes began to burn and my lungs began to scream. I was choking on fire. I dug frantically in my pack until I remembered that I'd left my handkerchief at my dorm that morning. My friend and I skipped behind a building in a meagre attempt to get out of the noxious wind. I was worried that, if in my retreat I came near the police, I would be arrested because they had moved out from behind a perimeter and were snatching solitary demonstrators. They even began blocking off the side streets that would have served as exit routes for us, funnelling the crowd in one direction—away from the wall and into the midst of the tear gas. (Bennett 50–51)

Stellan has characterized this sort of demonstration as a "war drama." The idea that violence can be seen as a form of communication, as a form of theatre, should not be new to you. We considered it in the case of state terror in the Southern Cone. There the manifest possibility of arbitrary arrest and torture was meant to eliminate in all citizens' minds the barrier between the torture cell and society, and to arrest all resistance in advance. We considered it in the case of the FLQ for whom violence dramatized the possibility of acting and writing one's own history. Here I want to consider the different "vocabularies" of violence at Quebec City.

Discourses of Violence

Consider how people dress for violence. Riot police are outfitted in black with thick body armour from which their limbs protrude like those of action figures or combat machines. Helmets, gas masks, visors, shields, jackboots, billyclubs all speak of war. In some engagements they beat their clubs against their shields like a heartbeat in fear.

The Black Bloc aesthetic, much in evidence at Quebec, speaks the same language. Some wear all black with stocking caps covering their faces like IRA gunmen. Others have do-it-yourself helmets, gas masks, and at Quebec, even shields and clubs. "Drums and music," writes one activist, "also play a fantastic role in rallying the crowd. On the overpass, hundreds of people bash stones and sticks against the railings to create an awesome cacophony, which ends up sounding like a heartbeat rhythm" (Grant).

Contrast this to dressing and ritually enacting non-violence. Clown noses were everywhere in Quebec. People walked precariously on stilts, and sported ragtag colours. Raging grannies put daisies in their hats and wore flowered dresses that recalled an era when women were anything but threatening. There were giant puppets and characters from the imagination, which were not menacing but hilarious or, at worst, sarcastic.

At night, in the face of police cordons, women danced in the street. An Argentine activist, who fled the dictatorship, was amazed: "They're dancing as though it was a party! They would never let us do that at home. Never. There, the police presence necessarily means confrontation.... Here, the young people dance!"

Vinthagen calls this "the carnival drama." In this mode of expression,

> ... activists try to undermine established definitions, discourses and social roles/relationships and creatively construct new ones. They use face masks, costumes and theatre equipment in order to become someone else and to make fun of conventional understandings. The carnival tradition display[s] for a short time the turning of the world up side down, to show how the powerful are without power and that another world is possible. (3)

Different discourses intermingled on the streets of Quebec City, even at the point of contact with the wall. Much of the demonstration at the wall was a parody of violence and a reproach to the militarization that the wall represents. Activists constructed a catapult that besieged the exclusion zone by lobbing teddy bears into it. Women's groups festooned it with ribbons, flowers, and handwritten testimonials of peace. They were bearing witness to the injustice of state coercion by staging a kind of "public reading" of state's own symbolism of coercion. In *View from the Summit*, a Latin American woman faces the camera through the steel of the fence and says, "For a long time we have waged an ideological struggle against the wealthy of the world. This is a powerful symbol that the fight has become more directly physical, more tangible."

Challenging the State to "Speak" in the Language of Violence

Other acts, of civil disobedience and direct action, are designed to force the state to "speak" in the language of violence. Remember from the sit-ins and freedom marches described in Chapter 3 that one form of this tactic relied upon passive defiance on the part of protesters. A violent state response like setting police dogs on Black marchers "reads" better as injustice in this case.

However, in the chapter on terrorism we saw a different version. Here protester violence, the "propaganda of the deed," was meant to force the state to drop its mask of democratic legitimacy and resort to naked force. What is supposed to change people's minds is the direct experience of indiscriminate state violence. There is no question that being attacked by police powerfully shaped people's understandings both at Quebec and Seattle. As one observer of Seattle put it, "... the response by the Police Department was one of the most significant turning points. It told everybody that all of you are slaves and you better get back in your cage" (qtd. in Freidberg and Rowley).

For some the script was for the state to "speak"; for others it was to force the state into silence. In other words, many held out the hope that they could "shut down" the discussions that were taking place among state and corporate representatives inside the security perimeter, just as activists had, or so they believed, shut down the WTO in 1999.

This could only have happened through physical blockade of the movements of delegates. Thousands would have had to stream through the breach in the security perimeter and—who knows?—maybe stormed the convention centre like the Bolsheviks stormed the Winter Palace. But then, given the predictable response of the police, the violence would have shifted from being communicative to become a literal military action.

THE VIRTUAL THEATRE OF VIOLENCE

The drama of modern demonstration takes place simultaneously on physical streets and on a virtual media stage. For global events, as Vinthagen puts it, summit cities become "*temporary global arenas* where global politics are made, displayed as a *power dramaturgy* between actors and structured by a[n] electronic *global mass media stage*" (Vinthagen 1). Tactical scripts do not always play the same way on the streets as on the mass media stage.

To begin with, the audiences are slightly different. Demonstrators share the physical stage with a bystander public who are invited to participate. Much of the ritual of the event is designed around the experience of participation; it is as much for the demonstrators themselves as for a wider audience. Summit delegates are also an important audience. Demonstrators seek physical co-presence with these brokers of power. Even if they cannot meet face to face, it helps to know that the targets of their demonstration can see and hear them and feel their collective power.

Ideological Work of the Media

The electronic media are not neutral in the way that they structure the power dramaturgy. Activists learned from Seattle the limits of their control over this structuring, over how their performance is interpreted. Mainstream news reports showed selective bias and outright misrepresentation in the way that they portrayed protester versus police violence. *This Is What Democracy Looks Like* quotes actual news footage of the event. "We have not used tear gas," one reporter assures viewers after the first day of clashes, "and we will not be using tear gas." "How many civilians were injured?" asks one reporter near the end of the demonstrations, to which the chief of police responds, amazingly, "less than 20." No doubt he has a special definition of what it means to be "injured." Just before his officers start wielding truncheons, ripping off gas masks, and spraying pepper spray directly in people's faces a police sergeant assures peaceful, locked-down protesters that he has no intention of hurting them, but that they will be the subject of "chemical and pain compliance."

A different language is applied to police violence and a different framework is invoked for understanding it. News reporters insist on the prior violence of the demonstrators. "I think our officers are exercising remarkable restraint," a police spokesperson is quoted as saying. "It was the actions of protesters, the demonstrators," concludes the reporter, "that led them to take the actions they did." Indeed, police actions almost disappear in the face of protester responsibility: "Anyone [who] wants to stand down here and be in the way, I guess they're inviting trouble upon themselves." Despite the fact that protester violence is not aimed at human targets, an effort is made to represent property damage in terms of human pain. "We share in the anguish and the pain," says one police spokesperson, "to see windows boarded up on dozens of businesses."

The alternative press, including the film *This Is What Democracy Looks Like,* makes a counter-argument. *Democracy*'s first image of violence is a police attack on peaceful demonstrators. A scene of a Starbucks window being smashed highlights the intervention of other protesters to prevent it. Hooded figures with face masks form a line to protect the storefront and shouts of "Quit breaking shit! Why are you guys breaking shit?" can be heard.

The camera moves across a map of the city with a voice-over detailing the prior "violence" against people: sweatshop workers, who make the clothing for another of the demonstrators' targets—Nike. After vandalizing a bank (the Canadian Imperial Bank of Commerce) in Quebec City, a black-clad anarchist leaves a parting message: "Banks don't bleed, protesters have" (Stewart 140).

While a new breed of video and Web activists have taken media production into their own hands and can make their own stories available worldwide, they are still only narrow-casting. They are speaking to the relative few who search out indymedia Web sites or read *Z-Net* or *International Worker* online. The presence of these alternative channels may help to keep the mainstream press honest, but it is still the mainstream news sources that shape the message that reaches the majority. Quebec anarchists can spray-paint "Desinformation" across CBC press vehicles or kick in their windows, as they did in the anti-FTTA demonstrations, but these actions are not likely to change media sympathies.

Media Tactics of Authorities

Activists learned from Seattle, but so too did authorities. They were better prepared for the street battles as well as the propaganda war. Activists were put under surveillance long before the summit began. It has become easier to keep track of activist planning since so much of it takes place online. CLAC and Mobglob were quite open about promoting "diversity of tactics" in their public workshops and online discussion groups. Authorities made sure to publicize the "threat" in advance. *View from the Summit* replays a pre-summit news conference on the arrest of six would-be activists:

> ... they have been charged with conspiracy to commit life-threatening acts ... possession of explosive substances, as well as theft and possession of military supplies. This group conspired over several months with the intention of committing acts

endangering demonstrators, police and citizens.

Philippe Duhamel, of the non-violent, direct action group SalAMI (http://www.pmm.qc.ca/salami/ENGLISH/opers.html), is shown speaking to news reporters on the arrests:

> I have no proof, but I would suggest people remain skeptical. Arrests such as these on the eve of the summit, even though this group has been followed for several months, remind us of other fantastical stories of police infiltration in Quebec. It's easy to convince young people to buy compromising equipment. A well-prepared press conference was held just before the evening news, though these young people hadn't yet appeared in court.

The "fantastical stories" he refers to are the well-documented cases of criminal FLQ actions carried out by police agents provocateurs in the early 1970s. Activists continually make claims of "prior violence" on the part of agents provocateurs. These unsubstantiated and faintly conspiratorial allegations almost never make the news.

No matter how deftly video activists script the theatre of violence, the very diversity of views and tactics on the streets provide ample visual resources for "mainstream" editors to tell a different story. Despite activist arguments that protesters' actions are either defensive or aimed, never at people, but only at symbols of capitalism, the makers of *View from the Summit* were able to shoot a scene in which the Black Bloc attack police with clubs and hurl a steel barricade at them. Within this frame the police respond defensively, at least while the camera is rolling.

Vinthagen argues that demonstrators who play out the "war drama" are doomed to lose on the global media stage. Because they do not control media representation, they will inevitably fail to expose the illegitimacy of state violence or validate the cause of violent resistance. If he is right, then anti-globalization demonstrators face a new dilemma, which he does not address. That is, can the "carnival drama," colourful as it is, ever be enough to attract and sustain global media attention? Journalists themselves readily admit that when it comes to news stories, "If it bleeds, it leads." Is enacting the war drama demonstrators' best guarantee of entry onto the global virtual stage?

CIVIL SOCIETY

The street rituals of Seattle and Quebec City and their reverberations in the electronic ether are only small fragments of what people refer to as "global civil society." Nonetheless, these and similar "parallel summit" events hold part of the answer to questions that many theorists pose about what, concretely, we mean by the term. For this reason we will return to them in the following section. First, however, I want to review and expand what we already know concretely about civil society.

Civil Society: Review/Definition

In the chapter on state terror we saw how totalitarian states attempted to eradicate all checks and balances to state power first by undermining the independence of the judiciary, then by undermining or eliminating any independent platforms for political organization within civil society. We saw how the remnants of civil society formed the nucleus for eventual resistance. Of what did these remnants consist?

Organizations/Networks

In part they were networks of individuals linked by bonds of trust and histories of common struggle. They also included non-governmental organizations. NGOs are typically legal entities, incorporated to act as collective bodies on a not-for-profit basis. They also have physical assets. So, for instance, their premises were in some cases made available as free spaces for network organizing or to provide asylum for those fleeing state repression. Public space was important at least as a platform for, if not a component of, civil society. In Argentina, where so few independent NGOs survived, the Plaza de Mayo offered a place for the Madres to gather and publicly bear witness to state injustice in the disappearances of their sons and daughters.

As corporate bodies, NGOs have a kind of visibility to those at a distance who might be inclined to assist in their cause. People and organizations abroad that became aware of the human rights situation channelled support through organizations like Comité de Cooperación para la Paz en Chile (COPACHI) or the Vicaría de la Solidaridad (Vicariate of Solidarity). More recently, when people sought to assist victims of the 2004 Asian tsunami, they looked for organizations such as Médecins sans Frontières (www.msf.org) or Direct Relief International (www.directrelief.org) through which to donate money, supplies, or volunteer labour. These international links between organizations and individuals, as well as the growing number of international NGOs, such as Médecins sans Frontières, Amnesty International (www.amnesty.org) or OXFAM (www.oxfam.org), constitute another of the threads of global civil society.

Culture of "Universal Jurisdiction"

In these examples we see not just organizations and networks, but an emerging spirit of common concern that crosses borders. Recall that human rights NGOs have been working to construct an international legal regime with "universal jurisdiction" that would allow trials of state terrorists like Pinochet in courts outside of Chile. This impulse arises from a prior sense of *moral* "universal jurisdiction" that also motivated offers of assistance to torture victims in Chile and tsunami victims in Indonesia.

Between Civil Society and the State

On the basis of the Southern Cone case study, we tentatively defined civil society as "public, political activity organized independently of the state." However, case studies in other chapters have brought into question how clearly this line can be drawn between state and supposedly independent organizations. Consider co-ops. These are usually conceived of as NGOs that make up part of civil society, yet states created the special legal framework that allowed them to operate. States also set up special government departments and hired officials to promote their organization. States have attempted to use co-ops to shape political action within civil society. In Canada, the idea was to direct working-class political energies away from militant unionism.

We also saw how, more recently, NGOs and civil society have figured in neoliberal theories of how states should govern with minimal resources. Environmental NGOs, for example, were supposed to partner with socially responsible businesses, or seek funds from charitable foundations in order to solve environmental problems. Governments were supposed to set the agenda and provide guid-ance for this activity, but withdraw from the actual work as well as from the commitment of resources that that involves. It is true that well-funded international NGOs like Greenpeace (www.greenpeace.org) or the more conservative IUCN (www.IUCN.org) and WWF (www.wwf.org) act almost like "environmental departments" for states whose own capacity for environmental governance has been devastated by neoliberal SAPs.

The idea that civil society consists of political action organized independently of the state will always be problematic since states are perpetually interested in projects of co-opting civil society organizations. This is part of the nature of modern governance. In order to draw our rather arbitrary line, let us say that "independent" means that policy is not dictated by states and that the bulk of funding does not come from states. This relative independence might not be enough for NGOs to evade co-optation. Nonetheless, they may use it to take political directions at odds with state agendas, as the co-op movement did for a while in Saskatchewan.

Between Civil Society and the Market

The fact that corporations are increasingly "partnering" with NGOs and, as we saw in Chapter 9, occasionally masquerading as citizens' organizations, raises the question of independence from corporate control. At the international level, corporate rather than state co-optation may be the greater risk for NGOs that want to pursue an independent agenda. You may be surprised to learn that Direct Relief International gets much of its funding from large pharmaceutical companies, or that the IUCN gets at least some of its corporate support from oil companies like Shell and British Petroleum, automakers like BMW, and even pulp and paper companies. How might these corporate involvements influence the kind of medical aid or environmental intervention that these NGOs engage in?

Suppose we draw the line between civil society and the market (and market players like corporations) in the same way we drew the line between civil society and the state. Civil society would include only those organizations whose policy was not dictated by firms (or market logic) and the bulk of whose resources did not come from firms or market activity. The B.C. Forest Alliance, since it was entirely funded by forestry companies, would not be part of civil society by this definition. Nor would any corporate front groups.

What about the pro-free trade Canadian Alliance for Trade and Job Opportunities (CATJO)? It was created and funded by the Canadian Manufacturers' Association (CMA) and the Business Council on National Issues. The funding for both of these was largely corporate (the Council may have had foundation funding). The policies of the CMA were dictated by its member firms. What about CATJO? Does its additional step of remove from direct corporate control qualify it as "civil society?" You decide.

Civil Society: Conceptual History

Now we are defining civil society as "public, political activity organized independently of the state and the market." (Try the definition out on some difficult cases: Share groups in B.C., the UN, the NDP, the CBC.) Some political scientists will tell us that this is too easy. They know too much about the tortuous history of the concept. For example, for John Locke the term was associated with the peaceable "social contracts" on which, as he understood it, modern *states* were based.

Adam Ferguson, like his contemporary Adam Smith, saw it in the way that legal

contracts linked together people increasingly separated by the division of labour. The coordinating principle that made this atomistic behaviour coherent was the market, or what Marx derisively called the "cash nexus." Ferguson actually worried that this "civil society" would atomize people and pacify them with material comforts, thereby making societies more *vulnerable* to being overtaken by military dictatorship.

Neither theorist had a clear idea of what a coherent sociation independent of the state and market might look like. In working-class neighbourhoods, Marx actually observed new autonomous forms of social order emerging, which Locke and Ferguson were too early to observe and perhaps too middle class to take note of. However, he would never have used the words "civil society" to describe them. From reading Ferguson, as well as his one-time mentor Friedrich Hegel, Marx had come to associate the term with the "bourgeois" cash nexus. It was de Tocqueville in his book *Democracy in America* who brought concrete examples of independent organizations to the notice of liberal theorists. In many European countries such independent political associations were banned, so he had to travel to America to see them in action.

De Tocqueville marvelled at what he called the American "art of associating together." Here he is talking more about civic organizations and lobby groups than the informal networks of mutual aid, working men's clubs, and unions that Marx was so interested in.

> As soon as several inhabitants of the United States have taken up an opinion or a feeling they wish to promote in the world, they look for mutual assistance; and as soon as they have found one another out, they combine. From that mo-

ment they are no longer isolated men, but a power seen from afar, whose actions serve for example and whose language is listened to. (de Tocqueville, qtd. in Anheier, Glasius, and Kaldor 13)

It was de Tocqueville who most clearly articulated the idea that this sort of independent organization was essential to prevent democracies from falling prey to tyranny. The independent voices of civil society could criticize governments and call them to account. The organizational capacity that individuals developed through association enabled them to compete effectively for political power when governments became corrupt or ignored the will of the people.

Gramsci was one of the first to make a persuasive case that Marxists should reconsider the term. While he believed that most organizations of civil society were within the orbit of a hegemonic capitalist state, Gramsci also perceived the possibility of a war of position in which truly working-class organizations, of the type that Marx was interested in, might take a leadership role. When Marxists defined civil society, they were much more interested than liberals in drawing the line between civil society and the cash nexus.

The definition we are using draws both from de Tocqueville and Gramsci and locates civil society between state and market. However, the definition need not be tied to a Marxist political project of working-class hegemony within civil society. Nor need it be tied to a project of promoting liberal democracy. Here is a difficult problem. Consider Islamist or fascist organizations that want to establish totalitarian states. Should they be considered part of civil society?

CIVIL SOCIETY AND GLOBAL GOVERNANCE

Anheier, Glasius, and Kaldor make the case that there has been a quantitative increase in global civil society in recent decades (Anheier, Glasius, and Kaldor 4–6). They focus on what can easily be measured: numbers of organizations, membership, and formal links between organizations. The number of international NGOs dramatically increased in the 1990s from 31,000 to 37,000 in 2000 (Anheier Table R23b). This number does not include the hundreds of national NGOs in hundreds of countries that began to network with one another across borders and with international NGOs to oppose the neoliberal revolution. During this same period, the membership of international NGOs grew by over a third. Formal links between them grew by a similar amount. If what we saw in the previous chapter on coalitions is characteristic, then behind these formal links are networks of ties between people that act relatively independently of formal organizations.

Our case study of the Canadian coalition against NAFTA, the MAI, and the WTO demonstrated that this global turn in civil society is driven in part by opposition. These national and international coalitions were forged to stop the surrender of power from nation-states to global markets and global economic actors like the World Bank, the WTO, and multinational corporations. Power has shifted nonetheless, and many of these organizations have also sought to fill the vacuum of social governance at the global level.

The anti-sweatshop movement has tried to use consumer boycotts to bring social accountability to the transnational apparel industry. The fair trade movement constructs alternative supply chains, mostly in agriculture, that circumvent agribusiness and favour locally controlled co-operatives that pay fair wages and observe environmental practices. Organizations like Médecins sans Frontières and scores of "development" NGOs assist nations crippled by government cutbacks with their social welfare infrastructure, services, and "capacity building." The IUCN funds and manages the nature conservation programs in such nations.

These and myriad other NGO projects are examples of non-state governance. The UN, beginning from a much earlier period, has played a role in encouraging civil society organizations to see themselves as partners in global governance. As an organization whose funding and policy direction come entirely from member states, the UN is neither an NGO nor a "member" of civil society.

However, it has developed its own organizational culture, and follows a set of directives, spelled out in the various international treaties it is responsible for, that are often at odds with the practice of member states, but resonant with civil society values. The UN, for example, promotes the Universal Declaration of Human Rights and various environmental and labour treaties admired by international NGOs but routinely violated by UN member states.

The UN has cultivated NGO input in international forums in order to strengthen its own governmental authority. The idea has been to co-opt civil society to UN governance projects, strengthening the governance capacity of weak states and focusing popular pressure on corrupt or non-compliant states. As we saw in the case of the global indigenous movement, the UN has, since the 1970s, provided the infrastructure and resources for NGOs to act on the global stage.

While not strictly part of global civil society, the UN's New York and Geneva offices, staff, and resources have served as one of the main platforms upon which global civil society has coalesced and expanded. As the indigenous case also shows, these NGOs at the nations' table have not always bent to the UN's will.

Still, many observers are profoundly suspicious of this complicity of civil society in governance projects. Some deal with it by making a distinction between civil society and more genuine "people's organizations." We considered this argument in Chapter 9. It goes something like this. Civil society is made up of NGOs that have full-time staff and large budgets that they must finance through donations from states, corporations, or foundations. These organizations consequently tend to be implicated in the governance projects of states or corporations. They speak more in the interests of such projects than the interests of the people they supposedly serve or represent. People's organizations, by contrast, are spontaneous, self-organized, and volunteer. They consist of people speaking in their own voice.

Organizations do vary on these dimensions. Perhaps there are pure forms of grassroots organization. Perhaps the cyberanarchists will devise a way to make unmediated political action flourish and remain viable across spans of space and over time. However, the reality is that most popular organizing, on closer inspection, turns out to be mediated in some way. Remember that even the anti-toxics movement, that most grassroots example of popular environmentalism in America, mobilized with support from organizations funded by foundations. The need for organizational infrastructure and material resources increases at the transnational level as distances across which people must meet and coordinate action widen.

Mediation increases the risk of co-optation. However, I suggest that we avoid building the presumption that civil society organizations are co-opted into our definition of civil society. Co-optation can be addressed as a separate issue to be evaluated through critical case study. Of course, you are free to disagree, and by this time, so close to the end of this book, you should have a good basis for independently formulating and defending your own views.

In summary, global civil society is public political activity organized independently of the state and market and in which the players act across national borders. In an effort to picture what it is concretely, we have invoked the idea of formal organizations, the physical spaces and resources at their disposal, and the formal exchanges between them. Civil society also involves networks of people linked abstractly by common frameworks of understanding as well as feelings of trust, and concretely by transportation and communications infrastructure.

There is probably no "master frame" for people within these networks, but there are at least widely held understandings around the values of "universal jurisdiction" and "popular sovereignty." Civil society is also criss-crossed by social movements, such as the counter-globalization movement, that have less formal, quantifiable dimensions. These tend to be visibly embodied in parallel summits where transitory teams show up, and elements of transnational movement cultures—the puppets, the slogans ("People before Profits!"), the revolutionary chic—are manifest. It is to the parallel summit, as instantiation of global civil society, that we return in the next section.

LOGIC OF PARALLEL CIVIL SOCIETY SUMMITS

Here we return to a question posed at the beginning of the chapter: For those social movements that seek to act on the global stage, and civil society organizations that want a voice in emerging global governance, how crucial is it that they have access to global public space—the cities that serve as the physical platforms for global summits? What is the value of physical public space? What exactly takes place among people who converge en mass in the flesh and how does this contribute to the project of building a movement or building civil society?

Public Space and Open Discourse

Much of the preparation for both Seattle and Quebec City took place online. Scores of anti-corporate organizations like CorpWatch (www.corpwatch.org), Global Exchange (www.globalexchange.org), Public Citizen (www.citizen.org), and Third World Network (www.twnside.org.sg) published news and analysis on their Web sites. These functioned like public teach-ins online through which many affinity groups and would-be transitory team members armed themselves with knowledge of the issues.

Many had been engaging in political action through signing online petitions (e.g., MoveOn.org), or writing letters of protest initiated by the Campaign for Labor Rights (www.clrlabor.org) or Amnesty (www.amnesty.org). Others engaged in political discussions and planning through listservs, like Mobglob (https://lists.resist.ca/mailman/listinfo/mobglob-discuss) and the Student Activist Network (www.civilrights.org/campaigns/student_activist/) or on interactive news sites like Indymedia (www.indymedia.org).

While some online forums were open only to known and trusted circles of activists, most of this activity was public. That is, it was open to anyone with Internet access. However, it lacked an important feature that theorists associate with genuine public space. These online venues were effectively walled off from the daily traffic of the Internet. To find them you would have to either know in advance where to look or else track them down through a search engine.

The physical world parallel is a public talk or discussion that takes place in a classroom or meeting room in a library basement. The public will never see it unless they learn of the time and place in advance. These are open access, but spatially walled off or compartmentalized events.

Truly public spaces are both open access and spatially transparent. They allow for random encounters. On a university campus, in a public square, or pedestrian promenade, people going about their private daily pursuits might notice a poster stapled to a power pole, be handed a political pamphlet, or witness a speech, rally, or other political event.

These spaces of serendipitous encounter can provide a gateway to compartmentalized public events in the physical or the virtual world. You may learn from the pamphlet handed to you that Vandana Shiva will be talking about biopiracy later that day on campus or be directed to the Etc. Group Web site (www.etcgroup.org) to learn more about the environmental risks of nanotechnology.

The only unsolicited encounters you are likely to have online in your daily pursuit of MP3 downloads, online banking, or whatever your particular cyber-pleasure are commercial banner ads, or perhaps the news and sports that AOL sees fit to post on its Internet portal. Many theorists worry that physical space, particularly in automobile-dependent North American cities, is becoming similarly compartmentalized and commercialized.

Automobile-dependent people see billboards on the freeway. Convenience draws them to places where parking is easy, like shopping malls. Here they can actually walk among throngs of people and be exposed to unscripted encounters, but these are more likely to be promotions for a new perfume or credit card than for a political cause. Malls are privately owned "public" spaces where postering, leafleting, and participating in political demonstrations are prohibited. These are pseudo-public spaces that are physically open, but in which the rights of free speech and assembly can legally be denied (Kohn 71–72).

BOX 12.1:

WHOSE PUBLIC SPACE?

Public space is a kind of physical "mainstream." Think of the places in cities that seem always to attract vibrant street life. Some people are there just to pass through on their way to offices, subways, or theatres; some are there for the shops, cafés, or galleries; some are there just to people-watch or be part of the scene. There is a constant stream of people. Unlike media mainstreams, these are open to anyone who wanders by. Here people tell their stories just by their physical presence. The panhandlers and the Lincoln Navigators are actors in a free documentary about the social conditions in the city.

These are also sites where those who cannot afford billboards or TV ads or who do not have the public authority to attract coverage in the newspapers or electronic media come to have their voices heard. People rarely stand on soapboxes and harangue the crowd. They are much more likely to hand out leaflets or put up posters that say, "Here is the issue. If you want to know more, read this or come to a meeting at such and such place and time." Public spaces offer free "mainstream" advertising to marginal voices. The thing about marginal voices is that most people do not want to hear them. City governments make repeated attempts to silence them.

Some city councillors in Toronto want to ban postering. They see do-it-yourself handbills stapled in layers on utility poles or pasted to construction hoardings as unsightly and annoying. Advocates for public space like Matthew Blackett argue that they are no more annoying than corporate advertising, which takes up far more public space. "It just seemed wrong to ban posters for garage sales, lost dogs, indie rock bands, and ESL lessons while the city allowed the proliferation of massive corporate advertising. Somehow the idea got into some people's head that a Room for Rent poster was a horrible blight on the urban landscape, but massive iPod ads covering entire subway stations was just a-okay." Activists see postering as essential to political organizing and a right of free speech.

"The anti-postering bylaw is a blatant attack on human rights and is unconstitutional," writes Dylan Penner of the Toronto Coalition to Stop the War (TCSW). "Postering is critical to TCSW's efforts to end the illegal occupation of Iraq; we are using posters to organize an upcoming demonstration on March 19, for example" (Harpham). The Supreme Court of Canada agrees (*Peterborough v. Ramsden*, 1998) that banning posters would be a violation of Canada's Charter of Rights. The principle here is that the majority (represented by elected city councillors) cannot silence minority voices. However, the Court allowed that cities could regulate postering. So the new question becomes whether the regulations of postering proposed by city councils are so limiting or so onerously difficult as to limit free speech.

In 2002 Toronto was proposing to limit poster size to 11 by 17 inches and location to 4,000 specially designated poles. In addition, posters would have to be taken down after a certain time. Blogger Andrew Rowell points out that 4,000 is only 2 percent of the utility poles in the city and that competition for postering space is so great that "... whatever someone puts up will likely be covered up within a couple of hours." "If this bylaw were to come into force," argues Penner, of TCSW, "and the coalition continued postering for future demonstrations, we would be faced with fines of hundreds of thousands of dollars per demonstration.... If that isn't an attack on free speech, what is?" (Harpham). Clearly there will always be those who think that any restriction on public discourse is illegitimate and should be challenged. The further question that Penner raises is how heavily such dissent should be penalized.

Graffiti is a type of free public, and often political, expression. Along with the "liberation" of the streets of Paris in 1968 came an explosion of graffiti: "Humanity will not be happy until the last capitalist is hung with the entrails of the last bureaucrat." "Be realistic, demand the impossible!" In Latin American countries, people spray-paint stencilled images of revolutionary heroes or revolutionary "logos" on the walls, or devote whole murals to political subjects. In Zimbabwe, where free speech has been ruthlessly repressed, graffiti has become the most popular form of speaking out. In the United States, "freeway bloggers" (see www.freewayblogger.com) have been posting their opinions ("I'm tired of hearing what rich people think," says one) on the "mainstream" of the American freeway. For some, graffiti is political speech; others see it as the art of the disenfranchised (for some truly beautiful examples of street art, see www.streetsy.com).

For others, of course, it is "vandalism," an attack on public and private property. In 2006 the London, Ontario, city council attempted to combat it by banning the sale of marking pens and spray paint to people under the age of 18. The law is a milder version of a recent New York law that makes it illegal for anyone under the age of 21 to even possess these offending items. Remember, what is being banned here is not the act of graffiti, but the tools that make it, as well as a whole series of other benign uses. Councillor David Winninger has called the London bylaw "ludicrous." "It's an offence to the Charter of Rights," he says, "It's not reasonable that it can be justified in a free and democratic society" (CBC). What do you think?

Sources: Matthew Blackett, "Anti-postering By-law Not So Anti Anymore," *Spacing Wire*, 2006. May 20, 2006, http://spacing.ca/wire/?p=582; CBC, "Anti-graffiti Crackdown Bans Spray Paint Sales to Minors," CBC News Online, 2006, May 19, 2006, www.cbc.ca; Bruce Harpham, "Proposed Poster Ban 'Attacks Free speech,'" *The Varsity*, March 17, 2005. May 20, 2006, www.thevarsity.ca/media/storage/paper285/news/2005/03/17/News/Proposed.Poster.Ban.attacks.Free.Speech-896631.shtml?norewrite200605201639&sourcedomain=www.thevarsity.ca.

At parallel summits not all of the civil society action takes place on the streets. NGOs, sometimes in collaboration with the official summit organizers, book venues for parallel "people's summits." Like the official summits, these involve talks, workshops, and discussions. Just as indigenous peoples have done at UN forums, people come to bear witness to their experiences of oppression. Meeting and listening to a maquiladora worker gives the anti-sweatshop struggle an immediacy and human face for those unaware of it, as well as for those aware only at a distance and in the abstract.

The compartmentalized public space of the conference venue works well for fleshing out online convictions, commitments, and personal connections through face-to-face contact. People network, renew and strengthen old bonds, and forge new ones. Threads of contact weave between virtual and physical space. People trade e-mail and Web addresses, or bump into cyber-contacts in the flesh. "As I was leaving and introduced myself to the young woman I had been speaking with," recounts a Net activist at Quebec City, "another student turned to me and said, 'Did you say Janet Eaton? Don't you post to the Student Activist Network?'" (Eaton).

Public Space and the Ritual Embodiment of Civil Society

Face-to-face dialogue is a component in building trust and strengthening informal networks. Something richer and more emotionally moving happens in the streets, not so much through dialogue as through ritual. We have seen this before in the reclaiming and transforming of institutional space that happened in 1960s occupations of buildings and the Gay Pride parades of the 1970s. These were ritual enactments of the idea that another world is possible. We have already seen examples from Quebec City of parody of the existing order—its barriers, borders, and military exclusions—in what Vinthagen calls the "festival drama." Both in Quebec and Seattle there were also dramatizations of inclusive acceptance, caring, and mutual aid.

Kevin MacKay describes how activists "expressed their political vision through paintings, music and dance, while a tireless contingent of Food Not Bombs activists from Winnipeg staffed a free kitchen, providing vegetarian meals to thousands of protestors" (MacKay 15). Sharing food is an ancient human ritual of affirming social bonds. Here, the rite that Durkheim called "alimentary communion" is not for a select circle but open to anyone and everyone. It is an eloquent statement of what Marx once called the "brotherhood of man."

Everywhere in Seattle and Quebec City, volunteer "street medics" were on hand to give assistance to people overcome by pepper spray or tear gas or injured by rubber bullets. They would hold victims' heads, flush their eyes with water, calm and reassure them. In what more tangible way could people express the values of human commitment and mutual aid that so many feel are absent from the neoliberal agenda?

Two of the most moving moments in *This Is What Democracy Looks Like* are similar acts of communion. In one shot a group of protestors is blocking a city street, resolved to sit and wait for arrest. A woman, obviously afraid, looks desperately to a companion for reassurance. He encircles her in his arms in a primordial gesture of protectiveness. Another is at the solidarity action outside the King County jail. One of the lawyers from the volunteer legal team is speaking to the crowd through a megaphone. She asks people to hold hands and repeat after her, ritually dramatizing their connection and the idea of speaking in "one voice." She gives updates on the negotiations for the prisoners' release, talks about the fact that some of them have been beaten while in prison. Then she tells the assembled crowd, "The people inside can hear you!" A cheer goes up from the crowd, and hands appear waving from behind the smoked glass windows high on the prison wall. This fragile but intense need to reach out, to touch, to make physical contact is unaccountably moving.

From dancing in the street to jail solidarity actions, ritual is about physical, collective co-presence. The collective dimension conveys a power and intensity of meaning that the one-on-one interaction involved in networking, important as it is, can never

quite match. On the street, instant and abstract bonds of trust and allegiance take shape. What I mean by "abstract" is not that they are in some way intellectual, but that they are not directed to a specific individual or identifiable set of people. "Anonymous" might be a better term.

Interestingly, some of the more powerful ritual experiences are those of opposition and defence that are made possible by the "war drama." Without it, the medics and jail solidarity would be meaningless. For all the difficulty of framing the "war drama" on the virtual media stage, it can play very effectively to the crowd on the streets when they indiscriminately become the targets of police repression.

MacKay argues that it created solidarity across the tactical divides. He quotes a union member from a public sector union, who was won over, even to Black Bloc tactics.

> The thud of tear gas was continuous. The canisters would fly in a high arc and then crash down to the ground. We would try to chart the parabola and avoid being hit. When the canisters smashed onto the ground they would bounce and spin, spewing out poison. Then, something amazing would happen. A black-clad figure with a gas-mask would appear from nowhere and hurl the bomb back over the fence at the police. Every time one was lobbed back, a huge cheer went up from the crowd.
>
> I guess these "bomb disposal teams" were the anarchists—CLAC, the Black Bloc. Usually they were like ghosts, invisible, and then they would suddenly appear and deal with tear gas. Other times, they would snake in a line through the protest, heading towards the fence. The crowd would part and

let them through. As the afternoon continued, our admiration for them steadily grew. (qtd. in MacKay 29)

It certainly was the sort of tangible demonstration of commitment that helped people feel embraced across racial lines. Black activist Hop Hopkins describes jail in Seattle as a positive experience. Even though he was one of the few people of colour,

> ... it was good experience to be there in jail to recognize, hey, no matter where these people are coming from, right? ... they decided that they had had enough and that they were willing to lay what ever they had—which at that time was really their body—down for the cause. And to be with the group of people no matter where you were coming from is [a] very powerful thing. (qtd. in Freidberg and Rowley)

Similarly, a Canadian protestor of Filipino descent describes being

> ... especially touched and hopeful when I see and hear stories of thousands of students and workers around the world who are willing to endure arrests, tear gas and rubber bullets to fight for change. The image of students in Seattle raising their hands in peace signs nearly two years ago at the World Trade Organization demonstrations, and again in Québec City as they confronted rows of police in riot gear, will remain with me for a long time. (qtd. in MacKay 30)

In both cases it is the demonstration of bodily commitment and sacrifice that carries such emotional weight.

The voice-over in *This Is What Democracy Looks Like* records a bodily experience of an awakening power:

> ... when we filled the streets of Seattle, there was a power in our bodies that we didn't know we had. In this city, for this moment, our lives were our own. Who can say at what precise location and at what exact hour and date this global movement began? In Seattle we were only a small part of the movement, but in the gas and bullets our memory returned. For a moment our history was made clear to us; we felt the edges of our skin marked by global and historical struggle. We stopped waiting for our world to be legislated or prescribed to us; this time we did not ask for permission to be free.

The cumulative effect is euphoric. MacKay aptly invokes Durkheim's term "collective effervescence" to describe it. He quotes the description given by a labour marcher of the spirit of the Quebec City demonstrations.

> Griselda can't stop smiling. Her dark eyes are glowing. She is full of life. She jumps to see what is going on up front of the parade.... Now, she is marching, holding hands with people she has never met before. It doesn't matter—they are sisters and brothers in the struggle...
>
> I'm happy here. Maybe more, I'm exultant, radiant, thrilled. I cannot stop chanting. Shouting. "so-so-solidarité, so-so-so solidarité!" My throat is hurting, it doesn't matter. "The people, united, will never be defeated!" Some friends want to join our group, so I give away my steelworker vest and hat. I keep the flag

and wrap it over my shoulders—part
political marcher, part soccer fan.
(qtd. in MacKay 32)

For Durkheim, collective effervescence was about not just "revivifying" connections among an aggregate of people. "[A] society," he wrote in 1915, "is not made up merely of the mass of individuals who compose it, the ground which they occupy, the things which they use and the movements which they perform, but above all is the idea which it forms of itself." The creation of this idea "... is the act by which it is periodically made and re-made" (470).

Durkheim understood that the physical spaces of public assembly and procession were necessary sites for the ritual embodiment of our abstract conceptions of "society." Or, to borrow Benedict Anderson's term, public ritual in these spaces is a technique for making tangible those anonymous, translocal "imagined communities" of which we are a part. Could this be what was happening in the streets of Seattle and Quebec City: giving tangible, emotional shape to the idea of not a national society but a global civil society that is more extensive and anonymous than the collection of individuals assembled at those places at those particular moments?

BOX 12.2:

THE HUMONGOUS FUNGUS

In 1992 the discovery of the first humongous fungus (*Armillaria bulbosa*) was published in the journal *Science*. Since then, other and even larger fungi have been documented. The most impressive to date is an *Armillaria astoyae* in the Blue Mountains of Oregon thought to be as old as 8,500 years and covering an area of over 9.65 square kilometres (equivalent to 6,000 hockey rinks for those of you who think in these terms). All that you can see are little mushrooms, like the ones you find on your pizza, that pop up briefly on the surface of the forest floor. The rest of this huge organism consists of a tangle of filaments, or rhizomorphs, that weave blindly in all directions and spread out over vast distances beneath the surface of the soil.

When I first learned of the humongous fungus, I thought it an apt metaphor for global civil society. The rhizomorphs are like the translocal networks of activists and NGOs whose ongoing work is normally invisible to the casual observer. The mushrooms are like parallel summits, demonstrations, and other public events where civil society pops to the surface in visible, tangible embodiments. Each of these events, no matter how large and inclusive, is only a fragment of the underlying reality, but it can stand for that reality in our minds.

Thomas J. Volk, one of the first scientists to document the scale of these life forms, describes the subterranean rhizomorphs as being "... able to transport food and other materials long distances, thus allowing the fungus to grow through nutrient poor areas located between large food sources such as stumps." Think of places like Argentina, Chile, or Uruguay under the dictatorships as nutrient-poor areas for civil society, and the translocal links to international NGOs as rhizomorphs of global civil society fuelling the efforts of the few tentative "mushrooms" attempting to survive there. "The rhizomorphs," Volk continues, "can also act as 'scouts' for the rest of the thallus, searching for new food sources. These proliferative rhizomorphs apparently permit *Armillaria* colonies to spread and become quite large." The parallel here is not perfect, but consider the way in which planning for and siting large civil society events in various locales helps to enlarge and reinforce contacts and build local organizational capacity.

"Rhizome" and "rhizomatic" have also become popular terms in cultural studies and the social sciences. While "rhizomes" and "rhizomorphs" are not the same biological entities, they are similar enough in structure and function to bear the same metaphorical connotations. Deleuze and Guattari, in their 1987 book *A Thousand Plateaus: Capitalism and Schizophrenia*, explain, rather obscurely, the potential of the rhizome concept. Consider how well you think it applies to global civil society. The rhizome, they tell us, embodies six principles.

Principles 1 and 2 are "connection and heterogeneity." Rhizomes consist of networks in which numerous parallel connections open up multiple routes to any point. There is no hierarchy of switching stations to channel flows, and no "choke points" from which to control access. There is no single, uniform set of communications protocols, "... only a throng of dialects, patois, slangs, and specialized languages."

Principle 3 is "multiplicity." "There is no unity," write Deleuze and Guattari, "to serve as a pivot in the object, or to divide in the subject." To flesh out their rather obscure meaning, they use the metaphor of puppets connected to puppets, their strings a tangled weave that neither one pulls as the "puppeteer." (Normally the puppet would be the object, under the control of the puppeteer—the subject.) There is no central command point and no overall unifying subject. Applied to civil society, this might mean that there is neither a homogeneous "collective identity" nor leading "revolutionary subject."

Principle 4 is "asignifying rupture." Of this they write, "transversal communications between different lines scramble the genealogical trees.... The rhizome is an anti-genealogy." Picture a genealogical chart listing your family tree. This is a hierarchical structure in which, we suppose, a genetic "idea" (your great-grandmother's DNA, let's say) flows one way in time. Your guess may be as good as mine, but I take them to mean that the generative ideas of the rhizome cannot simply be traced through a history of "development" (they are implicitly taking aim at the historical, "genealogical" method of Foucault), but are subject to surprising cross-fertilizations acting laterally, in the moment.

Principles 5 and 6 are "cartography and decalcomania." The rhizome, they tell us, "... rejects any idea of pretraced destiny, whatever name is given to it—divine, anagogic, historical, economic, structural, hereditary, or syntagmatic." There is no teleology, no laws of history that can predict how rhizome structures will unfold over time.

What do you think? Is the rhizome or the humongous fungus or perhaps the rhizomatic humongous fungus a useful metaphor for global civil society? The translocal networks of global civil society are non-linear. Social scientists are still grappling with how to conceive of them and what they are likely to become. The value of Deleuze and Guattari's difficult, metaphorical language may simply be to help disturb our habitual conceptual paths and think laterally and creatively about this new problem.

Source: Gilles Deleuze and Félix Guattari, *A Thousand Plateaus: Capitalism and Schizophrenia* (Minneapolis: University of Minnesota Press, 1987); Tom Volk, "The Humongous Fungus—Ten Years Later," 2002. May 19, 2006, http://botit.botany.wisc.edu/TOMS_FUNGI/apr2002.html.

CHANGING SPATIAL LOGIC OF PARALLEL SUMMITS

Since the turn of the century, all of the global players that host summits and attract parallel summits—the WTO, the World Economic Forum, the FTAA, the EU, and even the UN—have become increasingly hostile toward demonstrations of civil society. States and city governments have obliged by enclosing public space, walling it off, or clearing it out through the kinds of draconian legislation and policing that in the U.S. came to be known as the "Miami Model."

When the FTAA meetings were held in Miami in 2003, the city passed an ordinance banning many of the props of demonstration, including wood thicker than ¼ inch, spray paint, pointed objects (e.g., scissors), on the grounds that they could be used as weapons, as well as anything that demonstrators could use to defend themselves against police violence: body armour or anything that "would protect the respiratory tract and face against irritating, noxious or poisonous gasses" (TEXT of Miami City Ordinance).

The security panic post-9/11 enabled authorities to introduce new legislation and police to push the boundaries of that legislation at the cost of civil liberties. Despite what you might expect, however, public demonstrations on the global stage have only increased in scale. True, in the United States for a time, patriotic rallying around the president's War on Terror had a chilling effect on demonstrations. Organized labour and some of the more institutionalized NGOs became leery of being seen on the streets with the anti-globalists and peace activists (Huber and McCallum). However, the focus of action shifted to anti-war demonstrations centred in Europe and summits often parallel in time with official events but in separate cities away from metropolitan centres in Europe and North America.

The World Social Forum: Temporally Parallel/Spatially Separate

The World Social Forum (WSF), held for the first time in 2000 in Porto Alegre, Brazil, was an attempt to refocus the agenda of civil society activism. For some years a power elite—representatives of major states, corporations, and multilateral agencies—had been meeting and helping to set the global agenda in what they called the World Economic Forum in Davos, Switzerland. Instead of denouncing this forum and the vision of globalization it represented, the idea of the Social Forum organizers was to formulate constructive alternatives. Their slogan was "Another world is possible."

The spatial remove, half the globe away from Davos, would preclude the deployment of military street tactics and would make little sense as a stage for the confrontational "war drama." If there was to be confrontation, it should be the confrontation of images and ideas juxtaposed on people's TV screens or in the news. Regardless of distance, the two temporally parallel events could be linked through what McLuhan called the electronic sensorium.

Despite MacKay's argument about the potential of the war drama to weld labour and Black Bloc in solidarity, serious splits were developing over "diversity of tactics." *View from the Summit* follows ongoing exchanges between Tania Halle and Jaggi Singh of CLAC and Philippe Duhamel and Myreille Audet of SalAMI as they prepare for Quebec City. SalAMI is organizing civil disobedience and its members expect to get arrested, but they want to avoid inciting violence. "Can I assure my mother and other relatives," Duhamel asks Singh, "that they won't be hit by Molotov cocktails? Will there be bombs? We haven't debated the limits of 'diversity.'" Of course the anarchists cannot speak for others or give an itemized list of what others may or may not do.

As it turns out, Molotov cocktails were thrown (by agents provocateurs—who knows?). Later that summer a protester at the G8 summit in Genoa was shot dead by police. Despite the effort to designate "green zones" in Quebec City, the police did not respect them and filled them with tear gas and stray rubber bullets nonetheless. At one particularly chaotic point during the demonstrations, Audet and Duhamel ambush Singh on camera.

> *Audet:* "I was dragged here willy-nilly. I'm seven months pregnant. I was carried along by people running like maniacs."
> *Jaggi:* "We had a green zone."
> *Duhamel:* "It was predictable...."
> *Audet:* "... anything happens to me, I'll hold you personally responsible."
> *Duhamel:* "She's pregnant. There are children here, all kinds of people."
> *Audet:* "You knew! Don't be hypocritical."
> *Singh:* "You're being demagogic. We had nothing to do with it.... You and Myreille have done the most demagogic thing that I seen recently; you're not novices.... You come here when a camera is running! You come here when a camera is running to tell us this.... You do stage-managed things...."
> Halle: "You guys are all fucked up."

The argument that is implicitly being made here is that CLAC, by licensing violence, is imposing that tactic and its consequences on others. It is not a discursive imposition—anarchists never dictate in this way to others—but it is a situational imposition. If you are there when they initiate violence, it spills out uncontrollably in all directions, and you, despite yourself, are forced to become part of it.

In Porto Alegre the police have to be pro-demonstrator. Both the city and the state governments are run by the Brazilian Workers' Party (Partido dos Trabalhadores), which is unabashedly socialist. It was refreshing, writes Naomi Klein, for people "accustomed to being met with clouds of pepper spray, border strip searches and no-protest zones" instead to be "welcomed by friendly police officers and greeters with official banners from the tourist department" (Klein, "Fete"). Public space was made freely available and people used it primarily for the lectures, discussions, and round tables of formal summitry. There were also "carnival dramas" in the streets, as well as examples of state-sponsored spectacle.

Klein was among the first to identify a new risk in this context, that of being co-opted by statist conceptions of socialism. The most promising discussions about new models of democracy were, in her view, anarchist influenced.

> The ideas flying around included neighbourhood councils, participatory budgets, stronger city governments, land reform and cooperative farming—a vision of politicized communities that could be networked internationally to resist further assaults from the IMF, the World Bank and World Trade Organization. For a left that had tended to look to centralized state solutions to solve almost every problem, this emphasis on decentralization and direct participation was a breakthrough. (Klein, "Hijacking of the WSF")

However, she saw signs that socialist heads of state like Brazil's recently elected Lula da Silva and Venezuela's Hugo Chávez were interested in the forum as a platform for their own visions of socialist democracy.

When the forum was hosted by Chávez in 2006, local anarchists felt it necessary to organize an *Alter-Foro* (Alternative Forum) in order to raise their concerns about the lack of independent civil society within Venezuela and ways in which they felt Chávez was attempting to bask in the appearance of active civil society support while exercising an old style *caudillo* or strongman authoritarian style of governance (Uzcategui 15; Decali 11).

Whatever Chávez's intent, the very fact of hosting an international civil society event no doubt strengthened local civil society. Local NGOs may not have gained as much as they could have in organizational capacity since much of the forum logistics was provided by the military, but they certainly benefited from face-to-face networking.

This is one of the benefits of locating civil society summits in cities of the South. Wherever a civil society summit is held, close to half of the NGOs involved come from the host country. The overwhelming majority come from the region, with minimal representation from other continents, with the possible exception of western Europe.

When the UN Conference on Environment and Development was held in Rio in 1992, a large handful of African NGOs had delegates present, but there were thousands of Latin American NGOs. When the follow-up World Summit on Sustainable Development was held 10 years later in Johannesburg, the pattern was reversed. The World Social Forum attempted to expand its representation in 2006 by holding a "polycentric" event in three continents of the South: Caracas, Venezuela (South America); Bamako, Mali (Africa); and Karachi, Pakistan (Asia).

World Social Forums are globally connected thorough the Internet. For example, the 2002 forum Web site hosted a half a million visitors a day (Karliner). However, they are largely invisible through the other electronic media. The North American mainstream media that headlined Seattle, Quebec City, and Genoa virtually ignore the WSF. Perhaps it is arrogant disinterest in events that take place in the developing world. Admittedly the UN-sanctioned environmental summits in Rio and Johannesburg attracted the global media spotlight, but all the key heads of state were present alongside civil society.

The fact that heads of state are meeting in Davos does not mean that media crews will also be flown to Porto Alegre. Perhaps, and this could be the sad dilemma for civil society, the only guarantee that the global media stage will light up for civil society demonstrations is if the demonstrators are close enough to threaten heads of state or to invoke the war drama.

Global Hybrids of Virtual/Physical Space

There are ways around this dilemma. In fact, despite all obstacles, civil society networks mobilized the largest street demonstration in human history in 2003, this time to full global media coverage. Some argue that the "Porto Alegre camp" was the initiating force. (Walgrave and Verhulst, cited in "February 15, 2003 Anti-War Protest"). This may be true, but at the same time support for the idea spread rhizomatically from multiple directions, taking multiple routes. While many media of communication were involved, the most rapid and rhizomatic was undoubtedly the Internet.

Eventually thousands of local networks in 800 cities and uncounted towns around the globe were preparing marches, rallies, and speeches for February 15, against the war in Iraq. The mitochondrial filaments of this "humongous fungus" reached all the way to the Antarctic where polar scientists staged their own tiny demonstration. Communist China was the only country with no recorded response.

Many Europeans organized to bus people from the small towns to demonstrations in major cities. The streets of Rome were filled with 3 million people, more than any recorded single demonstration and more than police could possibly have controlled even if they had hoped to. (Remember, Seattle was only 50,000.) In Antigonish, the small town where I teach, a few made the long trip to Halifax. However, it was a bitterly cold February and many were not in the mood for long road trips, so the rest, 200–300 people (massive for a conservative town of 7,000), held a march down Main Street and a rally in the United Church hall. When speakers relayed the news of demonstrations around the world—half a million here, a million there, perhaps 10 or 12 million worldwide (later estimates went as high as 30 million)—we really felt like we were part of something huge and truly global.

We were—in the sense of being linked at multiple points, through our personal acquaintances and contacts in town and beyond to that invisible global network. The translocal events unfolding on the streets, animated first through network channels then reflected back to us through the global media, was a physical demonstration of that. A rumour sprang up, whether true or not does not matter, that Nelson Mandela had asked people who could not take part in the streets to place a lighted candle in their windows. It brought an image to my mind of not just small places like Antigonish, but "microsites" of private homes whose occupants were linked in ritual demonstration, like millions of Deleuze and Guattari puppets connected by uncountable horizontal filaments. Might this intertwining of the virtual and the embodied be the shape of public rituals in the future?

In these hybrids the scope and strength of virtual networks might facilitate flexible, spontaneous, and surprising ways to route around physical and legislative constraints. Recall Rheingold's model of the smart mob that through mobile peer-to-peer networking, such as text messaging with cellphones, learns and self-organizes actions on the fly. He shows how the reflexive feedback that this allows enabled Philippine demonstrators in 2001 to assess their own strength prior to assembling in the capitol, Manila. Knowing in advance the capacity of their numbers to intimidate police lowered the "action threshold" for would-be participants. In Seattle a broader range of electronic communications tools were networked to create "a pulsing infosphere of enormous bandwidth, reaching around the planet via the Internet" (de Armond 211). The Direct Action Network was able to use it to coordinate its tactical movements vis-à-vis police.

My own experience in Johannesburg at the 2002 World Summit on Sustainable Development confirms the potential of such virtual linkages. Johannesburg is a divided, privatized city with few public spaces that are either safe or legally open access. Parallel summit venues were ghettoized in compartmentalized public spaces widely dispersed throughout the city. Official planning was unreliable. Without a public transit system, physical movement between venues was difficult, but delegates worked around these limitations by networking constantly through text messaging and logging on at free Internet portals made widely available.

Authorities had hoped to discourage any large anti-neoliberal demonstrations. Both the South African government and the UN faced mounting popular opposition to the neoliberal drift of their policies. Nonetheless, a core of civil society activists was able to mobilize a hugely successful protest demonstration from Alexandria, a poor Black township, to Sandton, the glittering site of the official UN summit. Their tools were the "pulsing infosphere" that overcame physical barriers to communication as well as the eye of the global media that made the South African authorities reluctant to appear overtly oppressive against an international civil society demonstration (Bantjes 22).

CONCLUSION

In this chapter we have looked at the parallel summits in which NGOs and social movement actors have shadowed the meetings of global decision makers. We have treated the parallel summit as one spatial instantiation of the phenomenon that people have been calling "global civil society." Two sorts of global action take place at these parallel events: civil society conferences or "people's summits" and demonstrations. In order to accommodate huge convergences of people, these events demand the physical space and logistical capacity that only world-class cities can afford. While civil society conferences can be sequestered in private conference venues or walled-off public spaces (what we have called "compartmentalized public space"), global demonstrations require genuine, open-access public space. In addition to the mainstream visibility of streets, boulevards, and public squares, they require, in order to be truly global, visibility on the global media stage.

World-class cities have, however, become increasingly hostile to global demonstrations. Authorities have sought through physical barriers, border exclusions, restrictive laws, and policing to "enclose" public space. This 21st-century trend raises ethical questions regarding the acceptable limits to civil rights of assembly and free speech. It also raises theoretical and tactical questions for emergent global civil society. One such

question has to do with the value of street drama for realizing in concrete terms the abstraction of global civil society.

Face-to-face interaction helps to cement virtual connections and extend networks of collaboration. However, the collective effervescence of open public assemblies adds an emotional intensity to these connections that mere conferencing cannot. Physical ritual, touch, collective acts of sharing, and spontaneous gifts of mutual aid all contribute to often euphoric experiences of communion and trust. Ritual events evoke these sensations in those physically assembled, but also *represent* communion with distant anonymous others who comprise global civil society as an "imagined community."

MacKay has pointed out how clashes with police, in what we have called the "theatre of violence," help to intensify bonds among demonstrators. Vinthagen, by contrast, has argued that invoking what he calls the "war drama" is always a losing tactic. Demonstrators hope to expose and de-legitimate state violence. However, they have little control over how events will be represented in the "electronic *global mass media stage.*" In this arena, tremendous ideological work is invested in portraying protester, rather than police, violence as illegitimate.

This situation presents a dilemma for demonstrators, for, as the experience of the World Social Forum (WSF) has shown, global media attention is less likely to be drawn to demonstrations without the lurid threat of violence. Media disinterest has weakened the power of the WSF strategy of holding civil society summits that are parallel in time but not physically proximate to state/corporate summits. The two have not tended to be linked in the imaginations of a wider public through the electronic sensorium.

The temporally parallel, physically separate summit is one strategy for overcoming the enclosure of public space. We briefly considered other models for organizing and staging global demonstrations that at least point to new potentials for working around physical and legal restrictions on public assembly. The massive anti-war demonstration of February 15, 2003, used rhizomatic virtual channels to coordinate activities and flood every available public arena on the globe. The result was a peaceful mega-demonstration whose unprecedented scale made it impossible for the global media to ignore.

The Johannesburg example illustrated the potential of the "pulsing infosphere" not just for mobilizing across physical barriers, but doing so rapidly, flexibly, in ways that outpace attempts at containing them. Finally, the February 15 event pointed to a possibility that not only the mobilization for but the demonstration itself might function as a virtual/physical hybrid in which countless "microsites" might be coordinated in ritual action. These microsites need not be classic examples of public space—the requisite scale and openness can instead be created by virtual links.

In addition to discussing the role of physical platforms and performances in concretely realizing global civil society, we have also attempted to define what, concretely, global civil society is. Abstractly defined, it is "public, political activity organized independently of the state and market and in which the players act across national borders." Its tangible expressions include NGOs, formal and informal networks, and the physical infrastructure that sustains them. They also include the parallel summits that serve as a visible, public embodiment of these often invisible networks. Parallel summits also ritually embody social movement cultures and provide a platform for the affinity groups and transitory teams that loosely affiliate with these cultures.

We have tried not to burden the definition of civil society with any particular political project—the hegemony of an anti-capitalist working class as envisioned by Gramsci, or the building of liberal democracy on the pluralistic model of de Tocqueville. However, we have noted that at this particular historical moment there may be an emerging "master frame" for global civil society around the values of "universal jurisdiction" and "popular sovereignty."

Throughout this text I have highlighted social movements' turn to the global. The coalescence of the rhizomatic connections that have built up throughout the 20th century into something that people want to call global civil society is one of the most interesting and important developments of the 21st century. I know I will be curious to see how it unfolds. In particular, I will be interested to see whether and how links develop in the Muslim world and China, and whether the civil society project continues to be anti-neoliberal and with what effect on the current brokers of global power. These are issues for active engagement, but also study and debate, and this, at least, I hope you will add your voice to.

REFERENCES

Anheier, Helmut. "Measuring Global Civil Society." *Global Civil Society 2001*, edited by Helmut Anheier, Marlies Glasius, and Mary Kaldor. London: London School of Economics, 2001. May 20, 2006, www.lse.ac.uk/Depts/global/Publications/Yearbooks/2001/2001chapter910b.pdf.

Anheier, Helmut, Marlies Glasius, and Mary Kaldor. "Introducing Global Civil Society." *Global Civil Society 2001*, edited by Helmut Anheier, Marlies Glasius, and Mary Kaldor. London: London School of Economics, 2001. May 20, 2006, www.lse.ac.uk/Depts/global/Publications/Yearbooks/2001/2001chapter1.pdf.

Bantjes, Rod. "The Geography of 'Global' Representation." 6th Nordic Conference on Environmental Social Sciences (NESS), 2003. May 20, 2006, www.stfx.ca/people/rbantjes/texts/civilspace_03%20_1_.pdf.

Bennett, Jennifer. "Anishinaabe Girl in Quebec." *Resist!: A Grassroots Collection of Stories, Poetry, Photos, and Analysis from the FTAA Protests in Québec City and Beyond: Words and Images of Activists, Writers, Artists, Filmmakers, Journalists, Students, and Workers from across Canada and the United States*, edited by Jen Chang et al. Halifax: Fernwood, 2001.

Blackett, Matthew. "Anti-postering By-law Not So Anti Anymore." *Spacing Wire*, 2006. May 20, 2006, http://spacing.ca/wire/?p=582.

CBC. "Anti-graffiti Crackdown Bans Spray Paint Sales to Minors." CBC News Online, 2006. May 19, 2006, www.cbc.ca.

de Armond, Paul. "Netwar in the Emerald City: WTO Protest Strategy and Tactics." *Networks and Netwars*, edited by John Arquilla and David F. Ronfelt. Santa Monica, California: Rand, 2001. November 16, 2006, www.rand.org/pubs/monograph_reports/MR1382/MR1382.ch7.pdf.

Decarli, Humberto. "Militarismo: Garante Del Populismo Latinoamericano." *Alterforo* (February 2006): 11.

Deleuze Gilles, and Félix Guattari. *A Thousand Plateaus: Capitalism and Schizophrenia*. Minneapolis: University of Minnesota Press, 1987.

Durkheim, Emile. *The Elementary Forms of the Religious Life*. 1915. New York: Free Press, 1965.

Eaton, Janet M. "Reporting Back from Quebec City!!" Global Action News, 2001. May 19, 2006, http://nadir.org/nadir/initiativ/agp/a20/janet.htm.

"February 15, 2003 Anti-war Protest," http://en.wikipedia.org/wiki/February_15,_2003_anti-war_protest. 25 May 2006.

Ferguson, Adam. "An Essay on the History of Civil Society." *The Civil Society Reader*, edited by Virginia Hodgkinson and Michael W. Foley. Hanover: University Press of New England, 2003.

Freidberg, Jill, and Rick Rowley. *This Is What Democracy Looks Like*. Prod. Seattle Independent Media Center and Big Noise Films. Dir. Jill Freidberg and Rick Rowley. Seattle Independent Media Center and Big Noise Films, 2000.

Gramsci, Antonio. *Selections from the Prison Notebooks*, edited and translated by Quintin Hoare and Geoffrey Nowell Smith. New York: International Publishers, 1979.

Grant, Alex. "A Change in Consciousness: Quebec City Protests, April 20th–22nd, 2001." May 19, 2006, www.newyouth.com/archives/protests/a_change_in.asp.

Harpham, Bruce. "Proposed Poster Ban 'Attacks Free Speech'." *The Varsity*, March 17, 2005. May 20, 2006, www.thevarsity.ca/media/storage/paper285/news/2005/03/17/News/Proposed.Poster.Ban.attacks.Free.Speech-896631.shtml?norewrite20060520163 9&sourcedomain=www.thevarsity.ca.

Huber, Emily, and Jamie McCallum. "Anti-globalization, Pro-Peace?" Mother Jones Online, 2001. May 19, 2006, www.motherjones.com/news/feature/2001/10/peace.html.

Karliner, Joshua. "Globalizing Hope: Another World Is Still Possible," 2002. May 19, 2006, www.corpwatch.org/article.php?id=1708.

Klein, Naomi. "A Fete for the End of the End of History," 2001. May 19, 2006, www.nologo.org.

————. "The Hijacking of the WSF," 2003. May 19, 2006, www.nologo.org.

Kohn, Margaret. "The Mauling of Public Space." *Dissent* 48, no. 2 (2001): 71–77. ABI/INFORM Proquest. Angus L. Macdonald Library, Antigonish. August 29, 2004, http://libmain.stfx.ca/newlib/electronic/databases/.

Lapointe, Paul, Germaine Ying Gee Wong, and Jacques Ménard. *View from the Summit*. Prod. Les Productions Érézi Inc. National Film Board of Canada, 2001.

Mckay, Kevin. "Solidarity and Symbolic Protest: Lessons for Labour from the Québec City Summit of the Americas." *Labour/Le Travail* 50 (Fall 2002): 21–72. May 19, 2006, www.historycooperative.org/journals/llt/50/mackay.html.

The People's Lenses Collective. *Under the Lens of the People: Our Account of the People's Resistance to the FTAA, Québec City, April 2001*. Toronto: People's Lenses Collective, 2003.

Powell, Andrew W. "Shame in the City: The Anti-postering By-law," March 10, 2005, Greater Toronto Area Bloggers. May 25, 2006, www.gtabloggers.com/blog/_archives/2005/3/10/416949.html.

Rebick, Judy. "Qatar Reveals Impact of Sept. 11 on Trade Battle." Z-Net Daily Commentary, 2001. May 19, 2006, www.zmag.org/sustainers/content/2001-11/17rebick.cfm.

Simard, Francis. *Talking It out: The October Crisis from the Inside*. Prose Series 4. Montreal: Guernica, 1987.

Stewart, Darren. "A Generation That Knows the Taste of Tear Gas." *Resist!: A Grassroots Collection of Stories, Poetry, Photos, and Analysis from the FTAA Protests in Québec City and Beyond: Words and Images of Activists, Writers, Artists, Filmmakers, Journalists, Students, and Workers from across Canada and the United States*, edited by Jen Chang et al. Halifax: Fernwood, 2001.

"TEXT of Miami City Ordinance," September 11, 2003. Portland Indymedia. May 25, 2006, http://portland.indymedia.org/en/2003/09/272405.shtml.

Uzcategui, Rafael. "WSF Caracas: Shroud for Venezuela's Social Movements." *Alterforo* (February 2006): 15.

Vinthagen, Stellan. "Globalisation from Below: Understanding Global Social Movements Challenging Corporate Globalisation from Above—A Theoretical Framework." *The Possibilities of Nonviolence*. Gothenburg: Swedish Peace and Arbitration Society, 2002. November 26, 2004, www.svenskafreds.se/konflikthantering/ickevald/Vinthagen.PDF.

Volk, Tom. "The Humongous Fungus—Ten Years Later." 2002. May 19, 2006, http://botit.botany.wisc.edu/TOMS_FUNGI/apr2002.html.

Walgrave, Stefaan, and Joris Verhulst. "The February 15 Worldwide Protests against a War in Iraq: An Empirical Test of Transnational Opportunities. Outline of a Research Programme." May 25, 2006, http://nicomedia.math.upatras.gr/conf/CAWM2003/Papers/Verhulst.pdf.

Zoll, Daniel. "NGOs Unwelcome at Forum." World Trade Observer, November 30, 1999. May 25, 2006, www.globalpolicy.org/ngos/99deb/wto.htm.

CRITICAL THINKING QUESTIONS

1. How much does dissent depend upon access to physical public space? To what extent can virtual space compensate for enclosures of physical public space?

2. The films *This Is What Democracy Looks Like* and *View from the Summit* make different arguments about the nature of protester violence. Compare the two and consider *how* the filmmakers visually and discursively construct their arguments. *View from the Summit* is much more critical of protesters' role in instigating violence. Is this an artifact of the filmmakers' perspective, or did protesters in Quebec City behave differently from those in Seattle?

3. Were the actions of protesters at Quebec City "terrorist" according to the definition in the USA PATRIOT Act and/or Canada's Bill C-36? What of the actions of the police?

4. Is Vinthagen right that playing into the "war drama" is always a losing strategy for demonstrators?

5. Is CATJO a part of civil society according to the definition given in this book? If you think the definition is ambiguous in this or other cases, how would you clarify it?

6. Would the definition of "global civil society" discussed in this chapter include al Qaeda? If so, do you think the definition should be changed? If so, how and why?

FURTHER READING

Anheier, Helmut, Marlies Glasius, and Mary Kaldor. "Introducing Global Civil Society." *Global Civil Society 2001*, edited by Helmut Anheier, Marlies Glasius, and Mary Kaldor. London: London School of Economics, 2001. May 20, 2006, www.lse.ac.uk/Depts/global/Publications/Yearbooks/2001/2001chapter1.pdf.
Most of the publications of the Centre for the Study of Global Governance are worth reading. This one provides an introduction to the concept of global civil society that is theoretically sophisticated and empirically grounded.

Kohn, Margaret. "The Mauling of Public Space." *Dissent* 48, no. 2 (2001): 71–77.
Kohn argues that public space, which she thinks is essential for democratic discourse, is disappearing from North American cities. Automobile-dependent cities shift public life to private malls where rights of free speech and assembly do not apply.

MacKay, Kevin. "Solidarity and Symbolic Protest: Lessons for Labour from the Québec City Summit of the Americas." *Labour/Le Travail* 50 (Fall 2002): 21–72. May 19, 2006, www.historycooperative.org/journals/llt/50/mackay.html.
This is an excellent case study of a parallel civil society demonstration. While his main focus is on the forging of alliances between anti-globalization activists and labour, MacKay shares our interest in how the global is made tangible in such events.

Naughton, John. "Contested Space: The Internet and Global Civil Society." *Global Civil Society Yearbook 2001*, 2001. November 26, 2004, www.lse.ac.uk/Depts/global/Yearbook/outline.htm.

Those who think that the answer to Kohn's problem is a shift to "virtual" public spaces should read Naughton. He outlines the threats of privatization and state regulation to formerly "free" internet spaces.

Pianta, Mario. "Parallel Civil Society Summits." *Global Civil Society Yearbook 2001*, 2001. August 29, 2004, www.lse.ac.uk/Depts/global/Yearbook/outline.htm.

Pianta offers a clear conceptualization of the significance of parallel civil society summits as well as the best available summary of the data on their growth over the past decades.

RELEVANT WEB SITES

Centre for Civil Society
www.lse.ac.uk/collections/CCS/

The London School of Economics' Centre for Civil Society is one of the best research sites on global civil society. Check out their yearbook and working papers series.

Civicus—World Alliance for Citizen Participation
www.civicus.org

Civicus is a coalition of organizations dedicated to strengthening global civil society. It hosts its own platform for civil society networking and exchange of ideas—the World Assembly—which is considerably smaller than the World Social Forum.

Spacing Wire
http://spacing.ca/wire/

This is a hip Toronto-based news and discussion site on the politics of public space.

World Social Forum
www.forumsocialmundial.org.br

The World Social Forum is meant to be a site where the forces of "globalization from below" gather to work on alternatives to the neoliberal model of "globalization from above." Find out who attends these meetings, and what has come of them.

WTO History Project
http://depts.washington.edu/wtohist/

The University of Washington has compiled a documentary archive on the Battle of Seattle. This is a good place to learn more about the events of that historic event. You could also check out the Global Policy Forum's page of articles and links (www.globalpolicy.org/ngos/role/globdem/stlindx.htm).

COPYRIGHT ACKNOWLEDGMENTS

Chapter 4

Photo: Andre Monteiro, "602737_strong_line, from Stock Xchng.

Mara Loveman, "High-Risk Collective Action: Defending Human Rights in Chile, Uruguay, and Argentina," from *The American Journal of Sociology* 104(2) (1998): 477-525. Copyright © University of Chicago Press, 1998. Reprinted by permission of University of Chicago Press.

Box 4.1: Maher Arar, "Maher Arar: statement," from *CBC News Online, INDEPTH*. http://www.cbc.ca/news/background/arar/arar_statement.html. Reprinted by permission of Maher Arar Support Committee.

Box 4.2: Human Rights Watch, "Will Pinochet Answer for His Crimes?" Adapted from *The Pinochet Case—A Wake-up Call to Tyrants and Victims Alike.* http://www.hrw.org/campaigns/chile98/precedent.htm.

Chapter 5

Photo: Liz Fagoli, "589857_thinking_1," from Stock Xchng. Reprinted by permission of Liz Fagoli.

Gary Kinsman, "The Regulation of Desire Sexuality in Canada," from *The Regulation of Desire Sexuality in Canada* (Montreal: Black Rose Books Ltd, 1987): 187. Copyright © Black Rose Books Ltd, 1987. Reprinted by permission of Black Rose Books Ltd.

Elizabeth A. Armstrong, *Forging Gay Identities Organizing Sexuality in San Francisco, 1950-1994*, (Chicago: University of Chicago Press, 2002): 56, 62, 69, 70. Copyright © University of Chicago Press, 2002. Reprinted by permission of University of Chicago Press and Elizabeth A. Armstrong.

Myrna Kostash, *Long Way From Home: The Story of the Sixties Generation in Canada*. (Toronto: James Lorimer & Company Ltd, 1980): 168, 171, 184, 224, 225, 238. Copyright © James Lorimer & Company Ltd, 1980. Reprinted by permission of James Lorimer & Company Ltd.

Box 5.2: Kevin McDonald, "From Solidarity to Fluidarity: Social Movements Beyond "Collective Identity"—the Case of Globalisation Conflicts Social," from Social Movement Studies 1(2) (2002): 109-28. Reprinted by permission of Taylor & Francis Ltd.

Chapter 6

Photo: Richard Simpson, "Teargas #86431," from Stock Xchng. Reprinted by permission of Richard Simpson.

Pete Townshend (Composer), "Won't Get Fooled Again," from *Polydor Records*. Copyright © BMG Music Publishing—USA, 1971.

Helen M. Brown, "Organizing Activity in the Women's Movement: An Example of Distributed Leadership," from *International Social Movement Research: Organizing for Change: Social Movement Organisations in Europe and the United States*, Bert Klandermans ed., (Greenwich, Conn.: JAI Press): 225, 228-230, 233. Copyright © JAI Press, 1989.

Box 6.1: "Wikipedia on Anarchism." Adapted from http://en.wikipedia.org/wiki/Anarchism_today.

Box 6.2: Chris DiBona, Sam Ockman, and Stone, Mark, *Open Sources: Voices from the Open Source Revolution.* http://www.oreilly.com/catalog/opensources/. Reprinted by permission of O'Reilly & Associates, Inc.

Chapter 7

Photo: Penny Mathews, "588877_a_way_out," from Stock Xchng.

Francis Simard, "Talking It Out: The October Crisis from Inside," translated by David Homel from, *Prose Series 4* (Montreal: Guernica Editions, 1987): 13-21, 24, 26, 27, 29-31 33. Copyright © Guernica Editions, 1987. Reprinted by permission of Guernica Editions.

Chapter 8

Photo: Jason Cangialosi, "Stocks and Stripes #404575," from Stock Xchng.

Naomi Klein, *No Logo:Taking Aim at the Brand* (Toronto: Random House, 2000): 22-24, 46, 61, 65, 112, 114, 115. Copyright © Naomi Klein, 2000. Reprinted by permission of Knopf Canada.

Box 8.1: "Don't Buy SFI." Adapted from *Rainforest Action Network*.

Box 8.2: Naomi Klein, "No Logo: Taking Aim at the Brand Bullies" from *No Logo: Taking Aim at the Brand Bullies* (Toronto: Random House, 2000): xx, 20, 211, 213, 407-408. Copyright © Naomi Klein, 2000. Reprinted by permission of Knopf Canada.

Chapter 9

Photo: Brad Harrison, "Logging #466469," from Stock Xchng. Reprinted by permission of Beaver River Media.

Sharon Beder, "Global Spin the Corporate Assault on Environmentalism," from *Global Spin the Corporate Assault on Environmentalism* (Dartington, Totnes, Devon, United Kingdom: Chelsea Green Publishing, 2002): 23,28,27, 34, 36, 42, 44, 51. Reprinted by permission of Green Books Ltd.

Michael Gismondi and Mary Richardson, *Discourse and Power in Environmental Politics: Public Hearings on a Bleached Kraft Pulp Mill in Alberta, Canada.* (Abingdon, United Kingdom: Taylor & Francis Ltd): 51, 52, 60, 61. Copyright © Taylor & Francis, 1991. Reprinted by permission of Taylor & Francis Ltd.

Thomas Dunk, "Talking About Trees: Environment and Society in Forest Workers' Culture," from *Canadian Review of Sociology and Anthropology 31(1)* (1994): 14-34. Reprinted by permission of Canadian Sociological Association.

Michael Gismondi, Joan Sherman, and Mary Richardson, "Winning Back the Words: Confronting Experts in an Environmental Public Hearing," from *Winning Back the Words: Confronting Experts in an Environmental Public Hearing* (Toronto: Garamond Press): 17, 29, 33, 34, 37, 38, 40, 41, 135, 144. Copyright © Garamond Press, 1993.

Alexander Simon, "Backlash! Corporate Front Groups and the Struggle for Sustainable Forestry in British Columbia," from *Capitalism, Nature, Socialism 9(4)* (1998): 19-20. Copyright © Taylor & Francis Ltd, 1998. http://www.tandf.co.uk/journals. Reprinted by permission of Taylor & Francis Ltd.

David Helvarg, *The War Against the Greens: The "Wise-Use" Movement, the New Right, and the Browning of America* (Boulder, CO: Johnson Books, 1997). Copyright © David Helvarg, 1994.

Chapter 10

Photo: Chris Petescia, "Fading Afternoon @ LM 2 #243758," from Stock Xchng. Reprinted by permission of Chris Petescia.

Box 10.1: David Cohen, "Identity And Virtual Culture." Adapted from slums.surfing.com.

Chapter 11

Photo: Paul Le Comte, "10233_protest3," from Stock Xchng.

Jeffrey McKelvey Ayres, "Defying Conventional Wisdom Political Movements and Popular Contention Against North American Free Trade," from *Studies in Comparative Political Economy and Public Policy* (Toronto: University of Toronto Press, 1998): 34, 43, 58, 78, 106. Copyright © University of Toronto Press, 1998. Reprinted by permission of University of Toronto Press.

Jill Freidberg and Rick Rowley, *This Is What Democracy Looks Like.* Copyright © Seattle Independent Media Center and Big Noise Films, 2000.

Box 11.1: Terry Cook, "Thousands of workers in South Korea strike against repressive labour laws." Adapted from *World Socialist Website* http://www.wsws.org/articles/2003/nov2003/kore-n19.shtml. "Korea Is a Law-Abiding Country—Firebombers Should Not Be Tolerated." Adapted from *Korean Times.* http://www.wsws.org/articles/2003/nov2003/kore-n19.shtm.

Chapter 12

Photo: Lorena Molinari, "peace&love #18490," from Stock Xchng.

Jennifer Bennett, "Anishinaabe Girl in Quebec," from *Resist!: A Grassroots Collection of Stories, Poetry, Photos and Analysis From the FTAA Protests in Québec City and Beyond.* (Halifax, Canada: Fernwood Publishing Co. Ltd, 2001): 50-51. Reprinted by permission of Fernwood Publishing Co. Ltd.

Kevin MacKay, "Solidarity and Symbolic Protest: Lessons for Labour From the Quebec City Summit of the Americas," from *Labour /Le Travail* 50 (2002): 29, 30, 32. Reprinted by permission of Canadian Committee on Labour History.

Box 12.2: Deleuze Gilles and Felix Guattari, "The Humongous Fungus." Adapted from *A Thousand Plateaus: Capitalism and Schizophreni.* http://botit.botany.wisc.edu/TOMS_FUNGI/apr2002.html.

INDEX

Abbreviations: FLQ (Front de Libération du Québec); NGO (non-governmentalorganization); PR (public relations); UN (United Nations); WTO (World Trade Organization). In addition, abbreviations for provinces and states have been used where appropriate.

A

Abalone Alliance, 341

Aboriginal peoples

    see also indigenous peoples; UN, as platform for indigenous peoples

    activism by. *See* indigenism

    and Alpac pulp mill public hearing, 278, 281–282

    assimilation of, 299

    and Clayoquot Sound clear-cutting, 235, 236, 241–242, 243

    collective rights of, as undermined by state, 299, 301

    cultural hybridity of, 299, 301

    displacement and migration of, 308

    languages of, as accessible on Internet, 300

    and need for treaty rights protection, 301

    organizations of, 302

    and self-determination, 305–307

    and sovereignty, 307–308

    territory of, 308

    Web sites of, 300, 310

Aboriginal peoples, and James Bay hydroelectric project. *See* Grand Council of the Crees; Great Whale hydroelectric project; James Bay Cree

affinity groups, 157–159, 180–181, 186

affluence, postwar, 72–73

    see also New Left; peace movement

    and consumer alienation, 74–75

    and military activity, 78–83

    role of, in success of social movements, 85–86

    and worker alienation, 73, 77–78

agency and structure, dialectic of, 148–149, 162–163

agriculture

    under capitalism, 8, 16, 47–48

    postwar decline of, 73

    subsistence economy of, 51–52, 54

al Jazeera, 208

al Qaeda, 113, 114, 203, 207–208, 209, 222

    as abstract principle, 208, 222

    discourse surrounding, 203–204, 206, 207

    as including all races, 216

    and Islamic prohibitions on violence, 217

Forest Stewardship Council (FSC)
certification, 243-244
Foucault, Michel, 46-47, 370. *See also*
governance
frame analysis, 136-137, 146-149, 162-163
France, 22, 23, 78-79, 221, 306
see also Situationists
and "great refusal" of 1968, 77-78, 92,
193, 220, 324
free trade, 25-26, 215, 327-328
see also Canadian nationalism;
globalization; neoliberalism
coalition against, 329-335, 345
Free Trade Agreement, Canada-U.S. (FTA),
327, 334, 335, 345
Free Trade Agreement, North American
(NAFTA), 177, 229, 335, 345, 361
Free Trade Area of the Americas (FTAA), 327,
352, 371
Quebec City summit of, 215, 219, 350-351
Friends of Clayoquot Sound (FOCS),
235, 236, 237, 240, 243, 275-276. *See
also* Clayoquot Sound
Front de Libération du Québec (FLQ), 83, 219
see also October Crisis
acts of, as dialogue with state, 199-200,
200-201
cells of, 192, 194, 202
compared to Cuban revolutionaries,
196-197
discourse of/against, 204
failure/decline of, 201, 222, 223
and international urban terrorism, 196
manifesto of, 192, 195-196, 200, 201
and moral implications of murder,
197-199
police infiltration of, 202-203, 357
and postal truck drivers' strike, 194, 196,
220
and Quebec's history of colonization/
abjection, 192, 194, 196
and revolutionary action as moral
obligation, 193-195, 196
and state violence/oppression of 1960s,
192

and violence against civilians, 197-199
working-class backgrounds/struggle of,
194-195, 196
front groups, corporate anti-environment,
231-233, 258, 259-260, 262, 298, 360
Fundación de Ayuda Social de las Iglesias
Cristianas (FASIC), 116, 121, 124, 127
Future Forest Alliance, 239, 258

G
Gallin, Dan, 27
Gandhi, Mahatma, 68, 104, 306
gay liberation movement, 150-155
see also culture; identity politics
and act of "coming out," 151, 152-153
and adaptation of New Left principles, 151
and borrowings from Black/feminist
struggles, 151-152
and challenge to capitalism, 154
consciousness raising by, 152
co-operative businesses of, 154
and "gay pride," 151-152, 153, 154
lesbian experiences in, 152, 153, 154
and Marxism, 156, 159-160, 163
and masculine lifestyle/culture, 151
as "pure" identity politics, 154-155, 162
spaces/neighbourhoods claimed by,
153-154, 162
"zaps," as used by, 152
General Agreement on Tariffs and Trade
(GATT), 327
General Electric, 14, 18
Geneva Convention on treatment of prisoners
of war, 219
Genoa, G8 summit in, 372, 373
Ghana, cocoa farmers' co-operative in, 60
Gibbs, Lois, 260-261, 264, 273
Global Climate Coalition (industry group),
232, 258, 260
globalization, 21
see also anti-globalization movement;
neoliberalism
and free trade, 25-26, 215, 327-328
and indigenous culture/language, 299-
300, 308-310

and invocation of War Measures Act,
200, 201, 219, 222
Keable Commission on, 202, 203
and later suspension of civil liberties,
201–202
and public support for state power, 201,
206, 222
as way to target social dissent, 202, 219
official discourse, of terrorism, 204, 206
"Ohio" (Young), 83
"old-growth" forests, 234, 242, 243. *See also*
Clayoquot Sound
oligarchy, 170–171, 177–178. *See also*
bureaucracies; networks; women's
centres
One Gigantic Prison (Inter-Church Committee
on Human Rights in Latin America), 122
Open Source movement, 181–184
and Linux operating system, 181–183, 186
oppositional discourse, of terrorism, 204
"Orangeburg Massacre," 83, 105
organization, of workers, 12–14, 21–24, 170,
210, 262. *See also* labour unions
Ottawa Citizen, 89–90
Our Bodies, Ourselves (Boston Women's
Health Book Collective), 145
Owen, Robert, 12, 44–45
Oxfam, 60, 122, 248, 358

P
Palestine Liberation Organization (PLO), 196,
209
Palestinian struggle with Israel, 216, 222
parallel summits, of civil society, 375
see also civil society; public space; Quebec
City; Seattle
media coverage of, 373, 375
online preparation for, 363–364
personal connections made through, 366,
375
physical spaces for, 364, 366, 371–375
promotion of, 364
and rituals of humanity, 366–367, 375
and virtual space, 373–375
Paris Commune, 13

Parti Québécois (PQ), 214, 306–307
Patriot Act, 2001 (U.S.), 219–220
peace movement, 78–83
and Canadian complicity in U.S.
military/foreign policy, 80–81
transitory teams within, 81–82, 87,
92–93, 185
violence and, 82–83, 89
women's, as non-hierarchical/
democratic, 173, 175
Pentagon, 77, 203
Peruniak, Merilyn, 282–283
petty bourgeoisie, 14, 24
see also bourgeoisie
farmers, as part of, 52, 55, 57, 59, 61–62
Philip Morris, 244
Philippines, fall of government in, 184, 374
Pinochet, Augusto
see also Chile
and fight for trial/conviction of, 123–124,
359
military coup/rule of, 102, 106, 109,
115–117, 122
Playboy, 245–246
police
see also state repression; state terror; state
violence
covert operations by, against New Left,
103–105
extra-legal killings by, 104–105
police violence
see also state repression; state terror; state
violence
against civil rights movement, 68–69, 70,
83, 89, 104–105, 355
against dispossessed, 352
against New Left, 77–78, 82–83, 91, 103,
104–105, 193
against protesters, in Quebec City, 353–
354, 355, 367–368, 372
against protesters, in Seattle, 338–340,
350, 355, 356, 368
Political Parties (Michels), 170
"political space," and resistance to state
terror, 116, 118, 129